D0725402

THE ROUGH GUIDE TO
BALI & LOMBOK

This ninth edition updated by
Iain Stewart

Based on original text by
Lesley Reader and Lucy Ridout

ROUGH GUIDES

Contents

Introduction to
Bali & Lombok

Part of the Indonesian archipelago, Bali and Lombok boast dramatically rugged coastlines, gloriously sandy beaches and world-class surf. Both islands are small – Bali extends less than 150km at its widest point, Lombok a mere 80km – and dramatically volcanic, graced with swathes of extremely fertile land, much of it sculpted into elegantly terraced rice paddies. Culturally, however, they could hardly be more different. Bali is Southeast Asia's only Hindu society, and religious observance permeates every aspect of life here; the Sasak people of Lombok, on the other hand, are Muslim, like the vast majority of Indonesians.

Bali landed on the tourist map over ninety years ago and is today an incredibly popular destination, drawing everyone from backpackers to high-end travellers, divers to sun-worshippers, package groups to people seeking spiritual healing. Visitor numbers plunged after the terrorist attacks of 2002 and 2005 but they have boomed in recent years, fuelled by a huge increase in Asian tourists, particularly from China. The island boasts stunning hotels, amazing restaurants and world-class spas but lacks the infrastructure to cope with this new influx, and traffic congestion and commercialization have affected swathes of Southern Bali.

That said, the island's original charm is still very much in evidence once you leave the densely populated southern strip, with evocative temples and vibrant festivals set off by the verdant landscapes of the interior. Just to the east of Bali, **Lombok** plays host to far fewer foreign travellers, but numbers are steadily increasing thanks to the island's many unspoilt beaches, terrific surf and forested mountain slopes. Blessed with such natural beauty, the island has a burgeoning reputation as a more adventurous destination than its illustrious neighbour.

Until the nineteenth century, both Bali and Lombok were divided into small **kingdoms**, each ruled by a succession of rajas whose territories fluctuated so much

ABOVE REEF, NUSA PENIDA **RIGHT** BALINESE FAMILY IN TRADITIONAL DRESS that, at times, parts of eastern Bali and western Lombok were joined under a single ruler. More recently, both of the islands have endured years of colonial rule under the Dutch East Indies government, which only ended when hard-won **independence** was granted to Indonesia in 1949. The Jakarta-based government has since tried hard to foster a sense of national identity among its vast array of extraordinarily diverse islands and peoples, both by implementing a unifying five-point political philosophy, the Pancasila, and through the mandatory introduction of Bahasa Indonesia, now the lingua franca across the whole archipelago. Politically, Bali is administered as a province in its own right, while Lombok is the main island in West Nusa Tenggara.

TRADITIONAL DRESS

It is customary for Balinese men and women to wear **traditional dress** to attend temple festivals, cremations, weddings, birth rites and other important rituals; men also wear temple dress if playing in a gamelan orchestra and occasionally for *banjar* (neighbourhood) meetings too.

Many **women** wear a vividly coloured bustier under the *kebaya* (blouse), and some don flamboyant hair accessories as well. For big festivals, women from the same community will all wear the same-coloured *kebaya* to give their group a recognizable identity.

Men also wear a type of sarong (*kamben sarung*), a knee-length hip-cloth (*saput*) and a formal, collared shirt (generally white but sometimes batik) or a starched jacket-like shirt. The distinctive headcloth (*udeng*) can be tied according to personal taste, but generally with a triangular crest on top (shops sell ready-tied *udeng*). As with the sash, the *udeng* symbolically concentrates the mental energies and directs the thoughts heavenwards via the perky cockscomb at the front.

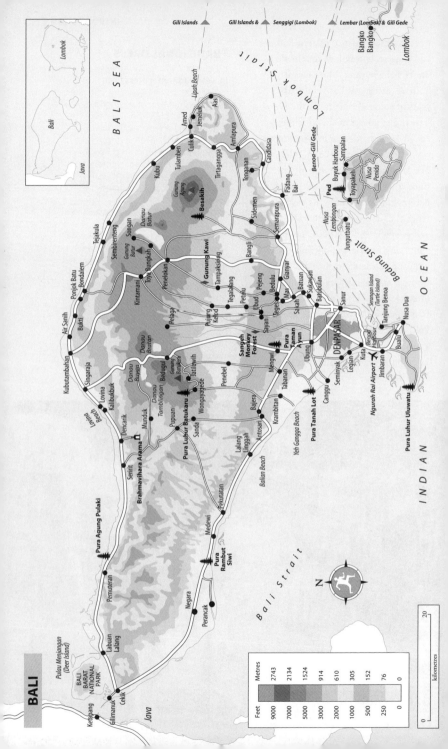

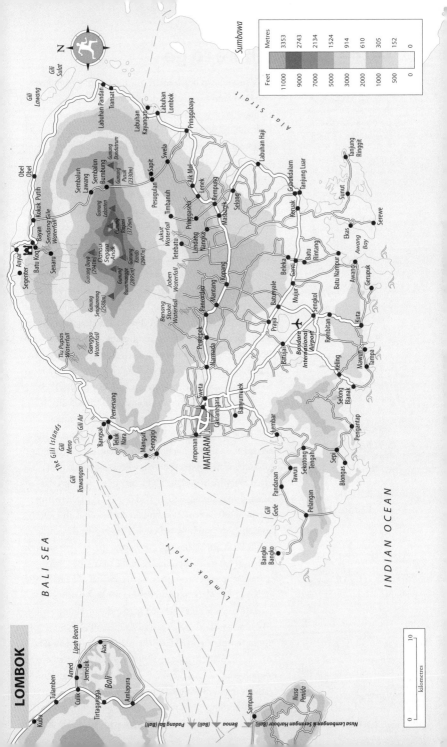

FACT FILE

- **Bali** (almost 5800 square kilometres in size with a population of over 4.4 million) and **Lombok** (just over 4700 square kilometres in size and with a population around 3.4 million) make up two of the 34 provinces of the Republic of Indonesia, an ethnically diverse democracy of around 260 million people.

- The Balinese traditionally celebrate their new year, known as **Nyepi** and generally falling in March/April, with a day of silence and meditation. By contrast, the night before features a deafening cacophony designed to scare away evil sprits.

- Every November/ December, Muslim and Hindu communities on Lombok take part in the **Perang Topat**, or **Ketupat War**, a ceremonial mock-battle at Pura Lingsar featuring copious rice- and egg-throwing.

- The **Wallace Line** that runs through the 35km-wide Lombok Strait, which separates the two islands, was long thought to mark the boundary between the distribution of Asian and Australasian wildlife.

- Both Bali and Lombok are **volcanic**: large eruptions killed thousands in the twentieth century and occasionally close the islands' airports.

Where to go

Bali's best-known beach resort, the **Kuta–Legian–Seminyak** strip is an 8km sweep of golden sand that draws an incongruous mix of holidaying Australian families, weekending Jakartans, backpackers, a loyal gay clientele and design-conscious visitors drawn by its fashionable restaurants and boutiques. Travellers seeking more relaxed alternatives generally head north to the beaches around and beyond Canggu, across the southern peninsula to **Sanur** or offshore to **Nusa Lembongan**; to sedate **Candidasa** or **Amed** further east; or to the black volcanic sands of **Lovina** on the north coast. Quieter, smarter seaside options can be found at **Jimbaran** in the south and **Pemuteran** in the northwest. On Lombok, the trio of white-sand **Gili Islands** draw the biggest crowds; there are quieter islands off the **Sekotong** peninsula, a wide range of resort accommodation around **Senggigi** and a series of extraordinarily beautiful beaches near **Kuta** in the south. All these resorts make comfortable bases for **divers** and **snorkellers** and are within easy reach of the islands' many reefs. **Surfers** have countless swells to choose from, including the famously challenging Uluwatu on Bali and Desert Point on Lombok, as well as many more novice-friendly breaks.

Most visitors also venture inland to experience more traditional island life. On Bali, the once-tiny village of **Ubud** has become a hugely popular cultural centre, still charming but undeniably commercialized, where traditional dances are staged every night and the streets are full of organic cafés, art galleries, yoga studios and myriad purveyors of alternative therapies. **Tetebatu** on Lombok occupies a similarly cool position in the foothills, although, like the island as a whole, it lacks Bali's artistic heritage. In general, the villages on both islands are far more appealing than the towns, but Bali's capital, **Denpasar**, the historic district capital of **Semarapura**, and Lombok's **Mataram** conurbation are each worth a day-trip for their museums, markets and temples.

Bali's other big draw is its proliferation of elegant Hindu **temples**, particularly the island temple of **Tanah Lot**, the dramatically located **Uluwatu** and the extensive **Besakih** complex on the slopes of Gunung Agung. Temple **festivals**, most of which are open to tourists, are also well worth attending.

CLOCKWISE FROM TOP LEFT TEMPLE OFFERINGS; PURA ULUN DANU BATUR, BALI; KUTA BEACH, BALI; FARMER SIFTING RICE

Both islands hold a number of **hiking** possibilities, many of them up **volcanoes**. The best is undoubtedly the climb to the summit of Lombok's **Gunung Rinjani**, which at 3726m is one of Indonesia's highest peaks. The ascent of Bali's **Gunung Agung** (3142m) is shorter and slightly less arduous. The climb up **Gunung Batur** (1717m) is much less taxing and therefore more popular. Bali's sole **national park**, Bali Barat, has relatively few interesting trails, but is good for **birdwatching**, as is the area around **Danau Bratan** in the centre of the island. Even if you don't want to go hiking, it's worth considering a trip to an inland village for the change of scenery, views and refreshing temperatures; the villages of **Sidemen**, **Tirtagangga**, **Sarinbuana** and **Munduk** are all good bases.

When to go

Just eight degrees south of the equator, **tropical** Bali and Lombok enjoy fairly constant year-round temperatures, averaging 27°C in Bali's coastal areas and the hills around Ubud and 22°C in the central volcanoes around Kintamani. Both islands are hit by an annual **monsoon**, which brings rain, wind and intense humidity from October through to March.

The **best time to visit** is outside the monsoon season, from May to September, though monsoons are, like many other events in Indonesia, notoriously unpunctual, and you should be prepared to get rained on in Ubud at any time of year. However, the prospect of a daily rainstorm shouldn't put you off: you're far more likely to get an hour-long downpour than day-long drizzle. Mountain-climbing, though, is both unrewarding and dangerous at monsoon time (the authorities close Rinjani for six months or so every year for safety reasons).

You should also be aware of the peak **tourist seasons**: resorts on both islands get packed out between mid-June and mid-September and again over the Christmas–New Year period, when prices rocket and rooms can be fully booked for weeks in advance.

AVERAGE MONTHLY TEMPERATURES AND RAINFALL

	Jan	Feb	March	April	May	June	July	Aug	Sept	Oct	Nov	Dec
KINTAMANI												
°C	22	22	22	22	22	21	21	21	22	22	22	22
mm	444	405	248	174	72	43	30	21	35	50	166	257
KUTA (BALI)												
°C	28	28	28	28	27	27	26	26	27	27	28	28
mm	394	311	208	115	79	67	57	31	43	95	176	268
MATARAM												
°C	27	27	26	26	26	25	25	25	26	27	27	27
mm	253	254	209	155	84	67	38	21	36	168	250	209
SINGARAJA												
°C	27	27	27	27	28	28	27	27	28	29	28	28
mm	318	318	201	123	57	36	31	7	21	54	115	180
UBUD												
°C	27	27	27	27	27	26	26	26	26	27	27	27
mm	412	489	274	224	101	172	128	132	142	350	374	398

Author picks

Our authors covered every corner of Bali and Lombok – from soaring volcanic peaks to underwater havens, bustling city markets to ancient temples – to research this new edition. Here are a few of their favourite experiences.

Beach bars The coastline between Seminyak and Canggu is loaded with fine places for a sundowner from the uber-luxe environs of *Potato Head* (p.72) to beach shack haven *Warung 707* (p.72)

Stunning views On Bali, the jaw-dropping seascape from Pura Luhur Uluwatu is out of this world; views of impossibly green rice terraces don't get much better than around Ubud (p.116), Sidemen (p.166) and Tirtagangga (p.180). Lombok's rice-paddy scenery is impressive too, especially at Tetebatu (p.270).

Off the beaten track Lombok's southeast peninsula (p.274) may only be a bumpy ninety-minute drive from the airport, but it feels like the end of the world. The southwest peninsula (p.254) is better connected but also very remote. On Bali, get your explorer kicks at the narrow and winding Amed coastal road to Ujung (p.183).

Underwater vision The vibrant coral reefs around the Gili Islands (p.284) are perfect both for snorkelling right from the beach and for shallow scuba diving. For dramatic pelagic life including manta rays, Nusa Penida (p.105) excels, while Pulau Menjangan (p.235) has lots of reef sharks.

World-class waves Lombok is a sensational place to surf, whatever your skill level: learn the basics in Kuta's fabulous bays (p.275) or hit some of the world's best waves at nearby Gerupuk (p.280).

> Our author recommendations don't end here. We've flagged up our favourite places – a perfectly sited hotel, an atmospheric café, a special restaurant – throughout the Guide, highlighted with the ★ symbol.

FROM TOP LOMBOK SURFING; BEACH BAR, SEMINYAK; GUNUNG RINJANI'S HOT SPRINGS

23

things not to miss

It's not possible to see everything that Bali and Lombok have to offer in a single trip – and we don't suggest you try. What follows is a selective taste of the islands' highlights, including memorable places to stay, outstanding beaches and spectacular hikes. All highlights are colour-coded by chapter and have a page reference to take you straight into the Guide, where you can find out more.

1

1 SUNRISE FROM GUNUNG BATUR

Page 195

Climb this ancient volcano before dawn and you'll be rewarded with the most extraordinary panoramas on Bali.

2 TEMPLE FESTIVALS

Page 32

Every one of Bali's twenty thousand Hindu temples holds at least one annual festival to entertain the gods with processions and offerings.

3 THE AMED COAST

Page 183

Memorable diving and snorkelling close to Bali's shore and a breathtakingly dramatic coastline.

4 SOUTH LOMBOK BEACHES

Page 274

The wild and glorious Kuta coastline has some of the most beautiful white-sand bays on the islands.

16

21

22

18 BALINESE DANCE
Page 319

From acutely choreographed solo dances to unforgettable choruses of more than fifty men in the Kecak, watching a Balinese dance performance never fails to enchant.

19 CLIMBING RINJANI
Page 266

The most challenging and rewarding climb on the islands takes in a dramatic crater lake with its own volcano rising from the waters.

20 NUSA LEMBONGAN
Page 98

Laidback island life, fine coastal scenery and exceptional diving and snorkelling are all just a short boat ride from Bali's mainland.

21 FINE DINING
Page 30

Splash out on creative gourmet cuisine at ultra-chic restaurants on Bali.

22 COCKTAILS AT SUNSET
Pages 72 & 294

On Bali, head to Seminyak or Canggu for DJ bars and sundowners on the beach, or to the west coast of Gili Trawangan.

23 GILI ISLANDS
Page 284

Dazzlingly white sand, turquoise waters and zero road traffic – the three Gilis are real desert islands.

Itineraries

The following itineraries feature a mix of popular and off-the-beaten-path attractions, taking you right across Bali and Lombok, from volcanic foothills to cultural hubs, from idyllic tropical islands to bustling cities. You may not have time to complete a full list, but even doing a partial itinerary – or mixing and matching elements from different ones – will give you a wonderful insight into the two islands.

THE GRAND TOUR

You'll need around three to four weeks to complete this comprehensive trip around Bali and Lombok, though there are numerous places that will tempt you to extend your stay.

❶ **Bukit Peninsula** Expect spectacular views, world-class surf, the magnificent Pura Uluwatu temple and a fine choice of stylish homestays and hotels in this emerging region. **See p.75**

❷ **Kuta–Legian–Seminyak** This busy south Bali conurbation has something for all tastes, with rowdy Kuta, chic Seminyak and the more family-friendly Legian. **See p.54**

❸ **Canggu** Bali's most fashionable district is a semi-rural region replete with gorgeous bars, destination restaurants and surf beaches. **See p.63**

❹ **Pura Tanah Lot** This spectacularly sited temple – perched on a rocky crag overlooking a black-sand, wave-lashed beach – is a favourite sunset spot for tourists. **See p.225**

❺ **Ubud** Bali's artistic, musical and cultural hub, laidback Ubud has an array of tempting boutique hotels, restaurants, shops and spas that makes it an easy place to linger. **See p.110**

❻ **Gunung Batur** There are stupendous views from the summit of this volcanic cone,

especially at sunrise – and after descending, you can sink into one of the hot springs beside the turquoise Danau Batur lake. **See p.192**

❼ **Gunung Agung and Besakih** Bali's highest peak, the dramatic, 3142m Gunung Agung volcano, is home to a number of important religious sites, most notably Besakih, the Mother Temple. **See p.162 & p.164**

❽ **The Gili Islands** From Padang Bai hop on a fast boat to the Gili Islands. This trio of blissfully traffic-free islands boasts beautiful beaches and reefs. Choose between pumping nightlife on Gili Trawangan, sheer tranquillity on Gili Meno, or the more local feel of Gili Air. **See p.284**

❾ **Gunung Rinjani** The climb up the 3726m Gunung Rinjani is the most challenging and rewarding trek on either Bali or Lombok. **See p.266**

❿ **Kuta and south coast Lombok** This stunning stretch of coastline, with its giant white-sand bays remains – for now – largely undeveloped. **See p.274**

SAND, SCUBA AND SURF

You'll need around three weeks to visit all of these destinations, though many people end up staying longer in the Gili Islands, in particular, than they originally planned.

ABOVE TRADITIONAL BOATS

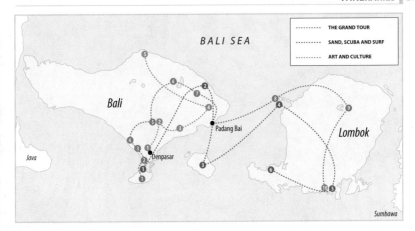

❶ **South Bali** Learn to surf on Kuta Beach or in Canggu. If you're more experienced head to the adrenaline-pumping breaks at Uluwatu, Dreamland, Bingin and Padang Padang. See p.54

❷ **Liberty wreck** Just off the coast of Tulamben, the wreck of the *Liberty*, a US steamship torpedoed in 1942, is Bali's most popular dive site. See p.189

❸ **Nusa Lembongan and Nusa Penida** These two relaxed islands have a very different feel to the mainland. Divers regularly encounter manta rays and sunfish. See p.98 & p.105

❹ **The Gili Islands** From Lembongan, catch a boat to the Gilis. The dive sites surrounding these islands are some of the best in Lombok – turtles, sharks and moray eels are all common – and there are some great beaches too. See p.284

❺ **Kuta, Lombok** This little town is fast emerging as a prime tourist centre, with some of Indonesia's most spectacular beaches and world-class surf close by. See p.275

❻ **Sekotong and the southwest peninsula** An isolated region dotted with white-sand islets that's a haven for snorkellers, divers, surfers and sunseekers alike. See p.254

ART AND CULTURE

This itinerary can be completed in as little as a week and a half, if you have your own vehicle, though a more leisurely timescale allows for a more contemplative exploration and makes it easier to travel by public transport.

❶ **Bali Museum** This museum in Bali's capital, Denpasar, provides an excellent introduction to the island's cultural heritage. See p.88

❷ **Ubud** Watch a traditional dance or gamelan performance, admire paintings by Balinese and expat artists, or learn a new skill – from woodcarving to silversmithing. See p.110

❸ **Semarapura and the Nyoman Gunarsa Museum** The town of Semarapura is a centre of classical Balinese art, while nearby is the enlightening Nyoman Gunarsa Museum. See p.159 & p.161

❹ **Taman Tirtagangga Water Palace** Built in 1946 by the last raja of Karangasem, this palace has a riot of pools, moats and fountains. See p.181

❺ **Pura Meduwe Karang** This grand temple on Bali's northern coast features exquisite carvings and reliefs. See p.215

TRADITIONAL FOOD MARKET, UBUD

Basics

Getting there

There's no shortage of international and domestic flights to Bali's only airport, Ngurah Rai Airport (see p.64) – officially referred to as Denpasar (DPS), though it's actually 3km south of Kuta. Bandara Internasional Lombok (see p.248), in the south of the island, also has a range of domestic and a few international flights.

The most expensive times to fly to Bali and Lombok are during **high season**, which for most airlines runs from the beginning of July through to the middle or end of August and also includes most of December and the first half of January. During these peak periods flights should be reserved well in advance.

Flights from the UK and Ireland

There are no nonstop flights **from the UK or Ireland** to Bali or Lombok. Singapore Airlines, Emirates and Garuda offer some of the fastest London–Denpasar flights; all require a brief transfer, but can get you to Bali in as little as seventeen hours. They are often competitively priced against the other major airlines that serve Bali, most of which require longer transit times and can take up to 22 hours. From London and Manchester low-season return **fares** rarely cost less than £575 including tax, rising up to around £900 in high season. Flying from Ireland, you'll need to add on the return fare to London.

To Lombok

Lombok is served by a far smaller range of international flights operated by Singapore Airlines/Silk Air and Garuda; from the UK and Ireland, you can expect to pay around £100–250 more than to Bali. Alternatively, take the cheapest available flight to Bali or Jakarta, from where you can take an inexpensive domestic flight to Lombok (see p.248).

Flights from the US and Canada

There's a big choice of flights to Bali **from North America**, although none are direct. Flights leaving from the **west coast** cross the Pacific to Asian hubs such as Taipei, Seoul, Tokyo, Hong Kong, Singapore or Kuala Lumpur, with connections to Bali. The best journey times are around 24 hours (crossing the Pacific in one hop), although considerably more than this is not unusual; slower journeys touch down midway, perhaps in Honolulu and/or Guam, while some schedules involve overnighting en route. From the **east coast**, airlines take a northern trajectory "over the top"; for example, New York–Tokyo is typically fourteen hours' flying time, New York–Bangkok is seventeen hours. Typically you'll be looking at a **fare** of US$1000-plus in low season and US$1800 or more in high season from either starting point.

Round-the-world or **Circle Asia** multi-stop **tickets** put together by consolidators can cost little more than the return prices quoted above. Another possibility, which could also work out cheaper, is One World's "**Visit Asia Pass**", which can offer very good value for flights from North America.

Flights from Australia, New Zealand and South Africa

Scores of flights operate every day **from Australia to Bali**, with the best deals on low-cost carriers such as Jetstar and Air Asia; Garuda also flies major routes. Return fares from Western Australia and the Northern Territory, including Perth (4hr) and Darwin (2hr 30min), start at around Aus$275 including tax, or about Aus$450–550 in high season. Flights from Sydney (5hr 30min), Melbourne (6hr), Adelaide (5hr), Brisbane (6hr) and Townsville (5hr 30min) start at Aus$400.

Air New Zealand has (seasonal, May to October) direct flights to Bali from Auckland (9hr) from NZ$1400. Virgin, Jetstar and Qantas offer good deals and fast connection times from Auckland and Christchurch via Brisbane, Sydney or Melbourne all year round, prices start at around NZ$800 inclusive in low season, NZ$1300 in high season and flight time is around 11 hours. Alternatively, shop around for the cheapest Sydney flight then change onto one of the budget airlines listed above.

At the time of writing there were no direct flights to **Lombok**; travel via Bali.

A BETTER KIND OF TRAVEL

At Rough Guides we are passionately committed to travel. We believe it helps us understand the world we live in and the people we share it with – and of course tourism is vital to many developing economies. But the scale of modern tourism has also damaged some places irreparably, and climate change is accelerated by most forms of transport, especially flying. All Rough Guides' flights are carbon-offset, and every year we donate money to a variety of environmental charities.

There are no nonstop flights **from South Africa** to Bali or Lombok but it's possible to reach Bali in around 18 to 22 hours with Singapore Airlines via Singapore and Emirates via Dubai. Return fares start from ZAR9600.

TRAVEL AGENTS AND TOUR OPERATORS

For specialist diving and surfing tours it can work out cheaper to contact Bali- and Lombok-based operators direct.

Ampersand Travel UK ☎ 020 7819 9770 ⓦ www.ampersand travel.com. Specialises in off-beat luxury trips using boutique lodges in extraordinary locations and plenty of cultural interest.

Asian Pacific Adventures US ☎ 1 800 825 1680, ⓦ asianpacific adventures.com. Small-group tours including "Bali: Through an Artist's Eye", fourteen days based mostly in Ubud concentrating on art, music and culture.

Audley Travel ⓦ www.audleytravel.com. Well-planned luxury tours around Bali and Lombok utilising choice accommodation.

Backroads US ☎ 1 800 462 2848, ⓦ backroads.com. Cycling tours including an eight-day "Bali Biking" tour that takes in cooking classes and snorkelling.

ebookers UK ☎ 020 3320 3320, ⓦ ebookers.com; Republic of Ireland ☎ 01 4311 311, ⓦ ebookers.ie. Low fares.

Flight Centre US ☎ 1 877 992 4732, Canada ☎ 1 877 967 5302, UK ☎ 0870 499 0040, Australia ☎ 13 31 33, New Zealand ☎ 0800 243 544, South Africa ☎ 0860 400 727; ⓦ flightcentre.com. Guarantees to offer the lowest airfares; also sells package holidays and adventure tours.

Hello World Travel Australia ☎ 1300 722 501, ⓦ helloworld.com. au. Sells flights and package tours with all the big operators.

Imaginative Traveller UK ☎ 0845 077 8802, ⓦ imaginative -traveller.com; Australia ☎ 1300 135 088, ⓦ imaginative-traveller .com.au. Small-group adventure tours to Bali and Lombok, including treks to the crater rim on Rinjani.

Intrepid Travel US ☎ 1 800 970 7299, Canada ☎ 1 866 915 1511, UK and Ireland ☎ 0203 147 7777, Australia ☎ 1300 364 512, New Zealand ☎ 0800 600 610; ⓦ intrepidtravel.com. Well-regarded, small-group adventure tour operator, their 12-day Bali & Lombok takes in rafting, hiking and snorkelling.

North South Travel UK ☎ 01245 608 291, ⓦ northsouthtravel .co.uk. Travel agency whose profits support projects in the developing world.

STA Travel UK ☎ 0871 2300 040, US ☎ 1 800 781 4040, Australia ☎ 134 782, New Zealand ☎ 0800 474 400, South Africa ☎ 0861 781 781; ⓦ statravel.com. Worldwide specialists in independent travel; good discounts for students and under-26s.

Sunda Trails Lombok, Indonesia ☎ +62 (0)370 647390, ⓦ sundatrails.com. Highly regarded tour operator based in **Ampenan**, Lombok with tours of Lombok, Bali and Nusa Tenggara on foot, by bicycle or motorbike as well as diving and trekking packages.

Surf Travel Company Australia ☎ 02 9222 8870, ⓦ surftravel .com.au. Flights and accommodation packages – resort-based or on yachts – to the best surf spots in Bali and Lombok.

Symbiosis Expedition Planning UK ☎ 0845 123 2844, ⓦ symbiosis-travel.com. Unusual tailor-made holidays plus small-group specialist trips to Bali focusing on diving and cycling.

Trailfinders UK ☎ 0845 058 5858, Ireland ☎ 01 677 7888, Australia ☎ 1300 780 212; ⓦ trailfinders.com. One of the best-informed agents for independent travellers.

Travel CUTS US ☎ 1 800 592 2887, Canada ☎ 1 866 246 9762; ⓦ travelcuts.com. Budget travel specialist.

USIT Ireland ☎ 01 602 1906, Northern Ireland ☎ 028 9032 7111; ⓦ usit.ie. Discounted and student fares.

Visas

Indonesia **visa laws** change frequently so always check the latest situation before travelling. All visitors must have a passport that is valid for at least six months from the date of arrival, and have proof of onward or return passage.

Currently citizens from 169 countries qualify for 30-day **visa-free** entry. The list includes all European countries, USA, Canada, Australia, New Zealand, South Africa and India. This visa-free arrangement is *non-extendable*.

If you want to stay longer than 30 days you have two choices. You can apply in advance for a visa (30 or 60 days) from an Indonesian embassy (see above); fees vary per country. It's an (absurdly) complicated process in some countries and may require a recent bank statement showing a minimum balance (the UK specifies £1000), a recent letter from your employer, educational establishment, bank manager, accountant or solicitor certifying your obligation to return home/leave Indonesia by the designated date.

Alternatively, citizens of 61 countries (including most EU nations, UK, USA, USA, Canada, Australia, New Zealand and South Africa) can pay for a 30-day visa on arrival (which are extendable for another 30 days) at one of the country's 44 **designated gateway ports**. Both Bali and Lombok's airports are visa-issuing gateways. The fee is $35, payable in US dollars or other hard currencies.

Visa extensions can be arranged at **immigration offices** (*kantor imigrasi*) in Denpasar (see p.92), Kuta (see p.75) and in Mataram on Lombok (see p.252); you need to apply at least a week before your existing visa expires. The extension price is Rp250,000, with an extra charge levied locally if you want your paperwork fast-tracked. At the time of writing the fastest standard processing time was in Mataram (24hr, or less than 3hr for the fast-track option); other offices can take a week. You will need to fill out various forms, submit two passport photos and pay to have relevant passport pages photocopied. Travel agents in Bali and Lombok can do all this for you, for a fee of course.

Penalties for **overstaying your visa** are severe.

TYING THE KNOT

If you fancy the idea of getting married in Bali, the options are mind-boggling. Many hotels will organize the whole thing for you, as will any number of wedding planners. They will also advise on the paperwork and formalities, which are significant, so start planning early. Prices vary enormously and it is important to check exactly what is included. It's also a good idea to check out postings on travel forums for locations and planners. Attractive **boutique hotels** that host weddings include *Desa Seni* (see p.70) and *Puri Taman Sari* (see p.226). Using a villa as a setting can also be very cost-effective.

Indonesian embassies and consulates abroad

For comprehensive listings of **Indonesian embassies and consulates** around the world, see the "Mission" page of the website of the Indonesian Ministry of Foreign Affairs at Ⓦ kemlu.go.id.

FOREIGN EMBASSIES AND CONSULATES

Most countries maintain an **embassy** in the Indonesian capital, Jakarta, and some also have **consulates** in Bali; there are none on Lombok. Your first point of contact should always be the Bali consulate.

Australia Consulate Jl Letda Tantular 32, Renon, Denpasar Ⓣ 0361 2000100, Ⓦ bali.indonesia.embassy.gov.au.

Australia Embassy Jakarta Ⓣ 021 2550 5555, Ⓦ indonesia .embassy.gov.au.

Canada Consulate Contact the Australian consulate in Denpasar first.

Canada Embassy Jakarta Ⓣ 021 2550 7800, Ⓦ canada international.gc.ca.

Ireland Contact the UK consul in Sanur first.

Malaysia Embassy Jakarta Ⓣ 021 522 4947, Ⓦ www.kln.gov.my.

New Zealand Consulate Contact the Australian consulate in Denpasar first.

New Zealand Embassy Jakarta Ⓣ 021 2995 5800, Ⓦ nzembassy .com/indonesia.

Singapore Embassy Jakarta Ⓣ 021 2995 0400, Ⓦ mfa.gov.sg/jkt.

South Africa Embassy Jakarta Ⓣ 021 574 0660, Ⓦ www.dirco .gov.za/jakarta.

UK Consulate Jl Tirta Nadi 2 no. 20, Sanur Ⓣ 0361 270601.

UK Embassy Jakarta Ⓣ 021 2356 5200, Ⓦ www.gov.uk /government/world/indonesia.

US Consulate Jl Hayam Wuruk 188, Renon, Denpasar Ⓣ 0361 233605, Ⓔ amcobali@indosat.net.id.

US Embassy Jakarta Ⓣ 021 3435 9000, Ⓦ id.usembassy.gov.

Customs regulations

Indonesia's **customs regulations** allow foreign nationals to import one litre of alcohol, two hundred cigarettes or 25 cigars or 100g of tobacco, and a reasonable amount of perfume. Laptops and video cameras are supposed to be declared on entry and re-exported on departure. Import restrictions cover the usual banned items, including narcotics, weapons and pornographic material, and foreigners are also forbidden to bring in amounts of Rp5,000,000 or more in Indonesian currency. Indonesia is a signatory to the Convention on International Trade in Endangered Species (CITES), and so forbids import or export of products that are banned under this treaty, which includes anything made from turtle flesh or turtle shells (including tortoiseshell jewellery and ornaments), as well as anything made from ivory. Indonesian law also prohibits the export of antiquities and cultural relics, unless sanctioned by the customs department.

Getting around

Bali and Lombok are both small enough to traverse in a few hours by road (there's no rail transport on either island), although the lack of street names, traffic congestion (in Southern Bali) and route numbers can make things confusing if you are driving yourself. The major roads are good, carrying at least two-way traffic, and are fairly well maintained, although they see a lot of large trucks. On less-frequented routes, the roads are narrow and more likely to be potholed, while off the beaten track they may be no more than rough tracks.

The state of the road is a reasonable indication of the frequency of **public transport**, which is generally inexpensive, but offers little space or comfort and very few travellers bother with it. **Tourist shuttle buses** operate between major destinations on Bali and Lombok, and although these are more expensive, they are convenient. If you prefer to drive yourself, bicycles, motorbikes, cars and jeeps are available to rent throughout the islands, or you can rent cars or motorbikes with a driver. App-based taxi services, including Uber, are in Bali and inexpensive, but are not always available, see p.26.

Getting **between Bali and Lombok** is easy by plane or boat (see p.248).

Tourist shuttle buses

Most travellers use private shuttle buses to get around. The most established **operator** is Perama (🌐 peramatour.com), serving all major tourist destinations. Fares generally work out at least double that of public transport, but the service is usually direct and there's likely to be room for luggage, wheelchairs, buggies and surfboards. For example, fares from Kuta, Bali are Rp60,000 to Ubud and Rp125,000 to Lovina. It's best to book the day before.

There are several **rival companies** operating on both Bali and Lombok who advertise throughout tourist areas and offer a similar service, but are not as high profile. These are worth checking out if, for example, the Perama office is inconveniently far from the town centre (as in Lovina and Ubud).

Bemos and buses

On both Bali and Lombok, public transport predominantly consists of buses and bemos. **Bemos** are minibuses of varying sizes. **Buses** operate long-distance routes such as Denpasar to Singaraja, Denpasar to Amlapura, and Mataram to Labuhan Lombok. Because of the rise in motorbike ownership, bemos are declining on the islands year on year making public transport ever more time-consuming. Bemos don't really have fixed timetables, generally leaving every hour or so (or when full).

You can pick up a bus or bemo from the **terminal** in bigger towns or flag one down on the road. Fares are paid to the driver or conductor, if there is one. You can't buy tickets in advance.

No local person negotiates a **fare**. When they want to get off they yell "Stoppa", hop out and pay the fixed fare. Note tourists can be charged several times the local fare, and you may be charged extra for a bulky rucksack.

Ferries and boats

Huge inter-island **ferries** connect Bali and Lombok with the islands on either side, from Gilimanuk to Java (see p.237), from Padang Bai to Lembar on Lombok (see p.170) and from Labuhan on Lombok to Sumbawa (see p.248). They run frequently and regularly, day and night.

Many small, expensive **fast boats** connect the Balinese mainland with the Gili Islands, Nusa Lembongan, Nusa Penida and Bangsal in Lombok. There are also smaller, slower boat services to Nusa Lembongan from Bali and from mainland Lombok to all three Gili Islands. A regular ferry runs from Padang Bai on Bali to Nusa Penida.

Taxis

The taxi trade in Bali is notorious, and its workings very complicated. Essentially there are three kinds of taxi: local drivers who almost never use a meter; taxis like Blue Bird which always use a meter; and Uber/Grab app-taxis that you order on your smartphone (but you can pay for in cash). In some areas, like Kuta or Denpasar, you've a choice of all three kinds of taxi. In Ubud, the local taxi cartel attempts to block all others, while in other regions it's a grey area. In Lombok there's less hassle. There were no app-taxis here at the time of research and Blue Birds operated freely in the Senggigi and Mataram areas. Wherever you are, hotel and restaurant staff will know the score and be able to advise.

Local taxi drivers tout for business on street corners, and many villages and towns have an organised cartel of drivers who effectively monopolize the local taxi business (and intimidate cheaper rivals like Uber, and Bluebird). You'll see signs all over the island with "No Uber" or "No Grab". These local drivers set their own (high) tariffs, which you'll have to use. Some expats refer to them as 'taxi mafia'. They'll usually allow rival cabs to drop-off customers but not pick up from their patch.

Metered **taxis** have a "Taxi" sign on the roof. They cruise for business in Kuta, Sanur, Nusa Dua, Jimbaran and Denpasar on Bali, and around Mataram and Senggigi on Lombok. The best company is the highly efficient light-blue Blue Bird Bali/Lombok taxis (Bali ☎ 0361 701111, Lombok ☎ 0370 627000, 🌐 bluebird group.com). Blue Bird rates are reasonable and drivers courteous. A trip from Kuta to Denpasar is around Rp75,000 or Rp120,000 to Sanur.

App taxis are quite new in Bali (and not yet available in Lombok). Uber and Grab are the two main companies. Rates vary on demand, but are a lot cheaper than using local drivers, and usually quite a bit less than a Blue Bird. Note that local drivers try to ban Uber cabs in many areas of Bali to protect their own trade.

Cidomo

The traditional form of transport in Lombok was the horse and cart (cidomo). Today they survive in the Gili Islands (where all motorized vehicles are banned). Prices are fixed, and very expensive.

Rental vehicles

There's a big selection of vehicles available for rental on the islands; think about your itinerary before you decide what you need. In the mountains, you need power for the slopes and on rougher terrain clearance is vital.

Renters must produce an **International Driving Permit**. On major public holidays (like Galungan and Nyepi) vehicles are snapped up quickly, so make arrangements in advance. Rental vehicles need to have both Balinese and Lombok registration to travel on both islands, so you must tell the rental agency if you intend to take the vehicle between the islands, and check with them exactly what paperwork is required.

Local and international rental companies operate – see the Arrival and Departure and Getting Around sections for the major resorts in the Guide chapters, or enquire at your hotel. Typical daily **rates** are around Rp180,000–200,000 for a Suzuki Jimny or Toyoto Avanza, a bit more for a Kijang. Discounts are available for longer rentals.

Some outfits offer partial **insurance** as part of the fee; typically, the maximum you'll end up paying in the event of any accident will usually be $200–500. The conditions of insurance policies vary considerably and you should make certain you know what you're signing. Bear in mind that under this system, if there is minor damage – for example if you smash a light – you'll end up paying the whole cost of it.

Before you take a vehicle, **check** it thoroughly and record any damage that has already been done, or you may end up being blamed for it. Most vehicle rental agencies keep your passport as security, so you don't have a lot of bargaining power in the case of any dispute. Wherever you get the vehicle from, take an emergency telephone number to contact if your car breaks down.

On the road

Traffic in Indonesia drives **on the left**, and there's a maximum speed limit (except on tollways) of 70km/hr (though you'll be lucky to average 30km/hr in traffic-choked south and west Bali). Foreign drivers need to carry an **International Driving Permit** and the **registration documents** of the vehicle or are liable to a fine. Seatbelts must be used. The police carry out regular spot checks and you'll be fined for any infringements.

Occasionally police stop foreign drivers for supposed infringements and "fine" them on the spot in what is essentially an extortion racket. If it happens to you, the best advice is to keep calm and have some easily accessible notes well away from your main stash of cash if you have to hand some over.

It's worth driving extremely defensively. **Accidents** are always unpleasant, disagreements over the insurance situation and any repairs can be lengthy, and many local people have a straightforward attitude to accidents involving tourists – the visitor must be to blame. Don't drive at **night** unless you absolutely have to, largely because pedestrians, cyclists, food carts and horse carts all use the roadway without any lights. There are also plenty of roadside ditches.

Note that many **petrol stations** are cash-only.

Hiring a driver

Hundreds of drivers in tourist areas offer **chartered transport** – this means you rent their vehicle (generally cars or jeeps) with them as the driver. Ojeks (single-passenger motorbike taxis) are also common. You're expected to pay for the driver's meals on all trips and accommodation if the trip takes more than a day, and you must be very clear about who is paying for fuel, where you want to go and stop, and how many people will be travelling. With somebody driving who knows the roads, you've got plenty of time to look around and fewer potential problems to worry about, but it's very difficult to guarantee the quality of the driving. If you're hiring a driver just for the day, you'll generally pay Rp500,000–600,000 for the vehicle, driver and fuel. Try to get a personal recommendation of reliable drivers – we've listed our recommendations in Senggigi (see p.260). Alternatively, check the Bali and Lombok Travel Forum (ⓦ travelforum.org/bali).

Motorbike and bicycle rental

Motorbikes available for rent vary from scooters through small 100cc jobs to more robust trail-bikes. Prices start at around Rp50,000 per day without insurance, with discounts for longer rentals. Officially you're supposed to have an **international motorcycle licence**, and if you're stopped by the police without one expect to pay a fine of Rp50,000 or more. Conditions on Bali and Lombok are not suitable for inexperienced drivers, with heavy traffic on major routes, steep hills and difficult driving off the beaten track. There are increasing numbers of accidents involving tourists, so don't take risks. All motorcyclists, both drivers and passengers, must wear a helmet; these will be provided by the rental outlet, but most aren't up to much.

In most tourist areas, it's possible to rent a **bicycle** for around Rp25,000 a day; check its condition before you set off and carry plenty of water.

Helmets, puncture repair kits and locks may or may not be provided so, if you intend to cycle a lot, it would be wise to take your own. There is occasional bag-snatching from bicycles in less populated areas, so attach your bag securely to yourself or the bike. Ubud is a popular area for cycling day-trips and guided rides (see p.126) and they are available in Lombok (see p.260); on the Gili Islands cycling is the only way to get around, other than walking or in a horse and cart.

Flights

Tickets for all domestic flights can be booked online, or there are ticket sales counters in airports. Typical fares between Bali and Lombok are from US$25 and there are at least eight daily flights.

Accommodation

Whatever your budget, the overall standard of accommodation in Bali and Lombok is very high. Even basic lodgings are generally enticing, nearly always set in a tropical garden and with outdoor seating. Interiors can be a bit sparse – and dimly lit – but the verandas encourage you to do as local people do and spend your waking hours outdoors.

Most budget places to stay are classed as **losmen**, a term that literally means homestay but most commonly describes any small-scale and inexpensive operation. Some offer the option of hot water and air conditioning, and many include **breakfast** (*makan pagi*) in the price of the room. Very few losmen offer **single rooms** (*kamar untuk satu orang*), so solo travellers will normally be given a double room at 75–100 percent of the full price. Hostels, with dorm beds and a social vibe, are also becoming part of the accommodation

BALI AND LOMBOK'S TOP 5 PLACES TO STAY
Ubud's green haven: *Bambu Indah*. See p.139
Stylish seaside resort: *Qunci Villas*. See p.262
Fantasy island hotel: *Tugu*. See p.266
Home from home: *Yuli's Homestay*. See p.278
Pererenan elegance: *FC Residence*. See p.70

scene in key backpacker hangouts like Kuta Bali and Gili Trawangan.

Nearly all other accommodation falls into the **hotels** category, most of which offer air conditioning and a swimming pool. Rooms in both losmen and hotels are often in **"cottages"** (sometimes known as **"bungalows"**), which can be anything from terraced concrete cubes to detached rice-barn-style chalets (*lumbung*). Bali in particular does **boutique hotels** very well: small, intimate places, often with gorgeous rural views and tasteful Balinese furnishings. The islands' **super-luxury hotels** tend to give you more for your money than similarly priced hotels in the West, especially when suites come with private plunge pools and living areas.

Villas are luxurious private holiday homes with pools and kitchens; they're especially good for families. They can be rented by the day or week and often include the services of a housekeeper and cook. Be aware, though, that a growing number of villas operate illegally, without government licences, which means they could get closed down at any time; you may be able to check a villa's licence online, and licences must be displayed prominently on the premises. Online villa-rental **agencies** include ⓦ balion.com and ⓦ balivillas .com. Airbnb (ⓦ airbnb.com) also has a wide selection of villas and apartments.

ACCOMMODATION PRICES

Unless stated otherwise, all the accommodation prices in this Guide are based on the cost of the cheapest double room in high season, including tax; when a hotel offers both fan and a/c rooms, the former is the cheapest option and the price that's quoted. Rates in low season may be up to fifty percent lower and booking via online agencies at any time may give you significant discounts. Many losmen and hotels quote their rates exclusive of government **tax** (ten or eleven percent); many of the more expensive hotels add an extra five or ten percent **service charge** (in hotel-speak, these supplements are usually referred to as "plus-plus").

The smartest hotels quote their rates in **US dollars**, or sometimes in **euros**, and usually accept cash and credit cards, but will also convert to rupiah. In the Guide, we have quoted accommodation prices in the currency used by the establishment.

BATHROOMS

Most losmen and hotel rooms have en-suite **bathrooms** (*kamar mandi*). **Toilets** (*wc*, pronounced *way say*) are usually Western style, though flushing is sometimes done manually, with water scooped from an adjacent pail. The same pail and scoop are used by Indonesians to wash themselves after going to the toilet (using the left hand, never the right, which is for eating), but most tourist bathrooms also have toilet paper.

Many Balinese and Sasak people still **bathe** in rivers, but indoor bathing is traditionally done by means of the scoop and slosh method, or **mandi**, using water that's stored in a huge basin. This basin is not a bath, so never get in it; all washing is done outside it and the basin should not be contaminated by soap or shampoo. Many losmen and all hotels in the bigger resort areas provide showers as well as *mandi*. Outside the bigger resorts, the very cheapest rooms may not have hot water (*air panas*).

In the more stylish places, bathrooms can be delightful, particularly if they are designed to be open to the sky and bedecked with plants. These "**garden bathrooms**" often have showers and *mandi* fed by water piped through sculpted flues and floors covered in a carpet of smooth, rounded pebbles. However, they're not to everyone's taste, especially as they can also attract squadrons of bloodthirsty mosquitoes.

Camping is not popular in Bali: it's not easy to get permission to camp in Bali Barat National Park and it's considered inappropriate to camp on the slopes of Bali's most sacred mountains, although camping on Lombok's Gunung Rinjani is normal practice and tents and sleeping bags can be rented for the climb.

Room rates in all classes of accommodation can vary considerably according to demand. During **low season** (Feb–June and Sept–Nov) many moderate and expensive hotels also offer good discounts on walk-in rates. In **peak season** (July, Aug and the Christmas holidays), however, rates can rise dramatically, especially in Amed, Canggu and on the Gili Islands; rooms are at a premium during these months so it's advisable to **reserve** ahead. **Check-out time** is usually noon.

Food and drink

Bali and Lombok cuisine is spicy, sweet and incredibly varied with rich curries, fragrant soups, delicious noodle dishes, steamed vegetables and Chinese-style stir-fries all competing for your tummy's attention. The more local you go, the more authentic the meal. In the main tourist regions, most restaurants tend to serve more generic Indonesian food and a multitude of Western and Asian dishes. For really genuine Balinese and Sasak food, head to night markets and warung (simple local cafés).

At the inexpensive end of the scale, you can get a bowl of *bakso ayam* (chicken noodle soup) for around Rp6000 from one of the **carts** (*kaki lima*) on the streets and at night markets after dark. Slightly smarter are **warung** and rumah makan (eating houses), ranging from a few tables and chairs in a kitchen to fully fledged **restaurants**. There's usually a menu, but in the simplest places it's just rice or noodle dishes on offer. Most places that call themselves restaurants cater for a broader range of tastes, offering Western, Indonesian and Chinese food, while others specialize in a particular cuisine such as Mexican, Japanese or Italian. The multinational fast-food chains have also arrived in the tourist and city areas.

Vegetarians get a good deal, with tofu (*tahu*) and *tempeh*, a fermented soybean cake, alongside plenty of fresh vegetables.

Restaurant **etiquette** is pretty much the same as in the West, with waiter service the norm. If you're eating with friends, don't count on everyone's meal arriving together.

Prices vary dramatically depending on the location rather than the quality of the meals. In the humblest local warung, a simple dish such as *nasi campur* is about Rp12,000–22,000, while basic tourist restaurant prices start at around Rp30,000–40,000 for their version of the same dish with the sky the limit in the plushest locations. If you choose non-Indonesian food such as pizza, pasta and steak, prices start at around Rp50,000 in tourist restaurants and again become stratospheric for imported steaks with all the trimmings in swanky locations. Bear in mind that restaurants with more expensive food also have pricier drinks and, in addition, most places add anything up to 21 percent to the bill for tax and service.

BALI AND LOMBOK'S TOP 5 RESTAURANTS
Mozaic Ubud. See p.131
One Eyed Jack Canggu. See p.72
Sardine Kerobokan. See p.71
Pituq Café Gili Trawangan. See p.294
Sage Ubud. See p.131

In the Language section of the Guide there is a menu reader of dishes and a list of common terms (see p.340).

Styles of cooking

Throughout Bali and Lombok **Indonesian** rice- and noodle-based meals are most widely available, followed closely by **Chinese** (essentially Cantonese) food, as well as a vast array of other Asian (Thai and Japanese especially) and **Western** food in the resorts. Native Balinese food on Bali, and Sasak food on Lombok, is something you'll need to seek out. Should you wish to learn more about local food, check out the cookery schools for visitors (see p.44).

Indonesian food

Based on rice (*nasi*) or noodles (*mie* or *bakmi*), with vegetables, fish or meat, **Indonesian food** is flavoured with chillies, soy sauce (*kecap*), garlic, ginger, cinnamon, turmeric and lemongrass. You'll also find chilli sauce (*sambal*) everywhere.

One dish available in even the simplest warung is **nasi campur**, which is boiled rice with small amounts of vegetables, meat and fish, often served with *krupuk* (huge prawn crackers) and a fried egg. The accompanying dishes vary from day to day, depending on what's available. Other staples are **nasi goreng** and **mie goreng**, fried rice or noodles with vegetables, meat or fish, often with fried egg and *krupuk*. The other mainstays of the Indonesian menu are **gado-gado**, steamed vegetables served with a spicy peanut sauce, and **sate**, small kebabs of beef, pork, chicken, tofu, goat or fish, barbecued on a bamboo stick and served with spicy peanut sauce.

Fish is widely available: grilled, kebabed, baked in banana leaves or in curries. However, although tasty, by Western standards a lot of it is overcooked.

Inexpensive, authentic and traditionally fiery **Padang** dishes are sold in rumah makan Padang in every sizeable town. Padang food is pre-cooked, served room temperature and displayed on platters. There are no menus; when you enter you either select your composite meal by pointing to the dishes on display, or just sit down and let the staff bring you a selection – you pay by the number of plates you have eaten from at the end. Dishes include *kangkung* (water spinach), *tempeh*, fried aubergine, curried eggs, fried fish, meat curry, fish curry, potato cakes and fried cow's lung.

Balinese food

The everyday **Balinese** diet consists of a couple of rice-based meals, essentially *nasi campur*, eaten whenever people feel hungry, supplemented with snacks such as *krupuk*. The full magnificence of Balinese cooking is reserved for ceremonies. One of the best dishes is **babi guling**, spit-roasted pig, served with *lawar*, a spicy blood mash. Another speciality is **betutu bebek**, smoked duck, cooked very slowly – this has to be ordered in advance from restaurants.

The Balinese rarely eat desserts but **bubuh injin**, black rice pudding, named after the colour of the rice husk, is available in tourist spots. The rice is served with a sweet coconut-milk sauce, fruit and grated coconut. Rice cakes (*jaja*) play a major part in ceremonial offerings but are also a daily food.

Sasak food

According to some sources, the name "Lombok" translates as "chilli pepper" – highly appropriate considering the savage heat of traditional **Sasak food**. It's not easy to track down, however, and you'll find Indonesian and Chinese food far more widely available on Lombok. Traditional Sasak food uses rice as the staple, together with a wide variety of vegetables, a little meat (although no pork), and some fish, served in various sauces, often with a dish of **chilli sauce** on the side in case it isn't hot enough already. Anything with *pelecing* in the name is served with chilli sauce. Taliwang dishes, originally from Sumbawa, are also available on Lombok, consisting of grilled or fried food with, you've guessed it, a chilli sauce. All parts of the animals are eaten, and you'll find plenty of offal on the menu.

Fine dining

Just as it's possible to get by spending a dollar or less for a meal in Bali or Lombok, you can also enjoy some superb **fine dining** experiences on the islands. Plenty of innovative chefs, some Western, some Asian, have imported and adapted modern international gourmet cooking. They offer menus that are creative and imaginative and, best of all, taste great. Restaurants serving this food are invariably stylish, with excellent service, charging $30 or more per head.

BETEL

One habit that you'll notice in villages, mainly among older people, is the chewing of **betel**. Small parcels, made up of three ingredients – areca nut wrapped in betel leaf that has been smeared with lime – are lodged inside the cheek. When mixed with saliva, these are a stimulant as well as producing an abundance of bright red saliva, which is regularly spat out on the ground and eventually stains the lips and teeth red. Other ingredients can be added according to taste, including tobacco, cloves, cinnamon, cardamom, turmeric and nutmeg. You may also come across decorated boxes used to store the ingredients on display in museums.

Fresh fruit

The range of **fresh fruit** available on Bali and Lombok is startling. You'll see **bananas**, **coconuts** and **papaya** growing all year round, and **pineapples** and **watermelons** are always in the markets. Of the citrus fruits, the giant **pomelo** is the most unusual to visitors – larger than a grapefruit and sweeter. **Guavas**, **avocados** (served as a sweet fruit juice with condensed milk), **passion fruit**, **mangoes**, **soursops** and their close relative, the **custard apple**, are all common. Less familiar are seasonal **mangosteens** with a purple skin and sweet white flesh; hairy **rambutans**, closely related to the lychee; **salak** or **snakefruit**, named after its brown scaly skin; and **star fruit**, which is crunchy but rather flavourless. **Jackfruit**, which usually weighs 10–20kg, has firm yellow segments around a large stone inside its green bobbly skin. This is not to be confused with the **durian**, also large but with a spiky skin and a pungent, sometimes almost rotten, odour. Some airlines and hotels ban it because of the smell, but devoted fans travel large distances and pay high prices for good-quality durian fruit.

Drinks

Bottled water (see p.35) is widely available throughout the islands (Rp3000–5000 for 1.5 litres in supermarkets), as are international brands of **soft drinks**; you'll pay higher prices in restaurants. There are also delicious **fruit juices**, although many restaurants automatically add sugar to their juices so you'll need to specify *tampa gulah* (without sugar) if you don't want that.

Indonesians are great **coffee** (*kopi*) and **tea** (*teh*) drinkers. Locally grown coffee (*kopi Bali* or *kopi Lombok*) is drunk black, sweet and strong. The coffee isn't filtered, so the grounds settle in the bottom of the glass. If you want milk added or you don't want sugar, you'll have to ask (see p.340). Increasing numbers of espresso machines have arrived in the swisher tourist restaurants along with imported coffee, so lattes and flat whites are readily available if you want one. One coffee you could consider avoiding is *kopi luwak*, which is an expensive blend made from coffee beans that have been ingested by, and then secreted by civets. Most of these captive civets are kept in cramped, inhumane conditions.

Alcohol

Locally produced **beer** includes Bintang, a light, reasonably palatable lager. Expect to pay around Rp25,000 for a 620ml bottle from a supermarket or Rp32,000 and upwards in a restaurant or bar. Draught beer is available in some places. There are four varieties of locally brewed organic Storm beer from the palest (like a British bitter ale) to the darkest (a stout).

Many tourist restaurants and bars offer an extensive list of **cocktails** (generally Rp50,000 upwards) and imported spirits; the cheaper cocktails are invariably made with local alcohol.

Wine and spirit lovers should be aware that punitive taxes make drinking extremely expensive in Bali or Lombok: expect to pay at least Rp75,000 for a glass and upwards of Rp325,000 for a bottle of wine. Locally produced **wine** is available on Bali, made from grapes grown in the north of the island by Hatten Wines – their Aga White, rosé and sparkling wines are very drinkable. Other companies, including L'Artisan, Two Islands and Cape Discovery, use imported Australian grapes to produce wines. Imported spirits are available in major tourist areas, where wines from Australia and New Zealand, California, Europe and South America are also available.

Local liquor include *brem*, a type of rice wine, *tuak*, palm wine brewed from palm-tree sap, and

METHANOL WARNING

Be aware that **methanol-related deaths** occur most years in Bali and Lombok. Incidents are rare but have occurred in bars popular with backpackers, when cheap cocktail buckets have been tainted with methanol. Stick to beer if in any doubt.

powerful *arak*, a palm or rice spirit that is often incorporated into highly potent local cocktails.

Happy hours are common in tourist areas.

Festivals and events

Religious ceremonies and festivals remain central to Balinese life and anyone spending more than a few days on the island is likely to spot local people heading to or from temples. Visitors are welcome as long as they follow certain rules of etiquette (see p.38). Hindus on Lombok adhere to the same customs. On top of these, an array of non-religious festivals are equally appealing.

Balinese festivals

Bali has a complex timetable of religious ceremonies and festivals both local and island-wide, made even more complicated by Bali having two **traditional calendars**; the *saka* calendar, with 354–356 days, is divided into twelve months and runs eighty years behind the Gregorian year, while the *wuku* calendar is based on a 210-day lunar cycle. One of the biggest is **Galungan**, an annual event in the *wuku* calendar. This ten-day festival celebrates the victory of good over evil and the ancestral souls are thought to visit earth. Elaborate preparations take place: *penyor* – bamboo poles hung with offerings – arch over the road. Galungan day itself is spent with the family. The final and most important day is **Kuningan**, when families once again get together, pray and make offerings as the souls of the ancestors return to heaven.

The main festival of the *saka* year is New Year, **Nyepi**, generally in March or April, the major purification ritual of the year. The night before Nyepi the evil spirits are frightened away with drums, gongs, cymbals, firecrackers and huge **papier-mâché monsters** (*ogoh-ogoh*). On the day itself, everyone sits quietly at home to persuade any remaining evil spirits that Bali is completely deserted. Visitors are expected to stay quietly in their hotels.

Every temple has an annual **odalan**, an anniversary and purification ceremony. The majority of these are small, local affairs, but the celebrations at the large directional temples draw large crowds. There are also local temple festivals related to the moon, some associated with full moon and some with the night of complete darkness.

Another annual event, **Saraswati**, in honour of the goddess of knowledge (see p.313), takes place on the last day of the *wuku* year. Books are particularly venerated and the faithful are not supposed to read, while students attend special ceremonies to pray for academic success. Other annual festivals are **Tumpek Kandang**, when all animals are blessed, and **Tumpek Landep**, a day of devotion to all things made of metal, including tools, motorbikes, cars and buses.

Nonreligious anniversaries that are celebrated in Bali include April 21, **Kartini Day**, commemorating the birthday in 1879 of Raden Ajeng Kartini, an early Indonesian nationalist and the first female emancipationist. Parades, lectures and social events are attended by women, while the men and children take over their duties for the day. September 20, the anniversary of the **Badung puputan** in Denpasar in 1906 (see p.306), is commemorated each year by a fair in Alun-alun Puputan. November 20 is **Heroes Day** in Bali, in remembrance of the defeat of the nationalist forces led by Ngurah Rai at Marga in 1946 (see p.308).

The huge month-long **Arts Festival** (Ⓦ baliarts festival.com) celebrates all Balinese arts including traditional music, gamelan recitals and film and documentary screenings. It's held annually at Denpasar's Taman Werdi Budaya Arts Centre from mid-June. Watersports competitions and parades are the highlights of the **Kuta Karnival**, which runs for a week, usually in October. In Ubud, there's the **Bali Spirit Festival** of world music, dance and yoga every March (Ⓦ balispiritfestival.com) and the **Ubud Writers and Readers Festival** (Ⓦ ubud writersfestival.com), with over two hundred events, talks and workshops from an international cast of writers, every October.

Lombok's festivals

Lombok's festivals are a mixture of Hindu, Muslim and local folk events. **Ciwaratri** (in Jan) is celebrated by Hindus in West Lombok, where followers meditate without sleeping or eating for 24 hours to redeem their sins. A far more public occasion is **Nyale** (see box, p.275) which takes place every February or March near Kuta and along the south coast, attracting thousands of people to witness the first appearance of the sea worms. **The Anniversary of West Lombok**, a formal government event, takes place on April 17. **Harvest festival** is celebrated by Balinese Hindus in March/April at Gunung Pengsong, when they give thanks for the harvest by the ritual slaughter of a buffalo. **Lebaran Topat** occurs seven days after

Ramadan, when Sasak people visit family graves and the grave of Loang Baloq on the edge of Mataram.

In November or December comes **Perang Topat**, informally known as the **Ketupat War** (see p.253), a riotous and spectacular public rice-throwing battle between local Hindus and Wetu Telu followers that takes place at Pura Lingsar in Mataram. Also around this time, offerings are made at Gunung Rinjani's crater lake, Segara Anak, to ask for blessings, known as **Pekelem**, and the **Pujawali** celebration is held at Pura Kalasa temple at Narmada, at Pura Lingsar and at Pura Meru in Mataram. December 17 marks the anniversary of the political **founding of West Nusa Tenggara**. Finally, **Chinese New Year** (Imlek) sees many Chinese-run businesses closing for several days in January or February.

Health

Most travellers to Bali and Lombok experience no health issues. Traveller's diarrhoea ("Bali belly") will affect some. However, serious illness and accidents (including surfers' mishaps) can't be ruled out. All visitors should have travel insurance in case private health care and medical evacuation is needed (see p.46).

Discuss your trip with your **doctor** or a specialist travel clinic (see p.35) as early as possible to allow time to complete courses of **inoculations**. If you've come directly from a country with yellow fever, you'll need to be immunized and you should carry the immunization certificate. Apart from this no inoculations are legally required for Indonesia. However, inoculations against the following should be discussed with your medical adviser: diphtheria, hepatitis A, hepatitis B, Japanese encephalitis, polio, rabies, tetanus, typhoid and tuberculosis.

If you have any medical conditions, are pregnant or are travelling with children, it is especially important to get advice. If you need regular medication, carry it in your hand baggage and carry a certificate/letter from your doctor detailing your condition and the drugs – it can be handy for overzealous customs officials.

Treatment in Bali and Lombok

You'll find **pharmacies** (apotik), village **health clinics** (klinik) and **doctors** across the islands and **public hospitals** in each district capital and in Denpasar, supplemented by **specialist tourist** **clinics** in the main tourist areas. In local facilities the availability of English-speaking staff and their ability to tackle accidents and common tourist ailments varies from area to area. Most Balinese use local facilities together with traditional healers (balian) as they believe that physical symptoms are a sign of spiritual illness (see p.332).

If you need an **English-speaking doctor**, seek advice at your hotel (some of the luxury ones have in-house doctors). For more serious problems, you'll want to access private **clinics** in the main resorts. A couple of places on the outskirts of Kuta and Seminyak have good reputations for dealing with expat emergencies: Bali International Medical Centre (BIMC) and International SOS (see p.75) offer consultations at the clinic, doctor call-out and ambulance call-out; prices depend on the time of day or night and distance from the clinic. The only **recompression chamber** on Bali is located in Denpasar (see p.92) and there is another on Lombok (see p.287). Details of local medical facilities including **dentists** (doctor gigi) are given in the Directory section of each city account in the Guide.

Major diseases

Bali and Lombok are home to a range of diseases endemic to tropical Southeast Asia, most of which are not a threat in travellers' home countries. Inoculations are therefore strongly advised.

Most Western travellers will have had inoculations against **polio**, **tetanus**, **diphtheria** and **tuberculosis** during childhood. Travellers should check that they are still covered against them and have booster injections if necessary.

Typhoid can be lethal and is passed through contaminated food or water. It produces an extremely high fever, abdominal pains, headaches, diarrhoea and red spots on the body. Dehydration is the danger here as with all intestinal problems, so take rehydration salts and get medical help urgently. Inoculation and personal hygiene measures (see p.34) offer the best protection.

Avoid contact with all animals, no matter how cute, especially street dogs. Rabies is spread via the saliva of infected animals, most commonly cats, dogs or monkeys; it is endemic throughout Asia and all visitors to Bali should be aware of the disease. Bali was rabies-free for ten years until 2008 but since then the disease has re-established itself and it's now present throughout the island. If you see a suspicious dog you can contact the Bali Animal Welfare Association (W bawabali.com, ☎ 081 138 9004).

Hundreds of people have died in the last decade despite a major culling and vaccination programme. If you get bitten, wash the wound immediately with antiseptic and get medical help. Treatment involves a course of injections, but you won't need all of them if you have had a course of pre-departure jabs. Lombok was officially rabies-free in 2016, but given its proximity to Bali the same precautions should be taken.

Japanese encephalitis is a serious viral illness causing inflammation of the brain. It is endemic across Asia and is transmitted from infected birds and animals via mosquitoes. Inoculation is available for those planning extended periods in rural areas who are most at risk, although it is rare among travellers. The symptoms are variable but flu-like headache, fever and vomiting are common and the best advice is to seek medical help immediately if you develop these.

There are several strains of **hepatitis** (caused by viral infections) and vaccines can offer some protection against some strains. Symptoms in all of them are a yellow colouring of the skin and eyes, extreme exhaustion, fever and diarrhoea. It's one of the most common illnesses that afflicts travellers to Asia and can last for months and can also lead to chronic illness. Hepatitis A is transmitted via contaminated food and water or saliva. Hepatitis B is more serious and is transmitted via sexual contact or by contaminated blood, needles or syringes, which means that medical treatment itself can pose a risk if sterilization procedures are not up to scratch.

Malaria

Both Bali and Lombok are within **malarial zones**. Information regarding the prevalence, prevention and treatment of malaria is being constantly updated so you must seek medical advice at least a month before you travel. Current advice suggests that there is very little risk of malaria in Bali, but a low risk in Lombok. The latest information shows an increase in the most serious form of malaria across Asia and there are reports of resistance to certain drug treatments by some strains. Pregnant women and children need specialist advice.

Malaria, which can be fatal, is passed into humans in mosquito bites (one is all it takes). The appropriate prophylactic drug depends on your destination but all are taken to a strict timetable beginning before you enter the malarious area and continuing after leaving. If you don't follow instructions precisely, you're in danger of developing the illness. The symptoms are fever, headache and shivering, similar to a severe dose of flu and often coming in cycles, but a lot of people have additional symptoms. Don't delay seeking help: malaria progresses quickly. If you develop flu-like symptoms at any time up to a year after returning home, you should inform a doctor of your travels and ask for a blood test.

However, none of the antimalarial drugs is a hundred percent effective and it is vital to try to stop the mosquitoes biting you: sleep under a **mosquito net** – preferably one impregnated with an insecticide especially suited to the task – burn mosquito coils, and use **repellent** on exposed skin. The most powerful repellents should be brought from home; DEET is effective but can be an irritant and natural alternatives are available containing citronella, eucalyptus oil or neem oil.

Dengue fever

Another reason to avoid mosquito bites is **dengue fever**, caused by a virus carried by a different species of mosquito, which bites during the day. There is no vaccine or tablet available to prevent the illness – which causes fever, headache and joint and muscle pains among the least serious symptoms, and internal bleeding and circulatory system failure among the most serious – and no specific drug to cure it. Outbreaks occur across Indonesia throughout the year, but particularly during the rainy season. It is vital to get an early medical diagnosis and obtain treatment to relieve symptoms.

AIDS/HIV

Bali has a high rate of HIV/AIDS cases; bear in mind, as well, that other travellers may be infected. Many people with HIV are also infected with hepatitis. **Condoms** can be bought on both islands, but it's advisable to bring your own too.

General precautions

Precautions while you are travelling can reduce your chances of getting ill. Personal hygiene is vital and it pays to use some discretion about choosing where to eat – if the bits you can see are filthy, imagine the state of the kitchen. Avoid **food** that has sat around in the heat in favour of freshly cooked meals; food prepared in fancy tourist places is just as likely to be suspect as that from simple street stalls. **Ice** is supposedly prepared under regulated conditions in Indonesia, but it's impossible to be sure how it has been transported or stored since leaving the factory. If you're being really careful, avoid ice in your drinks – a lot easier said than done in the heat. Treat even small cuts or scrapes with antiseptic. Wear flip-flops or thongs in the bathroom rather than walk around barefoot.

Water hygiene

Do not drink untreated tap **water** on Bali or Lombok, as it is likely to contain disease-causing micro-organisms. **Bottled water** is available every-where and refilling facilities are becoming more widespread (cutting down on plastic waste). Or you can buy **purifying tablets**, **water filters** and **water purifiers** from travel clinics (see below) and specialist outdoor-equipment retailers.

Heat and skin problems

Travellers are at risk of **sunburn** and **dehydration**. It's wise to bring your own sunscreen, which is available in Bali (less so in Lombok) but more expensive than in the West. Limit exposure to the sun in the hours around noon, use high-factor sunscreen and wear sunglasses and a hat. Make sure that you drink enough as you'll be sweating mightily in the heat. If you're urinating very little or your urine turns dark (this can also indicate hepatitis), increase your fluid intake. When you sweat you lose salt, so add some extra to your food or take oral rehydration salts (see below).

A more serious result of the heat is **heatstroke**, indicated by high temperature, dry skin and a fast, erratic pulse. As an emergency measure, try to cool the patient off by covering them in sheets or sarongs soaked in cold water and turn the fan on them; they may need to go to hospital, though.

Heat rashes, **prickly heat** and fungal infections are also common; wear loose cotton clothing, dry yourself carefully after bathing and use medicated talcum powder or antifungal powder if you fall victim.

Intestinal trouble

The priority with an **upset stomach** is to prevent dehydration. Start drinking **rehydration solution** as soon as the attack starts, even if you're vomiting as well, and worry about a diagnosis later. Rehydra-tion salts (such as Oralit and Pharolit) are widely available in pharmacies but it makes sense to carry some with you. The home-made form of these consists of eight teaspoons of sugar and half a teaspoon of salt dissolved in a litre of clean water.

Stomach upsets can either be a reaction to a change of diet or can signal something more serious. You should seek medical advice if the attack is particularly severe, lasts more than a couple of days

or is accompanied by constant, severe abdominal pain or fever, blood or mucus in your diarrhoea or smelly farts and burps.

Drugs such as Lomotil and Imodium, which stop diarrhoea, should only be used if you get taken ill on a journey or must travel while ill; they are not a cure, and simply paralyse your gut, temporarily plugging you up, at a time when your insides need to get rid of the toxins causing the problem.

Many travellers find locally available charcoal remedies effective against diarrhoea.

Cuts, bites and stings

Divers should familiarize themselves with potential **underwater hazards** and the appropriate first aid, although you're more at risk from bad diving practices and coral scrapes than from tangling with sharks, sea snakes, stingrays or jellyfish. All cuts should be cleansed and disinfected immediately, covered and kept dry until healed.

On the land, there are poisonous **snakes** on both Bali and Lombok, although they're only likely to attack if you step on them – they are most often encountered in ricefields, so if you are exploring these look where you're stepping. In jungle areas wear long thick socks to protect your legs when trekking and walk noisily. If you're bitten, try to remember what the snake looked like, move as little as you can and send someone for medical help. Under no circumstances do anything heroic with a Swiss army knife. There are also a few poisonous **spiders** in Bali and Lombok, and if you're bitten by one you should also immobilize the limb and get medical help. If you get **leeches** attached to you while trekking in the jungle in the rainy season, use a dab of salt, suntan oil or a cigarette to persuade them to let go, rather than just pulling them off.

MEDICAL RESOURCES FOR TRAVELLERS

Canadian Society for International Health ☎ 613 241 5785, 🌐 csih.org. Extensive list of travel health centres.

CDC ☎ 1800 232 4636, 🌐 cdc.gov/travel. Official US government travel health site.

Hospital for Tropical Diseases Travel Clinic UK 🌐 www.thehtd.org/TravelClinic.aspx

International Society for Travel Medicine US ☎ 1404 373 8282, 🌐 istm.org. Has a full list of travel health clinics.

MASTA (Medical Advisory Service for Travellers Abroad) UK 🌐 masta-travel-health.com

Tropical Medical Bureau Ireland ☎ 01 2715 200, 🌐 tmb.ie.

The Travel Doctor 🌐 traveldoctor.com.au. Lists travel clinics in Australia, New Zealand and South Africa.

Outdoor activities

The sea and the mountains are the two great focuses of outdoor activities in Bali and Lombok. Both islands have world-class surf breaks, excellent diving and spectacular volcano hikes.

Surfing

Bali's volcanic reef-fringed coastline has made the island one of the world's great **surfing** centres, with a reputation for producing an unusually high number of perfect and consistent tubes and waves. There are also plenty of gentler beach breaks, which are ideal for beginners.

From April to October, the southeast trade winds blow offshore, fanning the waves off **Bali**'s southwest coast and off Nusa Lembongan. This is both the best time of year for surf and the pleasantest, as it's also the dry season. The most famous and challenging of the southwestern breaks are around **Uluwatu** on the Bukit Peninsula – at **Balangan** (see p.78), **Dreamland** (see p.79), **Bingin** (see p.79), **Padang Padang** (see p.80) and **Suluban** (see p.80). These are tough, world-class breaks and get very crowded, particularly from June to August; small, surfer-oriented resorts have grown up around each one. **Nusa Lembongan**'s breaks can be less busy but are also challenging (see p.98). Novice and less confident surfers generally start with the breaks around **Kuta** (see p.59), **Canggu** (see p.63) and **Medewi** (see p.235). From November to March, the winds blow from the northwest, bringing rain to Bali's main beach breaks, though the lesser breaks off eastern Bali, around **Sanur** (see p.92) and **Nusa Dua** (see p.82), are still surfable at this time of year.

On **Lombok**, Bangko Bangko's **Desert Point** (see p.255) is rated as one of the world's top breaks, but there are plenty of other good breaks for all levels of experience around **Kuta** on the south coast (see p.275), including at **Gerupuk**, **Mawi**, **Ekas** and **Selong Blanak**.

Bali and Lombok have so many different breaks that it's worth doing your homework and being selective if you're a novice; even pros find the tougher breaks very challenging.

Equipment, lessons and information

The main **surf centres** are Kuta, Bali and Kuta, Lombok. In both these resorts you'll find shops that rent **boards** from around Rp50,000 per day, sell new boards and international-brand equipment, and repair boards. The coastline is dotted with surf instructors (a local guy who might charge US$15 per hour) and professional **surf schools** (lessons from around $50 per half-day). There is also a women-only luxury surf camp, Surf Goddess Retreats (Ⓦ surf goddessretreats.com), in Seminyak. For detailed reviews of surf breaks, see the **book** Indo Surf and Lingo, widely available in Bali and from Ⓦ indosurf. com.au (this website is also a good source of information), as is Bali Waves Ⓦ baliwaves.com).

Many **airlines** will take boards in the hold for free as long as your total luggage weight doesn't exceed 20kg, but call to check if they require special insurance. Board bags with straps are a good idea, as some breaks are only accessible by motorbike. Some **tourist shuttle buses** on Bali and Lombok refuse to carry boards, though Perama buses will take them for an extra fee. You may be best off renting a car or a motorbike to get to the breaks. In the main centres, it's easy to rent **motorbikes** with special surfboard clips already attached.

Diving and snorkelling

Bali and Lombok are encircled by reefs that offer excellent and varied year-round **diving and snorkelling**. The main **dive resorts on Bali** are at Amed (see p.183), Candidasa (see p.172), Nusa Lembongan (see p.98), Padang Bai (see p.168), Pemuteran (see p.238) and Tulamben (see p.188); the beach resort of Sanur (see p.92) also has many dive operators but is further from the best dive sites. The Gili Islands are another hugely popular dive destination, with many established schools and diving right offshore. Lombok's southwest peninsula and islands (see p.254) are growing in popularity with divers, and there are a few dive sites on the island's south coast that dive shops in Kuta (see p.66) head to for advanced divers only.

Most of these dive sites are also rewarding for **snorkelling**, though obviously the shallowest reefs are best. Many hotels and boat captains offer dedicated snorkelling trips from about Rp200,000 per person, including gear. Some dive centres will also take accompanying snorkellers for a reduced rate.

Freediving schools based in Amed (see p.186) and the Gili Islands (see p.287) offer professional tuition and internationally recognized courses for those who want to experience the thrill of breath-hold diving.

Dive centres and courses

There are dozens of **dive centres** on Bali and Lombok. If possible, get recommendations from other divers as well, and check the centre's PADI

(Wpadi.com) or SSI (Wdivessi.com) accreditation. Most are highly professional but there a few dodgy dive operators in Bali and Lombok that fake their PADI credentials, and others that are not PADI dive centres, though their staff may be individually certified.

Technical diving using gases other than compressed air is gaining in popularity in Bali and Lombok; the relevant associations are Technical Diving International (Wtdisdi.com) and IANTD (Wiantd.com). Avoid **booking** ahead online without knowing anything else about the dive centre, and be wary of any operation offering extremely cheap courses: maintaining diving equipment is an expensive business in Indonesia, so any place offering unusually good rates will probably be compromising your safety. Ask to meet your instructor or dive leader, look at their qualifications, find out how many people there'll be in your group (four divers to one dive master is a good ratio) and whether they're a similar level to you, and look over the equipment, checking the quality of the air in the tanks yourself and also ensuring there's an oxygen cylinder on board. Dive centres that use their own boats, rather than renting one with a crew, tend to take better care of equipment.

Most dive centres charge similar **rates**. One-day **dive trips** usually cost from $50–100 including equipment, PADI Open Water courses are $350–500 (dive shops must include the dive manual and exam papers in this price). Most dive centres also run PADI's introductory Discover Scuba course for novice and Scuba Review for those needing a refresher.

In the Gilis all divers contribute a one-off payment of Rp50,000 to the Gili Eco Trust Fund which goes towards the maintenance of buoys on dive sites, patrols against illegal fishing and reef clean-ups.

Safety and information

When planning your trip, note that as you shouldn't go anywhere that's more than **300m above sea level** for eighteen hours following a dive, you'll have to be careful neither to fly straight after your dive, nor to go into the highlands of Bali or Lombok. Specifically that means the Kintamani (Batur) region, Wongayagede and Sanda are all temporarily out of bounds on Bali, as are Senaru and Rinjani on Lombok.

Bali's **recompression chamber** is at Sanglah Public Hospital (see p.92) but any reputable dive centre should organize treatment for you in the very unlikely event that you need it. There is also a recompression chamber on Lombok (see p.287). Make sure your travel insurance covers you, as treatment can cost upwards of $4000.

Hiking

The most challenging **hikes** on Bali and Lombok take you up the islands' towering volcanoes, but there are also lots of gentler treks through ricefields in the interior. The biggest undertaking is the ascent of Lombok's **Gunung Rinjani** (see p.266), which involves at least one night on the mountain, or more time if you want to reach the summit and the crater lake; guides are obligatory for this. Bali's holiest peak, **Gunung Agung** (see p.162), also involves a very strenuous guided climb, but the ascent and descent can be managed in one day. **Gunung Batur** (see p.192), also on Bali, is a much easier proposition and by far the most popular of the volcano walks; don't be put off by this, though, as the sunrise from the top is glorious. **Gunung Batukaru** is less commonly hiked but guides are available at the several starting points (see p.228).

The most popular centre for **ricefield treks** is Ubud (see box, p.116), but arguably more rewarding are the smaller and far less busy tourist centres on Bali at Sidemen (see p.166), Candidasa (see p.172), Tirtagangga (see p.180), Munduk (see p.203), Wongayagede (see p.228), Sarinbuana (see p.229) and Sanda (see p.241). There are good hikes inside the Taman Nasional Bali Barat (see p.234) too. In Lombok, Senaru (see p.269) and Tetebatu (see p.270) are the main hiking centres.

Rafting and kayaking

Whitewater rafting on Bali's rivers ranges from Class 2 to Class 4, so there are routes for first-timers as well as the more experienced; you can book trips in all the major coastal resorts as well as in Ubud. It's also possible to go **kayaking** on the gentler rivers, as well as on Danau Tamblingan and off Gili Trawangan; overnight kayak trips can be arranged from Senggigi.

Cycling and horseriding

Bali and Lombok both offer terrific **cycling**, and there are several tour companies that can get you off the beaten track, riding through spectacular volcanic scenery, rice paddies and craft villages. Ubud and Kintamani are hotspots for tours. Bali Bike Baik (Wwww.balibike.com) and Banyan Tree Cycling (Wwww.banyantreebiketours.com) are two good operators.

There's good **horseriding** in Kerobokan near Seminyak, at Yeh Gangga, in Kuta (Lombok) and on Gili Trawangan.

Spas, traditional beauty treatments and yoga

Herbal medicines or *jamu* (see p.134) and massages using oils and pastes made from locally grown plants have long played an important role in traditional Indonesian health care. In the last few years, this resource has been adapted for the tourist market, with dozens of spas and salons now offering traditional beauty treatments to visitors.

The biggest concentrations of hotel **spas** and traditional beauty salons are in Seminyak/Petitenget (see p.74) and Ubud (see p.134) but there are many more across Bali and Lombok: browse Bali Spa Guide (Ⓦbalispaguide.com) for a comprehensive database.

Treatments

The most famous traditional treatment is the Javanese exfoliation rub, **mandi lulur**, in which you're painted and then massaged with a turmeric-based paste. Such is its apparent power to beautify that Javanese brides are said to have a *lulur* treatment every day for the forty days before their wedding ceremonies. Another popular body wrap is the **Balinese boreh**, a warming blend of cloves, pepper and cardamom that improves circulation and invigorates muscles. Most scrub treatments include a gentle Balinese-style massage and a moisturizing "milk bath"; prices (/hr) vary from around Rp130,000 to more than Rp1,200,000, depending on the poshness of

> ### YOGA AND HOLISTIC THERAPIES
> Ubud-based Bali Spirit (see p.134) is an excellent resource for all things **holistic** in Bali; the website (Ⓦbalispirit.com) carries a detailed programme of all upcoming yoga retreats. Regular **yoga sessions and courses** are held all over Bali, including Kuta, Seminyak, Canggu (see p.67), Ubud (see p.135), Sanur (see p.95), Munduk (see p.204), Gili Air (see p.98) and in Lombok in Gili Trawangan (see p.290), Senggigi and Kuta (see p.277). There are also good pilates studios near Canggu (see p.67) and Ubud (see p.135).

the venue. Prices for a simple massage start at around Rp60,000 for a half-hour rub on the beach but may cost Rp750,000 or more at a top hotel. On Bali, some massage centres also run massage **courses**, such as in Seminyak (see p.67).

Culture and etiquette

The people of Bali and Lombok are extremely generous about opening up their homes, temples and festivals to interested tourists but, though they're long-suffering and rarely show obvious displeasure, they do take great offence at certain aspects of Western behaviour. The most sensitive issues on the islands are Westerners' clothing – or lack of it – and the code of practice that's required when visiting holy places.

Religious etiquette

Anyone entering a **Balinese temple** (*pura*) is required to show **respect** to the gods by treating their shrines with due deference (not climbing on them or placing themselves in a higher position) and by **dressing modestly**: skimpy clothing, bare shoulders and shorts are all unacceptable, and in many temples you'll be required to wear a sarong (usually provided at the gate of the most-visited temples). In addition, you should wear a **ceremonial sash** around your waist whenever you visit a temple. These can be bought cheaply at most shops selling sarongs, and can be of any style; they too are provided for visitors to popular temples.

When attending special **temple ceremonies**, cremations and other village festivals, you should try to dress up as formally as possible: sarongs and sashes are obligatory, and shirts with buttons are preferable to T-shirts. Don't walk in front of anyone who's praying, or take their photo, and try not to sit higher than the priest or the table of offerings. Never use a flash.

At temples, you'll be expected to give a **donation** towards upkeep (Rp10,000 or so is an acceptable amount) and to sign the donation book.

Because the shedding of blood is considered to make someone **ritually unclean** (*sebel*) in Balinese Hinduism, women are not allowed to enter a temple, or to attend any religious ceremonies, during **menstruation**, and the same applies to

BALINESE CASTE AND NAMES

Balinese society is structured around a hereditary **caste system**, which, while far more relaxed than its Indian counterpart, does nonetheless carry certain restrictions and rules of etiquette, as ordained in the Balinese Hindu scriptures. Of these, the one that travellers are most likely to encounter is the practice of **naming** a person according to their caste.

At the top of the tree is the **Brahman** caste, whose men are honoured with the title **Ida Bagus** and whose women are generally named **Ida Ayu**, sometimes shortened to **Dayu**. Traditionally revered as the most scholarly members of society, only Brahmans are allowed to become high priests (*pedanda*).

Satriya (sometimes spelt Ksatriya) form the second strata of Balinese society, and these families are descendants of warriors and rulers. The Balinese rajas were all Satriya and their offspring continue to bear telltale names: **Cokorda**, **Anak Agung**, **Ratu** and **Prebagus** for men, and **Anak Agung Isti** or **Dewa Ayu** for women. The merchants or **Wesia** occupy the third most important rank, the men distinguished by the title **I Gusti** or **Pregusti**, the women by the name **I Gusti Ayu**.

At the bottom of the heap comes the **Sudra** caste, the caste of the common people, which accounts for more than ninety percent of the population. Sudra children are named according to their position in the family order, with no distinction made between male and female offspring. Thus, a first-born Sudra is always known as **Wayan** or, increasingly commonly, **Putu**, or **Gede** (male) or **Ilu** (female); the second-born is **Made** (or **Kadek**, or **Nengah**); the third **Nyoman** (or **Komang**) and the fourth **Ketut**. Should a fifth child be born, the naming system begins all over again with Wayan/Putu, and so it goes on. In order to distinguish between the sexes, Sudra caste names are often prefaced by "**I**" for males and "**Ni**" for females, for example I Wayan. Some Wayans and Mades prefer to be known by their second names, and many have distinctive nicknames, but you will come across many more Wayans than any other name in Bali.

Unlike their counterparts in the far more rigid Indian caste system, the Sudra are not looked down upon or denied access to specific professions (except that of *pedanda*), and a high-caste background guarantees neither a high income nor a direct line to political power.

anyone bearing a fresh wound. Under the same precepts, new mothers and their babies are also considered to be *sebel* for the first 42 days after the birth (new fathers are unclean for three days), and anyone who has been recently bereaved is *sebel* until three days after burial or cremation. These restrictions apply to non-Balinese as well, and are sometimes detailed on English-language notices outside the temple.

Mosques

On the whole, the **mosques** of Lombok and Bali don't hold much cultural or architectural interest for non-Muslim tourists, but should you have occasion to visit one, it's as well to be aware of certain Islamic practices. Everyone is required to take off their shoes before entering, and to wear long sleeves and long trousers; women should cover their shoulders and may also be asked to cover their heads (bring your own scarf or shawl). Men and women always pray in separate parts of the mosque, though there are unlikely to be signs telling you where to go. Women are forbidden to engage in certain religious activities during menstruation, and this includes entering a mosque.

During the month of **Ramadan** (see p.50), devout Muslims neither eat, drink nor smoke in daylight hours. If visiting Lombok during this time, you should be sensitive to this, although you'll certainly be able to find places to eat. Adherence varies across the island at this time: it is most apparent in the south and the east, but something you might not even notice in Senggigi or the Gili Islands.

At any time of year it's highly offensive to drink alcohol near a mosque, including on the Gili Islands. If you're in a bar or restaurant compound where alcohol is served, that's fine, but drinking on the street outside a mosque is a no-no.

The body

Despite tolerating skimpy **dress** in the beach resorts, most Indonesians are extremely offended by topless and nude bathing, and by immodest attire in their towns and villages. You'll command a great deal more respect if you keep your shortest shorts, vests and bare shoulders for the seaside. This is especially true in central and eastern Lombok.

The Balinese and Sasak people themselves regularly expose their own bodies in public when

bathing in rivers and public bathing pools, but they are always treated as invisible by other bathers and passers-by. As a tourist you should do the same: to photograph a bathing Balinese would be very rude indeed. If you bathe alongside them, do as they do – nearly all Balinese women wash with their sarongs wrapped around them – and take note of the segregated areas: in public pools, the men's and women's sections are usually clearly defined, but in rivers the borders are less obvious.

According to Hindu beliefs, a person's body is a microcosm of the universe: the **head** is the most sacred part of the body and the feet the most unclean. This means that you should on no account touch a Balinese person's head – not even to pat a small child's head or to ruffle someone's hair in affection; nor should you lean over someone's head or place your body in a higher position than their head without apologizing. You should never sit with your **feet** pointed at a sacred image (best to sit with them tucked underneath you) or use them to indicate someone or something. Balinese people will never walk under a **clothes line** (for fear of their head coming into contact with underwear), so you should try not to hang your washing in public areas, and definitely don't sling wet clothes over a temple wall or other holy building. The **left hand** is used for washing after defecating, so Indonesians will never eat with it or use it to pass or receive things or to shake hands.

Social conventions

As elsewhere in Asia, Indonesians dislike **confrontational behaviour** and will rarely show anger or irritation. Tourists who lose their cool and get visibly rattled tend to be looked down on rather than feared. A major source of irritation for foreigners is the rather vague notion of **time-keeping** in Indonesia: lack of punctuality is such a national institution that there is even a word for it – *jam karet*, or rubber time.

Since the downfall of Suharto in 1998, and the subsequent democratic elections, Indonesian people seem to have become much more confident about discussing **political issues** and voicing critical opinions of the state. This is mirrored by a more open press. Religious beliefs, however, are a much more sensitive issue, and it would be bad form to instigate a debate that questions a Balinese person's faith.

You will probably find Balinese and Sasak people only too eager to find out about your **personal life** and habits. It's considered quite normal to ask "Are you married?" and to then express sorrow if you say that you aren't, and the same applies to questions about children: marriage and parenthood are essential stages in the life of most Balinese and Sasaks.

Public **displays of affection** are subdued – you're more likely to see affectionate hand-holding and hugging between friends of the same sex than between heterosexual lovers.

Tipping

It's becoming increasingly common to **tip** on Bali and Lombok, generally about ten percent to waiters (if no service charge is added to the bill), drivers and tour guides; a few thousand rupiah to bellboys and chambermaids in mid-range and upmarket hotels; and a round-up to the nearest Rp5000 for metered-taxi drivers. In non-touristy areas tipping is not expected.

Photography

While Bali and Lombok are both incredibly photogenic, not all local people want to be the subject of visitors' holiday snaps; always ask by word or gesture whether it is OK to take a photograph, and respect the answer. Be especially sensitive during religious events such as cremations and take care never to get in the way of worshippers.

Shopping

Shopping can easily become an all-consuming pastime in Bali: the range and quality of artefacts is phenomenal, and although the export trade has dulled the novelty, the bargain prices are irresistible. Bali also has a well-deserved reputation for its elegant modern designs in everything from fashion to tableware; key locations for contemporary goodies are Legian, Seminyak and Ubud. On Lombok, Senggigi has the widest choice of shops, but the real pleasure is visiting the island's pottery and textile villages.

Remember that touts, guides and drivers often get as much as fifty percent **commission** on any item sold to one of their customers – not only at the customer's expense, but also the vendor's. Many shops will organize **shipping**, but be prepared for a huge bill; the minimum container size is one cubic metre, which will set you back at least $175, even to Australia. For parcels weighing under 10kg, use the postal system (see p.50).

Arts and crafts

Locally produced arts and crafts include traditional and modern **paintings**, **pottery**, **textiles**, **basketware**, **stone sculptures** and **woodcarvings**. Though the big resorts stock a wide range of all these artefacts, there's much fun and better bargains to be had, at least on the high-quality versions, at the craft-producing **villages** themselves.

There are a couple of practical points to note when choosing **woodcarvings**. Be warned that not all "sandalwood" (*cendana*), which is an extremely expensive material, is what it seems as the aroma can be **faked** with real sandalwood sawdust or oil. In either case, the smell doesn't last that long, so either buy from an established outlet or assume that it's faked and reduce your price accordingly. **Ebony** is also commonly faked. Compare its weight with any other wood: ebony is very dense and will sink in water. Most tropical woods **crack** when exported to a less humid climate: some carvers obviate this by drying the wood in kilns, while others use polyethylene glycol (PEG) to fill the cracks before they widen. Always check for cracks before buying.

Some **stonecarvings** are also not what they seem, though shops rarely make a secret of this. Specifically, the cheapest lava-stone *paras* sculptures are usually mass-produced from moulded lava-stone paste rather than hand-carved. They're sometimes referred to as "**concrete**" statues but can still be very attractive.

Soft furnishings, clothing and jewellery

Designers make beautiful use of the sumptuous local fabrics for luxurious and unusual **soft furnishings**, including cushions, bedspreads, sheets, curtains, drapes and tablecloths. Seminyak, Legian, Canggu, Sanur and Ubud have the best outlets.

Bali also produces some great **clothes**. Kuta–Legian–Seminyak and Canggu have the classiest and most original boutiques, along with countless stalls selling beachwear. Brand-name surfwear and urban sportswear is also good value here, as are custom-made leather shoes, boots and jackets.

Bali's small but thriving **silver** and **gold** industry is based in the village of Celuk, where silversmiths sell to the public from their workshops. For more unusual jewellery, you're better off scouring the jewellery shops in Kuta, Ubud, Lovina and Candidasa, where designs tend to be more innovative and prices similar, if not lower. Lombok is known for its bargain-priced imported freshwater **pearls**, and for its home-grown South Sea pearls; shops in Mataram are best for the latter, while Senggigi vendors sell the imports.

WHERE TO SHOP

Basketware In Lombok: Sayang-Sayang. In Bali: Tenganan; Pengosekan.
Beaded bags, **necklaces**, **shoes** Penestanan; Kuta (Bali); Ubud.
Books Ubud.
Ceramics Pejaten; Jimbaran.
Fashion Kuta–Legian–Seminyak; Canggu; Ubud; Sanur; Gili Trawangan.
Furniture Modern furniture in Kerobokan; Seminyak. Repro antique furniture from Batubulan, Mas, Seminyak and Senggigi, Lombok.
Interior decor and soft furnishings Seminyak; Legian; Canggu; Ubud; Sanur; Tegalalang–Pujung road.
Jewellery and silver Celuk is Bali's main silver-producing village; shops in Kuta, Seminyak, Canggu, Ubud, Lovina and Candidasa. Gold shops on Jl Hasanudin, Denpasar. Freshwater and South Sea pearls in Mataram and Senggigi, Lombok.
Leather shoes and jackets Kuta (Bali).

Markets and pasar seni In Bali: Sukawati; Ubud; Denpasar. In Lombok: Mataram; Senggigi.
Masks Mas; Singapadu.
Paintings Ubud area; Batuan; Kamasan.
Pottery In Lombok: Mataram; Senggigi; Banyumulek; Gili Meno; Penakak.
Puppets Sukawati.
Stone sculptures Batubulan.
Textiles Traditional *ikat* in Tenganan, Gianyar, Sidemen and Singaraja in Bali; and in Mataram and Sukarara in Lombok. Traditional Sumba and Flores textiles in Kuta (Bali), Ubud and Candidasa. Batik and dress fabrics in Denpasar, especially Jl Sulawesi. Mass-produced and hand-printed batik sarongs in *pasar seni* and tourist shops in Kuta (Bali), Sukawati, Ubud, Lovina, Sanur, Candidasa and Senggigi.
Woodcarvings Unpainted figurines from Mas, Ubud and Nyuhkuning. Painted wooden artefacts from villages along the Tegalalang–Pujung road.

Furniture

Several shops in Bali and Lombok advertise, quite ingenuously, "Antiques made to order". The **antiques** in question generally either come from Java or are **reproductions** of mostly Javanese items, chiefly **furniture**, screens, carved panels, window shutters and doors. Weatherworn or fashionably distressed, most of the furniture is heavy, made from hardwoods like teak. Check items for rot and termite damage (genuine teak is resistant to termites).

There is an increasing demand for contemporary **modern furniture** on Bali. The best place to browse is the region north of Seminyak, around Kerobokan.

Travelling with children

The Balinese make a great fuss of their own and other people's children, and permit them to go pretty much anywhere.

One peculiar cultural convention you might encounter, though, is that the Balinese abhor young children crawling on the ground – a practice that's considered far too animal-like for young humans – and so in their early months kids are **carried** everywhere, either on the hip or in slings made from sarongs. Don't be surprised if your child gets scooped off the ground for the same reason.

Activities for kids

There's plenty on Bali and Lombok to appeal to children. Aside from the beach and other water-based activities in the southern resorts, Bali's Waterbom Park is fun for all ages (see p.61). In the north of the island, Bali Treetop Adventure Park (see p.201) has ziplines and a climbing wall.

Active children may also enjoy **learning to surf**, **mountain-biking**, **whitewater rafting**, **horse-riding** and **wildlife attractions** such as the Bird and Reptile parks in Batubulan (see p.141) and the Bali Safari and Marine Park in Gianyar (see p.156). Many **dive centres** will teach PADI children's scuba courses: their Bubblemaker programme is open to 8-year-olds and the Junior Open Water course is designed for anyone over 10.

Ubud (see p.110) is especially child-friendly, with a huge amount on offer that they will love, including chances to try their hand at jewellery-making, batik, gamelan and dancing, and a multilingual kids' library. The colour and dynamism of the **dance and music** shows could almost be tailor-made for children – from the beauty and grace of Legong to the drama of the Barong. Older, more fashion-conscious children will relish the varieties of brand-name **clothing** on offer, while parents will appreciate the bargains to be had in the children's sections of department stores in Kuta and Denpasar and the specialist children's clothing stores.

Practicalities

When choosing a resort, beaches in Sanur, the north coast of Bali (including Lovina), and the Gili Islands enjoy calm waters most of the year whereas waves can be huge and potentially dangerous on the ocean-battered shoreline in southern Bali (Kuta-Legion-Seminyak and Canggu) and south Lombok.

Many top-end **hotels** provide extra beds for one or two under-12s sharing a room with their parents and the best ones have a kids' club as well, and may also offer babysitting services. The Tuban area of south Kuta is particularly strong on family-oriented hotels, many of which have grounds that run right down to the sea.

On the whole, children who occupy their own seat on **buses** and **bemos** are expected to pay full fare. Most **domestic flight** operators charge two-thirds of the adult fare for children under 14, and ten percent for infants.

Although you can buy **disposable nappies** (diapers) in the supermarkets of Kuta, Sanur, Denpasar and Ubud, the Balinese rarely use them, so prices are inflated. Bring a **changing mat**, as there are precious few public toilets in Bali and Lombok, let alone ones with special baby facilities (though posh hotels are always a useful option). For touring, child-carrier **backpacks** are ideal. Opinions are divided on whether or not it's worth bringing a **buggy** or three-wheeled **stroller** – pavements are bumpy at best, and there's an almost total absence of ramps; sand is especially difficult for buggies, though less so for three-wheelers. Buggies and strollers do, however, come in handy for feeding and even bedding small children, as highchairs and cots are only provided in the most upmarket hotels. Taxis and car-rental companies never provide baby seats. A child-sized **mosquito net** might be useful. **Powdered milk** is available in every major tourist centre, but sterilizing bottles is a far more laborious process in Indonesian hotels and restaurants than it is back home.

Food in the main resorts of Bali and Lombok is generally quite palatable to children as it's toned down for western tastes and rarely too chilli-hot. In 'local' places (particularly in Lombok) the food is usually much spicier. It's probably wise to avoid unwashed fruit and salads, and dishes that have been left uncovered.

Thundering **traffic** is another hazard, as is the tropical **sun**. Many beaches have little shade so sun hats, sunblock and waterproof suntan lotions are essential, and can be bought in the major resorts (though are usually more expensive than in the west). You should also make sure, if possible, that your child is aware of the dangers of **rabies** (see p.33); keep children away from animals, especially dogs and monkeys, and ask your doctor about rabies jabs.

Information and advice

The Bali for Families **website** (W baliforfamilies.com) is run by parents who have lots of first-hand experience of travelling in Bali; as well as child-friendly recommendations, there's also a travellers' forum.

Charities and volunteer projects

Despite the glossy tourist veneer, Bali and Lombok are part of a poor country with limited resources to provide high-quality education and health care to its citizens, whose opportunities, quality of life and very survival are compromised as a result. Below are some suggestions for charities that welcome help from visitors; most of their websites include information on volunteer work.

CHARITIES AND VOLUNTEER WORK

AdoptASchool W adoptaschool.org.au. Established as a dressmaking cooperative run by and for women who were widowed by the 2002 Kuta bombing, with a small shop in Candikuning, Bedugul (see p.213), the organization also administers the sponsorship of pupils in Bali and runs English clubs.

Bali Hati Foundation T 0361 974672, W balihati.org. Promotes access to education for all, provides student scholarships and sponsorship, offers community education and health care and runs an acclaimed school in Mas. Their spa centre, Spa Hati, in Ubud (see p.135), helps fund the work.

BAWA Jl Raya Ubud, Ubud T 081 138 9004, W bawabali.com. Working to improve all aspects of animal welfare on Bali including the vaccination, as opposed to culling, of dogs as a response to rabies on the island.

Crisis Care Foundation T 0812 377 4649, W balicrisiscare.org. Provides free health care for local people both in the clinic near Lovina and as outreach and is run on charitable donations, which are always needed. There's more information and a Wish List on the website; donations can be made online.

East Bali Poverty Project T 0361 410071, W eastbalipoverty project.org. Helps isolated mountain villages on the arid slopes of Gunung Agung and Gunung Abang in a number of ways, including education, nutrition, health and sustainable agriculture.

Gili Eco Trust Gili Trawangan T 0813 3960 0553, W giliecotrust .com. Works to promote sustainable tourism in the Gili islands. Projects include growing new coral reefs, recycling programmes, caring for horses and environmental education in schools. Visitors can participate in their monthly beach clean-up and they run courses on Biorock reef restoration (see box, p.239).

IDEP Foundation T 0361 294993, W idepfoundation.org. An Ubud-based NGO that promotes sustainable-living programmes across Indonesia, including permaculture, micro-credit, fair trade and disaster response projects.

Kupu-Kupu Foundation W kupukupufoundation.org. Encourages sponsors and volunteers to help improve the lives of disabled people in Bali. Sells inexpensive, high-quality handicrafts and jewellery made by disabled craftspeople at its shop in Ubud (see p.133). They also have cottages for rent.

Peduli Anak W www.pedulianak.org. Centre set up to help street children, with a health clinic and education programme. Volunteers are needed. It's on the outskirts of Mataram, Lombok (see p.249).

Pondok Pekak Library and Learning Centre Jl Dewi Sita, Ubud T 0361 976194, W pondokpekaklibrary.com. A free library service in Ubud that offers all local children access to books and educational activities. Visitors can support the project by using the excellent adult-oriented library of English-language books (see p.133), by taking cultural classes or Indonesian lessons here (see p.127) and by donating books and funds.

Sjaki-Tari-Us Foundation Off Jl Dewi Sita, Ubud W sjakitarius.nl. Works with disabled children and their families offering education, training and job opportunities.

Yayasan Senyum T 0361 233758, W senyumbali.org. Dedicated to helping fund operations for Balinese people with craniofacial disabilities such as cleft palate. Visitors can assist by donating secondhand goods to their two Ubud charity outlets, the Smile Shop (see box, p.133).

Travel essentials

Addresses

Because the government has outlawed the use of English-language names, demanding that Indonesian names be used instead, a number of streets in resort areas such as Kuta (Bali) are known by two or more names (see box, p.65). Because of haphazard planning, frequent rebuilding and superstitions about unlucky numbers, street numbers are not always sequential – and may not be present at all. It's also quite common to use "X" where an adjacent property has been added, with the original building being, say, Jl Raya 200 and the new one becoming Jl Raya 200X.

Cookery and cultural classes

Short courses in Indonesian cookery are available in Ubud (see p.127), Petitenget (see p.67), Tanjung Benoa (see p.85), Gili Trawangan (see p.290), Lovina (see p.209), Sidemen (see p.168), Munduk (see p.204) and at the *Alila Manggis* near Candidasa (see p.175). Ubud is the most popular place to take workshops in art, dance, music, carving and other Balinese arts and crafts (see p.127).

Costs

Foreign tourists visiting Bali and Lombok, wherever they come from, invariably find that hotel rooms at all levels of comfort, goods and services are relatively inexpensive when compared with their home countries. However, the range of accommodation, restaurants and other opportunities means that it is just as easy to have a fabulously extravagant experience as a budget one.

If you're happy to eat in local places, stay off the beer, use the public transport system (or rent a bicycle) and stay in simple accommodation, you could scrape by on a **daily budget** of £15–20/$25–35 per person if you share a room. For around £35/$55 a day per person if you share a room, you'll get quite a few extra comforts, like the use of a swimming pool, hot water and air conditioning, three good meals and a few beers; and you'll be able to afford tourist shuttle buses or the odd taxi to get around. Staying in luxury hotels and eating at the swankiest restaurants and chartering transport, you're likely to spend from £70/$125 per day. The sky's the limit at this end of the market, with $1000-a-night accommodation, helicopter charters, dive or surf safaris and fabulous gourmet meals all on offer.

Government-run museums and the most **famous temples** charge around Rp15,000 per person and **private art museums and galleries** Rp30,000–50,000. Tourist attractions can be pricey. Youth and student **discounts** are rare but can be fifty percent where available. All visitors to any temple are expected to give a small donation (minimum about Rp10,000).

Bargaining

Bargaining is one of the most obvious ways of keeping your costs down. Except in supermarkets, department stores, restaurants and bars, the first price given is rarely the real one, and most stallholders expect to engage in some financial banter before finalizing the sale; on average, buyers will start their counterbid at about thirty to forty percent of the vendor's opening price and the bartering continues from there. Pretty much everything, from woodcarvings to car rental is negotiable, and accommodation rates can often be knocked down outside high season, from the humblest losmen through to the top-end places.

Bargaining is an art, and requires humour and tact – it's easy to forget that you're quibbling over a few cents or pennies, and that such an amount means a lot more to an Indonesian than to you.

Crime and personal safety

While incidents of crime are relatively rare on Bali and Lombok, the importance of tourism to the economy, and the damage that adverse publicity could do, means that the true situation may be kept conveniently obscured. Certainly, the majority of visitors have trouble-free trips, but there have been instances of theft and assault on tourists.

It makes sense to take a few **precautions**. Carry vital documents and money in a concealed money belt: bum-bags (aka fanny packs) are too easy to cut off in a crowd. Make sure your luggage is lockable (there are gadgets to lock backpacks) and be aware that things can quickly be taken from the back pockets of a rucksack while you're wearing it without your knowing. Beware of pickpockets on crowded buses or bemos and in markets. They usually operate in pairs: one will distract you while another gets what they can either from your pockets or your backpack.

Check the **security** of a room before accepting it, make sure doors and windows can be locked, and don't forget to check if access could be gained via the bathroom. Make sure there are no peepholes through into neighbouring rooms. Some guesthouses and hotels have safe-deposit boxes, which neatly solves the problem of what to do with your valuables while you go swimming.

Keep a separate **photocopy** of your passport and airline ticket, or scan them in and store them online, so you can prove who you are and where you are going if you need to get replacements.

It's never sensible to carry **large amounts of cash**, and on Bali it's not necessary. However, on Lombok you may need to carry more than you would like because of the scarcity of moneychangers outside the resort areas. It's wise to keep a few dollars hidden somewhere away from your main stash of cash so that if you get your money stolen you can still get to the police and buy essentials while you sort everything out. There are a number of potential rip-offs when you're changing money (see box, p.48).

Something else to watch out for on Bali is being approached on the street by somebody wanting to ask a few questions about your holiday. These seemingly innocuous questionnaires provide information for **time-share companies**, who have a reputation for hassling visitors once they've divulged their details. Another ruse is for the "researchers" to offer you a prize as a reward for participating – usually a free dinner or tour – which invariably involves a trip to the time-share company's office. Advice on this is to never sign anything unless you've thought about it extremely carefully, examined all the small print – and then thought about it some more.

It's also worth being alert to the possibility of **spiked drinks** and to be aware that **gambling** is illegal in Indonesia and problems can arise from foreigners getting involved in this.

It is foolish to have anything to do with **drugs** in Indonesia. The penalties are very tough, even for simple possession, and you won't get any sympathy from consular officials. The horrendous fate that awaits foreigners arrested for drug use is described in *Hotel K: The Shocking Inside Story of Bali's Most Notorious Jail* (see p.336).

If you're arrested, or end up on the wrong side of the law for whatever reason, you should ring the **consular officer** at your embassy immediately (see p.25).

It's worth being aware that if you're **driving** the chance of entanglement with the police increases somewhat (see p.27).

Women travellers

Bali and Lombok do not present great difficulties for **women travellers**, either travelling alone or with friends of either sex; basic issues of personal security and safety are essentially the same as they would be at home. Women should take similar responsibility for their own safety, especially in bars and large parties.

However, an image of Western women as promiscuous and on holiday in search of sex is well established on both islands, although attitudes on Bali are a little more open-minded than most places on Lombok.

Observe how local women **dress** both on the streets and on the beach. While topless sunbathing is popular among tourists – and it's unlikely that local people will say anything directly – it's worth being aware how far outside the local dress code such behaviour is. Whatever you do on the beach, you should cover up when you head inshore, and

visits to temples or festivals carry their own obligations regarding dress (see p.38).

There's a large population of **young men** on both Bali and Lombok known variously as Kuta Cowboys, mosquitoes (they flit from person to person) or gigolos, whose aim is to secure a Western girlfriend for the night, week, month or however long it lasts. Check out the documentary Cowboys in Paradise (Ⓦwww.journeyman.tv/film/4910) for more on this. Older women are increasingly targeted for attention. The boys vary considerably in subtlety and while the transaction is not overtly financial, the woman will be expected to pay for everything. You'll see these couples all over the islands, and if a Western woman and a local man are seen together, this is the first assumption made about their relationship. Local reaction is variable, from hostility in the more traditional villages through acceptance to amusement.

Sex outside marriage is taboo in the Muslim religion, and young girls on Lombok are expected to conform to a strict moral code. On Bali things are changing and while sex outside marriage is not actually approved of, it is accepted that it happens – although marriage is still expected should the girl become pregnant.

Male travellers

In Kuta, Bali there are large numbers of prostitutes touting for business in nightclubs, bars and on the street. Western men can expect to be approached by **sex workers** on scooters late at night in Kuta. Some of these prostitutes (both female and ladyboys) target drunken men for business, and groups of ladyboys also patrol the backstreets of Kuta in the early hours intent on pickpocketing inebriated male tourists.

Reporting a crime or emergency

If you have anything **lost** or **stolen** you must get a **police report** for insurance purposes, so head for the nearest police station (these are marked on the maps in the Guide). In areas without local police, such as the Gili Islands off the coast of Lombok, ask for the local village headman, *kepala desa* or *kepala kampung* in smaller villages, whose job it is to sort out the problem and take you to the nearest police. The police will usually find somebody who can speak some English, but it's a good idea to take along someone who can speak both Indonesian

EMERGENCY NUMBERS

In an emergency, call the police (☎110), ambulance (☎118) or fire service (☎113).

and English, if you can. Allow plenty of time for any bureaucratic involvement with the police. If you're unfortunate enough to be the victim of violent crime, contact your consulate (see p.25) at once.

Electricity

Usually 220–240 volts AC, but outlying areas may still use 110 volts. Most outlets take plugs with two rounded pins.

Insurance

It is vital to arrange **travel insurance** before travelling to Bali or Lombok, covering for medical expenses due to illness or injury, the loss of baggage and travel documents plus cancellation or curtailment of your journey. Most exclude so-called dangerous sports unless an extra premium is paid: in Bali and Lombok, this can mean scuba diving, kayaking and whitewater rafting.

Before buying a **policy**, check what cover you may already have. Your home-insurance policy may cover your possessions against loss or theft even when overseas; in addition, many credit cards include some form of travel cover and some private medical schemes, especially in Canada and US, may include cover when abroad. However, in many cases the coverage from these sources is pretty meagre and you'll need to extend your cover or buy a new policy.

Specialist travel insurance companies usually offer the most comprehensive and competitive policies, or consider the travel insurance deal we offer (see box below). Many policies can be chopped and changed to exclude coverage you don't need. With regard to medical coverage, ascertain whether benefits will be paid as treatment proceeds or only after your return home, and be sure to carry the 24-hour medical emergency number and the policy number with you at all times. Always make a note of the policy details and leave them with someone at home in case you lose the original. When securing

baggage cover, make sure that the per-article limit – typically under £500/$900 – will cover your most valuable possession.

It can be more economical for couples and families travelling together to arrange joint insurance. Older travellers or anyone with health problems is advised to start researching insurance well in advance of their trip.

If you need to make a claim, you should keep receipts for medicines and treatment, and, if possible, contact the insurance company before making any major payment (for example, on additional convalescence expenses). In the event you have anything stolen, you must obtain an official report from the police.

Internet

Free **wi-fi** is common in restaurants, bars and virtually all accommodation options. There are also cybercafés in the main resorts on Bali and Lombok. The cheapest way to get mobile internet on your phone in Bali and Lombok is by buying a prepaid local 3G or 4G SIM card (see p.50).

Language lessons

Indonesian language lessons are available in Seminyak (see p.67) and Ubud (see p.127).

Laundry

Most hotels and losmen have laundry services. In tourist centres there are plenty of laundries outside the hotels as well.

Left luggage

Most losmen and hotels will store luggage. Bali's Ngurah Rai Airport has a left-luggage facility (see p.64) and the shuttle-bus operator Perama will store luggage for its customers.

ROUGH GUIDES TRAVEL INSURANCE

Rough Guides has teamed up with WorldNomads.com to offer great travel insurance deals. Policies are available to residents of more than 150 countries, with cover for a wide range of adventure sports, 24hr emergency assistance, high levels of medical and evacuation cover and a stream of travel safety information. Roughguides.com users can take advantage of their policies online 24/7, from anywhere in the world – even if you're already travelling. And since plans often change when you're on the road, you can extend your policy and even claim online. Roughguides.com users who buy travel insurance with WorldNomads.com can also leave a positive footprint and donate to a community development project. For more information, go to ⓦ roughguides.com/travel-insurance.

LGBT travellers

As members of a society that places so much emphasis on marriage and parenthood, the Balinese are generally intolerant of homosexuality within their own culture, to the point where gay Balinese men will often introduce themselves to prospective lovers as hailing from Java, so as not to cause embarrassment to their own people. It's not uncommon for men to lead a gay lifestyle for ten or fifteen years before succumbing to extreme social pressure around the age of 30, getting married and becoming fathers. Lesbians are even less visible, but subject to similar expectations.

On the positive side, it's much more common in Bali and Lombok to show a modest amount of physical affection to friends of the same sex than to friends or lovers of the opposite sex, which means that Indonesian and foreign **gay couples** generally encounter less hassle about being seen together in public than they might in the West. Indonesian law is relatively liberal: the legal **age of consent** for both gay and heterosexual sex is 16.

Despite the indigenous aversion to LGBT culture, Bali's tourist industry has helped establish the island as one of the two main gay centres of Indonesia (the other being Jakarta). Young gay men from islands as far afield as Borneo gravitate to Bali in search of a foreign partner, and most end up in southern Bali, where Seminyak has become the focus of the island's small but enduring **scene**. Here, Jalan Camplung Tanduk has several established gay bars and clubs (with drag shows, go-go dancers, theme nights and the like). A mixed gay crowd of Indonesians and foreigners congregates in certain other Kuta venues, where they're welcomed without a problem. Everything is a lot quieter and less overt on **Lombok**, where Senggigi clubs offer the best chance of access to the local gay scene.

A lot of gay visitors and expatriates do have **affairs** with Indonesian men, and these liaisons tend to fall somewhere between holiday romances and paid sex. Few Indonesians would classify themselves as rent boys – they wouldn't sleep with someone they didn't like and most don't have sex for money – but they usually expect to be financially cared for by the richer man (food, drinks and entertainment expenses, for example), and some do make their living this way.

The Utopia website (Ⓦutopia-asia.com) is an excellent **resource** for LGBT travellers in Bali and the rest of Indonesia. The Bali-based tour agencies Bali Friendly (Ⓦbalifriendlyhotels.com) and Bali Gay (Ⓦbaligay.net) recommend gay-owned and LGBT-friendly hotels, spas and package tours, while the umbrella organization for gays and lesbians in Bali and Lombok is Gaya Dewata (☎0361 780 8250, Ⓦgayadewata.com).

Living and working in Bali and Lombok

Bali has a large and lively expat community, with significant numbers of foreigners choosing to make their homes in and around Ubud, Seminyak, Canggu and Sanur in particular; on Lombok, Senggigi and Gili Trawangan are the main centres. Visa regulations are complicated (see Ⓦkemlu.go.id) but some expats manage to work as English-language teachers in Kuta (Bali) and Ubud, or as dive instructors in south Bali resorts or on the Gili Islands. Others export Indonesian fabric, clothes, jewellery, artefacts and furniture. The Living in Indonesia website (Ⓦexpat.or.id) is a good resource on expat life, and the *Bali Advertiser* (Ⓦbaliadvertiser.biz) has employment adverts.

Maps

The best are published by Periplus Travel which publishes maps to *Bali* (1:250,000) and *Lombok & Komodo* (1:175,000) as well as the impressive *Bali Street Atlas*, which is exhaustively indexed and good for drivers.

The media

Online and updated daily, *The Bali Times* (Ⓦthebali times.com) is highly informative; there's a printed version published weekly. For Indonesian news, the English-language daily *Jakarta Globe* (Ⓦjakartaglobe .id) and *The Jakarta Post* (Ⓦthejakartapost.com) are both reliable. For more incisive journalism, check out the weekly **news magazine** *Tempo* (Ⓦtempointer active.com), published in both Indonesian and English versions. The online quarterly *Inside Indonesia* (Ⓦinsideindonesia.org) runs hard-hitting articles on social and political change.

Most hotels have satellite TV; channels include CNN, HBO and sometimes BBC World, ABC and National Geographic as well as French and German channels.

Hard Rock FM Bali (87.8 FM; Ⓦhardrockfm.com) is a music station with English-speaking DJs.

Money

The Indonesian **currency** is the **rupiah** (abbreviated to Rp). Notes commonly in circulation are Rp1000 (blue), Rp2000 (grey), Rp5000 (green and brown),

MONEYCHANGING SCAMS

Some unscrupulous exchange counters try to rip customers off, and there are several well-known **moneychanging scams** practised in the bigger resorts, in particular in Kuta and Sanur on Bali.

SOME COMMON RIP-OFFS

- Confusing you with the number of **zeros**. It's easy for staff to give you Rp100,000 instead of Rp1,000,000.
- Giving you your money in Rp10,000 **denominations**, so that you lose track.
- Tampering with the **calculator**, so that it shows a low sum even if you use it yourself.
- **Folding notes** over to make it look as if you're getting twice as much as you are.
- Turning the lights out or otherwise **distracting** you while the pile of money is on the counter.
- **Stealing** some notes as they "check" it for the last time.
- Once you've rumbled them and complained, telling you that the discrepancy in the figures is due to "**commission**".

SOME ADVICE

- **Avoid** anywhere that offers a ridiculously good rate. Stick to banks or to exchange desks recommended by other travellers. Authorized moneychangers should display a green logo with "PVA Berizin" written on it.
- Work out the total amount you're expecting beforehand, and write it down.
- Always ask whether there Is commission.
- Before signing your cheque, ask for notes in **reasonable denominations** (Rp10,000 is unreasonable, Rp50,000 is acceptable), and ask to see them first.
- **Count your money** carefully, and never hand it back to the exchange staff, as this is when they whip away some notes without you noticing. You should be the last person to count the money.

Rp10,000 (pink or purple), Rp20,000 (green), Rp50,000 (blue) and Rp100,000 (pinky red). They are all clearly inscribed with English numbers and letters. You'll commonly come across Rp100 (silver-coloured plastic), Rp500 (larger, round, bronze) and Rp1000 (large, round, bronze with silver rim) coins. Don't be surprised if cashiers in supermarkets give you sweets instead of small-denomination coins as change.

At the time of writing the **exchange rate** was $1 to Rp13,335, €1 to Rp14,435 and £1 to Rp16,425. However, the exchange rate does change quite a lot. For the current rate check out the useful "Travellers Currency Cheat Sheets" at ⓦoanda.com.

Generally you will use rupiah for day-to-day transactions. Many tourist businesses, including hotels, dive operators, tour agents and car-rental outlets, however, quote for their goods and services in **US dollars** while a few use **euros**; in the Guide, where dollars are mentioned they are always US dollars. Even where prices are displayed in US dollars or euros, though, you have the option of paying with cash, credit or debit cards or rupiah.

Cash

There's no need to get **cash** rupiah before you travel. There are exchange counters and ATMs in both Bali's and Lombok's airports. Some cash in **US dollars or Euros** is useful to take with you, but take crisp new notes.

In tourist centres, **exchange counters** are the most convenient places to exchange money cash. They open daily from around 10am to 10pm and rates compare favourably with those offered by the banks. However, be wary of moneychanging scams (see box above), particularly in Kuta, Bali.

Normal **banking hours** are Monday–Thursday 8am–2pm, Friday 8am–noon and, in some branches, Saturday 8–11.30am, but these do vary. However, in many banks the foreign-exchange counter only opens for a limited period. Banks in smaller towns don't have foreign-exchange facilities.

Plastic

Major **credit cards**, most commonly Visa and MasterCard, are accepted by most mid- to top-end hotels and tourist businesses. However, outlets often add fees for using cards (typically three to five percent), bumping costs up.

ATMs are very widespread in all Bali's and Lombok's biggest tourist centres, towns and some villages. Virtually all accept international Visa and MasterCard credit and **debit cards**.

Be aware that your home bank may well block your card when you initially try to use it abroad, even if you've warned them of your trip, and it may take a couple of phone calls to sort this out – take the relevant telephone number with you.

Be careful when using your card – unlike machines at home, some of the Bali and Lombok machines only return your card *after* they've dispensed your cash, making it easier to forget it. Prepaid travel cards are useful: they work like a debit card in ATMs, hotels and other businesses and allow you to top up as and when you wish.

Wiring money

If you get into financial trouble, getting money wired to you from home is fast but expensive. Money should be available for collection in local currency from the company's local agent within twenty minutes of being sent via Western Union (Ⓦwesternunion.com) or Moneygram (Ⓦmoney gram.com). Both charge on a sliding scale, so sending larger amounts of cash is better value. Money can be sent via the agents, by telephone or, in some cases, through the websites themselves. Check the websites for locations and opening hours. Getting money wired from a home bank to a local bank on Bali or Lombok can be tortuous and is best avoided.

Opening hours and public holidays

Opening hours are not straightforward in Bali and Lombok, with government offices, post offices, businesses and shops setting their own timetables.

Generally speaking, **businesses** such as **airline offices** open at least Monday to Friday 8am to 4pm, Saturday 8am to 1pm, with many open longer, but have variable arrangements at lunchtime. Normal **banking hours** are Monday to Thursday 8am to 2pm, Friday 8am to noon and, in some branches, Saturday 8 to 11.30am, but these do vary and foreign-exchange-counter opening hours are often shorter.

> ### MUSLIM FESTIVAL DATES
> **Ramadan begins** May 16, 2018; May 6, 2019; April 24, 2020.
> **Idul Fitri** June 15, 2018; June 5, 2019; May 24, 2020.
> Note that Islamic festivals depend on local sightings of the moon; actual dates may vary by a day or two.

> ### NATIONAL PUBLIC HOLIDAYS
> **January 1** New Year's Day (Tahun Baru).
> **January/Febuary** Chinese New Year.
> **February/March** Maulid Nabi Muhammad, birth of the Prophet.
> **March/April** Balinese New Year (Nyepi).
> **March/April** Good Friday and Easter Sunday.
> **April/May** Waisak Day, anniversary of the birth, death and enlightenment of Buddha.
> **May/June** Ascension of Jesus Christ (Isa Almasih).
> **May/June** Al Miraj, Ascension Day.
> **July/August** Idul Fitri, celebration of the end of Ramadan.
> **August 17** Independence Day (Hari Proklamasi Kemerdekaan).
> **November** Muharram, Muslim New Year.
> **November/December** Idul Adha, the Muslim day of sacrifice.
> **December 25** Christmas Day.

In tourist areas, **shops** open from around 10am until 8pm or later, but local shops in towns and villages open and shut much earlier with the exception of supermarkets in shopping centres, which are generally open from at least 10am to 10pm. Local **markets** vary; some start soon after dawn with business completed by 10am, others only close up towards the end of the afternoon.

Government offices are widely reported as being open Monday to Friday 8am to 4pm; in fact there is much variability in different areas and departments – most close early on Friday and you'll generally be most successful if you turn up between 9am and 11.30am. Official government hours shorten during Ramadan; the best advice is to ring offices at that time to check before you make a long journey.

National public holidays

In addition to **national public holidays** celebrated throughout Indonesia (see box above) there are frequent local **religious festivals** occurring throughout the Muslim, Hindu and Chinese commu-nities. Each of Bali's twenty thousand temples also has an anniversary celebration once every *wuku* year, or 210 days, local communities host elaborate **marriage** and **cremation** celebrations, and both islands have their own particular secular holidays.

All major **Muslim festivals** are national holidays. These, based on a lunar calendar, move backwards against the Western calendar, falling earlier each year. The ninth Muslim month is **Ramadan**, a month of fasting during daylight hours. It is much more apparent on Muslim Lombok than on Hindu Bali. Followers of the Wetu Telu branch of Islam on Lombok (see box, p.266) observe their own three-day festival of **Puasa** rather than the full month. Many Muslim restaurants, although not tourist establishments, shut down during the day so it can be hard to get a meal in central and eastern parts of Lombok where you should not eat, drink or smoke in public at this time. However, in all other areas of Lombok and the Gili Islands you'll find Ramadan much less apparent. **Idul Fitri**, also called Hari Raya or Lebaran, the first day of the tenth month of the Muslim calendar, marks the end of Ramadan and is a national holiday. In fact, many businesses across Indonesia shut for a week and many hotels on Bali and Lombok get booked out with visitors from across the archipelago.

Phones

The cheapest way to make **international calls** is generally via Skype or an app such Viber, Whats App or Facebook Messenger/Facetime. Some local mobile phone networks also offer very inexpensive rates for international calls: as low as Rp1000/min to Australia, for example. If you buy a local SIM card ask the vendor what the best access code is for the cheapest international calls as they vary depending on your network provider.

If you don't have internet access or a local SIM, use one of the privately run "telephone shops", or **wartel**, which are found all over Bali and Lombok; most open long hours, typically from 7am to 10pm. A **local call** (*panggilan lokal*) should cost in the region of Rp100/min; calls to all other domestic destinations with a different area code are classed as **long-distance calls** (*panggilan inter-lokal*) and will cost more.

Bali is divided into several **code zones**, and Lombok has two codes. Calls to **mobile phones** – whose numbers begin ☎08 – are more expensive.

> ### INTERNATIONAL CALLS
> To **phone abroad** from Indonesia the international access code varies according to the network you're using; Telkomsel uses ☎001.
> To **call Bali and Lombok from abroad**: dial your international access code + 62 for Indonesia + number (minus its initial zero).

Mobile phones

Most mobile phones will work fine in Indonesia. Virtually all travellers these days choose not to use international roaming (as costs can be prohibitive) but use a **local SIM card**, which will provide 3G or 4G mobile internet. A local SIM can cost as little as Rp5000, while data packages start at around Rp50,000. Mobile coverage is excellent in Bali and Lombok and there are phone shops everywhere. Staff may have to unblock your phone first and will also advise on the best SIM card for your needs, bearing in mind local and international coverage. Top-up cards are sold at mobile-phone stalls everywhere.

Post

Every town and tourist centre on Bali and Lombok has a **General Post Office** (GPO; *kantor pos*) where you can buy stamps (*perangko*) and aerogrammes (*surat udara*), and can post letters (*surat*) and parcels (*paket*) Most *kantor pos* keep official government office **hours** (Mon–Thurs 8am–2pm, Fri 8–11am, Sat 8am–1pm; closed on festival days and public holidays). In larger towns and resorts, you can also buy stamps and send letters and parcels from **postal agents**. Post boxes aren't widespread, so it's best to post letters at GPOs or postal agents.

If the *kantor pos* doesn't offer a **parcel-packing service**, there will be a stall next door for getting your stuff parcelled up; don't bother packing it yourself as the contents need to be inspected first. *Kantor pos* won't handle any parcels over 10kg or more than 1m long, but most shops can arrange **shipping**.

Time

Bali and Lombok are on **Central Indonesian Time** (GMT+8, North American EST+13, Australian EST-2). There's no daylight saving.

Tourist information

Indonesia has a few **tourism officers** scattered around the world; consult ⓦ www.indonesia.travel /en/travel-guidance/visit-indonesia-tourism-office.

District capitals across Bali and Lombok all maintain their own **government tourist office** (Mon–Thurs 8am–3pm, Fri 8am–noon; those in the main tourist centres keep longer hours) but they're generally of limited use to travellers. The Ubud office is an exception, with well-informed staff.

GOVERNMENT TRAVEL ADVICE

Most Western governments maintain websites with travel information detailing some of the potential hazards and what to do in emergencies.

Australian Department of Foreign Affairs Ⓦ dfat.gov.au.
British Foreign & Commonwealth Office Ⓦ redirects to www .gov.uk.
Canadian Department of Foreign Affairs Ⓦ international.gc.ca.
Irish Department of Foreign Affairs Ⓦ dfa.ie.
New Zealand Ministry of Foreign Affairs Ⓦ mfat.govt.nz.
US State Department Ⓦ www.state.gov
South African Department of Foreign Affairs Ⓦ www.dirco .gov.za

LISTINGS MAGAZINES AND TOURIST PUBLICATIONS

Plenty of **free tourist magazines** supply information on Bali's and Lombok's sights, activities and events; they're generally available online as well as in hotels and restaurants in the main tourist centres.

Agung Ⓦ www.agungbali.com. Periodical all about eastern Bali from Padang Bai to Amed.

Bali Plus Ⓦ baliplus.com. Compact monthly that covers tourist attractions and lists and reviews restaurants, clubs, shops and spas.

The beat Ⓦ thebeatbali.com. Bali's premier nightlife listings magazine covers gigs, parties and clubs plus a few bars and restaurants. Fortnightly.

The Lombok Guide Ⓦ thelombokguide.com. Runs interesting features and general information on all aspects of visiting Lombok and the Gili Islands.

My Lombok Glossy monthly magazine with articles on culture, events, travel and food.

Sanur Weekly Ⓦ sanurweekly.com. News, events and listings in the Sanur area.

The Yak Ⓦ theyakmag.com. Lifestyle quarterly magazine for the Seminyak expat community and visitors.

WEBSITES AND FORUMS

Bali Bible Ⓦ balibible.guide. Comprehensive online guide with reviews and useful Top Ten lists.

Bali Discovery Ⓦ balidiscovery.com. Weekly tourism-related news from Bali, plus hotel and tour booking.

Bali Paradise Online Ⓦ bali-paradise.com. Features and links on everything from traditional architecture to car rental and the weather forecast. Also has a busy travellers' forum.

Bali Travel Forum Ⓦ balitravelforum.com. Active forum with lots of expert posters.

The Bud Ⓦ thebudmag.com. Focusing on Ubud and the surrounding area.

Gu Guide Ⓦ cangguguide.com. Deals with everything from nightlife to spas in and around Canggu.

What's New Bali Ⓦ whatsnewbali.com. Listings of club and live music events, dance performances and major festivals, plus restaurant and shopping recommendations.

Travellers with disabilities

Indonesia makes few provisions for its disabled citizens, which clearly affects **travellers with disabilities**, although the situation is definitely improving year on year.

At the physical level, kerbs are usually high (without slopes) and pavements/sidewalks uneven, with all sorts of obstacles; access to most public places involves steps (very few have ramps); public transport is inaccessible to wheelchair users (although Perama tourist buses will take them); and the few pedestrian crossings on major roads have no audible signal. On the positive side, many hotels consist of bungalows in extensive grounds and/or have spacious bathrooms, while the more aware are increasingly making an effort to provide the necessary facilities. These hotels are highlighted in the Guide and the Bali Paradise site (see below) carries a roundup of accessible hotels.

For all of these reasons, it may be worth considering an **organized tour** or holiday – the contacts listed here (see below) will help you start researching trips to Bali and Lombok. Note that a medical certificate of your fitness to travel, provided by your doctor, can be extremely useful; some airlines or insurance companies may insist on it.

Be sure to carry your complete supply of **medications** whenever you travel (including on buses and planes), in case of loss or theft. It's also a good idea to carry a doctor's letter about your drugs prescriptions with you at all times, particularly when passing through customs at airports, so you don't get hauled up for narcotics transgressions. Assume that if anything happens to equipment, such as a wheelchair, spares will be hard to find, and a small repair kit may well come in very handy.

CONTACTS FOR TRAVELLERS WITH DISABILITIES

Bali Access Travel Jl Danau Tamblingan 31 ☎ 0851 0051 9902, Ⓦ baliaccesstravel.com. Specialists in wheelchair-accessible travel in Bali, Lombok and Java, including equipment rental, accessible vehicles, all-inclusive tours and home-care services.

Bali Paradise Ⓦ bali-paradise.com. Follow the Special Needs Traveler link for detailed local information, suggestions and tips.

Emerging Horizons Ⓦ emerginghorizons.com. Magazine with a huge range of worldwide travel information and inspiration for wheelchair users and slow walkers.

Thorntree Forum Ⓦ lonelyplanet.com/thorntree. The "Travellers with Disabilities" forum is useful.

South Bali

SURFING IN PADANG PADANG

1

South Bali

The mainly flat land that makes up the south is among the most densely populated in Bali. This is where you'll find the island's major tourist resorts: at Kuta and Jimbaran in the west, and Sanur, Nusa Dua and Tanjung Benoa in the east. The area is a surfers' paradise, pounded by some of the most famous and challenging breaks in the world. The vast majority of visitors head straight for the brash, commercial coastal sprawl of Kuta–Legian–Seminyak, famous for its shopping and nightlife, but the neighbouring area just to the north, around Canggu, is far more attractive and less built-up.

Bali's administrative capital, **Denpasar**, is also here, and while most tourists treat the city as little more than a transit point for cross-island journeys, it holds the island's best museum and makes an interesting contrast to the more westernized beach enclaves.

Across on the southeast coast, beach life is quieter and less frantic at **Sanur** and more luxurious and manicured at **Nusa Dua** and **Tanjung Benoa**, home to many luxury hotels. Offshore lie three islands: escapist but little-visited **Nusa Penida**; tiny **Nusa Ceningan**; and resolutely relaxed **Nusa Lembongan**, with exceptional diving and easy access from Sanur. South of Kuta, the **Bukit Peninsula** offers peaceful, upmarket beachfront hotels at **Jimbaran** and fabulous **surf** and lively beach bases beneath the cliffs in and around **Uluwatu**, also the site of an important clifftop temple.

Kuta–Legian–Seminyak

The biggest, brashest resort in Bali, the **KUTA–LEGIAN–SEMINYAK** conurbation expands relentlessly out from its core on the southwest coast, 10km southwest of Denpasar. Packed with thousands of hotels, restaurants, bars, clubs, shops, spas and tour agencies, the 10km-long coastal strip plays host to millions of visitors each year who come to party, shop, surf or simply laze a week away, and sucks in ever-more Indonesians for work. It's a hectic place: noisy, full of touts and busy with constant building work. The area's road network is totally insufficient, so prepare yourself for the horrific traffic: all the main routes are rammed with cars, motorbikes and fumes and the pollution can be punishing. It's often quicker to walk.

Infrastructure aside, the resort does retain a tropical charm. It's still largely low-rise, and coconut palms and splashes of colour from frangipani trees and bougainvillea help soften the urban scene. And though Kuta-Legian-Seminyak is very much an international resort – *McDonald's*, Rip Curl, *Hard Rock* and most of the usual corporate suspects are all present – a distinctly Balinese character endures. Villagers still live and work here, making religious offerings, attending *banjar* meetings and holding temple

BINGIN

Highlights

❶ Canggu This still largely rural region, blessed with fine surf beaches, endless ricefields and dotted with cool cafes and yoga schools is Bali at its boho best: it draws a cast of characters from across the globe. **See p.63**

❷ Dining in Seminyak and Kerobokan Top international chefs plus moneyed tourism equals one of Asia's most dynamic dining destinations. **See p.70**

❸ Kuta–Legian–Seminyak beach clubs Choose from style-magazine chic, hipster cool or beach shack and lose a day with sounds, sustenance and sand all in one place. The fun beach holiday in a nutshell. **See p.72**

❹ Bingin Rickety bamboo bars on stilts, surf and a villagey vibe – welcome to the finest escape on the Bukit Peninsula. **See p.79**

❺ Surf beaches Even non-surfers should visit Uluwatu for its grandstand view of one of the most legendary waves in the world. Bingin and Padang Padang also offer powerful breaks. **See p.79 & p.80**

❻ Pura Luhur Uluwatu This important temple complex enjoys an utterly magical clifftop location, particularly at sunset. **See p.80**

❼ Nusa Lembongan Twenty kilometres from Bali, twenty years away in ambience, this laidback island offers great diving with manta rays and mola mola, and escapism in spades. **See p.98**

HIGHLIGHTS ARE MARKED ON THE MAP ON PP.56–57

1

SWIMMING IN KUTA

The waves that make Kuta such a great beach for surfers can make it treacherous for **swimming**, with a strong undertow as well as the rollers to contend with. The current is especially dangerous at the Canggu beaches. Always swim between the red-and-yellow striped flags, and take notice of the warning signs that dot the beach. If you need extra discouragement, note that Bali's lifeguards are involved in dozens of rescues some months, and there are fatalities every year. **Lifeguards** are stationed in special towers all along Bali's southwest coast from Uluwatu on the Bukit to Seseh near Pererenan; the central lifeguard post is on the beach at the corner of Jalan Pantai Kuta.

festivals. Each morning and afternoon women still place **offerings**, which litter the pavements and streets.

The reason everyone is here is the vast **beach**. Even if not quite so glorious as it once was, it is still a gentle curve of pale sand that stretches for 8km from Tuban to Canggu, its breakers luring amateur and experienced surfers alike. It's also the venue for the much-lauded Kuta sunsets; at their blood-red best in April, but streaky-pink at any time of year and the stuff sundowners are made of – whether cocktails in a hip bar or just a cold Bintang on plastic seats.

Brief history

For centuries, Kuta was considered by the Balinese to be an infertile stretch of coast haunted by malevolent spirits and a dumping ground for lepers and criminals. In the seventeenth and eighteenth centuries it operated as a **slave port** when the Balinese rajas sold hundreds of thousands of people to their counterparts in Java and beyond. By the mid-nineteenth century, however, life had become more prosperous – thanks in part to the energetic Danish business trader **Mads Lange**, who set up home here in 1839. Lange's political influence was also significant and, thanks to his diplomatic skills, south Bali avoided falling under Dutch control until 1906.

In 1936 the Americans **Bob and Louise Koke**, spotting Kuta's tourist potential, built a small hotel and, until the Japanese invasion of 1942, the place flourished. World War II and its aftermath stemmed the tourist flow until the 1960s, when young travellers established Kuta as a highlight on the **hippie trail**. Homestays were eventually joined by smarter international outfits, and Kuta–Legian–Seminyak has since evolved into the most prosperous region of the island, drawing workers from across Bali as well as the rest of Indonesia.

The flood of fortune-seekers from other parts of Indonesia raised the ugly spectre of religious tension, but no one could have anticipated the **October 12, 2002 bomb**

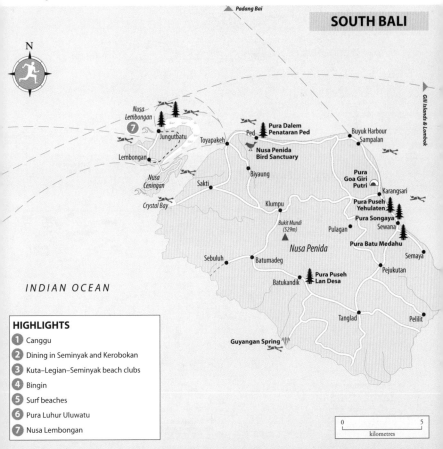

▲ *Padang Bai*

SOUTH BALI

N

Gili Islands & Lombok

Nusa
Lembongan
⑦
Jungutbatu
Ped
**Pura Dalem
Penataran Ped**
Buyuk Harbour
Sampalan
Toyapakeh
Lembongan
**Nusa Penida
Bird Sanctuary**
Biyaung
**Pura
Goa Giri
Putri**
Karangsari
Nusa
Ceningan
Sakti
Crystal Bay
Klumpu
**Pura Puseh
Yehulaten**
Pura Songaya
Sewana
*Bukit Mundi
(529m)*
▲
Pulagan
Nusa Penida
Pura Batu Medahu
Semaya
Sebuluh
Batumadeg
Pejukutan
INDIAN OCEAN
Batukandik
**Pura Puseh
Lan Desa**
Tanglad
Pelilit
Guyangan Spring

HIGHLIGHTS
1. Canggu
2. Dining in Seminyak and Kerobokan
3. Kuta–Legian–Seminyak beach clubs
4. Bingin
5. Surf beaches
6. Pura Luhur Uluwatu
7. Nusa Lembongan

0   5
kilometres

1

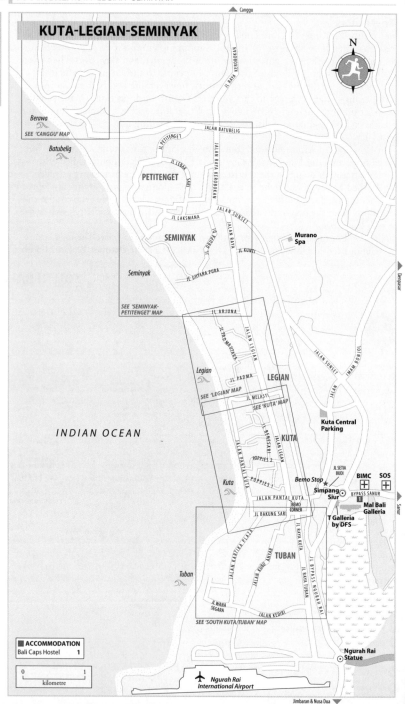

KUTA-LEGIAN-SEMINYAK

Canggu

N

Berawa
SEE 'CANGGU' MAP

Batubelig

JALAN BATUBELIG

JL PETITENGET

JL LEBAK SARI

PETITENGET

JALAN RAYA KEROBOKAN

JL RAYA KEROBOKAN

JALAN SUNSET

JL LAKSMANA

SEMINYAK

JL DRUPADI

JALAN RAYA

JL KUNTI

Murano
Spa

Seminyak

JL DHYANA PURA

SEE 'SEMINYAK-
PETITENGET' MAP

JL ARJUNA

JL PURA MAHATMA

JALAN LEGIAN

Legian

JL PADMA

LEGIAN

SEE 'LEGIAN' MAP

JL MELASTI

SEE 'KUTA' MAP

JALAN SUNSET

IMAM BONJOL

Denpasar

JL BENESARI

JALAN LEGIAN

KUTA

Kuta Central
Parking

JALAN PANTAI KUTA

POPPIES 2

POPPIES 1

Kuta

JALAN PANTAI KUTA

BEMO
CORNER

JL SETIA
BUDI

Bemo Stop

Simpang
Siur

BIMC

SOS

BYPASS SANUR

Mal Bali
Galleria

Sanur

INDIAN OCEAN

JL BAKUNG SARI

T Galleria
by DFS

JALAN KARTIKA PLAZA

JALAN KUBU ANYAR

JL RAYA KUTA

TUBAN

JL BYPASS NGURAH RAI

JL RAYA TUBAN

Tuban

JL WANA
SEGARA

JALAN KEDIRI

SEE 'SOUTH KUTA/TUBAN' MAP

Ngurah Rai
Statue

■ **ACCOMMODATION**
Bali Caps Hostel   1

0   1
kilometre

✈ Ngurah Rai
International Airport

Jimbaran & Nusa Dua ▼

KUTA–LEGIAN–SEMINYAK ORIENTATION

It's now impossible to recognize the demarcation lines between the once-separate villages of Kuta, Legian and Seminyak. We've used the common perception of the **neighbourhood borders**: Kuta stretches north from the Matahari department store in Kuta Square to Jalan Melasti; Legian runs from Jalan Melasti as far north as Jalan Arjuna; and Seminyak extends from Jalan Arjuna to *The Oberoi* hotel, where Petitenget begins. Petitenget feeds into Kerobokan and then north up to the string of Canggu area beaches, not strictly within the Kuta boundaries but close enough to share facilities. Kuta's increasingly built-up southern fringes, extending south from Matahari to the airport, are defined as south Kuta/Tuban.

The resort's **main road**, which begins as Jalan Legian and becomes Jalan Raya Seminyak, runs north–south through all three main districts, a total distance of 5km. The bulk of resort facilities are packed into the 600m-wide strip between Jalan Legian in the east and the coast to the west, an area crisscrossed by tiny *gang* (alleyways) and larger one-way roads.

The other main **landmark** is Bemo Corner, a minuscule roundabout at the southern end of Kuta that stands at the Jalan Legian–Jalan Pantai Kuta intersection.

attack (see p.310), in which Muslim extremists from Java detonated two bombs at Kuta's most popular nightspots, *Paddy's Irish Bar* and the *Sari Club*. Three years later, on October 1, 2005 (see p.310), bombs at Kuta Square and in Jimbaran killed twenty. The **Monument of Human Tragedy**, dedicated to the 202 people from 22 countries known to have been killed in the 2002 attack, now occupies the "Ground Zero" site of the original *Paddy's Irish Bar* on Jalan Legian. *Paddy's* has been rebuilt just down the road.

Kuta and Tuban

Young, fun and frequently trashy, **KUTA** is the original Balinese mass resort. It's hard to believe that as late as the early 1980s, eating and accommodation options were fairly limited here. Today it's frantic, jam-packed with shops – from tiny outlets to big-brand megastores – and hugely popular with travellers on a budget or visiting for a party – chiefly backpackers, surfers and young Australians. It's almost a surprise to see a temple squeezed between the endless T-shirt and sunglasses outlets in the traffic-choked lanes. The two main lanes, Poppies 1 and 2, and the winding alleys around and between them are the accommodation hubs. Jalan Legian is the 4km-long shopping strip. However, the beach is the real reason everyone is here – often crowded, but a long stretch of fine biscuit-coloured sand.

Just beyond Kuta Square's Matahari department store, Kuta Beach officially becomes **Tuban**, or **South Kuta**, and things quieten down. This area is often the choice of families or older couples, many of whom stay in the resort hotels that have direct access to the beach. No bemos run this way but the beachfront promenade runs from the lifeguard post near the corner of Jalan Pantai Kuta to the fence of the airport and it's about a thirty-minute walk from Kuta Square to the final resort hotel, owned by *Holiday Inn*.

Turtle hatchery

Kuta beach, access Jl Pantai Kuta • No set hours • Free • ⓦ baliseaturtle.org

Despite the crowds, Olive Ridley and some green **turtles** (see box, p.84) return to Kuta's shores every year between March and September to lay eggs late at night. To protect them from poachers a **hatchery** has been established by the ProFauna organization and the Satgas community police. Positioned beside the community police office on the beach near the corner of Jalan Pantai Kuta, the hatchery is basic, just a kiosk with information

1

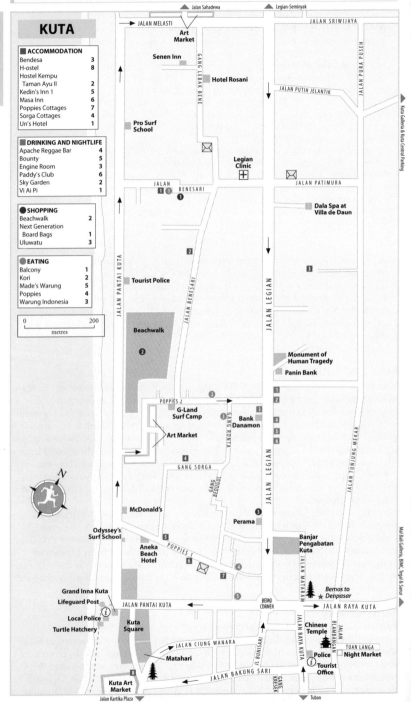

KUTA

■ **ACCOMMODATION**
Bendesa	3
H-ostel	8
Hostel Kempu	
Taman Ayu II	2
Kedin's Inn 1	5
Masa Inn	6
Poppies Cottages	7
Sorga Cottages	4
Un's Hotel	1

■ **DRINKING AND NIGHTLIFE**
Apache Reggae Bar	4
Bounty	5
Engine Room	3
Paddy's Club	6
Sky Garden	2
Vi Ai Pi	1

● **SHOPPING**
Beachwalk	2
Next Generation	
Board Bags	1
Uluwatu	3

● **EATING**
Balcony	1
Kori	2
Made's Warung	5
Poppies	4
Warung Indonesia	3

0 _____ 200
metres

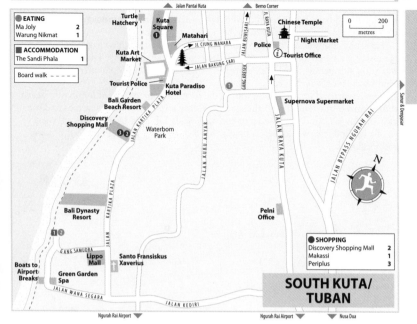

boards and, in season, sand containers that hold the eggs. The hatchlings are released the following day into the ocean.

Waterbom Park

Jl Kartika Plaza, Tuban • Daily 9am–6pm • Adults Rp520,000, children aged 2–11 Rp370,000; two-day passes to be used within a week Rp880,500/Rp620,000 • Ⓦ waterbom-bali.com

Kuta's **Waterbom Park** is a hugely popular aquatic adventure park, with water slides, a 150m-long macaroni tube, a lazy river with inner tubes and the Climax ride, which features a 60m near-vertical drop before you slingshot around a tight loop. You top up a pay-wristband first to pay for stuff on-site. However, it's not a cheap day out.

Legian

Calmer than Kuta with less-crowded sands, **Legian** is popular with families and tourists who are seeking a more relaxed, easy-going version of Kuta. Geographically and in atmosphere, it is midway between raucous Kuta and more upmarket Seminyak, with plenty of shops (generally more interesting than those in Kuta) and restaurants, and a wider choice of mid-range hotels than Kuta. If you've got your eye on a beachfront hotel in Legian, note that the shorefront road between Jalan Melasti and Jalan Arjuna is open only to toll-paying cars and is very quiet.

Seminyak, Petitenget and Kerobokan

Given the excesses of Kuta and growing development in Legian, expats and style-conscious tourists have been gradually heading north to escape the masses. **Seminyak** and **Petitenget** peaked in popularity with the jet set and hipsters around 2005, but over-development and an increasingly Kuta-esque sprawl has lead to a further exodus and today Seminyak is a pretty mainstream resort with a slew of midrange hotels, bars, clubs, restaurants and shops. Most of the style cognoscenti, and the best independent

1

boutiques and bars, have now shifted north to neighbouring **Kerobokan** and on to the Canggu area, a further 7km or so to the north.

That said, Seminyak still has plenty of appeal, particularly for those in need of a good night out or a meal: there's a glut of restaurants along Jalan Kayu Aya (aka Jalan Laksmana) and at the northern end of Jalan Petitenget. Seminyak's Jalan Camplung Tanduk is the area's centre for gay nightlife.

Vegas has arrived on the beach, too, in the form of a smattering of bombastic **beach clubs** north of the temple at Petitenget, providing a venue for rich Jakartans and the like to lounge around over food and cocktails while DJs spin beats. Here and there you'll also find less swanky beach shacks, for the simpler pleasures of a cool Bintang and local grub.

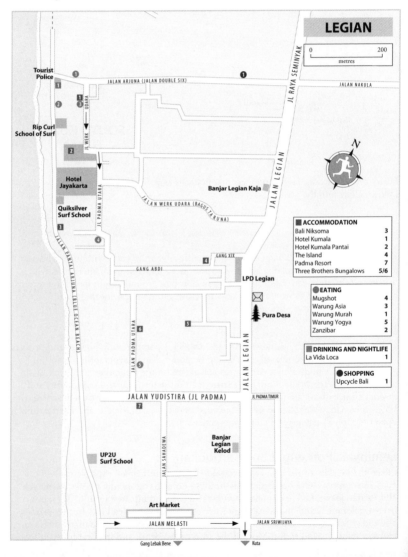

LEGIAN

ACCOMMODATION	
Bali Niksoma	3
Hotel Kumala	1
Hotel Kumala Pantai	2
The Island	4
Padma Resort	7
Three Brothers Bungalows	5/6

● EATING	
Mugshot	4
Warung Asia	3
Warung Murah	1
Warung Yogya	5
Zanzibar	2

■ DRINKING AND NIGHTLIFE	
La Vida Loca	1

● SHOPPING	
Upcycle Bali	1

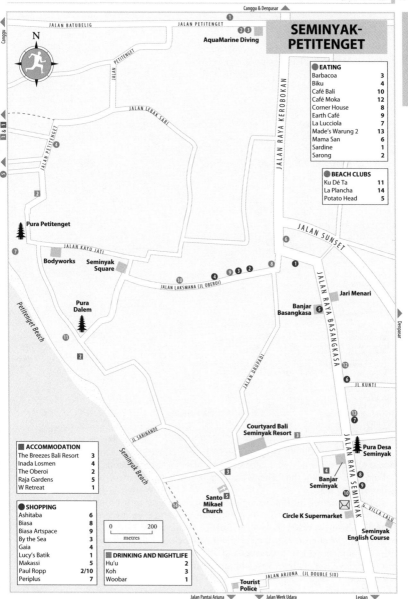

SEMINYAK-PETITENGET

● EATING

Barbacoa	3
Biku	4
Café Bali	10
Café Moka	12
Corner House	8
Earth Café	9
La Lucciola	7
Made's Warung 2	13
Mama San	6
Sardine	1
Sarong	2

● BEACH CLUBS

Ku Dé Ta	11
La Plancha	14
Potato Head	5

■ ACCOMMODATION

The Breezes Bali Resort	3
Inada Losmen	4
The Oberoi	2
Raja Gardens	5
W Retreat	1

● SHOPPING

Ashitaba	6
Biasa	8
Biasa Artspace	9
By the Sea	3
Gaia	4
Lucy's Batik	1
Makassi	5
Paul Ropp	2/10
Periplus	7

■ DRINKING AND NIGHTLIFE

Hu'u	2
Koh	3
Woobar	1

Canggu

North of Kerobokan, the coastline unfurls in a succession of surfing beaches and dramatic coastal panoramas at Batubelig, Berewa, Batu Bolong, Echo Beach (Batu Mejan) – all can be dangerous for swimming. This area is loosely referred to as **Canggu** and in recent years it has become *the* name to drop among "connected" visitors: think stylish hotels, uber-luxe villas, *nouveau*-warung, pilates studios and an epidemic of hipster barber shops where beard grooming is an art form.

1

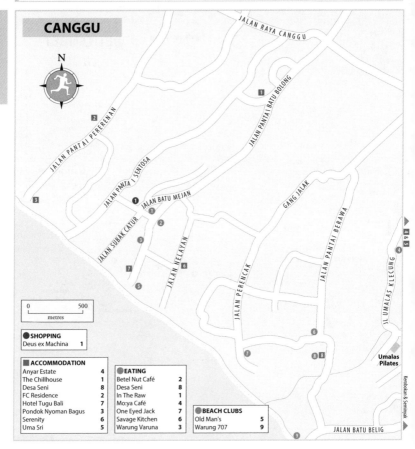

CANGGU

N

● SHOPPING
Deus ex Machina	1

■ ACCOMMODATION
Anyar Estate	4
The Chillhouse	1
Desa Seni	8
FC Residence	2
Hotel Tugu Bali	7
Pondok Nyoman Bagus	3
Serenity	6
Uma Sri	5

● EATING
Betel Nut Café	2
Desa Seni	8
In The Raw	1
Mo:ya Café	4
One Eyed Jack	7
Savage Kitchen	6
Warung Varuna	3

● BEACH CLUBS
Old Man's	5
Warung 707	9

Umalas Pilates

But as all the action is well dissipated, with places scattered among ricefields and behind wild beaches, the Canggu area retains a delightfully (neo)rustic feel – there's no urban sprawl at all.

Echo Beach and Batu Bolong are the real hubs. As ever across southern Bali, traffic can be trying. There's virtually no public transport and even once-quiet backroads like Jalan Betubelig from Kerobokan can now be traffic clogged. Never take the Tanah Lot highway in the afternoon, which is total roadblock. Locals and resident expats tend to use a bumpy network of little lanes and dirt pathways that are not plotted on maps, but even these can get bumper-to-bumper with mopeds as sunset approaches.

Inevitably, change is happening lightning-fast in Canggu and what was once a surfer bolthole is now developing at terrifying pace. Get there soon.

ARRIVAL AND DEPARTURE   KUTA–LEGIAN–SEMINYAK–CANGGU

BY PLANE

Bali's only airport, Ngurah Rai Airport (☎ 0361 751011 ext 5273 or ☎ 0361 751020 ext 5123, ⍟ ngurahrai-airport .co.id), is situated 3km south of Kuta. You'll find the usual ATMs and currency exchange booths in the baggage claim hall and just outside the Arrivals building, along with

car rental outlets. The 24hr left-luggage offices (Rp25,000/ day/item) are tucked away outside, between International Arrivals and Departures, to the right of Domestic Arrivals. **Prepaid taxis** The easiest way of getting away from the airport to Kuta–Legian–Seminyak is by pre-paid taxi. The counter is outside International Arrivals to the left, or just outside Arrivals in the domestic terminal. Fares are fixed: currently Rp55,000 to Tuban; Rp70,000–80,000 to Kuta; Rp95,000 to Legian; Rp110,000 to Seminyak; Rp150,000 to Kerobokan; Rp225,000 to Canggu.

Metered/app taxis Metered taxis are around twenty percent cheaper than prepaid. They're not licensed to pick up inside the compound, so wait on the road outside the airport gates (turn right outside International and walk about 500m). Blue Bird taxis are recommended. Uber and Grab app-taxis operate to some areas of southern Bali; rates are about half those charged by airport cabs. However it can be difficult to get one to pick you up from the airport due to opposition by local drivers.

Bemos Dark-blue public bemos often wait for customers on Jl Airport Ngurah Rai outside the airport gates during daylight hours, then run to Kuta. However, given that schedules are random and there can be extra charges for bags very few travellers bother with them.

Hotel pick-ups Many hotels offer pick-up from (and travel to) the airport for prices just above those charged by taxis.

BY SHUTTLE BUS

Private tourist shuttle buses run to all tourist destinations on Bali, including Lombok and the Gili Islands. There are many operators but Perama has the best reputation. Drop-offs are usually at the operator's office at the destination rather than specific hotels.

Perama Based 100m north of Bemo Corner at Jl Legian 39 (daily 6am–10pm; ☎0361 751875, ⓦperamatour.com); for an extra Rp25,000 you can be picked up (and dropped off) from/at your hotel. Typical fares include Rp35,000 to Sanur, Rp60,000 to Ubud, Rp125,000 to Lovina and Rp450,000 to the Gili Islands (including boat transfer).

Destinations Amed (daily; 3hr 15min); Bedugul (daily; 2hr 30min–3hr); Candidasa (4 daily; 2hr 15min); Gili Islands (daily; 9hr 30min); Kintamani (daily; 2hr 30min); Lovina (daily; 4hr); Nusa Lembongan (daily; 2hr 30min); Padang Bai (4 daily; 2hr); Sanur (7 daily; 30min); Senggigi, Lombok (daily; 9hr); Ubud (6 daily; 1hr–1hr 30min).

BY BEMO

Public bemos in south Bali ply limited routes through the Kuta area. From Denpasar's Tegal terminal (see p.89), the dark-blue Tegal–Kuta–Legian bemo goes via Bemo Corner and runs clockwise via Jl Pantai Kuta, Jl Melasti and north up Jl Legian as far as Jl Yudistira (Jl Padma), before returning back down Jl Legian to Bemo Corner again. If you're staying in south Kuta, note that drivers generally drop passengers on the eastern edge of Jl Bakung Sari – a 5min walk from Bemo Corner. Coming by bemo from Jimbaran, you'll probably be dropped off at the same place. Arrival from elsewhere in Bali by bemo almost always entails going via Denpasar.

Destinations Denpasar (Tegal terminal; 35min); Jimbaran (30min); Ngurah Rai Airport (20min); Nusa Dua (Bali Collection; 40min).

BY BUS

There are two useful bus services. Kura Kura (ⓦkura2bus .com) runs a/c minibuses (with wi-fi) across southern Bali (Rp50,000) and to Ubud (Rp70,000) via its depot in T-Galleria, Jl By Pass Ngurah (east Kuta); from here regular buses arrive/depart for Kuta beach, Legian and Seminyak (all Rp20,000). Alternatively, Trans Sarbagita buses do not have a great reputation for reliability or punctuality but operate two routes: Batubulan bemo terminal–Sanur Bypass–Kuta Central

ALTERNATIVE ROAD NAMES

As if the confusion of lanes wasn't enough, the resort of Kuta–Legian–Seminyak plays fast and loose with **road names**. Many roads were named after their first or biggest hotel or restaurant and although they have been given official names (indeed, often several in succession over the years), many local residents, taxi drivers and maps stick to older versions, and street signs are rarely consistent. The following are the most confusing examples. The **official name** is given in bold.

Jalan Kayu Aya (Petitenget) Previously called Jalan Laksmana and Jalan Oberoi – now sometimes known as "Eat Street" because of its many restaurants.

Jalan Camplung Tanduk (Seminyak) Also known as Jalan Dhyana Pura and Jalan Abimanyu, and sometimes as Jalan Gado-Gado, after the restaurant at the western end.

Jalan Arjuna (Legian) Commonly referred to as Jalan Double Six after the famous nightclub located on the beach.

Jalan Yudistira (Legian) Until very recently this was Jalan Padma.

Jalan Pantai Arjuna (Legian) Also known as Jalan Blue Ocean Beach, after one of its hotels.

Jalan Werk Udara (Legian) Formerly called Jalan Bagus Taruna, and sometimes known as Jalan Rum Jungle, after a restaurant.

Jalan Bakung Sari (south Kuta/Tuban) Previously known as Jalan Singo Sari.

1

Parking–Jimbaran–Nusa Dua; and Puputan Square (Renon)–Udayana University Campus (near Jimbaran)–GWK. In theory buses run every 30min from 5am–9pm. Current flat-rate fares are Rp3500.

GETTING AROUND

By bemo Public bemos are in decline (see p.65), so unless you're on a very tight budget or bloody-minded enough to wait, a taxi is often easier. Kuta bemos are dark-blue. Local trips cost around Rp5000.

By taxi The most reliable taxis are the light-blue Blue Bird taxis (☎0361 701111; ⍟bluebirdgroup.com) which you can order online or via their app. Uber and Grab app-taxis also operate in this part of Bali.

BY BOAT
Private agents such as Perama (see p.65) offer integrated bus and boat tickets to Lombok, Nusa Lembongan and other Indonesian islands.

By car, bike or motorbike Countless tour agents offer car and motorbike rental. Many also offer bicycles – arguably the best way to get around, though not for the faint-hearted. Such is the traffic that a car is more hassle than it's worth within the resort. Where it is legal to park beside the road, attendants charge Rp2000 to wave you in and out and guard your vehicle.

INFORMATION AND ACTIVITIES

Adventure activities operators Bali Adventure Tours (☎0361 721480, ⍟baliadventuretours.com) and See Bali Adventures (☎0361 794 9693, ⍟seebaliadventures.com) offer mountain-bike trips from the rim of Gunung Batur volcano, plus trekking and elephant tours. Sobek (☎0361 768050, ⍟balisobek.com) specializes in cycling and rafting/kayaking tours on the Grade II–III rapids of the Ayung River. All provide free transfers in southern Bali.

Diving AquaMarine Diving, Jl Petitenget 2A, Kuta (☎0361 738020, ⍟aquamarinediving.com) and Manta Manta Diving, Jl Padma, Legian (☎0812 3787 0200, ⍟manta manta-diving.com) both run dive trips to southern Bali sites such as Nusa Penida, including transport from the Kuta–Legian–Seminyak area.

Kitesurfing Operators Sanur (see p.95) provide pick-ups from the Kuta area.

Tourist information There's an official tourist office at Jl Raya Kuta 2 (in theory Mon–Sat 9am–7pm; ☎0361 766188).

SURFING IN KUTA

They say **surfing** was introduced to Bali by American hotel-owner Bob Koke in 1936. Today it is huge in the Kuta strip; the beach, Poppies 2, Poppies 1 and Jalan Benesari are crammed with board rental and repair shops and surfwear outlets. Surf championships are regular events.

As Kuta is a sandy beach with no coral or rocks to wipe out on, it's a **great place to learn** to surf. However, while Kuta may have launched many a surfer's lifetime hobby, don't underestimate the power of waves on bigger days. First-timers should book a preliminary lesson to guarantee their safety. Slightly more advanced breaks can be found further south in Tuban, accessed by boats from the lot at the west end of Jalan Wana Segara. North of Seminyak, in the Canggu area, there are reef breaks at Batu Bolong, Echo Beach and Pererenan. The best **time of year** for surfing off Kuta is during the dry season (April–Oct); at other times surfers head east to Sanur and Nusa Dua.

SURF SCHOOLS

Surfing **lessons** are offered throughout the resort, but choose your instructor carefully; personal recommendation is always good, and bear in mind that established **surf schools** are accredited and have insurance. In these, prices average $45 for a half-day introduction in a group. Freelance instructors hang out on all the main beaches, charging around $15/hr including board rental.

Odyssey's Surf School Mercure Kuta Bali, Jl Pantai Kuta ☎0815 5821 8778.

Pro Surf School Jl Pantai Kuta ☎0361 744 1466, ⍟prosurfschool.com. Accommodation (including dorms) is available on site.

Rip Curl School of Surf Blue Ocean hotel, Jl Pantai Arjuna, Legian ☎0361 750459, ⍟ripcurlschoolof surf.com. Also offers wakeboarding, kitesurfing, windsurfing and stand-up paddleboard lessons as well as equipment rental and has a base in Sanur.

UP2U Surf School Jl Pantai Kuta, Legian ☎0812 3699 7504, ⍟up2usurfschool.com. Beginner group lessons cost Rp300,000; private lessons are Rp500,000.

COURSES AND CLASSES

1

Once you tire of sea, sun, sand and shopping, you will be able to find more cultural and spiritual pastimes amid the hedonism.

Balinese cookery *Saté Bali* restaurant (Jl Kayu Aya 22A, Petitenget ☎ 0361 736734, ✉ satebali@yahoo.com) offers 3hr classes, led by expert chef Nyoman Sudiyasa (9.30am–1.30pm; Rp400,000 including lunch).

Indonesian language Seminyak Language School (Jl Seminyak 7 ☎ 0819 9949 3275, ⊛ learnindonesianinbali .com) runs short courses for tourists, family courses and longer 40hr courses, one-to-one or in groups. Also has a branch in Canggu.

Massage Jari Menari (Jl Raya Basangkasa, Seminyak ☎ 0361 736740, ⊛ jarimenari.com) is a well-known massage centre offering one- and twelve-day courses (Tues 9am–3.30pm;

one day, Rp2,363,000/person).

Yoga, Pilates and meditation There are more than a dozen yoga schools in this region. Up to five drop-in sessions a day in numerous styles are run at the *Desa Seni* hotel (Jl Subak Sari 13, Canggu ☎ 0361 844 6392, ⊛ desaseni .com) as well as longer retreats and yoga training. *The Island* hotel (Gang IX, off Jl Legian ☎ 0361 762722, ⊛ theisland hotelbali.com) offers daily classes of hatha and "surf" yoga. Umalas Pilates (Jl Umalas Klecung 33, Kerobokan ☎ 0818 1918 0630, ⊛ facebook.com/Umalaspilatesstudio) is a professional studio equipped with reformers.

ACCOMMODATION

You're spoilt for choice for accommodation here. Most in Kuta is of the cheap and cheerful variety: hostels, losmen and somewhat dated mid-range places. The accomoodation in Legian, Seminyak and Kerobokan is more expensive and more chic. Canggu has more villas for rent than hotels or guesthouses, but there are some highly characterful places.

KUTA AND TUBAN

Bali Caps Hostel Jl Bypass Ngurah Rai 9A, ☎ 0361 849 6665 ⊛ balicaps.com; map p.58. Large, well-designed new hostel which feels more like a minimalist hotel; cleanliness is excellent and the modern dorms (with single or double beds) are spacious and supremely comfortable. There's a pool table and dartboard, free breakfast and shuttle service to the beach and airport. Dorms **Rp110,000**

Bendesa Jl Legian ☎ 0361 754 366, ⊛ bendesa accommodation.com; map p.60. A cut above most of the competition, with a range of decent-sized rooms in a large, leafy complex around a pleasant pool, and friendly staff. **Rp200,000**

★ **H-ostel** Kuta Square E8, ☎ 361 475 2387, ⊛ h-ostel .com; map p.60. Very centrally located, this contemporary hostel is close to vibrant nightlife, shopping and 200m from the beach. All dorms (mixed and female) are a/c and bunks are equipped with charging sockets, reading lights and lockers. There's a great roof terrace, cafe, speedy wi-fi and breakfast is included. Dorms **Rp150,000**

Hostel Kempu Taman Ayu II Jl Benesari ☎ 0361 754376, ⊛ homestaykempu.com; map p.60. As basic as it gets in the cheapest fan-only rooms – there's a bed, a rudimentary bathroom with hot water and outside seating – and things are a mite shabby, if clean. But if you want a rock bottom price, it fits the bill. **Rp170,000**

Kedin's Inn 1 Poppies 1 ☎ 0361 756771, ⊛ facebook .com/KedinsInn; map p.60. Backpackers' favourite with simple rooms arranged around quiet gardens and a pool. It's in the thick of the action, though you'd never know it. You'll pay an extra Rp50,000 for a/c, and more still for hot water. **Rp250,000**

Masa Inn 31 Poppies 1 ☎ 0361 758507, ⊛ masainn .com; map p.60. With two pools and a pretty garden, this long-running family-run place has a traditional, Balinese feel with a/c, mid-range rooms and a restaurant. Singles (Rp325,000) are competitively priced too. **Rp500,000**

Poppies Cottages Poppies 1 ☎ 0361 751059, ⊛ poppies bali.com; map p.60. The attention to detail and genuinely warm welcome from the staff (many have worked here for decades) has served this place well, for it's full of visitors who return every year. Twenty charming, traditionally styled thatched cottages are scattered in a tropical garden around a lovely pool. Reserve ahead. **$127**

★ **The Sandi Phala** Jl Wana Segara ☎ 0361 753780, ⊛ thesandiphala.com; map p.61. Accommodation in lofty thatched rooms and suites that marry modern style with traditional design, mature gardens with a pool, faultless staff and a beach location that feels like it's on another island and not a mere 20min walk to central Kuta. **$122**

Sorga Cottages Gang Sorga, off Poppies 1 ☎ 0361 751897, ⊛ hotelsorgakuta.com; map p.60. On a quiet alley, yet within firing range of the clubs on Jl Legian, these dated-but-decent rooms are comfortable, if something of a 1980s timewarp. There's a small pool and restaurant. **Rp265,000**

Un's Hotel Jl Benesari ☎ 0361 757409, ⊛ unshotel .com; map p.60. Antique furnishings, art and traditional architecture plus a lovely small garden with pool combine to provide a good-value stay with Balinese character. All rooms have hot-water en-suites but you'll pay about Rp40,000 more for a/c. **Rp457,000**

1

LEGIAN

Bali Niksoma Jl Padma Utara ☎ 0361 751946, ⓦ bali niksoma.com; map p.62. Crisp Balinese minimalism in an award-winning boutique hotel bang on the beach. Deluxe rooms are worth the extra expense for their style and space. Also has a spa, a pool overlooking the breakers and faultless service. **$225**

Hotel Kumala Jl Werk Udara ☎ 0361 732186, ⓦ hotel kumala.com; map p.62. A five-minute walk from the beach, and with lots of cafes and restaurants close by, this fine-value hotel has real Balinese flavour thanks to a scattering of statuary and carvings. Avoid the standard rooms which are very plain; the others are spacious and well-furnished, all with a/c, hot water and modern bathrooms. There's a pool and restaurant. **Rp375,000**

Hotel Kumala Pantai Jl Werk Udara ☎ 0361 755500, ⓦ kumalapantai.com; map p.62. Popular with families and couples, this resort hotel has comfortable classic-modern a/c rooms with balconies, cable TV, bath and shower, in three-storey buildings on the seafront road. There are also two pools, one of which is big enough for laps. **$85**

★ **The Island** Gang XIX off Jl Legian ☎ 0361 762722, ⓦ theislandhotelbali.com; map p.62. Great little place tucked in an alley that has the feel of a secret retreat. Nine small, stylish rooms are set around a little pool or alternatively there are two of the poshest dorms in town. The atmosphere is chilled and friendly and there's a nice lounge to hang out in. Dorms **Rp227,000**, doubles **Rp552,000**

Padma Resort Jl Yudistira 1 ☎ 0361 752111, ⓦ padma resortbali.com; map p.62. Smart resort hotel whose extensive tropical gardens run down to the beach. Accommodation, all near or with direct access to a pool, is in the hotel wings or larger deluxe "chalets" – some wheelchair-accessible – and there's a fine spread of facilities: restaurants, bars, pools, a spa, a complimentary kids' club and tours office. **$240**

★ **Three Brothers Bungalows** Jl Legian ☎ 0361 751566; map p.62. This place, in a mature garden setting with a pool, resembles a temple complex more than a hotel. Airy accommodation (rooms and two-storey cottages) boast Balinese carvings – "Deluxe" have four-poster beds and semi-outside bathrooms (they're worth the extra). **$58**

SEMINYAK, PETITENGET AND KEROBOKAN

★ **Anyar Estate** Jl Bumbak Dauh, Umalas ☎ 0361 736 559, ⓦ anyarestate.com; map p.64. Gorgeous pool villas, with two to five bedrooms, all with stylish Balinese furnishings and a contemporary feel in a tranquil village location on the east side of Kerobokan. Breakfast is cooked to order and there's plenty of space to entertain and relax. **$320**

The Breezes Bali Resort Jl Camplung Tanduk 66 ☎ 0361 730573, ⓦ thebreezesbali.com; map p.63. Good-quality resort hotel near the beach, where tasteful modern rooms gather around a split-level lagoon-style pool – the big draw here, especially for families. Also has a tennis court, on-site spa, gym, cinema and daily activities, plus shuttle buses to Legian. Rates drop to $100 or so during quiet times. **$156**

Inada Losmen Gang Bima 9, off Jl Camplung Tanduk and Jl Raya Seminyak ☎ 0361 732269, ⓔ putuinada @hotmail.com; map p.63. This cheapie run by a helpful Indonesian/Japanese couple has a dozen basic rooms: a bed, a desk, a fan, a bathroom with hot water – and that's your lot. **Rp180,000**

The Oberoi Jl Kayu Aya ☎ 0361 730361, ⓦ oberoihotels .com; map p.63. The *grande dame* of local luxury hotels provides beautiful, traditional-style rooms and villas – think thatched roofs meet marble bathrooms – all privately secluded in gorgeous beachfront grounds. To its credit, the ambience remains distinctly Balinese despite the finest international standards (to which numerous awards and celebrity guests testify). **$355**

Uma Sri Gang Kerta Rahayu 9, Kerobokan ☎ 0811 399 513, ⓦ umasribali.com; map p.64. Set in a peaceful Kerobokan location, these attractive a/c rooms (with terrace or balcony) in two-storey blocks overlook a large pool and restaurant area. Staff can be a little distracted but it's good value given the facilities and location. **$33**

Raja Gardens Jl Camplung Tanduk ☎ 0361 730494, ⓔ jdw@eksadata.com; map p.63. A real haven, this small setup has nine rooms in a beautiful garden a moment's walk from the beach. The brick bungalows are all white rattan and bleached-wood furnishings, some with open bathrooms. Peaceful, family run and good value. **Rp475,000**

★ **W Retreat** Jl Petitenget ☎ 0361 300 0106, ⓦ wretreatbali.com; map p.63. A kind of resort city for hipsters featuring a blend of glamour and playfulness in open-plan public areas, stylish bars and restaurants, all gathered around a multi-tiered pool of simply staggering dimensions. At night it feels more like an ultraspacious cool club than a hotel. Choose between 159 well-appointed rooms or 79 stunning garden villas with pools. **$315**

CANGGU AND PERERENAN

The Chillhouse Jl Kubu Manyar 22, Canggu ☎ 0812 3958 3056, ⓦ thechillhouse.com; map p.64. Laidback surf-inspired style – think designer lampshades, a crisp colour scheme and surf photos – in a small garden hotel. Accommodation, in rooms, bungalows and a treetop loft, is all a/c and set in a lovely garden with a pool and restaurant. Offers surfing as well as massage and yoga packages. It's 500m from the beach; bikes are available. Doubles **$138**, bungalows **$182**

1

Desa Seni Jl Subak Sari 13, Canggu ☎0361 844 6392, ⓦdesaseni.com; map p.64. A New Age "village resort", this place consists of lovely old wooden houses sourced from across the Indonesian archipelago, rebuilt and exquisitely furnished with antiques and colourful flair. There are daily yoga classes among an array of mind-body-spirit programmes, a spa, complimentary bicycles and a saltwater pool. $150

★**FC Residence** Jl Pantai Pererenan ☎0821 4412 2023, ⓦfc-bali.com; map p.64. Gorgeous boutique hotel on the exquisitely peaceful northern side of Pererenan, fringed by ricefields and managed by a welcoming Anglo-French couple. The very generously sized and stylish rooms are grouped around a 30m pool, and there's a lovely open-sided restaurant with elevated views over the countryside. Rates drop to as low as $125 in low season. $200

★**Hotel Tugu Bali** Jl Pantai Canggu ☎0361 473 1701, ⓦtuguhotels.com; map p.64. Evoking Indonesian tradition like nowhere else on the island, this Canggu original has ambience, class and history. You stay in polished-teak houses set back from the beach, all beautifully furnished with antiques and many with private plunge pools. Communal areas are equally fabulous, from the restaurant set in a seventeeth-century Chinese temple (moved here brick by brick) to the *Calon Arang* bar, gorgeous pool and spa. $373

Pondok Nyoman Bagus Pantai Pererenan ☎0361 848 2925; map p.64. This friendly, family-run beachside losmen, set just behind the Pererenan surf break, has been pepped up with cheerful bright linen and modern bathrooms in the rooms, all of which have a/c. Deluxe options have sea views and you can check out the waves from a rooftop infinity pool. Rp480,000

Serenity Jl Nelayan ☎0361 747 4625, ⓦserenity ecoguesthouse.com; map p.64. This easy-going place built largely from bamboo has a certain ramshackle, rambling charm. The homely rooms have fan or a/c, and massage and yoga are on offer. There's a backpackers' annexe down the road. Free tea and coffee, bikes for rent and horseriding can be arranged. Good value. Dorms Rp160,000, doubles Rp200,000

EATING

This part of Bali is bursting with restaurants: from tiny **warung** to cutting-edge "**dining experiences**". The most sophisticated (and expensive) are in Seminyak, Petitenget, Canggu and especially Kerobokan; there's often little to differentiate the tourist restaurants in Kuta and Legian (we've selected some of the standouts). If rupiah are precious, Kuta's main **night market** (*pasar senggol*), on Jl Blambangan at the southern edge of Kuta, offers mains from Rp15,000.

KUTA AND TUBAN

Balcony Jl Benesari ☎0361 750655, ⓦthebalconybali .com; map p.60. This airy place segues from good breakfasts (such as Swiss bircher muesli or herb omelette) to mains (from Rp49,000) such as pork rib burger, grills and surfer-friendly Indonesian dishes. Also has magazines to browse. Daily 7am–midnight.

Kori Poppies 2 ☎0361 758605, ⓦkorirestaurant.co.id; map p.60. A lovely garden setting off Poppies 2 plus good food make this old-timer one of Kuta's standouts. Indonesian standards include *bebek goreng bumbu pedas* (crispy duck with spicy sambal, Rp145,000) and sates, while Thai and international dishes are also on the menu (though there's not a lot of choice for vegetarians). It's a lovely spot for a quiet evening drink, too. Daily noon–11pm.

Ma Joly Jl Wana Segara ☎0361 753780, ⓦwww .ma-joly.com; map p.61. The beachside restaurant of *The Sandi Phala* hotel scores for romance and light international-Asian dishes that live up to the location: most mains are Rp200,000 to 250,000 but there are pasta and risotto dishes for half that. Five-course menus (Rp590,000) offer good value for a splurge. Daily 8am–10pm.

Made's Warung Jl Pantai Kuta ☎0361 755297, ⓦmades warung.com; maps p.60 & p.63. The original tourist warung from 1969, now a Kuta institution that appeals for its simplicity and great classic Indonesian dishes such as *nasi campur* and Balinese specials such as duck (Rp55,000–180,000). The portions are large, the quality excellent. There's an offshoot on Jl Raya Seminyak in a rather more elegant setting. Daily 8am–midnight.

Poppies Poppies 1 ☎0361 751059, ⓦpoppiesbali .com; map p.60. A Kuta institution, established in 1973, which christened the road. And this haven from the hustle still packs 'em in for a huge Indonesian menu (*gado gado* is Rp43,000 or *nasi goreng* Rp65,000) and international menu (Rp50,000 and up) of well-cooked and well-presented food, all served beneath bougainvillea-draped pergolas. Daily 8am–11pm.

Warung Indonesia Gang Ronta ☎0361 759817; map p.60. In the thick of things, this relaxed warung is more authentic than most in the area, and attracts Indonesians too – always a good sign. Pick and mix your own veg and non-veg *nasi campur* (Rp30,000 will fill up most people) or order Indonesian staples and great value juices (around Rp15,000). Daily noon–midnight.

Warung Nikmat Gang Biduri 6A (off Jl Kubu Anyar) ☎0361 764678; map p.61. Javanese warung of the plastic stools persuasion where you can assemble a terrific *nasi campur* from around thirty spicy dishes – fried fish, beans with chilli, curried eggs, *urap* (steamed vegetables with spiced coconut), *tempeh* and much more for around Rp28,000. Daily 8am–9pm.

LEGIAN

Mugshot Jl Padma Utara ☎ 0361 750335; map p.62. Excellent flat white, long black, macchiato and piccolo latte coffees from an Australian-managed café, plus pastries, patisserie and Aussie-style pies (Rp40,000), as well as free use of computers and wi-fi. Daily 6am–6pm.

Warung Asia Jl Wekudara 5 ☎ 0361 742 0202, Ⓦ warungasia.com; map p.62. An airy upstairs café great for *Pad Thai* (Rp46,500), delicious palate-tingling curries (Rp59,000), Vietnamese spring rolls and satay. Daily 9am–11pm.

Warung Murah Jl Camplung Tanduk ☎ 0361 732082; map p.62. Hits the mark for thrifty diners, especially for lunch: select a *nasi campur* medley from curries, *tempeh*, fritters and vegetable dishes (from Rp20,000), or choose from the small menu featuring the usual Indo-Chinese suspects (from Rp25,000). Also serves organic wheatgrass shots and good juices. Daily 8am–11pm.

Warung Yogya Jl Padma Utara 79 ☎ 0361 750835; map p.62. A simple warung renowned for its unpretentious, cheap food: most dishes – such as *nasi pecel* (rice and veg with peanut sauce) – are just Rp20,000, or fill up on *nasi campur* (veg or non-veg) for Rp25,000. Daily 9am–10pm.

Zanzibar Jl Pantai Arjuna ☎ 0361 733528, Ⓦ zanzibar bali.com; map p.62. Boasts a raised terrace and breezy upper deck with views of the waves and a large, tourist-friendly menu, which includes good breakfasts (try a Spanish omelette), wood-fired pizza (from Rp50,000), pasta, steak and seafood. Daily 7.30am–10.30pm.

SEMINYAK, PETITENGET AND KEROBOKAN

Barbacoa Jl Petitenget 14 ☎ 0361 739233, Ⓦ barbacoa -bali.com; map p.63. Argentinian-style place with a spectacular warehouse-style dining room, and dishes roasted on an open fire. Highlights include grilled chorizo (Rp190,000), charcoal-grilled octopus (Rp110,000) and the frozen margaritas. Daily noon–3pm & 6pm–midnight.

★ **Biku** Jl Raya Petitenget 888 ☎ 0361 857 0888; map p.63. Tasty breakfasts and great lunches and dinners, taking in Indonesian food, posh burgers, salads featuring the likes of rocket, pumpkin, pear and feta (Rp52,000) and home-made pies (Rp68,000). Dining in the old Joglo provides a wonderful atmosphere, too. Reservations recommended. Daily 8am–11pm.

Café Bali Jl Laksmana ☎ 0361 736484; map p.63. With its mildly distressed furniture, pretty lampshades and lace tablecloths, this place has more charm than its cooler neighbours. The long, eclectic menu includes quesadillas and sushi rolls, pasta and grills, Indian and Indo faves. Daily 7am–midnight.

Café Moka Jl Raya Seminyak ☎ 0361 731424, Ⓦ cafemokabali.com; map p.63. A modern a/c French patisserie offering filling set breakfasts, fine crusty pies and quiches (try the pumpkin and broccoli, Rp34,000) plus pastries, cakes, sandwiches, salads, tapas and more. Daily 7am–10pm.

Corner House Jl Laksmana 10A ☎ 0361 730276, Ⓦ corner housebali.com; map p.63. Stunning café-restaurant in an a/c loft-like space that's great for brunch, grilled meats and salads (virtually all dishes are Rp70,000 to Rp90,000). There's a kids' menu too. Daily 7am–11pm.

Earth Café Jl Laksmana 99 ☎ 0361 736645, Ⓦ earth cafebali.com; map p.63. Tasty vegetarian dishes, predominantly organic, including the likes of quinoa coconut curry (Rp52,000), Arabic salad with tahini (Rp55,000) and delicious smoothies and juices in a buzzy little vegetarian café. Daily 7am–11pm.

La Lucciola On beach beside Pura Petitenget car park, off Jl Petitenget ☎ 0361 730838; map p.63. Saffron risotto with seafood and a dash of chilli typifies the high-end Mediterranean flavours in this open beach restaurant; mains are Rp80,000–170,000. It's a popular spot for sunset cocktails as much as romantic dinners. Daily 9am–11pm.

Mama San Jl Raya Kerobokan 135 ☎ 0812 3634 3386, Ⓦ mamasanbali.com; map p.63. A hip warehouse-style space with eclectic retro leanings – love that painted mural. Food-wise it's sizzling Southeast Asian, with Thai, Malay and Indonesian dishes such as crispy salted pork with yellow bean, garlic, chilli and *gailan* (Rp150,000). Nice lounge bar above, too. Reservations recommended. Mon–Sat noon–3pm & Sun 6–11pm.

★ **Sardine** Jl Petitenget 21 ☎ 0361 738202, Ⓦ sardine bali.com; map p.63. Gorgeous imaginative cuisine in a bamboo *bale*-style structure beside a ricefield. Fish and seafood dominate the menu, with the dishes changing daily depending on the catch – miso-grilled mahi-mahi (Rp180,000), Jimbaran-style fish and organic salads are typical. Daily 11.30am–11pm.

Sarong Jl Petitenget 19X ☎ 0361 473 7809, Ⓦ sarong bali.com; map p.63. Sophisticated South Asian flavours to tingle the tastebuds – Aceh lamb cooked over a coconut chargrill and fluffy naan bread – in a consistently excellent high-end Kerobokan restaurant. With its plush neocolonial style and open sides, the elegant dining area is a delight by candlelight. Daily 6pm–midnight.

CANGGU

Betel Nut Café Jl Batu Bolong 60 ☎ 0821 4680 7233 (SMS only); map p.64. Popular travellers' hangout split between a small a/c interior and an airy upper deck. Either way, you're here for a healthy menu: whole coconuts, fresh juices, salads, wraps and a great selection of burgers (Rp50,000) – fresh fish, veggie and beetroot patties. Tues–Sun 7am–10pm.

Desa Seni Jl Kayu Putih 13, Pantai Berewa; map p.64. Fresh and organic are watchwords in the restaurant of this quirky eco-resort; many of the vegetables are grown on site, while dishes such as seafood in coconut milk and lemongrass (mostly Rp65,000) are delicious. Also offers salads and pastas in the same relaxing setting. Daily noon–11pm.

In The Raw Jl Batu Bolong ☎0812 3749 6861; map p.64. Hip Brit-owned cafe perfect for cold-pressed juices (Rp36,000), smoothies, raw foods – "love bowls" (fruit smoothies topped with granola), nori rolls and salads – and other nutritious snacks. Coffee and teas are also available. Daily 7am-5pm.

Mo:ya Café Jl Bumbak Dauh 91X, Kerobokan ☎0822 3707 3880; map p.64. Boho chic café-restaurant with tables bordering ricefields and a tempting menu that takes in perfectly prepared breakfasts (Rp50,000 including eggs, bacon, sourdough bread, fruit salad and orange juice), western and Indonesian mains, and healthy delights such as a papaya "boat" filled with dragon fruit, banana, almond, walnut, pumpkin seed and cashews. Daily 8am–7pm.

★**One Eyed Jack** Jl Pantai Berawa ☎0819 9929 1888, ☎oneeyedjackbali.com; map p.64. Established by an ex-Nobu chef, One Eyed Jack features stupendous Japanese fusion cooking. Choose from the small plates menu, with highlights including crispy soft-shell crab sliders (Rp75,000), black cod tacos (Rp65,000), kelp salad and yakitori bites. There's a good choice of sake too. The premises are deceptively humble given the quality of the cuisine – expect to pay around $40 a head for a memorable feed. Daily 5pm–midnight

Savage Kitchen Plaza Club, Jl Raya Pantai Berawa ☎0819 1641 4541, ☎thesavagekitchen.com; map p.64. Raw and wild, this uber-healthy café-restaurant serves creative organic cuisine at pretty moderate rates for the area. You pick a salad (all Rp55,000; try the green papaya and rustic cabbage) then add some protein (meat or fish), sauce or side order if needed. Wash it all down with a "phytonutrient" juice, young coconut water or (whisper it) even a beer. Daily 6.30am-9.30pm.

Warung Varuna Jl Batu Bolong 89; map p.64. Surfers' hangout with chunky wooden tables and paint-smeared walls. Serves up a mean nasi campur for about Rp24,000, depending on dishes selected. There's a useful noticeboard for yoga classes and community events. Daily 8am–10pm.

BEACH BARS AND CLUBS

For lazy days and balmy nights enjoying food and drink beside the breakers, Bali's **beach clubs** are very popular indeed. But choose carefully, as some of these places have become oversized, Vegas-style and soulless – Finns take note. Relaxed little beach **bar-shacks** endure here and there too. **Entrance charges** vary greatly according to the venue and night. The mainstream Kuta clubs are usually free to get in. More upmarket venues in Seminyak and elsewhere tend to charge Rp75,000–100,000 entrance; more if there's a big DJ or band playing.

Ku Dé Ta Jl Kayu Aya 9 ☎0361 736969, ☎kudeta.com; map p.63. Globally famous venue that remains a cut above the competition for sophisticated dining and relaxing beachside. The sea views are as breathtaking as the prices on the dinner menu (Rp280,000 for parmesan- and sumac-crusted pork). Often hosts club nights too. Daily 8am–1pm.

La Plancha Seminyak Beach; map p.63. With its blast of colour, this little beach shack feels more Mexico than Bali. Alongside lazy beach vibes and beats, it serves a small menu of tapas favourites (Rp55,000) plus chicken and seafood (from Rp70,000). Come early to bag a cushion on the beach. Daily usually 7am–11pm but occasional parties until 3am.

★**Old Man's** Jl Batu Bolong, Canggu ☎0361 846 9158, ☎oldmans.net; map p.64. A no-nonsense, wildly popular Canggu beach bar with tables by the waves that draws an eclectic, incongruous crowd of surfers, expats, boozers, boozing surfer expats, yogis and even the odd local. Check out its "Dirty Wednesday" parties, live music on Fridays and regular events. Beer is cheap and the ambience is social and relaxed. Daily 7am–11pm

★**Potato Head** Kerobokan beach, off Jl Petitenget ☎0361 473 7979, ☎ptthead.com; map p.63. With an exterior clad in old shutters, this effortlessly hip beach club shouts style. Eclectic retro furnishings tap into the glamour of Fifties Miami, but really it's about great modern food, great chilled beats and great views of the waves as you laze by the pool on a day bed. Daily 11am–2am.

Warung 707 Batu Belig Beach; map p.64. The perfect beach hangout with bean bags and a shack for a bar serving simple drinks. Musically it's far more sophisticated than some of the mega beach clubs, with DJs playing deep house, reggae and funk to a boho clientele.

NIGHTLIFE

Bali has a vibrant nightlife scene, with the vibe very much depending on the area. **Kuta**'s bars and clubs are loud and laddish – this is the drunken home of the jam jar (pint-sized cocktails of multiple spirits) and countless happy hours. Start at Paddy's Club and follow the crowds from one to the next. The scene is more sophisticated in **Legian**, **Seminyak** and **Kerobokan**, with an ever-changing choice of lounge bars, plus occasional nights at beach clubs (see above). Many clubs stage **live music** and special events, detailed in the free fortnightly **magazine** the beat (☎thebeatbali.com).

1

KUTA AND LEGIAN

Apache Reggae Bar Jl Legian 146 ⊕0361 761213; map p.60. Tucked in what seems to be a Balinese barn beside *Bounty*, Kuta's reggae spot is all heavy bass. Features talented live bands every night, and resident DJs. Daily 8pm–3am.

Bounty Jl Legian, near Poppies 2 junction; map p.60. Infamous hub of bare-chested boozy excess, centred around a replica of Captain Bligh's ship. Expect mainstream dance, cover bands on live music stages, themed foam parties and much drunkenness. A love-or-loathe experience. Daily 10am–4am.

Engine Room Jl Legian ⊛engineroombali.com; map p.60. Occupying several levels, this established club is the place to come for pumping R&B, hip-hop and house. Drinks are cheap and it's popular with a party-loving international crowd. Daily 9pm–3am.

La Vida Loca Pantai Arjuna 7; map p.62. Salsa, Nu Yorica, Cuban son and the occasional burst into Brazilian samba in a small rather scruffy nightspot just behind the beach, with a live band nightly around 11pm. Daily 8pm–3am.

Paddy's Club Jl Legian 66, near Poppies 2 junction ⊕0361 726666; map p.60. This place – Part of the *Bounty* complex – is huge and open-sided but still manages to get crammed; think chart sounds, drinking competitions and organized merriment for a young crowd. Daily 5pm–3am.

Sky Garden Jl Legian 61, across from Poppies 2 ⊛sky gardenbali.com; map p.60. Spread over four floors, this multibar/club venue is loud, lively and fun, with various rooms pumping out different sounds, and terraces with views across the resort. Draws top DJs like Afrojack. Daily 5pm–3am.

Vi Ai Pi Jl Legian 88 ⊕0361 752355, ⊛viaipibali.com; map p.60. Smart restaurant-bar-club with live music most nights from 9pm, and bands playing pop and rock anthems. From midnight DJs take over, playing the latest electronic dance sounds. Daily 11am–3am.

SEMINYAK, PETITENGET AND KEROBOKAN

Hu'u Jl Petitenget ⊕0361 473 6576, ⊛huubali.com; map p.63. There's style and atmosphere at this hip drink 'n' dine place that's quiet midweek but rocking at weekends. Think sofas in a candlelit garden with a swimming pool and dancing in a loft-style bar. Musically it's got a little more commercial in recent years, but it's still a fun night out. Mon–Fri 11am–1am, Sat & Sun 11am–2am.

★Koh Jl Camplung Tanduk 15X, Seminyak ⊛facebook .com/kohbali; map p.63. For more of an underground vibe, this credible club has tech house, deep house and progressive DJs, a mean sound system and an industrial feel. Artists who have performed here include Bushwacka, Skream and Ralph Lawson. Thurs 10pm–4am, Fri & Sat 11pm–5am.

Woobar Jl Petitenget ⊕0361 300 0106, ⊛wretreatbali .com; map p.63. The glossy bar of the *W Retreat* hotel (see p.68) is very Ibiza/Miami club-cool – start beachside on the terrace with sunset cocktails (around – gulp – Rp150,000), then move into the main bar area, all soundtracked by lounge and disco-house. A small downstairs club opens for occasional international DJs. Mon–Thurs & Sun noon–1am, Fri & Sat noon–2am.

SHOPPING

Kuta–Legian–Seminyak is retail dreamland, especially for clothes, surfing gear, homeware and souvenirs. There's a 6km strip from Bemo Corner up Jl Legian into Seminyak that takes in everything from cheap, mass-market stuff to style and substance around Seminyak where Jl Kayu Aya has several designer stores. Things get quirkier and more independent the further north you go: Kerobokan and Canggu have many intriguing little stores selling unusual clothing and craft products.

ART, BOOKS, DVDS AND MUSIC

Biasa Artspace Jl Raya Seminyak 34 ⊕0361 730308, ⊛biasagroup.com; map p.63. Part of the clothing store next door (see opposite), this light commercial gallery specializes in exhibitions of modern Indonesian art. Daily 9am–9pm.

Periplus Made's Warung 2, Seminyak; Discovery Shopping Mall, Tuban ⊛periplus.com; map p.61. This outstanding chain of English-language bookshops has branches throughout the resort and features novels and plenty of books about Bali and Indonesia among an eclectic nonfiction range, plus international magazines. All daily 10am–9pm.

CLOTHES, JEWELLERY AND ACCESSORIES

Stylish boutiques are concentrated on the northern end of Jl Legian, Jl Raya Seminyak and up in Kerobokan and Canggu. Surfwear shops abound, though prices for genuine clothing is rarely any cheaper than in Australia or the UK.

★Biasa Jl Raya Seminyak 36, Jl Raya Seminyak 34 ⊕0361 730308, ⊛biasagroup.com; map p.63. Two adjacent stores with elegant, tasteful clothing from natural fabrics for men and women, plus scarves and a sophisticated take on Indonesian jewellery. Daily 9am–9pm.

By The Sea Jl Laksmana 20C ⊕0361 732198, ⊛bythe seatropical.com; map p.63. Relaxed, casual beach fashions for men, women and children; think loose-fitting, unfussy designs in navy, white, pale grey and cream. Daily 10am–10pm.

Gaia Jl Kayu Aya 88, Seminyak ⊕0812 3676 2266, ⊛gaia .co.id; map p.63. This "house of shades" stocks a fine range of sunglasses including designs by Le Specs, Ksubi, DITA, House Of Holland and Karen Walker. Daily 10am–10pm.

1

Paul Ropp Jl Laksmana 68, Raya Seminyak 39 ☎0361 735613, ⊛paulropp.com; map p.63. If you want to make a statement, these zesty boho-chic fashions hand-tailored from brightly coloured silks and cotton are just the ticket. Daily 9am–9pm.

Uluwatu Two branches on Jl Legian, also at Jl Pantai Kuta, Jl Laksmana ☎0361 751933, ⊛uluwatu.co.id; map p.60. White and black handmade Balinese lace and cotton clothes in modern styles that make a virtue of simplicity. Also some bedding. Daily 8am–10pm.

DEPARTMENT STORES, SUPERMARKETS AND SHOPPING CENTRES

Beachwalk Jl Pantai Kuta ⊛beachwalkbali.com; map p.60. This cathedral to consumer culture is the antithesis of the neighbouring stalls – its multistorey venue has cooling mists, the full gamut of international chains from Accessorize to Zara and Gap, plus cafés like *Starbucks* and even a cinema. You'll love it or loathe it. Daily 10am–midnight.

Discovery Shopping Mall Jl Kartika Plaza, Tuban ⊛discoveryshoppingmall.com; map p.61. A colossal place on the seafront that's a good one-stop shopping destination, with scores of international and local brand-name clothing stores, including Indonesian department stores, a bookshop or two, plus several cafés. Daily 10am–10pm.

HANDICRAFTS, SOUVENIRS AND HOMEWARES

The so-called art markets and stalls in Kuta are generally full of tourist tat; mass-produced batik and handicraft souvenirs from all over Indonesia. As with clothing, the better-made items are in Legian and Seminyak. The cheapest places to buy everyday rayon and mass-produced cotton sarongs are the street stalls and art markets of Kuta and Jl Arjuna.

Ashitaba Jl Raya Seminyak 6 ☎0361 737054; map p.63. Intricate *ata*-grass goods crafted in the Bali Aga village of Tenganan, fashioned into everything from place mats and bowls to baskets and clutches, all sold at fixed prices. Daily 9am–9pm.

Deus ex Machina Jl Batu Mejan 8, Canggu ☎0361 217 1076, ⊛deuscustoms.com; map p.64. Way of life store-café-hangout which sells surfboards, skatewear, art and the coolest customised motorcycles in Asia. Grab a coffee or a bite while you browse. Daily 8am–10.30pm

★**Lucy's Batik** Jl Raya Basangkasa 88, Seminyak ☎0361 736098, ⊛lucysbatik.com; map p.63. Stunning Javanese batik sarongs and scarves, from stamped cotton wraps up to exquisite hand-drawn silk versions (which cost millions), plus some homewear (from recycled wood and shells), accessories and kids' clothing. Daily 9.30am–9pm.

★**Makassi** Jl Raya Basangkasa, Kuta Square D18 ☎0361 733764 or ☎0361 754955, ⊛makassi.com; map p.61. Colourful, kitsch bags, clutches, gifts and some clothing. Items can be customized to your own design from a photo for example. Daily 9am–8pm.

Next Generation Board Bags Jl Benesari; map p.60. This workshop will produce your perfect board bag from a selection of designs; plain or patterned, some with a dash of Indo kitsch. All board lengths and shapes catered to. Turnaround time is two to three days. Daily 10am–9pm.

Upcycle Bali Jl Arjuna ☎0813 9674 9986, ⊛navehmilo .com; map p.62. Styling itself as a "green museum shop", this delightfully offbeat store stocks bags made from playing cards and wrappers, hats from measuring tape and lots of other curios.

SPAS AND BEAUTY TREATMENTS

Cheap and cheerful **day spas** abound, offering massages, pedicures and manicures from dawn until well after dark, and you'll doubtless be offered a kneading on the beach from one of Kuta's conical-hatted massage women. In addition, most **high-end hotels** listed in the Guide have a spa open to non-residents.

Bodyworks Jl Kayu Jati 2, Petitenget ☎0361 733317, ⊛bodyworksbali.com. Set around a courtyard, this long-running and well-regarded treatment centre offers an extensive menu of massages (from Rp260,000) including Balinese, Javanese (*mandi lulur*), Thai, hot stone, exfoliation and aromatherapy. Beauty treatments are also available. Daily 9am–10pm.

Dala Spa Villa de Daun, Jl Raya Legian ☎0361 756276, ⊛dalaspa.com. Award-winning spa offering fabulous pampering in plush, luxurious surroundings just a short walk from Jl Legian. The signature two-hour treatment (Rp845,000) takes in foot massage, aromatherapy and a facial. Daily 9am–10pm.

Jari Menari Jl Raya Basangkasa 47, Seminyak ☎0361 736740, ⊛jarimenari.com. *Jari Menari* means "dancing fingers" and this all-male massage centre certainly lives up to that, with professional massages (from Rp385,000/ 1hr 15min) and courses. Reservations advisable. Daily 9am–9pm.

Murano Spa Jl Dewi Saraswati III (also known as Jl Kunti II), Seminyak ☎0361 738140, ⊛muranospa .com. Well-regarded, excellent-value spa – it's tucked away a bit, so take advantage of the free pick-up service. Massages (from Rp100,000/hr), reflexology and packages are available. Daily 10am–8pm.

1

DIRECTORY

Banks and exchange ATMs are everywhere. Be careful at exchange counters: there are several well-known scams (see box, p.48). A recommended moneychanger is PT Central Kuta, which has many bureaux in the Kuta–Legian–Seminyak region, including several on Jl Legian. If you do get caught in a moneychanging scam, contact the community police (see below).

Dentist Bali Dental Clinic 911, 2nd Floor, Mal Bali Galleria, Simpang Siur roundabout, Jl Bypass Ngurah Rai (☎0361 766254, ⬥bali911dentalclinic.com). In addition, International SOS (see below) has a dentist.

Embassies and consulates See p.25.

Hospitals and clinics Two reputable, private 24hr hospitals on the outskirts of Kuta have English-speaking staff, A&E facilities, ambulance and medical evacuation services: Bali International Medical Centre (BIMC), Jl Bypass Ngurah Rai 100X (☎0361 761263, ⬥bimcbali.com) and International SOS, Jl Bypass Ngurah Rai 505X (☎0361 710505, ⬥internationalsos.com). For quicker (and cheaper) consultations, Legian Clinic, Jl Benesari,

Kuta (☎0361 758503) offers 24hr services and consultations from Rp575,000.

Immigration office Jl Ngurah Rai, Tuban (☎0361 751038).

Left luggage Hotels and losmen will store your luggage if you reserve a room for your return; some charge a nominal fee. There's also left luggage at the airport (see p.64) and, for Perama customers, at the Perama office, Jl Legian 39, Kuta (daily 6am–10pm; Rp15,000/week or part thereof; ☎0361 751875).

Police Community police, Satgas Pantai Desa Adat Kuta, are English-speaking and in 24hr attendance at their office on the beach in front of *Inna Kuta Beach Hotel* (☎0361 762871). Tourist police are further north on Jl Pantai Kuta. The government police station is at Jl Raya Kuta 141, south Kuta (☎0361 751598).

Post offices The General Post Office for poste restante is in Denpasar. Smaller postal agents elsewhere in the resort can handle parcels and postcards (remember them?); see maps for other locations.

The Bukit Peninsula

After it narrows to a sliver of land at Jimbaran, the **Bukit Peninsula** dangles off the south of Bali. Officially called **Bukit Badung** (*bukit* means "hill" in Bahasa Indonesia), the high limestone plateau has more in common with infertile Nusa Penida than with the lush paddies elsewhere. Known for its dry climate and thin dusty soils, the typical **Bukit landscape** is one of cracked earth and kapok trees, brightened only by the occasional bougainvillea, perhaps a strip of cassava tubers (used to make tapioca flour) and grass-like sorghum, whose seeds are also pounded into flour.

Given that farming is almost impossible here, its discovery by **surfers** in the late 1960s was a godsend for the local economy. An alchemy of open-ocean swell and

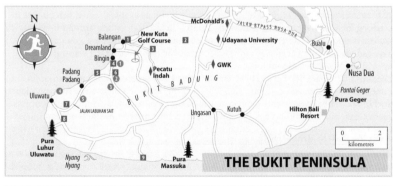

■ ACCOMMODATION		The Gong		**8**	Pink Coco	**5**	Drifter Surf Shop Cafe	
Alchemist	**3**	Leggies	**4**	Pondok Indah Gung	**4**	and Gallery	**2**
Alila Villas Uluwatu	**9**	Medori Putih Homestay	**6**	The Temple Lodge	**4**	Jiwa Juice	**3**
Balangan Sea View Bungalow	**1**	Mick's Place	**4**			Single Fin	**4**
Bali Bule	**7**	Naturela Homestay	**2**	● EATING		Yeye's Warung	**5**
Flower Bud Bungalows I and II	**1**	Mu	**4**	The Cashew Tree	**1**		

1

SURFING OFF THE BUKIT PENINSULA

Views aside, the greatest assets of the Bukit are its **surfing beaches**. Heavy ocean swells strike the gorgeous craggy shoreline to produce the most revered breaks in Bali. Balangan, which receives the most shelter, is generally the most forgiving wave, while Uluwatu, the most exposed, is for advanced surfers only – it's a wave that demands respect. Board rental is widely available throughout the area and the **breaks** are at their best from April to October. Finally, a word of warning: while the beaches are stunning, **swimming** can be dangerous because of rips and reefs. If swell directions play ball, Balangan provides shelter at its southern end, Bingin has lifeguards in season and Padang Padang is calm since waves detonate on the reef outside.

coastal alignment produces Bali's most famous and most challenging breaks. And in the last decade or so everyone else has caught on to the extraordinary beauty of the coastline. While most beaches remain nicely ramshackle, development is expanding at a crazy pace as **luxury resorts** and **villas** take advantage of the glorious clifftop views. No one begrudges poor farmers the chance to cash in as their infertile land is re-evaluated as prime retail estate. The sustainability – and sensitivity – of such development is another matter.

Fishing town-turned-resort **Jimbaran**, a couple of kilometres south of the airport, kicks off the luxury hotels, spread behind a fine beach. Continuing beyond, the **surf beaches** begin on the east coast: **Balangan**, **Bingin**, **Padang Padang**, then **Uluwatu**, the latter a world-class left-hander that is as legendary as any break in Hawaii. Uluwatu is also home to one of Bali's major clifftop temples, perched on the island's tip. On the east coast is **Nusa Dua**, a purpose-built resort that is deluxe but dull, and **Tanjung Benoa**.

GETTING AROUND   **THE BUKIT PENINSULA**

Public transport in the Bukit is sporadic at best and to see it properly you'll need your **own wheels**. Incidentally, be aware that parking charges of around Rp5000/car or Rp3000/scooter are standard to access Bukit beaches.

Jimbaran

With its crescent of golden sand and upmarket hotels, **JIMBARAN** is a quieter alternative to Nusa Dua. Easy access to the airport makes it a handy first- or last-night destination.

Tourism aside, its raison d'être, however, is **fish**. Every morning at dawn the town's fishermen return with hundreds of kilos for sale at an enjoyable covered **fish market** in Kedonganan, at the northern end of Jimbaran beach. It's at its best around 6–7am, but stays open all day – the stallholders are used to sightseers. Even if you don't see it, you can taste the day's catch when it is served at the dozens of beach warung that specialize in **barbecued seafood**.

Other than lazing in the sun by day and eating fish at night, there's little to do in Jimbaran, although you can rent boogie boards on the beach or surf the Airport Rights **surf break**, halfway down the Jimbaran side of the airport runway; most surfers access it from Kuta, but you should be able to charter a fishing boat from the beach.

ARRIVAL AND INFORMATION   **JIMBARAN**

By plane For a taxi from the airport (see p.64) to Jimbaran you'll pay around Rp100,000.

By bemo There's a sporadic bemo service from Denpasar's Tegal terminal to Jimbaran, via Kuta's eastern fringes and then on to Nusa Dua.

Destinations Denpasar (Tegal terminal; 50min); Kuta (30min); Ngurah Rai Airport (15min); Nusa Dua (30min).

By bus Kura Kura minibuses (ⓦkura2bus.com), hourly

until 5pm, connect Jimbaran with Kuta and onto other destinations in Southern Bali. Trans Sarbagita also provides an hourly bus service to Batubulan bemo terminal in Denpasar and on to Sanur and Kuta.

By taxi A taxi from Kuta will cost about Rp95,000.

Banks, exchange and internet ATMs, moneychangers and internet places are strung along Jl Raya Uluwatu.

ACCOMMODATION

Bali Breezz Hotel Jl Pantai Sarai 23 ☏ 0361 708524, ⓦ balibreezzhoteljimbaran.com. While Standard rooms are compact, accommodation in this family hotel is modern, bright and clean. There are two pools, attractive gardens and the beach is less than 100m away. <u>Rp550,000</u>

★**Jimbaran Puri Bali** Jl Yoga Perkanti ☏ 0361 701605, ⓦ jimbaranpuribali.com. Contemporary, well-designed hotel with 42 cottages and gorgeous villas with pools, all with marble and teak interiors and in fabulous grounds – understated sophistication rules here. There's also a large pool and spa. <u>$496</u>

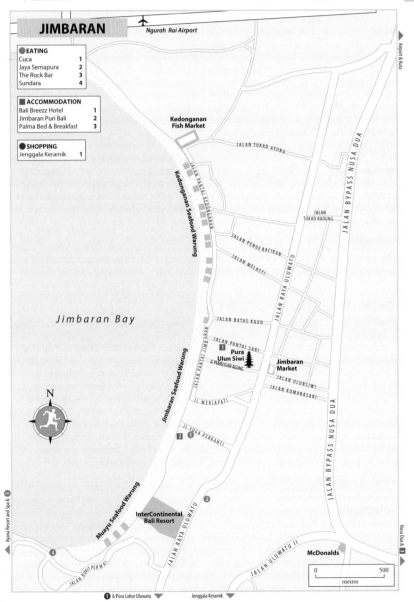

JIMBARAN

Ngurah Rai Airport

● EATING
Cuca	1
Jaya Semapura	2
The Rock Bar	3
Sundara	4

■ ACCOMMODATION
Bali Breezz Hotel	1
Jimbaran Puri Bali	2
Palma Bed & Breakfast	3

● SHOPPING
Jenggala Keramik	1

Kedonganan
Fish Market

Kedonganan Seafood Warung

JALAN PANTAI KEDONGANAN

JALAN TUKAD AYUNG

JALAN BYPASS NUSA DUA

JALAN TUKAD BADUNG

JALAN PENGERACIKAN

JALAN MELASTI

JALAN RAYA ULUWATU

Jimbaran Bay

JALAN BATAS KAUH

JALAN PANTAI SARI

Pura
Ulun Siwi

JL PEMELISAN AGUNG

Jimbaran Seafood Warung

JALAN PANTAI JIMBARAN

Jimbaran
Market

JALAN ULUNSIWI

JALAN KUMARASARI

JL MERJAPATI

N

JL YOGA PERKANTI

JALAN BYPASS NUSA DUA

Muayu Seafood Warung

InterContinental
Bali Resort

JALAN RAYA ULUWATU

JALAN BUKIT PERMAI

McDonalds

JALAN ULUWATU II

0	500
	metres

& Pura Luhur Uluwatu   Jenggala Keramik

Airport & Kuta

Ayana Resort and Spa &

Nusa Dua &

Palma Bed & Breakfast Jl Danau Batur Raya Taman Griya 53 ☎ 0361 847 9788, ⓦ palmabedandbreakfast .blogspot.co.uk. Perfect for a cheap bed near the airport, with decent mixed (fan-cooled or a/c) dorms and comfy privates. It's locally owned and welcoming, though 2.5km inland from the beach. Dorms Rp95,000, doubles Rp250,000

EATING AND DRINKING

Jimbaran's **famous seafood warung** are in three clusters on the beach: north, middle and south. The setup is similar throughout – a few tables above and on the sand and a menu of lobster, prawns, fish, squid and crab grilled in the warung behind – so simply select whichever takes your fancy. The caveat is that some offer set prices, while others price dishes by weight (determine the price before cooking starts). Food is served from noon, but the warung are at their **liveliest from sunset**. Most also offer simple Indonesian dishes and grilled meat.

★ **Cuca** Jl Yoga Perkanthi ☎ 0361 708066, ⓦ cucaflavor .com. With a "globally inspired, locally sourced" menu, *Cuca* is a thoroughly modern culinary experience – its acclaimed Canadian chef has worked in three-star Michelin restaurants including Spain's *El Bulli*. Think fine dining from a tapas-style menu – ceviche (Rp90,000) or black squid risotto (Rp150,000) – and expect to eat three plates/ person. The garden is a lovely spot for a pre- or post-meal drink. Daily noon–midnight.

Jaya Semapura Jl Raya Uluwatu 33 ☎ 0361 999 3420. A no-frills warung with a long menu of Chinese and Indonesian dishes – lots of chicken and seafood, with the likes of *ayam goreng* (fried chicken) with spicy *sambal* and *ikan bakar* – most priced below Rp25,000. Daily 9am–9pm.

The Rock Bar Ayana Resort and Spa, Jl Karang Mas Sejahtera ☎ 0361 702222. Perched 20m above the waves at the base of the Bukit cliffs, this is one of Bali's most celebrated bars – with queues to match. And since access is via a lift, there are also queues to leave. Still, it's impressively arranged over several terraces with DJs stoking the atmosphere later on. Mon–Thurs 4pm–1am, Fri–Sun 4pm–3am.

Sundara Four Seasons Resort Bali at Jimbaran Bay ☎ 0361 708333, ⓦ sundarabali.com. A spectacularly sited beachside bar/restaurant; there's a 57m infinity pool above the waves, a bar for cocktails, live music five days a week, and international cuisine in a spectacular restaurant including great seafood and Bali's longest Sunday brunch (book ahead). Daily 11am–1am.

SHOPPING

Jenggala Keramik Jl Uluwatu II house ☎ 0361 703311, ⓦ jenggala.com. The flagship store and factory of this ceramic specialist offers sophisticated and simple designs, as well as table linen and cutlery. Daily 8am–8pm.

Garuda Wisnu Kencana (GWK)

Jl Raya Uluwatu, Badung • Daily 8am–10pm • Rp100,000; children Rp60,000, plus parking: Rp5000/Rp10,000 scooter/car • ☎ 0361 700808, ⓦ gwkbali.com

Off the main Jimbaran–Uluwatu road, the monumental **Garuda Wisnu Kencana** cultural park, or **GWK** (pronounced "Gay Way Kah"), is a massive project (most would say eyesore) that's being carved out of the hillside. The focal point is a towering copper statue of the Hindu god Vishnu astride his sacred vehicle, the half-man, half-bird Garuda – by early 2017 it was over 40m high and visible from across southern Bali, but when complete it should be a staggering 120m in height, 68m across and weigh 4000 tonnes. Critics have deplored the commercial rather than religious motivation of the venture and muttered about Bali as a Hindu theme park – a comment that resonates with concerns about the "touristification" of Balinese culture (see p.333). So far it's been a failure, as the empty car parks and scruffy commercial space attest. GWK also hosts rock concerts: Iron Maiden played here in 2011. We suggest you walk on by.

Balangan

Given its proximity to the luxury resorts of Jimbaran – even the hulking resort of Dreamland, just around the headland (see box opposite) – **BALANGAN** is a surprise. It's the bit the developers haven't got round to yet; a wonderful cove beach of golden sand that draws travellers and surfers. Above the beach are some ramshackle surfer warung and a cluster of guesthouses, with new accommodation opening all the time in the hills around. The shallow reef offshore powers a speedy left-hand break at high tide but can

KICKING THE BUKIT: FROM DREAMLAND TO NEW KUTA

Around Balangan's southern point, **Dreamland Beach** sums up the perils of unregulated development on the Bukit Peninsula for many Balinese and expats. Once it was known solely for its great surf – a fast left and right peak with long rides – and gloriously white sands. Yet like much of the surrounding land, its raw nature was "improved" in 2009 with concrete walkways and restaurants, masseurs and spas, in a multimillion-rupiah project by a development company. The company rebranded it as New Kuta Beach in 2010. A focus for the controversy is the huge *Pecatu Indah Resort* which stacks against the cliff behind the eighteen-hole New Kuta Golf Course (☎ 0361 848 1333, ⦿ newkutagolf.com). An ostentatious development which blights the coast, say critics. A valuable source of income and employment for the Bukit, counter its supporters.

make swimming dicey; depending on the swell direction, the far southern end of the beach usually provides most shelter.

ARRIVAL AND DEPARTURE   BALANGAN

By car or motorbike Road access to Balangan is via 6km of twisting lanes from the main Jimbaran–Uluwatu road.

There's no public transport.

ACCOMMODATION

Alchemist Jl Pantai Balangan ☎ 0858 5719 6504; map p.75. A couple of clicks inland from the beach, this gorgeous place has beautifully crafted wood cabins, treehouses and a bar built around an ancient kapok tree. There's a pool and fresh, healthy food in the café-restaurant which is open to non-guests. $55

Balangan Sea View Bungalow Jl Pantai Balangan ☎ 0361 780 0499, ⦿ balanganseaviewbungalow.com; map p.75. This attractive place has lovely thatched *lumbung* cottages, posh bungalows and decent fan or a/c

rooms that draw a young crowd who come to loaf around its pool. Rp350,000

Flower Bud Bungalows I and II ☎ 0361 8572062, ⦿ flowerbudbalangan.com; map p.75. From the rusty hurricane lanterns hung on the gate to the lush gardens, this Balinese-owned spot ticks all boxes for rustic escapism. You stay in traditional bungalows with large verandas; the cheapest are cold water-only. *Flowerbud II* has family-sized accommodation and a pool. Rp570,000

Bingin

Though fast developing into the liveliest of the Bukit surf beaches, **BINGIN** remains an oversized village of quiet lanes and astonishing scenery, whether you are admiring the superb coastal views from the cliffs or from the rickety warung that line the beach. It's a lovely backwater, which has its own rewarding **surf breaks** – the short left-hand tubes close to shore and the long and peeling left-handers of "Impossibles" surf break further out are the reason to come for many visitors. There's even a dedicated lifeguard in season. And where it trumps surrounding destinations is in its choice of accommodation. Access to the beach is via two sets of steep steps.

ARRIVAL AND DEPARTURE   BINGIN

By car Take the coastal road, Jl Labuhan Sait, which is signed west off the main Uluwatu road, then, 500m beyond

Jiwa Juice turn right onto a side road marked Pantai Bingin for the 2km drive to the parking area.

ACCOMMODATION AND EATING

Bingin has a burgeoning number of accommodation options, mostly midrange and above, with several boutiquey places opening in recent years. The cheapest places to stay are the beach warung, many of them built hard against the rock; expect to pay from Rp150,000 for a basic bamboo-walled room in high season.

Leggies ☎ 0361 854 4330, ⦿ leggiesbungalows.com; map p.75. Popular surfers' setup, with seventeen good-value,

though plain, fan- and a/c-cooled rooms set around a large garden with a small swimming pool. Rp500,000

1

Mick's Place ☎ 0361 847 0858, ⓦ micksplacebali.com; map p.75. Barefoot luxe is the word here. The seven contemporary-styled circular huts each have bamboo blinds that open to reveal a stunning position on the cliff edge, and the small pool on the very lip is truly spectacular. Book the spectacular Honeymoon Bungalow ($390) for 180-degree ocean views. Very popular, with a two/three night minimum stay in high season, and no children under 12. Behind the hotel a new annexe, *Acacia Bungalows*, offers similar bungalows at similar rates. $150

Mu ☎ 0361 895 7442, ⓦ mu-bali.com; map p.75. This French-run boutique place has a touch of castaway cool in its gorgeous, individually furnished thatch huts (all with a/c) spread behind a saltwater pool (and jacuzzi) on the cliff. Facilities include a spa, a small resort shop and a resident troupe of (wild) monkeys! $130

Pondok Indah Gung Bingin clifftop ☎ 0361 847 0933; map p.75. Family-run, this welcoming lodge has a really Balinese feel with its carved doors and architecture. There's a dozen tasteful fan-cooled rooms set round a leafy compound, some of them in pretty coconut-wood-and-thatch bungalows. **Rp320,000**

★ **The Temple Lodge** ☎ 08573 901 1572, ⓦ thetemple lodge.com; map p.75. Romance, eclecticism and a stunning location combine in this hideaway, where reclaimed pieces and Indonesian antiques lend bohemian flair to the six bungalows — some boasting sea views (from $190), and a new villa with a private pool that is perfect for a family or a group. There's an infinity pool, yoga sessions (at 8am daily, extra cost), a spa, and Mediterranean cuisine in a superb restaurant serving fresh healthy dishes. $95

EATING

More and more new places are opening all the time, many with menus that raid the globe for inspiration.

The Cashew Tree ☎ 0859 5378 9675; ⓦ bit.ly /CashewTreeBingin; map p.75. A relaxed garden café that serves creatively prepared healthy food, with lots of options for vegans and veggies: *Buddha Bowl* with cashew nuts and *tempeh*, greens and brown rice is deeply satisfying. Also offers detox juices and less saintly cakes. *The Cashew Tree* hosts a weekly party with live acts and a DJs, plus yoga sessions. Daily 10am–10pm.

Drifter Surf Shop Cafe and Gallery Jl Labuansait 52, 1km inland from the beach, ☎ 081 755 7111, ⓦ driftersurf .com; map p.75. Huge surf store well stocked with boards and wave essentials, plus yoga mats and lots of clothing. There's a great cafe for espresso coffee, cakes, snacks and meals. Browse their books while you're here. Daily 8am–9pm.

Jiwa Juice Jl Labuan Sait ☎ 0361 895 7562; ⓦ facebook .com/jiwa.juice; map p.75. Set on the main road before the Bingin turn-off, this little café serves soul food – "jiwa" translates as soul, life or energy – including Mediterranean-style mains such as prawns *pil pil* (served sizzling with chilli and garlic; Rp32,000). Daily 7am–10pm.

Padang Padang and Uluwatu

Padang Padang is a gorgeous cove notched in the Bukit's high cliffs that's safe for swimming. Nothwithstanding its use as a location in the film *Eat, Pray, Love* (Julia Roberts meets her beau here), its fame – and the reason for all the restaurants and guesthouses – is the eponymous **surf break**, one of the most exciting waves in Indonesia, not least because of a kink in the final section. Access to the waves and beautiful sands is via steps by the bridge.

Arguably the most impressive break hereabouts, however, is at **Pantai Suluban**, 2km beyond Padang Padang. The **Uluwatu surf breaks** (named after the nearby temple) that wrap around the cliffs on the Bukit's tip are legendary. There are five left-handers, all consistent and surfable from two to fifteen feet, though crowds can be heavy and locals' priority enforced – this is no place for a novice. Even if you don't access the breaks via the steep steps beside the *Blue Point Bay Villas and Spa*, you can head to the warung that cling to the cliff for an astonishing grandstand view of turquoise water and crashing white surf.

Pura Luhur Uluwatu

2km east of Uluwatu surf breaks • **Temple** Daily 8am–7pm • Rp30,000, including sarong and sash rental • **Kecak and Fire Dance** Daily 6–7pm (weather permitting) • Rp100,000 • No public transport, but this is a fixture on many tourist agency tours in south Bali (around Rp250,000, including sunset dance)

One of Bali's holiest temples and most iconic sights, **Pura Luhur Uluwatu** is superbly sited on the edge of a sheer promontory that juts out 70m above the foaming surf at the island's tip. Views over the serrated coastline are stunning and this is a favourite spot at sunset, especially with coach-tour groups. Indeed, the setting is all: the temple itself is relatively small and for the most part unadorned.

Accounts of Uluwatu's early **history** are vague, but the Javanese Hindu priest Empu Kuturan almost certainly constructed a *meru* (multitiered thatched shrine) here in the tenth century. Pura Luhur Uluwatu is now sanctified as one of Bali's sacred **directional temples**, or *kayangan jagat* – state temples that have influence over all the people of Bali, not just the local villagers or ancestors. It is the guardian of the southwest, dedicated to the spirits of the sea and its festivals are open to all; during the holy week-long period of Galungan, Balinese from all over the island come here to pay their respects.

Climbing the frangipani-lined stairway to the temple's **outer courtyard**, you're likely to meet Uluwatu's resident troupe of macaques, brazen thieves of many a pair of earrings and sunglasses, even cameras. Images of the elephant god Ganesh flank the temple entrance. Only worshippers are allowed inside but the temple extends to the cliff edge and the famous three-thatched *meru* is visible from along the cliff. A tiny courtyard in the temple contains a locked shrine housing an ancient statue which is thought by some to be Nirartha, the influential sixteenth-century priest from Java, who possibly achieved his own spiritual liberation (or *moksa*) on this spot.

You'll get some of the best **views** of Pura Luhur Uluwatu's dramatic position from the tracks that wind along the cliff edge to the left and right of the temple for a few hundred metres, affording fine, silhouetted vistas of the three-tiered *meru* perched atop the massive, sheer wall of limestone.

ACCOMMODATION AND EATING

PADANG PADANG

Medori Putih Homestay Jl Pemutih 1A, 1km inland from beach ☎0361 895 7377, ⓦmedoriputihhomestay .com; map p.75. A ten-minute walk from the beach, this fine-value place has twenty clean, orderly rooms, all with a/c and hot-water en-suites and a small pool for chilling. Breakfast is not included. **Rp300,000**

Pink Coco Jl Labuan Sait, about 400m before bridge ☎0361 895 7371, ⓦpinkcocobali.com; map p.75. "La casa del surfero" reads the sign, which may explain the hint of Mexico about this place; think rust-red colours in international-standard rooms with chunky moulded shelves and polished concrete floors. Also has a spa and two pools. **$78**

Yeye's Warung 500m beyond bridge ☎0361 742 4761; map p.75. Popular for a beer or a bite, this Balinese place with an attractive terrace has good local and western food (try the beer-battered calamari) and fresh-pressed juices. Service can be slow when busy – all dishes are cooked to order – but this is a fine spot to spend an evening. Daily noon–midnight.

ULUWATU

★**Alila Villas Uluwatu** ☎0361 848 2166, ⓦalila hotels.com; map p.75. On the cliff at the southern end of the Bukit with stunning contemporary villas and a sublime infinity pool that merges into the horizon (and has graced the cover of many a glossy magazine). Check out the yoga deck, which is suspended above the ocean. Non-guests can enjoy the unique setting in one of its

PADANG PADANG AND ULUWATU

restaurants: *Warung* for Indonesian dishes or *Cire*, serving "MediterAsian" food. **$775**

Bali Bule Jl Pantai Padang Padang ☎0361 769979, ⓦbalibulehomestay.com; map p.75. A 10min walk from the breaks, this is a great-value option, with twelve hugely spacious modern bungalows, all with a/c and nice verandas arranged around a pool in manicured gardens. **Rp550,000**

The Gong Jl Labuan Sait, 1km west of Pantai Suluban ☎0361 769976, ⓦthegonguluwatubali.com; map p.75. Long-running family-run budget place that remains a good choice: relaxed and with twelve clean rooms (including bunks), some with distant sea views, and a pool. There's a popular warung here serving big portions at low rates. **Rp220,000**

Naturela Homestay Jl Labuan Sait, ☎0361 557 2110, ⓦnaturelahomestay.blogspot.co.uk; map p.75. A good new place with clean, tiled rooms (some with a/c) that have decent quality mattresses. There's a pool and a café (meals from Rp35,000), with tables set in a pretty little garden. Staff are helpful and rent scooters at cheap rates. **Rp250,000**

★**Single Fin** Pantai Suluban ☎0361 769941; map p.75. There are other options for wave gazing, but none has the credentials of this surfer-owned place that spreads over several terraces. The extensive menu takes in pizzas, pasta and Indo curries (mains Rp75,000–150,000), and their cocktails (around Rp110,000) go down a treat. There's a great acoustic night on Wednesdays while the Sunday session rolls and rolls until 1am. Mon–Sat 10am–10pm, Sun till 1am.

1

Nusa Dua and Tanjung Benoa

Bali's most carefully designed high-end beach resort luxuriates along a coastal stretch of reclaimed mangrove swamp some 14km southeast of Kuta. A manicured, gated enclave, **NUSA DUA** was purpose-built to indulge upmarket tourists while simultaneously protecting local communities from the impact of mass tourism (see p.333). Though it has succeeded, it feels fairly soulless after the colour of genuine island life; sort of like Bali for people who don't really want to be there. What draws most visitors here is

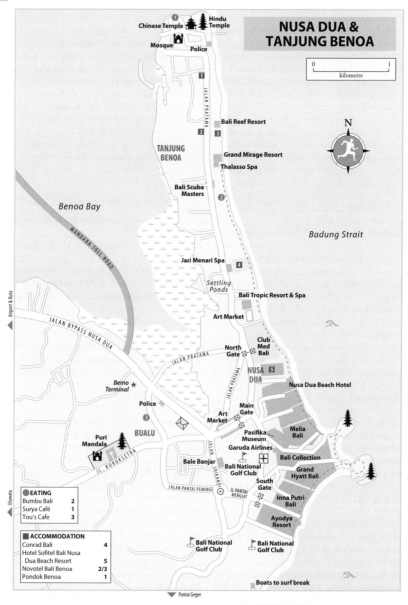

NUSA DUA & TANJUNG BENOA

0   1
kilometre

N

Chinese Temple
Hindu Temple
Mosque
Police

Bali Reef Resort

TANJUNG BENOA

Grand Mirage Resort
Thalasso Spa

Bali Scuba Masters

Benoa Bay

MANDARA TOLL ROAD

Badung Strait

Jari Menari Spa

Settling Ponds

Bali Tropic Resort & Spa

Art Market

Airport & Kuta

JALAN BYPASS NUSA DUA

Club Med Bali

North Gate

NUSA DUA

Nusa Dua Beach Hotel

Bemo Terminal

Police

Art Market

Main Gate

BUALU

Pasifika Museum

Melia Bali

Puri Mandala

JL. KURUKSETRA

Garuda Airlines

Bali Collection

Bale Banjar

Bali National Golf Club

South Gate

Grand Hyatt Bali

JALAN PANTAI PEMINGE

JL PANTAI MENGIAT

Inna Putri Bali

Ulluwatu

EATING
Bumbu Bali   2
Surya Café   1
Tou's Cafe   3

Ayodya Resort

ACCOMMODATION
Conrad Bali   4
Hotel Sofitel Bali Nusa
  Dua Beach Resort   5
Novotel Bali Benoa   2/3
Pondok Benoa   1

Bali National Golf Club

Bali National Golf Club

Boats to surf break

Pantai Geger

the **beach**: a long ribbon of mostly pale gold sand, though a reef is exposed at low tide. Halfway down the shoreline, the land blossoms out into two little clumps, or "islands" (Nusa Dua means "Two Islands"), with a temple standing on each one.

Real life of a sort resumes north of Nusa Dua on the narrow sand bar known as **Tanjung Benoa**, though this, too, is a strip of yet more swanky hotels, tourist restaurants, shops and watersports facilities. Continue on to the very top of the peninsula, however, and village life returns in areas that can be fun to explore.

Pasifika: Museum Pacific Asia

Complex Bali Tourism Development Corporation (BTDC) Area Block P • Daily 10am–6pm • Rp70,000 • ☎ 0361 774935, ⓦ museum-pasifika.com

To venture beyond Nusa Dua's beach, you could pay a visit to **Pasifika: Museum Pacific Asia**, north across the access road from the Bali Collection, which houses a wide-ranging and reasonably interesting display of art and artefacts from Asia and the Pacific, including a decent gallery of Balinese paintings.

Bualu

Just outside the gates of Nusa Dua the village of **BUALU** is where you'll find the densest concentration of *banjar*, temples, warung, family homes and commerce, particularly along Jalan Srikandi. It's the sort of scene common to any small Balinese town, but a worthwhile target if you want to explore beyond the rarefied confines of Nusa Dua itself.

Pantai Geger

About a 1km drive from the golf course or a 20min walk along the beach from *Ayodya Resort* – without your own transport take a metered taxi to Pantai Geger; an informal service will take you back

For a day out from the beach that fringes Nusa Dua head south towards the *Hilton Bali Resort* and follow signs for **Pantai Geger**. The broad, white-sand beach is quieter than that in Nusa Dua, although much of the southern end, below the clifftop temple, Pura Geger, is given over to seaweed farming.

Tanjung Benoa

Not to be confused with **Benoa Harbour** just north of **TANJUNG BENOA**'s tip, the beach here is more activity-based than the groomed stretches of Nusa Dua, somewhere for the happy hordes to go banana-boating, parasailing or windsurfing. It also has the dubious distinction of being the centre of Bali's turtle trade (see box, p.84).

Inland Tanjung Benoa has a few points of interest. At the northern tip, there's an impressive coral-carved **Hindu temple**, a gaudy red-painted **Chinese temple** and the restrained contours of a mosque within a few hundred metres of each other. Follow any of the lanes running west from the middle stretch of Jalan Pratama to find typical Balinese warung, fruit and veg stalls and family compounds.

ARRIVAL AND INFORMATION

NUSA DUA AND TANJUNG BENOA

By taxi If you've splurged on a few nights' luxury here you're unlikely to be hauling your bags on a bemo or bus – a prepaid taxi from the airport (see p.64) costs Rp140,000, or expect to pay around Rp120,000 in a metered taxi from Kuta.

By bus Kura Kura buses (ⓦ kura2bus.com/line/nusa_dua) connect Kuta with Nusa Dua (Rp50,000) every two hours between 9am and 10pm.

Banks and exchange ATMs are on Jl Pratama in Tanjung Benoa. Big hotels offer exchange.

Hospitals and clinics Most Nusa Dua hotels provide 24hr medical service; there are also expat-oriented clinics near Kuta (see p.75) and hospitals in Denpasar (see p.92).

GETTING AROUND

The resorts, restaurants and shops are strung over some 6km from the northern tip of Tanjung Benoa to southern Nusa Dua, so getting around can be a hot business.

By shuttle bus A free shuttle bus to the Bali Collection shopping centre loops around the big hotels and shops (approximately hourly, 10am–9pm). Some hotels also run their own free transport.

1

TANJUNG BENOA AND THE TURTLE TRADE

Indonesia is one of the world's most important countries for **marine turtles** and home to six out of the seven marine turtle species, all endangered due to the destruction of habitat and **nesting sites**, illegal trade and accidental capture by fishing nets. Female turtles only lay eggs on the beaches where they were born; on Bali these include those at **Kuta**, **Sanur**, **Nusa Dua**, **Tanjung Benoa**, **Jimbaran** and **Pemuteran**. All of these have been affected by tourist development; turtles will not come ashore if there's too much light or noise, and hatchlings can get confused by the bright lights and head inshore rather than out to sea.

Traditionally, turtles were slaughtered on Bali for human consumption and religious sacrifice. It is estimated that between 1969 and 1999 **thirty thousand turtles** per year were landed in Tanjung Benoa, plunging the population into severe decline. However, in 1999 Indonesia implemented a **turtle trade ban** amid threats of a tourism boycott of Bali and in 2005 the Hindu Dharma Council of Indonesia decreed that substitutes could be used for any endangered species in religious rituals.

The change in attitudes means that neither turtle flesh nor products are offered anymore in Tanjung Benoa. Some say the trade has just shifted **underground**; newspapers still report illegal trading of animals poached elsewhere in Indonesia. It's certainly a profitable business; a single turtle can fetch up to $600.

Several groups have established **turtle hatcheries** on Bali, including on Kuta Beach (see p.59) and Reef Seen Aquatics in Pemuteran (see p.238). For further information and to support **conservation efforts** contact Turtle Foundation (🌐 turtle-foundation.org), ProFauna Indonesia in Denpasar (☎ 0361 808 5800, 🌐 profauna.org) and the Jakarta branch of the World Wide Fund for Nature (☎ 021 576 1065, 🌐 wwf.or.id).

By taxi Metered taxis circulate constantly.
By bike The flat terrain makes cycling a good option; large hotels provide rental.

On foot The shortest route between hotels is nearly always via the paved beachfront walkway; it takes around 2hr to walk the entire length.

ACTIVITIES

Birdwatching An early morning at the ponds around the mangrove swamp to the north and west of Nusa Dua's North Gate can yield several species of kingfisher, as well as lots of water birds including white-vented Javan mynahs, Sunda teals and white-browed crakes.
Diving There are several PADI Dive Centres: Bali Scuba Masters is at Jl Pratama 85 (☎ 0361 777156, 🌐 baliscuba masters.com) and runs day-trips to Nusa Penida (two dives US$110).
Snorkelling Local sites such as White Tower reef (where fish are fed bread) are not that inspiring for snorkelling trips

but there are coral patches and reasonable numbers of fish.
Surfing The main Nusa Dua surf break is a right-hander about 1km offshore (accessible by boat from a signposted point south of the golf course), while further north, a short paddle beyond the *Club Med Bali*, "Sri Lanka" is a short, speedy right-hander.
Watersports Tanjung Benoa is south Bali's watersports playground, with parasailing, water-skiing, jet-skiing, kayaking, wakeboarding, banana-boating and all the rest offered by at least a dozen shorefront watersports centres. Prices are uniformly Rp250,000–400,000/15min session.

ACCOMMODATION

NUSA DUA

Hotel Sofitel Bali Nusa Dua Beach Resort ☎ 0361 849 2888, 🌐 sofitel.com. There's a real sense of contemporary style evident at this landmark resort, which boasts three restaurants, two bars, a gorgeous pool, fine spa and kids' club. Rooms are beautifully appointed, many with oblique seaviews and some have private plunge pools. **$280**

TANJUNG BENOA

Conrad Bali Jl Pratama 168 ☎ 0361 778788, 🌐 conrad bali.com. Modern architecture, strong, uncluttered lines, pale cream stone and dark wood give this deluxe chain

hotel enormous style. A 33m lagoon pool dominates a complex that has numerous restaurants, a spa, kids' club, daily yoga and tennis among many other offerings. Some rooms are wheelchair-accessible. **$256**
Novotel Bali Benoa Jl Pratama ☎ 0361 772239, 🌐 novotelnusaduabali.com. Offers the best value in the area, though it's not the newest, with accommodation in a low-rise hotel spread over both sides of the road. Cheaper non-beachside rooms, all with a balcony or small garden, are near a quiet pool. Beachside options include tropical terrace bungalows with gardens and fabulous bathrooms by a larger pool. **$115**

★**Pondok Benoa** Jl Pratama 99 ☎ 0896 7138 7329, ⓦ pondok-benoa.com. For a personal touch and home-stay ambience, this welcoming place 100m from the beach has comfortable a/c rooms and studios with kitchenettes, all with attractive furnishings and contemporary bathrooms, hot water and a/c, some with terraces, overlooking pretty gardens with a pool. It's great value and staff can organize scooter hire. **Rp280,000**

EATING AND DRINKING

Bumbu Bali Jl Pratama, Tanjung Benoa ☎ 0361 774502, ⓦ balifoods.com. Founded and managed by renowned expat chef and food writer Heinz von Holzen, this famous courtyard restaurant serves classy Balinese cuisine such as marinated diced fish grilled in banana leaf (Rp160,000), and there's lot of choice for vegetarians. The *Bumbu* empire includes a second restaurant *Bumbu Bali 2*, 500m away, and a cooking school. Daily 11am–11pm.

Surya Café Jl Segara 21, Tanjung Benoa ☎ 0361 772016. Fish and seafood priced by weight and fresh from the tank in a restaurant open to the theatre of boats whizzing past. Try the crab (Rp32,000/100g) served with chilli and black pepper sauce. Not cheap, but fun to sit and watch the life on the water. Daily 11am–10pm.

Tou's Cafe Jl Siligita 18 Nusa Dua ☎ 0811 386 4840, ⓦ facebook.com/tousfoodcoffee. The perfect antidote to swanky high-end Nusa Dua, this a/c roadside café has very affordable breakfasts (from Rp30,000) and meals, plus great espresso coffee – a flat white is Rp25,000. Daily 7am–10pm.

Denpasar

Despite the traffic congestion, despite the ever-expanding sprawl, Bali's capital remains a rather pleasant city at heart. Downtown **DENPASAR** is centred on a grassy square, **Alun-alun Puputan**, and has just a few major shopping streets in its core. Department stores and air-conditioned malls are mushrooming in southern districts – modern Denpasar is epitomized by **Jalan Teuku Umar**, a neon-lit strip crammed with restaurants and shopping centres – which leaves these central older neighbourhoods rather bereft of modern life. Maybe that's the appeal – these areas are still dominated by family compounds grouped into traditional *banjar* (village association) districts. There is also a marked influence of the sizeable immigrant communities, notably Javanese Muslims, Sasaks from Lombok and Chinese-Indonesians, who together constitute a **large minority** of the city's population of almost 900,000.

Most tourists whizz in on a day-trip from the southern resorts, lingering just long enough to tour the **Bali Museum** and neighbouring state temple, **Pura Agung Jagatnata**, and perhaps to browse the traditional **markets** such as **Pasar Badung**, a huge covered affair beside the Badung River. Very few stay overnight. While these are its main sights as such, handily all within walking distance of each other, the relative dearth of tourists – and accompanying hoopla – is appealing in itself.

Sunday is a particularly good day to visit as traffic is light and many main streets are closed in a car-free initiative that sees joggers and cyclists reclaim the city.

Brief history

Until the early twentieth century, control of the city – then known as **Badung**, like the regency it governed – was divided among several rajas, most notably those at the courts of Pemecutan (southwest Denpasar) and Kesiman (east Denpasar). Supremacy was wrested from them, however, by the insatiably expansionist Dutch. On the pretext of alleged piracy in Sanur, the colonizers marched on the raja on September 20, 1906, and massacred the local court. After Indonesia won independence in 1949, the island's administrative **capital** was moved to Badung from the north-coast town of Singaraja and the city was renamed Denpasar. Almost fifty years later Denpasar's status was upgraded again when, in 1992, it became a self-governing municipality, no longer under the auspices of Badung district. Since 2000 the city has continued to sprawl in every direction, and its southern suburbs now merge into the Kuta-Legian-Seminyak district, forming a huge conurbation.

1

Kerobokan, Kuta & BaliMed Hospital

Kuta

DENPASAR

1, Ubung bemo terminal, Tanah Lot & Gilimanuk   Sangeh

JALAN PATIMURA

Pura
Satriya

JALAN SETIABUDI

JALAN SUTOMO

JALAN KARTINI

JALAN NAKULA

JALAN YUDISTIRA

JALAN VETERAN

Pasar
Burung

JALAN KEDONDONG

Wangaya
Bemo
Terminal ★

Pasar Seni

Bog Bog

Gunung
Agung Bemo
Terminal

JALAN GUNUNG AGUNG

JALAN WAHIDIN

Pura Maospahit 2

JALAN ABIMANYU

JALAN RAMBUTAN

JALAN ARJUNA

JALAN KARNA

2

JALAN VETERAN

JALAN DURIAN

JALAN GN. MERAPI

Statue

4

JALAN GAJAH MADA

Bank
Bali

JALAN SURAPATI

JALAN M. H. THAMRIN

Pasar
Badung

JALAN SUMATRA

Catur
Muka
Statue

JALAN UDAYANA

Pura Agung
Jagatnata

Pasar
Kumbasari

Alun-alun
Puputan

Pura Tambang
Badung

Jalan Sulawesi

Puri Pemecutan

JALAN SULAWESI

JALAN BELITON

Bali
Museum

JALAN IMAM BONJOL

JALAN HASANUDIN

JALAN SUGIANYAR

Garuda Airlines

JALAN DEBES

JALAN BUKIT TINGGAL

Suci Bemo
Terminal

The gold
quarter

Dept.
Store

Tegal Bemo
Terminal

JL G. MANDALA WANGI

JALAN G. MANDALA WANGI

Badung River

JALAN DIPONEGORO

Tiara
Dewata
Shopping
Centre

Hospital

JALAN SURDIRMAN

Ramayana
Mal Bali
Shopping
Centre

Police

JALAN YOS SUDARSO

JALAN IMAM BONJOL

JALAN NUSAKAMBANGAN

JALAN TEUKU UMAR

Robinson
Dept. Store

Bank
Duta

Bank
Bali

JALAN DEWI SARTIKA

JALAN P.B. SUDIRMAN

Denpasar
Junction

Matahari
Dept. Store

JALAN DIPONEGORO

Hero
Supermarket
(Libi Plaza)

SIMPANG
ENAM

JALAN P. TARAKAN

Sanglah
Hospital

JL. P. NIAS

Kuta

Benoa

Alun-alun Puputan

Grassy **Alun-alun Puputan**, or Taman Puputan (Puputan Square), commemorates the
fateful events of September 20, 1906, when the Raja of Badung marched out of his
palace gates, followed by hundreds of his subjects, and faced the invading Dutch.
Dressed entirely in holy white, with each man, woman and child clasping a golden *kris*
(dagger), the people of Badung had psyched themselves up for a **puputan**, or ritual fight
to the death (see p.306). The final death toll was reported to be somewhere between four

Batubulan bemo terminal, Catur Eka Bodhi & Stage Uma Dewi

hundred and two thousand. The palace itself, just across Jalan Surapati on the north edge of the modern square, was razed and has since been rebuilt as the official residence of Bali's governor. The huge bronze statue depicting figures bearing sharpened bamboo staves and *kris* on the northern edge of the park is a memorial to the citizens who died in the *puputan*; it's an image that you'll see across the island. The traffic island here is topped with a huge stone **statue of Catur Muka**, the four-faced, eight-armed Hindu guardian of the cardinal points, indicating the exact location of the city centre.

1

Puputan Square hosts a commemorative **fair**, with food stalls and *wayang kulit* shows, every year on September 20.

Bali Museum

Jl Mayor Wisnu 1 • Mon–Thurs, Sat & Sun 7.30am–3.30pm, Fri 7.30am–1pm; closed public holidays • Rp20,000, children Rp10,000 • ☎ 0361 222680 • On the turquoise Kereneng–Ubung bemo route

The great repository of Balinese culture, the **Bali Museum** (Museum Negeri Propinsi Bali) is Denpasar's top attraction and provides an excellent introduction to the island's culture, past and present. Instigated, ironically, by the very Dutch colonial settlers who spelled the demise of traditional lifestyles, the ethnography museum is housed in an appealing compound divided into traditional courtyards, complete with *candi bentar* (split gates), *kulkul* (bell) tower, shrines patterned by lichen and flower gardens. You don't really need one of guides who approach as you arrive – labels within are in English.

Much of the appeal of a visit is of going on a treasure-hunt through island culture. The two-storey **Gedung Timur** at the back of the entrance courtyard features archeological finds downstairs, including a massive second-century BC **stone sarcophagus**, and an upstairs gallery given over to traditional **paintings and woodcarvings**. Through the traditional gateway left off the entrance courtyard, the **Gedung Buleleng** holds fine Balinese **textiles**, including the rare Kain *geringsing*, a complicated material created through an intricate dyeing and weaving technique practised only by the villagers of Tenganan (see p.177).

Built to resemble the long, low structure of an eighteenth-century Karangasem-style palace, the **Gedung Karangasem** introduces Balinese **spiritual and ceremonial life** – the cornerstone of an islander's day-to-day existence – and is the most interesting section of the museum since it details the religious ceremonies of Balinese Hinduism. The Balinese **calendars** on the right-hand wall are immensely complex and still widely used to determine events from temple festivals to when to start building a new house.

Music and dance is tackled in the **Gedung Tabanan**, a replica of a Tabanan regency palace. Exhibits include masks, shadow puppets and costumes, including Barong costumes like the shaggy **Barong Ket**, a cross between a lion, a pantomime horse and a Chinese dragon, that symbolizes the forces of good.

Pura Agung Jagatnata

Jl Mayor Visnu • Daily dawn–dusk • Entry by donation includes sarong and sash

Just over the north wall of the Bali Museum, the modern state temple of **Pura Agung Jagatnata** is set in a garden of pomegranate, hibiscus and frangipani trees. Founded in 1953, it is dedicated to the supreme god, Sanghyang Widi Wasa, who is here worshipped in his role as "Lord of the World", or Jagatnata.

Carvings of lotus flowers and frogs adorn the tiny stone bridge that spans the moat around the temple's central gallery (access at festival times only) and scenes from the Hindu epics the Ramayana and Mahabharata decorate the gallery's outer wall. The temple's focal point is the looming five-tiered **padmasana** tower in the inner courtyard, balanced on a huge cosmic turtle. Built from blocks of white coral, the tower is carved with demons' heads and the bottom level displays the face and hands of Bhoma, the son of the earth, whose job is to repel evil spirits from the temple. The lotus throne at its summit is left empty for Sanghyang Widi Wasa to fill when descending to earth at festival times – the god is represented in a gold relief embossed on the back. In the southeast corner of the outer compound stands the **kulkul** tower, its split wooden bell still used to summon locals to festivals, meetings and temple-cleaning duties.

Twice a month, on the full moon and new (or dark) moon, **festivals** are held here and *wayang kulit* shows are sometimes performed, from around 9pm to 11pm; ask at the nearby tourist office for details.

Taman Werdi Budaya Arts Centre

Jl Nusa Indah • Daily 7.30am–3pm • Reached via a 15min walk from the Kereneng bemo terminal, or direct on a Sanur-bound bemo

Marooned in the suburbs of east Denpasar, the **Taman Werdi Budaya Arts Centre** was designed in 1973 by one of Indonesia's most renowned architects, Ida Bagus Tugur. It consists of a number of performance spaces and is the location of the spectacular annual **Arts Festival** (usually between mid-June and mid-July; ⓦbaliartsfestival.com), with a spectacular array of special exhibitions, competitions and shows.

That aside, the reason to visit is a small **museum** (same hours; free) on the history of Balinese arts. On show is an overview of Balinese **painting**, including the classical *wayang* style plus works from the Ubud, Batuan and Young Artists styles (see box, pp.122–123) and modern works, as well as a small display of woodcarving, masks, dance costume, shadow puppets and jewellery.

Bajra Sandhi

Renon; entrance just off Jl Raya Puputan • Daily 9am–5pm • Rp10,000 • Renon is served by Sanur-bound bemos

The government administrative district, **Renon**, on the southeastern edge of the city, is another world from downtown Denpasar, all landscaped gardens, broad tree-lined boulevards and space galore. Among the offices is the huge grey lava-stone **Bajra Sandhi** ("Balinese People's Struggle") monument, at the heart of the **Lapangan Puputan Margarana** park. Designed by Taman Budaya's architect, Ida Bagus Tugur, to resemble a priest's bell, the monument's structure also symbolizes the date of Indonesia's Declaration of Independence – August 17, 1945 – with its eight entrances, seventeen corners and height of 45m. The upper floor contains a series of 33 dioramas illustrating edited episodes from Balinese history. Climb the spiral stairs and you're rewarded with a panoramic view across Denpasar's rooftops.

ARRIVAL AND DEPARTURE — DENPASAR

BY PLANE

Ngurah Rai Airport (see p.64) is 13km south of Denpasar. A prepaid taxi from the airport to Denpasar will cost around Rp100,000.

BY BEMO

Bemos arrive at one of four terminals on the edges of town. All times are (very) approximate depending on traffic, and prices are a guide only. As most Balinese prefer motorbikes, frequencies on all these routes is falling due to low demand.

Batubulan Batubulan terminal, on the far-flung north-east fringes, runs regular services to Ubud (40min–1hr 20min; Rp15,000), east Bali, parts of north Bali and Nusa Dua via Sanur (dropping passengers on the outskirts at the *Sanur Paradise Plaza* hotel) and the eastern outskirts of Kuta.

Kereneng Kereneng terminal off Jl Hayam Wuruk, in east central Denpasar covers Sanur (15–25min; Rp8000); services are fairly erratic.

Tegal Located on Jl Imam Bonjol, in the southwest corner, Tegal covers routes south of Denpasar, including Kuta

(25min; Rp12,000), Legian (Rp12,000), Tuban/airport (40min; Rp15,000), Jimbaran (50min; Rp18,000), Nusa Dua (Rp20,000) and Sanur (25min; Rp8000).

Ubung Ubung, northwest of city on the main road to Tabanan, runs frequent transport to north and west Bali, as well as to Padang Bai (for Lombok) and Java.

Other terminals There are smaller bemo terminals on Jl Gunung Agung, for transport to Canggu and Kerobokan (Rp8000); near the Sanglah hospital, for Benoa Harbour and Suwung; at Wangaya for Sangeh and Pelaga; and at Suci for Pulau Serangan.

BY BUS

Bali's public Trans Sarbagita buses run from Denpasar, though it's not a very reliable or punctual service. The routes are: Batubulan bemo terminal–Sanur bypass–Kuta Central Parking–Jimbaran–Nusa Dua; and Puputan Square (Renon)–Udayana University Campus near Jimbaran–GWK. In theory buses run every 30min from 5am–9pm and cost Rp3500. Less frequent feeder minibuses link the Tegal terminal to the airport via Central Parking Kuta.

GETTING AROUND

By bemo Very, very few travellers even attempt to take on Denpasar's bewildering bemo system as app-taxis like Uber are so affordable. But it's possible; the city has four main terminals – Tegal, Kereneng, Batubulan and Ubung – which are linked by circuitous routes. Be prepared to wait for a bemo to fill at each transit point (anything from 5min

1

to 1hr). All bemos are colour-coded. Prices are higher for foreigners: expect to pay Rp10,000 for a cross-city ride or Rp12,000 to Batubulan. For impartial advice on routes and prices, ask at the controller's office at each terminal. Useful routes include: the Tegal–Nusa Dua bemo (dark blue) via Renon, and the Kereneng–Ubung bemo (turquoise) via Jl Gajah Mada, past the Bali Museum.

By taxi Metered and app-taxis taxis circulate around the city. Blue Bird taxis (☎0361 701111, ⊛bluebirdgroup.com) and Uber/Grab are all reliable.

INFORMATION AND ACTIVITIES

Tourist office Near the Bali Museum at Jl Surapati 7 (Mon–Thurs 7.30am–3.30pm, Fri 6am–1pm; ☎0361 226302). Useful for transport and festivals information, and they've a decent city map, but don't expect much more.

Dance performances Tourist performances (about 2hr; adult/child Rp100,000/50,000) of the Barong (daily 9.30am) take place at the Catur Eka Budhi on Jl Waribang, in Denpasar's eastern Kesiman district, while the Kecak (daily 6.30pm) is performed at the Stage Uma Dewi, also on Jl Waribang, about 300m south of the Barong dance stage.

Music and dance lessons Lessons and workshops in gamelan and Balinese dance at Mekar Bhuana Conservatory, Jl Gandapura III No.501X, Kesiman Kerthalangu (☎0361 464201, ⊛balimusicanddance.com).

ACCOMMODATION

★**Nakula Familiar Inn** Jl Nakula 4 ☎0361 226446, ⊛nakulafamiliarinn.com. Eight well-maintained rooms with a balcony and either a fan or a/c in a welcoming family-style losmen. It's less than a 10min walk from the Bali Museum and about a 15min walk from Tegal bemo terminal.

The only downside is traffic noise at rush-hour. **Rp200,000**

Niki Rusdi Jl Pidada, just behind Ubung bus and bemo terminal ☎0361 416397. This little hotel has clean fan and a/c rooms and is handily located for bus departure/arrivals, though its location is quite noisy. Doubles **Rp150,000**

EATING

There are few tourist-oriented restaurants in Denpasar, so this is a good chance to sample Bali's cheap, authentic neighbourhood places to eat. Note that smaller restaurants generally shut by 7pm. Renon is the eating destination of choice for middle-class locals and expats but it's a fair haul from the hotels in the city centre.

Babi Guling Jl Sutomo 20. Serves just one dish – roast suckling pig (*babi guling*), considered by some to be the best in the city and only Rp30,000/plate. Best for lunch, as they sometimes run out by mid-afternoon. There's no sign, but it's just north of Pura Maospahit. Daily 10am–5pm.

Bhineka Jaya Kopi Bali Jl Gajah Mada 80 ☎0361 224016, ⊛kopibali.com. At this modest-looking outlet of Indonesia's Butterfly Globe Brand, you can sample a cappuccino or Bali coffee (Rp6000) then choose which grade of island beans to take home. Mon–Sat 9am–4pm.

Pasar Malam Kereneng Just off Jl Hayam Wuruk, adjacent to Kereneng bemo terminal. More than fifty vendors convene at this night market from dusk to dawn every night, dishing out super-cheap soups, noodle and rice dishes from Rp15,000, including *babi guling*, fresh fruit juices and cold beers. Daily roughly 6pm–4am.

Warung Be Pasih Renon Jl Pemuda ☎0361 237755. Renowned for delicious Balinese-style fish and seafood, this local place is inexpensive and has good *paket* (set meals). Try the *ikan goreng* (fried fish, Rp23,000) or barbecued prawns (Rp33,000), which come with soup and sambal sauce.

Warung Wardani Jl Yudistira 2 ☎0361 224398. The finest *nasi campur* you'll eat in Denpasar (from Rp35,000) – a delicious, complete feed that might take in *sate lilit*, beef curry, salted egg and a vegetable dish or two. Other options including *nasi soto ayam* and *gado-gado* are also available. No pork though. Daily 8am–4pm.

SHOPPING

Perhaps the second-best reason to visit Denpasar after the museum is the city's selection of **markets**. Tourists find them picturesque; to locals they're for mundane day-to-day purchases, and most Balinese prefer the growing number of **shopping malls**.

MARKETS

The gold quarter Not far from Jl Sulawesi is the city's gold quarter. Centred on the stretch of Jl Hasanudin that runs west from Jl Diponegoro to the river, this market has lots of jewellery outlets, but designs cater to local tastes rather than tourist ones and it pays to do some homework on the price of gold before embarking on the obligatory bargaining. Generally daily 9am–4pm.

Jalan Sulawesi Just to the east of Pasar Badung, this narrow thoroughfare, running from Jl Hasanudin in the south to Jl Gajah Mada in the north, is devoted to fabric of all descriptions, much imported by Middle Eastern and

Indian merchants but including batik, *songket* brocades and sari silks. Generally daily 9am–4pm.

★ **Pasar Badung** The biggest market and the best occupies a three-storey covered *pasar* beside the river. Trading takes place almost 24hr a day – the main action is around 4–6am, and there's a lull in early afternoon – with buyers and sellers pouring in from all over Bali. You'll find fruit, veg and spices on lower floors, while those upstairs sell everything from buckets to boots and shoes to shovels. Daily 4am–11pm.

Pasar Kumbasari Directly across the Badung River from Pasar Badung. This four-storey art market stocks clothes, souvenirs, textiles, woodcarvings, paintings and sarongs – all the stuff on sale in Kuta but without the crowds and generally at cheaper prices. Daily 7am–5pm.

DIRECTORY

Embassies and consulates See p.25.

Hospitals, clinics and dentists Sanglah Public Hospital (Rumah Sakit Umum Propinsi Sanglah, or RSUP Sanglah) at Jl Kesehatan Selatan 1, Sanglah (☎ 0361 227911) is the main provincial public hospital, with an emergency ward and some English-speaking staff. It also has Bali's only divers' recompression chamber (☎ 0361 257361 or mobile ☎ 0812 465 5281). BaliMed Hospital is a private hospital at Jl Mahendradatta 57X (☎ 0361 484748, ⊛ balimedhospital .co.id). Most expats use BIMC or International SOS, both near Kuta (see p.75).

Immigration office Corner of Jl Panjaitan and Jl Raya Puputan, Renon (Mon–Thurs 8am–4pm, Fri 8–11am; ☎ 0361 227828).

Police There are police stations on Jl Patimura and Jl Diponegoro; the main police station is in the far west of the city on Jl Gunung Sanghiang (☎ 0361 424346).

Post office Denpasar's poste restante (Mon–Sat 8am– 6pm) is at the General Post Office on Jl Raya Puputan in Renon. The Sanur–Tegal and Kereneng–Tegal bemos pass the front door.

Sanur

If Kuta–Legian–Seminyak is too frantic and Nusa Dua too manufactured, **SANUR** could well be your sort of place. It's a low-key destination strung behind 5km of fine beach, with a laidback atmosphere and an appealing lack of hustle. Traffic is light, there's little air pollution to content with, it's leafy and boasts a fine promenade. While it's true Sanur is somewhat lacking in clubbing and all-night partying venues (some nickname it "Snore"), for many visitors that is decidedly a good thing. With calm shallow water it's a safe spot for the kiddies, and there are also two surf breaks and some so-so diving. You could use it as a base to explore nearby – Kuta is 15km (about 45min) southwest and Ubud an hour or so's drive north, while chilled Nusa Lembongan is a short boat ride away.

It could all have ended so differently. Sanur was the site of Bali's first major beach hotel in the 1960s. The lumpish, concrete **Grand Bali Beach** (currently part of the *Inna* hotel group) did not go down well locally and led to a Bali-wide edict against building anything higher than a coconut tree. That edict has slipped (or there are some seriously high coconut trees in Bali), but the ethos against high-rises remains. Sanur's other claim to fame is as the source of some of Bali's most powerful **black magic** and as the home of the most feared sorcerers and respected healers, or *balian*. Not so long ago it was not uncommon to hear stories of police enquiries that used the black-magic practitioners of Sanur to help track down criminals.

The beach

The length of Sanur's 5km **shoreline** is fronted by a shady, paved esplanade. There are far worse ways to while away a day than to wander (or cycle) down the coast in search of your personal paradise, stopping off for lunch at the abundant warung and restaurants, then pausing for a cool sunset Bintang on the return. The busy patches of beach are around the *Inna Grand Bali Beach* in the north and, further south between the Sindhu Art Market and the *Tandjung Sari Hotel*. The empty stretch just south of Beujimbar is the quietest. Wherever you end up, the **views** are great: on a clear day, the profile of Gunung Agung soars northeast while out to sea you might just make out the cliffs of Nusa Penida.

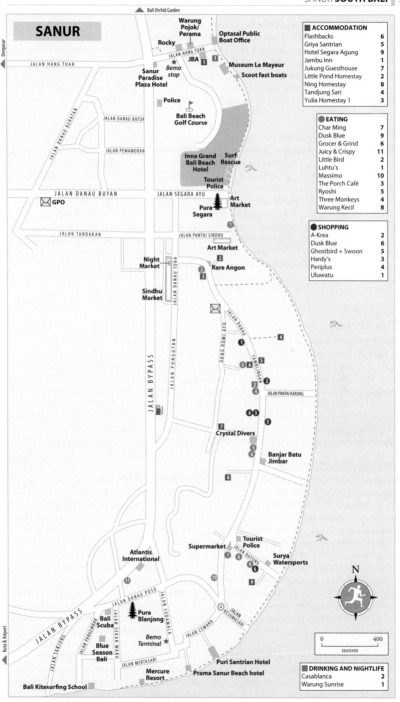

SANUR

Bali Orchid Garden

Warung
Pojok/
Perama

Optasal Public
Boat Office

Rocky

JALAN HANG TUAH

JBA

Bemo
stop

Museum Le Mayeur

Scoot fast boats

Sanur
Paradise
Plaza Hotel

Police

Bali Beach
Golf Course

JALAN DANAU BATUR

JALAN PEMAMORAN

Inna Grand
Bali Beach
Hotel

Surf
Rescue

Tourist
Police

JALAN SEGARA AYU

Art
Market

GPO

Pura
Segara

JALAN DANAU BUYAN

JALAN TANDAKAN

JALAN PANTAI SINDHU

Art Market

Night
Market

Rare Angon

Sindhu
Market

JALAN DANAU TOBA

GANG BUMI AYU

JALAN DANAU

JALAN PUNGUTAN

JALAN BYPASS

TAMBLINGAN

JALAN PANTAI KARANG

Crystal Divers

Banjar Batu
Jimbar

Tourist
Police

Supermarket

JALAN DUYUNG

Surya
Watersports

Atlantis
International

Bali
Scuba

Pura Blanjong

JALAN DANAU POSO

JALAN SEKAR WARU

JALAN SUDAMALA

Bemo
Terminal

JALAN CEMARA

JALAN RESUMASARI

Blue
Season
Bali

JALAN PANGEMBAK

JALAN TANDJUNG

JALAN MERTASARI

Mercure
Resort

Puri Santrian Hotel

Prama Sanur Beach hotel

Bali Kitesurfing School

Denpasar

Kuta & Airport

N

0   400
metres

■ ACCOMMODATION	
Flashbacks	6
Griya Santrian	5
Hotel Segara Agung	9
Jambu Inn	1
Jukung Guesthouse	7
Little Pond Homestay	2
Ning Homestay	8
Tandjung Sari	4
Yulia Homestay 1	3

● EATING	
Char Ming	7
Dusk Blue	9
Grocer & Grind	6
Juicy & Crispy	11
Little Bird	2
Luhtu's	1
Massimo	10
The Porch Café	3
Ryoshi	5
Three Monkeys	4
Warung Kecil	8

● SHOPPING	
A-Krea	2
Dusk Blue	6
Ghostbird + Swoon	5
Hardy's	3
Periplus	4
Uluwatu	1

■ DRINKING AND NIGHTLIFE	
Casablanca	2
Warung Sunrise	1

A huge expanse of Sanur's shore is exposed at low tide and a reef lies about 1km offshore at high tide. This offers three mid- to high-tide surf breaks – one in front of the *Inna Grand Bali Beach* hotel, one opposite the *Tandjung Sari* hotel and another 2km offshore the *Bali Hyatt* – but the **currents** beyond it are strong. They're all at their best Sept–March, when the northwest winds blow offshore.

The shallows within are fine for paddling at low tide and swimming at other times, as well as providing a venue for numerous watersports.

Museum Le Mayeur

Entrance from beach 50m south of Jl Hang Tuah • Mon–Thurs, Sat & Sun 7.30am–4pm, Fri 7.30am–1pm • Rp50,000 • ☎ 0361 286201

Sanur's cultural sight, the **Museum Le Mayeur**, is former home of artist **Adrien-Jean le Mayeur de Merprés** (1880–1958). Having arrived in Singaraja in 1932, the 52-year-old Belgian settled in Sanur and set up his easel, painting canvases of 16-year-old beauty Nyoman Pollok and her friends; "the beauty and splendid figure of Ni made the painter enjoy his stay", the museum notes drily. Married three years later, the couple lived in the floridly carved house where around eighty of his works now hang: Impressionist early paintings from his travels in Europe, North Africa and India and romanticized canvases of Ni and her friends from the 1950s. Imagine French Impressionism channelled by Gauguin and you're close. The 1930s house is also interesting for its carving and for the couple's furniture – Ni donated the property to the government on her death in 1985.

Bali Orchid Garden

3km north of Sanur on Jl Bypass, just beyond the junction with the coast road to Pantai Saba and Kusamba • Daily 8.30am–6pm • Rp100,000 • ⓦ www.baliorchidgardens.com

The Balinese love their tropical gardens and many buy their plants from the nurseries that line the roads between Sanur and Denpasar. This enterprising nursery has turned itself into a paying attraction as the **Bali Orchid Garden** and encourages tourists to discover the beautiful flowers for a charge. The grounds are pleasingly landscaped and alongside the huge variety of orchids are other tropical lovelies, including heliconias, bromeliads and tree ferns. However the entrance fee is certainly steep and the wannabe guides tip-hungry.

ARRIVAL AND DEPARTURE · SANUR

By plane From Ngurah Rai Airport (see p.64) a prepaid taxi is about Rp145,000 to Sanur.

By shuttle bus The fastest, most direct transport is usually tourist shuttle bus. The drop-off point for the biggest operator, Perama, is Warung Pojok minimarket, Jl Hang Tuah 31 in north Sanur (☎ 0361 285592, ⓦ perama tour.com); you can pay an extra Rp15,000 for a hotel drop-off (or pick-up), or bemos or taxis will take you onward. Sample fares include Rp35,000 to Kuta/the airport, Rp50,000 to Ubud, Rp75,000 to Padang Bai, Rp125,000 to Lovina and Rp175,000 to Amed.

Destinations Amed (daily; 3hr); Bedugul (daily; 2hr–2hr 30min); Candidasa (4 daily; 2hr 30min–3hr); Gili Islands (daily; 9hr); Kintamani (daily, min 2 people; 2hr 30min–3hr); Kuta/Ngurah Rai Airport (7 daily; 40min–1hr); Lovina (daily; 3–4hr); Padang Bai (4 daily; 2hr–2hr 30min); Senggigi, Lombok (daily; 8hr 30min); Ubud (7 daily; 45min–1hr).

By bemo Arrival and departure by bemo is from the Denpasar terminals at Kereneng or Tegal (see p.89). Dark-green bemos from Kereneng run to the Jl Bypass/Jl Hang Tuah junction in north Sanur, then Jl Danau Beratan and Jl Danau Buyan, before continuing down Jl Danau Tamblingan to Semawang. Dark-blue bemos from Tegal run direct to Sanur then follow the same route as the Kereneng ones. Leaving is easy – bemo drivers along Jl Danau Tamblingan and the Jl Bypass will honk to pick you up.

By bus Kura Kura minibuses (ⓦ kura2bus.com) connect Sanur with Kuta (Rs50,000) four times daily between 10am and 4pm. You can change at their depot in Kuta's T-Galleria mall for services to Seminyak and Nusa Dua. Or Trans Sarbagita buses run from Batubulan bemo terminal–Sanur Jl Bypass–Kuta Central Parking–Jimbaran–Nusa Dua. In theory, buses (Rs3500) run every 30min from 5am–9pm.

By boat Sanur is the main departure point for boats to Nusa Lembongan and also has services to Nusa Penida.

From a jetty in north Sanur public and private ferries run to Jungutbatu (more than 14 daily; 30min–2hr) and Mushroom Bay (8 daily; 40min–2hr) in Lembongan. For Penida there are 12 scheduled boats daily to Toya Pakeh, Buyuk and Sampalan. Benoa Harbour (Pelabuhan Benoa), 5km southwest of southern Sanur, is the arrival and departure point for many sailing trips and tourist boats, including fast boats to the Gili Islands (see p.284) and day-trips to Nusa Lembongan (see p.98), as well as for all Pelni ships from elsewhere in Indonesia.

By taxi A taxi ride from central Kuta or Denpasar should cost about Rp110,000, or Rs65,000 in an Uber/Grab.

GETTING AROUND

By bemo The green and blue public bemos to and from Denpasar's terminals can be useful for buzzing up and down the main streets; the tourist price is about Rp7000 for a local ride.

By taxi Blue Bird taxis (☏0361 701111) are reliable; a short hop in Sanur won't cost more than Rp12,000. If you're planning a long trip, consider negotiating a fee with one of the roadside transport touts.

By car or motorbike Transport touts also rent cars and motorbikes, as do many hotels and tour agencies. JBA is one of the few Sanur agencies to sell car insurance, and will also supply a car with driver; it's located at Jl Danau Toba 1 (☏0361 369 8902).

By bike Sanur is a good bet for cyclists; most hotels and travel agents along Jl Danau Tamblingan have them for rent (around Rp20,000–30,000/day).

INFORMATION AND ACTIVITIES

Information Check out the website ⊚sanurweekly.com for reviews, information and all things Sanur.

Golf It wouldn't excite Tiger Woods, but Sanur has the nine-hole Bali Beach Golf Course in front of the *Inna Grand Bali Beach* (☏0361 287733, ⊚balibeachgolfcourse.com); it's not cheap, though, at Rp1,385,000 a round.

Kitesurfing Bali Kitesurfing School, Pantai Mertasari (☏0851 0089 9013, ⊚bali-kitesurfing.org) on Sanur beach offers lessons for beginners and advanced pupils (from Rp950,000 for 2hr), plus gear rental and kitesurf tours.

Spas and beauty treatments Most of Sanur's more expensive hotels have luxurious spas open to the public and offer a range of treatments including aromatherapy, reflexology, traditional Balinese massages, the Javanese *mandi lulur* exfoliation scrub (see p.38), facials and hair treatments. Alternatively, there's always the massage-and-manicure ladies who hang out on the beach, charging around Rp100,000/hr.

Surfing There is little in the way of surfboard and boogie board rental; a couple of stalls south of the Sindhu art market provide rent gear.

Watersports Parasailing, glass-bottomed boats, banana boat rides, jet skis, sit-on kayaks, even fishing trips in traditional boats – there's little that Sanur's enterprising agents won't offer. Beachfront outlets rent out equipment, or contact one of the larger operators such as Surya Watersports, Jl Duyung 10B (☏0361 287956, ⊚balisuryadivecenter.com) in south Sanur.

Yoga Power Of Now Oasis at Jl Merta (☏0878 6153 4535, ⊚powerofnowoasis.com) offers up to six daily hatha and vinyasa flow classes and Yoga Alliance-accredited teacher training courses.

ACCOMMODATION

There are beds to suit every budget in Sanur and few dud stays – quality is generally high and you get more space and better facilities for your rupiah or dollar here than in Kuta–Legian–Seminyak. Obviously, places with direct access to the beach command a premium.

Flashbacks Jl Danau Tamblingan 110 ☏0361 281682, ⊚flashbacks-chb.com. Lovely intimate bolthole with nine rooms and bungalows, some with a/c and one with a kitchenette. Style is a sort of budget rustic boutique – think stone floors, carved bedsteads and ikat textiles – all in a lush garden compound with a saltwater pool. It's just behind *Porch* café. Doubles **Rp270,000**, bungalows **Rp585,000**

Griya Santrian Jl Danau Tamblingan 47 ☏0361 288181, ⊚santrian.com. There's plenty of space and no shortage of beach views at this large well-run hotel, with spacious rooms in a garden compound that runs down to the shore. You'll also find an art gallery, good seafront restaurant and three pools (one shoreside). **$186**

Hotel Segara Agung Jl Duyung 43 ☏0361 288446, ⊚segaraagung.com. Offering fine value and a peaceful location a couple of minutes' walk from the beach, this hotel has inviting a/c rooms and suites, a garden, pool and warm welcomes. Doubles **Rp444,000**, suites **Rp812,000**

Jambu Inn Jl Hang Tuah 54 ☏0361 286501, ⊚jambuinnsanur.com. A convenient option for early boats to/from Nusa Lembongan with sixteen spacious rooms in a mismatch of styles, set in a garden with pool. Hot water, cable TV and a/c come as standard. **Rp375,000**

Jukung Guesthouse Gang Penjor ☏0812 3968 0629, ⊚jukungguesthouse.com. Stylish little guesthouse where the attractive a/c rooms have traditional tiled floors, soft white linen, hot-water en-suites, tea or coffee making

DIVING AND SNORKELLING AROUND SANUR

Despite the abundance of diving operators, Sanur's **reef dives** are only really of interest for beginners or as a refresher. The coral is unspectacular, the visibility so-so, and dives rarely descend beneath 12m. However dive trips to Nusa Penida and Amed are offered by several schools and **snorkelling** trips (around $25/person/hr, including gear) are also popular. Recommended dive centres in Sanur include:

AquaMarine Diving Jl Petitenget 2A ☎ 0361 738020, 🌐 aquamarinediving.com. UK-run PADI five-star resort.

Atlantis International Jl Bypass Ngurah Rai 350, Sanur ☎ 0361 284312, 🌐 balidiveaction.com. PADI five-star IDC Centre. Operates courses in English, French, Spanish, German and Indonesian.

Bali Scuba Jl Danau Poso 40, Blanjong, Sanur ☎ 0361 288610, 🌐 baliscuba.com. PADI five-star IDC

centre that's known for its technical diving.

Blue Season Bali Gang Wanasari, off Jl Danau Poso ☎ 0361 270852, 🌐 baliocean.com. PADI CDC centre. UK-Japanese-run.

Crystal Divers Jl Danau Tamblingan 168, Batujimbar ☎ 0361 286737, 🌐 crystal-divers.com. PADI CDC centre. Established for 20 years and also runs tailored dive safaris all over Bali.

---

facilities, minibars and whitewashed wooden furniture. Balconies overlook a pool area scattered with giant beanbags. Rp350,000

★**Little Pond Homestay** Jl Danau Tamblingan 19, Sindhu ☎ 0361 289902, 🌐 littlepondbali.com. The fifteen small bright rooms grouped around a pool have a choice of fan or a/c and are a cut above the usual losmen, each with verandas, hot-water bathrooms and a homely feel. Once you factor in that this is quiet and close to the main road and beach, you'll realize you've got a bargain. Rp175,000

★**Ning Homestay** Gang 3, off Jl Kesari 1 ☎ 0823 3910 7639, ✉ ningtyas.homestay@gmail.com. Sanur's best hostel is well-organized, with clean accommodation and a sociable vibe: the eight-bed dorm is a/c and bunks have reading lights, lockers and power sockets while the double room is fine value for Sanur. There are plenty of spots to relax and chat with other guests around the garden, the restaurant has well-priced drinks and meals, there's free

drinking water and communal bathrooms are kept tidy. Dorms Rp100,000, doubles Rp200,000

Tandjung Sari Jl Danau Tamblingan 41, Sindhu ☎ 0361 288441, 🌐 tandjungsarihotel.com. Today a delightful, intimate and classy hotel, this was once a private beach house for an English/Javanese couple. There are beautifully furnished cottages of varying sizes, each with a courtyard garden; expect antique floor tiles and tasteful batik furnishings. Add in a large pool, fitness centre, library, a garden that runs to the shore and faultless service and this is a fine choice for a relaxing stay. $216

Yulia Homestay 1 Jl Danau Tamblingan 38, Sindhu ☎ 0361 288089, 🌐 facebook.com/yulia1homestay. A very welcoming family-run cheapie with twenty fan-cooled or a/c rooms, some with hot water, all well maintained and comfortable if a little old-fashioned. Owner Ketut is a mine of information about Bali and there's a small pool to enjoy. Rp200,000

EATING

Beachfront café-restaurants abound between Sindhu and Batujimbar but none stands out for cuisine, so stroll the promenade and take your pick. The most authentic Indonesian food and cheapest eats are beyond the main drag; the night market (6pm–midnight) inside the Sindhu Market at Jl Danau Tamblingan/Jl Danau Toba, and the surrounding lanes, are good hunting grounds.

Char Ming Jl Danau Tamblingan 97 ☎ 0361 288029, 🌐 charming-bali.com. Glorious formal restaurant housed in a high-ceilinged *bale* with wooden carvings and statues. The East-meets West menu includes pan-grilled John Dory fillets (Rp125,000) or for a splurge, the two-person, ten-dish *rijsttafel* platter (Rp365,000). Call for a complimentary ride (and return trip). Daily 6–11pm.

Dusk Blue Jl Duyung 3 ☎ 0811 398 5611, 🌐 duskblue bali.com. Looking like somewhere you'd find in Santorini, this powder blue-and-white café has a pretty front terrace that's a relaxed spot for a coffee (including Vietnamese drip-style, Rp30,000), juice or a Med-inspired meal. Daily 7.30am–9pm.

Grocer & Grind Jl Danau Tamblingan 152 ☎ 0361 270635, 🌐 grocerandgrind.com. Set back from the main drag, this outpost of Aussie metropolitan cool is your spot for good coffee and pastries, cakes and fine sandwiches, falafel (Rs74,000) or a pulled pork sub (Rs94,000). Not cheap, but portions are generous and service accomplished. Daily 7.30am–10pm.

★**Juicy & Crispy** Jl Tirta Nadi 5 ☎ 0812 3615 3336, 🌐 juicyandcrispy.com. A meat feast par excellence – buzzing, busy J&C has a mercifully short menu, specializing in super-succulent spare ribs (from 5pm only) and rotisserie chicken (from Rp42,000) though they'll also knock up a *nasi* *goreng* should you choose. It's a tiny, cramped space so book ahead for seating, or grab and go. Daily noon–9pm.

Little Bird Jl Danau Tamblingan 34 ☎0361 745968. Hugely likeable little warung, partly due to a mellow vibe, partly due to good Indonesian food that's more zingy than most in Sanur and comes at lower prices: specials are chalked up outside and might include *nasi goreng ayam* (Rp35,000). Daily 8am–11pm.

Luhtu's Sindhu Beach ☎0812 388 8448. Likeable beachfront cafe that serves up great breakfasts, sandwiches and salads (Rp35,000–40,000) and a mean *soto ayam* (chicken soup). There's also a counter of fresh cakes to go with it – try the lemon cheesecake. Daily 7am–9pm.

Massimo Jl Danau Tamblingan 228 ☎0361 288492. The finest Italian cooking in Sanur, produced by a native chef: excellent antipasti such as *frittura de calamari* (squid with alioli) thin-crust pizza and pasta (Rp53,000–75,000) plus mains including the catch of the day, marinated, grilled and served with a chilli shellfish sauce (Rp69,000). There's a kids' menu and takeaway *gelato* are a lifesaver on hot days. Daily 11am–11pm.

The Porch Café Jl Danau Tamblingan 110 ☎0361 281682. A well-run Aussie-owned cafe with a/c interior and small front terrace that offers a good range of breakfasts, home-made fresh pies (Rp58,000), veggie dishes, the full gamut of espresso coffee combinations and endless varieties of fresh juice. Daily 7am–10pm.

Ryoshi Jl Danau Tamblingan 150 T0361 288473, ⓦryoshibali.com. Fine value and perfect if you're fed up with *nasi goreng* and the like. The Japanese food here is divine – try the sashimi, sushi (nine pieces Rp65,000) or beef teriyaki (Rs60,000). Daily 11am–midnight.

Three Monkeys Jl Danau Tamblingan 116 ☎0361 286002, ⓦwww.threemonkeyscafebali.com. "Hot food, cool jazz" is the motto, minimalism is the style of this dining room/lounge bar. Food-wise, expect probably the best range of salads on the east coast (organic garden salad Rs60,000), plus delicious slow-roast pork belly and upmarket Asian favourites (from Rp70,000) such as tasty prawn *laksa* (spicy noodle soup with coconut). Daily 11am–11pm.

Warung Kecil Jl Duyung ☎0361 202 0002. Tiny modern warung with both Indo and Western food. Grab a panini, salad or a *nasi campur* (Rp27,000) and slurp on a fresh juice. There are a few books to browse too. Daily 8am–9.30pm.

NIGHTLIFE AND ENTERTAINMENT

There's not much here – this is "Snore", remember? If you don't fancy the cover bands at beachside restaurants on the main drag, you'll have to make do with so-so sports bars and "Irish" pubs favoured by expats.

Casablanca Jl Danau Tamblingan 120 ☎0361 287263, ⓦfacebook.com/casablanca.dine. It's certainly not hip, but the self-styled "most colourful place in Sanur" is definitely lively with live rock, reggae, indie and soul bands entertaining the holiday crowds. Daily 10am–1am.

Warung Sunrise Jl Hang Tuah. Beachside bar with chairs on the sand, live reggae three nights a week, gregarious staff and strong cocktails (from around Rp40,000). Daily 10am–late.

SHOPPING

A-Krea Jl Danau Tamblingan 51 ☎0361 286102. Great little outlet of a Balinese mini-chain whose woven and batik handmade bags and purses, homewares, clothes and cute kidswear and toys are all crafted tastefully in simple modern designs. Daily 9am–9pm.

Dusk Blue Jl Duyung 3 ☎0811 398 5611, ⓦduskblue bali.com. Gorgeous design store selling well-chosen homeware including woven bags and zany little placemats. Doubles as a café (see opposite). Daily 7.30am–9pm.

Ghostbird + Swoon Jl Danau Tamblingan 75 ☎0821 4425 4110, ⓦghostbirdswoon.com. A class above every other fashion boutique in Sanur, this high-end store sells stunning handmade clothing from local designers (dresses start at around Rp700,000) and select artworks. Tues–Sun 11am–7pm.

Hardy's Jl Danau Tamblingan 136 ☎0361 285806. You'll find mass-produced crafts if you rummage among the souvenir tat on the top floor of Sanur's only department store. The ground floor sells more Bali souvenir T-shirts than you knew possible. Daily 8am–10pm.

Periplus Jl Danau Tamblingan 136 ☎0361 282790. The excellent English-language Periplus bookstore has a branch in Hardy's department store. It sells a good selection of national and international media, plus a wide selection of fiction and nonfiction, including much on island life and culture. Daily 8.30am–10pm.

Uluwatu Jl Danau Tamblingan ☎0361 288037. A large outlet of the Balinese chain, which sells elegant white or black handmade lace and flowing cotton clothes – plus bed linen and some jewellery. Daily 8am–10pm.

DIRECTORY

Banks and exchange There are ATMs and exchange counters all over Sanur.

Embassies and consulates See p.25.

Hospitals and clinics All the major hotels provide 24hr medical service. The Guardian Pharmacy by Hardy's supermarket also has a doctor on call. For major international

1

clinics, see Kuta–Legian–Seminyak.

Pharmacies Several on Jl Danau Tamblingan.

Police There's a 24hr Tourist Police post on Jl Danau Tamblingan, just south of the *Bali Hyatt* hotel. The police station (☎ 0361 288597) is on Jl Bypass in north Sanur, just south of the *Sanur Paradise Plaza* hotel.

Post office Sanur's General Post Office is on Jl Danau Buyan, Sindhu.

Nusa Lembongan and Nusa Penida

It's amazing what 20km of sea will do. Even compared to Sanur, the islands of **Nusa Lembongan**, **Nusa Ceningan** and **Nusa Penida** across the Badung Strait seem a throwback to the Bali of twenty years ago – the Bali of laidback villages and bumpy lanes winding through mangroves; of fine white sand and turquoise water; of spectacular sunsets on the beach as time slips by at a lovely lazy pace. Small wonder many people come for two days and find themselves on the return boat two weeks later.

Of course, there's more to these islands than idle days scrunching white sand between your toes. Encircled by superbly clear water and healthy reef, they offer outstanding **diving** – Nusa Penida's sites are world-class – and challenging **surfing**. There's even industry of sorts – seaweed farming is still a source of income for many islanders.

Of the trio, **Nusa Lembongan** has nearly all the facilities. Even though it's developing rapidly, it remains relaxed, with most accommodation slotted in between homes. Activities providers offer trips both on foot and on two wheels. Tiny undeveloped **Nusa Ceningan** is best seen as an afterthought to Nusa Lembongan – it's linked by a bridge – and has few sights. **Nusa Penida** is the largest of all and more rugged than Nusa Lembongan. Apart from a few guesthouses and the odd simple tourist warung, it remains almost entirely undeveloped – ripe for a few days' exploration for the adventurous.

Nusa Lembongan

Yes, there are now boutique hotels. And each visit reveals a new patch of scrub cleared for yet another homestay or yet more motorbikes on the lanes. But **NUSA LEMBONGAN** retains its village ambience – you can sense the island atmosphere as soon as you wade off the boat. Even the hawkers are half-hearted. Tourism has most definitely arrived – around seventy percent of the seven thousand population are engaged in tourism to some degree – yet it's largely restricted to **Jungutbatu** village in the north (which has the most accommodation), **Mushroom Bay** on the west side and the **Lembongan** area in the south, where the hotels tend to be more upmarket.

Previously, the island earned a crust by **seaweed farming** in the aquamarine shallows. A source of **agar** vegetable gel and **carrageenan** used in cosmetics and foodstuffs, seaweed is grown on chequerboard bamboo frames and harvested after 45 days – hard, physical work with unpredictable financial rewards. Mangroves, meanwhile, fringe much of the north and east coast. This makes much of the coast so-so for swimming, but there are some pretty white-sand bays that are good for a dip so long as you heed local warnings about currents. Unfortunately trash is a huge problem all over the island, with discarded building waste and household rubbish spoiling the scenery. Project Aware (⬤ projectaware.org) is one organization trying to clean things up.

There are near zero cars, so **getting around** means joining villagers on motorbikes or bicycles, which are widely available for rent. The island is just 4km long and less than 3km wide, so if you are supremely keen you could walk around it in a long hot day. Good luck with that.

Jungutbatu and Mushroom Bay

Strung out along the northwest coast, the slightly scruffy village of **JUNGUTBATU** spreads out along the beachfront from its core of accommodation and restaurants. The sandy **beach** is lovely and though it is no great shakes for swimming, it looks gorgeous

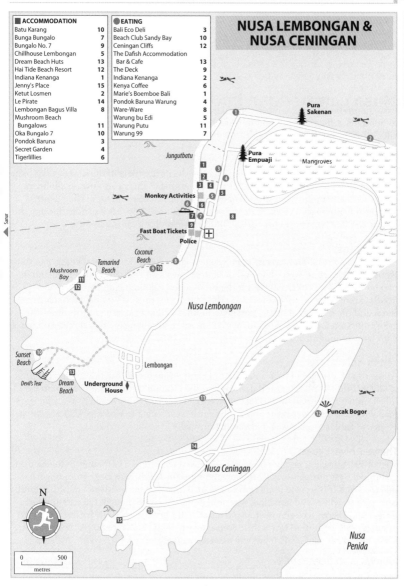

NUSA LEMBONGAN & NUSA CENINGAN

■ ACCOMMODATION	
Batu Karang	10
Bunga Bungalo	7
Bungalo No. 7	9
Chillhouse Lembongan	5
Dream Beach Huts	13
Hai Tide Beach Resort	12
Indiana Kenanga	1
Jenny's Place	15
Ketut Losmen	2
Le Pirate	14
Lembongan Bagus Villa	8
Mushroom Beach Bungalows	11
Oka Bungalo 7	10
Pondok Baruna	3
Secret Garden	4
Tigerlillies	6

● EATING	
Bali Eco Deli	3
Beach Club Sandy Bay	10
Ceningan Cliffs	12
The Dafish Accommodation Bar & Cafe	13
The Deck	9
Indiana Kenanga	2
Kenya Coffee	6
Marie's Boemboe Bali	1
Pondok Baruna Warung	4
Ware-Ware	8
Warung bu Edi	5
Warung Putu	11
Warung 99	7

at low tide, a strip of coarse golden sand that arcs before an aquamarine sea filled with wooden boats. It's an ideal place for sunset drinks or for losing days gazing out to Gunung Agung on the northwestern horizon. For a bit more activity, you can walk 1km south to Mushroom Bay in 30–45 minutes via a scenic **west-coast path** that begins at the steps at the far southern end of the beach. You'll have to improvise a path at points – just keep the coast on your right – but the reward is a couple of small beaches en route. A crescent of white sand behind a turquoise bay, **Mushroom Bay** is small and lovely. The downside is that it's often crowded with boats, huge offshore

1

> ### A MANGROVE SAFARI
> Given Nusa Lembongan's focus on diving and surf, a trip into the **mangrove swamps** that fringe the northeast coast is one of the more unusual diversions on a visit. It's an eerie experience: boats are punted with bamboo, so there's no engine noise to disturb the crabs and birds that inhabit the muddy forest floor – the trip is best at low tide when the roots are exposed.

party pontoons and day-trippers. If you ask locally, you should be able to find a path to Sunset Beach and its restaurant, though the easiest access is by road via Lembongan village (see below).

The north coast
Village life and seaweed farming dominates on the **northern tip of the island**, a flat 3km that's easily covered by bicycle from central Jungutbatu. There's also the possibility of exploring the mangrove forest that fringes the northeast coast. Most of the warung beyond the unremarkable sea temple, **Pura Sakenan**, will organize a paddle through the mangroves (see box above) for Rp100,000 per person for a 20-minute trip.

The east coast
A fork in the road 200m west of Pura Sakenan takes you down the **east coast**, past **Pura Empuaji** (700m southwest; dawn till dusk; free; own sash and sarong required) and its two monumental ficus trees – this is the most venerated temple on the island and you'll need a sarong and sash if you want to visit. The road wends its way between mangrove forest and the occasional house, and after another 5.5km reaches the turn-off for the bridge to Nusa Ceningan. From here it's 2km up to Lembongan village, then another 3km back to Jungutbatu.

Lembongan
At the top of a steep hill 3km southwest of central Jungutbatu the tidy settlement of **LEMBONGAN** is the largest on the island and the location of the **Underground House** (open on request; Rp20,000). Dug between 1961 and 1976 by Made Byasa, a local man who is said to have been inspired by the Mahabharata (see box, p.321), it consists of several dank rooms, a well and ventilation shafts.

The southwest coast
Two of Bali's loveliest beaches lie on the southwest coast. From Lembongan, follow the main road west through to a T-junction and signs for Mushroom Bay, 750m down a side road. A left turn here leads 1km to **Dream Beach**, one of the island's most beautiful bays with its white sand and clear, turquoise water – beware though, the currents are dangerous. There's accommodation and a restaurant here (see p.103). It's just a few minutes' walk beyond to lovely little **Sunset Beach**, with its own resort. At both beaches, it can be too risky for a swim but you can use the pools for a fee.

ARRIVAL AND DEPARTURE   NUSA LEMBONGAN

What with the private fast boats, tourist shuttle and slow boats, there are over twenty **daily services** to Jungutbatu and eight to Mushroom Bay. All leave from the end of Jl Hang Tuah in north Sanur (see p.94). In Lembongan, offices are on the seafront of southern Jungutbatu. Note that all boats anchor just off the beach, so you're required to **wade** ashore; a porter may offer to carry your luggage (Rp20,000). On arrival at Lembongan "beach guides" may offer to show you to accommodation for free (hotels pay commission). They'll also offer motorbikes to transport you between bays for steep fees (around Rp50,000), though if you reserve ahead hotel staff should meet you.

FROM AND TO SANUR
By fast boat No fewer than 11 private operators run speedy boats from Sanur to Lembongan. Operators include

Scoot (☎0361 285522, ⓦscootcruise.com) and Rocky (☎0361 801 2324, ⓦrockyfastcruise.com), which both run four times a day in each direction (30min; around

DIVING AND SNORKELLING AROUND NUSA LEMBONGAN

Protected as a marine conservation area, the reefs around Nusa Lembongan and Nusa Penida attract **divers** from all over the world, not least for the chance to swim with manta rays and the one-tonne legendary local giant, the **mola mola** (oceanic sunfish; see box, p.104), from early July to the end of October. The diving here is unquestionably the most dramatic in Bali, but also rarely benign, as currents and waves can be fierce. Many of the reefs are rewarding for **snorkelling**, too.

Of the fourteen main dive sites, the most famous are **off Nusa Penida** and can get very crowded in peak season. The aptly named **Manta Point** is renowned for manta rays and pelagics (whale sharks are occasionally encountered here) and is the site that everyone wants to experience. It's also the most exposed, being subject to huge swells and currents, and should only be dived when conditions are favourable – choose a reputable dive company. The famous manta "cleaning station" is at 8m in depth, and if you're lucky you'll encounter a procession of mantas banking in the water (like airplanes circling the sky waiting to land) and then swooping down to the station to get cleaned of parasites by waiting reef fish. Alternatively, juvenile manta rays (still over 2m!) can often be encountered at neighbouring Manta Bay where the sea is usually calmer. **Crystal Bay** is known for its clear waters – visibility can be 40m – and is one of the sites which attracts pelagic mola mola or sunfish from late July to October. Mola mola, manta rays and tuna also frequent the huge coral boulders and pillars of **Toyapakeh** reef, which is an incredibly rich site, teeming with fishlife, macro interest such as nudibranches and other curiosities (stonefish included). Sekolah Desar is an excellent drift dive past the healthy reefs of north Nusa Penida, particularly rich in sponges, and where white-tip reef sharks and huge schools of damselfish are present.

Prime **snorkelling** spots off Nusa Lembongan that are accessible from the shore if the tide is right are **Mangrove Corner** and **Mushroom Bay**. Off Nusa Penida they include **Crystal Bay** (see p.107), the **Penida Wall**, Manta Bay and **Malibu Point**. Virtually every guesthouse and hotel in the island can organize a trip (from Rp250,000) as can World Diving and Monkey Activities.

DIVE CENTRES

The seas around Penida and Lembongan are affected by cold upswells (down to 18C) and are known for treacherous **currents**, so dive with experts – some sites are for experienced divers only. There are a number of reputable **dive centres** on Nusa Lembongan (and one in Ceningan) including those listed below. Prices average around $40 per dive, with cheaper deals for longer dive packages. All centres offer tuition.

Big Fish Diving Secret Garden bungalows, Jungutbatu ☎ 0813 5313 6861, ⓦ bigfishdiving.com.
Ceningan Divers ☎ 0821 4585 5934, ⓦ ceningandivers.com. Five-star PADI dive school in Nusa Ceningan.
Monkey Activities Beachfront Jungutbatu ☎ 0821 4614 7683, ⓦ monkeyactivities.com. SSI freediving training (3-day Level 1 course is $330) and snorkelling excursions (half-day $16).
World Diving Lembongan Pondok Baruna, Jungutbatu ☎ 0812 390 0686, ⓦ world-diving.com.

Rp285,000/Rp450,000 one-way/return). Scoot also has a combination ticket with Gili Trawangan and Lombok (Rp600,000/one-way). Both have offices on Jl Hang Tuah. Perama (☎ 0361 751875, ⓦ peramatour.com) operates a shuttle boat from Sanur that connects with its island-wide shuttle bus services from Sanur, Kuta and Ubud. It runs to Jungutbatu (daily at 10.30am; 1hr 30min; Rp140,000); book a day in advance.

By public boat From Sanur there's supposed to be a daily 8am slow boat for Jungutbatu (Rp60,000; 2hr) and Mushroom Bay (Rp80,000; 90min), but it has become very unreliable and is frequently cancelled.

FROM AND TO EAST BALI
Demand willing, there are occasional services between Padang Bai and Jungutbatu, Lembongan.

GETTING AROUND

By bike or motorbike Not necessary around the villages but a good bet around the island – set off in a clockwise direction to avoid a killer climb south of Jungutbatu if cycling. The road is tarmac, although very broken in places. Both bikes (from Rp25,000) and motorbikes (Rp60,000) can be rented through your accommodation

1

By buggy Hotels rent out electric golf carts for Rp800,000 per day.

By pick-up Some isolated restaurants in the south offer free transport with a reservation.

On foot None of the best west-coast beaches is more than 90min from Jungutbatu.

ACTIVITIES

Spa and massage Su B (☎ 0813 3838 9062; 10am–9pm), behind the shore at the south end of Jungutbatu, is the expats' tip for the best massage on the island – he or his wife offer aromatherapy massage and reflexology (Rp100,000/hr). For more of a luxe spa environment, Lulur Spa Lembongan (☎ 0366 559 6377, ⊛ lulurspalembongan.com) in the Batu Karang resort offers scrubs, aromatherapy and massages (Rp440,000/hr).

Surfing Surfing around Nusa Lembongan is famously challenging. The best months for surfing are from May to September when southeast winds blow offshore. The breaks peel off the reef before Jungutbatu – from south to north: Playgrounds (the most forgiving break); the well-named, heavy Lacerations; and Shipwrecks. You can paddle out the 400m or rent a boat (around Rp70,000/Rp100,000 one-way/return). Board rental is available on the seafront at Jungutbatu and costs around Rp100,000/2hr – Monkey Surfing (☎ 0821 4614 7683, ⊛ monkeysurfing.com) offers the best selection and can provide lessons (Rp600,000/ beginners).

ACCOMMODATION

Jungutbatu has the widest choice of accommodation, much of it fronting the beach. Rooms elsewhere tend to be pricier. A word of warning: the island is packed from April to October so reserve ahead during this time.

JUNGUTBATU

Batu Karang ☎ 0366 559 6377, ⊛ batukarang lembongan.com. Set on the hillside overlooking the bay of Jungutbatu, these luxurious suites and villas are all limestone floors and outdoors bathrooms and contemporary cool around the pools (there are three). Facilities include a small gym and lovely spa. Minimum stay of three nights in high season. Doubles $250, villas $310

Bunga Bungalo ☎ 0366 559 6421, ⊛ bunga-bungalo .com. There are just six rooms in this French-owned place on the seafront, whose hippie beach aesthetic – carved doorways or a giant clam shell for a basin – suggest escapism despite the central location. Those on the upper floor have seaviews. As ever, a/c costs extra (Rp60,000). Rp305,000

Bungalo No. 7 ☎ 0366 559 6421, ⊛ bungalo-no7.com. Sixteen good-value rooms beside the beach in the heart of the village. Gathered around a pool, they all have en-suite bathrooms and verandas; splash out extra for a/c, hot water and sea view. Rp275,000

★**Chillhouse Lembongan** Jl Dusun Kelod 1 ☎ 0821 4500 6892, ⊛ facebook.com/chillhouselembongan. Set back from the shore in the village, these neat, very clean and well-presented a/c rooms have good king-sized beds, hot-water bathrooms, flat-screen TVs and verandas. The owner Gede is a super-helpful soul who will arrange snorkelling trips, scooter rentals and is full of island info and history. Rp230,000

Indiana Kenanga ☎ 0366 24471, ⊛ indiana-kenanga -villas.com. A design-conscious boutique resort right on the beach, with vaguely baroque-meets-contemporary decor. Standard suites are in private garden compounds, while family villas sleep four in two bedrooms. Has two pools, a spa and is home to a gastronomic restaurant (see opposite). Doubles $319, villas $696

Ketut Losmen ☎ 0813 3784 6555, ⊛ ketut.net. There's a wide choice of rooms (some very smart with a/c and hot water) at this locally owned place which has a traditional Balinese feel thanks to carved furnishings and doors, plus paintings in rooms. There's a small beachside pool but no restaurant. Rp250,000

Lembongan Bagus Villa ☎ 0812 3746 7740. A fine-value new setup run by local Made and his family, with five lovely a/c wooden bungalows that feature outdoor bathrooms and either twin or double beds. It's on the edge of the village, 400m from the sea. A pool and restaurant are planned. Rp450,000

Oka Bungalo 7 Hillside ☎ 0828 368 1443, ⊛ bungalo -no7.com. Five rooms and a couple of *lumbung* cottages, all with a/c, that enjoy sweeping bay views and represent good value for the location. There's a plunge pool for cooling off. Rp550,000

Pondok Baruna ☎ 0812 390 0686, ⊛ world-diving.com. There are three options in this local empire: simple yet attractive fan-cooled beachfront rooms with full-frontal seaviews; just behind, smarter a/c "Garden" rooms around a pool; and a newer "Frangipani" block, with modern international-hotel-standard a/c accommodation around a large pool down the street. Beachfront Rp350,000, "Garden" Rp450,000, "Frangipani" Rp550,000

★**Secret Garden** ☎ 0813 5313 6861, ⊛ bigfishdiving .com/stay. A relaxed hideaway, this small, peaceful place has nine spacious fan-cooled bungalows set around a pool in the garden, 100m from the beach. Also hosts the YogaShack and conservation-focused Big Fish Diving (see box, p.101). Great value. Rp250,000

Tigerlillies ☎ 0877 6174 1486. The romance of a simple Balinese beach hut meets boutique style in an Australian-owned retreat amid lush tropical gardens. Expect floaty drapes and pops of colour in pretty thatched cottages with semi-outdoor bathrooms (one room does not have an en-suite). No children under 12. $\overline{5}$71

THE REST OF THE ISLAND
Dream Beach Huts Dream Beach ☎ 0361 743 2344 (booking only) or ☎ 0813 3873 7344, ⓦ dreambeach lembongan.com. Above the fantastic Dream Beach, these rooms and *lumbung*-style thatch-roof huts have bamboo beds, fans and cold-water garden bathrooms; Deluxe offer the most romance and space. There's also a two-bed family house, two-tier pool over the breakers and a restaurant/

bar. Quite isolated, though that's half the point. **Rp750,000**
Hai Tide Beach Resort Mushroom Bay ☎ 0361 720331, ⓦ haitidebeachresort.com. A beautifully designed, small-scale resort with eighteen charming thatched *lumbung* (some with ocean views) and a two-bed villa (with private pool). Kayaks, SUPS and snorkelling gear are available to guests, and there's a good restaurant by the shore. $\overline{5}$146
Mushroom Beach Bungalows Mushroom Bay ☎ 0366 24515, ⓦ mushroom-lembongan.com. Good-quality, spacious rooms in a splendid location on the headland at the eastern end of Mushroom Bay, just a 2min walk from a pretty small beach. Has a small pool. $\overline{5}$65

EATING AND DRINKING

JUNGUTBATU
Bali Eco Deli ⓦ baliecodeli.net. Attractive open-sided roadside café with plenty of space to enjoy a coffee and chat. Famous for its cakes (try the chocolate, cashew and coconut, Rp26,000) which are all baked on the premises. Healthy meals, fruit salads and ice-pops are also offered and you can refill drinking water bottles here for free. Daily 7am–9pm.
The Deck ☎ 0366 559 6376, ⓦ thedecklembongan .com. This café-bar-resto in the hillside *Batu Karang* hotel is *the* spot in town for a sundowner (happy hour 5–6.30pm) when cocktails and beers are discounted. It's also a good bet for grub such as gourmet baguettes, paninis and fish tacos (Rp85,000). Their Sunday Session features live DJs spinning funky house and lounge vibes. Daily 8am–10pm.
Indiana Kenanga ☎ 0828 9708 4368, ⓦ indiana -kenanga-villas.com. The only gastro address on the island, run by Clement Fouqueré, a French chef who has worked in Michelin-starred restaurants in Paris. There's a casual day menu with dishes such as shrimp ceviche (Rp90,000) or gourmet burgers while the evening menu really delivers a punch with winning plates such as scallops with a coriander coulis, gnocchi and clam sauce (Rp205,000). Daily 8am–10pm.
Kenya Coffee Beachfront. Great little café offering well-made espresso, cappuccino and fancy options such as green tea lattes. Tables enjoy perfect bay views and the wi-fi is relatively speedy for Lembongan. Daily 7am–10pm.
★**Maria's Boemboe Bali** Bamboo benches, feet in the sand and a view over seaweed fields to Gunung Agung – this basic warung provides Lembongan's most escapist meal. The signature dish on the home-cooking menu is Boemboe Bali – tuna, calamari or prawns cooked with herbs (Rp33,000). Daily 7am–8pm.
Pondok Baruna Warung ☎ 0812 390 0686. Popular for

Indonesian cooking in more comfortable surrounds than your average warung: the menu takes in well-cooked dishes including tasty pork sate with sweet soy sauce (Rp37,000) and chicken curry with cumin, cardamom and coconut milk (Rp40,000). Daily 7am–10pm.
Ware-Ware ☎ 0812 397 0572. On a waterside deck with an excellent panorama over surf breaks, boats and beach to Gunung Agung, this is a good choice for food with a view. Fresh seafood is the choice on a large menu, especially the likes of barbecue tuna or mahi-mahi fillets (Rp95,000). Daily 7.30am–10pm.
Warung bu Edi Famous for its *nasi campur*, this simple place attracts a stream of expats and locals who come for a feast that might include spicy chicken, yellow rice and stir-fried veg, all for around Rp22,000. Daily 9am–8pm.
Warung 99 A good local option with views of the bay, serving inexpensive Indonesian and Indo-Chinese dishes. Portions are generous: a filling *nasi campur* is Rp38,000 while *fu yung hai* (omelette with vegetables, chicken or shellfish) is Rp24,000. Daily 8am–11pm.

THE REST OF THE ISLAND
Beach Club Sandy Bay Sunset Beach, a 5min walk from Dream Beach ☎ 0828 9700 5656, ⓦ sandybaylembongan .com. This chic spot is a fine place to spend a day. Seafood is good or try the Peking duck salad with shredded Asian vegetables; most mains are Rp80,000–120,000. Spend Rp100,000 during the day and you can use the sunloungers and pool. SMS or phone for free transport. Daily 8am–11pm.
Warung Putu ☎ 0813 7745 4706. A great spot around sunset, this warung serves inexpensive local nosh, particularly seafood – try snapper with spicy sweet-and-sour sauce (around Rp45,000) – or they'll also rustle up a burger if needed. It's on the south side of the island, 150m west of the suspension bridge. Daily 10am–9.30pm.

DIRECTORY

Banks and exchange There are several ATMs dotted around Jungutbatu. Moneychangers, guesthouses and hotels will change money (at poor rates) and offer credit card

advances (eight percent commission, passport required).
Health centre The island's health centre (*klinik*) is on the main road in Jungutbatu.

1

MOLA MOLA

Between July and October the waters around Nusa Lembongan and Nusa Penida offer the best chance most people will ever have of spotting a **mola mola** (oceanic sunfish), one of the most elusive and startling of underwater creatures. The heaviest bony fish in the world, it has an average weight of 1000kg. Some specimens weigh more than double that and grow up to 3m long, roughly the size of a small car. *Mola* is Latin for millstone, which it resembles in being huge, grey, rough and rounded in shape – it has no tail. Fortunately it is docile and no danger to divers, as it eats jellyfish and other gelatinous marine life. Much remains unknown about this gentle giant but it is thought to spend most of its life well below 200m.

For some reason the annual shift of ocean currents brings mola mola up to shallower waters for a few months each year, which is when enthusiasts and the merely curious head to the seas around these small islands in the hope of spotting one. They are usually encountered when upswells bring cool water from the depths to the surface, so if sea temperatures are balmy they are very rarely seen.

Nusa Ceningan

At the point where the channel between Nusa Lembongan and **NUSA CENINGAN** is narrowest, a **bridge** links the islands. This suspension bridge only dates from 2017, replacing another, which collapsed (killing several worshippers who were travelling to a temple ceremony). You can cycle or ride a motorbike across for a look at this totally rural island, just 4km long by 1km wide, but it's quite a challenge: the road is very rough in places, there are no signs and gradients are steep, including one killer climb. Forested and hilly, the island depends on seaweed farming and lacks swimmable beaches, though there is a famous **surf break**, Ceningan Point. You get great views of the break, plus Lembongan and Bali's southeast coast, from the top of the precipitous **Puncak Bogor** hill (unsigned), where there's a café from where you can drink in the breathtaking views over Penida. Ceningan's growing reputation for escapism among surfers and adrenaline-junkies who cliff-jump off a ledge at the southwestern tip (it can't be stressed enough – follow local guidance and do not attempt this alone) means that tourist development is increasing. There's also a new PADI dive school, Ceningan Divers (⒲ceningandivers.com), in a very peaceful location in the mangroves.

ACCOMMODATION AND EATING   NUSA CENINGAN

Tourist facilities on Ceningan are few: hotel restaurants aside, eating is limited, though there are a couple of warung about 500m southwest of the bridge. As well as the hotels listed, overnight **homestays** can be organized by the village ecotourism network, JED (⒯0361 737447, ⒲jed.or.id).

Ceningan Cliffs ⒯0821 4443 0807. Better for a beer (Rp35,000 for a small Bintang) or a juice than the so-so food, this isolated café-restaurant sits high, high above Nusa Penida on Ceningan's southern cliffs. It's one of the most dramatic locations in all Bali, with the deep Penida channel straight ahead, and distant ocean on the horizon. Note the access road is very steep indeed, but just about doable on a scooter. Daily 9am–7.30pm.

The Dafish Accommodation Bar & Cafe ⒯0821 4704 1189, ⒲dafishceninganbali.com. A welcoming place with a pool and stylish, spacious wooden bungalows with verandas, a/c and outdoor bathrooms. The restaurant serves tasty Balinese and Western food and it's close to the cliff-jump. ¬$35¬

Jenny's Place ⒯0812 3627 7650, ⒲jennysplace lembongan.com. Occupying a magnificent position right in front of Ceningan Point surf break, this supremely relaxed stay has six bungalows and a couple of rooms with awesome views of Lembongan and Bali. In atmosphere, it feels like a home from home, and there's a lovely infinity pool but limited food menu. ¬$48¬

Le Pirate ⒯0361 741 6833, ⒲lepirate.com. A French-owned mini-resort that suggests the Caribbean in the bright colours of its cute (though tiny) thatched "Beach Box" huts; with options for a/c and bunk beds. The pool and restaurant make good use of the seashore location and aside from surfing or snorkelling there's a movie room, petanque and board games to play. ¬Rp450,000¬

Nusa Penida

Dominated by a dry central limestone plateau either side of beaches in the north and by towering sea cliffs in the south, the handsome island of **NUSA PENIDA** feels quite different from mainland Bali. It was once used as a penal colony, a sort of Siberia for transgressive Balinese, and is famous as the home of the legendary demon I Macaling; its temple, **Pura Dalem Penataran Ped**, is an important pilgrimage site for Hindus from all over Bali. Islanders have their own dialect and many live off seaweed farming, fishing and growing tough crops such as corn; it's too dry for rice.

Despite offering first-class **diving** (see box, p.101), superb scenery and a chance to see the endangered **Bali starling**, Nusa Penida has limited tourist facilities and gets few foreign visitors; local rumour suggests island elders are reluctant to approve tourism development, though a sprinkling of new places are opening and infrastructure and access are slowly improving. While some may feel unnerved by the lack of facilities, more adventurous visitors will find reward in the opportunity to visit a destination almost free of tourist glitz – the welcome in villages is genuinely warm.

On a day-trip from nearby Nusa Lembongan you can get a taste of Penida on a circuit that takes in Pura Dalem Penataran Ped, **Pura Goa Giri**, a view of the south-coast cliffs and **Crystal Bay**, as well as the island's main towns, **Toyapakeh** and **Sampalan**. Ideally, at least two days' exploration provides a better impression of an island that feels far larger than its 20km by 16km because of the steep inclines and dizzy back roads. Take to the latter and you'll get lost, of course. But maybe that's half the point.

Toyapakeh

Boats from Nusa Lembongan dock at **TOYAPAKEH**, spread behind a crescent of white-sand beach. There's nothing particular to see, just a small daily market and a tiny mosque, but there are a couple of basic warung and usually a hawker or two to meet you. Still, it's a mellow spot – or is unless one of the day-tripper party boats from Sanur has moored to a pontoon just offshore.

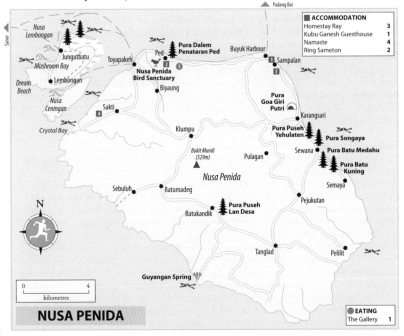

■ ACCOMMODATION	
Homestay Ray	3
Kubu Ganesh Guesthouse	1
Namaste	4
Ring Sameton	2

● EATING	
The Gallery	1

NUSA PENIDA

1

Pura Dalem Penataran Ped

Ped village, main road • Daily dawn–dusk • Free; own sash and sarong required to visit

Every day **Pura Dalem Penataran Ped** attracts worshippers from across Bali, bearing copious offerings. The temple complex is always dressed to receive them, its dazzlingly smooth white limestone walls and fantastic carvings draped in ceremonial cloths of black-and-white *poleng* and gold-brocade *songket*. The temple is regarded as *angker*, a place of evil spirits; it is the home of the dreaded **I Macaling**, also known as **Ratu Gede** and **Jero Gde**, who brings disease, floods and ill-fortune to the mainland and requires regular appeasement. There are actually four temples within the compound, one of which is dedicated to I Macaling; another has a dramatic sculpture of the half-fish, half-elephant deity of the sea, Gajah Mina.

Nusa Penida Bird Sanctuary

Western edge of Ped, a few hundred metres west of the temple • Daily dawn–dusk • Donation appreciated • ☎ 0361 977978 or ☎ 0361 0828 9760, ⓦ fnpf.org

Thanks to an innovative, community-focused programme run by the Friends of the National Parks Foundation (ⓦfnpf.org), the endangered, fluffy white **Bali starling** (*jalak putih Bali*), or Rothschild's mynah (*Leucopsar rothschildi*), is now flourishing on Nusa Penida, with over a hundred birds microchipped and free to flutter around the island. The easiest place to spot them is at the **Nusa Penida Bird Sanctuary**, where they congregate for food; staff will lead you round the small site. The foundation also accepts volunteers for its starling programme and more island conservation projects.

Sampalan

The largest village on the island, **SAMPALAN**, 4km from Ped, is a metropolis by local standards, with several ATMs, warung, shops and a central **market** (daily 6–11am) all spread out behind the coast. The bemo terminal is in the middle of the village.

Pura Goa Giri Putri

Karangasari • Daily dawn–dusk • Donation around Rp20,000, includes sash and sarong

It's a spectacular ride south from Sampalan on a coast-hugging road that offers views of *prahus* on beaches and seaweed-farming plots, as well as vistas of Lombok ahead. About 10km south, in the village of **Karangasari**, a steep flight of steps leads up to the limestone bat-cave temple of **Pura Goa Giri Putri**. Squeeze through a narrow gap in the rock and you enter a 300m-long cavern which houses several small shrines, countless bats and a meditation cave. Walk past the lot and you'll emerge blinking into sunlight at the far end having walked right through the hill. Balinese people consider this a very powerful spiritual site.

The south coast

Turning inland at Sewana (or Suana), from Pura Goa Giri Putri, you climb to the central plateau and eventually reach the village of **Batukandik**. A long winding trip should eventually see you wind up on the **south coast**, where spectacular limestone cliffs rise sheer out of the ocean. A side road leads 7km south to the edge of the cliffs and a precipitous 200m descent to the **Guyangan freshwater spring** at their base. This is typical of the whole southern coast of the island; there are several spots where equally hairy descents to the sea are possible.

Beyond Batukandik, turn left at Batumadeg to **Sebuluh**, where the road ends 200m beyond the village green and numerous paths run through the village to the cliffs. There are two **temples** here, one on a promontory linked to the mainland by an exposed ridge, and the other at the bottom of a path that winds down the cliff to a freshwater spring.

Returning to Batumadeg, the road skirts close to the summit of **Bukit Mundi**, at 529m the highest point on the island, crowned with wind turbines, then descends from the plateau, dropping through the village of Klumpu and on to **Sakti**.

Crystal Bay

From Sakti it's 3km southwest down a very steep hill to **Crystal Bay**, a postcard-perfect nook of white-sand beach and outstandingly clear water. It's a popular dive site with operators from Nusa Lembongan – most come in the morning, so if you are here in the afternoon, you're likely to have the water to yourself – but there's good snorkelling here too and a shrine on an offshore islet. That said, currents in the bay can be fierce in certain tide states. It's a gorgeous spot simply to admire the view in the shade beneath palms for now. There's some construction ongoing here, and a resort may open soon.

ARRIVAL AND DEPARTURE   NUSA PENIDA

From Nusa Lembongan A public boat from Jungutbatu to Toyapakeh departs early in the morning – 6am at the time of research (30min; Rp75,000). Other boats go roughly hourly (dependent on passenger numbers) from the bridge between Nusa Ceningan and Nuta Lembongan (15min; Rp40,000 each way). For all trips, bear in mind that swells and currents in the channel can disrupt sailing.

From Bali From Sanur there are twelve daily scheduled boats (though again heavy seas can mean cancellations). The best service is Maruti Express (☎0338 754 848,

Ⓦmarutigroupfastboat.com), leaving three times a day (30min; Rp300,000/Rp550,000 one-way/return) to Toyapakeh. Mola Mola boats (☎0361 895 6430, Ⓦmola -molaexpress.balipromotion.net) are also fairly reliable, sailing twice daily (Rp125,000, 45min) to Sampalan. Other companies operate boats to Toyapakeh and Buyuk harbour which is very close to Sampalan. From Padang Bai to Buyuk Harbour there's one daily ferry at noon (Rp30,000, 1hr 30min) and occasional fast boats according to demand.

GETTING AROUND

By bemo A sketchy public bemo service operates between Toyapakeh and Sampalan, via Ped, between about 6am and 9pm.

By motorbike The best way to get around is by motorbike. Motorbike drivers/guides wait at Toyapakeh harbour to meet arrivals from Lembongan, and will offer to guide;

Rp250,000 is a reasonable price for a full day of riding and guiding. You can also rent your own bike here for about Rp60,000/day – try Rod (☎0818 0533 3747), who speaks excellent English (the chances are he'll find you). The island is a maze of remote lanes and signposts are few. That said, getting lost may be half the fun.

ACCOMMODATION AND EATING

Sampalan has the most guesthouses, most of which are simple fan-cooled affairs (roughly Rp150,000). Eating options are largely limited to restaurants in the hotels and simple warung. Be warned: the further south you go, the more limited your options for food – it's packet snacks only in the deep south. Daily 7.30am–10pm

The Gallery Jl Raya Bodong, Sampalan ☎0819 9988 7205. Community café serving a wide range of western food, including vegan and vegetarian dishes, great breakfasts with home-made muesli, fine coffee and wonderful rosella (red hibiscus) iced tea. Owner Mike and his wife Kadek are very informative about the island and it's a good spot to meet others. Doubles as a store selling local crafts. Daily 8am–8pm.

Homestay Ray Opposite the market, Sampalan ☎0366 559 6674 or ☎0878 6021 8955, Ⓦfacebook.com/ray. nusapenida. Offering comfortable but plain accommodation, these clean and quiet fan rooms designed in traditional style with carved pillars and Kamasan paintings are set around a courtyard (with caged birds). The odd grotto-style bathrooms may appeal. There's wi-fi. **Rp275,000**

★ **Kubu Ganesh Guesthouse** Geria Tengah, Sampalan ☎0822 3617 7717, Ⓦkubuganesh.blogspot.co.uk. A five-minute walk from the harbour for boats to/from Bali

this conveniently located guesthouse is run by a welcoming French host and his local team who are a mine of local info and can arrange scooter and sightseeing trips. The villas are beautifully built and have sea views from their terraces, food is great (meals Rp75,000) and there's snorkelling right offshore. **Rp1,065,000**

Namaste Sakti ☎0813 3727 1615, Ⓦnamaste -bungalows.com. A small French-owned retreat with a pool, en route to Crystal Bay. Rough luxe is the style in the ten bungalows, with artfully distressed furniture, fine bed linen and minimalist bathrooms – "deluxe" (Rp650,000) come with a/c. Prices drop in the low season. **Rp545,000**

Ring Sameton Ped ☎0361 785 3464, Ⓦringsameton -nusapenida.com. Well-kept business-style hotel with smart rooms that make up in space and mod cons for what they lack in character; all have a/c and hot water. The restaurant (8am–10pm) serves a good seafood curry (Rp45,000). **Rp600,000**

Ubud and central Bali

TRADITIONAL BALINESE DANCERS

Ubud and central Bali

2

The inland town of Ubud and its surrounding area form Bali's cultural heartland, home to a huge number of temples, museums and art galleries, where Balinese dance shows are staged nightly, a wealth of craft studios provide absorbing shopping, and traditional ceremonies and rituals are observed daily. The centre of town is increasingly congested but once you get away from the main thoroughfares Ubud's lovely location is apparent, set amid lush, terraced rice paddies, and there's plenty of scope for hikes and bicycle rides. To get a real sense of traditional Bali, visit the nearby settlements of Penestanan and Peliatan, for example, or Pejeng, which still boasts relics from the Bronze Age.

Ubud lies within the boundaries of **Gianyar district**, formerly an ancient kingdom. Gianyar itself (see p.154), 10km east of Ubud, lies on the main route into east Bali. Roads around Ubud tend to run north–south down river valleys, making it difficult in places to travel east–west, and subsequently traffic jams and pollution affect Ubud's centre.

Ubud and around

Ever since the German artist Walter Spies arrived here in 1927, **UBUD** has been a magnet for any tourist with the slightest curiosity about Balinese arts and traditions. It is now a fully fledged tourist destination, visited by nearly every holidaymaker on the island, even if only as part of a day-trip.

Although it's fashionable to characterize Ubud as the "real" Bali, especially in contrast with Kuta, it bears little resemblance to a typical Balinese town. The core village has expanded to take in several neighbouring hamlets and there are now dozens of organic cafés, riverside bungalows and craft shops, spas and alternative treatment centres, chic expat homes and boutique hotels overlooking panoramic scenery. There's even a Starbucks.

That said, traditional practices are still fundamental to daily life and the atmosphere is an appealing blend of ethnic integrity and tourist-friendly comforts. The local people really do still paint, carve, dance and make music, and hardly a day goes by without some kind of religious festival. Appropriately, Ubud is a recognized centre of **spiritual tourism**, a place where visitors can get stuck into yoga and meditation, and visit local healers.

BATIK PAINTING

Highlights

❶ A walk through the rice paddies Enjoy classic vistas of emerald terraces and coconut groves, framed by distant volcanoes, on this walk through the countryside surrounding Ubud. **See p.116**

❷ Neka Art Museum This museum houses the finest collection of Balinese paintings on the island. **See p.117**

❸ Cultural classes Return home with a new skill in batik painting, silversmithing, Balinese cookery or innumerable other activites. **See p.127**

❹ Traditional dance performances Gods and demons flirt and fight by torchlight, to the sounds of the gamelan, at these evocative shows in and around Ubud. **See p.132**

❺ Mind, Body and Spirit Ubud is one of Asia's leading yoga centres and you can also visit a local healer, have a massage or learn to meditate. **See p.134**

❻ Bali Bird Park This vast and beautifully landscaped aviary has elusive Bali starlings in residence. **See p.141**

❼ Gunung Kawi Descend 315 steps to reach these impressive eleventh-century rock-cut "tombs" in the valley of the sacred Pakrisan River. **See p.146**

HIGHLIGHTS ARE MARKED ON THE MAP ON P.112

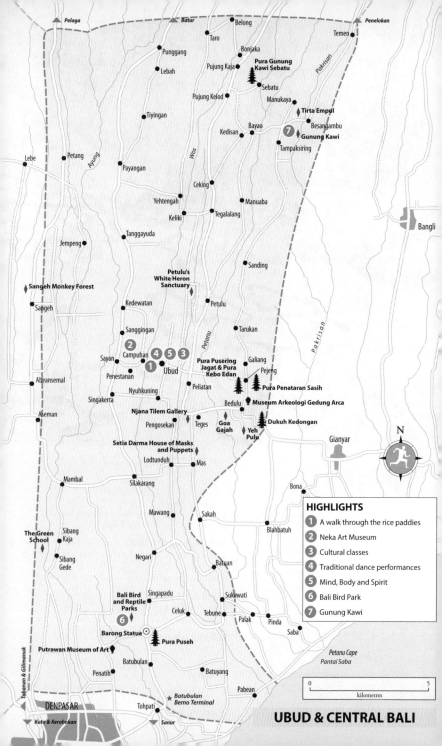

UBUD & CENTRAL BALI

HIGHLIGHTS

1. A walk through the rice paddies
2. Neka Art Museum
3. Cultural classes
4. Traditional dance performances
5. Mind, Body and Spirit
6. Bali Bird Park
7. Gunung Kawi

Shopping is a major pastime too, with Balinese carvers and painters selling their wares alongside expat fashion designers and artists. Ubud's **restaurants** and **accommodation** set the town apart as well: imaginative menus are the norm here, and hotels and homestays tend to be small and charming. The surrounding region, meanwhile, gives ample opportunity for exploration.

Sadly the town's new prosperity has led to one of Bali's worst traffic problems and Ubud is in desperate need of a pedestrianization programme and bypass before clouds of exhaust fumes suffocate the town's appeal and drive away the yogis and healers to somewhere less polluted.

Brief history

Ubud's emphasis on the arts really evolved at the beginning of the twentieth century; before then its energy had been concentrated on fighting other Balinese kingdoms and then the Dutch. In 1900 the Ubud court was obliged to join its neighbour, the Gianyar royal family, in asking for the protection of the Netherlands Indies government against other land-hungry rajas. As a Dutch protectorate with no more wars to fight, the ruling Sukawati family and the people of Ubud were free to follow creative and musical pursuits. **Cokorda Gede Agung Sukawati** (1910–78) cultivated the arts, and actively encouraged foreign artists to live in his district. The most significant of these was the artist and musician **Walter Spies**, who established himself in the hamlet of Campuhan in 1927. Over the next decade or so, Spies introduced fresh ideas to Ubud's already vibrant **artistic community**. A crowd of other Western intellectuals followed in his wake, including the Dutch artist Rudolf Bonnet and the Canadian musician Colin McPhee, who between them injected a new vigour into the region's arts and crafts, which have thrived ever since.

Central Ubud

Covering the area between Jalan Raya Ubud in the north and the Monkey Forest in the south, and between the Campuhan bridge in the west and the General Post Office in the east, **Central Ubud**'s chief draws are its restaurants and shops. However, it does hold a few notable sights, including Ubud's oldest art museum, **Puri Lukisan**, and the **Threads of Life** textile gallery.

Museum Puri Lukisan

Jl Raya Ubud • Daily 9am–6pm • Rp85,000 includes drink, children under 15 free • ☎ 0361 971159, ⓦ museumpurilukisan.com

The **Museum Puri Lukisan** is best visited as an adjunct to the far superior Neka Art Museum, just over 2km west in Sanggingan (see p.117). Set in well-maintained gardens, Puri Lukisan ("Palace of Paintings") was founded in 1956 by the Ubud *punggawa* (local administrator) Cokorda Gede Agung Sukawati, the member of the Ubud royal family who focused his energies on developing the arts (see above), and the Dutch artist Rudolf Bonnet.

The **North Pavilion**, Pitamaha Gallery, located at the top of the garden, is largely given over to prewar Balinese paintings, mostly black-and-white **Batuan-style** and early **Ubud-style** (see box, pp.122–123) pictures depicting local scenes. There's also a good selection of distinctive drawings by I Gusti Nyoman Lempad (see box, p.115). Several fine **woodcarvings** from the 1930s to the 1950s are also here, including the surreal

---

FESTIVALS IN UBUD

Ubud hosts an annual literary **festival**, the Ubud Writers and Readers Festival (ⓦ ubudwriters festival.com), every October, and the Bali Spirit Festival of world music, dance and yoga every March (ⓦ balispiritfestival.com).

2

Ubud Sari Health Resort & Threads of Life

Ubud Botanic Garden ▲ & Rumah Lingkungan

CENTRAL UBUD & PADANG TEGAL

Campuhan & Neka Art Museum

Museum Puri Lukisan

Pura Taman Saraswati

Sari Api

Smile Shop

Café Lotus

Pura Desa

Ubud Palace

JALAN KAJENG

JALAN SUWETA

JALAN SRIWEDARI

JALAN RAYA UBUD

JALAN SANDAT (JALAN TIRTA TAWAR)

Lempad's House

Bemo Stop

BAWA

Ary's Buisness & Travel Service

Market

JALAN RAYA UBUD

Highway @

Peliatan

FNPF

JALAN BISMA

Nirvana Batik

@

Black Beach

JALAN SUGRIWA

JALAN JEMBAWAN

Honeymoon Guesthouse

JALAN KARNA

JALAN GOOTAMA

JALAN MARUTI

Jungle Shop

Balinese Traditional Healing Centre

SHOPPING

Blue Stone	12
The Drum Factory	4
Galaxyan	8
Ganesha Bookshop	5
Ikat Batik	20
Kado	13
Kafe	17
Kou Cuisine/Kou	9/11
Kupu-Kupu	3
Macan Tidur	6
Mitra Bali Fair Trade	19
Periplus	2/10
Pondok Bamboo	21
Pondok Pekak Library and Learning Centre	14
Rio Helmi	1
Sjaki's Warung	15
Studio Perak	7
Tegun	16
Ubud Organic Food Market	18

JALAN MONKEY FOREST (JALAN WANARA WANA)

JALAN DEWI SITA

Football Field

Pondok Pekak Library & Learning Centre

Stage

JALAN HANOMAN

EATING

Bali Buda	9
Bollero	11
Café des Artistes	4
Casa Luna	3
Clear	7
Gelato Secrets	6
Ibu Oka	1
Ibu Rai	10
Kafe	15
Locavore	12
Locavore to Go	13
Monsieur Spoon	16
Nomad	5
Seniman Coffee Studio	2
Sjaki's Warung	14
Warung Enak	17
Warung Lokal	8

Banjar Ubud Kelod

Ubud Bodyworks Centre

Nur Salon

JALAN MONKEY FOREST (JALAN WANARA WANA)

Café Wayan

Pertiwi

Pura Desa Padang Tegal

JALAN SUGRIWA

JALAN HANOMAN

ACCOMMODATION

Artja Inn	1
Jati Homestay	7
KajaNe Mua	9
Komaneka Resort at Monkey Forest	8
Nick's Pension	6
Nirvana Pension	3
Sama's Cottages	2
Sania's House	4
Sayong House	5

Warung Sopa

N

DRINKING AND LIVE MUSIC

Laughing Buddha Bar	3
No Mas Ubud	4
Night Rooster	1
Shisha XL Lounge	2

0   150
metres

Monkey Forest Sanctuary

PADANG TEGAL

The Yoga Barn

Perama Shuttle Bus
Perama

Nyuhkuning

ARMA

LEMPAD

Many of Ubud's most important buildings – among them Puri Lukisan, Pura Taman Saraswati and Ubud Palace – are associated with the venerable sculptor, architect and artist **I Gusti Nyoman Lempad** (c.1862–1978). Lempad came to Ubud with his family at the age of 13, where he found favour in the court of the Sukawatis, for whom he worked for most of his life. A versatile **artist** who designed temples, carved stone reliefs, built cremation towers and produced ink drawings, Lempad was an influential figure and an important member of the Pita Maha arts association, which he cofounded with his friends Cokorda Gede Agung Sukawati and Rudolf Bonnet. A **traditionalist** in certain matters, Lempad would only work on propitious days and is said to have waited for an auspicious day on which to die; by that time he was thought to be approximately 116 years old. The best places to see his drawings are the Neka Art Museum and Museum Puri Lukisan.

For more than a century, Lempad lived on Jalan Raya Ubud, diagonally opposite the market, in a **house** that still belongs to his family, and which is open to the public as a **showroom** for artists working under the "Puri Lempad" by-line (daily 8am–6pm; free).

2

earth-goddess *Dewi Pertiwi* by Ida Bagus Nyana (see box, p.138), the sinuous *Dewi Sri* by I Ketut Djedeng and I Cokot's much-emulated *Garuda Eating Snake*.

In the **West Pavilion**, to the left on the way up the garden, the Ida Bagus Made (1915–99) Gallery showcases the artist's work alongside other postwar Balinese paintings, including those in the naive expressionist **Young Artists** style that originated in nearby Penestanan in the 1960s. Also in this pavilion you'll find paintings in the **Ubud style**, including *Balinese Market* by Anak Agung Gede Sobrat, as well as works in the so-called **modern traditional** style, such as I Made Sukada's *Battle between Boma and Krishna*.

In the **East Pavilion**, to the right on the way up the garden, the Wayang Gallery houses a collection of **wayang-style** paintings as well as temporary exhibitions.

There's a good cafe (daily 10am–9pm) for local and Western food in the **South Pavilion**, which is used for temporary exhibitions and a bookshop.

Pura Taman Saraswati

Jl Raya Ubud • Generally sunrise–sunset • Free

Commissioned in the 1950s by Cokorda Gede Agung Sukawati, **Pura Taman Saraswati** is the work of the prolific royal architect and stonecarver I Gusti Nyoman Lempad, who set the temple complex within a delightful lotus-pond garden. It's dedicated to Saraswati, the goddess of learning, science and literature.

Access to the temple is via a lane between *Café Lotus* and *Starbucks*: walk between the lotus ponds to the red-brick *kori agung* (temple entrance). The straight route into the temple courtyard is blocked by an unusual **aling-aling** (the wall device built into nearly every temple to disorient evil spirits), which is in fact the back of a rotund statue of a *raksasa* (demon guardian). Inside the **courtyard** the main lotus-throne **shrine** is covered with a riot of *paras* (volcanic tuff) carvings, with the requisite cosmic turtle and *naga* (a snake/dragon deity) forming the base, while the tower is a swirling mass of curlicues and floral motifs.

Only visitors in Balinese dress are allowed inside, there's a stall close by which rents out traditional clothing.

Threads of Life Indonesian Textile Arts Center and Gallery

Jl Kajeng 24 • Daily 10am–7pm • Free • ☎ 0361 972074, ⊕ threadsoflife.com

The small **Threads of Life Indonesian Textile Arts Center and Gallery** is devoted to exquisite hand-woven textiles from across the islands of Indonesia, including Bali, Sumba, Timor, Java and Sulawesi. Though they were all produced using natural dyes and ancient methods, the textiles are modern works, commissioned by the Threads of

2

A RICE-PADDY WALK THROUGH UBUD KAJA

Running east of, and almost parallel to, the Campuhan ridge walk (see box, p.118) is an almost circular **rice-paddy walk** that begins and ends in the northern part of Ubud known as **Ubud Kaja** (*kaja* literally means "upstream, towards the mountains"). The complete walk takes about two and a half hours and is flat, though there's not much shade. About 800m into the walk the *Sari Organik* café (see p.131) makes a good place for a break, and you can refill water bottles here too.

The walk begins from the western end of **Jalan Raya Ubud**, just before the overhead aqueduct, where a track leads up to the *Abangan Bungalows* on the north side of the road. Head up the slope and, at the top, follow the track, which bends to the left before straightening out, passing *Gusti's Garden 2* bungalows and heading north to *Sari Organik*. From here the route is straightforward, following the track, which is paved in places, for about 3km as it slices through gently **terraced ricefields** fringed with coconut palms; you should see scores of beautifully coloured dragonflies and plenty of **birdlife**, including, possibly, iridescent blue Javanese kingfishers. There are a number of art shops/studios where you can get a drink en route.

After about an hour and a quarter, the track ends at a sealed road. For the most straight-forward version of the walk, turn around here and retrace your steps. Alternatively, if you want a bit of an adventure, turn right onto the road, which rises, curves and then falls to cross the river. The **southbound track** starts almost immediately after the bridge and runs east of the river. After five minutes of following the track through the village, it forks; take the right fork, keeping the water channel on your right. Another five minutes later a dirt path heads up into the paddy fields to your left; take this path. At this point the southbound track becomes totally indistinct and for the next thirty minutes you should try to follow the narrow paths along the top of the ricefield dykes, sticking roughly to a southerly direction and keeping the river in view on your right. You'll inevitably wind in and out on the paths through the paddies rather than being able to head straight-as-an-arrow south. Don't forget to look back at the amazing **views of Gunung Agung** (cloud cover permitting): with the mountain in the background and the conical-hatted farmers working in the glittering ricefields, these views are perfect real-life versions of the Walter Spies-style paintings you see in the museums and galleries of Ubud. After thirty minutes or so you'll see a rough path about 5 or 6m below you to the right on the riverbank. Scramble down some rough-cut muddy steps to reach the path. This will lead you back to Ubud through some light forest and then paddyfields.

Twenty-five minutes after the scramble down you'll reach the **outskirts of Ubud**. When the path forks, take the left fork steeply down to a stone bridge. The road bends right, passes a school and becomes Jalan Kajeng, a little road paved with graffiti-covered stones that runs down to Jalan Raya Ubud in ten minutes or so. The stones are inscribed with the names, messages and doodlings of everyone who helped finance the paving of the lane.

Life foundation in an attempt to keep Indonesia's historic textile art alive. This is a complex and highly skilled art, and severely endangered, not least because a single weaving can take two years to complete. The gallery displays superb weavings alongside exhibits on natural dyes, spinning and weaving techniques. Beautiful, if pricey, textiles are for sale and there are regular classes and **workshops** on traditional textile appreciation (see p.127), weaving and dyeing.

Campuhan and Sanggingan

Sited at the confluence of the rivers Wos Barat and Wos Timor, the hamlet of **CAMPUHAN** (pronounced *cham-poo-han*) extends west from Ubud as far as the *Hotel Tjampuhan*, and is famous as the home of several of Bali's most charismatic expatriate painters, including the late **Antonio Blanco**, whose house and gallery have been turned into a museum; the late **Walter Spies**, whose villa is inside the *Hotel Tjampuhan* compound; and **Symon**, who still paints at his studio-gallery across the road from the hotel.

North up the hill, Campuhan turns into **SANGGINGAN** (though few people bother to distinguish it from its neighbour), and it's here that you'll find Bali's best art gallery, the **Neka Art Museum**.

Blanco Renaissance Museum

Just off Jl Raya Campuhan, next to the Penestanan turn-off • Daily 9am–5pm • Rp50,000 including drink • ☎ 0361 975502 • Phone ahead for free transport

The former home of the flamboyant Catalan artist **Antonio Blanco** – complete with gilded pillars and sweeping Spanish balustrades – is open to the public as the enjoyably camp **Blanco Renaissance Museum**. Dubbed "the Bali Dalí", Blanco (1911–99) specialized in **erotic paintings** and drawings, in particular portraits of Balinese women in varying states of abandon. Blanco fell for a local girl, Ni Ronji, soon after arriving in Ubud in 1952, singling her out as his top model and later marrying her. There are sweeping views from the roof, which has four gilded statues.

Blanco's collection also includes multimedia pieces, plus lots of idiosyncratic picture frames created from unorthodox materials. The museum **garden** contains a small aviary and there's a restaurant where you can enjoy your complimentary drink.

Neka Art Museum

Jl Raya Sanggingan, about 2.5km northwest of central Ubud • Mon–Sat 9am–5pm, Sun noon–5pm • Rp75,000 • ☎ 0361 975074, Ⓦ museumneka.com • Take any westbound bemo from the market in Ubud

Boasting the island's most comprehensive collection of paintings from across Bali's various artistic styles (see box, pp.122–123), the **Neka Art Museum** is housed in a series of pavilions alongside the main Campuhan/Sanggingan road. English-language labels are posted beside the paintings, with Balinese, expatriate and visiting artists all represented. The museum shop sells a couple of recommended **books** about the collection, notably *Neka Art Museum: The Heart of Art in Bali* by Suteja Neka and Garrett Kam, which is essentially a catalogue of the highlights of the collection, and *Perceptions of Paradise: Images of Bali in the Arts* by Garrett Kam.

First Pavilion: Balinese Painting Hall

The first pavilion surveys the three major schools of **Balinese painting** from the seventeenth century to the present day. Some of the earliest works are "puppet style"

WALTER SPIES IN CAMPUHAN

The son of a German diplomat, **Walter Spies** (1895–1942) left Europe for Java in 1923, and relocated to Bali in 1927. He set up home in Campuhan and devoted himself to the study and practice of Balinese art and music. He sponsored two local gamelan orchestras and was the first Westerner to attempt to record **Balinese music**. Together with the Canadian composer Colin McPhee, he set about transposing gamelan music for Western instruments, and with another associate, Katherine Mershon, encouraged Bedulu dancer I Wayan Limbak to create the enduringly popular dance-drama known as the **Kecak** (Monkey Dance).

Spies was an avid collector of Balinese **art**, and became one of the founding members of the Pita Maha arts association in 1936. He is said to have inspired, if not taught, a number of talented young Ubud artists, among them the painter Anak Agung Gede Sobrat, and the woodcarver I Tegelan. Characteristic of Spies's own Balinese works are dense landscapes of waterlogged paddies, peopled with conical-hatted farmers – a distinctive style that is still much imitated. There's currently only one Walter Spies painting on show in Bali; it's at the Agung Rai Museum of Art in Pengosekan (see p.124).

In 1937 Spies retired to the village of Iseh in the east, turning his Campuhan home into a **guesthouse**, the first of its kind in the Ubud area. He died in 1942, drowning when the ship deporting him as a German national in World War II was bombed in the Indian Ocean. The guesthouse became *Hotel Tjampuhan*.

2

THE CAMPUHAN RIDGE WALK

Campuhan means "the place where two rivers meet" and the confluence of the Wos Barat and the Wos Timor is marked by **Pura Gunung Lebah** (also known as Pura Campuhan). The track that extends north along the grassy spine behind Pura Gunung Lebah forms part of a pleasant two-hour circular **walk** around the outskirts of Campuhan and Sanggingan. Alternatively, if you continue the complete length of the ridge, you'll eventually reach **Keliki** (7km) and **Taro** (13km) before joining the Sayan road to **Kintamani** (32km). All routes are feasible on a **mountain bike**, but be prepared for some significant undulations and a few steps.

If you're starting **from central Ubud**, walk (or take a bemo) west from Ubud market almost as far as the Campuhan bridge, turning north off the main road about 100m before the bridge, into the entrance of the *Ibah* hotel, where an immediate left fork takes you down some steps to the Pura Gunung Lebah. The track heads right around the temple walls and climbs up onto the ridge, where it undulates for a stretch before levelling out along the flattened **ridgetop** between the two river valleys. The perspective from this section is breathtaking: to the left lie the steep banks of the Wos Barat valley; to the right, the eastern panorama across the Wos Timor valley is of savanna, coconut groves, the rocky river gorge and Gunung Agung in the distance. You'll walk through a seemingly endless carpet of **alang-alang grass** swaying in the breeze – a valuable resource used for thatching houses and shrines.

About twenty minutes from Pura Gunung Lebah, the track passes through the first ridgetop settlement, site of the *Klub Kokos* hotel and, beyond, about 1500m of sculpted ricefields before reaching the traditional hamlet of **Bangkiang Sidem**. Just beyond the village temple, you arrive at a larger sealed road; turn left on the road for the round trip back to Campuhan road, or continue straight on for Keliki.

Once you've turned left, the road cuts a swathe through ricefields, drops down steeply towards the Wos Barat and then climbs up through the hamlets of **Payogan** and **Lungsiakan** before reaching **Jalan Raya Sanggingan**. From here you can either flag down any bemo heading east for the ten-minute ride into Ubud, or continue walking for twenty minutes east down to the Neka Art Museum, or twenty minutes west to Kedewatan and the main Kintamani road.

---

paintings that depict narrative scenes from Balinese and Javanese literature. Fine examples of **Kamasan style** include works from contemporary artists such as Ida Bagus Rai in *Rajapala Steals Sulasih's Clothes* and *The Pandawa Brothers in Disguise*, in which classical elements are fused with a more modern sensuality. These are followed by art representing the **Ubud style**, including *The Bumblebee Dance* by **Anak Agung Gede Sobrat**. Finally come the dark and densely packed **Batuan-style** canvases, including the dramatic *Busy Bali* by **I Wayan Bendi**, which delineates the effect of tourism on the island, and **I Made Budi**'s 1987 work, *President Suharto and his Wife Visit Bali*.

Second Pavilion: Arie Smit Pavilion

The top floor of the second pavilion is devoted to the hugely influential Dutch expatriate artist **Arie Smit**. His work is instantly recognizable by the bold, expressionist tone; many of the paintings, including *A Tropical Garden By the Sea*, have a breathtakingly beautiful Cézanne-like quality.

The ground-floor hall is given over to **contemporary Balinese art**, which includes expressionist, figurative and abstract works – a clear indication of the vibrancy of modern art on the island. The styles range widely from the huge abstract canvases of I Made Sumadiyasa to the unsettling wooden sculptures of I Made Supena.

Third Pavilion: Photography Archive Center

The third pavilion houses an archive of black-and-white **photographs** from Bali in the 1930s and 1940s, taken by the American **Robert Koke**. He and his wife Louise founded the first hotel in Kuta in 1936. His photographic record includes village scenes, temple festivals and cremations, but its highlights are the pictures of the dance performances and the portraits of the Kebyar dancer Mario and of the Kecak choreographer I Wayan Limbak.

Fourth Pavilion: Lempad Pavilion

The late **I Gusti Nyoman Lempad** (see box, p.115) is the subject of the fourth pavilion, which holds the largest collection of his pictures in Bali. Among his best-known works is a series on **Men and Pan Brayut**, the well-known folk story about a poor couple and their eighteen children (see box, p.161).

Fifth Pavilion: Contemporary Indonesian Art Hall

The fifth pavilion focuses on works by formally trained Indonesian artists, whose style is often labelled "Academic". Outstanding examples include large oils by Javanese-born **Anton Hwang** (Anton Kustia Widjaja), who moved to Ubud in 1969, and **Abdul Aziz**'s much-reproduced diptych entitled *Mutual Attraction*.

Sixth Pavilion: East–West Art Annex

The upstairs galleries feature the paintings of **foreign artists in Bali**, including the Dutch painter **Rudolf Bonnet**'s sensual portraits: *Temptation of Arjuna* is particularly impressive. The bright Gauguin-esque oils of Swiss-born **Theo Meier** draw on the vivid light and sultry ambience of Bali, in contrast to the Dutch **Willem Gerard Hofker**'s minutely observed crayon studies of temples, such as *Temple at Campuhan, Ubud*. Also on show are some erotically charged portraits by the Catalan-born **Antonio Blanco**, whose studio-gallery is nearby (see p.117); the Australian **Donald Friend**'s charmingly fanciful Chagall-esque evocations of his Sanur home, including *Batujimbar Village*; and the Dutch **Han**. Not all the impressions of Bali come from outside Asia: the dynamic *Gabor-Pendet Dance* is by **J. Elizalde Navarro** from the Philippines, while the striking works *Barong and Rangda Dance* and *Balinese Fishing Boats* are by the Javanese expressionist **Affandi**.

Penestanan

West of Campuhan is the still-traditional hamlet of **PENESTANAN**, which became famous in the 1960s for its so-called **Young Artists** (see box, pp.122–123), who forged a naive style of painting that's since been named after them. Some are still painting, but Penestanan's current niche is **bead-making**, and the village has several shops selling intricately decorated items.

Penestanan is accessible from the side road that turns off beside the Blanco Museum, but the most atmospheric approach is via the steep flight of steps a few hundred metres further north along Jalan Raya Campuhan. The steps climb the hillside to a narrow westbound track, which passes several arterial north–south paths leading to panoramic **views** (many of which have been appropriated by new villas), then drops down through ricefields into the next valley, across a river and through a small wooded area, before coming to a crossroads with Penestanan's main street. Go straight across (west) if you're heading for Sayan (600m away), right for *Taman Rahasia* hotel after 200m (see p.130), or left for the circular walk back through the village to the Blanco Museum in Campuhan (1.5km). There are several places to eat en route, including *Made's Warung* (see p.131).

Monkey Forest Sanctuary

Jl Monkey Forest; the entrance is a 15min walk south of Ubud's central market • Daily 8.30am–6pm • Rp40,000, children Rp30,000 • ☏ 0361 971304, 🖰 monkeyforestubud.com

Ubud's best-known tourist attraction is the **Monkey Forest Sanctuary**, which occupies the land between the southern end of Jalan Monkey Forest and the northern edge of Nyuhkuning. It is the focus of numerous day-tours because of its six resident troupes of

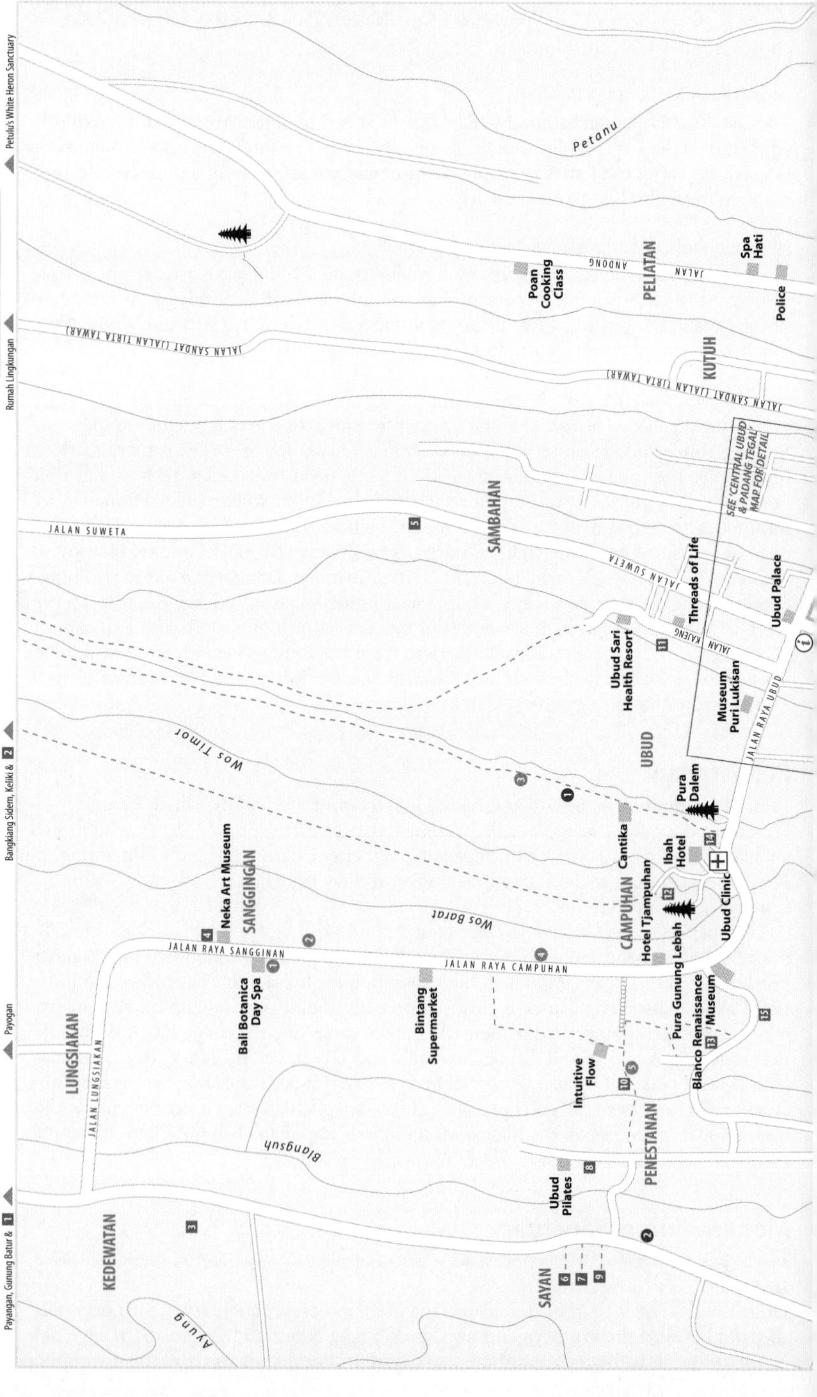

2

Petanu

◄ Petulu's White Heron Sanctuary

Poan Cooking Class

JALAN ANDONG

PELIATAN

Spa Hati

Police

KUTUH

JALAN SANDAT (JALAN TIRTA TAWAR)

JALAN SANDAT (JALAN TIRTA TAWAR)

◄ Rumah Lingkungan

SEE 'CENTRAL UBUD' & PADANG TEGAL' MAP FOR DETAIL

JALAN SUWETA

SAMBAHAN

5

JALAN SUWETA

Threads of Life

Ubud Palace

1

Ubud Sari Health Resort

JALAN KAJENG

Museum Puri Lukisan

JALAN RAYA UBUD

UBUD

◄ Bangkiang Sidem, Keliki & **2**

Wos Timor

3

1

Pura Dalem

17

Neka Art Museum

SANGGINGAN

Cantika

Ibah Hotel

CAMPUHAN

Hotel Tjampuhan

12

Wos Barat

Ubud Clinic

14

JALAN RAYA SANGGINAN

16

2

JALAN RAYA CAMPUHAN

4

Pura Gunung Lebah

Bali Botanica Day Spa

◄ Payangan

LUNGSIAKAN

Bintang Supermarket

JALAN LUNGSIAKAN

Blanco Renaissance Museum

13

15

Intuitive Flow

10

5

Blangsuh

Ubud Pilates

8

◄ Payangan, Gunung Batur & **11**

KEDEWATAN

3

PENESTANAN

SAYAN

6

7

9

2

Ayung

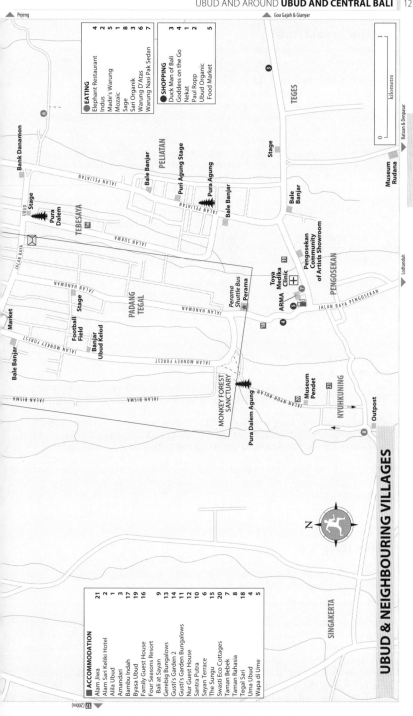

UBUD & NEIGHBOURING VILLAGES

● EATING
Elephant Restaurant	4
Indus	2
Made's Warung	5
Mozaic	1
Sage	8
Sari Organik	3
Warung D'Atas	6
Warung Nasi Pak Sedan	7

● SHOPPING
Duck Man of Bali	3
Goddess on the Go	4
Nekat	1
Paul Ropp	2
Ubud Organic Food Market	5

■ ACCOMMODATION
Alam Jiwa	21
Alam Sari Keliki Hotel	2
Alila Ubud	1
Amandari	3
Bambu Indah	17
Byasa Ubud	19
Family Guest House	16
Four Seasons Resort	
Bali at Sayan	9
Gerebig Bungalows	13
Gusti's Garden 2	14
Gusti's Garden Bungalows	11
Nur Guest House	12
Santra Putra	10
Sayan Terrace	6
The Sungu	15
Swasti Eco Cottages	20
Taman Bebek	7
Taman Rahasia	8
Tegal Sari	18
Uma Ubud	4
Wapa di Ume	5

2

BALINESE PAINTING

Art historians group **Balinese painting** into six broad **schools**: *wayang* (also known as classical or Kamasan), Ubud, Pengosekan, Batuan, Young Artists and Modern or Academic.

WAYANG OR KAMASAN STYLE

The earliest Balinese painters drew their inspiration from the *wayang kulit* shadow plays, using two-dimensional figures to depict episodes from the same religious and historical epics that were played out on the stage. Variously known as the **wayang style**, the **classical style** or the **Kamasan style** (after the east Bali village where the most famous *wayang*-style artists came from), this is the most traditional genre of Balinese art, and the one that's been the least influenced by Western techniques and subjects. The oldest surviving examples are the eighteenth-century temple banners, calendars and astrological charts housed in the **Nyoman Gunarsa Museum** near Semarapura (see p.161). To see Kamasan art in situ you need to visit the old palace in Semarapura, where the ceilings of the **Kerta Gosa** and **Bale Kambung** pavilions retain their *wayang*-style painted ceilings; they were done by artists from Kamasan in the early nineteenth century but have been retouched several times (see p.159).

All *wayang*-style pictures are packed full of people painted in **three-quarter profile**, with caricature-like features and puppet-like poses. There is no perspective, and stylized symbols indicate the location; pictures are often divided into scenes by borders of mountains, flames or walls. Traditional *wayang* artists limit their palette to red, blue, yellow, black and white.

As with the *wayang* puppets, the **characters** in the paintings are instantly recognizable by their facial features and hairstyles and by their clothes, stance and size. Convention requires, for example, that "refined" characters (heroes, heroines and others of noble birth) look slightly supercilious, and that their bodies be svelte and elegant. "Coarse" characters, on the other hand, such as clowns, servants and demonic creatures, have bulbous eyes, prominent teeth and chunky bodies.

The *wayang* style is still popular with modern artists and continues to be centred on the village of **Kamasan**, which has many studios open to the public.

UBUD STYLE

By the 1930s, Balinese painters were starting to experiment with more **naturalistic techniques**, including perspective and the use of light and shadow, and to reproduce what they saw at the market, at the temple and in the ricefields. The village of Ubud was at the heart of this experimentation so the style has been dubbed **Ubud style**. Expatriate artists **Walter Spies** and **Rudolf Bonnet**, both resident in the Ubud area in the 1930s, are said to have had a big influence; they also helped set up the **Pita Maha arts foundation**, whose mission was to promote innovation and individual expression.

Though the Ubud style is more naturalistic than *wayang* art, the pictures are still unrealistically crammed with busyness and **activity**, every corner filled with detail. Every palm leaf and blade of grass is painstakingly delineated, every sarong pattern described, but people are rarely given much individuality, their faces usually set in a rather stylized expression.

Most of the best-known Ubud-style artists are represented in the major Ubud art museums, among them the highly rated **Anak Agung Gede Sobrat**.

PENGOSEKAN STYLE

During the 1960s, a group of young painters working in the Ubud style and living in the village of Pengosekan on the outskirts of Ubud came up with a new approach, subsequently known as the **Pengosekan style**. From the Ubud-style pictures, the Pengosekan school isolated

more than five hundred malevolent but photogenic **long-tailed macaques** (they will swiftly hunt out any food or drink you might have on your person, and bites and scratches are not uncommon, so beware). There is a first-aid station in the sanctuary, and note that plastic bags are officially banned.

The forest itself is small and has many mature trees, with over a hundred species present including the Majegan tree used for the building of Balinese shrines. A stroll around the forest works well with an exploration of Nyuhkuning. Five minutes into just a few components, specifically the **birds**, **butterflies**, **insects** and **flowering plants**, and magnified them to fill a whole canvas. The best Pengosekan paintings look delicate and lifelike, generally depicted in soothing pastels, and reminiscent of classical Japanese flower and bird pictures.

BATUAN STYLE

In contrast to the slightly romanticized visions of events being painted by the Ubud-style artists in the 1930s, a group of painters in nearby Batuan were taking a more quizzical approach. Like the *wayang* artists, **Batuan-style** painters filled their works with scores of people, but on a much more frantic scale. A single Batuan-style picture might contain a dozen apparently unrelated scenes – a temple dance, a rice harvest, a fishing expedition, an exorcism and a couple of tourists taking snapshots – all depicted in fine detail that strikes a balance between the naturalistic and the stylized. By clever juxtaposition, the best Batuan artists, such as the Neka Art Museum exhibitors **I Wayan Bendi**, **I Made Budi** and **Ni Wayan Warti**, can turn their pictures into amusing and astute comments on Balinese society. Works by their precursors, the original Batuan artists **Ida Bagus Made Togog** and **Ida Bagus Made Wija**, focused more on the darker side of village life, on the supernatural beings that hang around the temples and forests, and on the overwhelming sense of men and women as tiny elements in a forceful natural world.

YOUNG ARTISTS STYLE

A second flush of artistic innovation hit the Ubud area in the 1960s, when a group of teenage boys from **Penestanan** started producing unusually expressionistic works, painting everyday scenes in vibrant, non-realistic colours. Encouraged by Dutch artist and Penestanan resident **Arie Smit**, who gave them materials and helped organize exhibitions, they soon became known as the **Young Artists**, a tag now used to describe work by anyone in that same style. The style is indisputably childlike, even naive: the detailed, mosaic-like compositions of scenes from daily life are crudely drawn with minimal attention to perspective, outlined in black like in a child's colouring book, and often washed over in weird shades of pink, purple and blue.

All the major museums have works by some of the original Young Artists from the 1960s, the most famous of whom include **I Ketut Tagen**, **I Wayan Pugur**, **I Nyoman Londo**, **I Nyoman Mundik** and **I Nyoman Mujung**. The Neka Art Museum in Ubud devotes a whole gallery to Arie Smit's own work (see p.118).

ACADEMIC AND BALI MODERNISM

Bali's Modern artists, both indigenous and expatriate, are sometimes labelled as **Academic**, meaning that they've studied and been influenced by Western modernism but have settled in Bali and paint Balinese subjects. Many of the best known are graduates from the Yogyakarta Academy of Fine Arts in Java, and some are or have been part of the **Sanggar Dewata Indonesia** art movement, whose style – loosely defined as Balinese Hindu abstract expressionism – has been the dominant form of modern Balinese painting since the 1970s. Although the style has been somewhat devalued by the countless poor-quality abstracts sold in souvenir shops across Bali, works by the most famous Academics – including **Affandi**, **Anton H** and **Abdul Aziz**, all from Java, the Sumatran-born **Rusli**, and **Made Wianta**, **Nyoman Gunarsa**, **Nyoman Erawan** and **Made Budiana** from Bali – are on show at the Ubud museums and the Nyoman Gunarsa Museum near Semarapura (see p.161). Of these important modern artists, Made Wianta is probably the best known internationally; he represented Indonesia in the Venice 2003 Biennale, with a video installation on the Kuta bombings.

the forest, you'll come to **Pura Dalem Agung Padang Tegal**, the temple of the dead for the *banjar* (neighbourhood) of Padang Tegal (you can borrow the requisite sarong and sash at the temple entrance, for which a small donation is requested). You'll find half a dozen stonecarved images of the witch-widow **Rangda** (see p.320) flanking the main stairway – hard to miss with her hideous fanged face, unkempt hair, metre-long tongue and pendulous breasts. Two of the Rangda statues are depicted in the process of devouring children – a favourite occupation of hers.

2

Nyuhkuning

South of the Pura Dalem Agung Padang Tegal is the woodcarvers' village of **NYUHKUNING**, a pleasingly quiet place for a wander and the site of several charming hotels and cafes. The road is dotted with shops selling the carvers' handiwork but the atmosphere is relaxed and more workshop-oriented than in the more famous woodcarving centre of Mas – and prices are better too. Many of the carvers will give woodcarving lessons to interested tourists. Works by the famous Nyuhkuning carver, the late I Wayan Pendet, are exhibited in the tiny **Museum Pendet** (daily 10am–5pm; free). Just beyond the museum, beside the football field, the road branches. Heading straight on, along the **main street**, you'll pass walled family compounds for the 600m to the main road. A left turn here leads into the next village of **Pengosekan** (1km to the east). If you turn right towards *Sage* restaurant, a right turn north again leads back up to the football field at the top of the village, from where you can head back to the Monkey Forest and central Ubud.

Pengosekan

At the southern end of Jalan Hanoman, about a thirty-minute walk from central Ubud or a short hop on a Ubud–Batubulan bemo, the road enters the small hamlet of **PENGOSEKAN**, home to the excellent **Agung Rai Museum of Art**, as well as an interesting artist community. The Pengosekan painters developed a distinct style (see box, pp.122–123) and their art also features on carved picture frames, boxes and small pieces of furniture.

Agung Rai Museum of Art (ARMA)

JI Raya Pengosekan • Daily 9am–6pm • Rp80,000, includes drink • ☎ 0361 975742, ⓦ armabali.com

Pengosekan's main attraction is the impressive **Agung Rai Museum of Art**, or **ARMA**. Founded by Ubud art dealer Anak Agung Rai, its collection nearly matches that of the Neka Art Museum; there's also an excellent public-access **library** and research centre here, plus an open-air dance stage, spa, bookstore, restaurant and hotel.

If you drop by in the mid-afternoon (usually 3–5pm) you may chance upon a Balinese dance practice or a gamelan orchestra rehearsal. There are also regular evening dance performances, check the ARMA website for details.

Bale Daja pavilion

From the main entrance, pass through the temporary exhibition hall and across the garden to the large **Bale Daja pavilion**. The downstairs area celebrates the life and work of Walter Spies (see box, p.117) and includes life-size reproductions of his work along with some typical Ubud-style paintings such as I Ketut Sepi's *Cremation Ceremony* and Anak Agung Gede Sobrat's *Baris Dance*. The upstairs gallery gives a brief survey of the development of Balinese art, though the labels aren't that helpful. Historically speaking, you should begin with the **wayang-style** canvases that are hung high up on the walls overlooking the central well; they are in typical seventeenth-century style, though experts think that they date from much later. Ida Bagus Belawa's *Cock Fighting* is thought to have been painted in the 1930s and is a good example of a modern subject done in traditional two-dimensional style.

Also on this floor, the **Batuan-style** art focuses on real life too; the works are instantly recognizable by their extraordinary detail. *The Island of Bali* by the popular I Wayan Bendi is a fine example: crammed with archetypal Balinese scenes, it's also laced with satire, notably in the figures of long-nosed tourists poking their camera lenses into village events. If you look closely you'll find a surfer in the picture too. Look out also for the pen-and-ink cartoons of I Gusti Nyoman Lempad, an important Ubud character (see box, p.115).

Bale Dauh pavilion

Across the garden, the **Bale Dauh pavilion** is dedicated to works by expatriate artists, including Rudolf Bonnet, Miguel Covarrubias, Donald Friend, Theo Meier, Antonio Blanco, Arie Smit, Malaysia's Chang Fee Ming and Damas Mangku of Java. The highlight is *Calonarang* (1930) by **Spies** himself, a dark portrait of a demonic apparition; this is the only Spies painting currently on show in Bali. The other major work is the *Portrait of a Javanese Nobleman and his Wife* (1837) by the Javanese artist **Raden Saleh**, considered to be the father of Indonesian painting. The rest of the floor is given over to modern Indonesian painting, including works by **Affandi** and some strikingly powerful abstracts by I Made Sumadiyasa.

2

Petulu's white heron sanctuary

1.5km off Jl Andong • No fixed opening hours • Rp20,000 • Follow Jalan Andong north from the T-junction at the eastern edge of Ubud for about 1.5km, then take the left-hand (signed) fork for a further 1.5km; lots of public bemos ply Jalan Andong, but you'll have to walk the section from the fork

Every evening at around 6pm, hundreds (sometimes thousands) of herons fly in from far and wide to roost in the village of **PETULU**, immediately northeast of Ubud – quite a spectacle. Birdwatchers might be able to distinguish the four species of wading birds that frequent the heronry – the **Javan pond heron**, the **plumed egret**, the **little egret** and the **cattle egret** – but for everyone else the sheer volume of birds is impressive enough. From the upper floor of the community centre you'll get a good perspective over the scene and local guides are at hand to help you spot the different birds (and sell you beer).

It isn't clear why the birds have chosen to make their home in Petulu, though locally it's claimed that the birds are **reincarnations** of the tens of thousands of men and women who died in Bali's civil war (1965–66; see p.308). Many of the victims were buried close by, and the birds are said to have started coming here only after an elaborate ceremony was held in the village in memory of the dead.

ARRIVAL AND DEPARTURE **UBUD AND AROUND**

Most Ubud **travel agents** sell Perama bus and boat tickets for the Gili Islands and Lombok, as well as international and domestic airline tickets. Ary's Business and Travel Service, Jl Raya Ubud (☎0361 973130, ✉arys_tour@yahoo.com) provides transport and travel agency services, as does Perama (see below).

BY PLANE
The easiest way to get to/from Ngurah Rai Airport (see p.64) is by shuttle bus (around Rp60,000) or taxi (Rp280,000–325,000).

BY SHUTTLE BUS
Perama Bali's ubiquitous shuttle-bus operator, Perama, serves all major tourist destinations on Bali and Lombok. Perama's head office (daily 7am–10pm; ☎0361 973316, ⓦperamatour.com; tickets are also available from the tourist office and some travel agencies) is inconveniently located in Padang Tegal at the far southern end of Jl Hanoman, 2.5km from the central market. There's no local bemo or metered taxi service from here; you can either take your chances with touts offering free transport to whichever accommodation they're promoting or pay one of the drivers that hang about outside (around Rp50,000 to central Ubud).
Destinations airport (3 daily; 1hr 15min–1hr 45min); Amed (1 daily; 2hr 30min); Bedugul (1 daily; 1hr 30min); Candidasa (3 daily; 1hr 30min–2hr); Gili Islands (daily;

8hr); Kintamani (1 daily; 45min); Kuta (6–7 daily; 1hr–1hr 30min); Lovina (1 daily; 1hr 45min–2hr); Nusa Lembongan (1 daily; 2hr 30min); Padang Bai (3 daily; 1hr–1hr 30min); Sanur (6 daily; 45min–1hr); Senggigi (Lombok; 2 daily; 7hr 30min–11hr 30min).

Other services Other shuttle-bus companies may offer more convenient services: the tourist office keeps an up-to-date list of operators and sells tickets. The alternative is the transfer service offered by transport touts and some losmen and hotels. For Pemuteran, Gilimanuk and other parts of northwest Bali, take a shuttle bus to Lovina and then change on to a westbound bemo for the last coastal stretch.

BY BEMO
Only a limited number of direct bemo services run from Ubud, normally departing every 30min or so from about 6am until around 2pm, then at least hourly until about 5pm. They all leave from the central market on Jl Raya Ubud. If coming from Batubulan (Denpasar) you can alight in Peliatan en route; if heading for Campuhan, Sanggingan

or Penestanan, you can connect on to a westbound service at the market. For Nyuhkuning, you'll either have to walk from the market (about 30min) or negotiate a ride with a transport tout. Change in Batubulan (see p.141) for services across Denpasar and convoluted connections to southern resorts, the southwest and Java. Change in Gianyar for connections to Candidasa.

Destinations Campuhan/Sanggingan (5–10min); Celuk (40min); Denpasar (Batubulan terminal; 50min); Gianyar (20min); Goa Gajah (10min); Kedewatan (10min); Kintamani (1hr); Mas (15min); Peliatan (5min); Pujung (25min); Sukawati (30min).

GETTING AROUND

By bemo It's possible to use the public bemos for certain short hops (from Rp5000): to get to the Neka Art Museum, flag down any bemo heading west; for Pengosekan or Peliatan take any bemo heading for Batubulan; and for Petulu use the orange bemos to Pujung or the brown bemos to Tegalalang and Kintamani.

By taxi There are no metered taxis in Ubud, so you have to bargain with the transport touts who hang around on every corner; typically, you can expect to pay around Rp50,000 from the Perama office to the central Ubud hotels/market in a car (less by motorbike). Most outlying hotels provide free transport in and out of central Ubud. Bluebird, Uber and Ola cabs do not circulate in Ubud (the local transport touts prevent them from operating).

By car or motorbike Most transport touts and tour agencies in central Ubud offer car and motorbike rental. A reputable and efficient place is Ary's Business and Travel Service (☏ 0361 973130, ✉ arys_tour@yahoo.com) on Jl Raya Ubud. Note that if you're driving northwards, i.e. uphill, to Kintamani or to the north coast, it's worth getting something more powerful than the cheapest Jimny.

By bike Bicycles are an excellent way to get around if you avoid the busier roads; they can be rented from numerous outlets along Jl Raya Ubud, Jl Monkey Forest and Jl Hanoman (from Rp20,000/day).

On foot The most enjoyable way of seeing Ubud and its immediate environs is on foot via the tracks through the rice paddies and the narrow *gang* that weave through the more traditional *banjar*.

INFORMATION

Tourist information Ubud's tourist office (daily 8am–8pm; ☏ 0361 973285) is centrally located just west of the Jl Raya Ubud/Jl Monkey Forest intersection. Staff provide schedules of dance performances and festivals, sell tickets for dance shows, run inexpensive day-trips to local sights and sell shuttle-bus tickets for Perama and their competitors. You can pick up useful local magazines here. Consult ✆ ubudnowandthen.com

for good cultural information.

Maps and specialist guides If you're planning to do any serious walking or cycling around the area, buy the worthwhile *Bali Pathfinder* map from any local bookstore or the widely available *Bali Street Atlas* (Periplus). Another good investment, though less widely available, is the slim volume, *Bali Bird Walks*, written by the local expat ornithologist Victor Mason, who also runs tours (see opposite).

TOURS

Although the Ubud tourist office and all travel agencies offer programmes of **standard tours** (generally from Rp225,000/ person; minimum 2 people), it's usually more rewarding (and no more expensive if there's at least a couple of you) to hire your own driver and **design your own itinerary**, something that generally costs Rp350,000–500,000/day. Recommended freelance drivers include Nyoman Suastika (☏ 0813 3870 1962, ✆ nyoman-suastika.tripod.com), or you can arrange one through almost any car-rental outlet or hotel. Most tour agencies advertise inclusive trips to local festivals and cremations (see p.331), although you can simply check the details at the tourist office and attend independently. Note that whether you go to a temple ceremony with a group or on your own, formal dress (sashes and sarongs) is required.

Bicycle tours Downhill rides from Gunung Batur (see p.192), via villages, temples and traditional homes, cost Rp350,000–450,000. Recommended operators include the following: Bali Bike Baik Cycling Tours (☏ 0361 978052,

✆ balibike.com); Bali Eco Cycling (☏ 0361 975557, ✆ baliecocycling.com); Banyan Tree Bike Tours (☏ 0813 3879 8516, ✆ banyantreebiketours.com); Greenbike Tour (☏ 0851 0169 9692 ✆ greenbiketour.com); Happy Bike

VOLUNTEERING AROUND UBUD

The Ubud area hosts a number of **charitable foundations** (see p.43) that can use a helping hand for varying lengths of time. Sjaki-Tari-Us Foundation (✆ sjakitarius.nl) at *Sjaki's Warung* and BAWA, Jl Raya Ubud (✆ bawabali.com) both welcome volunteers; contact them in advance.

Cycling Tour (☎ 0819 9926 0262, ⓦ happybiketour.com); and Jegeg Bali Cycling Tours (☎ 0812 3677 9429, ⓦ jegeg balicycling.com).

Bird walks Bird-spotting walks in the Campuhan area, organized by expat author Victor Mason (☎ 0812 391 3801, ⓦ balibirdwalk.com; Tues, Fri, Sat & Sun 9am; Rp500,000, including lunch and conservation donation).

Cultural and ecological walks Guided walks with an emphasis on learning about traditions and local life from Rp250,000: Bali Nature Walks (☎ 0817 973 5914, ⓦ balinaturewalks.net); Bali Off Course (☎ 0361 369 9003, ⓦ balioffcourse.com); Keep Walking Tours (☎ 0361 973361,

ⓦ balispirit.com/tours/bali_tour_keep_walking.html).

Sunrise mountain treks Gunung Batur (from Rp550,000) and Gunung Agung (from Rp1,100,000). Try Bali Sunrise Trekking and Tours (☎ 0818 552669, ⓦ balisunrisetours.com); Keep Walking Tours (see below); or Jegeg Bali (see above).

Traditional medicine walks Traditional herbalists Ni Wayan Lilir and I Made Westi show how to identify native medicinal plants in the Ubud countryside (☎ 0812 381 6024, ⓦ baliherbalwalk.com; Rp200,000).

Whitewater rafting and kayaking On the Ayung River just west of Ubud, Sobek's 2hr courses cover about 8km and cross Class 2 and 3 rapids (see p.66).

COURSES AND WORKSHOPS

With so many creative types in residence, Ubud is a great place to learn something new: there are tourist-oriented **courses** in everything from batik to yoga. In addition to the more formal venues listed below, it's always worth asking advice from the more traditional homestays, whose managers are often dancers, musicians or painters. Unless otherwise stated, all of the places below are in central Ubud.

ARTS, CRAFTS, MUSIC, DANCE AND TRADITIONAL CULTURE

ARMA Cultural Workshops Jl Raya Pengosekan, Pengosekan ☎ 0361 976659, ⓦ armabali.com. Museum-endorsed classes (mostly 2hr; Rp300,000–600,000) in ancient Balinese culture, Balinese painting, woodcarving, batik, gamelan, dance and theatre, silver, basket-weaving, traditional architecture, Hinduism, astrology and making offerings.

Five Art Studio Jl Raya Keliki ☎ 0878 6198 4083, ⓦ five artubud.com. Well-regarded batik painting, and wood- and stone-carving classes. Free transport in the Ubud area.

Museum Puri Lukisan Cultural Workshops Jl Raya Ubud ☎ 0361 971159, ⓦ museumpurilukisan.com. Reputable classes (Rp125,000–500,000) at Ubud's oldest art museum covering batik, woodcarving, beadwork, classical painting, basketry, kite-making, mask-painting, shadow puppet-making, gamelan and Balinese dance.

Nirvana Batik Course Jl Gootama 10 ☎ 0361 975415, ⓦ nirvanaku.com. Renowned batik artist I Nyoman Suradnya runs one- to five-day courses in batik painting (Rp485,000/day, including materials).

Nyuhkuning woodcarving shops Nyuhkuning. There are plenty of willing teachers in this village of woodcarvers; just ask at any of the shops.

Pondok Pekak Library and Learning Centre Jl Dewi Sita ☎ 0361 976194, ⓦ pondokpekaklibrary.com. Beginners' classes in dance, gamelan, painting, woodcarving, making offerings and jewellery (Rp150,000–300,000). Book ahead.

Sari Api Jl Suweta ☎ 0361 977917, ⓦ sariapi.com. Courses (from Rp500,000) in ceramics-making from the Canadian ceramicist Susan Kohlik.

Sehati Guesthouse Off the southern end of Jl Monkey Forest, Padang Tegal ☎ 0361 976341. Learn the elements of Balinese dance from a graduate of Denpasar's prestigious

school of performing arts (from Rp100,000/hr).

Studio Perak Jl Hanoman ☎ 0361 974244, ⓦ studio perak.com. Courses in silversmithing: in half a day you can produce your own ring or pendant (Rp350,000 inclusive of 5g of silver).

Threads of Life Indonesian Textile Art Center Jl Kajeng 24 ☎ 0361 972187, ⓦ threadsoflife.com. Classes (Rp100,000; minimum four people) on different aspects of Indonesian and Balinese textiles and natural dyes; also hosts regular lectures.

COOKING AND LANGUAGE

Alam Indah/Café Wayan Jl Monkey Forest ☎ 0361 975447, ⓦ alamindahbali.com. There are seven choices of lessons (2hr; Rp350,000) featuring various menus, given at *Café Wayan*'s sister restaurant *Laka Leke* in Nyuhkuning village.

Casa Luna Jl Raya Ubud ☎ 0361 977409, ⓦ casaluna bali.com/cooking-school. Famous, long-running half-day Balinese cooking workshops (from Rp400,000) run by *Fragrant Rice* author Janet deNeefe.

Paon Cooking Class Laplapan village ☎ 0813 3793 9095, ⓦ paon-bali.com. Well-regarded classes (from Rp350,000) with free pick-up in the Ubud area.

Pondok Pekak Library and Learning Centre Jl Dewi Sita ☎ 0361 976194, ⓦ pondokpekaklibrary.com. Intensive Indonesian language courses and individual lessons (Rp175,000/1hr 30min), plus Balinese lessons.

Tegal Sari Jl Hanoman, Padang Tegal ☎ 0361 973318, ⓦ tegalsari-ubud.com. Half-day courses in Balinese and Indonesian cuisine (Rp330,000 including lunch).

Warung Enak Jl Pengosekan, Padang Tegal ☎ 0361 972911, ⓦ warungenakbali.com. Classes (Rp475,000, including pick-up from the Ubud area) come with a different set menu on each day; vegetarian options available on request.

ACCOMMODATION

Ubud has an incredible choice of **accommodation**. Most family homestays are in traditional compounds and have real Balinese charm. Midrange hotels often have pools and a dash of artistic style, while upscale options are wonderfully luxurious, many with rice-paddy or river views. For a stunning river valley location, the Ayung River hotels (see p.139), 6km or so west of Ubud, are perfect. For **house rental** opportunities, check the noticeboards at *Bali Buda* café, Jl Jembawan; Bintang Supermarket, Jl Raya Sanggingan; and *Kafe*, Jl Hanoman.

CENTRAL UBUD

The 1km-long Jl Monkey Forest is the most central and commercial part of town, while the smaller roads, such as Jl Karna, Jl Maruti, Jl Gootama, Jl Kajeng and Jl Bisma, for example, retain a more peaceful atmosphere and have less traffic. Jl Hanoman, to the east, is marginally quieter than Jl Monkey Forest but still has plenty of shops and restaurants.

Artja Inn Jl Kajeng 9 ☎ 0856 379 4777; map p.114. Set away from the road behind a home compound in a cute garden, this family-run place offers a handful of neat, inviting rooms in a modern block and older, spartan, bamboo-walled cottages. The owners are very hospitable and there's free wi-fi. **Rp175,000**

Gusti's Garden 2 Jl Abangan, about 150m walk north from Jl Raya Ubud ☎ 0361 971474, ⓦ gustigarden bungalows.com; map pp.120–121. Overlooks rice paddies on the western fringes of central Ubud and its seven nicely designed rooms are deservedly popular. Boasts a grotto-like swimming pool. **Rp325,000**

Gusti's Garden Bungalows Jl Kajeng 27 ☎ 0812 465 1441, ⓦ gustigardenbungalows.com; map pp.120–121. Sixteen pleasant rooms, with fan or a/c, set around a small swimming pool in a peaceful location just north of Pura Tamen Saraswati. **Rp325,000**

Jati Homestay Jl Hanoman, Padang Tegal ☎ 0361 977701, ⓦ jatihs.com; map p.114. These homely fan-cooled rooms – all with bamboo furniture and private bathrooms – are run by a family of painters; it has an art gallery on site and art lessons are available. **Rp250,000**

★**KajaNe Mua** Jl Monkey Forest ☎ 0361 972877, ⓦ kajane.com; map p.114. Popular resort with villa compounds offering one to four rooms, all with private pools in addition to the inviting main pool. The chic modern Balinese or antique-themed interiors come with good facilities; service is excellent and there's a small gym and a DVD library for rainy nights in. **$146**

Komaneka Resort at Monkey Forest Jl Monkey Forest ☎ 0361 976090, ⓦ komaneka.com; map p.114. Beautifully designed, this contemporary hotel offers large, fabulously stylish a/c bungalows, some with private pools. There's also a stunning lap pool and beautiful spa. Three other wonderful resorts are offered in and near Ubud – check the website for details. **$221**

Nick's Pension Jl Bisma ☎ 0361 975636, ⓦ nickshotels-ubud.com; map p.114. Efficiently run place with a wide choice of rooms (all with private bathrooms, verandas and plenty of space). There's a decent pool, and a bridge that acts as a handy shortcut between Bisma and Monkey Forest streets (guests only). You pay more for a rice paddy view. The same owners also run a couple of other hotels in Ubud (see website for details). **Rp600,000**

Nirvana Pension Jl Gootama 10 ☎ 0361 975415, ⓦ nirvanaku.com; map p.114. Comfortably furnished and artistically decorated rooms, all with fan and hot water, in the traditional house compound of painter and batik teacher Nyoman Suradnya (see p.127). **Rp350,000**

Nur Guest House Jl Abangan ☎ 0361 479 2614, ⓦ nursalonubud.com; map pp.120–121. This lovely place has gorgeous traditional wooden bungalows set amongst ricefields. It's a short walk from central Ubud yet feels very rural and the complimentary breakfast is outstanding. **$60**

Sama's Cottages Jl Bisma ☎ 0361 973481, ⓦ samas cottagesubud.com; map p.114. Tranquil hideaway, just 10min from central Ubud with charming cottages (with either fans or a/c) built on steep tiers in a river gully. There's a small pool, and breakfast is brought to your private veranda each morning. **$44**

Sania's House Jl Karna 7 ☎ 0361 970003, ⓔ sania _house@yahoo.com; map p.114. Well-maintained fan or a/c rooms (some in multistorey buildings) close to the market, and there's a small pool. **Rp250,000**

Sayong House Jl Maruti ☎ 0361 973305, ⓔ sayong _ubud@yahoo.com; map p.114. Ten simply furnished rooms, all with hot water, terraces and either fans or a/c, set around a garden. There's also a swimming pool just across the road. **Rp340,000**

TEBESAYA, PELIATAN, PENGOSEKAN, NYUHKUNING, PADANG TEGAL AND SAMBAHAN

Tebesaya is a residential area around 15min walk east from Ubud market. Further east again, the neighbourhood of Peliatan harbours a couple of excellent places to stay. Nyuhkuning, Padang Tegal and Pengosekan are peaceful southern settlements. Sambahan is just north of central Ubud.

★**Alam Jiwa** Nyuhkuning ☎ 0361 977463, ⓦ alam indahbali.com; map pp.120–121. Run by a hospitable family, the spacious accommodation here is located by a small river, affording dramatic views of ricefields and Gunung Agung. There's a pool, and free transport into Ubud. This is one of a small local chain of delightful *Alam* hotels. **$85**

Byasa Ubud Jl Made Lebah ☎0813 3842 9363, ⓦbyasa-ubud.com; map pp.120–121. Set off the road, this small hotel has nine plush rooms in a delightfully peaceful location overlooking paddy fields and a lovely pool. Staff really go the extra mile here. **Rp550,000**

★**Family Guest House** Jl Sukma 39, Tebesaya ☎0361 974054, ⓦfamilyubud.com; map pp.120–121. Friendly place offering well-maintained bungalows in the family compound, all of them with stylish furniture, fans, hot water and large verandas. The more expensive options are huge and especially good value. Rates include breakfast, tea/coffee (all day) and an afternoon snack. **Rp300,000**

Swasti Eco Cottages Nyuhkuning ☎0361 974079, ⓦbaliswasti.com; map pp.120–121. Eco hideaway with spacious, tastefully decorated accommodation in rooms (with either fans or a/c) and delightful Javanese Joglo-style cottages. There's a pool and spa, yoga sessions, and an excellent organic restaurant, which offers French, Thai, Indian and Indonesian cuisine. **Rp480,000**

★**Tegal Sari** Jl Hanoman, Padang Tegal ☎0361 973318, ⓦtegalsari-ubud.com; map pp.120–121. An excellent, ecologically conscious place that's solar powered and has a waste-recycling programme. Rooms are fine value and tastefully furnished, all with terraces and a/c; the deluxe options (from Rp550,000) are very stylish indeed. Service is thoughtful and there are massage facilities, a pool, free local transport and opportunities for cookery classes, day-treks and village visits. Book well ahead. **Rp330,000**

★**Wapa di Ume** 1.8km north along Jl Suweta from Ubud market, in the hamlet of Sambahan ☎0361 973178, ⓦwapadiume.com; map pp.120–121. The attention to detail is flawless at this beautiful natural chic hotel where each room has a rice-paddy view. There's a fine pool, spa, restaurant with stunning vistas and free daily yoga class. Regular shuttles into central Ubud are available. **$196**

SANGGINGAN, PAYANGAN AND KELIKI
West of central Ubud, the hotels in Sanggingan are reached via busy Jl Raya Ubud; some hotels offer free transfers. If you're staying in Keliki or Payangan you'll probably need transport.

Alam Sari Keliki Hotel Keliki ☎0361 981420, ⓦalam sari.com; map pp.120–121. The inviting accommodation here overlooks ricefields and coconut groves about 10km north of Ubud. Facilities include a fine restaurant, spa and swimming pool. A kids' programme, art and culture classes, bike tours, village visits and shuttle service are offered. Doubles **$78**, villas **$150**

Alila Ubud Payangan ☎0361 975963, ⓦalilahotels .com; map pp.120–121. Boasts a wonderful position overlooking the jungle-rich Ayung Valley and has spacious and stylish rooms and bungalows that make the most of the stunning views. There's a superb restaurant, professional spa with an extensive range of treatments, and perhaps Ubud's best infinity pool. **$272**

Uma Ubud Jl Raya Sanggingan, Sanggingan ☎0361 972448, ⓦcomohotels.com/umaubud; map pp.120–121. Fabulous resort of white-walled compounds containing Japan-influenced accommodation set along the side of the Wos River. Part of the top-end *COMO* group, they put an emphasis here on wellbeing, with complimentary daily yoga classes and morning walks. **$292**

PENESTANAN
Many of Penestanan's villas can be rented and there are some good mid-range accommodation options up here and in the village below; places in the latter are referred to as *kelod* (away from the mountain) or *kaja* (towards the mountain) in the following listings. Ridgetop access is by foot or motorbike, while village accommodation has the advantage of road access.

Gerebig Bungalows Penestanan Kelod ☎0813 3701 9757, ⓦgerebig.com; map pp.120–121. Appealing rooms and bungalows, all with fans, fridges and some with kitchen facilities, set amid local ricefields. The swimming pool is a bit further out in the fields. A three-bedroom house (Rp1,000,000) is also available. **Rp460,000**

Santra Putra Ridgetop ☎0361 977810, ⓦfacebook .com/santraputraKAS; map pp.120–121. A fusion of art gallery and guesthouse offering a charming selection of

---

PLASTIC FREE BALI

Discarded plastic bottles don't decompose and are expensive and wasteful to manufacture. The Bali Cantik Tanpa Plastik (**Plastic Free Bali**) Campaign is working to get rid of *all* plastic, including bags. Their Facebook page is ⓦwww.facebook.com/groups/44297661289. In the meantime, to help minimize the rubbish problem, you can **refill** your plastic water bottle with the filtered water supplied at certain clued-up outlets in Ubud for less than what it would cost to buy a replacement. These include:

Jl Dewi Sita *Tutmak* restaurant; Pondok Pekak Library and Learning Centre; and *Sjaki's Warung*.
Jl Hanoman *Kafe* restaurant.
Jl Jembawan *Bali Buda* café.
Rice-paddy walk *Sari Organik* café.

2

rooms with kitchenettes and great verandas or balconies overlooking the garden. There's a wide range of courses on offer too. Accessible on foot via the Campuhan steps or by motorcycle from the Penestanan side. **Rp375,000**

The Sungu Penestanan Kelod ☎0361 975719, ⓦthe sunguresort.com; map pp.120–121. A fine selection of spacious rooms and villas in pretty, leafy grounds with a pool. Offers excellent breakfasts and a free shuttle service to central Ubud. Check their website for special offers and package deals. **$72**

Taman Rahasia Penestanan Kaja ☎0361 979395, ⓦtamanrahasia.com; map pp.120–121. A classy, family-run boutique hideaway in the heart of the village. The large a/c rooms here are attractively furnished with tasteful artworks and local fabrics and have deep verandas or balconies. There's a restaurant, small pool, good spa and charming garden. Also has a cooking school for in-house guests. Not recommended for children. **$106**

EATING

If you like your food vegan, organic and raw, Ubud will be heaven: it's probably Asia's healthy eating epicentre. Or if barbecued meats and pizza are more to your taste, well, you'll eat well here too. Factor in Japanese, Chinese, Italian, French, a slew of delis, and of course, Indonesian and Balinese restaurants and there's an amazing selection. Many restaurants outside central Ubud offer free pick-ups if you call up in advance.

CENTRAL UBUD

Bali Buda Jl Jembawan 1 ☎0361 844 5935, ⓦbalibuda.com; map p.114. Offers a vast menu of healthy drinks (most Rp22,000–34,000), sandwiches made with traditional or rye, spelt and red-rice breads, raw-food meals, pizza and salads, soups and main courses (Rp28,000–78,000), as well as cakes and pastries. There's a shop around the corner, plus a noticeboard for yoga and language classes and houses for rent. Daily 7am–10pm.

Bollero Jl Dewi Sita ☎0361 972872; map p.114. An airy restaurant dishing up nicely cooked and presented Balinese, Asian and international dishes (mains Rp52,000–92,000) in relaxed surroundings decorated with black-and-white prints. The desserts are extremely tempting, and there are also cocktails and a small wine list (happy hour 4–8pm). Daily noon–10.30pm.

Café des Artistes Jl Bisma 9X ☎0361 972706, ⓦcafedesartistesbali.com; map p.114. Sophisticated place with exhibitions by local artists and a tasty menu that features half a dozen steak dishes (try tenderloin with blue cheese), pastas, *escargots* and *moules* (mains from Rp65,000) plus a good-value monthly four-course special. It also offers more than forty imported wines (glasses from Rp90,000) and Belgian beers. Daily 11am–11pm.

Casa Luna Jl Raya Ubud ☎0361 977409, ⓦcasaluna bali.com; map p.114. Long-running, justly popular restaurant-bakery serving fine international cuisine (mains from Rp60,000). The weekend brunch (served until 3pm) is particularly good and there's live jazz on Thursday and Sunday evenings. However service can be distracted at times. *Casa Luna's* owners also run cooking classes (see p.127). Daily 8am–10.30/11pm.

Clear Jl Hanoman ☎0361 889 4437, ⓦclearcafebali .com; map p.114. Offers an excellent range of organic raw, vegan, vegetarian and seafood dishes, drawing culinary inspiration from across the globe (though many ingredients are sourced in Bali). The design (bamboo screens, high ceiling, wonderful aged wooden door) is eye-catching too. Mains start at around Rp50,000. Daily 8am–11pm.

Gelato Secrets Jl Monkey Forest ⓦgelatosecrets.com; map p.114. Serving the best ice creams and sorbets in central Ubud, this gelateria sources its ingredients from across the Indonesian archipelago and makes its cones in-house. Daily 10am–10.30pm.

Ibu Oka Just off Jl Suweta; map p.114. This open-sided warung attracts queues of diners for its flavoursome *babi guling* (suckling pig, from Rp55,000), though the crackling could be crispier. There are a couple of other branches around town too. Daily 11am–5.30pm (or until the babi guling runs out).

Ibu Rai Jl Monkey Forest ☎0361 973472; map p.114. Serves up artfully presented Indonesian, Asian and inter-national dishes in bustling surroundings (mains Rp51,000–110,000). Daily 8am–11pm.

Kafe Jl Hanoman 44B ☎0811 324 9747, ⓦkafe-bali .com; map p.114. The vast and enticing "organically inspired" menu (most mains Rp41,000-79,000) includes Mexican dishes, soups, stir-fries, noodles and sandwiches supplemented by healthy juices and smoothies, top coffee, and scrumptious cakes and desserts. *Garden Kafe* is a small branch at The Yoga Barn (see p.132). Daily 7.30am–11pm.

★Locavore Jl Dewi Sita ☎0361 977733, ⓦwww .locavore.co.id; map p.114. A serious gastronomic experience, this acclaimed restaurant (with an open kitchen) has really raised the bar in Ubud with its highly innovative (and expensive) Modern European cuisine. Their five- or seven-course tasting menus (from Rp575,000) change every month and include a veggie option; there's no à la carte menu. The more casual *Locavore to Go* across the street is open all day and serves posh comfort grub including the best burger in town. Mon–Sat noon–2.30pm & 6–11pm.

★Monsieur Spoon Jl Hanoman 10 ☎0361 973263, ⓦmonsieurspoon.com/shops; map p.114. Perhaps Ubud's best continental-style café, serving perfectly baked pastries, brioches, cakes (try the salted caramel) as well as breakfasts, quiches and great coffee in all the combinations you could care for. There are well-chosen tunes on the stereo. Daily 7am–9pm.

Nomad JI Raya Ubud 35 ☎0361 977169; map p.114. Serves local, Asian fusion and international dishes with style from a small but inviting menu (mains from Rp42,000) including satay, Malaysian *laksa* and Balinese-style tapas. There are plenty of cocktails, too. Daily 10am–11pm.

★Seniman Coffee Studio JI Sriwedari 5 ☎0812 3607 6640, ⓦsenimancoffee.com; map p.114. Coffee (Rp22,000–32,000) is elevated to an art form at this hip café-roastery-design shop, which has a range of equipment that would look more in place in a science lab. The menu features five regular, single-origin coffees, plus weekly "guest beans", as well as British- and Indonesian-style breakfasts, top cakes and pleasing oddities like Argentine *alfajores* (*dulce de leche*-filled biscuits). Daily 8am–10pm.

Sjaki's Warung Off JI Dewi Sita ☎0813 5718 1122, ⓦsjakitarius.nl; map p.114. Overlooking the football field, this warung serves up cheap, good-quality Indonesian mainstays and some Western dishes (around Rp30,000). Daily 10am–10pm.

Warung Enak JI Pengosekan ☎0361 972911, ⓦwarungenakbali.com; map p.114. Raiding virtually the entire Indonesian archipelago for dishes, this atmospheric, modish place is sure to satisfy. The *rijsttafel* is the way to hit all the highlights, or try the well-cooked soups, sates, curries, noodles and rice dishes (mains from Rp50,000). Daily 11am–1pm.

Warung Lokal JI Gootama 7; map p.114. This Balinese warung offers *cap cai*, *nasi campur*, *nasi goreng* and the like at good prices (main meals mostly Rp15,000–20,000), attracting a clientele of savvy foreigners and locals. Daily 10am–10pm.

NYUHKUNING AND PELIATAN

★Sage JI Nyuh Bulan ☎0361 976528, ⓦfacebook .com/sagerestobali; map pp.120–121. Located on a corner plot, this vegan place has an outstanding selection of healthy dishes including "Go Jolly Green salad" (with kale, spinach and tempeh, Rp70,000), great jackfruit tacos (Rp60,000) and wonderful juices. The attractive premises are light and airy and staff are sweet. Daily 8am–9.30pm.

Warung D'Atas JI Gunung Sari, Peliatan 777 ☎0361 908 0345; map pp.120–121. Sizzling up a storm, this unpretentious, open-sided place is a carnivore's delight with expertly spiced pork ribs, home-made sausages and kebabs

at moderate prices. Their meat combo plate (Rp100,000) is almost enough for two. Daily 9.30am–10pm.

CAMPUHAN, SANGGINGAN, PENESTANAN AND PENGOSEKAN

Elephant Restaurant JI Raya Sanggingan ☎0851 0016 1907, ⓦelephantbali.com; map pp.120–121. Offering vistas over the Tjampuhan ridge, this vegetarian restaurant with an international menu is a wonderful spot to enjoy a delicious meal. Mains (around Rp60,000) include *polenta alla griglia* (grilled polenta with pesto) and there are good smoothies, coolers and juices. It's in the *Hotel Taman Indrakila*. Daily 8am–9.30pm.

Indus JI Raya Sanggingan ☎0361 977684, ⓦcasaluna bali.com; map pp.120–121. Boasts great daytime views across the Campuhan ridge and draws a loyal clientele for its eclectic menu: healthy breakfasts, Balinese, Asian and Western cuisine (main courses from Rp55,000) and a fresh fish dish on Fridays. There's free transport from *Casa Luna* (see opposite) and a daily happy hour with free tapas (5–7pm). Daily 8am–10.30/11pm.

Made's Warung Penestanan ridge ☎0361 977885; map pp.120–121. One of several excellent options along the Penestanan ridge, serving well-priced travellers' favourites (from Rp25,000), including inexpensive juices, good *nasi campur* and (with 24hr notice) Balinese smoked duck (Rp195,000 for two). Daily 8am–10pm.

Mozaic JI Raya Sanggingan ☎0361 975768, ⓦmozaic -bali.com; map pp.120–121. This multi-award-winning restaurant showcases the talents of French-American chef Chris Salans. The French- and Asian-inspired dishes change regularly but include favourites such as Kintamani suckling pork with Javanese pomelo purée or splash out on a *grand menu* (from Rp600,000). Reservations essential. Daily 6–11pm.

Sari Organik (aka Bodag Maliah) Off JI Abangan, about 800m walk north from the aqueduct on western JI Raya Ubud ☎0361 972087; map pp.120–121. Situated about 20min into the Ubud Kaja ricefield walk (see box, p.116), this café has gorgeous views and good home-grown organic produce. The menu (most dishes Rp45,000–70,000) includes great veggie kebabs, chicken and salads. Expect to wait a while. Daily 8am–8pm.

Warung Nasi Pak Sedan JI Raya Pengosekan; map pp.120–121. Some of the most economical food (dishes around Rp10,000) in and around Ubud is served at the low-key *Warung Nasi Pak Sedan*: try the tasty house speciality, *nasi campur ayam* (the classic *nasi campur* with the addition of chicken). Daily 7.30am–5pm.

NIGHTLIFE AND ENTERTAINMENT

Ubud is no hotbed of hedonistic nightlife. Most tourists go to an early-evening **Balinese dance performance** before catching last orders at a restaurant at around 9pm. The bar scene is pretty sedate, so choose a **live music night** at one of the town's restaurants or bars to be sure of a decent crowd.

2

DANCE AND DRAMA IN UBUD

The Ubud region is an important centre of **Balinese dance** (see p.319) and **gamelan** and boasts dozens of performance groups. Between them they stage up to nine different dance shows every night in the area; the tourist office publishes the schedule (which is also available at ⓦ ubud.com) and arranges **free transport** to outlying venues. **Ticket prices** are fixed and cost Rp75,000–100,000 from the tourist office or touts and on the door. Performances generally start between 7pm and 8pm, and there's unreserved seating so arrive early for the best spot.

The **Kecak** (Monkey Dance) and the **Barong** (Lion Dance) are the most accessible and visually interesting, while the **Legong** is more refined and understated. Unusual shows worth seeking out include the unique **all-female** Kecak Srikandhi.

If you have only one evening to catch a show, consider seeing whatever is playing at **Puri Saren Agung (Ubud Palace)**, opposite the market in the centre of Ubud. The setting is atmospheric, with the courtyard gateway and staircase furnishing a memorable backdrop. The Kecak that's staged twice a month on the nights of the full and dark moon at the **ARMA** in Pengosekan (see p.124), the Cak Rina, is also worth a special effort to catch, as it's an unusually fiery and humorous version.

BARS AND LIVE MUSIC VENUES

Laughing Buddha Bar Jl Monkey Forest ☎0361 970928, ⓦlaughingbuddhabali.com; map p.114. There's live music (from blues to reggae) every night at this small, relaxed bar in the heart of Jl Monkey Forest. You'll find a long drinks menu plus plenty of nibbles and tapas. Happy hour stretches from 4pm to 7pm. Daily 8am–midnight.

No Mas Ubud Jl Monkey Forest ☎0361 908 0800, ⓦnomasubud.com; map p.114. Stylish bar with a social vibe, vintagey decor, live bands, DJs and killer cocktails (try a Pickleback – whisky and home-made juice, Rp60,000). Daily 5pm–1am.

Night Rooster Jl Dewi Sita ☎0361 977733, ⓦwww .locavore.co.id/nightrooster; map p.114. Sleek new lounge bar from the Locavore team, with outstanding cocktails (Rp130,000ish), fine wine by the glass, and superb sharing platters: try their charcuterie spread. Daily 4pm–midnight.

Shisha XL Lounge Off Jl Monkey Forest; map p.114.

Chilled place overlooking the football field that stays open late and features DJs and live music. Food tends to be disappointing so stick to ice-cold beers or suck on a shisha pipe. Daily 10am–2am.

CINEMA

Black Beach Jl Hanoman ☎0361 971353, ⓦblack beach.asia. This restaurant shows arthouse European films on its rooftop terrace at 8pm on Wednesday and Thursdays. Free admission.

Paradiso Ubud Jl Goutama Selatan ☎0361 783 5545, ⓦparadisoubud.com. A professional set-up with HD projector and Dolby surround-sound system. Screens classics, documentaries, cult movies and kids' flicks.

The Yoga Barn Southern end of Jl Hanoman in Padang Tegal ☎0361 971236, ⓦtheyogabarn.com. Hosts an eclectic programme of "Monday Night Movies" every other Monday from 7.30pm (Rp30,000, or Rp85,000 including dinner from 6pm).

SHOPPING

Shopping for arts and crafts is a major pastime in Ubud: there are outlets in all its neighbourhoods, but if you're short on time the **market** in central Ubud is a good one-stop venue and overflows with stalls. For a shopping excursion around the central area, Jl Monkey Forest, Jl Hanoman and Jl Dewi Sita are the best roads. You might also want to explore the specialist "craft villages" of Celuk, Sukawati, Batuan and Mas that lie south of Ubud along the Denpasar–Ubud road (see p.136). The 24hr **minimarts** that dot the Ubud streetscape stock essentials, from suntan lotion to beer. Many Ubud shops can organize shipping if required. Unless otherwise stated, all of the places below are in central Ubud.

ART

Nekat Just off the path to Sari Organik restaurant; map pp.120–121. This gallery in the middle of the paddies displays the striking and deceptively simple pop-naive paintings by the idiosyncratic Pandi. Daily 10am–5pm.

Rio Helmi Jl Suweta 6b ☎0361 972304, ⓦriohelmi .com; map p.114. Gallery of the respected Indonesian

photographer. Limited edition prints cost $125–2250, while mass-market prints start at around $5. There's a good a/c veggie cafe here too. Daily 7am–7pm.

BOOKS

Ganesha Bookshop Jl Raya Ubud, corner of Jl Jembawan ☎0361 970320, ⓦganeshabooksbali.com; map p.114. The best bookshop in Ubud, with a huge stock of new books on all things Balinese and Indonesian, plus maps and fiction. Daily 9am–9pm.

Periplus North end of Jl Monkey Forest and Jl Raya Ubud ☎ 0361 975178, ⓦ periplus.com; map p.114. This well-stocked Bali-wide chain has two branches in central Ubud, each with a good collection of novels, non-fiction, coffee-table books, magazines and newspapers. Daily 9am–10pm.

Pondok Pekak Library and Learning Centre Jl Dewi Sita ☎ 0361 976194, ⓦ pondokpekaklibrary.com; map p.114. A great resource with around 30,000 books available for sale, rent (Rs2000 per day) and part-exchange. Daily 10am–8pm.

CLOTHING, JEWELLERY AND ACCESSORIES

Blue Stone Jl Dewa Sita ☎ 0361 970673, ⓦ bluestone botanicals.com; map p.114. Sells essential oils, aroma-therapy products, natural soaps and balms and even organic insect repellent. Daily 9am–8pm.

Galaxyan Jl Hanoman 3 ☎ 0361 971430; map p.114. Unusual and glorious (and gloriously expensive) range of jewellery made from silver, copper and gold wire, some of it crocheted into shape. A great antidote to much of the overly delicate jewellery on offer in Bali. Daily 9am–8pm.

Goddess on the Go Jl Raya Pengosekan, Padang Tegal ☎ 0361 976084, ⓦ goddessonthego.net; map pp.120–121. Features ecofriendly, travel-friendly, stylish clothes made from beech tree fibres. There's no hard sell and there are bags and jewellery as well. Daily 9am–8pm.

Kado Jl Dewi Sita ☎ 0361 886 3338, ⓦ saraswatipapers .com; map p.114. Outlet for Saraswati Papers, handmade in Bali from recycled papers and incorporating fresh flowers. The results are superb cards, notebooks, photograph albums, picture frames and wrapping papers. Daily 10am–8pm.

Kou Cuisine Jl Monkey Forest ☎ 0361 972319; map p.114. Stocks a fabulous range of home-made jams, Kusamba sea salt and lovely linen. Its sister shop around the corner on Jl Dewi Sita sells wonderful handmade soaps. Daily 9am–8pm.

Paul Ropp Jl Raya Sayan, Sayan ☎ 0361 974655, ⓦ paulropp.com; map pp.120–121. An excellent, though pricey, range of boho-chic hand-tailored clothing; dresses start at around $180. Daily 9am–9pm.

Studio Perak Jl Hanoman ☎ 0361 973371, ⓦ studio perak.com; map p.114. Stylish silver jewellery to suit all tastes from the folks who run the silversmithing courses (see p.127). It's also possible to purchase jewellery here produced by inmates at Kerobokan jail. Daily 9am–8pm.

CRAFTS, TEXTILES AND SOUVENIRS

Duck Man of Bali Jl Raya Goa Gajah, about 1.5km east along the road to Goa Gajah; map pp.120–121. Known for its phenomenal gallery of wooden ducks in all sizes and styles, carved by "the duck man", Ngurah Umum, and his assistants. Daily 9am–7pm.

Kafe Jl Hanoman 44B ☎ 0361 780802; map p.114. Well-selected handicrafts, books, food (including tea, coffee and chocolate), bags and toiletries. Daily 8am–11pm.

Kupu-Kupu Jl Tirta Tawar 22 ⓦ kupukupufoundation .org; map p.114. Inexpensive works produced by disabled woodcarvers, kite-makers, painters, bead-workers and weavers, under the auspices of the Kupu-Kupu foundation (see p.43). Staffed by the artists themselves. Daily 10am–6pm.

Ikat Batik Jl Monkey Forest ☎ 0361 975622, ⓦ ikat batik.com; map p.114. Gorgeous ikat and contemporary batik, many are hand-spun and hand-dyed pieces. Daily 9am–8pm.

Macan Tidur Jl Monkey Forest ☎ 0812 366 5669, ⓦ macantidur.com; map p.114. A stunning selection of arts, crafts, textiles and antiques from across Indonesia. Prices are at the top of the range but so is the quality. Daily 9am–8pm.

Mitra Bali Fair Trade Jl Monkey Forest ☎ 0361 972108, ⓦ mitrabali.com; map p.114. Support local craftspeople at this little shop, where a changing range of crafts is on offer. Daily 9am–8pm.

Sjaki's Warung Off Jl Dewi Sita ☎ 0813 5718 1122; map p.114. A small shop attached to the warung selling a range of items made by the young people with learning disabilities that the project helps; jewellery, art and small gifts are all on offer. Daily 10am–10pm.

Tegun Jl Hanoman 44 ☎ 0361 973361; map p.114. Tegun has Indonesian artefacts big and small from across the archipelago, including ikat, tribal statues, puppets, jewellery and wooden bowls and gifts. Daily 8am–9pm.

FOOD AND DRINK

Ubud Organic Food Market Opposite Pizza Bagus, Padang Tegal (on Sat) and opposite Zens Hotel Tebesaya, just west of central Ubud (on Wed) ⓦ www .ubudorganicmarket.com; map p.114. Stock up on picnic provisions at this twice-weekly market, which offers produce from local producers. Wed & Sat 9am–2pm.

TOO MUCH LUGGAGE?

Need to make room in your luggage for new purchases? Donate unwanted clothes, books, bric-a-brac and anything else "so long as it's not alive" to the Yayasan Senyum **charity shop**, the Smile Shop, at 12 Jalan Sriwedari (☎ 0361 233758, ⓦ senyumbali.org). Profits help fund operations for Balinese people with craniofacial disabilities such as cleft palate. You can, of course, also buy cheap secondhand stuff at the shop too.

MUSICAL INSTRUMENTS

The Drum Factory Jl Monkey Forest ☎0361 844 3107; map p.114. The largest hand-drum manufacturer in Indonesia offers more than two hundred percussion instruments, gongs and gamelan of all shapes and sizes. Some will even fit in your luggage. Daily 9am–8pm.

Pondok Bamboo Far southern end of Jl Monkey Forest, Padang Tegal; map p.114. Sells a full range of Balinese instruments made from bamboo, including *genggong* and the bamboo gamelan. The musician owner teaches music and is also a *dalang* shadow-puppet master; he performs here every Mon (Ramayana) and Thurs (Mahabharata) at 8pm (Rp75,000). Daily 10am–6pm.

SPA TREATMENTS AND ALTERNATIVE THERAPIES

Arty, spiritual-minded Ubud is Bali's centre for holistic practices and **alternative therapies**, and also offers plenty of traditional spa and **beauty treatments** (see p.38). For more information on holistic activities and therapies in Ubud and the rest of Bali, visit the website of the Bali Spirit network (ⓦbalispirit.com), which also runs Ubud's annual Bali Spirit Festival of world music, dance and yoga every March (ⓦbalispiritfestival.com). Unless otherwise stated, all of the places below are in central Ubud.

Bali Botanica Day Spa Jl Raya Sanggingan, Sanggingan ☎0361 976739, ⓦbalibotanica.com. Cute little day spa overlooking a small flower garden and river where the signature treatments are Ayurvedic and herbal massage. Massages start from Rp180,000 (1hr) and packages are available. Daily 9am–9pm.

Balinese Traditional Healing Centre Jl Jembawan 5 ☎0361 884 3042, ⊜balihealer@hotmail.com. Fourth-generation Balinese healer Ni Wayan Nuriasih uses a combination of local herbal medicine plus Chinese and Ayurvedic practices, massage and *jamu* to treat her clients. Her popularity has soared since the publication of Elizabeth Gilbert's best-selling spiritual memoir *Eat, Pray, Love* (see p.336), in which Wayan plays a major role. An initial consultation starts at Rp400,000, and rates escalate from there depending on which treatments are deemed necessary. No fixed opening times, contact in advance.

Cantika Jl Sok Wayah ☎0361 794 4425, ⓦindoline .net/santika. Located on the ricefield walk, en route to *Sari Organik* (see p.131). An hour's massage is Rp120,000 and facials, hair treatments, manicures and pedicures are also available using their own natural products. They also run workshops on making your own beauty products. Daily 9am–6pm.

Ubud Aura Jl Hanoman 888 ☎0361 972956, ⓦubud aura.com. This health retreat, with a pool, is affiliated

---

JAMU: HERBAL TONICS FOR HEALTH AND BEAUTY

Ubud has long been famous for its **herbal medicine** – *ubad* means "medicine" in Balinese – known both for the medicinal plants that flourish around the Campuhan river gullies and for the local healers who know how to use them.

The pills, pastes and potions distilled from medicinal herbs are collectively known as **jamu** and are widely used throughout Bali (and the rest of Indonesia), both in the treatment of serious ailments and for general wellbeing. Healers usually make their own *jamu* from herbs they may have picked or even grown themselves and will have a standard range of special, secret, mixtures to prescribe to their patients as pills or for use in infusions; often they'll custom-make *jamu* for particular conditions as well. Commonly used mainstream plants include turmeric, ginger, galangal and garlic, but there are countless others. Some *jamu* makers don't offer healing sessions but simply hawk their home-brews around the market in old glass bottles. Several Ubud spas and cafés also serve ready-made *jamu* drinks to tourists, including *Bali Buda* (see p.130).

Commercially produced *jamu* is also a huge industry and tends to focus more, but not exclusively, on the wellbeing side of things. Sex and beauty enhancers for men and women are predictably big sellers, as are diet and breast-enlargement elixirs, but there are also plenty of products for cleansing the blood, easing joint pain and muscle ache, improving circulation and dealing with skin conditions. The reputable brands use entirely natural ingredients, often to recipes that are familiar to those who make their own and, like home-made *jamu*, should have no side effects at all (though it's always best to seek local advice first). Pharmacies sometimes sell these commercial powders and pills but there are also dedicated *jamu* shops, like the one towards the eastern end of Ubud's Jalan Raya. Commercial *jamu* is distinctively packaged, often carrying a helpful graphic, like a pulsating knee joint (arthritis) or a smiling, muscular male (better sex), and the most vital information is usually also given in English.

with the Ubud Bodyworks Centre and offers a tranquil base for yoga, treatments and some good old pampering. Four-night yoga packages start at Rp3,700,000. Daily 8am–9pm.

Karsa Spa Campuhan Ridge ☎0813 5339 2013, ⊛karsaspa.com. Accessed via backroads or the Campuhan Ridge hiking trail, this professional spa has great massages (from Rp160,000) and tempting packages (full day of treatments including lunch is Rp950,000). Daily 9am–8.30pm.

Nur Salon Jl Hanoman 28 ☎0361 975352, ⊛nursalon ubud.com. Ubud's original massage and beauty salon still has a very good reputation; the *mandi lulur* treatments are especially famous. Massages start at Rp175,000 (1hr). The salon occupies a traditional Balinese compound and treatment rooms are designed in keeping. Uses male masseurs for male customers. Daily 9am–9pm.

Spa Hati Jl Andong 14, Peliatan ☎0361 977578, ⊛spahatibali.com. Small, unpretentious spa offering a select programme of massages (from Rp250,000) and *lulur* treatments (from Rp150,000), plus use of a jacuzzi and cute little swimming pool. Profits help fund the work of Bali Hati Foundation community projects (see p.43). Daily 9am–9pm.

Ubud Bodyworks Centre Jl Hanoman 25 ☎0361 975720, ⊛ubudbodyworkscentre.com. Well-respected centre for massage and spiritual healing where you can book an appointment with master healer Ketut Arsana or with one of his staff. Also offers traditional baths and massages, beauty treatments, acupressure, energy balancing, herbal healing, reflexology and yoga sessions, and sells essential oils. Daily 9am–9pm.

Ubud Sari Health Resort Jl Kajeng 35 ☎0361 974393, ⊛ubudsari.com. Boasts an on-site swimming pool and health restaurant. Treatments (from $10) include massage, reflexology, reiki, sports massage and yoga. You can also book an all-inclusive healing week ($1480). Daily 8am–8pm.

2

YOGA, PILATES & MEDITATION

Ubud is one of Asia's foremost **yoga communities**, with many resident and visiting devotees. You'll find over a dozen schools in the area and there are possibly hundreds of instructors. Check websites for exact schedules.

Honeymoon Guesthouse Jl Bisma ☎0361 973282, ⊛casalunabali.com. Offers beginners' and intermediate sessions in the morning that are a blend of Hatha and Vinyasa yoga, plus early evening yin yoga sessions.

Intuitive Flow Ridgetop, Penestanan ☎0361 977824, ⊛intuitiveflow.com. Many yoga styles are taught here, as well as meditation and healing therapies. Classes are at the centre on the Penestanan ridgetop with brilliant views from the studio windows. Also runs yoga teacher-training courses.

Taksu Yoga Jl Goutama Selatan ☎0361 971490, ⊛taksuyoga.com. Offers vinyasa, hatha gentle yoga and private classes. Their drop-in rate is Rp120,000, with package discounts available. Daily 9am–5.30pm.

Ubud Aura Jl Hanoman 888 ☎0361 972956, ⊛ubud aura.com. This retreat, with a pool, is affiliated with the Ubud Bodyworks Centre and offers a tranquil base for yoga and treatments. Four-night yoga packages cost Rp3,700,000.

Ubud Pilates Off Jl Raya Campuhan, Penestanan ☎0813 5334 9900, ⊛ubudpilates.com. Offering small-group classes (from beginners to advanced) from an experienced instructor in a beautiful location.

Ubud Yoga House Jl Subak Sokwayah ☎0821 4418 1058, ⊛ubudyogahouse.com. Located in the ricefields leading to the Campuhan Ridge, the Yoga House offers a busy programme of hatha, vinyasa flow and gentle yoga sessions. Guided meditation classes are also available.

The Yoga Barn Southern Jl Hanoman, Padang Tegal ☎0361 971236, ⊛theyogabarn.com. Runs a big programme of yoga classes (Rp110,000) in various disciplines along with pilates, capoeira, dance and meditation. It also offers yoga retreats and yoga teacher-training. Daily 7am–9pm.

DIRECTORY

Banks and exchange There are ATMs and moneychangers throughout central Ubud. Be aware of some ongoing scams (see box, p.48). PT Central Kuta is a recommended exchange counter in the Circle K supermarket opposite Museum Puri Lukisan.

Embassies and consulates See p.25.

Hospitals, clinics and dentists Ubud Clinic at Jl Raya Campuhan 36 (☎0361 974911, ⊛ubudclinic.co.id) is open 24hr, staffed by English-speakers and will respond to emergency call-outs; it also has a dental service. For anything serious, the nearest hospitals are in Denpasar (see p.92).

Internet access Most hotels, restaurants and bars offer free wi-fi. The best internet café is *Highway* on Jl Raya Ubud (open 24hr; Rp30,000/hr).

Libraries The Pondok Pekak Library and Learning Centre off Jl Dewi Sita (daily 9am–9pm) has lots of books about Bali, English-language novels, a comfortable upstairs reading room and a children's library. The Agung Rai Museum of Art (ARMA) has the island's best library of books about Bali, including famous esoteric works and language books.

Police The main police station is on the eastern edge of town, on Jl Andong. There's a more central police booth at the Jl Raya Ubud/Jl Monkey Forest crossroads.

Post office The main office, at Jl Jembawan 1 (Mon–Sat 8am–5pm, Sun & holidays 9am–4pm), has a parcel-packing service at the back. There are postal agents throughout Ubud where you can buy stamps and send mail and parcels.

South of Ubud

2

The stretch of road running 13km **south of Ubud** to Denpasar links a string of arts- and crafts-producing towns, all with long histories of creative activity: Mas, for example, is famed for **woodcarvings**, Celuk for **silverwork**, and Batubulan for **stone sculptures**. If you have private transport, the towns that lie on the main **bemo route** between Ubud and Denpasar's Batubulan terminal are easily visited as a day-trip from Ubud or from the southern resorts; access from Sanur (see p.92) is particularly easy, with Batubulan less than 10km from its northern outskirts.

When the main road from Ubud to Denpasar divides at Batubulan's Barong statue roundabout, the principal artery and bemo routes veer east to Celuk (see p.139), while the right-hand (north) prong narrows into a scenic **back road**, which cuts through a series of traditional villages as far as Sayan, a few kilometres west of Ubud, before continuing to Payangan and eventually to Kintamani. In addition, there are several other pleasantly rural and peaceful routes that run just north of Denpasar and take in some of the area's main attractions, such as the **Bali Bird Park** and **Bali Reptile Park** outside Batubulan, **The Green School** at Sibang Kaja and the **Putrawan Museum of Art** north of Penatih.

Museum Rudana

Teges: 800m north of the Nyana Tilem Gallery in Mas and about 1.5km south of the junction with Jl Peliatan • Mon–Sat 9am–5pm, Sun noon–5pm • Rp100,000 • ☎ 0361 975779, ⓦ museumrudana.com • From central Ubud, it's a 1hr walk

The chief reason to visit the village of **Teges**, sandwiched between Mas to the south and Peliatan to the north, is to see the contemporary Balinese paintings at the **Museum Rudana**. The exhibitions here change, and do not always focus exclusively on modern art, but the museum's core collection includes plenty of works by the big hitters of the contemporary scene. They include **Nyoman Gunarsa**, **Made Budhiana** and **Made Wianta**, all of whom are associated with the influential Sanggar Dewata Indonesia style (see box, pp.122–123).

Mas and around

Long established as a major **woodcarving** centre as well as for traditional *Topeng* and *wayang wong* masks, **MAS** is a rewarding place both to browse and to buy. However, be warned that it stretches 5km from end to end so exploration is gruelling, and its reputation means that prices are high.

Njana Tilem Gallery

Approximately halfway along the Mas–Ubud road, about 2km north of the baby Brahma statue • Daily 9am–5pm • Free • ☎ 0361 975099

The **Njana Tilem Gallery** is home to one of Bali's most famous woodcarving families. It displays the work of **Ida Bagus Nyana** (also spelt Njana) and his son, **Ida Bagus Tilem** (see box, p.138), whose descendants still run the workshop, shop and gallery displaying some of their finest originals. The quality and craftsmanship here is breathtaking, and dexterity of the woodcarvers (who use their feet to grip the carved wood) astonishing. Once you've seen the best, you're ready to browse the street, but be aware you'll need to bargain hard.

CLOCKWISE FROM TOP MASK-MAKER, MAS (P.140); NEKA ART MUSEUM (P.117); NORTHERN CASSOWARY IN BALI BIRD PARK (P.141) >

2

THE WOODCARVERS OF MAS

Woodcarving, like all the arts in Bali, was traditionally used only to decorate temples and palaces, but the early twentieth century saw a growing interest in **secular subjects** and a rise in creativity. Artists began to court the burgeoning tourist market with carvings of nudes, lifelike animals and witty portraits, and a whole new genre evolved in just a few years.

By the mid-1930s, however, creativity and standards were slipping, so a group of influential artists and collectors established the **Pita Maha** foundation to encourage Bali's best carvers to be more experimental. One of these carvers was **Ida Bagus Nyana**, from the village of Mas, who from the 1930s to the 1960s produced works in a range of innovative styles, including abstract elongated human figures, erotic compositions of entwined limbs, and smooth, rounded portraits of voluptuously fat men and women. His son, **Ida Bagus Tilem**, was particularly famous for his highly expressive pieces fashioned from contorted roots and twisted branches. Works by both artists are on show at the Njana Tilem Gallery in Mas (see p.136). The Jati artist **I Nyoman Cokot** developed a "free-form" style that turned monstrous branches into weird, otherworldly creatures, while his son, **Ketut Nongos**, lets his supernatural beings emerge from the contours of weatherworn logs and gnarled trunks.

The legacy of these trailblazers can be seen in almost every souvenir shop in Bali, many of which sell goods that suffer from the same lowering of artistic standards that those artists sought to combat. Few **contemporary woodcarvers** have attained the same status as the stars of the Pita Maha.

Setia Darma House of Masks and Puppets

Jl Br Tegan Bingin, to the east of the village on the way to Tengkulak • Daily 8am–4pm • Free • ☎ 0361 898 7493

The **Setia Darma House of Masks and Puppets** houses a huge collection of more than a thousand masks and 4700 puppets from around the world, with plenty from Bali and Indonesia, including a fine array of *Topeng* masks and *wayang kulit* puppets. A good selection is on show in the glorious antique houses from Java that comprise the museum, and there are explanations in English. The only feasible way to get here is with your own transport; it's about a 5km cycle ride from the bottom of Jalan Monkey Forest in Ubud.

ARRIVAL AND DEPARTURE   **MAS**

By bemo Mas is served by all Ubud–Batubulan bemos, which zip through the village and will stop anywhere on request.

ACCOMMODATION AND EATING

Taman Harum Cottages In the compound of Tantra Gallery, Jl Raya, southern Mas ☎ 0361 975567, ⊕ tamanharumcottages.com. The two-storey villas and suites are the best choice here, affording fine ricefield views from upstairs. All rooms have a/c and hot water and there are a pool, restaurant, spa and free transport to Ubud (20min). Non-guests are welcome to eat at the restaurant. Doubles ₹41, suites ₹88, villas ₹124

Batuan

A ribbon-like roadside development, **BATUAN** was the original home of the **Batuan style of painting** (see box, pp.122–123) and is now a commercial centre for all styles of Balinese art.

Batuan is dominated by large **galleries** lining the main road, while smaller studios are tucked away in the traditional neighbourhoods to the west; look out for "painter" signboards above their gateways. On the west side of the main road, the **I Wayan Bendi Gallery**, named after the most famous exponent of the Batuan style of painting, displays some of the great man's work, while the sprawling **Dewa Putu Toris**, another large commercial enterprise, is also worth a visit; it's located 250m west off the southern end of the main road, in the *banjar* of Tengah – turn west at the *raksasa* (demon-giant) statue and follow the signs. Just before the gallery you'll pass Batuan's main temple, **Pura Desa-Pura Puseh** (dawn–dusk; donation), graced with appropriately elaborate gold-painted woodwork.

At the northern limit of Batuan, a plump stone statue of a well-fed baby Brahma (officially known as Brahma Rare and unofficially as the **Fat Baby statue**) marks the Sakah turn-off to Blahbatuh and points east, while the main road continues north.

Sukawati

Southern Batuan merges into northern **SUKAWATI**, a lively market town and a major arts-and-crafts shopping destination. It's convenient for public transport as Ubud–Batubulan **bemos** stop in front of the town's **art market** (*pasar seni*), which trades every day from dawn till dusk inside a traditional two-storey building on the main road, Jalan Raya Sukawati. Here you'll find a tantalizing array of artefacts, paintings, fabrics, clothing and basketware, piled high on stalls that are crammed together. The scrum, and parking, are so bad that a second market, **Pasar Seni Guwang**, operates about 1km to the south, offering the same range of stuff but in slightly less frenetic surroundings.

Sukawati is also famous for its *wayang kulit*, or **shadow puppetry**, a traditional form of entertainment that's still popular across the island. The puppets (*wayang*) are made out of animal hide, perforated to let the light shine through in intricate patterns, and designed to traditional profiles that are instantly recognizable to a Balinese audience. To visit the workshops inside the homes of the makers look out for signs on Jalan Padma (the road that runs east off Jalan Raya, one block south of the *pasar seni*) and Jalan Yudisthira, which runs parallel to Jalan Raya a few hundred metres to the east.

Celuk

Known as the "silver village", **CELUK** is a major centre for **jewellery** production, and the silversmiths welcome both retail and wholesale customers – though designs are often less innovative than in Ubud or southern resort shops. Many of the outlets have workshops or factories where visitors can watch the silversmiths at work. The smaller, lower-key Celuk outlets are along Jalan Jagaraga (a back road to Singapadu), which runs north from the western end of the main road, Jalan Raya. Batubulan–Ubud **bemos** pass through Celuk, but the shops and workshops are spread out over a 3km stretch.

Singapadu and Sayan

The charming village of **SINGAPADU** is a classic central-Bali settlement of house and temple compounds behind low walls. Some of Bali's most expert **mask-carvers** come from this village (see box opposite), but there's little to buy locally.

Some 13km north of Singapadu the road runs through the village of **SAYAN**, located in the spectacular Ayung River valley, site of several top-notch hotels. Ubud is just 3km east of Sayan, via Penestanan and Campuhan.

ACCOMMODATION   KEDEWATAN AND SAYAN

Overlooking the spectacular Ayung river valley about 3km west of central Ubud, Sayan and nearby Kedewatan are famous for their **luxurious resorts**, all of which capitalize on the dramatic panoramas.

Amandari Jl Raya Kedewatan, Kedewatan ✆ 0361 975333, ⊛ aman.com; map pp.120–121. A true temple of luxury, the Aman's design evokes Balinese architecture and its bungalows and suites are wonderfully opulent, some with private pools. There's a library, and glorious jungle views from its idyllic main pool. Suites $700, villas $1200

★**Bambu Indah** Sayan ✆ 0361 974357, ⊛ bambu indah.com; map pp.120–121. Probably Bali's most unique place to stay, and the antithesis of the corporate five-star hotel. This is perhaps the most environmentally conscious hotel in Indonesia, built entirely from natural materials, while the 30m pool is river-fed and chlorine-free, and there are organic vegetable patches rather than

2

MASKS

Carved wooden **masks** play a crucial role in traditional Balinese dance-dramas. Many are treated as sacred objects, wrapped in holy cloth and stored in the temple when not being used, and given offerings before every public appearance. There's even an annual festival day for all masks and puppets, called Tumpek Wayang, at which actors and mask-makers honour their masks with offerings. The main centres of mask-making on Bali are **Singapadu** and **Mas**. Such is the power generated by certain masks that some mask-makers enter a trance while working.

Traditional masks fall into three categories: human, animal and supernatural. Most **human** masks are made for performances of the Topeng, literally "Masked Drama" (see p.323), while **animal** masks are generally inspired by characters from the Hindu epic the Ramayana. Most sacred of all are the fantastical **Barong** and **Rangda** masks, worn in many dramas by the **mythical creatures** representing the forces of good and evil.

manicured gardens. Guests get to revel in the epic views over the Ayung valley and stay in traditional Javanese teak houses, or startling mod-meets-trad bamboo creations. There's fine food, attentive service and a wonderful chillout zone by the riverbank below. Houses $\underline{\$155}$, two-bed houses $\underline{\$268}$

Four Seasons Resort Bali at Sayan Sayan ☎ 0361 977577, ⓦ fourseasons.com/sayan; map pp.120–121. One of Bali's top hotels, the *Four Seasons* is built on several levels in the Ayung valley; the two-tier pool and other communal areas are stunning. Its suites and villas are beautifully appointed and fabulously comfortable, and villas have private pools. Suites $\underline{\$465}$, villas $\underline{\$755}$

Sayan Terrace Sayan ☎ 0361 974384, ⓦ sayanterrace resort.com; map pp.120–121. These enormous rooms and villas with fans and a/c, all with huge windows and verandas, make the most of the fine Ayung river views. There's an inviting pool and a restaurant, and transport to central Ubud. Doubles $\underline{\$81}$, villas $\underline{\$136}$

Taman Bebek Sayan ☎ 0361 975385, ⓦ tamanbebek bali.com; map pp.120–121. Atmospheric accommodation built in airy colonial style with sliding screens and carved doors. Lush foliage obscures some of the Ayung river views but the atmospheric garden is a winner. There's a pool, spa and transport to Ubud (10min), and meals can be provided. Doubles $\underline{\$92}$, suites $\underline{\$166}$, villas $\underline{\$227}$

The Green School and Community

Sibang Kaja, about 13km from Ubud • Daily tours; book in advance • Rp190,000 to visit the Green School only; various tour packages ($30–47) are available, including lunch • ☎ 0361 469875, ⓦ greenschool.org • Accessible by motorcycle or bicycle (via Silakarang and Mambal Market)

North from Denpasar at Sibang Kaja, the **Green School** makes a fascinating excursion. Opened in 2008 by John and Cynthia Hardy, owners of a successful jewellery business and Bali residents for more than forty years, the school was established to educate pupils (aged 3–17) in emotional, spiritual and environmental issues alongside the more traditional subjects. Interesting from an **educational** point of view, the school is also fabulous architecturally as it consists entirely of open-sided **bamboo structures**; the main bridge and multistorey Heart of School are quite simply works of art. There's a great café here too, open to all.

Tours of the school can be extended with visits to other parts of the Green School family. These include a fascinating **bamboo factory** nearby where bamboo, mostly from the north of Bali, is prepared for construction use (it's boiled, soaked in saltwater, washed, treated and dried) for export across the world. Alternatively visit the **KulKul Farm**, an impressive permaculture operation, or the **Kembali** recycling centre where new objects are made out of discarded materials. Undoubtedly the most spectacular part of the entire operation is the utterly astonishing **Green Valley** (ⓦ greenvillagebali.com), a bamboo community consisting of eighteen dramatic bamboo houses (costing a cool $750,000 or so) built on a steep slope overlooking the jungle-clad Ayung river valley. Visitors get to enter a couple of these bamboo houses as part of a guided tour.

Batubulan and around

Barely distinguishable from the northeastern suburbs of Denpasar, **BATUBULAN** is the capital's terminal for public transport heading east and northeast, the home of famous Barong **dance troupes**, and respected across the island for its **stonecarvers**. There's also a **bird park** and a **reptile park** here. The town is strung out over 3km along the main road, bound by the bemo/bus station in the south and the huge **Barong statue** at the Singapadu/Celuk junction in the north.

Roadsides throughout Batubulan are crowded with ranks of **stone statues** in front of dozens of workshops and galleries. Most of these shops deal in a range of images and stone types. Some sell carvings imported from Java, and most also deal in cheaper, mass-produced artworks that are moulded (rather than carved) from lava-stone "concrete".

Pura Puseh

250m east off the main road, from a signed junction about 250m south of the Barong statue • No fixed opening times • Free

As you'd expect in a town so renowned for stonecarving, the main temple, **Pura Puseh**, is exuberantly decorated. Its unusual design features a five-tiered gateway tower inspired by Indian religious architecture, as well as a number of Buddha images not normally associated with Bali's Hindu temples. The rest of the iconography, however, is characteristically and flamboyantly Balinese: a grimacing Bhoma head overlooks the main gateway and, to his right, the god Wisnu poses astride a bull; to the right of him, Siwa stands ankle-deep in skulls and wears a string of them around his neck.

Bali Bird Park and Bali Reptile Park

Taman Burung, 5km northwest of Batubulan bemo terminal • Daily 9am–5.30pm • Joint ticket for both parks: adult Rp431,200; family packages available; book online for discounts • ☎ 0361 299352, ⊕ bali-bird-park.com • All bemos or buses between Batubulan and Ubud or Gianyar can drop you at the Singapadu/Celuk intersection from where it's about 400m west

Both the Bali Bird Park and the neighbouring Bali Reptile Park are great fun. Home to some thousand birds from 250 species, the **Bali Bird Park** is beautifully landscaped

---

CARVED IN STONE: FOR GODS, RAJAS AND TOURISTS

The traditional function of **stonecarved statues and reliefs** was to entice and entertain the gods and to ward off undesirable spirits and evil forces. The **temples** in south Bali generally do this in a restrained way, being built mainly from red brick with just a few flourishes of carved volcanic tuff or *paras* (though Batubulan's Pura Puseh is an exception), but the northern temples, which are often built entirely from the easy-to-carve *paras*, are a riot of vivacious curlicues. Outstanding northern examples include the Pura Dalem in Jagaraga, Pura Beji and the Pura Dalem in Sangsit and, most famously, Pura Meduwe Karang at Kubutambahan. In the east, Bangli's Pura Kehen is not to be missed.

Rajas and high-ranking nobles also commissioned fantastic carvings for their **palaces** (*puri*). Few outlasted the early twentieth-century battles with the Dutch, but one notable survivor is the Puri Saren Agung in Ubud, the work of Bali's most skilful stonecarver, **I Gusti Nyoman Lempad** (see box, p.115). These days, **hotels** are the modern *puri*, and many of the older, grander ones were built in the Bali-baroque *puri-pura* style, with plenty of exuberant stonecarved embellishments. **Gateways** normally feature the most elaborate carvings, in keeping with their function as both a practical and symbolic demarcation between the outer and the inner world, whether they're leading to the inner temple courtyard or giving access to palace compounds or hotels.

Sculptures of *raksasa* (Hindu demon-giants) often guard temple and hotel gates, and most other freestanding stonecarvings destined for homes and gardens in Bali and abroad still take their inspiration from traditional subjects, including Hindu deities and mythological characters and creatures. The vast majority are made in the workshops of **Batubulan**, which is the best place to buy small or large sculptures.

2

TRADITIONAL DANCE SHOWS IN BATUBULAN

The spectacular **Barong dance**, which sees the lion-like Barong Ket pitted against the widow-witch Rangda, is performed for tourists at various venues around Batubulan (daily 9.30–10.30am; Rp100,000; ⦿ sahadewabarongdance.com), including the stage next to Pura Puseh and the Denjulan Barong and Kris stage, 300m south down the main Denpasar road from the Pura Puseh junction. Both stages are served by Ubud–Batubulan bemos. Additionally, in the evenings, there's a double bill of the **Kecak** and the **Fire Dance** (daily 6.30–7.30pm; Rp100,000) at the Barong Sahadewa stage on Jalan SMKI, signed off the main road about 500m south of the Pura Puseh junction.

around enormous aviaries. Highlights include birds of paradise, bright scarlet egrets, the rhino hornbill and iridescent blue Javanese kingfishers. And you shouldn't miss the severely endangered Bali starling, the Owl House or the daily "free flight" bird shows.

The highlights at the **Bali Reptile Park** include the highly poisonous green tree pit viper, which is very common in Bali, an 8m-long reticulated python and a Komodo dragon.

Putrawan Museum of Art

2km from Batubulan • Mon–Sat 9am–5pm, Sun noon–5pm • $3 • ☎ 0361 463737, ⦿ museumpuma.com • Situated inside the Alam Puri Resort, about 3km north of Denpasar

East of the main road to Ubud, more than 4km by road, the **Putrawan Museum of Art**, also known as **PUMA**, is a remarkable – though largely ignored – collection of tribal sculpture from across Indonesia including works from Flores, Nias, Kalimantan and Sumba, supplemented by jewellery and other artefacts. The *ana deo*, ancestral figures from Flores, and *tau tau*, effigies of the dead from Sulawesi, are especially compelling. Given that tourist shops are awash with reproductions of these, this is a fabulous chance to see the real thing.

ARRIVAL AND DEPARTURE   BATUBULAN AND AROUND

By bus and bemo Batubulan's bus and bemo station runs services across Denpasar and to destinations around Ubud, as well as to east and north Bali. It's at the far southern end of town and has clearly signed bays for each destination, including Amlapura via Candidasa, Kintamani, Nusa Dua, Padang Bai, Singaraja (for Lovina) and Ubud. All services run every 30min or so; after about 2pm services are sporadic at best; travel as early in the day as possible. Note that for rucksacks and other bulky baggage there's usually an extra charge on bemos; sometimes Rp5000–10,000, sometimes double the fare.

Destinations Amlapura (2hr 30min); Bangli (2hr 30min); Candidasa (2hr); Celuk (10min); Gianyar (1hr); Kintamani (1hr 30min); Klungkung (1hr 30min); Mas (35min); Nusa Dua (1hr); Padang Bai (for Lombok; 1hr 45min); Peliatan (45min); Semarapura (1hr 20min); Singaraja (Penarukan terminal; 3hr 15min); Sukawati (20min); Tegalalang (1hr 15min); Ubud (50min).

East of Ubud

Slicing through the region immediately **east of Ubud**, the sacred rivers Petanu and Pakrisan flow down from the Batur crater rim in parallel, framing a narrow strip of land imbued with great spiritual and historical importance. This 15km-long sliver has been settled since the Balinese Bronze Age, around 300 BC, and now boasts the biggest concentration of antiquities on Bali. From the stone sarcophagi and Bronze Age gong of **Pejeng** to the eleventh-century rock-hewn hermitage at **Goa Gajah** and fourteenth-century **Yeh Pulu reliefs**, these relics all lie within 7km of Ubud; Goa Gajah is crowded, while Yeh Pulu is often deserted. Access to this area by bemo is easy from Ubud – take any Gianyar-bound service – and similarly straightforward by bike or motorbike. This area also combines well with Tirta Empul and Gunung Kawi, 11km further north, and direct bemos connect the two.

Goa Gajah

3km east from Ubud's Jl Peliatan • Daily 8am–5pm • Rp20,000, children Rp10,000, including sarong rental

Thought to have been a hermitage for eleventh-century Hindu priests, **Goa Gajah** (Elephant Cave) is a popular tourist attraction largely because of its proximity to the main Ubud–Gianyar road. Besides the cave itself, there's a traditional bathing pool here and several ancient stone relics.

Descending the steps from the back of the car park, you get a good view of the elegant rectangular **bathing pool**. Such pools were usually built at holy sites, either at the source of a holy spring as at Tirta Empul or, like this one, near a sacred spot, so devotees could cleanse themselves before making offerings or prayers. The pool is now maintained for ornamental purposes only.

The carvings that trumpet the entranceway to the hillside cave are impressive, if difficult to distinguish. The **doorway** is a gaping mouth, framed by the upper jaw of a monstrous rock-carved head that's thought to represent either the earth god Bhoma or the widow-witch Rangda, or a hybrid of the two. It would have served both as a repeller of evil spirits and as a suggestion that on entering you were being swallowed up into a holier world. Early visitors interpreted it as an elephant's head, which is how the cave got its modern name.

Passing into the monster's mouth, you enter the dimly lit T-shaped **cave**, which served as meditation cells or living quarters for the priests or ascetics. Legend describes how the mythical giant Kebo Iwa gouged out the cells and the carvings here with his powerful fingernails in just one night.

Outside the cave, in a small pavilion to the left of the gateway, is a weatherworn statue of a woman surrounded by a horde of kids. This is the folk heroine **Men Brayut**, who has come to epitomize a mother's struggle against poverty (see box, p.161). Men Brayut is known as the goddess Hariti in Buddhist literature, and this statue, along with several other relics found nearby, has led archeologists to believe the site has a **Buddhist** as well as a Hindu history.

ARRIVAL AND DEPARTURE   GOA GAJAH

By bemo An Ubud–Gianyar bemo will drop you at the entrance.

By car The car park borders the main Ubud–Gianyar road.

On foot You can walk between Yeh Pulu and Goa Gajah through the ricefields, but you'll need to hire a guide (see p.144).

Yeh Pulu and around

East of Goa Gajah • Daily 7am–6pm • Rp20,000, children Rp10,000, including sarong rental

The rock-cut panels amid the ricefields at **Yeh Pulu** are delightfully engaging, and yet the site is rarely visited. Chipped away from a cliff face, the 25m-long series of **carvings** are said to date back to the fourteenth or fifteenth century. They are thought by some historians to depict a five-part story and while the meaning of this story has been lost, it's still possible to make out some recurring characters and to speculate on the connections between them; local people, however, simply describe the carvings as showing daily activities from times past.

The small **spring** after which the site is named (*yeh* means "holy spring", *pulu* "stone vessel") rises close by the statue of Ganesh that is carved into the final niche and is sacred – hence the need for all visitors to wear temple dress. The Balinese believe that all water is a gift from the spirits, so whenever the spring fails special ceremonies are required to restore a harmonious flow.

Dukuh Kedongan

Guides can take you on the two-hour return ricefield walk from Yeh Pulu to the rice temple **Dukuh Kedongan**, with the chance of a dip in the Petanu River (around Rp250,000); or there are longer variations (3–5hr), which continue either to the village of Segana or to the Durga Kutri temple, Pura Bukit Dharma Durga Kutri, in the village of Kutri (see p.154) or a trek of similar length to the village of **Tengkulak** via the Campuhan River. All of these cost around Rp400,000.

ARRIVAL AND DEPARTURE	YEH PULU AND AROUND

By bemo If you're using the Ubud–Gianyar bemo, get off at the Yeh Pulu signs just east of Goa Gajah or west of the Bedulu crossroads, then walk the 1km south through the hamlet of Batulumbang to Yeh Pulu.

By car When driving, follow the same signs through Batulumbang until the road peters out, a few hundred

metres above the stonecarvings.

On foot The prettiest approach to Yeh Pulu is on foot through the rice terraces behind Goa Gajah, but you'll need a guide – they wait for customers at both sites and charge around Rp200,000.

Pejeng

Inhabited since the Bronze Age, and considered a holy site ever since, the village of **PEJENG** and its immediate environs harbour a wealth of religious antiquities, from carvings and rock-cut *candi* to bronze artefacts and massive stone statues. Some of these have been left in their original location, alongside riverbeds or buried in the paddy fields, while others have been housed in local temples. Several have also been carted off to museums, here and in Denpasar, Jakarta and Amsterdam. The remains have rather an esoteric appeal, and the area gets relatively few visitors. Pejeng's three main **temples** all lie within a few hundred metres of each other on the Bedulu–Tampaksiring road and are clearly signposted.

Pura Penataran Sasih

Bedulu–Tampaksiring Rd • No fixed opening times • Free, but donation required; sarongs and sashes can be borrowed

Balinese people believe **Pura Penataran Sasih** to be a particularly sacred temple, because this is the home of the so-called Moon of Pejeng – hence the English epithet **Moon Temple**.

The moon in question is a **large bronze gong**, shaped almost like an hourglass, suspended high in its tower at the back of the temple compound. It probably dates from the Balinese Bronze Age, from sometime during the third century BC, and – at almost 2m long – is thought to be the largest such kettledrum ever cast. Legend tells how the gong once served as the wheel of a chariot that transported the moon through the skies, at which time the wheel shone just as brightly as the moon itself. The Balinese treat the Moon of Pejeng as sacred and make offerings to it whenever they need to move it.

The **temple** itself was once the most important in the area, and whatever the origins of the gong, it would have been used for the same purposes as the modern *kulkul* (bell-like drum) – to summon the people of Pejeng to ceremonies, to announce war, and also to invite rain to fall.

Pura Pusering Jagat

100m south of Pura Penataran Sasih • No fixed opening times • Free, but donation required; sarongs and sashes can be borrowed

Pura Pusering Jagat, the "Temple of the Navel of the World", is famous for its elaborately carved 1m-high **stone jar**, used for storing holy water. Carved in the fourteenth century from a single block of sandstone, the jar's reliefs are thought to depict a scene from the Hindu myth "The Churning of the Sea of Milk", in which the gods and the demons compete for the chance to extract, distil and drink the elixir of immortal life.

Housed in a nearby pavilion is another significant icon, the 1m-high phallic lingam and its female receptacle, the yoni – this is an important shrine visited by many newlywed and infertile couples.

Pura Kebo Edan

200m south of Pura Pusering Jagat • No fixed opening times • Free, but donation required; sarongs and sashes can be borrowed

Along with Pura Pusering Jagat, **Pura Kebo Edan** is also considered lucky for childless couples. The attraction here is the massive, lifelike phallus of the huge stone man, nicknamed the **Pejeng Giant**, who is nearly 4m tall and is depicted dancing on a prone female figure thought to represent the earth. He is said to possess six penises in all; aside from the one swinging out for all to see. His principal penis is pierced from front to back with a huge bolt-like pin, probably a realistic reference to an age-old Southeast Asian practice designed to increase women's sexual pleasure. The giant's identity is debatable; he is possibly Bhima, one of the chief characters from the Mahabharata, or the Hindu god Siwa, who harnessed enormous cosmic power whenever he danced.

Museum Arkeologi Gedung Arca

500m south of Pura Penataran Sasih • Mon–Thurs, Sat & Sun 8am–3pm, Fri 8am–12.30pm • Free, but a donation to your guide is expected

Pejeng's government-run **Museum Arkeologi Gedung Arca** houses an eclectic assortment of artefacts found in the area, ranging from Paleolithic chopping tools to bronze bracelets and Chinese plates, though labels are limited.

The most interesting exhibits are the huge **sarcophagi**. These massive coffins, up to 3m long and fashioned from two fitted sections of hollowed-out stone, probably date back to about 300 BC. They were designed to hold adult skeletons (those placed in the smallest vessels would have been flexed at knees, hips and shoulders), and only the more important members of a community would have merited such an elaborate burial. Bronze jewellery, coins and weapons were found in some of the sarcophagi.

ARRIVAL AND DEPARTURE   **PEJENG**

By bemo Coming from Ubud, take a Gianyar-bound bemo to the Bedulu crossroads and then either wait for a Tampaksiring-bound bemo, or walk the 1km to the temples.
By bike The alternative route from Ubud – by bike or motorbike – is the fairly scenic but severely undulating 5km-long back road that heads east from the Jl Raya Ubud/

Jl Peliatan junction at the eastern edge of Ubud, passes the *Maya Ubud* hotel, and then zigzags through paddies and small villages before finally emerging at the market on the main road, just 25m north of Pura Penataran Sasih (turn right for the temple).

North of Ubud

All three major roads **north of Ubud** lead eventually to Gunung Batur and its huge crater (see p.192). Whether you go via **Payangan** to the west, **Tegalalang** directly to the north, or **Tampaksiring** to the east, the villages and paddy fields along each route make for a pleasant drive. Distances are comparable, about 40km to Batur whichever way you go, but the most significant tourist sights are located along the most easterly route, around the Tampaksiring area.

Although there's little of specific interest on the **westerly route**, which takes you via Campuhan and Payangan, this is the quietest, least congested and prettiest of the three, and the best if you have **private transport**. The villages on the way are picturesque and in Payangan you pass the village's famously huge roadside banyan tree. The road eventually brings you to Pura Ulun Danu Batur (see p.197) on the Batur–Kintamani road, about 5km west of Penelokan.

The **central route** up to Gunung Batur begins at the eastern edge of Ubud, from the point where Jalan Raya Ubud intersects with Jalan Peliatan (if you're heading up here on a bicycle, you might prefer the more peaceful route that starts on central Ubud's Jalan Suweta).

By bemo The most frequent and reliable bemo service running north from Ubud is on the central route via Tegalalang and Pujung; there are frequent bemos along the first section of the westerly route, as far as Payangan, but only some of them continue as far as Kintamani. For the easterly route via Tampaksiring, you'll need to change bemos at the Bedulu crossroads, just over 5km from the market in Ubud by road.

Tegalalang and Ceking

Seven kilometres north of Ubud, the village of **TEGALALANG** and its environs produce a wide range of **handicrafts** and **home accessories**, and the entire length of the 12km-long Ubud–Tegalalang–Pujung road is lined with shops displaying their wares and some attractive artefacts. On a clear morning the **views** become increasingly spectacular as you pass through Tegalalang, with Bali's greatest mountains looming majestically ahead – Gunung Batur to the north and Gunung Agung to the east – and rice terraces providing the classic foreground. Just north of Tegalalang is the village of **CEKING**, which also has well-stocked souvenir shops along with several restaurants that make the most of the vistas.

Sebatu

North of Ceking, 18km along the main road you'll reach the Gunung Batur crater rim. Alternatively, a right turn at *Dewi Café* takes you along the scenic back road – to the village of **SEBATU**, 6km beyond, site of the uncrowded **Pura Gunung Kawi Sebatu** water-temple complex.

Pura Gunung Kawi Sebatu

Sebatu • Daily 8am–5pm • Rp15,000, including sarong rental

Not to be confused with the quite different and more-visited Gunung Kawi in nearby Tampaksiring, **Pura Gunung Kawi Sebatu** is built on the site of holy springs, whose water is channelled into seven walled **bathing pools** – four for public bathing and three, at the spring itself, for special cleansing rituals. Many of the temple's wooden shrines and *bale* are carved with exquisite, brightly painted floral motifs.

Tampaksiring and around

The most **easterly route** from Ubud to the mountains takes you along the Bedulu–Penelokan road, passing through Pejeng before reaching **TAMPAKSIRING**, 11km further on, a fairly nondescript town that's the access point for nearby **Gunung Kawi** and **Tirta Empul**.

Gunung Kawi

An easy walk north of the market in Tampaksiring; access is signed via Jl Bayubrata, which heads east off the main road a few hundred metres north of the market • Daily 8am–5.30pm • Rp15,000, children Rp7500, plus donation for sarong rental

Hewn from the rocky walls of the lush, enclosed valley of the sacred Pakrisan River, the eleventh-century royal "tombs" at **Gunung Kawi** occupy a lovely spot and are a lot quieter than most other archeological sites, not least because you have to descend 315 steps to reach them.

The *candi* are huge reliefs, chiselled from the riverside cliff face to resemble temple facades. Originally the surface would have been decorated with plaster carvings, but now all that's left are the outlines of a single false door on each one. The most likely **theory** about these "tombs", is that they were erected as memorials to the eleventh-century king Anak Wungsu and his queens. The four Queens' Tombs are thought to be for Anak Wungsu's minor consorts, while the five Royal Tombs across the river probably honour the king and his four favourite wives. The slightly higher *candi* at the far left end is believed to be Anak Wungsu's. As there are no signs of bones or ashes in the *candi*, it appears that they weren't actual tombs, yet over the false door of each were found inscriptions (most of them unreadable) thought to be names or titles.

The complex also contains an extensive **cloister**, which probably accommodated the tombs' caretakers. On the way back to the steps you can branch off left through the fields to reach the so-called **Tenth Tomb**, a five-minute walk away. Believed to have been erected in memory of an important member of the royal household, this *candi* stands on its own, framed only by rock-cut cloisters.

Tirta Empul

Signposted off the main Tampaksiring–Kintamani road, about 500m north of the turn-off to Gunung Kawi • Daily 7am–6pm • Rp15,000, children Rp7500 • You should be able to charter a bemo in the market

Balinese from every corner of the island make pilgrimages to **Tirta Empul**. They come to spiritually cleanse themselves and cure their physical ailments by bathing in the **holy springs**. Legend describes how the springs were first tapped by the god Indra during his battle with the evil Mayadanawa. Indra's spring was named Tirta Empul, and has been considered the holiest in Bali ever since the tenth century, if not longer. A **temple** was built around the springs and the complex is now an extremely popular destination, both for Balinese and foreign tourists.

The **bathing pools** are sunk into the ground of the temple's outer courtyard, the water from the springs in the inner sanctuary. Men, women and priests have segregated sections in which to immerse themselves, though most just splash their faces. However, for pregnant women and anyone who's just recovered from a long illness, Tirta Empul is one of three places in which they must bathe for a special ritual called *melukat*. This ceremony requires immersion in the waters of each of Bali's three holiest springs: the "holy waters of the mountain" at Tirta Bungkah, the "holy springs of the plain" here at Tirta Empul and the "holy springs of the sea" at Tirta Selukat at Pura Dalem Pingit.

ARRIVAL AND DEPARTURE · TAMPAKSIRING AND AROUND

By bemo Gianyar–Bedulu–Tampaksiring bemos terminate near the market in the centre of the long settlement. There's

no public bemo service between Tampaksiring and Penelokan, about 20km north, but you should be able to charter one.

East Bali

TAMAN TIRTAGANGGA WATER PALACE

East Bali

The east of Bali is dominated both physically and spiritually by the majestic, picture-perfect volcanic cone of Gunung Agung. The Balinese orientate their villages and homes towards this "Great Mountain" and after a few days in the region you'll probably fall under its spell too. Immediately beneath its awesome bulk unfurls a landscape of dense forests, narrow river valleys and sweeping rice terraces, making for a scenic drive or hike, whichever direction you travel in. By contrast, the land in the far east around the coastal centres of Amed and Tulamben is much drier, and their dark-sand beaches are drawing ever-increasing numbers of visitors.

3

Most of east Bali comes under the administrative district of **Karangasem**, where villagers still follow a traditional way of life, mostly living off the land or from the sea. There are tourist centres, but on a far smaller scale than in the south, and the lack of crowds and refreshingly unadulterated green vistas are a large part of the east's appeal. With Bali being relatively small, you can base yourself in this part of the island without missing any of the highlights.

The main tourist hubs are along the coast. **Candidasa** is a low-key resort with good facilities and handy transport connections. Nearby, funky little **Padang Bai** is a port for boats to the Gili Islands and Lombok, and also makes a decent base in its own right. The biggest-hitting **dive centres**, though, are in the northeast, at **Amed**, which has lots of accommodation and plenty of reef close to shore, and nearby **Tulamben**, site of a famous shoreside wreck.

Inland, **Gunung Agung** and its Mother Temple, **Besakih**, are major attractions. Climbing this most magnificent of volcanoes is a significant challenge, but a rewarding one. The temple, however, can disappoint, as much for its persistent touts as for its sometimes misty outlook.

You might find some of the region's other temples more satisfying, especially the venerable Pura Kehen in **Bangli**, with its splendid sculptures. The east also has a rich artistic heritage associated with its ancient courts: **Semarapura** and the nearby painters' village of **Kamasan** keep the traditional art of classical *wayang* painting alive, while there's a chance to enjoy palace architecture at the Puri Agung in **Amlapura**. The district capital of **Gianyar** is justly famous for its beautiful *endek* weaving, and there's even more exquisite textile art, in the form of the rare double *ikat*, produced at **Tenganan**, a traditional Bali Aga village that's home to descendants of the early inhabitants of Bali.

For classic rice-terrace vistas and village walks, it's hard to beat a stay in **Tirtagangga** or **Sidemen**, both offering attractive accommodation in tranquil settings.

RICEFIELDS WITH GUNUNG AGUNG IN THE DISTANCE

Highlights

❶ Nyoman Gunarsa Museum An exquisite (if dusty) collection of historic cloth paintings from Kamasan, and two floors of ethnographical exhibits. **See p.161**

❷ Gunung Agung Bali's highest and most important mountain looms majestically over every district of the east – everyone can enjoy the sight, and if you're seriously fit you can climb it. **See p.162**

❸ Sidemen There's great accommodation and classic rice-terrace scenery in this small upland village. It's also well placed for temple visits, rafting and hiking. **See p.166**

❹ Padang Bai. A small port town that's become a lively backpacker hub, it's fringed by pretty cove beaches. **p.168**

❺ Tirtagangga Enjoy glorious mountain and rice-paddy views, an attractive water palace and gentle treks through typical Balinese countryside. **See p.180**

❻ The Amed coast A dramatic coastline with steep cliffs, black-sand beaches, small bays packed with fishing boats, views of two volcanoes, and prime diving and snorkelling just offshore. **See p.183**

HIGHLIGHTS ARE MARKED ON THE MAP ON PP.152–153

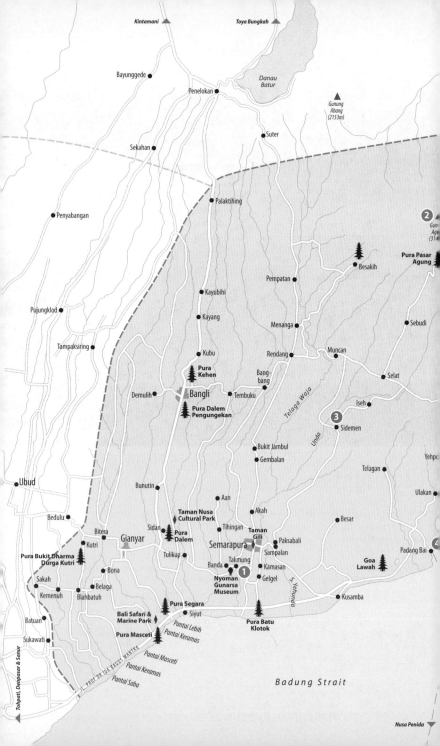

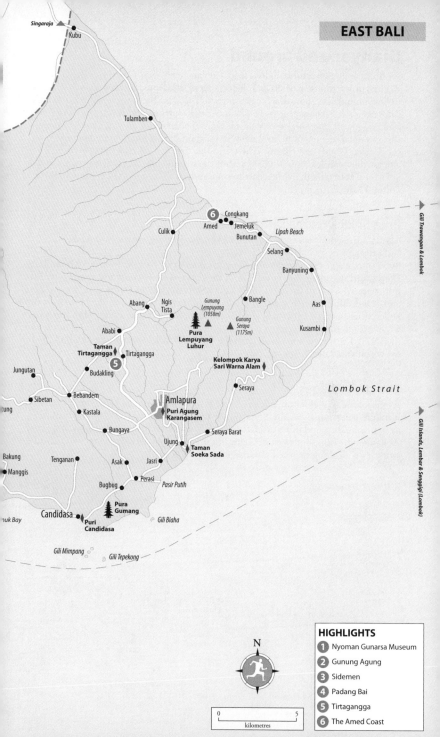

EAST BALI

HIGHLIGHTS

1 Nyoman Gunarsa Museum

2 Gunung Agung

3 Sidemen

4 Padang Bai

5 Tirtagangga

6 The Amed Coast

N

0 — 5
kilometres

Singaraja
Kubu
Tulamben
Congkang
Amed
Jemeluk
Lipah Beach
Culik
Bunutan
Selang
Banyuning
Aas
Abang
Ngis Tista
Gunung Lempuyang (1058m)
Bangle
Gunung Seraya (1175m)
Kusambi
Ababi
Pura Lempuyang Luhur
Taman Tirtagangga
Tirtagangga
Kelompok Karya Sari Warna Alam
Jungutan
Budakling
Seraya
Lombok Strait
Sibetan
Bebandem
Kastala
Amlapura
Puri Agung Karangasem
Bungaya
Seraya Barat
Ujung
Taman Soeka Sada
Bakung
Tenganan
Asak
Jasri
Manggis
Perasi
Pasir Putih
Bugbug
Pura Gumang
Candidasa
Puri Candidasa
Gili Biaha
nuk Bay
Gili Mimpang
Gili Tepekong

Gili Trawangan & Lombok

Gili Islands, Lembar & Senggigi (Lombok)

Gianyar and around

An immensely powerful kingdom from the late seventeenth century, Gianyar became a **Dutch protectorate** in 1900 and, being spared the depredations wreaked on other Balinese kingdoms, flourished as a centre for the arts. The district capital, also called **GIANYAR**, is still known for its handsome *endek* weaving, and for its delicious roasted suckling pig (*babi guling*) served at the night market, both of which merit a detour. But the town sees few tourists, being far outshone by its much more famous subdistrict, Ubud, just 10km to the west. There are several **craft villages** and worthwhile **temples** around Gianyar, but the region's biggest attractions are the **Bali Safari and Marine Park** by the coast to the south of town and the new **Taman Nusa Cultural Park** to the north.

Pura Bukit Dharma Durga Kutri

Daily 8am–6pm • Donation • Coming from Gianyar, the easiest way to get here is on a bemo bound for Denpasar's Batubulan terminal

Kutri, 4km west of Gianyar, is the site of an interesting temple, **Pura Bukit Dharma Durga Kutri**. Head up the staircase from the temple's inner courtyard to the top of the hill, where you'll find the statue of the many-armed goddess **Durga** slaughtering a bull and brandishing a conch shell, flames, bow and arrow, javelin and shield. Many people believe that the carving actually depicts **Mahendradatta**, the alter ego of the legendary widow-witch Rangda (see box, p.157), and that this is her burial place. An unusual way of visiting Kutri is to walk there from the Yeh Pulu rock carvings east of Ubud (3–5hr), for which you'll need a guide.

The craft villages

At the village of **Blahbatuh**, 5km south of Kutri, the main road is lined with **bamboo-furniture** workshops. Nearby, **Bona** and **Belaga** villages also make bamboo furniture, as well as **baskets** and other artefacts woven from rattan, palm and alang-alang grass. At **Kemenuh**, 7km southwest of Gianyar, the speciality is **woodcarving**, and there are workshops all along the road to Goa Gajah, 5km north.

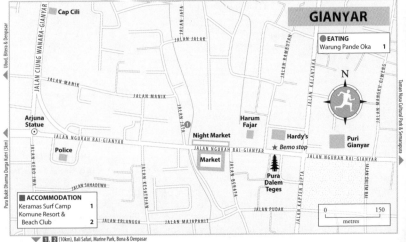

TRADITIONAL TEXTILES

Traditional **fabrics** are still fashionable for clothes and furnishings in Indonesia and continue to be hand-woven in some areas of Bali and Lombok. They also have **ritual functions**, with specific weaves used in certain ceremonies, such as the striped *bebali* produced in Pacung (see p.216). Hand-woven textiles are widely available for sale across Bali and Lombok and are often displayed to their best advantage on the special **carved wooden hangers** sold in some *ikat* and souvenir shops.

IKAT AND SONGKET

Easily recognized by the fuzzy-edged motifs it produces, **ikat** weaving is common throughout Indonesia, woven on backstrap, foot-pedal or, increasingly, on semi-automatic looms, from either silk, cotton or rayon. The word *ikat* derives from the Indonesian verb "to tie", and the technique is essentially a sophisticated tie-dye process. Bali is quite unusual in favouring **weft-ikat**, or **endek**, in which the weft yarn (the threads running across the fabric) is tie-dyed into the finished design before the warp begins. This produces the distinctive blurred edge to the predominantly geometric and abstract designs. **Gianyar** has several excellent *endek* showrooms and workshops (see box, p.156), and there's a highly regarded producer in **Sidemen** (see p.166); on Lombok, the weavers of **Sukarara** (see p.275) are the ones to seek out.

Warp-ikat (in which the threads that run lengthwise are tie-dyed) is more common elsewhere in Indonesia, including on Sumba and Flores, where the textiles typically feature bold humanoid motifs and images of real and mythological creatures. They are widely sold in Bali's resorts.

Warp- and weft-*ikat* are complicated enough, but **double ikat**, or **geringsing**, involves dyeing both the warp and the weft threads into their final designs before they're woven together; a double-*ikat* sarong can take five years to complete. There are just three areas in the world where this method is practised – India, Japan and **Tenganan** in eastern Bali. Not surprisingly, *geringsing* is exceedingly expensive to buy, and has acquired an important ritual significance. At first glance, *geringsing* can look similar to the warp-*ikat* of Flores, because both use the same dye combinations, but the Tenganan motifs have a highly charged spiritual meaning, and their geometric and floral designs are instantly recognizable to the people of Bali.

The art of embroidered *ikat*, or supplementary-weft weaving, is known as **songket**. This uses metallic gold and silver yarn to add tapestry-like motifs of birds, butterflies and flowers onto very fine silk (or, increasingly, rayon or artificial silk). *Songket* sarongs are worn on ceremonial occasions, and dancers wear *songket* sashes. **Sukarara** in Lombok is the best place to see *songket* being woven.

BATIK AND PERADA

Despite being more common than *ikat* for everyday and formal wear on Bali and Lombok, nearly all **batik** fabric is imported from Java. The batik process involves drawing patterns on the fabric in dye-resistant wax, then dyeing and re-waxing as necessary to create complex multicoloured designs that look the same on both sides. Screen-printed batik is generally inferior as the dyes don't penetrate to the reverse side.

A special type of batik called **perada** is used for ceremonial outfits and ornaments. This is the gold-painted cloth that you'll see fashioned into temple umbrellas, adorning some sacred statues, and worn in the Legong and other traditional dances. The background colour is nearly always bright green or yellow, sometimes purple, and onto this is painted or stamped a symbolic design (usually birds or flowers) in either gold-leaf paint or, more commonly today, a bronze- or gold-coloured pigment.

Pura Dalem

Sidan • Daily 8am–6pm; opened on request • Rp50,000 • The temple is 2km east of Gianyar then 1km north up the main Gianyar–Bangli road and served by bemos between the two towns

The widow-witch Rangda makes an especially gruesome appearance at the **Pura Dalem** in **Sidan**. This temple of the dead, dating from the seventeenth century, drips with grisly carvings and statues of the terrible Rangda squashing babies, along with depictions of

> ### GIANYAR'S TEXTILE WORKSHOPS
> The outstanding choice and quality of the hand-woven cotton and silk **endek** (tie-dyed weft *ikat*) produced in the **textile workshops** on the western outskirts of Gianyar town itself are well worth the trip. Prices range from around Rp170,000 to over Rp300,000 per metre, and you'll need about 2.25m for a sarong. You can also buy *endek* shirts, handbags, cushion covers and more. The best-known **showroom** is Setia Cap Cili (Jl Ciung Wanara 7; daily 9am–5pm; ☎0361 943409), which has a dyeing and weaving workshop on site; over twenty weavers are employed here.

the punishments that await evildoers in the afterlife – which include having your head sawn off and being boiled in a vat. As the entry fee is quite high, you may want to admire the external carvings, which are also impressive.

Taman Nusa Cultural Park

Jl Taman Bali, Banjarangka • Daily 9am–5pm • Adult/child $39/29, lunch $10 extra • ☎0361 952952, ⓦ taman-nusa.com • Located along a minor road leading to Bangli, Taman Nusa is signposted off the Gianyar-Semarapura road

The **Taman Nusa Cultural Park** is an impressive open-air museum with more than sixty traditional houses from across the nation and iconic Indonesian buildings overlooking a picturesque gorge. Most buildings are reconstructions including the pointed-roofed Sumba houses, while originals include the Minangkabau homes and the Nias house with its earthquake-proof beams. Don't miss the Honai, beehive-like huts of the Dani tribe of Papua, or the Dayak house with its elaborate carvings. You'll also see models of the Dutch-era Kota train station in Jakarta and the Buddhist temple of Borobudur. Tours by enthusiastic guides are included in the price, and there are music and dance shows, plus a couple of museums displaying crafts. You'll find two restaurants and seven cafés on site and there are golf carts for those that have mobility issues.

Bali Safari and Marine Park

1.5km east of Pura Masceti, 7km southeast of Gianyar and 15km east of Sanur, just off the coastal highway, Jl Bypass Prof Dr Ida Bagus Mantra • Daily 9am–5pm • From $74 including shuttle bus from Kuta/Sanur • ☎0361 751300, ⓦ balisafarimarinepark.com

The landscaped grounds of **Bali Safari and Marine Park** draw several thousand visitors a day who come to see animals from Indonesia, India and Africa (white tigers, Komodo dragons, hippos and Sumatra tigers among them). There's also an aquarium, a water park, the "Bali Agung" theatrical extravaganza, animal rides and shows. If you can deal with animals being treated as photo opportunities, it's worthwhile spending an entire day here. Note the marine park was still under construction at the time of research.

"Safari" buses take you around the park, passing the animal enclosures. There's a (somewhat dated) water park here too where you can cool off and take in a slide or two. It's an expensive day out, so check the various packages available (the buffet lunch offered is poor); some of these include a short elephant ride.

The coast south of Gianyar

The **coast south of Gianyar** is fringed with long, black-sand beaches and offers some fine views of Gunung Agung. It's mainly surfing territory here, and with a new four-lane coastal highway offering speedy connections to Sanur and the south, the region is developing fast.

Pantai Keramas

This slim dark-sand beach, 18km northeast of Sanur or 10km south of Gianyar, is one of the best surf spots on this shoreline, with a consistent right-hander that peels over a reef, creating some of the best tubes in Bali. For years Keramas was something of an

RANGDA, QUEEN OF THE WITCHES

Sporting a mane of unkempt hair, tusk-like teeth, a tongue that hangs to her knees and enormous, pendulous breasts, **Rangda**, Queen of the Witches, is a terrifying spectacle wherever you encounter her. And she is everywhere: on stage in religious dance-dramas, as a larger-than-life statue at temples, in paintings and on textiles. To the Balinese, she represents evil, death and destruction.

It's possible that Rangda is based on a real woman, **Mahendradatta**, a Javanese princess who married the Balinese prince Udayana and bore him a son, Erlangga, in 991 AD. According to legend, Udayana later banished Mahendradatta for practising witchcraft. When Udayana died, Mahendradatta, now a *rangda* (widow), used her powers to call a plague upon her son's kingdom. Erlangga duly dispatched a troop of soldiers to kill her, but they failed, despite stabbing her in the heart. In desperation, Erlangga asked for assistance from the holy man Empu Bharadah, who used Rangda's book of magic both to restore her victims to life and to destroy the witch by turning her own magic on herself. Both Mahendradatta and Empu Bharadah are thought to be associated with Bali's Mother Temple, Besakih (see p.164).

The Rangda story is widely enacted across Bali, most commonly during the **Barong** and **Calonarang** dramas (see p.320). She always speaks in the ancient Kawi language, spiced with plenty of grunts and cackles. Even in performances the figure of Rangda is believed to have remarkable powers, and prayers precede each show to protect the actors from the evil forces they are invoking.

in-the-know secret, but better road access and the arrival of the **Komune Bali resort** (see p.158), with its spotlights to enable night surfing, has put Keramas on the map. Note that a restaurant in the village here keeps captive dolphins in a swimming pool, a practice that has been condemned by environmentalists.

Pura Masceti

Jl Prof Dr Ida Bagus Mantra, Medahan, by the beach about 9km south of Gianyar, 20km northeast of Sanur • Daily 7am–6pm • Rp10,000

One of several important **temples** along the coast south of Gianyar, the ornate **Pura Masceti** is the directional temple, or *kayangan jagat* (see p.314), for the south. The setting on the coast is lovely, and regular festivals see dozens of worshippers setting off for purification rituals on the beach.

Pantai Lebih

2km northeast of Pura Masceti

Black-sand **Pantai Lebih** is crowded with fishing boats and famous for its dozen or so very popular warung serving **fresh seafood** (most are open daily until 10pm). Menu highlights include the local speciality *sate languan* (fish grilled with green coconut, spices and brown sugar), *ikan bakar* (charcoal-grilled fish in banana leaf) and *ikan pepes* (fish steamed in banana leaves); the warung are great value, with set meals from Rp20,000.

Pura Segara

Daily 8am–6pm

Across the highway from the sea, Lebih's **Pura Segara** (Sea Temple) is associated with magical forces, and holds an annual ceremony to placate the demon I Macaling, who is believed to bring disease and ill fortune from Nusa Penida across the Badung Strait (see p.98).

Pura Batu Klotok

7km east of Pantai Lebih • Daily 7am–6pm • Free

On the beach at Pantai Batu Klotok, **Pura Batu Klotok** is one of four highly revered state temples in Klungkung district. The sacred statues from the Mother Temple, Besakih, are brought here during the annual cleansing ritual of *malasti*. The temple boasts a tremendous outlook over a black-sand beach towards Lombok and is a fine location to witness sunrise.

By bemo Gianyar town has useful bemo services to and from Ubud and Denpasar's Batubulan terminal, both of which terminate near *Warung Pande Oka* restaurant, on the corner of Jl Ngurah Rai and Jl Jata. Most of the other services, including those to Candidasa and Batur, pick up

and drop off outside Hardy's on Jl Ngurah Rai.
Destinations Amlapura (1hr 20min); Bangli (20min); Batur (40min); Blahbatuh (30min); Candidasa (1hr); Denpasar (Batubulan terminal; 1hr); Semarapura (20min); Ubud (20min).

ACCOMMODATION AND EATING

Gianyar Market Jl Ngurah Rai, Gianyar town. The main daily market in a large building along Jl Ngurah Rai is best before noon. Daily 7am–4pm.
Keramas Surf Camp Pantai Keramas ☏0819 9908 7070, ⊛keramassurfcamp.com. Steps from the beach, bordering ricefields, this popular surfers' hangout is run by a friendly family and has attractive a/c bungalows with outdoor bathrooms, a beer garden and restaurant. Rp375,000
Komune Resort & Beach Club Pantai Keramas ☏0361 3018888, ⊛komuneresorts.com. Sleek, chic surf lodge with an oceanfront location, yoga sessions,

spa, a cool pool, healthy-eating cafe and lights to enable night surfing (book ahead). Accommodation is very stylish and offers all mod cons. Rooms $98, suites $139, villas $245
Warung Pande Oka Jl Jata, Gianyar town ☏0361 943351. Famous for its *babi guling*: roasted suckling pig stuffed with chillies, rice and spices, served with *lawar* (chopped meat, vegetables and coconut mixed with pig's blood); expect to pay about Rp27,000. They serve from early morning until they sell out; get there by noon to be sure of a feast, or try the night market after 4pm. Daily 8am–10pm.

Bangli and around

Situated between Gianyar and the volcanoes of Batur, the district capital of **BANGLI**, one of Bali's nine kingdoms until 1907, is a cool and spacious market town whose extravagantly carved **temples** are well worth making the effort to visit. In the pleasant town centre, meanwhile, you can shop and eat at the **market**, which mainly sells agricultural produce and crafts from the surrounding villages, or try regional snacks at the small but lively night market with several food stalls just south of the Trimurti statue. During the day, the market south of the Trimurti statue is also worth browsing for street food.

Pura Kehen

Jl Sriwijaya, 1.5km north of the centre • Daily 8am–6pm • Rp3500

Bangli's most famous sight is the ancient **Pura Kehen**, a gem among Bali's temples that is thought to have been founded in 1206. Rising in **terraces**, its mossy stairway is lined with statues of human and mythical creatures, led by a pair of elephants at the base, and crowned by a leering Bhoma above regal red-and-gold carved doors. In the **outer courtyard** a massive banyan tree hides a *kulkul* tower among its branches, and a small compound, guarded by *naga* under an old frangipani tree, houses a stone that reportedly glowed with fire when the site of the temple was decided. The **inner courtyard** contains an eleven-roofed *meru* dedicated to Siwa, and other shrines dedicated to mountain gods.

Across the road, the lavishly restored **Pura Penyimpenan** (Temple for Keeping Things) contains three ancient bronze inscriptions (*prasasti*) dating from the ninth century, which suggests Pura Kehen could be much older than some believe.

Pura Dalem Pengungekan

Jl Merdeka, 1.5km south of the centre • Daily 8am–6pm • Donation

From Pura Kehen it's a pleasant walk downhill to the temple of the dead, **Pura Dalem Pengungekan**, at the opposite end of town, where exuberant carvings cover the outside walls. Depicting the fate of souls in hell and heaven as witnessed by Bhima, one of the Pandawa brothers (see box, p.321), the carvings depict a riot of knives, pleading victims, flames and decapitated bodies. There are also appearances by the widow-witch Rangda and stories of Siwa, Ganesh, Uma and Rakshasha.

3

ARRIVAL AND INFORMATION

BANGLI AND AROUND

By bemo Bangli is served by bemos from Gianyar and is also on the Denpasar (Batubulan) to Singaraja (Penarukan) route.
Destinations Denpasar (1hr 30min); Gianyar (20min);

Singaraja (2hr 15min).
Banks and exchange There are ATMs near the Trimurti statue on Jl Nusantara.

Semarapura and around

Famous as a centre of classical Balinese art, Klungkung's district capital, **SEMARAPURA** (also frequently referred to as **KLUNGKUNG**), makes an enjoyable day out. The highlight is the rare painted ceiling of the **Kerta Gosa** pavilion inside the **Taman Gili** palace gardens. It overlooks the main crossroads marked by the Kanda Pat Sari statue, guarding the four cardinal directions. The lively **market** opposite is also a fun browse and there's more classical art on the outskirts: in the village of **Kamasan**, home to modern-day artists working in the *wayang* style, and at the **Nyoman Gunarsa Museum**, which houses Bali's best collection of historic Kamasan art.

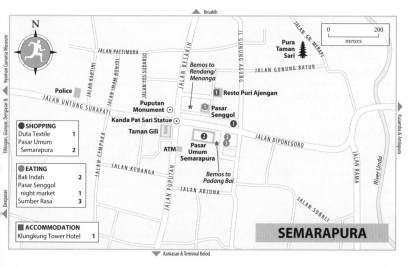

Brief history

Semarapura became a centre of the arts towards the end of the seventeenth century, when Bali's Majapahit rulers relocated here from their **court** at Gelgel, 4km to the south (Gelgel was believed to have fallen under a curse). The political power of the Majapahits was by then on the wane, with breakaway kingdoms such as Gianyar rising to prominence, but their sophisticated artistic and literary culture endured, its greatest legacy being the classical paintings that adorn the Kerta Gosa in Semarapura's palace grounds. The court remained at Semarapura until the early twentieth century and was one of the last two strongholds against the Dutch invasion. Rather than submit to the colonial power, on April 28, 1908, Semarapura's *dewa agung* (king) led two hundred members of his family and court in the traditional **puputan** (ritual suicide), marching into the line of fire. A monument opposite the Taman Gili commemorates this.

Taman Gili

Jl Untung Surapati • Daily 8am–6pm • Rp12,000

Built around 1710, and largely destroyed by the fighting in 1908, **Taman Gili**, or "Island Gardens", is all that remains of the original **Semarapura palace**. It's an attractive complex of lily ponds, pavilions and graceful statues, and its indisputable highlight is the superb painted ceiling of the **Kerta Gosa**. This is Bali's only example of *wayang*-style classical art still in situ and was painted by artists from nearby Kamasan (see box, pp.122–123), probably in the early nineteenth century. Despite its historical importance, the pavilion is open to the elements and located next to the city's busiest junction so the pictures are not in prime condition, though they have undergone several major restorations over the years.

The **Museum Daerah Semarapura** at the back of the Taman Gili grounds contains a motley collection including *kris* (daggers), textiles and Barong costumes.

Kerta Gosa

The **Kerta Gosa** is sometimes described as a criminal court, which adds poignancy to the pictures of gruesome punishments on the ceiling, but it's more likely to have been a debating chamber. It has nine levels of paintings. **Level one**, nearest the floor, shows scenes from an Indonesian version of the *Thousand and One Nights*, in which a girl, Tantri, weaves tales night after night. **Levels two and three** illustrate the "Bhima Swarga" story (part of the Mahabharata epic), and the punishments meted out to souls in the afterlife, such as having your intestines extracted through your anus for farting in public. Bhima is the aristocratic-looking chap with moustache, tidy hair, a big club and a long nail on his right thumb. **Level four** shows the "Sang Garuda", the story of the Garuda's search for *amerta*, the water of life. **Level five** is the *palalindon*, predicting the effects of earthquakes on life and agriculture, while **levels six and seven** continue the "Bhima Swarga" story. **Level eight** is the "Swarga Roh", which details the rewards the godly will receive in heaven; unfortunately, it's so far above your head that it's hard to see whether good behaviour is worth it. **Level nine**, the *lokapala*, right at the top, shows a lotus surrounded by four doves symbolizing good luck, enlightenment and salvation.

Bale Kambung

Near the Kerta Gosa, the **Bale Kambung** (Floating Pavilion), in the middle of the lotus pond, was the venue for royal tooth-filing ceremonies (see p.331). Its ceiling is slightly less finely drawn; six levels of paintings cover Balinese astrology, the tales of Pan Brayut (see box opposite) and, closest to the top, the adventures of Satusoma, a Buddhist saint.

Kamasan

As the home of the original nineteenth-century Kerta Gosa artists, and the source of subsequent generations of restorers and commercial artists, the suburb of **KAMASAN**,

THE TALE OF MEN AND PAN BRAYUT

Blessed – or lumbered – with eighteen children, **Men and Pan Brayut** ("Mother and Father Brayut") may be desperately poor, but their scrapes are typical of any Balinese family. So goes the popular Balinese folk tale that has inspired countless artists, including the mural painters of Semarapura's Bale Kambang hall, the Ubud artist I Gusti Nyoman Lempad (see box, p.115) and the stonecarvers of Pura Dalem Jagaraga, near Singaraja (see p.214). The fullest account of the couple's story is related in an **epic poem** called *Gaguritan Brayut*, housed in Singaraja's Gedong Kirtya library (see p.213).

According to one version of the **story**, the reason that Men Brayut has so many children is her uncontrollable appetite. When hungry, she gets irritable and rows with her husband, Pan Brayut. After fighting, the couple always make up in the time-honoured fashion – hence the constantly expanding clan. Another version puts the size of the family down to Pan Brayut's insatiable desire for his wife, which he acts upon regardless of place or circumstance.

Men Brayut is both full-time mother and part-time weaver, so her husband does most of the domestic chores; these scenes from daily life – cleaning the yard, cooking ceremonial dishes – feature in many paintings. Eventually, after all their hard parenting, Men and Pan Brayut **renounce the material world** and enter a retreat (still common practice, especially among elderly Balinese men), leaving their home and its contents to be divided among the children.

Although illustrations of the Brayut story always emphasize its **Hindu** elements, with lots of scenes showing offerings and temple ceremonies, Men Brayut is also associated with **Buddhist** lore. In this mythology she is said to have evolved from an evil ogress named Hariti who spent her time devouring children until she converted to Buddhism and became not only a protector of children but also a fertility goddess. Statues of Men Brayut in her Hariti manifestation can be found at Goa Gajah, near Ubud, and at the temple in Candidasa.

on the fringes of Semarapura, has given its name to the classical school of art with which it is so closely associated. Numerous artists have open studios in their homes here, particularly in the neighbourhood of **Banjar Sanging** (which is a kilometre southeast of Semarapura's Kelod bemo terminal). Among the most famous local names here are **I Nyoman Mandra** and **Ni Made Suciarmi**. Most of the work on sale is either inexpensive small cloth pictures or reproductions of traditional calendars, depicting mythological stories in muted classical colours.

Nyoman Gunarsa Museum

5km west of Semarapura, just beyond the village of Takmung on the Gianyar road • Mon–Sat 9am–4pm • Rp50,000 • Any Amlapura–Gianyar bemo will drop you outside

Try not to be discouraged by the dilapidated carbuncle of a building or the lack of air conditioning: the **Nyoman Gunarsa Museum** is well worth a lengthy browse. The big attraction is the large and rather special collection of Kamasan **cloth paintings**, some of which probably date back to the eighteenth century. Highlights include several 10m-long *ider ider* – ceremonial banners depicting mythological tales. Labels are informative and the art is supplemented by antique doors, carved gamelan ornaments and examples of *wayang kulit* puppets that echo the origins of the classical style. There are several paintings by the museum founder, **Nyoman Gunarsa**, one of Bali's foremost modern artists.

ARRIVAL AND INFORMATION

By bemo Semarapura is served by bemos from Padang Bai, Gianyar and Denpasar. Some Padang Bai bemos conveniently terminate on (and pick up from) Jl Nakula, just outside the market, but the main bus and bemo terminal, Terminal Kelod (also known as Terminal Galiron), is about 1km south of the town centre. If you're heading up to Besakih via Semarapura, you can pick up a bemo going

SEMARAPURA AND AROUND

to Rendang or Menanga on Jl Gunung Rinjani just north of the main crossroads in the centre of town.

Destinations Denpasar (1hr 30min); Gianyar (20min); Menanga (for Besakih; 45min); Padang Bai (30min); Rendang (30min); Sidemen (30min).

Banks and exchange There are ATMs east of the market building on Jl Nakula.

ACCOMMODATION AND EATING

All of the listings below are in central Semarapura.

Bali Indah Jl Nakula 1 ☎ 0366 21056. Mr Wong's family has been serving tasty Chinese food in this traditional shopfront restaurant since 1943. His specialities are the delicious *ko lo bak* sweet-sour pork for Rp30,000 as well as good chicken, beef and vegetarian dishes. Daily 8am–8.30pm.

Klungkung Tower Hotel Jl Gunung Rinjani 18 ☎ 0366 25637, ⊛ ktowerhotel.awardspace.com. Attractive a/c rooms with hot-water bathrooms and street-view verandas. There's a decent in-house restaurant and games room with pool table. Rp300,000

Pasar Senggol night market Jl Gunung Rinjani. The hot-food stalls of the lively night market occupy the western end of Jl Gunung Rinjani after dark. Daily 5–10pm.

Sumber Rasa Jl Nakula 5 ☎ 0366 25097. Canteen-like Chinese place opposite the market building with good *ko lo kee* sweet-sour chicken (Rp27,000). Daily 7am–7pm.

SHOPPING

Duta Textile Jl Diponegoro 71 ☎ 085 338566. Stocks exceptional textiles including silk and cotton sarongs, and shimmering *kebaya* material; staff are helpful and patient. Daily 8am–6pm.

Pasar Umum Semarapura Semarapura's important market, Pasar Umum Semarapura, is well worth a browse and best in the morning. It's essentially a non-touristy affair and at its largest and busiest every three days, but even on normal days it's a fun place to shop. Look out for fine *songket* fabric, as well as the usual sarongs and fruit and vegetables. Daily dawn–around 1pm.

Gunung Agung

Visible throughout eastern Bali and even from Nusa Lembongan and west Lombok across the sea, the classic volcanic cone of **Gunung Agung** is a majestic presence from any angle. It is the spiritual centre of the island: Balinese people believe the spirits of their ancestors dwell here, and several important temples, including **Besakih**, the Mother Temple, and **Pura Pasar Agung**, are sited on its slopes. Villages and house compounds are oriented towards the mountain, and many people sleep with their heads towards it. At 3031m, Gunung Agung is also Bali's highest peak and the focus of challenging **climbs** to its summit.

Two main **routes** lead up Gunung Agung; both are long and hard. One starts from Besakih and the other from further east, at the mountain's other main temple, Pura Pasar Agung. Whichever route you take, you'll need to set out in the middle of the night to be at the top for the **sunrise** (6–7am); clouds often obscure the view by late morning. A less-used route, from **Dukuh Bujangga Sakti**, inland from Kubu on the northeast coast, is offered by Mudi (see p.174). Starting out at an altitude of 300m, the climb is greater but not as steep as the other routes. You begin in the afternoon, camp on the mountain at 1750m and complete the three hours to the summit before dawn. The north of Bali is drier so is less often shrouded in cloud. You can walk round the rim to the absolute summit if you climb from this side and can see the sunrise on the horizon all year round.

The Pura Pasar Agung route

From **Pura Pasar Agung**, at an altitude of 1600m, it's at least a three-hour climb with an ascent of almost 2000m, so you'll need to set out by 3am from the temple, depending on how fit you are. The track initially passes through forest, ascending onto bare, steep rock. It doesn't go to the actual summit, but ends at a point on the rim that is about 100m lower. From here, the summit masks views of part of the island and, between April and September, the sunrise on the horizon, but you'll be able to see Lombok's Gunung Rinjani, the south of Bali and Gunung Batukaru, and look down into the 500m crater.

The Besakih route

From **Besakih** (950m), the climb is longer (5–7hr) and much more challenging; you'll need to leave between 10pm and midnight. This path leads to the **summit** of Agung, with breathtaking views in all directions, if skies are clear, including both Rinjani in Lombok to the east and Gunung Raung in Java to the west.

The initial climb is through forest, but the path gets very steep, very quickly, even before it gets out onto the bare rock, and you'll soon need your hands to haul yourself upwards. The descent is particularly taxing from this side and feels very precarious when you're already exhausted; allow at least five hours to get down.

INFORMATION   **GUNUNG AGUNG**

Consult the useful volcano trekking website ⊕ www.gunungbagging.com/agung for detailed information and tips before you attempt this climb. You'll need a **guide**, strong footwear, warm clothes for the summit, a good torch (ideally a headlamp) and water and snacks; for the descent, a stick is handy. Expect muddy conditions at the start of the trek and slippery rocks high up. Climbing is not permitted at **certain times of the year** because of religious ceremonies at Besakih or Pura Pasar Agung. The **dry season** (April to mid-Oct) is the best time to climb (particularly in July and Aug); at other times, especially between Dec and March, wind and rain can render the ascent too dangerous or may mean aborting an attempt. There have been fatalities due to a combination of slippery conditions and poor footwear.

TREKKING GUIDES

As this is a serious climb you need to have confidence in your guide and be able to communicate well with them. For these reasons it's strongly advised to climb with an established trekking guide; the freelance guides who hang round Pura Pasar Agung and Besakih tend to have very limited English and may not be as safety-conscious. In addition to the guides listed below, you'll find a wide choice of scenic accommodation and many guide services in the village of Sidemen, 18km from Pura Pasar Agung (see p.166); Selat (see p.166) and Tirtagangga (see p.180). In the resorts, there's Mudi Goes to the Mountain in

1963

The year **1963** is recalled as a time when the gods were displeased with Bali and took their revenge. Ancient texts prescribe that an immense ceremony, **Eka Dasa Rudra** – the greatest ritual in Balinese Hinduism – should be held every hundred years for spiritual purification and future good fortune. Before 1963, it had only been held a couple of times since the sixteenth century. In the early 1960s, religious leaders believed that the trials of World War II and the ensuing fight for independence were indicators that the ritual was once again needed, and these beliefs were confirmed by a **plague of rats** that overran the entire island in 1962.

The climax of the festival was set to take place at the Besakih temple complex (see p.164) on March 8, 1963, but on February 18, **Gunung Agung**, which had been dormant for centuries, started rumbling; fire glowed within the crater and ash began to coat the area. Initially, this was interpreted as a good omen sent by the gods to purify Besakih, but soon doubts crept in. Some argued that the wrong date had been chosen for the event and wanted to call it off. However, by this time it was too late: President Sukarno was due to attend, accompanied by a group of international guests.

By March 8, black smoke, rocks and ash were billowing from the mountain, but the ceremony went ahead, albeit in a decidedly tense atmosphere. Eventually, on March 17, Agung **erupted** with such force that the top 100m of the mountain was ripped apart. The whole of eastern Bali was threatened by poisonous gas and molten lava, villages were engulfed, between a thousand and two thousand people are thought to have died and the homes of another hundred thousand were destroyed. Roads were wiped out, some towns were isolated for weeks, and the ash ruined crops, causing serious food shortages and great hardship. Some villagers fled as far afield as Lombok.

Despite the force of the eruption and the position of Besakih high on the mountain, a relatively small amount of damage occurred to the temples, and the **closing rites** of Eka Dasa Rudra took place on April 20. Subsequently, many Balinese felt that the mountain's eruption at the time of the ceremony was an omen of the civil strife that engulfed Bali in 1965 (see p.308).

In 1979, the year specified by the ancient texts, Eka Dasa Rudra was held again, this time passing off without incident.

Candidasa (see p.174), Bali Sunrise Trekking and Tours in Ubud (see p.127) and Perama (bookable through their offices in most tourist centres or at ⊕peramatour.com).

Dartha Mount Agung Trekking Selat ☎0852 3700 8513, ⊕darthamountagungtrekking.com. This association was set up by Wayan Dartha who originates from a village in the foothills of Gunung Agung. Four routes are offered and professional guides are employed.

Gung Bawa Jl Tukad Pancoran IV/E 7, Denpasar ☎0812 387 8168, ⊕gungbawatrekking.com. Gung Bawa is a young, good-humoured, highly experienced and dependable guide who speaks excellent English. He charges Rp700,000/person (minimum two people) for a hiking package including guiding, food and drinks, accommodation and transport. He can supply a head torch, jacket and even shoes if necessary. He also offers an overnight option that leaves Selat at noon and camps at 2560m, and costs Rp1,500,000.

Besakih

Daily 6am–7pm • Rp15,000; sarong and sash hire is mandatory, available from information office for Rp20,000

The major draw in the east of Bali is undoubtedly the vast **Besakih** temple complex, the most venerated on the island. On a clear day it can be a magnificent sight, the multitiered shrines of the twenty-plus temples busy with worshippers in traditional dress bearing elaborate offerings and the whole complex framed against the stark grandeur of the sacred volcano. But Besakih also has a reputation as a place of unpleasant hassle, and its jumble of buildings, unremarkable in many ways, are closed to non-Hindus, who must stay outside the low walls; even the towering hulk of Gunung Agung is often invisible behind enveloping cloud. You might end up wondering why you bothered. If you do, arrive early morning or late afternoon to avoid the worst of the crowds. Note that there are cheap warung on the walk up to Besakih from the car park, but accommodation is very limited.

Brief history

It's likely that Besakih was a religious site long before the start of recorded history. Pura Batu Madeg (Temple of the Standing Stone), in the north of the complex, suggests megalithic connections through its ancient terraced structure based around a central stone. However, the present temple complex's founder is generally believed to be **Sri Markandeya**, a priest who came from eastern Java at the end of the eighth century. An important ceremony occurred in 1007, widely thought to be the cremation rites of **Queen Mahendradatta**, origin of the Rangda legend (see box, p.157). Already an important temple by the time of the **Majapahit** conquest of Bali in 1343, Besakih then became the **state temple** of the powerful Gelgel and Semarapura courts. An earthquake damaged the buildings in 1917 and renovations were needed after the 1963 eruption of Gunung Agung. As a result, the temples are a mix of old and new, and restoration work is always ongoing.

The temples

The **Besakih complex** consists of more than twenty separate **temples**, spread over a site stretching for more than 3km. It's a good idea to begin with **Pura Penataran Agung** (the

---

CEREMONIES AT BESAKIH

Every temple in Besakih has its timetable of **ceremonies**. The most important annual ceremony is the **Bhatar Turun Kabeh** ("The Gods Descend Together"), which takes place in March or April and lasts a month, with the high point on the full moon of the tenth lunar month. At this time, the gods of all the shrines are believed to come and dwell in Besakih, drawing worshippers from all over the island. Besakih's biggest ceremony is **Eka Dasa Rudra** (see box, p.163), held every hundred years. The **Panca Wali Krama** occurs every ten years and involves a 42km-long, three-day procession from the coast to the temple.

Great Temple of State), which is both the largest and the most dramatic. It's built on **six terraces**, with more than fifty *bale*, shrines and stone thrones inside; about half are dedicated to specific gods, while the others are for ceremonial purposes such as receiving offerings or accommodating the gods during festivals. A path skirts Pura Penataran Agung's perimeter wall, from which you can see most of the terraces (the best views are from the west side). A giant stairway, lined by seven levels of **carved figures**, leads to the first courtyard; the figures to the left are from the Mahabharata and the ones to the right from the Ramayana. As worshippers process through the first courtyard, they symbolically sever their connection with the everyday world before proceeding through the *kori agung* into the second courtyard, which contains the *padmatiga*, the three-seated lotus throne dedicated to Brahma, Siwa and Wisnu, where all pilgrims pray.

Beyond Pura Penataran Agung, the *meru* of **Pura Batu Madeg**, rising among the trees to the north, are enticing, while **Pura Pengubengan**, the most far-flung of Besakih's temples, is a good 2km through the forest. As you wander around the complex, look out for representations of the manifestations of the supreme god, in particular differently coloured **flags and banners**: black for Wisnu (the Preserver), red for Brahma (the Creator) and a multicoloured array for Siwa (the Destroyer).

ARRIVAL AND INFORMATION
BESAKIH

By bemo Bemos from Semarapura go as far as Menanga, from where you can hire an ojek to the temple. Bemos also run from Amlapura (via Selat and Muncan) to Rendang, with some continuing to Menanga. Most bemos run in the morning. There are no bemos north of Menanga to Penelokan, or between Rendang and Bangli.

Tours Without your own transport, the easiest way of getting to Besakih is to take an organized tour, but check how much time you'll have at the site; anything less than an hour isn't worth it.

Pura Pengubengan (2km) & route to Gunung Agung

BESAKIH

0   100
metres

Pura Peninjoan

Pura Gelap

Pura Ratu Penyarikan

Pura Batu Madeg

Pura Kiduling Kreteg

Pura Ratu Pande

Pura Penataran Agung

Pura Pedharman

Pura Ratu Pasek

Pura Basukian Puseh Jagat

Pura Jenggala

Pura Banua Kawan

Pura Merajan Kanginan

Pura Merajan Selonding

Pura Goa

Pura Ulun Kulkul

Pura Bangun Sakti

Souvenir shops and warung

i

Pura Manik Mas

P

Pura Dalem Puri

Pura Tirta Sudhamala

Pura Pesimpangan

Menanga

3

GUIDES AT BESAKIH

Besakih has established a terrible reputation over the last decade as a place of nonstop hassle. The problem stemmed from the hundreds of local men who styled themselves as **guides**, **guardians** or **keepers** of the temple, insistently attached themselves to tourists and then demanded large sums in payment for their "services". The official advice is to engage only properly badged guides; they can be found at the tourist office. In truth, guides are hardly needed: stick to the paths running along the walls outside the temples, wear a sarong and sash, and you'll be in no danger of causing any religious offence. If you do employ a guide, establish the **fee** beforehand: Rp50,000 is a reasonable amount. If you're escorted into one of the temples to receive a blessing you'll be expected to make a "donation" to the priest, the amount negotiable through your guide.

If you're on a **private tour**, your driver should be able to offer tips on how to negotiate these pitfalls, but he is forbidden to guide you or translate for you and won't be able to negotiate on your behalf.

3

Tourist information The Besakih tourist office (daily 7am–6pm), on the right just beyond the car park, is staffed by the local organization of guides who will pressure you to make a donation and engage their services, both of which are unnecessary (see box above).

Sidemen and around

The upland village of **SIDEMEN** sits within a quintessential Balinese setting of tiered rice terraces, coconut groves and the coursing Unda River beneath the looming profile of Gunung Agung. It makes a glorious base for a few days, with a burgeoning number of scenic places to stay, opportunities for gentle ricefield treks and easy access to Pura Pasar Agung for the challenging sunrise climb up Gunung Agung. It's also perfectly feasible to explore Besakih from here, and even Batur, which is just 48km, or a ninety-minute drive, to the northwest. Even if you don't intend to stay, you can appreciate some of the area's scenery from the road that begins at **Selat** (8km north of Sidemen) and drops down to Paksabali, 16km southwest of Sidemen on the main Semarapura–Kusamba road.

Artists Walter Spies (see box, p.117) and Theo Meier both lived in this area in the 1930s and 1940s, in **Iseh**, 3km to the north, and Anna Mathews wrote her evocative *The Night of Purnama* about her life in the village before and during the **1963 eruption** of Gunung Agung.

The main activity in these parts is **ricefield appreciation**, either from the comfort of your veranda or on a walk through the fields to nearby villages and temples. Guesthouses can supply a basic sketch map or you can take a guide for your first outing (Rp50,000/ group/hr). Alternatively, head up to the southern end of the main road for Sidemen's excellent **crafts shops**.

ARRIVAL AND DEPARTURE   SIDEMEN AND AROUND

By bemo Bemos drop passengers off along the main road through the village.

Destinations Semarapura (30min).

GETTING AROUND

By bemo In the morning, and less frequently in the afternoon, bemos connect Rendang with Amlapura and also serve Menanga to the north, for Besakih. Selat is served by bemos from Gianyar, Amlapura and Denpasar's Batubulan terminal (mornings only).

By car Recommended local drivers and guides are I Ketut Jana (☏ 0813 3806 2202) and Ketut Lagun (☏ 0812 362 2076, ✉ ketut_lagun@yahoo.com).
By scooter Widely available for rent (around Rp60,000).

INFORMATION AND ACTIVITIES

Tourist information Consult the website ⓦ sidemen -bali.com for local information.

Banks and exchange The nearest ATM is in Semarapura.
Walks and trekking Kedak Adita of Sidemen Tour and

Trekking (☎ 0819 3300 0775, ⓦ sidementourandtrekking .com) leads tours of the region including ricefield walks and hikes up Gunung Agung.

Whitewater rafting Trips down the Telaga Waja (see below) are organised by *Lihat Sawah* (see p.168).

Yoga Sidemen Yoga Center at Cepik Villa (☎ 0812 391 8700, ⓦ sidemenyogacenter.com) offers vinyasa flow and other

instruction from experienced Balinese teachers in beautiful surrounds.

Classes Several local women offer instruction about making *endek* and *songket* textiles. Sidemen Tour and Trekking can hook you with local weavers ($8/hr). *Warung Lihat Sawah* (see p.168) runs cooking courses.

ACCOMMODATION

The main accommodation area is west off the main road, in Dusun Tabola. The access road forks 400m west of the main road; the following listings give directions from the fork. Many places to stay are located in prime spots scattered across the ricefields. As it's reasonably cool here at night almost none have a/c; few have restaurants, either, but some have kitchenettes. Bring earplugs to muffle the cacophony of the nightly frog chorus. Non-guests can use the pool at *Suwah Indah* if you order a meal.

★ **Giri Carik** 800m along the left-hand fork ☎ 0819 3666 5821, ⓦ giricariksidemenbali.com Set in a pretty garden with a gorgeous pool, these five bungalows with verandas are excellent value, attractive and popular (book ahead). The in-house restaurant is good and the helpful staff can fix you up with everything from a scooter to a local masseur. $30

Great Mountain View Alas Tunggal, 5km north of Sidemen, 2km off the main road ☎ 0858 5701 3416, ⓦ greatmountainbali.com. Ten well-designed bungalows, most with full-frontal views of Gunung Agung across a gorgeous swathe of ricefields. There's a small pool and a new restaurant under construction. Pick-ups from Sidemen/ Selat possible. $60

Karma Loka 100m along the right-hand fork ☎ 0852 0511 0916, ⓦ lihatsawah.com. Also known as *Lihat Sawah*, this family-run hotel is a lively place to stay, with a dozen rooms, from simple cold-water options to very comfortable deluxe bungalows with hot water and pretty views; there's also a small pool and a villa. Activities include village walks and day-trips, there's an on-site restaurant (daily 7.30am–10pm) and staff are lovely. $30

★ **Khrisna Home Stay** 200m along the left-hand fork

☎ 0815 5832 1543, ✉ pinpinaryadi@yahoo.com. These four well-furnished en-suite rooms are set in a lovely garden, and have open showers, mozzie nets and private terraces. There's a small restaurant, too, with mains from Rp35,000 (daily 7am–9pm). Run by Sidemen's English-speaking nurse and his wife. R300,000

Kubu Tani 800m along the left-hand fork ☎ 0366 530 0519, ⓦ kubutani.com. Three beautiful, well-appointed two-storey villas built in wood and thatch to a sophisti-cated Bali-modern/traditional design. Verandas face a profuse garden and have great ricefield and Agung views. Each villa can sleep four. $55

Puri Agung Inn 1km west of the Sidemen road junction, Selat ☎ 085 235672. Ten basic fan-cooled rooms spread over in a quirky set of buildings that include a restaurant. The hotel is next to the main road, so ask for a quiet room at the rear. Rp220,000

Sawah Indah Villa 1km along the left-hand fork ☎ 0366 534 4455, ⓦ sawahindahvilla.com. Overlooking a fine amphitheatre of rice terraces, the large and stylishly decorated villa-style rooms here have picture windows, colour-washed bathrooms and prettily tiled floors. There's a lovely pool and the restaurant makes the most of the views. $50

THE RENDANG–AMLAPURA ROAD

From **Rendang**, 14km north of Semarapura on the main route to Kintamani, a picturesque **road** heads 32km east to **Amlapura**, running beneath Gunung Agung via ricefields, forest and deep river valleys. The scenery is good but the going is slow, the potholed road crowded with trucks bringing charcoal-coloured sand down from the mountain.

After crossing the River Telaga Waja, whose serpentine 14km-long descent is used by **whitewater rafting** companies such as Alam (ⓦ alam-amazing-adventures.com) and Bali Adventure Rafting (ⓦ baliadventuretours.com), you pass through Muncan, a possible base for climbing Gunung Agung (see p.162). From **Muncan**, a further 5km brings you to the western edge of **Selat**, an obvious base for treks up Gunung Agung, and the turn-off to the important **Pura Pasar Agung**, directional temple for the northeast. At 1600m above sea level this is one of the two main starting points for Gunung Agung ascents. The road to the temple is an ear-poppingly steep climb of 10km through bamboo stands and acacia forests, in countryside scored by deep lava-carved gorges. The temple itself, however, is probably not worth a special journey, though on a clear morning you do get fine views.

EATING

Warung Damah Jl Raya Sidemen ☎0366 555 1138. On the main drag, south of the fork, this roadside place offers both seafood and freshwater fish as well as a good *nasi campur* and noodle dishes. There's live music on Saturday nights, when there's an open mic. Daily 9am–9pm.

Warung Lihat Sawah Near Kubu Tani, 800m along the left-hand fork ☎0366 530 0519. This warung serves great Thai, Indonesian and European food at reasonable prices (most mains Rp35,000–45,000). Also runs cooking courses. Daily 8am–10pm.

SHOPS

Pelangi Southern end of Sidemen's main road ☎0853 3773 7555. Beautiful *endek* and *songket* (gold- and silver-thread) products (from Rp160,000/m). All textiles are made in Sidemen, and you can see the production process in the workshop behind the showroom where the staff dyes and dries threads before weaving the textile using foot-looms. Daily 9am–6pm.

3 Padang Bai and around

PADANG BAI, the tiny port village for boats to the Gili Islands and Lombok, has developed into a small, laidback travellers' centre and is also known as a base for **diving**. Its beaches are tiny, but its youthful vibe, funky cafés, cheap accommodation and live music bars may keep you lingering longer than you intended. There's a daily market and shops stocking basic necessities, but for anything major you'll need to head to Candidasa (20min away by bemo) or Semarapura (30min). The main local sight is the temple at **Goa Lawah**, on the way to Semarapura.

The beaches

Padang Bai's **village beach** is normally packed with *jukung* (traditional wooden outrigger boats), though you can swim here and it's often busy with local families on Sundays.

Most tourists head instead for the tiny whiteish-sand coves immediately over the headlands to the east and west, both within walking distance, meaning they get crowded and aren't always pristine. **Bias Tugal** (also known as **Pantai Kecil**) is a fifteen-minute walk south of the port via a steepish trail. The beach here is quite exposed to strong waves and has a few tiny warung.

Alternatively, a five-minute walk along the left fork just east of *Topi Inn* will bring you to the pretty but miniature cove of **Blue Lagoon**, not much more than 100m long. You can snorkel here at high tide but beware the serious undertow and watch the coral (which is just below the surface). The two restaurants rent snorkel gear (from Rp25,000) as well as sunloungers (around Rp40,000), and you're sure to find a couple of massage ladies and sarong-sellers in attendance.

Goa Lawah

7km west of Padang Bai • Daily 7am–6pm • Rp10,000 plus Rp3000 sarong rental • Goa Lawah is located right on the main road; any bemo between Padang Bai and Semarapura will drop you at the temple

As Bali's directional temple for the southeast, **Goa Lawah** (Bat Cave), by the coast, is always busy with worshippers who travel here in community groups to perform rites associated with significant life events. Discreetly watching the spectacle of the various **ceremonies**, both in the temple compound and at the shrine on the beach across the road, is part of the appeal of a visit. The other highlight is the **cave** at the base of the cliff, which heaves with fruit bats. It is supposedly the start of a tunnel that stretches 30km inland to Pura Goa in Besakih and is said to contain the cosmic *naga* Basuki. Watch out for pushy souvenir sellers and others offering "gifts" that you're pressured to buy. If you do engage a local guide, a Rp30,000 fee is reasonable.

ARRIVAL AND DEPARTURE   **PADANG BAI AND AROUND**

Hundreds of travellers pass through Padang Bai every day, and arranging onward transport is easy. Perama buses link Bali's main towns to Padang Bai, and there are frequent boat departures to the Gili Islands and Lombok. Any number of tour agencies will be keen to sell you tickets, often at highly fluctuating prices.

BY SHUTTLE BUS

Services depart from the Perama office near the port (daily 7am–5pm; ☎0363 41419, ⊛peramatour.com) to major destinations in Bali and Lombok. Other shuttle services are also available.

Destinations Candidasa (3 daily; 30min); Kuta/Ngurah Rai

DIVING AROUND PADANG BAI

There are half a dozen rewarding dive sites around **Padang Bai** and **Blue Lagoon**, whose hard and soft corals attract everything from eels, wrasses, turtles, lion fish and wobbegong sharks to leaf scorpion fish, ghost pipefish and pygmy sea horses; lobsters and crabs are frequently spotted on night dives. At nearby **Jepun** there's a decent artificial reef and the wreck of a 15m fishing boat, which is great for blue-spotted stingrays and reef fish. It's ideal for novice divers and macro photography, and good for **snorkelling** too. The dive sites of Tulamben, Amed, Candidasa and, further afield, Nusa Lembongan and Nusa Penida, are also within reach.

DIVE CENTRES

There are over a dozen dive outfits in Padang Bai, charging from $70 for two local dives including equipment, snacks and water. It's well worth choosing a dive centre carefully (see p.36); below are some long-established outfits.

Geko Dive ☎0363 41516, ⊛gekodivebali.com. Very professional Padi 5-star centre. Tech dives and training courses are offered.

Ok Divers ☎0811 385 8830, ⊛okdiversbali.com. Large school with a training pool that also offers Nitrox diving.

Water Worx ☎0363 41220, ⊛waterworxbali.com. Well-established German-run dive operator that also offers diving for people with disabilities.

3

Airport (3 daily; 2hr 30min); Sanur (3 daily; 1hr 30min); Tirtalannga (daily; 1hr); Ubud (3 daily; 2hr).

BY BEMO OR BUS

Bemos and buses from Amlapura, Candidasa, Semarapura and Denpasar's Batubulan terminal terminate at the port entrance about 300m from the main hotel area. Departures (mostly in the morning) run to Amlapura via Candidasa (Rp12,000) and Semarapura (Rp12,000).
Destinations Amlapura (45min); Candidasa (20min); Gilimanuk (3–4hr); Semarapura (30min).

BY BOAT

Car ferry to Lembar An hourly service operates 24hr and takes between four and five hours. Tickets are Rp40,000/person; motorbikes Rp112,000 (including two people); cars from Rp733,000 (including passengers). Perama (ⓦperamatour.com) runs a cheap and hassle-free daily car ferry-and-bus combo to Senggigi using this connection (9am; 6hr; Rp125,000). If you have a rental car let your agency know beforehand that you intend to travel between Bali and Lombok to ensure all requirements are met (see p.27).

Fast boats to the Gili Islands and mainland Lombok Five different operators offer connections to Gili Trawangan (1hr 30min–2hr; $20 to $52), and on to Bangsal, Teluk Kodek or Senggigi on mainland Lombok (same price), most leaving Padang Bai between 8.30am and 9.30am, with additional departures in high season. Some operators stop off at Gili Air as well. Scoot has two daily (high season only) boats to Nusa Lembongan (1hr). Tickets are sold online via the portal Gili Bookings (ⓦwww.gilibookings.com) and operators' websites, in shops and from freelance agents. It's good to check the safety record of unknown operators before purchasing a ticket, especially in rough weather. Sailings are cancelled during heavy seas. Reliable daily services include Blue Water Express (☎0361 895 1111, ⓦbluewater-express.com), Giligili (☎0361 763306, ⓦgiligilifastboat.com) and Scoot Cruise (☎0361 285522, ⓦscootcruise.com).

BY TAXI

Fixed-price taxis from Ngurah Rai Airport cost Rp315,000 (2hr); preordered pick-ups from Padang Bai will usually charge a bit more.

TOURS AND ACTIVITIES

Courses You can do courses in batik, *ikat*, basket-weaving, Balinese dance, wood carving, cooking, *wayang kulit* and more at *Topi Inn* (see p.172), from Rp160,000.
Tours Pak Pret is a recommended local driver and guide for east Bali excursions (Rp400,000/day); his tour agency

is located opposite the boat jetty on Jl Silayukti (daily 6am–9pm; ☎0813 3836 4551, ✉pakprettours@hotmail.com); he can also arrange car and scooter rental (Rp200,000/50,000/day).

ACCOMMODATION

Except for *Bloo Lagoon Village*, none of Padang Bai's accommodation is more than a 10min walk from the ferry port or jetty, or more than 200m from the sea (which also means that nowhere is out of earshot of the ferry announcements and foghorn blasts).

Bamboo Paradise Jl Penataran Agung ☎0822 6630 4330, ⓦfacebook.com/pg/bambooparadisebali. A cosy hostel and homestay with good fan-cooled dorms and a variety of basic private rooms. There's a great lounge for socializing. Dorms **Rp120,000**, doubles **Rp230,000**
Bloo Lagoon Village ☎0363 41211, ⓦbloolagoon.com. This village-like compound of 25 eco-conscious villas sits on top of a hill, a 2min walk from Blue Lagoon Beach. The two- and three-bedroom villas are all slightly different but all have big decks and coastal views, plus kitchenettes. There's a pool and restaurant and morning yoga classes are included. **$116**
Fat Barracuda Jl Segara ☎0822 3797 1212, ⓦfatbarracuda.com. A zany-looking, very well set up hostel with an excellent a/c ten-bed mixed dorm where each bunk has twin power points, reading light and locker and there's a hot-water en-suite. The (one) private room upstairs is fan-cooled and has a balcony. Chill out in the lounge which is loaded with beanbags. Dorms **Rp95,000**, double **Rp290,000**

Kembar Inn Jl Segara 6 ☎0363 41364, ⓦkembarinn.com. Old school guesthouse with nice staff, decent rooms on several floors and a generous breakfast. There are common sitting areas but no private balconies (and few external windows) except on the pricier top floor, which has a large terrace plus a/c and hot water. **Rp175,000**
★Lemon House Gang Melanting 5 ☎0812 4637 1575, ⓦlemonhousebali.com. Charming budget hotel in a yellow house up a flight of steep steps on the hillside west of the village. There are amazing views of the bay from the communal terrace. Two deluxe rooms enjoy these views as well, but are more exposed to noise; the quieter rooms at the back share facilities. You'll find books, magazines, DVDs and games for rainy nights. Dorms **Rp125,000**, doubles **Rp175,000**
Marco Inn Jl Segara ☎0818 0534 3897, ✉marco.inn.padangbai@gmail.com. A tiny, basic place with welcoming staff and clean, cheerfully-painted, cold-water rooms set round a courtyard off the harbour-front road.

Upstairs rooms have nice rooftop views down to the sea. Very cheap. **Rp120,000**

OK Divers Resort & Spa ☎ 0811 385 8830, ⓦ www .okdiversresort.com. A well-run place with stylish rooms in a whitewashed vaguely colonial-looking structure, some with sea views. There's a fine spa, pool (with swim-up bar) and dive shop and restaurant on site. Non-divers are very welcome. **$78**

Puri Rai Jl Silayukti 7X ☎ 0363 41385, ⓦ puriraihotels .com. Good-value hotel with an amazing three pools for its many large, comfortable if slightly dated a/c rooms; those upstairs are brighter. Wi-fi can be a bit spotty. **Rp550,000**

Topi Inn Jl Silayukti 99 ☎ 0363 41424, ⓦ topiinn.net. Long-running cheapie, social guesthouse and restaurant with simple rooms (some en suite) plus a common area that doubles as an open-plan dorm with mattresses and mosquito nets (security boxes are available). Breakfast is not included. Dorms **Rp65,000**, doubles **Rp170,000**

EATING

Fresh seafood is the speciality in Padang Bai's restaurants, especially mahi-mahi, barracuda, snapper and prawns. Head to the warung along the road just west of Goa Lawah (see below) for inexpensive fish dishes.

The Colonial Jl Silayukti ☎ 0360 341790, ⓦ www .okdiversresort.com. Located at *OK Divers*, this smart seafront place has good western dishes like Czech-style schnitzel, salads and a few Mexican dishes (mains from Rp40,000). There's lots of space to lounge around – just settle into one of their beanbags or sofas. Daily 7am–9pm.

Grand Café Padang Bai Harbour Jl Pantai Segara ☎ 0363 434 5043. Classy and popular harbour-view place with comfy rattan chairs, a dozen "bio" health juices and cappuccinos. The food is good and includes pizzas, mixed *sate campur*, grilled fish with garlic sauce, kebabs and steaks. Mains from Rp35,000. Daily 7am–10pm.

★**Martini's** Jl Segara ☎ 0818 0559 0450. The best warung in town, run by former beach hawker Martini and her ambitious children. Famous for its chicken sate, which comes with wonderfully rich peanut sauce but also serves good seafood dishes (from Rp35,000), soups (from Rp25,000) and delicious Balinese pancakes with palm syrup. Facing the car park. Daily 7am–11pm.

Topi Inn Jl Silayukti 99 ☎ 0363 41424, ⓦ topiinn.net. Classic travellers' cafe with great home-baked bread, cakes, cappuccinos and a ton of imaginative vegetarian dishes – including Mediterranean salads. Mains cost from Rp45,000; water refills are available too. Keep an eye out for the regular movie and party nights. Daily 7.30am–10pm.

★**Warung Lesehan Merta Sari** Jl Kresna, Desa Pesinggahan village. To find this highly rated seafood warung, turn off the main road 1.5km west of Goa Lawah and drive or walk straight for 1.2km. For a bargain Rp25,000 or so you get a delicious set meal of *sate lilit ikan* (minced fish sate), fish soup, steamed or grilled fish, rice, veg and side dishes. Daily 8am–7pm.

DRINKING AND NIGHTLIFE

Tiny live music bars open onto the car park inland from the jetty, with a battle of sound systems nightly from around 9pm,

Babylon Reggae Bar Jl Segara. Tiny, perennially busy late-night drinking and music venue with local musos playing covers every Tues, Thurs and Fri. Small Bintangs are Rp22,000, or try one of their cocktails. The barmen really make this place. Daily 5pm–3am.

Ozone Cafe Jl Silayukti ☎ 0817 470 8597. This lively bar-restaurant attracts a regular clientele of beer sluggers and has live music some nights. Daily 11am–11pm.

SHOPPING

Ryan Jl Segara. This bookshop offers fiction and non-fiction, including some good Indonesian titles, and books in several European languages.

DIRECTORY

Banks and exchange There are exchange counters in the village and several ATMs, with two near the Perama office.

Doctor Highly regarded, English-speaking Dr Nisa can be contacted via Water Worx Dive Centre (☎ 0811 380645). The nearest hospitals are at Semarapura or Denpasar.

Candidasa and around

East Bali's main tourist hub, **CANDIDASA** is a relaxed coastal resort with plenty of midrange and upmarket accommodation, some good restaurants, rewarding **diving** and lots of opportunities for day-trips. It's not a lively place, though, drawing an older crowd of visitors, and with hardly any nightlife. There's also little or no **beach**, which has eroded away since the reef was destroyed to produce lime for the tourist building boom, and the seafront is fronted by a phalanx of groynes and a sea wall. You can still swim in the sea here, and some hotels do have little patches of sand out front, but for anything approaching a beautiful beach you have to head 9km east to the lovely **Pasir Putih**.

Just 3km north of Candidasa is the famous traditional Bali Aga village and weaving centre of **Tenganan**, while to the east there's the locally important hilltop temple of **Pura Gumang**. Candidasa is also well placed for excursions to Besakih and Tirtagangga, and further afield to Amed.

Puri Candidasa

Jl Raya Candidasa • Daily 7am–7pm • Donation

Candidasa is an ancient settlement, and its temple **Puri Candidasa**, opposite the lagoon, is believed to have been founded in the eleventh century. The statue of the fertility goddess Dewi Hariti in the lower section of the temple, surrounded by children, is a focus for pilgrims (the name Candidasa originally derives from "Cilidasa", meaning ten children).

3

ARRIVAL AND DEPARTURE

By plane Candidasa is a 2hr drive from Ngurah Rai Airport (see p.64); airport taxis charge around Rp350,000. It's about Rp400,000 from Candidasa to the airport.

By shuttle bus Perama (☏ 0363 41114, ⍵ peramatour. com) does hotel pick-ups and runs shuttle buses to major Bali and Lombok destinations.

Destinations Amed (daily; 1hr 30min); Kuta/Ngurah Rai Airport (3 daily; 3hr); Lovina (daily; 3hr 30min); Padang Bai

CANDIDASA AND AROUND

(3 daily; 30min); Sanur (3 daily; 2hr); Tirtagangga (daily; 1hr); Tulamben (daily; 2hr); Ubud (3 daily; 1hr 30min).

By bemo or bus Buses and minibuses from Denpasar's Batubulan terminal pass through Candidasa en route to Amlapura. Bemos are also handy for travelling around Candidasa and can be flagged down anywhere en route.

Destinations Amlapura (20min); Denpasar (Batubulan terminal; 2hr); Gianyar (1hr); Padang Bai (20min).

GETTING AROUND

By taxi Gotya (☏ 0819 1613 4266, ⍵ candidasataxi .blogspot.de) charge around Rp500,000/day.

By car or motorbike Cars and motorbikes are best rented through your accommodation.

DIVING AND SNORKELLING AROUND CANDIDASA

The local reef is gradually rejuvenating and there is now **snorkelling** just offshore, stretching for about 1km westwards from the beach end of Jalan Puri Bagus. The **currents** can be hazardous, though, so don't venture too far out and stay aware of your position at all times. Jepun, near Padang Bai, is also rewarding. You can arrange snorkelling trips with local boat-owners: it's about Rp300,000 for two hours for up to three people, including equipment, to the islands off Candidasa or to Pasir Putih (see p.176).

Just off the coast, the rocky outcrops known as **Gili Tepekong**, **Gili Biaha** and **Gili Mimpang** offer excellent **diving**, although they're not suitable for beginners as the water can be cold and the currents strong. There are several walls, a pinnacle just off Mimpang, dramatic scenery at boulder-lined Tepekong Canyon and a cave at Gili Biaha. The current is too strong for the growth of big coral, but the fish include barracuda, tuna, white-tipped reef shark, mola mola (occasionally between August and October), turtles and sometimes even manta rays. **Prices** start at $75 for two local dives including equipment. Candidasa is also within day-tripping distance of the reefs at Padang Bai, the wrecks at Tulamben and Amed, and the challenging sites around Nusa Lembongan and Nusa Penida. It's worth choosing a dive centre carefully (see p.36); listed below are some well-regarded Candidasa options.

Bambu Divers ☏ 0363 41534, ⍵ bambudivers.com. Dutch-run dive school at the *Pondok Bambu*.

Shangrila Scuba Divers ☏ 0812 398 9239, ⍵ shangrilascubadivers.com. British-run centre at

Bali Palm Resort.

Zen Dive Jl Raya Candidasa ☏ 0363 41411, ⍵ zendive bali.com. Five-star PADI dive centre.

3

CANDIDASA

BUITAN

MENDIRA

ACCOMMODATION	
Alila Manggis	1
Amarta Beach Inn	4
Aquaria	11
Ari Homestay	6
Gedong Gandhi Ashram	10
Ida's Homestay	9
Lumbung Damuh	2
Pondok Pisang	3
Relax Beach Resort	8
Temple Café and Seaside Cottages	7
Watergarden (Taman Air)	5

BALI SEA

INFORMATION AND ACTIVITIES

Information Candidasa Network (⬥ candidasanetwork .com) is a free magazine with useful features and information available widely in the resort.

Massage and spas Try Salon & Accessories (☎ 0363 41834, massage from Rp125,000), opposite the *Watergarden* hotel. For a classy spa head to the *Alila Manggis* hotel (☎ 0363 41011; from Rp550,000).

Trekking and biking There's good trekking in the Candidasa area. One of the most popular routes begins at Kastala, near Tirtagangga, and takes you downhill to the Bali Aga village

of Tenganan, an easy 2–3hr walk with excellent rice-terrace views. A longer version begins in Tirtagangga and continues via the blacksmiths' village of Budakaling (5–6hr). Mudi Goes to the Mountain (☎ 0813 3815 3991, ⬥ mudigoestothe mountain.com) charges Rp350,000/person for the Kastala trek (minimum two people). He also organizes treks up Gunung Batur (Rp750,000/person); ascents of Gunung Agung (see p.162) and a 55km cycling tour from Muncan via Tirtagangga to the coast at Amed (Rp490,000/person, minimum two people).

ACCOMMODATION

Accommodation in central Candidasa is clustered along the main road. Further west, there's a decent beach at Mendira, beyond which the villages of Buitan and Manggis have some nice places to stay.

CENTRAL CANDIDASA

Aquaria Jl Puri Bagus ☎ 0363 41127, ⬥ aquariabali .com. In a tiny secluded shorefront compound at the edge of a banana grove, this chic place has ten contemporary terraced rooms and apartments and a couple of villas set around a striking little ionized pool. One of Candi's best restaurants is on site. **$84**

Ari Homestay Jl Raya Candidasa ☎ 0817 970 7339, ⬥ arihomestaycandidasa.com. Classic budget guesthouse with well-priced en-suites and bungalows, a book exchange and a tiny hot-dog café. Pay for a "superior double" (Rp320,000) and you'll get a/c and hot water. **Rp150,000**

Gedong Gandhi Ashram Jl Raya Candidasa ☎ 0363 41108, ⬥ ashramgandhi.com. Occupies a gorgeous location between the lagoon and the ocean and rents out a few simple, attractive bungalows. Guests can take part in the daily *puja*, yoga and meditation as much or as little as they wish; note that there's no smoking or drinking, and unmarried couples can't share a room. Volunteer placements (Rp100,000/ night) are also possible. Rates include three vegetarian or fish meals a day. **Rp450,000**

Ida's Homestay Jl Raya Candidasa ☎ 0363 41096, ⬥ facebook.com/Idas.Homestay.Candidasa. Old-school travellers' lodge in a coconut grove, offering six good-sized timber-and-thatch bungalows with mosquito nets, fans and cold-water garden bathrooms. There's a lovely shore-front deck and breakfast area plus a tiny patch of sandy beach. Book ahead as it's popular. **Rp250,000**

Relax Beach Resort Jl Raya Candidasa ☎ 0819 3645 4147, ⬥ facebook.com/relaxbeachresortcandidasa. Walk through the wonderful carved Balinese doors and you'll find an oasis of calm with an oceanfront pool and a selection of pretty a/c bungalows, each with generous veranda, traditional tiled roof and attractive interiors decorated with artistic flair. **Rp560,000**

Temple Café and Seaside Cottages Jl Raya Candidasa ☎ 0363 41629, ⬥ balibeachfront-cottages.com. The well-furnished bungalows here come in a range of standards and prices, from fan and cold-water versions to those with a/c, sea view, kitchenettes and very good hot-water bathrooms. Guests can use the pool at the *Watergarden* hotel opposite. **Rp200,000**

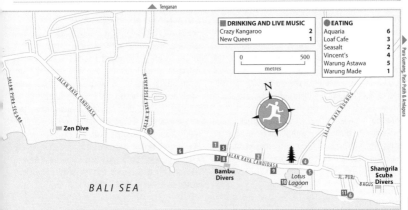

DRINKING AND LIVE MUSIC	
Crazy Kangaroo	2
New Queen	1

EATING	
Aquaria	6
Loaf Cafe	3
Seasalt	2
Vincent's	4
Warung Astawa	5
Warung Made	1

0 — 500 metres

3

★**Watergarden (Taman Air)** Jl Raya Candidasa ☎0363 41540, ⓦwatergardenhotel.com. Yes it's inland, but the Balinese garden setting is a dream, with lush tropical plants and a carp-filled lily pond. Bungalows are in several shallow tiers with the highest ones getting the most light; all have a/c but there are no TVs. There's a pretty swimming pool as well as a spa and a good restaurant. **$93**

MENDIRA
Accommodation in the village of Mendira fronts some of Candi's nicest beach but is several kilometres from the heart of the resort.

Amarta Beach Inn Jl Raya Mendira ☎0363 41230, ⓦamartabeachcottages.com. Enjoys a prime beachfront location, with white sand and clear water, while the rooms (fan or pricier a/c options) are delightful, with clean lines, modern decor and artwork, and all offering a sea view. The seaside restaurant has a good reputation, especially for fish, and there's a small pool. **Rp380,000**

Pondok Pisang Jl Raya Mendira ☎0363 41065, ⓦpondokpisang.com. A remote but lovely haven at the end of a sandy track, 1km from the main road. The quirky but elegant two-storey fan bungalows are furnished with driftwood, paintings and lovely textiles. Many guests come for yoga and meditation in the large open hall overlooking the sea; the sun can be worshipped from the beautiful decks jutting over the water, and there's good swimming. **Rp1,112,000**

MANGGIS
Around 6km west of central Candidasa, the village of Manggis offers several fine hotels.

★**Alila Manggis** Manggis ☎0363 41011, ⓦalilahotels .com. Good value given the facilities and attention to detail, this impressive hotel is situated in a shore-side coconut grove with rooms ranged around a gorgeous pool. Though the beach is stony, you can swim in the sea and there are imaginative cultural tours, kids' programmes, a classy spa and a variety of cooking courses. The excellent *Seasalt* restaurant is here (see p.176) and there are free shuttles to central Candidasa and Tenganan. **$178**

Lumbung Damuh Jl Pantai Buitan, Manggis ☎0363 41553, ⓦdamuhbali.com. A totally chilled, traveller-friendly little Balinese/European-owned hideaway of creatively designed *lumbung* beside a tiny patch of shore. Bedrooms are upstairs, with sitting areas and hot-water garden bathrooms below. A good breakfast is included and, though there is no restaurant, there are local warung. **Rp250,000**

EATING

There's a good range of restaurants in and around Candidasa, from cheap tourist-oriented warung to sophisticated hotel dining. Some offer free transport from hotels around the resort.

CENTRAL CANDIDASA AND JALAN PURI BAGUS
★**Aquaria** Jl Puri Bagus ☎0363 41127, ⓦaquariabali .com. Overlooking the pool, this impressive hotel restaurant serves delicious, inventive food such as mahi mahi with tamarind sauce, ginger-spiced prawns, rye-bread sandwiches and imported cheese. There's a good selection for vegans and a kids' menu; the veggies and herbs are organic. Daily noon–11pm.

Loaf Cafe Jl Raya Candidasa ☎0813 4629 9878. Excellent, buzzing a/c cafe with fine pies, sandwiches (with home-made bread), great cakes and all the coffee combos you could wish for, as well as fresh juices and smoothies. Daily 8am–6pm.

Vincent's Jl Raya Candidasa ☎0363 41368, ⓦvincentsbali.com. Very popular with expats, this landmark restaurant has a dining room, garden terrace and separate lounge bar. The menu is extensive and takes in European classics, fresh seafood, salads, Thai and local dishes – most mains are Rp80,000–150,000. Reserve for dinner (when there's often live jazz). Daily 11am–11pm.

Warung Astawa Jl Raya Candidasa ☎0363 41363. Fine-value streetfront place, with set three-course meals of Indonesian favourites, sizzling sate (served over charcoal coals) and flavoursome pork, chicken and fish dishes (mains from Rp45,000). Daily 7am–10pm.

BUITAN AND MANGGIS

★**Seasalt** Alila Manggis hotel, Manggis ☎0363 41011, ⓦalilahotels.com. The setting, in a lovely outdoor pavilion fringed by ponds, is wonderful at this acclaimed hotel restaurant, which features a delectable range of Asian, fusion and vegetarian dishes, with plenty of local specialities – right down to the salt (sourced from flats close by). Try the signature *megibung* eight-dish feast, which includes spicy beef, chicken sate and snapper with ginger (Rp360,000), which is more than enough for two. Daily 11am–11pm.

Warung Made Buitan, 4km west of central Candidasa. A simple place for good breakfasts, Indonesian and Western favourites and local seafood, try their *rendang babi* (slow-cooked pork stew, Rp35,000). Daily 7am–9pm.

DRINKING

Nightlife, mainly consisting of live music at different restaurants through the week, is low-key and things are usually pretty quiet by 10pm. Both of the below are in central Candidasa.

Crazy Kangaroo Jl Raya Candidasa ☎0363 41996, ⓦcrazy-kangaroo.com. This pub and restaurant has a pool table and an open kitchen serving good Indonesian and Western classics. There's live music (covers) on Tuesdays, while on Thursdays there's Balinese dancing. Free shuttle

service. Daily 10am–midnight.

New Queen Jl Raya Candidasa ☎0812 3653 1832, ⓦwww.newqueen.biz.nf. Popular tourist bar and restaurant (there are daily specials) with regular reggae and rock bands, and draught Bintang. Daily 9am–midnight.

DIRECTORY

Banks and exchange There are many ATMs in the central area, as well as a few moneychangers.

Doctor The Pentamedica clinic (Jl Raya Manggis 88 ☎0363

41909, ⓦpentamedica.com) is open 24hr. The nearest hospitals are in Amlapura, Semarapura and Denpasar.

Pura Gumang

Daily 7am–7pm • Donation • Bemos between Candidasa and Amlapura drive by the stalls at the temple staircase

At the top of the pass about 3km northeast out of Candidasa, on the way to Pasir Putih, monkeys crowd around roadside stalls at the point where worshippers begin their hour-long walk up to hilltop **Pura Gumang**. This is one of the most important temples in the area and affords a fine panorama inland to Gunung Agung, down to the coast and across to Gunung Rinjani on Lombok. Every two years, usually at full moon in October, four of the local villages – Bugbug, Bebandem, Jasri and Ngis – participate in a huge ceremony, complete with trance dances, that begins with a procession up to Pura Gumang. It attracts many thousands of people, especially new parents, who bring along hundreds of roast suckling pigs.

Pasir Putih

Everyone in Candidasa bemoans the loss of the beach, but there is a highly satisfying alternative, 9km northeast at the famously beautiful **Pasir Putih** (White Sand Bay). The less than straightforward access, via a steep and rutted track, is part of the appeal (kind of); en route you'll pass a gateway to pay an entrance fee (Rp10,000/person). The pale sand bay feels wild and remote, backed by palms and forest and sheltered by rocky headlands, with aquamarine water perfect for swimming. Offshore, small patches of coral reef offer decent snorkelling. The beach is lined with a dozen or so shacks providing meals and massage plus snorkel and sunloungers (usually free if you order drinks and food).

ARRIVAL AND DEPARTURE   **PASIR PUTIH**

By car or ojek Access is from the village of Perasi, immediately east of Bugbug on the road to Amlapura, about 6km from Candidasa. There are two routes from here: the first (unsigned) is immediately opposite a temple; the second is a few hundred metres further east and has a tiny sign for White Sand Beach, Jl Pasir Putih. Both lead 3km to the coast via a ticket barrier and a dauntingly rough track. An ojek will drive you there and back for around Rp100,000 from Candidasa, just text him when you want to be picked up; or car drivers charge around Rp250,000.

Tenganan Pegringsingan and around

One of the most famous Bali Aga villages (see box below) is **Tenganan Pegringsingan**, a wealthy settlement of over six hundred families set amid forest and hills 3km north of Candidasa. It's a major day-trippers' destination, known not only for its traditional architecture but also as the only place in Indonesia that produces the celebrated **geringsing** cloth. It's also the finishing point of a popular and scenic trek that begins in either Kastala or Tirtagangga (see p.180).

Laid out around three cobbled, vehicle-free avenues that run north–south, the village (admission by donation) rises in a series of terraces, its family compounds hidden behind high walls of thatch, adobe and brick. Communal activities and meetings take place in thatched *bale* on the main street and there are plenty of handicrafts stalls set out here too.

Tenganan's most famous craft is the unique and highly prized **geringsing** or double *ikat* (see box, p.155) that gives this village its name. Dyed in a limited natural palette of brown, deep red, indigo and tan, and designed with deeply symbolic motifs, *geringsing* is revered throughout Bali as sacred cloth, able to ward off evil and having an important role in tooth-filing and cremation ceremonies. Glossy, golden, tightly woven **basketwork** made from *ata* grass is another painstakingly crafted village product. The grass has to be split, woven, boiled, dried and then smoked, all of which means it can take a month to produce a single item. **Traditional calligraphy** is another attractive Tenganan craft. Pictures and symbols are incised on narrow lengths of *lontar* palm, which are then strung together to create a concertina-like book.

Tenganan Dauh Tukad

West across the river from Tenganan Pegringsingan, the twin Bali Aga settlement of **TENGANAN DAUH TUKAD** is smaller, and much less famous, but also worth a visit. Part of its appeal is that every visitor is accompanied by a local guide, which is a great chance to learn about village life and customs; their services are free but a tip is appreciated. Tenganan Dauh Tukad looks less traditional than its neighbour but it's also greener and more peaceful. It's also less commercial, because the village forbids inhabitants from displaying wares in the street.

WHO ARE THE BALI AGA?

When the Javanese Majapahit conquered Bali in 1343, imposing religious reforms and a caste system on the island, those that rejected the Javanization of Bali withdrew to their village enclaves to live a life based around **ritual and ceremony**. Nearly seven centuries later they are still a distinct group, known as the **Bali Aga** or Bali Mula, the "original Balinese", who adhere to a strict, archaic code in their social and religious lives.

The Bali Aga are followers of the Indra sect of Hinduism and trace their ancestral links to Orissa in India rather than to Java like most Balinese. Among other things, their exacting customary law determines on which of the three village streets they can live and whom they may or may not marry. Most of the daily rites are inaccessible to the public, but there are many **festivals** where visitors are welcome; see ⓦ www.tourism.karangasemkab.go.id for exact dates. One of the most dramatic is the month-long **Usaba Sambah**, generally in May and June, which includes ceremonial duelling known as *perang padan* or *mekare-kare*, in which bare-chested men fight each other with thorny pandanus leaves.

THE FOUNDING OF TENGANAN

In the days before the Majapahit invasion of Bali, **King Bedaulu** ruled the island. Legend has it that one day his favourite horse went missing, and so he offered a large reward for its return. When the horse was discovered – dead – near Tenganan, the king announced that he would give the local people the land within which the stench of the rotting animal could be smelled. One of the king's ministers was sent to adjudicate, and he and Tenganan's headman set out to decide the boundaries. The smell of the horse could be detected over a huge area. The lines were duly drawn and the minister departed. At this point, the devious village headman took out from under his clothes the piece of rotting horsemeat with which he had fooled the minister. The limits of the village lands are still the ones set at that time, and cover more than ten square kilometres.

ARRIVAL AND INFORMATION

By car or ojek A car from Candidasa costs about Rp50,000, ojek about Rp20,000.

On foot The road to Tenganan Pegringsingan is a pleasant 3km walk uphill from the western end of Candidasa. Tenganan Dauh Tukad is off the same road, partway up the hill. To walk between the two villages shouldn't take long

TENGANAN PEGRINGSINGAN AND AROUND

but you'll need a guide; going by road it's about 4km.

Tours To gain insight into daily life in the two Tenganan villages you'll need a guide, provided free of charge in Tenganan Dauh Tukad. Alternatively, consider joining a tour organized through the village ecotourism network, JED (☎ 0361 366 9951, ⊕ jed.or.id).

SHOPPING

Indigo Art Shop Tenganan Pegringsingan ☎ 0363 41168. One of the best-known village shops, run by I Wayan Kondri, whose family is still involved in every stage

of *geringsing* production. His exquisite weaves start at $125 for a scarf. Daily 8am–6pm.

Amlapura and around

Formerly known as Karangasem, **AMLAPURA** was renamed after the 1963 eruption of Gunung Agung, when the outskirts of the town were flattened by the lava flow. (Balinese people sometimes change their names after serious illness in the belief that it will bring about a change of fortune.) It's the capital of Karangasem district, and has a significant history, but the modern town is quiet, tidy and unhurried, with just enough to keep you busy for an hour or two. It also makes a handy pit stop on the popular day-trip circuit from Amed via the scenic coastal route, and there's accommodation and food close by at Jasri beach just south of town and **Seraya Barat** 6km east around the coast.

The main sights in and around town are associated with the **Karangasem court**. Once so powerful that in the seventeenth century it established Balinese rule over several Lombok principalities, Karangasem was later severely weakened by feuding between its rival factions and by the mid-nineteenth century was itself ruled from Lombok. Following the Dutch conquest of Lombok in 1894, **Anak Agung Gede Jelantik**, a member of the Lombok ruling family, was appointed regent of Karangasem by the colonialists. He was succeeded in 1908 by his nephew, **Anak Agung Anglurah**, the last raja of Karangasem before independence and famous as the architect of the water palaces at Tirtagangga and **Taman Soeka Sada** in Ujung. Their relatives continue to occupy the **Puri Agung Karangasem** palace in Amlapura and ties with Lombok are still strong: many Balinese in the west Lombok settlement of Cakranegara have family in Karangasem, and the sizeable Muslim community in Amlapura traces its ancestry back to the period when Karangasem was under Lombok rule.

Puri Agung Karangasem

Jl Sultan Agung • Daily 8am–5pm • Rp10,000

Built during the Dutch period at the end of the nineteenth century by the raja of Karangasem, Anak Agung Gede Jelantik, **Puri Agung Karangasem** is still home to descendants of the royal family and offers a rare chance to peek inside a palace. The structure is not in great shape today and is in need of renovation, but it does have some intriguing features (information sheets in English are available).

Areas open to the public include the elegantly airy **Maskerdam** guesthouse, which has beautiful doors carved with three-dimensional reliefs of birds, animals and foliage. It was used for greeting VIP guests; inside there are a few pieces of period furniture and a gallery of historic photographs. Elsewhere in the compact but artfully tranquil gardens is the **Bale Kambang** (Floating Pavilion), encircled by a lotus pond, which is for meetings, dancing and dining. Wander around the compound, via the edges of the current family quarters, for views down over the rest of the town and across to Lombok – at one time under Karangasem rule. The peaks of Gunung Agung and Gunung Lempuyang frame the vista.

Taman Soeka Sada (Ujung Water Palace)

5km south of Amlapura • Daily 7am–7pm • Rp50,000

In a rural location 5km south of central Amlapura stands the largest of the three extravagant water palaces conceived by the last raja of Karangasem, Anak Agung Anglurah. **Taman Soeka Sada**, also known as the **Ujung Water Palace**, dates from 1921 but was almost completely destroyed by the 1963 eruption of Gunung Agung. Renovations have recreated the stately tranquillity of its ponds, floating pavilions, ornamental bridges and pagodas, but the relief carvings and statuary are concrete. Nonetheless it's a serene spot, served by **bemos** from Amlapura, and worth a visit if you're en route to Amed via the scenic coastal route (see p.183), though the entrance fee is steep.

Jasri

Backed by coconut groves and ricefields, the slender shoreline around the beach at **JASRI**, just 2km south of Amlapura, consists of wave-polished grey stones and patches of dark sand. The sea can be choppy and too rough for most swimmers but the area retains a

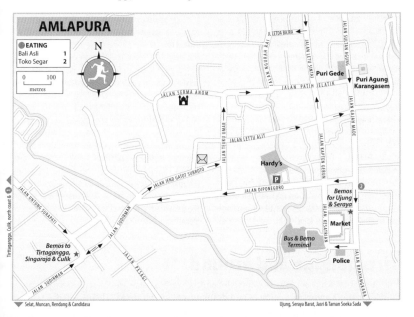

delightfully rural feel and it's a great spot to escape the mass tourism and crowds elsewhere in coastal Bali. A handful of lovely hotels and villas have emerged here in recent years.

Seraya Barat

The wild, dramatic black-stone shore at **SERAYA BARAT**, 1km east of Ujung, 6km from central Amlapura or 24km from Amed, has a few accommodation options. The sea here is usually too dangerous for reliable swimming but the gorgeous white sands of Pasir Putih are a twenty-minute drive away (see p.176) and the views to Nusa Penida and Lombok are awesome.

ARRIVAL AND INFORMATION   AMLAPURA AND AROUND

By bemo or bus Amlapura has useful bemo services (all most frequent in the morning). From the terminal in town services run to Padang Bai via Candidasa (orange), Gianyar, and Rendang via Muncan and Selat (green). Bemos to Culik via Tirtagangga leave from the turn-off on the outskirts of town, as do dark-red minibuses to Singaraja. Bemos to Ujung and occasional services to Seraya (blue) leave from the southern end of Jl Gajah Made, not far from the terminal.

Destinations Candidasa (20min); Culik (45min); Denpasar (Batubulan terminal; 2hr 30min); Gianyar (1hr 20min); Lovina (3hr 30min); Padang Bai (35min); Seraya (40min); Tirtagangga (20min); Tulamben (1hr); Ujung (20min).

Banks and exchange There are many ATMs in town.

ACCOMMODATION

JASRI

★**Aashaya Jasri** Jl Pantai Jasri, ☏0363 21045, ⓦaashayajasri.com. This beautiful guesthouse has real style thanks to the attention to detail evident in its traditional thatched buildings (with up to three bedrooms) which all boast batik textiles and classy wooden furnishings. There's a lovely pool, spa and its fine *Disini* restaurant is open to non-guests. **Rp900,000**

Villa Campuhan Jl Pura Mascima ☏0818 0538 6053, ⓦvillacampuhan.com. An astonishing hotel with six traditional structures of timber and thatch (four are Minangkabau-style with upturned boat-shaped roofs), largely built from recycled materials. There's a lovely pool, staff are great and the restaurant serves fine, creative cuisine. Apart from the surging of the waves over the slim pebble beach, it's utterly tranquil here. **$268**

SERAYA BARAT

Kebun Impian ☏0813 3872 1842, ⓦkebunimpian seraya.com. Attractive bungalows (fan or a/c options) in a garden by the sea, where there's a slither of a beach at low tide. The restaurant serves good food, including marlin steaks and fresh crayfish, and cooking classes are offered. Diners can also use the swimming pool. **$50**

Seraya Shores ☏0813 3841 6572, ⓦserayashores .com. A luxurious hideaway with gorgeous, individually designed Bali-style villas in a great seafront garden. It's popular with yoga groups, and has a lovely deck for practice, plus a beautiful shoreside pool. Breakfast is served any time you choose, but note that the restaurant isn't open to non-guests. **$87**

Villa Flow ☏0819 9945 4516, ⓦvillaflowbali.com. This elegant, environmentally friendly coastal retreat is the perfect place to get away from it all. Rooms in the main building are large and modern; the deluxe Coconut House beside the pool makes the most of the sea view. There's a spa, yoga classes (check website for packages) and a private beachfront garden just a few minutes' walk away. **$176**

EATING

AMLAPURA

★**Bali Asli** Gelumpang ☏0828 9703 0098, ⓦbaliasli .com.au. Wonderful Australian-run restaurant and cooking school with stunning views across ricefields to a volcano-filled horizon. The menu changes everyday, depending on the availability of market ingredients. Order the six-dish megibung feast (Rp195,000) for a really authentic taste of Bali. Follow the signs from the traffic lights on the Amlapura–Tirtagangga road. Daily 10am–6pm.

Toko Segar Jl Gajah Made 17. Shopfront warung near the palace in the centre of town that serves inexpensive Indonesian dishes (*mie goreng* is Rp20,000). Daily 8am–7pm.

Tirtagangga and around

Famous for its whimsical mid-twentieth-century **water palace** and its strikingly pretty landscape of plunging rice terraces and dramatic mountain peaks, **TIRTAGANGGA** is a

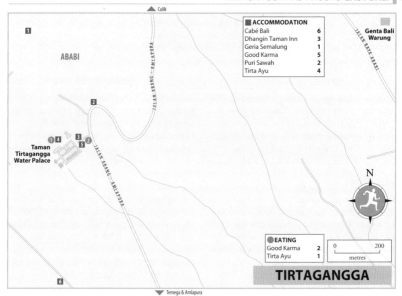

popular day-trip destination and a good base for walkers. It's significantly cooler than on the coast and there are countless possibilities for gentle **treks** or more strenuous full-day hikes or bike trips through the terraced ricefields, rambutan, vanilla and banana plantations, and tiny villages. Much of the accommodation enjoys fine panoramas, especially the quieter places in the neighbouring villages of **Temaga**, 1.5km to the south, and **Ababi**, 2.5km north. On a clear day you get fine views of Gunung Lempuyang to the east, on whose slopes stands **Pura Lempuyang Luhur**, a worthwhile local trip.

Taman Tirtagangga Water Palace

Daily 7am–7pm • Rp20,000 • ⓦ tirtagangga.com

Tirtagangga's only real sight, **Taman Tirtagangga Water Palace** was built in 1946 by Anak Agung Anglurah, the last raja of Karangasem, and is the finest manifestation of his obsession with pools, moats and fountains. Constructed on the site of a holy spring just off the main road, it's actually a water **garden** rather than a palace, a confection of terraced ponds, pretty shrubs and water burbling from the mouths of sculpted water buffaloes and nymphs, the pools flashing orange with very well-fed carp. Two of the upper-level pools are open to the public for **swimming** (Rp10,000, children Rp5000), mostly used by local kids.

Pura Lempuyang Luhur

Gunung Lempuyang • Daily 7am–7pm • Donation, sarongs for rent Rp10,000 • The temple car park is 8km from Abang, itself 3.5km north of Tirtagangga on the Culik road; bemos only cover the 2km from Abang to Ngis Tista, but go all the way during festivals

Visible to the northeast from Tirtagangga, less than 12km away, **Gunung Lempuyang** is a sacred peak and site of **Pura Lempuyang Luhur**, one of the *kayangan jagat* or directional temples of Bali, giving spiritual protection from the east. The temple gleams white on the mountain slopes and offers exceptional views. A daunting two-hour climb, up 1700 steps from the car park, will get you to the principal temple, which is believed to be the dwelling place of the god Genijaya, but the vistas, including of Gunung Agung perfectly framed in the temple gateway, make it all worthwhile. The **courtyard** contains a stand of bamboo, and on festival days the priest makes a cut in the bamboo to release holy water.

From the temple, a ninety-minute climb up another staircase brings you to the **summit** of Gunung Lempuyang (1058m), where there's another temple.

Festival days are the best time to visit, when the temple swarms with worshippers carrying offerings all the way up the staircase.

ARRIVAL AND INFORMATION   TIRTAGANGGA AND AROUND

By shuttle bus Perama (Ⓦ peramatour.com) run daily to/from Candidasa (Rp75,000; 45min) and destinations including Amed on demand.

By bus Tirtagangga is served by minibuses and buses plying the route between Amlapura and Singaraja.

Destinations Amlapura (20min); Culik (30min); Padang

Bai (1hr) Singaraja (2hr 30min); Tulamben (1hr).

By taxi Komang Gede Sutama (see below) can arrange transport on to Amed, Candidasa and Padang Bai.

Banks and exchange The nearest ATMs are in Amlapura, 6km south. There are moneychangers in the village but rates are better in Candidasa.

ACTIVITIES

Cycling Bungbung Cycle Tours runs back-road cycling tours from their office on the main road (Ⓣ 0812 3765 3467, Ⓦ sites.google.com/site/bungbungbikeadventure). Half-day tours include a long downhill ride (Rp350,000).

Massage I Made Putu Tungtang from Ababi is highly recommended (Ⓣ 0812 392 6321; Rp100,000/hr).

Trekking Every guesthouse can organise hikes. Specialist local guides include notably the reputable Komang Gede Sutama at *Good Karma* restaurant (see below) who covers the most options for around Rp60,000/person/hr, and

Nyoman Budiarsa, based at *Genta Bali Warung* on the main road (Ⓣ 0363 22436), who charges around Rp50,000/hr and who also sells a map of local walks (Rp5000). Choose from easy local hikes to longer versions that take you to Tenganan village above Candidasa (2–6hr depending on where you start the walk): the Kastala to Tenganan section (2hr) is a real highlight but can get busy in high season. More strenuous routes take you to Amed (Bunutan) via the mountaintop Pura Lempuyang (9hr; Rp1,000,000/guide), and up Gunung Agung (around Rp1,300,000).

ACCOMMODATION

Staying in central Tirtagangga puts you near a choice of warung but also within earshot of the busy road; staying further away means a greener and quieter location. Most accommodation has a restaurant attached.

Cabé Bali Temaga Ⓣ 0363 22045, Ⓦ cabebali.com. Encircled by ricefields with views to Gunung Agung and the sea, the four large bungalows enjoy glorious surroundings, including a pool. The genial German-Javanese hosts foster a relaxed atmosphere and the Indonesian food (served to guests only) is great. A 10min easy (flat) walk from Tirtagangga. Discounts for longer stays. **$78**

Dhangin Taman Inn Ⓣ 0363 22059. Close to the Water Palace, these are the cheapest beds in Tirtagangga. All rooms are simple, those with cold-water bathrooms are very spartan indeed but acceptable for a night, while the hot-water options (Rp200,000) are smarter. **Rp100,000**

Geria Semalung Ababi Ⓣ 0363 22116, Ⓦ geriasemalung .com. A forest hideaway of five attractively furnished hot-water bungalows, with fine views across to Gunung Lempuyang and down to the rice terraces below. It's a steep 15min walk down to Tirtagangga. **Rp380,000**

Good Karma Ⓣ 0363 22445, Ⓔ goodkarma .tirtagangga@gmail.com. A central spot to stay, set a decent distance back from the road, with four clean, tiled rooms in a small garden in the paddy fields. Fans and cold water only. **Rp258,000**

Puri Sawah Ⓣ 0363 22342. This fine British-Balinese-run place has a great restaurant, the *Rice Terrace Coffee Shop*, and spacious, nicely furnished rooms (one with hot water) in two-storey traditional-style structures. It's only a stone's throw from the Water Palace. **Rp275,000**

Tirta Ayu Ⓣ 0363 22503, Ⓦ hoteltirtagangga.com. Set inside the Water Palace compound, these five Bali-style villas are fit for a raja with very classy decor and furnishings, sunken bathtubs and grand verandas. Wake early and you can stroll the palace gardens at dawn before the public is admitted. **$130**

EATING

Good Karma Jl Abadi Ⓣ 0363 22445. A welcoming place where the long menu (mains from Rp40,000) takes in Western and Balinese specialities – try the *dendang be siap* (roast chicken, potatoes and spicy *bumbu* sauce). Service can be a tad slow at times. Daily 7am–10pm.

Tirta Ayu Ⓣ 0363 22503, Ⓦ hoteltirtagangga.com. For a unique experience head to this upmarket hotel restaurant with lovely views over the Water Palace grounds. The extensive menu offers an eclectic range of dishes including crispy duck and Balinese *megibung* dishes (Rp195,000 for two). Daily 7am–9.30pm.

The Amed coast

The entire 15km stretch of coast **from Culik to Aas** in the far east of Bali is known as **Amed**, although this is the name of just one village in an area of peaceful bays, clear waters and dramatically undulating topography. Long one of Bali's poorest regions, notorious for its dusty soil and subsistence economy based around fishing and salt production, Amed is steadily becoming an important tourism centre. Visitors are drawn by the region's impressive offshore reefs, which offer great **snorkelling** and **diving**, and facilities are mushrooming, with accommodation now available in every village bay.

Jemeluk, with its dive centres, restaurants and travellers' vibe, is a good choice if you don't have your own transport; **Bunutan** has some very nice places to stay; and **Banyuning** is great for snorkelling. If you're not here for the snorkelling or diving, you could enjoy some day-tripping possibilities, but be warned that the **beaches** are not Bali's finest, being mostly black, stony and shadeless (though they do get paler and sandier east of **Lipah**), and generally busier with traditional wooden outriggers (*jukung*) than sunloungers. The scenery, however, is magnificent: as the coast road crests one headland after another, the scalloped bays and aquamarine waters sparkle beneath the folds of the stark volcanic hills behind. It's a joy to explore on two wheels.

Amed, Jemeluk and Congkang

The eponymous **Amed** village, the westernmost of the coastal villages in the area, is just 3km from Culik. Its traditional occupations of fishing and salt production are slowly giving way to tourist development, but it retains a local feel.

With a decent spread of accommodation, a useful supply of tourist facilities and excellent diving and snorkelling just offshore, **Jemeluk** (6km from Culik) is much more of a tourist centre than Amed and makes a good base. Together with the adjacent hamlet of **Congkang**, it has plenty of accommodation, restaurants and a good dive shop along the narrow shrub-lined road. At low tide a swathe of beach is revealed here, and though there's almost no shade, there are sunloungers for rent. There's good snorkelling in front of many of the hotels, and especially beneath the headland by *Villa Coral Café* bungalows.

Bunutan

Continuing east over the headland from Congkang brings you first to **Bunutan**, 8km from Culik, which has some of the nicest accommodation along the Amed coast, many of the establishments enjoying great views. Places are quite spread out though, divided by a steep headland, so you'll probably need transport.

Lipah to Aas

Beyond Bunutan is **Lipah** beach, 10km from Culik, which has reasonable snorkelling. After Lipah, it's headland after headland to the peaceful little villages and their bays at **Lean** (11km from Culik), **Selang** (12km), **Banyuning** (13km) and eventually **Aas** (15km). These eastern beaches get progressively less stony and the sand gets paler; Banyuning has the area's best **snorkelling**, at the Japanese Wreck just offshore (see box, p.186). The beach at Banyuning also has some shade, plus snorkel rental, a couple of cheap warung and accommodation with restaurants at the north end.

The coast road from Aas to Ujung

One of the highlights of the Amed area is the **coast road** that connects **AAS**, the southernmost village of the Amed strip, with **UJUNG**, 25km to the southwest. It's a

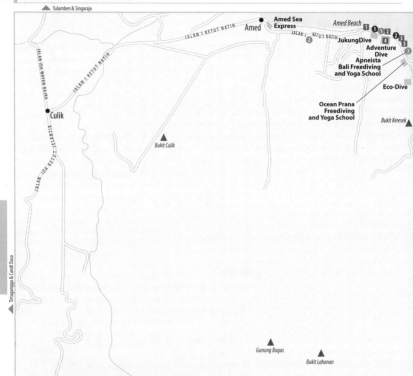

gloriously scenic high-level route that works well as part of a **day-trip loop** – via Amlapura and Tirtagangga, with a possible side trip to Pura Lempuyang Luhur, then back via Culik.

As you continue south and west around the coast from Aas, the scenery is breathtakingly dramatic, with hills sweeping up for hundreds of metres from the coast. The narrow, steeply undulating but paved road snakes through dry mountain land used in the wet season for growing peanuts, soya beans and corn, overlooked by the hulking profiles of Gunung Lempuyang and Gunung Seraya. It turns inland at **Kusambi**, about 4km from Aas and marked by a massive beacon; this is the most easterly point of Bali – on clear days Lombok is visible, 35km across the strait. At Seraya the road heads down to the coast, passing **Seraya Barat** (see p.180) and the **Ujung Water Palace** (see p.179) before reaching **Amlapura**.

Kelompok Karya Sari Warna Alam

Bungin, Seraya Timur • Daily 9am–5pm • Free • 📞 082 8368 8122

This weavers' cooperative lies 14km on from Kusambi, on the fringes of the small market centre of **Seraya**, and is well worth a stop. They grow their own cotton and dye it in the traditional way with indigo and bark harvested from the workshop garden; you can watch the spinners and weavers at work and then buy their beautiful scarves and sarongs, recognizable by their muted, natural tones.

ARRIVAL AND INFORMATION   THE AMED COAST

Access to Amed is via Culik, 12km northeast of Tirtagangga or 7km southeast of Tulamben. Tourist transport services are offered in almost every village, and through hotels, to all major destinations on Bali including the airport.

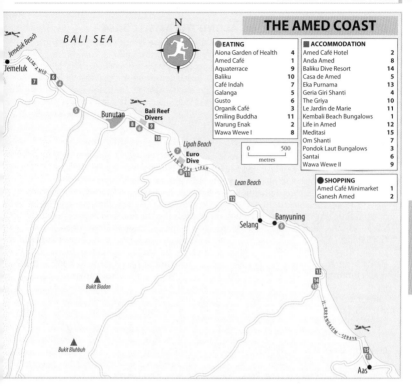

THE AMED COAST

● EATING			■ ACCOMMODATION	
Aiona Garden of Health	4		Amed Café Hotel	2
Amed Café	1		Anda Amed	8
Aquaterrace	9		Baliku Dive Resort	14
Baliku	10		Casa de Amed	5
Café Indah	7		Eka Purnama	13
Galanga	5		Geria Giri Shanti	4
Gusto	6		The Griya	10
Organik Café	3		Le Jardin de Marie	11
Smiling Buddha	11		Kembali Beach Bungalows	1
Warung Enak	2		Life in Amed	12
Wawa Wewe I	8		Meditasi	15
			Om Shanti	7
			Pondok Laut Bungalows	3
			Santai	6
			Wawa Wewe II	9

● SHOPPING	
Amed Café Minimarket	1
Ganesh Amed	2

3

By bus Perama (ⓦ peramatour.com) have regular mini-buses to several destinations in Bali from their office in Amed village.

Destinations Airport (daily; 2hr 45min); Candidasa (daily; 1hr 15min); Padang Bai (daily; 1hr 30min); Tirtagangga (2 daily, 30min); Ubud (daily; 2hr).

By bemo All public transport between Amlapura and Singaraja passes through Culik. From here, the odd bemo runs via Amed to Aas in the morning.

Destinations (from Culik) Aas (1hr 30min); Air Sanih (1hr 30min); Amed (10min); Amlapura (45min); Bunutan (45min); Jemeluk (30min); Lipah Beach (1hr); Selang (1hr 15min); Singaraja (Penarukan terminal; 2hr 30min); Tirtagangga (20min); Tulamben (20min).

By boat Fast boats run direct from Amed to the Gili Islands and Lombok but both operators (Amed Sea Express and Kuda Hitam) have a poor reputation for overcrowding and safety standards, and are best avoided.

Banks and exchange ATMs and moneychangers are in the main villages along the Amed coast.

GETTING AROUND

By car or motorbike Transport along the Amed coast is scant. For transport within the Amed area you'll either need to rent your own motorbike, available in every village for about Rp50,000/day, or use an ojek/driver. Car rental, with or without driver, is best arranged through your accommodation.

On a tour The most popular tours on dry land include the sightseeing loop via the spectacular coast road, Pura Lempuyang Luhur and inland hikes. Prices range from Rp275,000/person for a tour on the back of a motorbike to around Rp550,000 for a car plus driver. Treks up Gunung Agung can also be arranged from Amed (from Rp1,200,000).

ACCOMMODATION

In high season, villagers accommodate backpackers in their homes up tracks off the main road, asking around Rp150,000/couple.

JEMELUK AND CONGKANG

Amed Café Hotel (Pondok Kebun Wayan) Congkang ⓣ 0363 23473, ⓦ amedcafe.com. One of the biggest outfits in Amed, with 39 rooms plus a pool, dive centre, restaurant

DIVING AND SNORKELLING ALONG THE AMED COAST

Banyuning has the area's best **snorkelling**, at the **Japanese Wreck**, which lies in shallow water (6–12m) just 20m offshore; the small freighter is overgrown with soft corals and is frequented by pygmy seahorses, leaf scorpionfish and a number of nudibranchs. If you're staying elsewhere you can charter a boat to the wreck: from Jemeluk it's a forty-minute ride and costs Rp250,000 per two-person boat for the whole excursion. There's rewarding reef in **Jemeluk** too, especially in the (usually) very clear water around the headland beside *Villa Coral*, and also in a long stretch in front of *Amed Café* and *Ganesh Amed*. **Snorkel sets** can be rented everywhere.

DIVING

Amed's reefs are popular with divers from all over Bali and by late morning can be very crowded with day-trippers. Local dive operators tend to set off early in the day to get a head start on incomers, which is one of several good reasons to base yourself here.

The main diving area is at **Jemeluk**, where a massive sloping terrace of hard and soft coral leads to a wall dropping to a depth of more than 40m. Gorgonian fans, basket sponges and table coral are especially good, and there are plenty of fish (including schools of red-tooth trigger fish and sergeant majors), plus sharks, wrasses and parrotfish. Advanced divers rate **Gili Selang**, an islet off Bali's eastern tip, about 5km south of Aas, with its pristine reef and pelagics (hammerhead sharks are sometimes encountered here), but the currents are nearly always fierce. There are also the Japanese Wreck at **Banyuning** (see p.183) and a dramatic drift dive at **Bunutan**, with schools of barracuda and giant barrel sponges. **Tulamben** (see p.188) is a thirty-minute drive away and most dive centres offer safaris to sites further afield.

There are countless **dive centres** in the Amed area. All the established places will collect you from your accommodation. Prices average $75 for two dives around Amed or Tulamben and $85 at Gili Selang. There are also freediving schools for breathholding athletic types who hate underwater bubbles.

Adventure Divers ☎ 081 353136113, ⓦ adventure diversbali.com. At *Geria Giri Shanti*, Congkang.
Apneista Bali Freediving and Yoga School ☎ 0812 3826 7356, ⓦ apneista.com. Jemeluk.
Eco-Dive ☎ 0363 23482, ⓦ ecodivebali.com. Jemeluk.
Jukung Dive ☎ 0363 23469, ⓦ jukungdivebali.com. Congkang.
Bali Reef Divers ☎ 0363 23523, ⓦ diveamed.com. *Puri Wirata* hotel, Bunutan.
Euro Dive ☎ 0363 23605, ⓦ eurodivebali.com. Lipah.
Ocean Prana Freediving and Yoga School ☎ 0363 4301587, ⓦ oceanprana.com.

---

and minimarket. Rooms in all categories are spacious and nicely furnished; a/c is available but the cheapest have fans and cold water and are right by the road. **Rp350,000**

Casa de Amed ☎ 0363 430 1044, ⓦ casadeamed.com. A small, contemporary, impressively presented beachfront place with six well-appointed a/c rooms in two-storey buildings. There's a small café, cute pool and sundeck by the waves. **$75**

★ **Geria Giri Shanti** Congkang ☎ 0819 1665 4874, ⓦ geriagirishanti.com. A tropical garden hideaway, this well-run place has spacious, clean and thoughtfully outfitted bungalows (good mosquito nets, nice fabrics, lots of hangers and long mirrors) just above the road. All have fans and hot water. Also home to Adventure Divers. **$30**

Kembali Beach Bungalows Jemeluk ☎ 0817 476 8313, ⓦ kembalibeachbungalows.nl. Conveniently located on the beach with lots of bars and restaurants within walking distance, this well-managed hotel has eight lovely chalet-style bungalows with sea or garden views, verandas and attractive interiors. There's a pool and restaurant too. **Rp700,000**

★ **Pondok Laut Bungalows** Jemeluk ☎ 0813 3817 7324, ⓔ pondoklautamed@gmail.com. Quirky beachfront place offering a selection of lovely rooms with carefully mismatched furnishings – ceramics, ikat textiles and furniture – that combine Indonesia and Japanese influences. There's a small pool, a home-cooked, nutritious and delicious breakfast, and genial and attentive owners. **Rp450,000**

BUNUTAN

Anda Amed ☎ 0363 23498, ⓦ andaamedresort.com. A modern, well-thought-out British-run boutique hillside hotel with eleven generously-sized bungalows; all have ocean views, private gardens, bathtubs and a/c and some have funky kids' cubbyhole beds too. There's a large pool and innovative restaurant. Check their website for three-night special deals. **$108**

The Griya ☎ 0363 23571, ⓦ thegriya.com. This luxurious resort is perched on a headland so steep that golf carts are used to bring guests to their villas. Each villa has the latest electronic gadgets, a private infinity pool and great views over Lipah bay. The two restaurants and spa are top quality – but you'll need to walk a bit to get to the beach. Regularly hosts meditation workshops. **$202**

Om Shanti ☎0878 6135 6039, ⊛omshantibali.com. Offering fine value for money these four very attractive hillside cottages are supremely spacious with great terraces and contemporary bathrooms while their four-poster beds boast posh linen. It's about a ten-minute stroll down to the beach, there's a small pool and the spa has an excellent rep. **Rp400,000**

Santai ☎0363 23487, ⊛santaibali.com. Long-running beachfront resort with various types of a/c rooms in thatched bungalows. The furnishings are perhaps a tad dated in some ways but some have sea views. There's a small beach out front that's safe for children, with good snorkelling, and the on-site *Coconut Restaurant* is worth a visit. **$108**

Wawa Wewe II ☎0363 23522, ⊛bali-wawawewe .com. Beautifully located, good-value and family-friendly, these beachfront bungalows are always popular. Nearly all have loft spaces with kids' beds, a/c and partial or total sea views, and outdoor bathrooms. There's an infinity pool in the compact shorefront compound. **Rp400,000**

LIPAH, LEAN, SELANG, BANYUNING AND AAS

Baliku Dive Resort Banyuning ☎0363 430 1871, ⊛balikudiveresort.com. Luxuriously appointed and indulgently spacious villa-style bungalows – each with kitchenette, a/c, day bed and bathtub – in a steep plot across

the road from the Japanese Wreck. The veranda views of the reef, Lombok, and nearby hills are breathtaking. There's a pool and well-regarded restaurant. **$108**

Eka Purnama Banyuning ☎0828 372 2642, ⊛eka -purnama.com. Family-run, this is an excellent budget choice, especially for snorkellers, with robust bamboo bungalows from whose verandas you can practically see the reef fish across the road. Bungalows each have a single and double bed, fan, mozzie net and hot-water bathroom. **Rp400,000**

Le Jardin de Marie Lipah ☎0363 23507, ⊛lejardin demarie.sitew.fr. Set in a lush tropical garden, these four good-value, thatch-roofed fan and a/c bungalows are an excellent deal. The French owner is helpful and informed about the region. Book well ahead. **Rp400,000**

Life in Amed Lean ☎0363 23152, ⊛lifebali.com. Petite and pretty little beachside gem, where the a/c bungalows all have traditional carved doors, antique-style furniture, gorgeous tiled floors and extra beds in the loft. A couple of beachfront villas can sleep bigger groups. There are also a pool, restaurant and decent snorkelling on your doorstep. **$95**

Meditasi Aas ☎0828 372 2738, ⊛meditasibungalows .blogspot.com.au. Lovely isolated place with a social vibe (daily yoga classes at 5pm, cooking classes at 11am). There are eight large fan-cooled and simply decorated bamboo bungalows with huge sliding screens and private verandas, and four new luxury rooms (Rp700,000) with gorgeous wooden furniture. On-site organic restaurant, *The Smiling Buddha*, is excellent. No wi-fi, phone signal or TVs. **Rp400,000**

EATING

JEMELUK

Amed Café ☎0363 23473, ⊛amedcafe.com. Beachfront tables make this a pleasant place to refuel between snorkel forays. There's squid curry and fish sate (Rp60,000) on the standard menu, and Balinese classics such as *sate lilit* (minced seafood sate) if you order three hours ahead. They also run cooking lessons. Daily 7am–10pm.

Organik Café At Apneista Bali Freediving and Yoga School in Jemeluk. A relaxed café offering fresh salads, burritos and nachos, sandwiches and great cakes (try the orange chocolate cake) as well as espresso coffee. They also have a water refill service. Daily 8am–5pm.

Warung Enak About 750m west of Jukung Dive in Tukad Se ☎0819 1567 9019. Offers home-style Indonesian cooking including great *gado-gado* and very flavoursome chicken and beef rendang dishes. Expect reasonable prices (most mains are Rp35,000–60,000) and generous portions. Daily 8am–10pm.

BUNUTAN

Aiona Garden of Health ☎0813 3816 1730, ⊛aiona bali.com. This "holistic health resort" has an impressive vegetarian menu, with mains around Rp40,000, including

crisp salads, home-made pasta, wholemeal bread, hibiscus sorbet and chocolate cake, supplemented by aloe vera and *kombucha* (fermented tea) drinks. No alcohol. Reservations required. Daily noon–3pm & 6–10pm.

★**Galanga** ☎0819 1662 5048. The sign outside says "fusion food", but don't let that put you off – this is an outstanding cafe-restaurant serving great global food. Try a *nangka* curry (jackfruit cooked with coconut, Rp45,000), the perfectly cooked samosas or one of their memorable cakes and desserts (such as shortbread biscuit with pineapple and coconut mousse). There's great (though pricey) coffee and tea too. Daily 9am–9.30pm.

Gusto ☎0813 3898 1394, ⊛andaamedresort.com. A nicely designed Hungarian-run restaurant above the road, with great service and a good variety of freshly made Indonesian and central European dishes, including great beef goulash (Rp68,000) and Wiener schnitzel. *Gusto* also has an excellent bakery. Daily 3–10pm.

LIPAH, LEAN, SELANG, BANYUNING AND AAS

Aquaterrace Selang ☎0813 3791 1096, ⊛bbamed .exblog.jp. Enjoyable little café, which offers authentic

Japanese food like *okonomiyaki* (savoury pancakes, Rp39,000), sushi and teriyaki dishes as well as Balinese and international food. The dining area has good views over the bay. Daily 8am–10pm.

Baliku Banyuning ☏ 0828 372 2601, ⊛ balikudiveresort .com. Combine lunch at this hotel restaurant with free use of the pool and premier snorkelling across the road. The (quite pricey) menu is wide ranging and includes steak with peppercorn sauce, rendang and falafel. Daily 7am–9pm.

Café Indah Lipah ☏ 0363 23437. Use the pedestrian bridge at EuroDive to reach this neat warung right on the beach. *Indah* does excellent seafood, including great grilled mahi mahi as well as the usual Indonesian and European dishes. Expect to pay around Rp50,000–80,000 for a good meal. Daily 10am–10pm.

Smiling Buddha Aas ☏ 0828 372 2738. The restaurant at the *Meditasi* hotel has a gorgeous beach-facing location and offers fine local dishes (Rp75,000, including lots of seafood and good veggie choices). Balinese dancers serenade diners on full moon nights and they offer daily Indonesian cooking lessons. Daily 8am–9pm.

Wawa Wewe 1 Lipah ☏ 0363 23506, ⊛ bali-wawawewe .com. A lively restaurant and bar with sea views, serving Indonesian classics (around Rp35,000) and cocktails. It stages live music every Wednesday and Saturday. Daily 7.30am–10pm.

Tulamben

North of Amed, the parched landscape is cut with folds and channels, relics of the lava flow from the 1963 eruption of Gunung Agung, which rises dramatically inland. The main focus of tourist attention in these parts is the village of **TULAMBEN**, site of Bali's most popular dive, the **Liberty wreck**, which lies just 30m offshore. Over a hundred divers a day come to explore this most accessible of wrecks and, with several hotels and dive shops nearby, it's perfectly feasible to base yourself here for a few days. That way you can pick your dive times to avoid the crowds of day-trippers who clog the wreck between 11am and 4pm. The beach is black and stony and the village itself is dreary, so you want to choose one of the hotels just outside central Tulamben, or consider Amed (13km south) as a base.

ARRIVAL AND INFORMATION   TULAMBEN

By shuttle bus There are Perama shuttle buses from Candidasa (daily; 2hr; Rp100,000, minimum two people).

By bus or minibus Tulamben is about 10km northwest of Culik and served by Singaraja–Amlapura public buses and minibuses.

Destinations Air Sanih (1hr); Amlapura (1hr); Culik (30min); Singaraja (2hr); Tirtagangga (1hr).

Banks and exchange There's an ATM in central Tulamben, and several places can change money.

ACCOMMODATION

Most of the accommodation in central Tulamben is in a cluster between the sea and the Culik–Singaraja road. More upmarket places are scattered within a 5km radius east and west along the coast and will pick you up on request.

★**Batu Belah** 5km east of central Tulamben ☏ 0817 975 5214, ⊛ eastbaliresort.com. A family-run oasis in a superbly peaceful and panoramic spot right on the shore. The four bright, high-standard rooms are wheelchair-accessible and child-friendly and all have sea views, a/c, TV and hot water; there's also a family villa. There's a swimming pool and good restaurant (see opposite), glass-bottom boat trips to the reefs and snorkelling and fishing trips. €65

Liberty Dive Resort Central Tulamben ☏ 0813 3776 2206, ⊛ libertydiveresort.com. Just 200m up the lane from the *Liberty* wreck, the 32 rooms and cottages here have a/c, with large balconies and hot water throughout, plus a small pool and energetic staff. Rp650,000

DIVING AT TULAMBEN

Tulamben's underwater treasure trove, the **Liberty wreck**, lies on a sandy slope just 30m offshore, making this one of the most accessible wrecks in Southeast Asia and a gift for novice divers. There are plenty of entrances and some sections are in shallow water, making it a good **snorkelling** site, too. The wreck is encrusted with soft coral, gorgonians and hydrozoans plus a few hard corals, providing a wonderful habitat for around three hundred species of resident reef fish and another hundred species that visit from deeper water. Night dives are especially good. Built in 1915 in the US as a steamship, the 120m-long *Liberty* was carrying a cargo of rubber and rail parts when it was torpedoed on January 11, 1942, 15km southwest of Lombok. Attempts to tow the ship to port at Singaraja failed and it was beached at Tulamben, where it lay until 1963, when earth tremors accompanying the eruption of Gunung Agung shifted the *Liberty* into the water once more.

Although most people come to Tulamben for the wreck, there are plenty of other sites to explore. Many divers rate the **Tulamben Drop-off**, aka "The Wall", off the eastern end of the beach, at least as highly as the wreck itself. It comprises several fingers of volcanic rock that drop to 60m and are home to an enormous variety of fish, including unusual species such as comets, as well as black coral bushes. At **Batu Kelebit**, two huge boulders with coral-covered ridges are frequented by sharks, barracuda, jacks, manta rays and tuna. **Palung Palung** is suitable for beginners as well as experienced divers and has hard and soft coral, and an enticing variety of marine life from depths of 3m to 40m. **Tulamben Coral Garden** and **Shark Point** are self-descriptive, with black-tip reef sharks the draw at the latter. The locally famous muck dive at **Secret Seraya** (see below) is good for boxer crab, harlequin shrimp, ghost pipe fish and tiger shrimp.

DIVE CENTRES

Scuba dive centres in the area charge from $75 for two local dives and offer dive-and-accommodation packages as well as trips further afield, to Amed, Pemuteran and Nusa Penida. There's also a freediving school. The following centres are well established.

Apnea Bali ☎ 0822 6612 5814, ⓦ apneabali.com. Freediving school.
Tauch Terminal ☎ 0361 774504, ⓦ tulamben.com.
Tulamben Wreck Divers ☎ 0363 23400, ⓦ tulamben

wreckdivers.com.
Werner Lau Siddhartha resort (see below) ☎ 0363 23034, ⓦ wernerlau.com.

Puri Madha Central Tulamben ☎ 0363 22921, ⓦ puri madhabeachhotel.weebly.com. Set around an expansive shoreside garden right in front of the *Liberty* wreck. The priciest of the fifteen rooms (Rp500,000) are attractively furnished, with a/c and hot water as well as ocean views; the fan rooms are very basic. There's a pool and shoreside restaurant too. Rp200,000

Scuba Seraya Resort 3km east of central Tulamben ☎ 0363 4301288, ⓦ scubaseraya.com. Upscale dive resort with Bali-style maisonettes and villas in a spacious

beachside garden, plus a pool and dive centre. One of Bali's best muck dives, Secret Seraya, is just offshore. Rp950,000

Siddhartha Kubu, 3km west of central Tulamben ☎ 0363 23034, ⓦ siddhartha-bali.com. Classy dive resort with a dramatic contemporary design, elegant bungalows and villas, generous beachfront grounds and a spa. The house reef, a wreck, is just offshore and the in-house Werner Lau dive centre is well regarded. There's a spa, huge pool and free yoga sessions for guests. No children under 8. €140

EATING

Batu Belah 5km east of central Tulamben ☎ 0817 975 5214, ⓦ eastbaliresort.com. This oceanfront hotel restaurant makes a scenic stop on any trip along the coast, where you can indulge in British fish and chips and meat pie (mains Rp40,000–120,000) along with the usual Balinese dishes. Daily 7am–10pm.

Safety-Stop Central Tulamben ☎ 0812 4629 6152, ⓦ safety-stop-tulamben.com. Sited on the main drag in the village, this German-owned restaurant is very popular for its great grilled meat dishes, schnitzel, pasta (from Rp47,000), burgers (from Rp65,000) and huge portions. Daily 10am-10pm.

North Bali and the central volcanoes

PURA ULUN DANU BRATAN

North Bali and the central volcanoes

North Bali feels almost like a different island when compared to the crowded southern plains. A cool, less populated landscape of morning mists and forest, inland North Bali feels almost like a different island when compared to the crowded southern plains. It is an area defined by the volcanoes of Batur and Bedugul, where occasional puffs of smoke waft from black rock and market gardens line the shores of sacred volcanic lakes. Gunung Batur is Bali's most popular sunrise hike, but there are numerous other walks in the area. The Bedugul region around Danau Bratan is also defined by lakes and mountains, but it's on a smaller scale, with swathes of highland clove and coffee plantations around the little hilltown of Munduk and the important temple of Pura Ulun Danu Bratan, a popular destination for Balinese pilgrims.

For hundreds of years – possibly thousands – the north of Bali was most open to foreign influence as Indian, Chinese and Arab traders landed to do business here, most recently via the port and former Balinese capital of **Singaraja**. In the early twentieth century, the area became the island's tourist gateway, through the start of the KPM steamship service from Java in 1924. It was only when Ngurah Rai Airport opened in 1969 that the south became a focus for tourism and the axis of development shifted away from the north. Today, Singaraja remains north Bali's biggest city, capital of the administrative district of **Buleleng**, under whose jurisdiction the entire north coast falls.

The **coast** here is markedly quieter than its southern counterpart, receiving fewer visitors than the holiday conurbations in the south. Yet it is a rugged and, in places, impressive landscape, where flanks of the mountains drop steeply to black-sand beaches. The only resort that warrants the name is **Lovina**, a relaxed beach destination of family-owned guesthouses and funky cafés rather than pounding nightlife. It makes a decent base from which to explore the region on day-trips, to the temples and baths just west or to exuberant temple carvings and several large waterfalls around Singaraja.

GETTING AROUND   NORTH BALI AND THE CENTRAL VOLCANOES

By bemo or bus Public transport regularly serves the Singaraja–Gilimanuk road that runs along the north coast, taking in Lovina, and also the three main southbound roads through the mountains to Denpasar – from Seririt via Pupuan, Singaraja via Bedugul and Kubutambahan via Batur. This makes many of the sights in the north accessible by bus or bemo.

By car or motorbike You'll need your own transport to explore the scenic back roads.

Gunung Batur and around

Entry to the Batur area is Rp10,000/person, payable at booths on the access roads from Bangli and Ubud – you'll only pay once, so keep your ticket

On a clear day, no scenery in Bali can match that of the **Batur** area. With its volcanic peaks and silver-turquoise crater lake, the scale and spectacle of this

SEKUMPUL WATERFALL

Highlights

❶ Gunung Batur The hard-sell can infuriate, but Bali's most celebrated (and most active) volcano is worth the hassle for the spectacular panorama from its crater rim. To see it close up, trek up to the summit. **See p.192**

❷ Danau Bratan area This highland region harbours a trio of sacred crater lakes, a temple that is as beautiful as it is venerated and Bali's best botanical garden. **See p.201**

❸ Munduk The island's loveliest hill resort, a former Dutch colonial village with fine accommodation, enjoyable treks and hours to be lost simply enjoying the mesmerizing views. **See p.203**

❹ Lovina Although the beaches are not Bali's finest, the north coast's only mid-sized resort remains a laidback place, boasting a fine selection of hotels and restaurants. **See p.206**

❺ Sekumpul Waterfall Even on an island blessed by waterfalls, these seven cascades which tumble into a verdant valley are postcard-perfect. **See p.214**

❻ Pura Meduwe Karang The liveliest example of north Balinese temple carving, depicting vivid scenes from daily life and Hindu mythology. **See p.215**

HIGHLIGHTS ARE MARKED ON THE MAP ON P.194

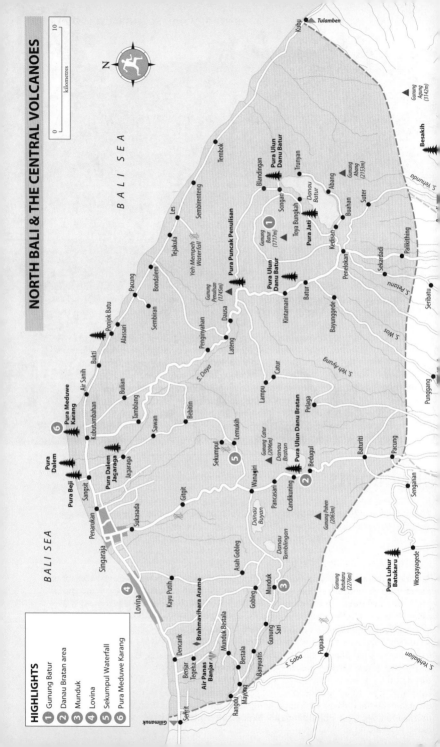

ERUPTIONS AT GUNUNG BATUR

Gunung Batur has **erupted more than twenty times** since 1800. In 1917, a major eruption killed over a thousand people, but the lava stopped just outside the temple of Batur village, which was then situated in the crater beside the lake. Considering this a good omen, the population stayed put until August 3, 1926, when another eruption engulfed the village and residents were relocated onto the rim. The **longest eruption** started in September 1963, a few months after the massive explosion of Gunung Agung (see box, p.163), and continued for eight months. At Yehmampeh, on the road around the base of the mountain, you'll see lava flows from an eruption in March 1974. The newest crater, Batur IV, was formed during the eruption that began on August 7, 1994, and continues to erupt periodically. It spewed ash 300m above the summit in 2000 and hiking trails were closed in 2009 due to more than a hundred **earthquakes**. It's startling to see the volcano still smoking, but locals believe it's better that Batur lets off a little steam regularly rather than saving it up for a major blow.

landscape is unrivalled; so much so that UNESCO listed it as a geopark in 2012. It was formed thirty thousand years ago when the eruption of a gigantic volcano created a vast outer caldera that spans 13.5km. **Gunung Batur** (Mount Batur; 1717m) at its heart is still active – wisps of sulphurous smoke still drift from smaller cones on its slopes. A major trans-Bali road runs along the west side of the crater rim, affording magnificent high-level views, and a side road gives access to the crater lake, **Danau Batur**, on its floor.

Given the scenery, it's no surprise that this is one of Bali's most popular tourist destinations. Hundreds of day-trippers come for lunch in the village of **Penelokan** and leave having experienced little except a wraparound panorama and a sloppy buffet lunch in the many coach-tour restaurants. Only by stopping overnight in one of the **villages by the lake** can you drink in the magic of this scenery. Many travellers base themselves locally to make the fairly straightforward sunrise trek up Gunung Batur, Bali's most climbed mountain. **Toya Bungkah** is popular and has some hot springs nearby while the village of **Kedisan** is an alternative, and also the departure point for ethically questionable boat trips to a Bali Aga cemetery at **Trunyan**. South of Kedisan, **Buahan** is the quietest spot of all, while **Songan**, at the northern end of the lake, is the start of other hikes up the crater rim.

The one downside to the awesome scenery is that the Batur area has a reputation for **hassle**. Persistent **hawkers** in Penelokan and aggressive hotel touts make those in Kuta seem relaxed, while a local trekking guide cartel makes it almost impossible to climb the mountain unguided (see box, p.197). Trust us: the remarkable views are worth it.

Routes up Gunung Batur

There's a choice of **routes up Gunung Batur**. If you have your own transport, the easiest option is to drive to **Serongga**, off the Yehmampeh road, west of Songan. From the car park, it's a stiff thirty minutes to an hour hike to the highest peak and largest of the caldera's inner craters, **Batur I**. Steam holes just below its rim confirm this volcano is far from extinct, although the crater has grassed over.

However, most people ascend up to Batur I from **Toya Bungkah** and **Pura Jati**, a steep climb but not too gruelling if you pace it steadily. The path from Pura Jati is shadeless and largely across old lava fields. From Toya Bungkah, numerous paths head up through the scrub – one starts just south of *Arlina's* guesthouse – before emerging onto bare lava slopes to ascend steeply through black volcanic sand to the tiny warung on the rim of Batur I. Allow two to three hours to get to the top from either starting point, and about half that time to get back down; sunrise treks up this route depart at

Pura Puncak Penulisan

Gunung
Penulisan
(1745m)

Pinggan

ACCOMMODATION

Bali Sunrise	1
Black Lava Hostel	4
Hotel Astra Dana	5
Hotel Baruna	8
Hotel Segara	6
Lakeview	7
Miranda	3
Volcano Terrace	2

Pura Bukit Mentik   Yehmampeh

Blandingan

Gunung Batur
(1717m)

Serongga

Kintamani   Pasar Umum
       Pura Ulun
       Danu Batur

Craters of Gunung Batur

Pura Ulun
Danu Batur

Songan

Kuban Cemetery

Association
of Mount Batur
Trekking Guides

Toya Bungkah

Toya Devasaya
Hot Spring

N

Batur

Pura
Jati

Batur Natural
Hot Spring

Trunyan

Danau Batur
(1031m)

Boats to
Trunyan

Abang

0   2
kilometres

Kedisan

Buahan

Penelokan

Gunung
Abang
(2153m)

Museum Gunungapi Batur

GUNUNG BATUR AND AROUND

Outer crater rim

Ubud   Tampaksiring   Bangli   Suter, Rendang & Besakih

about 4am. Though you could just as easily leave later and go for the view from halfway up – it's no less impressive.

A **medium-length trek** takes in Batur I, a walk around its rim, before descending by another route. The **long-trek** option, sometimes called the **Exploration** (about 8hr in total) involves Batur I, walking to the western side, then descending to Batur II, Batur III and down to Toya Bungkah or Yehmampeh.

Guides are not really necessary on the first two routes, but are definitely advisable if you're hiking at night (see box opposite). However, as the hard-sell and pressure from the guides' association is relentless, most hikers do hire a guide.

Penelokan, Batur and Kintamani

Spread along the crater rim's road for 11km, the scruffy villages of **Penelokan**, **Batur** and **Kintamani** virtually merge; the three are often named Kintamani after the largest settlement. The big attraction, of course, is the view, which is at its most sensational from Penelokan (1450m), literally meaning "Place to Look", and your spot for wraparound views of the volcanic landscape: Gunung Batur (on your left), Gunung Abang (2153m) opposite and between them Danau Batur lake as a shimmering skin of silver. To add context to the view, a recently expanded **museum** here offers a decent introduction to local geology and there are two very important **temples**, too. As you head north, the villages of Batur and Kintamani merge in a seamless sprawl of stalls and shops; the former was moved here from the crater beneath after it was obliterated in the 1926 eruption. There's a colourful morning market in Kintamani. Incidentally, bear in mind that you're at about 1400m above sea level up here, so nights are **chilly** – you might be glad of a sweater even in the daytime, especially if the mist descends.

Museum Gunungapi Batur

Jl Raya Penelokan, on Bangli road, just south of the junction with the crater-rim road • Mon–Thurs 8am–4pm, Sat & Sun 8am–2pm • Free • ☎ 0366 51152

Housed in a striking building that vaguely resembles a volcano, the **Museum Gunungapi Batur** (Batur Volcano Museum) summarizes the history, mythology and geology of Batur. Scale models show the changing face of the local topography, and there are informative computer animations on volcano systems and an exhibit on the Pacific's "Ring of Fire". From the top floor a telescope is directed at the smoking cone of Gunung Batur.

Pura Ulun Danu Batur

South Kintamani • Daily dawn–dusk • Rp35,000

The second most important temple on Bali after Besakih, **Pura Ulun Danu Batur** honours **Ida Batara Dewi Ulun Danu** (Dewi Danu for short), the goddess of the crater lake who is believed to control water for the irrigation systems throughout Bali. Her influential representative on earth is the temple's high priest, the Jero Gde, who is appointed on the death of his predecessor by a virgin priestess in a trance. He plays a vital role within Bali's sophisticated *subak* irrigation system and farmers consult him about plans and conflicts – his word is final.

Given its status and that it is one of the highly venerated *kayangan jagat*, or directional temples, which protects Bali from the north, it's perhaps surprising to learn that this temple is relatively new. It was relocated from the crater to its present position on the Kintamani–Penelokan border after the 1926 eruption (see box, p.195). The most significant of its countless shrines is the **eleven-roofed meru** in the inner courtyard, dedicated to both the goddess of the lake and the god of Gunung Agung. The drum in the *kulkul* tower is beaten 45 times each morning to honour the 45 deities worshipped in the temple.

Unfortunately gangs of aggressive, unholy scammers and guides spoil the experience for many. Yes, a sarong and sash are compulsory attire, but don't pay more than Rp20,000 or so to rent them from the pushy locals.

PLANNING A GUNUNG BATUR TREK

Batur remains **active** and the authorities sometimes close the mountain. Check the current situation at ⓦvsi.esdm.go.id – it's mostly in Indonesian but it is clear if any mountain is on alert. The **dry season** (April–Oct) is best for climbing.

Anyone who climbs Batur is put under intense pressure to engage a guide from the **Association of Mount Batur Trekking Guides**, or HPPGB (3am–3.30pm; ☎0366 52362), which has offices in Toya Bungkah and at Pura Jati. A guide is essential for all **sunrise treks**, which require route-finding in the dark – one solo foreign walker fell to his death in 2010 – and hugely advisable for longer hikes or less well-trodden paths. These routes are tricky and it's important to stay away from the most active parts of the volcano. If you are doing the climb in daylight either from Serongga or to Batur I from Toya Bungkah or Pura Jati, you don't really need a guide, but you will get intensely hassled, perhaps even intimidated, into hiring one anyway. On the plus side, a good guide will provide historical and cultural context to a walk.

Guide **prices** are displayed in the association's offices. At the time of research they were Rp350,000 per person for a four-hour sunrise trek; Rp500,000 to the main crater, Batur I (5hr); Rp800,000 up Gunung Agung (6hr) or up Gunung Abang (10hr). You'll probably have to pay extra for breakfast on the mountain – usually the novelty of boiled eggs cooked by geothermal energy – and transport to the trailhead, if required. Be absolutely clear which route you are doing.

Many **tour agencies** around Bali run sunrise hikes with pick-ups from hotels, albeit at times no tourist should have to see. Try Bali Sunrise Tours (ⓦbalisunrisetours.com), Pineh Bali Tours (ⓦpinehbalitours.com) or Mudi Goes to the Mountain (ⓦmudigoestothemountain.com).

However you ascend, you'll need sturdy footwear for the rough track and warm clothing for dawn treks.

Pura Puncak Penulisan

Sukawana (where road descends to coast) • Daily dawn–dusk • Donation sometimes requested for admission

Built on the summit of Gunung Penulisan (1745m), 5km north of Kintamani in the village of Sukawana, **Pura Puncak Penulisan** is the highest temple on Bali and one of the most ancient; it is named in ninth-century inscriptions. There are 333 steps to the top temple, **Pura Panarajon**, which is dedicated to Sanghyang Grinatha, a manifestation of Siwa and god of the mountains. Up here, *bale* shelter ancient lingam and statues from the eleventh to thirteenth centuries. Needless to say, when the clouds clear the views are spectacular.

Danau Batur and around

Filling the ancient crater, silver-emerald **Danau Batur** is not just the largest lake in Bali (8km by 3km), it is also one of the most impressive. As the home of Dewi Danu, the goddess of the crater lake, Danau Batur is especially sacred to the Balinese – it is believed to feed springs in other parts of the island. Several villages line the lake's shore, notably **Kedisan**, **Buahan** and **Toya Bungkah**, which have tourist accommodation, and **Songan**, site of an important temple and a footpath up the mountain. Nowadays, villagers survive on tourism and the simple things the gods provide: vegetables, which grow in the fertile soils along the shore, and fish.

Kedisan and Buahan

One of the first lakeside villages you'll come to, **KEDISAN** lies among the chilli, tomato, onion and potato plots at the bottom of the steep 3km road from Penelokan. The lakeside village is the departure point for boats to Trunyan cemetery (see below) and also kayaking and cycling trips around the lake.

Turning right at the T-junction in Kedisan brings you to the quietest and most attractive part of the lake, especially around and beyond the village of **BUAHAN**, 2km from Kedisan, where the eastern shore is lined with market gardens and fish-farming paraphernalia and offers some of the finest lake views of Gunung Batur.

Trunyan

TRUNYAN is among Bali's less edifying tourist destinations. It's one of the few remaining Bali Aga communities, inhabited by descendants of the "original Balinese" who rejected the Javanization of their island when the Majapahit invaded in 1343 and have maintained their distinctive customs ever since. The most famous is the village custom of leaving its dead to decompose in the open rather than cremating or burying them; cadavers are usually covered in a blanket and protected from animals within a bamboo cage (though human bones and even skulls are often visible). If you do decide to visit, expect demands for donations.

Visiting the **cemetery** is an uneasy experience and it can only be culturally sensitive if you attend with a responsible local guide. It's also not cheap: access is by chartered **boat** from a jetty in Kedisan (20min; 8am–5pm; from Rp450,000/boat for two people), then expect a hefty fee for a good guide (perhaps Rp250,000). We recommend that you skip it.

Toya Bungkah and around

The main tourist village on Danau Batur is **TOYA BUNGKAH**; though fairly shabby, it has the most accommodation around the lake and is the starting point for climbs up Gunung Batur, as well as a base of the Association of Mount Batur Trekking Guides (see box, p.197). It also has a couple of **hot springs** for soaking stiff limbs after a walk (see opposite). About 4km south of Toya Bungkah, **Pura Jati**, dedicated to the god Wisnu, has some fine carvings. One of the routes up the mountain starts near here.

Songan and around

At the northwestern end of the lake, 4km beyond Toya Bungkah, the village of **SONGAN** is the location of **Pura Ulun Danu Batur**, not to be confused with the bigger, newer temple on the crater rim. A ceremony is held here every ten years to honour the goddess of the lake, involving the ritual drowning of buffaloes, pigs, goats, chickens and geese, all adorned with gold ornaments. Locals speculate that the floor of the lake is littered with riches from hundreds of years of ceremonies – possibly more, since this is said to be built on the site of a pre-Majapahit temple. Not many bemos serve Songan and you may end up **walking** to or from Toya Bungkah, either along the road or a lakeside track.

Directly behind the temple in Songan, a **footpath** winds up onto the rim of the outer crater – you can follow tracks to explore farming villages of bamboo huts. There are some fine views down to the north coast and back to Abang, Agung and even Rinjani on Lombok. With a good supply of food and water, the more intrepid should be able to pick a route down to **Bali's northeast coast** to pick up public transport west to Air Sanih or east to Tulamben.

From the junction in central Songan, a **scenic road** runs for 26km around the base of Gunung Batur to Penelokan via the small village of **Yehmampeh**. It takes you past **Pura Bukit Mentik**, known as Lucky Temple because lava from the 1974 eruption surrounded it but caused no damage. By serendipity, the lava fields are now mined as building stone and sand, ferried from the area by a steady procession of trucks.

ARRIVAL AND DEPARTURE   GUNUNG BATUR AND AROUND

By bus or bemo The crater rim road is a main route between the north and south coasts, so public transport is frequent. Perama tourist shuttle buses run to and from Ubud, Kuta and Sanur. Occasional public bemos from Penelokan go as far as Songan on the western side of the lake and Abang on the eastern side; the tourist fare to any of the lakeside accommodation is about Rp10,000.

Destinations from Penelokan (add/subtract 20min for Kintamani to the north) Bangli (45min); Buahan (30min); Denpasar (Batubulan; 2hr 30min); Gianyar (50min); Singaraja (Penarukan; 1hr 30min); Songan (45min); Toya Bungkah (30min).

ACTIVITIES

Kayaking C Bali in Kedisan, Kintamani (☎0813 5342 0541, ⊚c-bali.com) offers morning-only kayaking trips (Rp530,000/person, minimum two) around Danau Batur, with good cultural input from local guides and free pick-ups from South Bali.

Mountain-biking Sobek (⊚balisobek.com) and Bali Adventure Tours (⊚baliadventuretours.com) both run downhill cycling trips (around $75) in the Batur area – usually down slopes and through rice paddies – including transport from tourist centres in south Bali. There's not much pedalling involved, mostly freewheeling.

Hot springs For a lovely spa-style experience head to the garden pools in Toya Devasya (daily 8am–7pm; Rp180,000; ⊚toyadevasya.com) in the village centre. Or just south of Toya Bungkah, Batur Natural Hot Spring (daily 7am–7pm; Rp150,000 including towel; ⊚baturhotspring.com) is a somewhat tatty place offering three pools filled with spring water up to 35°C – facilities are somewhat rundown.

ACCOMMODATION AND EATING

There are simple warung in the villages for Indonesian grub like *nasi campur* while the guesthouse restaurants tend to offer more varied menus, including fresh fish. All are open 8am–9pm. Note that hotels in this highland region, where many owners were subsistence farmers a generation ago, do not have as high standards as those in more mainstream tourist areas.

PENELOKAN, BATUR AND KINTAMANI

Lakeview Penelokan ☎0366 52525, ⊚lakeviewbali .com. It's overpriced and rooms need updating but you're paying for the finest panorama in the area – the balconies here seem almost to hang over the crater's lip. Food in the huge restaurant is a tad bland. $88

Miranda Kintamani ☎0366 52022, ⊚mirandahomestay .com. A basic homestay with functional, garishly furnished rooms (with *mandi* in cold-water rooms – hot water costs an extra Rp50,000), but this is a friendly little homestay that's handy for public transport and has good rates for single travellers. Owner Made Senter is a respected trekking guide. Rp220,000

DANAU BATUR AND AROUND

Bali Sunrise Songan ☎0818 552 669, ⊚balisunrisevillas .com. This hotel's name is generic but the three lovely villas and rooms are anything but, kitted out with gorgeous rattan

ROADS LESS TRAVELLED

It's 40km from Kintamani down through the foothills to **Kubutambahan** on the **north coast** (see p.211), from where Singaraja is 7km west and Air Sanih is 6km east. This road is one of Bali's main north–south routes, busy with trucks, cars and tourist buses, but it takes you through some pretty scenery.

If you have time to spare, an attractive quieter alternative route runs via the **back road to Bondalem**, a north coast village that's 15km east of Air Sanih and 4km west of Tejakula (see p.216). The narrow, twisting, very steep and very scenic 16km road is signed off the main Kubutambahan road at **Lateng**, 13km from the market at Kintamani, and 500m after the end of the village of Dausa. This back road is known locally as the **Tejakula road**. It initially descends through vegetable gardens and stands of cloves, cocoa, coffee and avocado with great views of neighbouring ridges and west towards Gunung Batukaru. After about 10km the temperature rises significantly, and coconut plantations stretch all the way to the north coast.

furniture and elegant beds and tasteful paintings. There's a fecund garden and the good restaurant has a terrace with dreamy lake views. **Rp500,000**

Black Lava Hostel Toya Bunkah ☎ 0813 3755 8998, ⓦ facebook.com/blacklavahostel123/info. Owned by a local trekking guide, this impressive, rustic hostel is just the place to hook up with other travellers in the Batur area. There are two mixed dorms (with lockers for shared bathrooms) and decent private rooms with en-suites. The restaurant serves affordable local food and has sweeping lake views. Dorms **Rp150,000**, doubles **Rp375,000**

Hotel Astra Dana 500m west of the T-junction, Kedisan ☎ 0366 52091, ⓔ astradana_kintamani@yahoo.com. Well located on the lake's shore, this friendly small place has two options: bright, comfy bungalows with floor-to-ceiling windows in the garden (Rp500,000) or a dozen ultrabasic rooms in the main losmen, with cold-water bathrooms but great views from the first floor. **Rp300,000**

Hotel Baruna Just east of Buahan ☎ 0366 51378, ⓦ barunacottages.com. This peaceful place has two bright bungalows; cosy, cabin-like *lumbung*-style huts; or, the pick of the bunch, four spacious bungalows on the shore (Rp500,000) with picture-windows onto the lake. Service can, however, be a little distracted at times. **Rp400,000**

Hotel Segara 300m west of the T-junction, Kedisan ☎ 0366 51136, ⓦ batur-segarahotel.com. Large place, set round a yard, with various grades of comfort: from basic cold-water Economy, via Standards with hot water (Rp300,000), to smart, newly renovated Superiors and Deluxes which are worth the extra rupiah if you have the budget. Traffic noise is an issue, however. **Rp250,000**

★**Volcano Terrace** Toya Bungkah ☎ 0822 3744 4410, ⓦ facebook.com/VolcanoTerraceBali. Beautifully designed new place with wonderful lake views from its four spacious minimalist rooms that boast comfort and imaginative decorative touches. It's run by a friendly local family who provide good meals and can arrange guides for the Batur hike and exploring the area. **Rp400,000**

Danau Bratan and around

At weekends, domestic tourists come by the coachload to munch strawberries, enjoy the cool temperatures and admire the lakes and cloud-capped hills around the upland resort region of **Bedugul** (altitude 700m-plus). The area takes its name from the village of Bedugul, one of several small settlements up here (and the most missable, incidentally). But it's also referred to as the **Danau Bratan** area after the largest and most visited of the three spiritually charged crater lakes around Bedugul.

On the lake's shores lies **Pura Ulun Danu Bratan**, not just an exceedingly photogenic temple but also an important pilgrimage site for the Balinese. Temples and fruit and vegetables aside, the other major sight here is the **Bali Botanic Gardens**, with their **Bali Treetop Adventure Park**.

For all the fuss made over it by islanders, **Candikuning** is not Bali's most inspiring base. More appealing for foreign visitors is the little hilltown of **Munduk**, 20km northwest; often misty, always mellow and a shining example of sustainable village tourism, with several good places to stay and a range of activities to while away a few lazy days. Munduk also offers the opportunity to walk around the area's smaller, less commercial lakes: **Danau Buyan** and **Danau Tamblingan**.

Danau Bratan

Lying just below Candikuning at 1200m above sea level, **Danau Bratan** is thought to be 35m deep in places. It is surrounded by forested hills, with the bulk of **Gunung Catur** (2096m), the caldera's highest peak, rising sheer behind. At weekends, the lake becomes frenetic with watersports, but the scenery more than compensates for the buzz of motorboats.

Candikuning

Sliced up by traffic, the village of **CANDIKUNING** above the western shores of Danau Bratan is the main base for the lake and Bali Botanic Gardens. Accommodation and restaurants line the highway through the village, as well as the side road to the gardens. The daily market in the centre is another fun, if touristy, stop, a mix of fresh local fruit, spices, temple offerings and mass-produced souvenirs. It's a good place to stock up for a picnic in the botanic gardens.

Bali Botanic Gardens and Treetop Adventure Park

Well signed off a mini-roundabout beside the market, then 700m down a side road • **Bali Botanic Gardens** Daily 7am–6pm (last entry 4pm) • Rp18,000, parking Rp6000 for cars, Rp3000 for motorbikes; driving in gardens an additional Rp12,000/car (motorbikes prohibited) • ☎ 0368 203 3211 • **Bali Treetop Adventure Park** Daily 9.30am–6pm • $24 ($25 before 10.30am), under-12s $16, family $65 • ☎ 0361 934 0009, ⊛ balitreetop.com

Spread back into the forested slopes, **Bali Botanic Gardens** (Kebun Raya Eka Karya Bali) conserves some two thousand species of tropical montane plants; from ferns and countless orchids to impressive cacti, medicinal plants, bamboo forests and an extensive collection of begonias. It's a tranquil place – often cool and misty due to its altitude of 1250–1450m – and at 1.58 square kilometres is large enough to lose half a day or more exploring. Do so and you may discover birdlife such as brown honeyeaters and grey-cheeked green pigeons – over a hundred species have been recorded here – or see monkeys on upper slopes. Given the park's size, some people drive around the gardens,

4

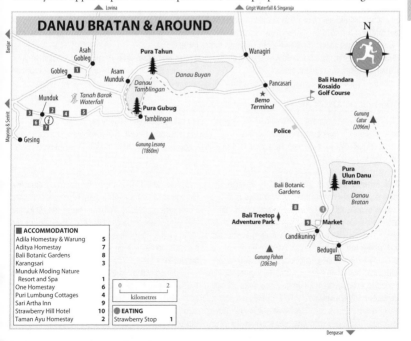

DANAU BRATAN & AROUND

N

Lovina   Gitgit Waterfall & Singaraja

Banjar

Asah
Gobleg

Gobleg ▮1

Munduk
Pura Tahun

Asam
Munduk

Danau
Tamblingan

Tanah Barak
Waterfall

Pura Gubug

Tamblingan

Danau Buyan

Wanagiri

Pancasari

Bemo
Terminal

Bali Handara
Kosaido
Golf Course

Gunung
Catur
(2096m)

Mayong & Seririt

Munduk ▮3 ▮2 ▮4 ▮5
▮6 ℹ7

Gesing

Gunung Lesong
(1860m)

Police

Pura
Ulun Danu
Bratan

Bali Botanic
Gardens

Danau
Bratan

Bali Treetop
Adventure Park

▮8

Gunung Pohon
(2063m)

Candikuning

●9 ▭ Market

Bedugul
▮10

■ ACCOMMODATION	
Adila Homestay & Warung	5
Aditya Homestay	7
Bali Botanic Gardens	8
Karangsari	3
Munduk Moding Nature Resort and Spa	1
One Homestay	6
Puri Lumbung Cottages	4
Sari Artha Inn	9
Strawberry Hill Hotel	10
Taman Ayu Homestay	2

0   2
kilometres

● EATING	
Strawberry Stop	1

Denpasar ▼

although you can also wander on foot. The gardens are a lovely spot for a picnic, which is a popular weekend activity. You can also stay in the gardens (see below).

A chance to go ape within the botanic gardens, the well-designed **Bali Treetop Adventure Park** allows you to swing (as well as slide and scramble) through the canopy of tall rasamala (*Altingia excelsa*) trees. The park, in the southwest corner of the botanical gardens, has seven circuits of ropeways, bridges, platforms, scrambling nets and zip lines constructed up to 20m off the ground. Mini-courses are designed to suit children from the age of four upwards, with some sections restricted to older children. Safety gloves and harnesses are provided, along with guides. Weekends are often very busy.

Pura Ulun Danu Bratan

1km north of Candikuning centre • Daily 9am–7pm • Rp50,000, children Rp25,000, parking Rp5000 • ☎ 0368 203 3050

Lake Danau and its goddess are worshipped in **Pura Ulun Danu Bratan**, a classical Balinese temple situated in a breathtaking lakeside location. Today it's a major tourist attraction, with car parks full of coaches from the coast, souvenir stands and the inevitable touts. Yet, despite the commercialization, the temple is also highly revered in Bali; especially at weekends, you'll see villagers dressed in their best to deliver offerings. Built in 1633 by the raja of Mengwi on a promontory on the western shore, it's dedicated to Dewi Danu, source of water and hence of fertility for the island and the Balinese. Shrines are dotted about the lake's shore and on islets – an impressive sight with the mountain slopes rising steeply behind. Closest to the shore, the eleven-roofed **meru** is dedicated to Wisnu and Dewi Danu. There's no public access to the shrines but, crowds and clouds permitting, they still look fabulous from the shoreline. Given the tourist circus, a quick photo opportunity is sufficient for most people.

ARRIVAL AND DEPARTURE

DANAU BRATAN AND AROUND

By shuttle bus Perama tourist shuttle buses pass through Candikuning on their Ubud–Lovina route and can drop you at any of the hotels on the main road for an extra Rp15,000; their office and pick-up point (☎ 0368 21011, ⊛ perama tour.com) is at *Sari Artha Inn*, just north of the market.
Destinations Kuta (daily; 2hr 30min–3hr); Lovina (daily; 1hr 30min); Sanur (daily; 2hr–2hr 30min); Ubud (daily; 1hr 30min); all destinations cost Rp75,000.

By bemo Candikuning sits on a main north–south road, so is served by bemo services to and from Denpasar and Singaraja. Local bemos also beetle around the area; the main terminal is north of Candikuning in Pancasari. No bemos go to Danau Tamblingan.
Destinations Denpasar (Ubung; 2hr); Singaraja (Sukasada); 1hr 30min).

By car and motorbike Danau Bratan is 53km north of Denpasar and 30km south of Singaraja on the main Denpasar–Mengwi–Singaraja road; no direct route links it to Batur.

ACCOMMODATION AND EATING

Because of the cool climate up here (down to 10°C at night), no accommodation offers fans or air-conditioning – you'll be more interested in thick quilts and hot water. Accommodation in the area can be quite run-down and overpriced – most foreigners prefer Munduk as a base. For a cheap feed, browse the abundant warung in the market, where there are always strawberries for sale.

Bali Botanic Gardens ☎ 0368 22050. Probably the most peaceful accommodation in Candikuning is at this hotel within the Botanic Gardens, which has comfortable hotel rooms (some with great garden views) and more modern cottages. Prices include entry to the gardens. **$52**
Sari Artha Inn Just north of the market, Candikuning ☎ 0368 21011. Cheap losmen, handy for public transport, with basic, hot- or cold-water rooms. It's located on the main road, so be prepared for some traffic noise. **Rp220,000**
Strawberry Hill Hotel Km 48, Bedugul ☎ 0368 21265, ⊛ strawberryhillbali.com. The best midrange choice for miles, this lovely lodge has seventeen stylish little bungalows kitted out with batik prints and attractive furnishings, while the brilliant pub-like bar-restaurant has a pool table, dart board, books to browse and even a log fire. You'll find Western and Indonesian favourites on the menu (dishes Rp22,000–70,000) and you can pick your own strawberries here too. **Rp550,000**
Strawberry Stop 1.5km north of the temple ☎ 0368 203 3100. Strawberries are grown in the allotments behind this place, and they feature in everything from ice cream and milkshakes to pancakes and waffles. Strawberries aside, Indo-European mains such as *nasi goreng* and *mie goreng* (Rp40,000) are also available. Daily 9am–6pm.

Munduk and around

Strung out amongst clove trees and coffee plantations along a steep valley spur, the village of **MUNDUK** is one of Bali's most appealing hill retreats. It remains a mellow, low-key settlement, with refreshingly cool temperatures and gorgeous vistas; the sort of place where you can arrive for a night and leave a week later. Cloud-gazing aside, days are spent **walking** to nearby villages and waterfalls, while dusks ease into nights to spectacular sunsets and a soundtrack of a million frogs. The **Dutch** administration were the first foreigners to relish Munduk's scenery, as well as its fertile soils and cooler climate at 500–700m above sea level. From 1910 they developed it as a summer retreat and cultivated coffee, cloves, vanilla and cocoa in the surrounding fertile soils. Some of their weekend homes are now used as guesthouses, but colonial **Dutch architecture** along the main street is hardly the point. (The village is barely 500m long, for a start.) Instead, see Munduk as a chance to kick back – slow travel has never been so beautiful.

Tanah Barak waterfall

The most accessible of several falls in the area is pretty **Tanah Barak waterfall**, also known as Red Coral waterfall or simply Munduk waterfall. Take a signposted track off the main road 1km east of Munduk, pay Rp3000 at an ad hoc booth (usually – it's not always manned) and you can take a short rainforest track to reach this impressive cascade which plumes into a lush gorge. There are several other falls in the area to make a half-day trip from central Munduk.

Danau Buyan

Car park Rp5000, although it's not always staffed

Danau Bratan may receive all the acclaim, but it's not the only lake in this highland region. In **Pancasari**, 4.5km north of Candikuning, at a small bemo terminal – it's busiest in the morning and is the junction for travel to Munduk – a turn-off tracks to **Danau Buyan** through allotments and gardens. More pothole than tarmac, the lane peters out at the lake's southern shore; a tranquil spot after the hubbub around Bratan, with little here except a ticket booth for a car park and a few fishermen in dugout canoes. It's a lovely place to relax – or you could embark from here on a good 4km track around the lake's shore and over a saddle to reach Danau Tamblingan.

Danau Tamblingan

Rp6000, plus Rp5000 parking if booth is manned

Danau Tamblingan is the smallest and most atmospheric of Bedugul's three lakes, once contiguous with Danau Buyan to the east (before a landslide in 1818), now separated by a forested shoulder of land. **Trekking** between the two lakes is a popular activity, you don't really need a guide as it's just a matter of keeping the lakes on your left-hand side. The path around the western shore is also renowned for **birdwatching** – sightings of babblers, woodpeckers, ground thrushes and malkohas are possible.

On the shore, **Pura Gubug** has eleven-, nine- and five-roofed *meru* and is dedicated to Dewi Danu, the goddess of the lake. Several other temples overlook the shoreline, including the ancient Pura Dalem Tamblingan on the east side. Villagers grow hydrangeas, marigolds and mandarins in the fertile, lake-watered soils, fish for carp, and rear cattle on the *tunjung* (lotus) that grows on the lake.

4

ARRIVAL AND INFORMATION	MUNDUK AND AROUND

Munduk is 8km west of Danau Tamblingan, 20km northwest of Candikuning and 20km southeast of Seririt. Access by public transport is possible but long and circuitous; bemos are most reliable in the early morning.

By shuttle bus Coming from southern resorts or Ubud, take the Perama shuttle bus to Bedugul (Pancasari), then change for a bemo to Munduk.

By bemo Bemos travel up to Munduk from Seririt, itself easily reached by bemo from Pemuteran or Lovina on the north coast. There are also bemos every couple of hours

THE CLOVE TRAIL

It was the search for **cloves**, among other spices, that first drove Europeans to explore the Indonesian archipelago, and for hundreds of years they were one of the region's most lucrative exports. Native to certain islands of the Moluccas (the original "Spice Islands"), cloves are now grown mainly in Maluku, Sumatra, Sulawesi and Bali. You'll spot the tall trees in the hills around Bedugul, Tamblingan and Munduk and if you're there during **harvest time**, from August to October, you'll see death-defying pickers on rickety ladders and huge piles of drying cloves beside the road – buds must be picked before the petals open, after which the amount of clove oil declines sharply.

Bali's cloves end up in Java for the manufacture of Indonesia's pungent **kretek cigarettes**. These consist of up to fifty percent cloves mixed with tobacco, and demand is so great that the former clove capital of the world now imports them from Madagascar and Zanzibar to supplement local production.

from Denpasar's Ubung terminal. Bemos on all routes are more frequent in the morning.

Destinations Denpasar (Ubung; 2hr 30min); Seririt (1hr).
By taxi Duta's Transport, at the east end of village (☎0819 3667 1141). Fixed-price fares are Rp250,000/car to Bedugul, Rp280,000 to Lovina or Rp450,000 to Ubud.
By motorbike Motorbikes are widely available for rent.
Banks and exchange There are no ATMs in Munduk, though a moneychanger is available.

ACTIVITIES

Activity tours Munduk Wilderness (☎0361 870 0001, ⓦ mundukwilderness.com) provides a number of off-road driving tours in 4WD buggies in the region ($99/person for two), as well as horseriding and two-day wilderness trips ($155/person includes twin-share room). Prices include transfers from major resorts in Bali.
Cooking lessons Both *Puri Lumbung Cottages* (see p.206) and *Chez Rico* (☎0852 0510 7928, ⓦ cocoricodebali@gmail .com) offer well-structured Indonesian and Balinese cooking lessons. The latter's cost Rp300,000.
Cultural workshops *Puri Lumbung Cottages* has an exceptionally diverse range of cultural workshops (from $15): as well as cooking lessons ($35) and yoga, it can run sessions in herbal medicine, Indonesian language, dancing, bamboo-instrument making and Balinese music classes.
Trekking and mountain biking Guesthouses arrange local guides; expect to pay Rp50,000–100,000/hr/guide

depending on whether you just have someone to show you the way or an expert English-speaking guide. Most treks are rural hikes through clove and coffee plantations, via market gardens growing blue hydrangeas (used for offerings), vanilla and mandarins, and through ricefields and villages. You're also likely to be offered treks to several waterfalls in the area, the closest being Tanah Barak (Munduk) waterfall (about 1km east of Munduk). Treks to and between lakes Tamblingan and Buyan are also well worth doing (see p.203), or you could try climbing Gunung Lesong (1860m). Munduk Trekking (☎0821 4729 4251, ⓦ mundukactivity.wordpress.com) offers good guided walks (half-day $35) past waterfalls and clove and coffee plantations. *Puri Lumbung Cottages* (see p.206) runs several half-day guided mountain bike rides including the "Pyramid Trail" past a pyramid made from recycled plastic, ricefields and Danau Tamblingan.

ACCOMMODATION AND EATING

The quality of accommodation in Munduk is generally high. Many places offer superb views and all have an attached restaurant (which is usually OK rather than particularly exciting). *Puri Lumbung Cottages* has the best in the area.

Adila Homestay & Warung ☎0819 3655 1226, ⓦ adilahomestay.com. Expert a warm welcome at this lovely place, where the four spotless rooms have four-poster beds, hot-water bathrooms and enjoy terrific vistas from their verandas. There's great local food in the warung and the owners are full of local information. Book ahead. Rp350,000
Aditya Homestay ☎0852 3888 2968, ⓦ adityahomestay

.com. Friendly homestay in a two-storey house with simply furnished but spotless comfortable modern rooms, all with hot water and a veranda. Another good reason to come are the views – some of the best in Munduk. $25
Karangsari ☎0821 4484 4844, ⓦ karangsari -guesthouse.com. This family-run place has bright rooms with modern Balinese furnishings opening onto a garden with views to the hills – upper rooms have the

best views. Older rooms in the Dutch-era "Bougainvillea" block beneath are spacious, but looking a little tired these days. Good rates for single travellers are available. **Rp250,000**

Munduk Moding Nature Resort and Spa Asah Gobleg village, 5km west of Danau Tamblingan ☎0361 700 5321, ⓦmundukmodingplantation.com. Hidden within a large plantation 10km from Munduk, this remote spa retreat is the perfect escape. Modern villas – all rich hardwood floors and crisp fine cotton – overlook beautiful forest; cheaper suite rooms are also available. Perhaps more impressive is the infinity swimming pool – rightly acclaimed as one of Asia's best – and the spa and hot tub are lovely too. Suites $144, villas $194

One Homestay Jl Selau ☎0852 3718 8980, ⓦfacebook .com/onehomestay.munduk. A cheapie but a goodie – *One Homestay* has four basic rooms with hot water over two floors of a family compound on a side road. The price and charming owner aside, the best reason to come is for the views across the valley. Breakfast is not included but there's an in-house warung for meals. **Rp140,000**

Puri Lumbung Cottages ☎0812 387 4042, ⓦpuri lumbung.com. This place has real character and wonderful vistas. Cosy *lumbung*-style cottages or spacious villas are set around ricefields with panoramas to the north coast, though interiors would benefit from some updating. On-site amenities include a spa, a sunset bar and the most extensive menu in the region (restaurant 8am–10pm), serving authentic Indonesian food and Western dishes (from Rp40,000). It also manages two Dutch-era homestays and eight forest cabins near Lake Tamblingan – if eco-isolation appeals and you don't need electricity, this is your place. Forest cabins $48, cottages $98, villas $130

Taman Ayu Homestay ☎0813 3755 6127, ⓦfacebook .com/taman.ayu.39. Traditional, welcoming family home-stay, where the simple rooms have mismatched furnishings, balconies over the valley and a basic bathroom with hot water. **Rp250,000**

Lovina and around

Northern Bali's primary beach resort, **LOVINA** remains a low-rise, low-key sort of place, especially when compared to its south Bali counterparts. Its shoreline is not startlingly attractive (the dark sand is not most people's vision of a tropical dream beach and there's some trash about) but Lovina does have a decidedly Balinese, non-international feel and this ensures an enjoyably mellow, local vibe.

Lovina is spread out along 8km of grey-sand beach, encompassing seven merged villages. **Kalibukbuk**, set between two side roads and lined with an oceanfront walkway, is the heart of Lovina, bursting with accommodation, restaurants and facilities. East of Kalibukbuk, the **Banyualit** side road, Jalan Laviana, runs down to the sea and is quiet and green, with banana palms still dotted between the various small warung and hotels. It's favoured by long-stay and older tourists from northern Europe. There's more of a backpacker vibe in the village of **Anturan**, 1.5km east of Banyualit, with most places on or very close to the village beach and a snorkellable reef offshore. Finally, Anturan peters out and ricefields take over and you're officially in the village of **Pemaron**.

Dolphin-spotting boat trips are wildly popular (though see warning below) and cultural activities including cooking classes are on offer. Lovina's proximity to good **snorkelling** and **diving** sites, and as a base for day-trips to nearby waterfalls and temples are another key appeal. The **Buddhist monastery** and **hot springs** at Banjar, 10km west, and temples and waterfalls east of **Singaraja** (see p.211) make a good day out. And with those ticked off, the crater lakes and hikes around Bedugul and Munduk are just under two hours away.

Brahmavihara Arama

Rarely closed; hosts a busy programme of meditation workshops and teachings (see website) • Donation for entry includes sarong rental • ☎0362 92954, ⓦbrahmaviharaarama.com • Catch any westbound bemo to Dencarik, where ojek wait to take you the last, steep 3km; if driving, head as for Air Panas Banjar hot springs and turn left at the central crossroads in Banjar Tegeha village

Bali's largest Buddhist monastery, the **Brahmavihara Arama** is 10km southwest of Lovina in the hills outside Banjar Tegeha village, so is a good combination trip with the hot springs at Banjar 3km away (see opposite). (Incidentally, if you ask for directions, bear in mind that locals know it as the "Buddis temple" rather than by its name.)

A DAY-TRIP DRIVE FROM LOVINA

For a day-trip from Lovina with your own transport, there's a scenic **inland drive** through the countryside south of Seririt (see p.241), 12km west of Lovina, initially along the Denpasar road. The road climbs through paddyfields then splits after 7km at **Rangdu**. The right-hand fork heads across the mountains via Pupuan to the south coast. However, the left goes through Mayong, home to *Bali Panorama* (see p.210), a small warung with scenic views, towards Munduk (see p.203) then on to Danau Tamblingan and Danau Buyan.

Just beyond Mayong, take a small left turn for "Desa Bestala", which leads to the village of **Bestala**. Turn left by the statue of the independence fighter, then wind down into the valley, across the river and up the other side to the hamlet of **Munduk Bestala**, famous for its durians; January and February are the main season. Turn right at the T-junction in the village, and if you have a decent map it's possible to navigate to **Pedawa** and **Sidetapa**, two traditional Bali Aga villages that still retain their narrow lanes and high-walled compounds.

Adjani in Lovina provides guided walks in the Sidetapa area, as well as transport (see p.209).

The monastery is a serene spot after the hurly-burly of everyday Balinese life. It's primarily a place of meditation, yet welcomes casual visitors, and its shrines and prayer halls afford good views to the coast. The centrepiece of the main temple is a Thai-style gold Buddha, but follow stairs in the peaceful grounds and you'll also find a Nepalese-style stupa (dome-shaped shrine). The most striking section is the (scaled-down) **lava-stone replica** of East Java's Borobodur temple in serene frangipani gardens at the summit of the complex. It houses a meditation hall with limestone reliefs of the life of the Buddha.

Air Panas Banjar hot springs

Daily 8am–6pm • Rp10,000, child Rp5000 • Coming from Kalibukbuk in Lovina, take the main road west for 8km, then follow signs south for 2.5km to reach the springs; the springs are also 3km from the Brahmavihara Arama Buddhist monastery, reached from the village crossroads; there's no public transport

The traditional-style **hot springs** at **Air Panas Banjar** are certainly picturesque: tiered over three pools and fed by water spouting from *naga* dragons' mouths, they sit enclosed in a dell of palm trees and tropical forest, 1.25km south of the market in Banjar Tegeha. The water, however, is another matter. Silky soft and slightly sulphurous, it is a rather murky green, but this doesn't stop the pools from being hugely popular with locals and tourists alike. Come in the morning to avoid the crowds; weekends are especially busy. There are lockers, (pretty filthy) changing rooms, and a small restaurant overlooking the pools. Note that women have reported being stared at when wearing swimwear.

ARRIVAL AND INFORMATION
LOVINA AND AROUND

Central Lovina is only 10km west of Singaraja, so there are plenty of transport services to major destinations across Bali, Lombok and Java, including those of Bali-wide Perama tourist shuttle buses.

By shuttle bus Perama tourist shuttle buses connect Lovina with tourist centres across Bali; their office is in Anturan (daily 8am–10pm; ☎0362 41161, ☺peramatour.com) but for an additional Rp15,000 you can be dropped off elsewhere.

Destinations All the following Perama services leave at 9am daily: Bedugul (1hr 30min); Candidasa (3hr–3hr 30min); Gili Islands, Lombok (8hr); Kuta/Ngurah Rai Airport (3hr 15min); Padang Bai (2hr 45min); Sanur (2hr 30min–3hr); Ubud (3hr 30min–4hr).

By bemo or bus From east Bali, you'll come via Singaraja: its

Banyuasri terminal is a 20min bemo ride away (Rp10,000). From Denpasar, there are Ubung–Singaraja services via Pupuan, and minibuses to Seririt for local bemo connections. Interisland buses from Java to Singaraja pass through Lovina, as do Gilimanuk–Singaraja and Amlapura–Gilimanuk services and all local buses and bemos from west Bali.

Destinations Amlapura (3hr 30min); Gilimanuk (2hr 45min); Seririt (20min); Singaraja (Banyuasri; 20min).

Tourist information Lovina's tourist office (Mon–Sat 8am–6pm; ☎0362 41910 mornings only) is on Jl Raya Kalibukbuk.

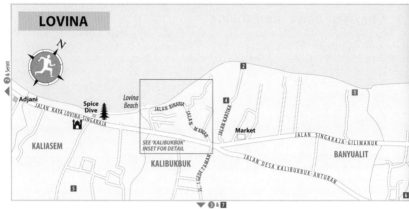

■ ACCOMMODATION	
The Damai	7
Frangipani Beach Hotel	2
Harris Homestay	10
Kubu Beach	3
Puri Bagus Lovina	1
Rambutan	9
Sananda Bungalows	6
Santhika Bed & Breakfast	5
Sea Breeze Cottages	8
Taman Lily's	11
Villa Taman Ganesh	4

■ DRINKING AND NIGHTLIFE	
Kantin 21	4
Poco Bar	3
Spunky's Bar and Restaurant	1
Zigiz	2

● EATING	
Akar Café	6
Bali Panorama	2
The Damai	3
Jasmine Kitchen	5
Le Madre	7
My Greek Taverna	4
Warung Bambu	1

GETTING AROUND

By bemo Bemos ply the main Lovina road, Jl Raya, fairly frequently during daylight hours (Rp5000 for a local ride within the Lovina area).

By car, motorbike or bike Cars or motorbikes are available everywhere – it's probably easiest to source

one through your accommodation. For bicycles, there are several travel agencies on Jl Mawar. Be very careful driving along the main drag Jl Raya Lovina which is the main route for a lot of Bali-Java traffic and is plagued by heavy traffic, including aggressive truck drivers, 24 hours a day.

ACTIVITIES

Buffalo races Lovina has a weakness for buffalo races (*sapi gerumbungan*) in Kaliasem, one of the few places on Bali where this colourful tradition can still be seen. They're usually staged on Independence Day (Aug 17), and in September (along with various other cultural performances) – source information at the tourist office.

Diving and snorkelling The local reef is pretty pedestrian for experienced divers, though there's decent fish life, a small wooden wreck and an artificial reef that's encouraging coral growth. Local dive shops run trips to Pulau Menjangan, Tulamben and Amed but these involve a lot of time on the road. Spice Dive (☎0362 41512, ⍟balispicedive.com), on the Kaliasem beachfront and on Jl Bina Ria, is a Five Star

PADI dive centre. It charges from $30 for local dives or $65–80 for trips to Menjangan, Tulamben or Amed. Snorkelling can be arranged through any hotel, with boat skippers on the beach (around Rp90,000/person for up to 2hr) or with dive centres. Spice Dive runs snorkelling day-trips to Menjangan and Tulamben.

Dolphin trips Lovina is famous (or should that be infamous?) for its dawn trips to spot the resident dolphins. And depending on who you talk to, they're either grossly overrated or one of the best things on Bali. A flotilla of traditional *prahu* head out to sea at sunrise, until one skipper spots a dolphin or two. On bad days the entire fleet (dozens of boats) chases after them – and despite regulations many boat owners harass the mammals by driving boats right through the pods and getting far too close. On good days there may be so many dolphins that the atmosphere is less frenetic and the hunt less aggressive. Boatmen charge around Rp60,000/person for the 2hr excursion, more if you want some snorkelling too; book directly with skippers on the beach or through your accommodation.

Scooter tours If you've always wanted to buzz about on a motorbike but would prefer someone else do the driving, Bali Vespa tours at Jl Kibarak 99 in Anturan (☎0877 6245 7772, ⓦbali-vespa-tour.com) offer fun excursions (half-day from Rp370,000) that take in waterfalls, some hiking and superb scenery.

Trekking The most interesting trek is the hike to Sekumpul Falls and nearby villages (see p.214), 30km east of Lovina. Any number of guides will be more than happy to provide a full-day outing for Rp320,000–450,000/person including lunch, depending on distances. Try Maha Nara (☎0362 27080, ⓦmahanara.com). Adjani (☎0812 3623 2019, ⓦadjanibali.com) leads half-day hikes ($35/person) in the hills around the traditional Bali Aga village of Sidetapa, including a visit to the Buddhist monastery and hot springs in Banjar (see p.207).

COURSES AND WORKSHOPS

Cookery classes Lovina has more than its fair share of cookery classes; most include transport to the morning market in Singaraja plus lunch (obviously). Adjani (☎0812 3623 2019, ⓦadjanibali.com; $35–40) runs classes in Kaliasem, including vegetarian cooking; and *Warung Bambu* restaurant in Pemaron (☎0362 31455, ⓦwarung -bambu.mahanara.com) offers various classes ($30), including one all about sweets.

Cultural classes *Warung Bambu* restaurant in Pemaron (details as above) can organize workshops in Balinese dance and gamelan on request.

SPA TREATMENTS

As an alternative to the massages offered by women on the beach, there are plenty of hotels and day spas offering treatments.

Araminth Spa Jl Mawar, Kalibukbuk ☎0362 41901. An extensive menu of massages and scrubs (from Rp120,000) plus more unusual treatments like water shiatsu.

Jaya Spa Puri Bagus Lovina, Pemaron ☎0362 21430, ⓦlovina.puribagus.net. One of the most luxurious options in town is the Jaya Spa. Its treatments in open *bale* structures range from warm stone therapy ($60) to foot reflexology ($20) or 150 minutes of "Lovina Heaven" ($73).

ACCOMMODATION

★ **The Damai** Kayu Putih ☎ 0362 41008, ⊛ thedamai .com. Elegance and luxury combine at this fine hotel, blessed with a supremely tranquil hillside location, 4km inland from Kalibukbuk. There are superbly appointed butler-serviced villas, some Bali-style with jacuzzis, others contemporary with a private pool. There's a spa, spectacularly sited pool, superb restaurant and shuttle service to Lovina. **$182**

Frangipani Beach Hotel Jl Kartika 99, Kalibukbuk ☎ 0362 343 5764, ⊛ frangipanibeachhotelbali.com. Seafront homestay where the rooms, all boasting clean modern lines and sleek bathrooms, are set round a lawn and pool just behind the shore. Located a 10min walk from central Kalibukbuk. **$68**

★ **Harris Homestay** Off Jl Bin Ria, Kalibukbuk ☎ 0362 41152. Sparklingly clean, exceptionally good-value German-run backpackers' accommodation with a real homely, welcoming ambience. The five spacious rooms (solo travellers pay Rp120,000) in the tiny compound are attractively simple and well maintained, with fans and cold-water bathrooms. Reservations recommended. **Rp150,000**

Kubu Beach Jl Seririt, Tukadmungga ☎ 0362 336 1159, ⊛ www.kububeachlovina.com. Sited about half-way between Kalibukbuk and Singaraja, this wonderful new beachfront place is outstanding value for money if you don't mind being away from central Lovina. Gorgeous contemporary rooms have high-quality wooden furniture, deep mattresses and lovely linen, minibar and TV, and tea and coffee making facilities. Generous balconies or terraces overlook the Java Sea and ricefields. There's a large pool and restaurant too. **Rp350,000**

Puri Bagus Lovina Pemaron ☎ 0362 21430, ⊛ lovina .puribagus.net. The chicest option in Lovina, offering large, airy, elegantly simple, well-appointed cottages in extensive beachside grounds – "Deluxe" buys a sea view – plus a lovely infinity pool and a wonderful spa. It's some distance from most restaurants and facilities, but the tranquillity really sets the place apart. **$158**

Rambutan Jl Mawar, Kalibukbuk ☎ 0362 41388, ⊛ rambutan.org. Impressive facilities – two pools, a spa, fitness centre, kids' areas and yoga room – give this UK-Balinese hotel real appeal. Rooms are in Balinese-style buildings and there are three spacious villas suitable for families. Standard fan-only rooms are far less inviting however. Doubles **Rp450,000**, villas **Rp950,000**

Sananda Bungalows Selat, 5km from Lovina ☎ 0362 700 0215, ⊛ www.sanandabungalows-bali.com. Swiss-owned place with attractive, very well-kept cottages, which feature a masala of Balinese furnishings and colourful fabrics, plus mosaics in great outdoor bathrooms and a hammock on the veranda. No pool. Best if you have your own transport. **$60**

Santhika Bed & Breakfast Jl Pandji Tisna, Kaliasem ☎ 0817 359 993, ⊛ facebook.com/santhikabnb. A quirky, sociable new travellers' base with artistic decor and lots of little zones for chilling and chatting. The dorm is mixed, fan-cooled and there are on-site yoga classes, plus a small spa and tiny pool for cooling off. All guests are welcomed with a drink, some fruit and a free foot massage. Dorms **Rp150,000**, doubles **Rp300,000**

Sea Breeze Cottages Beachfront, Kalibukbuk ☎ 0362 41138. Set in a great beachside position, this small outfit has seven rooms, five of them back-to-basics wooden cottages, all dark wood, bamboo walls and lazy days on the deck. All have hot water; the best are beside the small pool, with sea views. **Rp430,000**

Taman Lily's Jl Mawar, Kalibukbuk ☎ 0362 41307. Small Dutch/Balinese-run place with a row of six cute, clean and comfortably furnished bungalows in a lush garden. No pool, but all have hot water and minibars. Rooms are fan-cooled or have a/c (Rp280,000). **Rp240,000**

Villa Taman Ganesh Jl Kartika 45, Kalibukbuk ☎ 0362 41272, ⊛ taman-ganesha-lovina.com. Located in a residential area, this intimate homestay is owned by an accommodating and informed German artist (they're his paintings on the walls). There are four self-contained units, from a cosy studio to sweet family bungalows – all are beautifully furnished and set around a pool in gardens of frangipani trees. **Rp500,000**

EATING

Akar Café Jl Pantai Binaria, Kalibukbuk ☎ 0362 343 5636. Green in decor and ethics, this cute vegetarian café has a varied menu of imaginative food that includes Middle Eastern meze plates (Rp58,000), outstanding salads, plus health juices (try a "Greenpeace" with mint, lemon and honey), teas and ice creams. There's a garden terrace with river views at the rear. Daily 7am–10pm.

Bali Panorama Mayong ☎ 0821 4704 9827. While the Indonesian standards such as *gado-gado* (Rp25,000) are tasty and largely organic, the joys of this little roadside place are the lovely paddyfield views and relaxed ambience

– it makes a lovely lunch stop on a day-trip drive from Lovina (see box, p.207). Daily 9am–6.30pm.

★ **The Damai** The Damai hotel, Kayu Putih ☎ 0362 41008. The perfect place for a special meal, this creative, award-winning restaurant uses organic produce from its garden and the menu (three courses are Rp485,000) changes daily. There's an extensive wine list and free transport from the Lovina area. Daily 6–11pm.

Jasmine Kitchen Off Jl Bina Ria, Kalibukbuk ☎ 0362 41565. Dishes like Penang curry with prawns or red duck curry with pineapple and sticky rice typify the above-average Thai food in this small classy place. Most mains are Rp45,000–70,000. It's also a pleasant spot to enjoy a cappuccino or coconut ice cream. Daily 9am–11pm.

Le Madre Jl Mawar, Kalibukbuk ☎ 0362 343 5553. This small garden restaurant serves great home-made bruschetta and foccacia sandwiches, authentic pizzas, pasta (Rp35,000-65,000) plus great breakfasts: try the eggs Benedict. Daily 9am–10pm.

My Greek Taverna Jl Binaria, Kalibukbuk ☎ 0362 339 1503. With Aegean blue and white paintwork and a really hospitable ambience, this lively Greek-owned place has great salads (Rp30,000–45,000), lamb kebabs (Rp70,000), grilled fish and seafood specials, and super-tasty meze. Daily noon–10pm.

★**Warung Bambu** Jl Hotel Puri Bagus, Pemaron ☎ 0362 27080. Overlooking ricefields, this bamboo-built restaurant serves fine Balinese and Indonesian dishes – zingy curries as hot as you request, lots of seafood, traditional "Betutu style" Balinese duck or, for a blow-out, a twelve-dish *rijsttafel* (Rp195,000). There's Balinese dancing every Wednesday and Sunday evening and free transport in the Lovina area. Contact them about cooking classes. Daily 11am–11pm.

DRINKING AND NIGHTLIFE

Kantin 21 Jl Raya, Kalibukbuk ☎ 0362 343 5635. The bar "where the party never ends", apparently. Either way it's a nicely scruffy, laidback place that gets progressively more boozy (blame the cheap *arak* cocktails) as the night goes on. There are live bands every night in high season. Daily 6pm–1am.

Poco Bar Jl Binaria, Kalibukbuk ☎ 0362 41535. Raucous bar with live cover bands virtually every night, a dancefloor and moderate drinks prices: small beers are Rp30,000 and the happy hour ends at 9pm. Daily 6pm–1.30am.

Spunky's Bar and Restaurant Jl Starlight, Banyualit ☎ 0337 365094. The bar that sundowners are made of due to a superb shoreside location: settle into a bleached wood chair and sip juices, a chilled Bintang or cocktails from *arak*. Daily noon–10.30pm.

Zigiz Jl Pantai Binaria, Kalibukbuk ☎ 0857 3844 6086, ⓦ www.albe.net/de/zigiz/home.htm. A tiny, lively bar over two levels – upstairs provides a nice lounge area – with live acoustic music most evenings plus cocktails (with local/imported spirits around Rp40,000/70,000) and wine by the glass. Also shows major sports events. Daily 4pm–midnight.

DIRECTORY

Doctor Dr Made Widiadnyana has a practice on Jl Raya Lovina (Mon–Sat 4–8pm; ☎ 0362 41314). If you need a hospital, go to Denpasar (see p.92).

Immigration office Kantor Imigrasi, Jl Raya Pemaron (☎ 0362 32174); visa extensions take around a week (see p.24).

Police Jl Raya Banyualit (☎ 0362 41010).

Singaraja and around

The second-largest Balinese city after Denpasar, with a population of around 140,000, **SINGARAJA** is almost defiantly untouristy. It comes on as a typically Southeast Asian city, with a whirlwind of traffic in its streets and little concession to outsiders. Notwithstanding the occasional monument and the broad avenues, there are few obvious reminders of its past as the capital of Bali or of its role as the former seat of the Dutch administration for the Lesser Sunda Islands (which included Bali and all the islands east to Timor).

Today Singaraja has to content itself instead with being just the capital of the Buleleng district: images of **Singa Ambara Raja**, the winged lion symbol of Buleleng, appear all over the city – "Singa Raja" means "Lion King". Sights are few. The traditional market can be fun, while the specialist **Gedong Kirtya library** of books made from *lontar*-palm leaves is worth a visit. As it's very spread out, Singaraja makes for a sweaty, unrewarding time without your own transport.

A trio of otherwise unremarkable villages east of Singaraja – Sangsit, Jagaraga and Kubutambahan – have some of the most engaging **temple carvings** on Bali. Throw in a stop at the **Sekumpul** or **Gitgit waterfalls**, some of Bali's most beautiful falls, and you have the makings of a good day-trip from Lovina. The temple villages are served by bemos from Singaraja's Penarukan terminal (which is 3km east along Jalan Surapati from the Pelabuhan Buleleng waterfront).

4

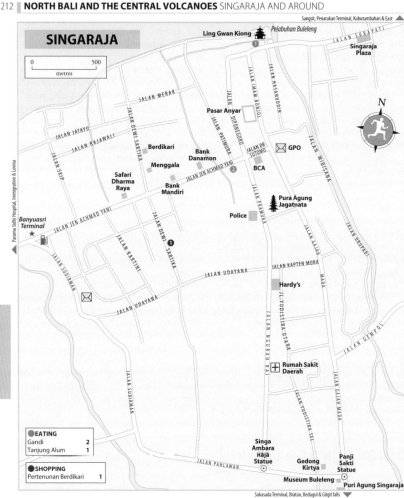

SINGARAJA

Ling Gwan Kiong

Pelabuhan Buleleng

Singaraja Plaza

0 — 500
metres

JALAN SURAPATI

JALAN HASANUDDIN

JALAN IMAM BONJOL

JALAN MERAK

JALAN JATAYU

JALAN RAWALI

JALAN DEWI SARTIKA

JALAN SKIP

Pasar Anyar

JALAN DIPONEGORO

JALAN PATIMURA

Berdikari

Bank Danamon

JALAN DR SUTOMO

GPO

Menggala

JALAN JEN ACHMAD YANI

BCA

Safari Dharma Raya

Bank Mandiri

JALAN WIJESANA

Pura Agung Jagatnata

Police

JALAN PRAMUKA

Banyuasri Terminal

JALAN JEN ACHMAD YANI

JALAN KARTINI

JALAN DEWI SARTIKA

JALAN UDAYANA

JALAN KAPTEN MUKA

Hardy's

JALAN GAJAH MADA

JALAN DRIPADI

JALAN SUDIRMAN

JALAN UDAYANA

JL-YUDISTIRA UTARA

JALAN NGURAH RAI

JALAN GEMPOL

Rumah Sakit Daerah

JALAN SUDIRMAN

JL-YUDISTIRA SEL

JALAN GAJAH MADA

JALAN PAHLAWAN

Singa Ambara Raja Statue

Gedong Kirtya

Panji Sakti Statue

Museum Buleleng

Puri Agung Singaraja

N

Parama Sidhi Hospital, Immigration & Lovina

EATING
Gandi	2
Tanjung Alum	1

SHOPPING
Pertenunan Berdikari	1

Brief history

When **Gusti Ngurah Panji Sakti** founded the kingdom of **Buleleng** in the seventeenth century, he built a new palace called Singaraja at the heart of his north-coast territory, then extended his dominion to Karangasem, Jembrana and parts of East Java. The regency's influence fluctuated over the next 150 years, culminating in eventual defeat at the hands of the **invading Dutch** in 1849, who had launched a series of extended campaigns against the north coast. The victorious colonialists took over the administration of Buleleng and set about building roads, improving irrigation systems and encouraging coffee as a cash crop in the region; European journalists, merchants and scholars began to settle in and around Singaraja, even as the south of the island was still battling the Dutch. As the Dutch strengthened their hold, the administrative importance of the north grew, and when the colonial power combined Bali and Lombok into one regency in 1882, Singaraja was established as the **capital**. During World War II, the invading **Japanese** also made their headquarters here, but Independence saw the Balinese capital move south to Denpasar.

Gedong Kirtya

Jl Veteran 20 • Mon–Thurs 8am–4pm, Fri 9am–12.30pm, Sat 9am–noon • By donation • ☎ 0362 22645 • Blue Sukasada–Penarukan bemos pass the entrance

Singaraja's best-known attraction is the esoteric **Gedong Kirtya**, the world's only library of **lontar manuscripts**. It holds over six thousand of these manuscripts – the text is written on *lontar* palm leaves and bound between wooden boards – covering Balinese religion, customs, philosophy, folklore, medicine, astrology and black magic. Such is the humidity, the books only last fifty to a hundred years, so decaying manuscripts are transcribed onto new *lontar* leaves, ensuring this ancient art survives. It's an inordinately lengthy process; leaves are soaked then boiled and pressed over many days before the precise, painstaking work of engraving the text can begin – it only becomes visible when rubbed with lamp black, the sooty residue from oil lanterns. The library also conserves *prasasti*, inscribed **bronze plates** from the tenth century, which are among the oldest written records on Bali. It's a scholarly place, but visitors are welcome; a member of the library staff will show you round.

Museum Buleleng

Jl Veteran 23 • Mon–Fri 8am–4.30pm • Donation welcome • ☎ 0362 21141

The same compound as the Gedong Kirtya – that of the palace of Puri Agung Singaraja (see below) – holds the **Museum Buleleng**. It's hard to get excited about its five rooms of local history; the 1930s typewriter formerly owned by Anak Agung Panji Tisna (1908–78), the **last Raja of Buleleng**, portraits of Buleleng heroes, including the kingdom's founding father, **Gusti Ngurah Panji Sakti** (see opposite) or local Stone Age tools and Bronze Age jewellery are hardly gripping. Moderately more interesting are the eighth-century Buddhist items found in Kalibukbuk in Lovina, which bear testament to north Bali's trading history.

Puri Agung Singaraja

Jl Veteran 23 • In theory Mon–Sat 9am–5pm, but often closed • Entry by donation

Behind the Museum Buleleng are the residential quarters of **Puri Agung Singaraja**, also known as Puri Gede Buleleng, the restored palace of the former royal family of Buleleng. Displays summarize the lives of previous rulers, in particular that of Anak Agung Panji Tisna (1908–78), the **last Raja of Buleleng**, founder of Lovina.

Pasar Anyar

Jl Diponegoro • Daily 6am–late afternoon

The commercial hub of traditional Singaraja is the covered **market**. It's at its busiest in the very early morning, around 5am, but at any time of day you can buy your live chickens or salted fish and stock up on temple offerings, sarongs and any number of handmade knives.

The waterfront

A few minutes' walk north of the market, **Pelabuhan Buleleng**, the **waterfront** is the site of the ancient harbour of Buleleng, although it's hard to imagine that this was once the busiest port on Bali. Today, it's notable for its restaurants, the statue of freedom fighter I Longtong pointing a defiant finger out to sea, and Chinese temple **Ling Gwan Kiong** (admission by donation), a red-and-white confection of shrines, statues and bridges.

Pura Beji and Pura Dalem Sangsit

Both daily 7am–6pm • Admission by donation (includes sarong rental)

Virtually an eastern suburb of the city, **Sangsit**, 2km from Singaraja's Penarukan terminal, is famous for its exuberant north Balinese temple carving. The pink-sandstone **Pura Beji**, 200m north off the main road, is dedicated to Dewi Sri, the rice goddess, and its every surface seems to writhe with carvings of animals, plants, masks, humans and monsters, both old and new.

From here you can just about glimpse the red roofs of **Pura Dalem Sangsit**, 500m northeast across a ricefield. Its front wall depicts the rewards that await the godly in heaven and, more luridly, the punishments lined up in hell: stone blocks on the head, women giving birth to strange creatures and sharp spikes descending through skulls.

Jagaraga

Around 4km south of Sangsit off the main road, **JAGARAGA** was the site of two immense battles between the Balinese and the Dutch. In 1848, the Balinese, led by local hero Gusti Ketut Jelantik, won with huge loss of life, their sixteen thousand troops fighting with lances and *kris* against three thousand well-armed Dutch. The two forces met here again in 1849, when the Dutch finally took control of the entire Buleleng regency (see p.304).

Pura Dalem Jagaraga

1km north of Jagaraga • Daily 7am–6pm • Rp15,000

Such was the bloodshed at Jagaraga that the sign for the **Pura Dalem Jagaraga** temple greets you with "Welcome to the temple of death". Though badly eroded in places, the lively late nineteenth- and early twentieth-century carvings of daily life before and after the Dutch takeover are among the most photographed in Bali. The best are on the outside front walls: on the left of the main gate is village life before the Dutch invasion – kite-flying, fishing, climbing coconut trees; next to them are the Dutch arriving by car, boat, plane and bicycle, destroying the community. There's also a much-reproduced carving of two Dutchmen in a Model T Ford being held up by bandits. Nearby, a statue of folk character Pan Brayut shows him being crawled over by some of his scores of children (see box, p.161). And inside the right-hand wall the crocodile eating the man is taken to represent the Dutch conquering Bali.

Gitgit Falls

South of Singaraja, 10km along the road to Bedugul • Daily 8am–5pm • Rp5000 at each • All buses between Singaraja (Sukasada terminal) and Denpasar via Bedugul pass Gitgit

The three well-signposted **waterfalls** at **Gitgit** are spread over a 3km stretch. Each gets busy and none of them is a patch on Sekumpul falls, but they're worth a look if you're passing by and willing to brave the persistent souvenir hawkers and wannabe guides (you don't need one). The main **Gitgit Falls**, a 40m single drop, is the one nearest to Singaraja; 2km south, the **Multi-Tiered Falls** has pools for swimming in; and 1km further towards Bedugul are the underwhelming **Twin Falls**.

Sekumpul Waterfall

Daily dawn–dusk • Rp15,000 • Access by own transport via Sekumpul, signed 9km south of Jagaraga; guided treks are possible (see box opposite)

The seven cascades of Bali's most gorgeous falls – the **Sekumpul Waterfall** – tumble 70m in a beautiful valley filled with clove, cacao and coffee trees. A ten-minute walk from the ticket booth and café, during which you gain a fantastic view over the waterfalls, then a steep, sometimes slippery flight of concrete steps leads you to the bottom of the chasm; water levels permitting, you can wade across the river and walk

---

TREKKING AROUND SEKUMPUL

Without your own transport the easiest way to visit the falls is to arrange **guided treks** between Sekumpul and Lemukih, via the falls, taking in the various plantations and rice terraces as well as a swim. Lovina agents offer this for Rp350,000–500,000 per person all inclusive (see p.209). If you visit by yourself, contact guide Kadek Ardita, the owner of a coffee stall on the path from Sekumpul (☎08523 704 4245, ✉kadek.ardita@yahoo.co.id; Rp200,000 for a group of up to three people for a three-hour trek), who offers trek guiding for two to four hours and charges.

---

another ten minutes to reach a swimmable pool beneath the falls. Ignore the pushy guides; you don't need one.

The falls are between two villages: **Sekumpul**, 11km south of Jagaraga (21km from Singaraja or about 30km from Lovina), and **Lemukih**, 2km further south up the same road.

Pura Meduwe Karang

300m east of the Kintamani road junction at Kubutambahan • Daily 7am–6pm • Donation requested, sarong rental included

Given that it is probably the most arresting temple in north Bali, **Pura Meduwe Karang** is surprisingly little visited. It lies 7km east of Singaraja's Penarukan terminal and is dedicated to Batara Meduwe Karang – the temple ensures divine protection for crops grown on dry land, such as coconuts, maize and groundnuts. It's certainly built on a grand scale: the terraces at the front support 34 figures from the Ramayana (see box, p.322), including the giant Kumbakarna battling with hordes of monkeys from Sugriwa's army.

Yet what the temple is famous for are the **carvings** of Balinese villagers, including elderly people and mothers with babies. In the inner courtyard, and typical of northern temples, a large rectangular base links the three central shrines, called the *bebaturan*. It is here, on the outer left wall, that you'll find one of the most famous reliefs on Bali: a rather psychedelic cyclist in floral shorts on a bike with a flowerhead wheel. He's sometimes named as W.O.J. Nieuwenkamp, a Dutch artist who explored Bali by bicycle in 1904.

4

ARRIVAL AND DEPARTURE SINGARAJA AND AROUND

By bus Singaraja is a major transit hub for travel to Java as well as Bali. Private operator Menggala at Jl Jen Achmad Yani 76 (☎0362 24374) operates daily night-buses to Surabaya (10hr) and other cities in Java; book ahead. The city's public bus and bemo terminals are in the outskirts: Sukasada (aka Sangket) south of the city; Banyuasri at its western edge and Penarukan in the east.

Destinations from Sukasada Bedugul (1hr 30min);

Denpasar (Ubung terminal; 3hr 15min); Gitgit (30min). Destinations from Banyuasri Gilimanuk (2hr 30min); Lovina (20min); Pemuteran, Seririt (40min). Destinations from Penarukan Amlapura (via Tulamben; 3hr); Culik (2hr 30min); Gianyar (2hr 20min); Kintamani, Kubutambahan (20min); Penelokan (1hr 30min; for the Batur area); Tirtagangga (2hr 30min); Tulamben (1hr).

GETTING AROUND

By bemo Small bemos ply main routes around town between terminals – cream between Banyuasri and Penarukan, dark-red between Sukasada and Banyuasri,

and blue between Sukasada and Penarukan. There are no metered taxis.

EATING

If looking for accommodation, it's better to make for Lovina, which is only 3km or so away.

Gandi Jl Jen Achmad Yani 25 ☎0362 21163. A dependable, venerable, inexpensive Chinese place where the decor could redefine the word "plain". The menu (dishes

are Rp15,000–45,000) has dozens of options, but home in on the seafood dishes such as *cap cay udang* (shrimp with stir-fried veggies). Daily 8am–8pm.

Tanjung Alum Dermaga Pelabuhan (waterfront) ☎0362 705 0696. There are four restaurants hanging over the sea on the old Dutch pier and this one specializes in fish and seafood – expect the likes of grilled squid or prawns for around Rp50,000. Daily noon–9pm.

SHOPPING

Pertenunan Berdikari Jl Dewi Sartika 42 ☎0362 22217. A traditional weaving centre and the only silk workshop in Bali. Silk *ikat* is hand-dyed and woven on foot looms. Fixed prices, cash only. Daily 7am–7pm.

The northeast coast

Beyond Kubutambahan, the black-sand beaches along the **northeast coast** are quiet and local; they tend to be slim and stony and trash can be an issue. If you have your own transport and fancy some tranquillity, you can check out a number of hotels here, especially in **Air Sanih**, and further east, en route to Tulamben (see p.188) at **Tejakula**, **Sembirenteng** and **Tembok**.

Air Sanih

AIR SANIH, 13km east of Singaraja's Penarukan terminal, is a locals' beach resort with some uninspiring cool **springs** (daily 6am–8pm; Rp8000). It's a popular getaway for Balinese couples who want a few private hours away from the village. Close by you'll find *Cilik's Beach Garden* (see opposite).

Symon's Studio

5km east of Air Sanih • Daily 9am–5pm • Free • ☎0361 974721, �𝕎 symonstudios.com

The studio-gallery (relocated recently from Ubud) of American-born artist **Symon** is packed with his paintings, sculptures and other creations. Symon has lived in Bali since 1978 and is best known for his vividly coloured portraits of sensual young Balinese men. Small oil paintings start at around $675 or there are Pop art screen prints from $250.

Ponjok Batu temple

Daily 7am–6pm • Free admission, though own sarong and sash required

About 12km east of Air Sanih, the road climbs a headland at **Ponjok Batu** with views along the coast. The impressive **temple** here was founded by the sixteenth-century Javanese priest Nirartha – the story goes that he used his powers to bring a shipwrecked crew back to life.

Surya Indigo Handweaving Centre

Pacung • Daily 10am–6pm • Free • ☎0812 362635, ⟨⟩ www.baliutaragaya.com

Less than 1km east of the temple at Ponjok Batu, the village of **Pacung** is worth a visit for the award-winning cooperative **Surya Indigo Handweaving Centre**, especially in the morning when you have more chance of seeing weavers in action. It's known for its striped *bebali* cloth, used in Balinese ritual, and you can see every stage of the process on site, from dyeing the silk and cotton with natural colours to weaving on *cagcag* (backstrap) looms. The art of hand-weaving *bebali* was revived here in 2000 but now the cooperative supplies cloth around the whole of Bali including some gorgeous indigo-dyed batik fabric from handspun organic cotton. Prices start at about Rp250,000 for a small cotton *bebali*. Since the cooperative launched, the owner Nymoman Sarmika has expanded to preserve other traditional handicrafts such as silversmithing, glassware and ceramics.

Les

Some 13km east of Pacung, the traditional fishing village village of **Les** makes a slightly scruffy but extremely friendly base for a few days away from Bali's booming tourism sector. There are no pushy trinket vendors and locals' use of English is minimal. Life in the village has always revolved around the ocean offshore, and in recent years the villagers have been cultivating coral and farming fish for the aquarium export trade. There's snorkelling offshore and homestays and warung in the village.

Yeh Mempeh Waterfall
Entrance Rp20,000

A sign directs you inland from Les to **Yeh Mempeh Waterfall**. It's 1.5km through the village to a parking area, then a twenty-minute walk through the forest to the falls and a pool deep enough to swim in during the wet season (Oct–March). Even in the dry season it is picturesque, as the water bounces down the rock face into a cold pool at the bottom.

ARRIVAL AND DEPARTURE   THE NORTHEAST COAST

By bemo Bemos from Singaraja's Penarukan terminal to Amlapura all pass this way. Similarly all bemos from east-coast hubs Amlapura (see p.178) and Candidasa (see p.172) to Singaraja will pass through here.

Destinations from Air Sanih Amlapura (2hr); Culik (1hr 30min); Gilimanuk (3hr); Singaraja (Penarukan; 30min); Tirtagangga (2hr); Tulamben (1hr).

ACCOMMODATION

Alam Anda Dive and Spa Resort Sembirenteng ☎0812 465 6485, ⓦalam-anda.de. This resort hotel is popular with divers due to its proximity to Tulamben and has a good house reef just offshore; Werner Lau manages the dive centre (ⓦwernerlau.com). Most accommodation is in a/c bungalows and villas, but there are two pleasant losmen rooms as well. There's also a large pool and spa. Doubles $68, bungalows $120

Cilik's Beach Garden Air Sanih ☎0819 1570 0009, ⓦciliksbeachgarden.com. Down at sea level, set in lush tropical gardens on the black-sand shore, this feels less like a hotel than a private stay, with just two huge Bali-style villas, an octagonal bungalow and one *lumbung*-style cottage, each eclectically furnished with antiques and modern pieces, and each secluded in its own clearing. *Lumbung* cottage $120, bungalow $145, villas $175

Gaia-Oasis Tejakula, 4km east of Bondalem ☎0362 343 6305, ⓦgaia-oasis.com. Secluded in a tranquil beachfront garden, eco- and socially conscious *Gaia-Oasis* offers bungalows with kitchenettes and a nice line in romantic decor. Facilities include free yoga sessions, a pool and spa. There's also a hillside retreat 6km inland under the same management. Hillside **Rp600,000**, beachside **Rp1,000,000**

★**Segara Lestari Villa** Les ☎0815 5806 8811, ⓦfacebook.com/lesvillagevilla. Owned and managed by the very hospitable Gede Yudarta, these four a/c seafront cottages are attractively decorated and have private verandas and hot-water bathrooms. Guests have access to a kitchen and the owner can arrange transport and snorkelling gear. **Rp325,000**

4

West Bali

RICE TERRACES NEAR JATILUWIH

5

West Bali

Sparsely populated and mountainous in places, west Bali stretches from the outskirts of Denpasar to Gilimanuk, 128km away at the island's westernmost tip. Once connected to Java by a now-submerged tract of land, the region has always had something of a Javanese character. When Java's Hindu Majapahit elite fled to Bali in the sixteenth century, the Javanese priest Nirartha started his influential preaching tour of Bali from the west – leaving the region with a trinity of stunning clifftop temples at Tanah Lot, Rambut Siwi and Pulaki. More recently, west Bali has acquired a significant Muslim population in the area west of Negara, giving it an above average number of mosques.

Apart from making obligatory visits to a trio of famous sights just west of Denpasar – **Pura Tanah Lot**, Mengwi's **Pura Taman Ayun** and **Sangeh Monkey Forest** are the main draws – few tourists linger in west Bali. You can see why: there aren't many visitor hubs here and few sights per se. Yet for a lazy week's touring, there's much to enjoy. The southwest coast has a wild black-sand coastline and good surf at **Balian Beach**, a mellow villagey resort near **Lalang Linggah**, and just down the road at **Medewi**, while the best of Bali's coral reefs lie off the northwest coast around **Pulau Menjangan**, near the little beach haven of **Pemuteran**. Bali's only national park, **Bali Barat National Park**, is also here – a good option if you're feeling adventurous, with its diverse birdlife and attractive coastline.. Inland, the island's second-highest peak, **Gunung Batukaru**, dominates the vistas and its southern slopes hold the most fertile paddies in Bali – none on the island are more spectacular than those around **Jatiluwih**, the focus for a famously scenic drive and heartland of the UNESCO-listed *subak* rice-growing culture which is celebrated in a museum in nearby **Tabanan**.

And one compensation for the lack of resorts in the west – arguably an attraction in itself if you enjoy getting off the beaten track, even if it does mean that all but a few restaurants are in **hotels** – is that there are several interesting places to stay in the area; from hideaways in the hills to rainforest retreats and gorgeous small spa stays on the coast.

GETTING AROUND   WEST BALI

By bemo or bus West Bali's southwest coast is served by public transport from Denpasar's Ubung terminal (see p.89) on Jl Cokroaminoto. West Bali's northwest coast is served from Singaraja. Southwest and northwest coast services terminate at Gilimanuk, from where car ferries shuttle across the Bali Strait to Java.

By car or motorbike As the main link between Denpasar and Java, traffic can be exceedingly heavy on the Tabanan–Gilimanuk road (most is single lane), with a higher than average quota of heavy trucks and kamikaze bus drivers. Plan for an average speed of 35km/hr and be very careful of oncoming reckless bus drivers when overtaking.

Tabanan and around

The former capital of the ancient kingdom of Tabanan and now administrative centre of Bali's most fertile district, **TABANAN** does little to encourage a protracted stop and has very few accommodation options. A midsize town with a traffic problem, it is best

CORAL REEF, PULAU MENJANGAN

Highlights

❶ Pura Tanah Lot Tour groups and souvenir stalls do nothing to cultivate spirituality, yet come early and you'll discover why Tanah Lot is Bali's most visited temple. **See p.225**

❷ Pura Luhur Batukaru Situated on Bali's second-highest mountain, Gunung Batukaru, this is one of the island's most atmospheric temples; all mossy carvings and *meru*, birdsong and bells, among tropical forest. **See p.228**

❸ Jatiluwih road Ancient rice paddies, farmers in straw hats and views to the coast – this sinuous route provides quintessential Balinese scenery. **See p.229**

❹ Rainforest retreats The antithesis of the hustle in resorts, eco-hillstays around Sarinbuana let you experience utter rural tranquillity. Slow down – take two nights. Better still, a week. **See p.229**

❺ Balian Beach Drop off the radar in this surfers' village, with consistent waves to ride, kilometres of beach to explore and relaxed, totally tropical ambience **See p.230**

❻ Diving and snorkelling off Pulau Menjangan With vibrant coral reefs and prolific marine life, this tiny island has some of the best diving in Bali. Try not to let on. **See p.235**

❼ Pemuteran The most relaxed resort on the north coast retains its laidback villagey ambience and has great diving and snorkelling, too. **See p.238**

HIGHLIGHTS ARE MARKED ON THE MAP ON PP.222–223

5

seen instead as a quick pit stop if you're interested in local culture: the **Subak Museum** here is dedicated to Bali's rice-growing culture.

To the north of the town, the **Bali Butterfly Park** and **Alas Kedaton Monkey Forest** offer quiet diversions and the visitor programme in the village of **Tunjuk** provides an insight into everyday rural living. To the east, reached on a northbound arterial route towards Bedugul and Singaraja, is the seventeenth-century temple complex at **Mengwi**, with a side road to the **Sangeh Monkey Forest**. No sight is particularly gripping, but with your own transport the modest sights combine into a decent day. The big draw in these parts, however, is the one on every tour group agenda – the coastal temple of **Pura Tanah Lot** south of Tabanan.

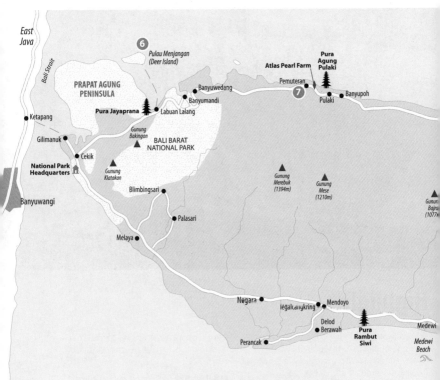

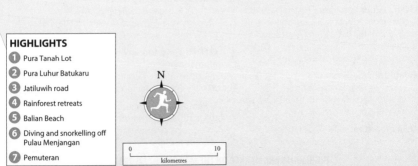

HIGHLIGHTS

1. Pura Tanah Lot
2. Pura Luhur Batukaru
3. Jatiluwih road
4. Rainforest retreats
5. Balian Beach
6. Diving and snorkelling off Pulau Menjangan
7. Pemuteran

N

0   10
kilometres

Other than the accommodation options listed below, the quiet coastal area of **Cemagi**, 5km southeast of Tanah Lot, also has a selection of luxury villas.

GETTING AROUND AND INFORMATION   TABANAN AND AROUND

By bemo or bus This area is not worth the hassle of touring without your own transport. However if you really want to give it a go, then Ubung (Denpasar)–Gilimanuk buses and bemos bypass Tabanan centre to drop passengers at the major Pesiapan terminal on the northwest edge of town (also serving Gilimanuk). Yellow city bemos shuttle into the town centre, 1.5km east. Regional services run to Kediri (for Tanah Lot and Taman Ayun in Mengwi), plus Yeh Gangga.

By car or motorbike Be aware that the main road to Pura Tanah Lot from Kuta–Legian–Seminyak via Kerobokan is perpetually clogged with traffic – expect at least an hour,

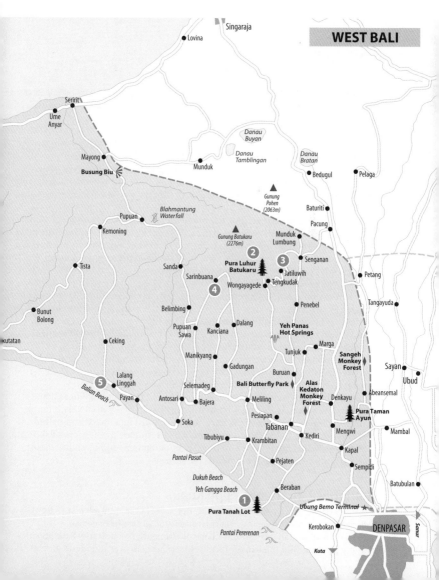

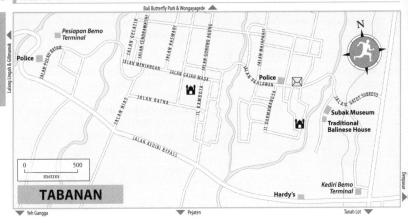

TABANAN

sometimes two to cover the 20km. You could also go direct from central Tabanan via Pejaten.

Information In Tabanan, banks, ATMs and the post office are on Jl Gajah Mada and its continuation, Jl Pahlawan. There's also an ATM plus several moneychangers near Pura Tanah Lot.

Subak Museum and traditional Balinese house

Jl Gatat Subroto, Desa Bajar Anyar • Mon–Thurs 8am–4pm, Fri & Sat 8am–noon • Rp15,000, children Rp10,000 • ☎ 0361 810315 • Signposted off the main Tabanan road in Banjar Senggulan, 1.5km east of Tabanan town centre and about the same distance west of the Kediri T-junction; if coming by bemo from Ubung (Denpasar), either alight at the Kediri junction and walk the 1.5km, or switch to a town-centre bemo at the Pesiapan terminal

Tabanan district has long been a major rice producer, and the **Subak Museum** or **Mandala Mathika Subak** celebrates the role of the island's 1200 rice farmers' collectives – the *subak* that control the distribution of irrigation water and shape the landscape. Rice is seen as a gift from the gods, so the *subak* follow a concept of blending the spiritual, human and natural worlds. It's such a distinctly Balinese philosophy that UNESCO added *subak* culture to its World Heritage list in 2012.

While the museum is hardly crammed with exhibits, one interesting display explains the complex **irrigation system** used by every *subak* on the island – an unmechanized process that has been in operation since the eleventh century at least. In a nutshell, a river is channelled to the *subak* area then dispersed by hundreds of small channels, with tiny dams to regulate the water flow and lengths of wood, called *tektek*, to determine the volume and direction of flow. It's also worth looking out for the **spiked wooden tweezers** used to catch eels from the waterlogged paddies at night, and the **wooden nets** to trap dragonflies, once prized as delicacies by the Balinese.

Less than 100m further along the lane, a purpose-built **traditional Balinese house** complements the Subak Museum by illustrating the layout of a typical village home (see p.329), comprising a series of thatched *bale* (pavilions) in a walled compound. Each *bale* has a specific function and its location is determined by the sacred Balinese direction *kaja* (towards the revered Gunung Agung mountain) and its counterpoint *kelod* (away from the mountain, or towards the sea).

Bali Butterfly Park (Taman Kupu Kupu)

Wanasari, on east side of road opposite village football pitch • Daily 8am–5pm, last entry 4.30pm • $8.50, children $4.50 • ☎ 0361 894 0595, ⊛ balibutterflypark.com • No public transport; try chartering a taxi from central Tabanan or Pesiapan terminal

Located 5km north of Tabanan, in the village of Wanasari, **Bali Butterfly Park** houses a good variety of butterflies (plus insects and spiders) from all over Indonesia in its small, pretty garden. Look out in particular for the impressive birdwing butterfly with a wingspan of around 30cm. The butterflies are at their most active in the morning.

Yeh Gangga Beach

Heading west from Tabanan, nearly every minor road south leads to the coast, a barely developed stretch of black sand notable for weird rock formations offshore. The most appealing (and developed) section is at **YEH GANGGA**, 10km southwest of Tabanan, which has emerged into something of a luxury hideaway in recent years. The currents make the sea too dangerous for swimming, but it's a dramatic scene, punctuated by huge rocks, and the **beach** stretches for kilometres in both directions. If you're really keen, you could walk along the coast to Tanah Lot in around two hours. Yeh Gangga and Pantai Gangga are signposted off the main road about 4km west of the Kediri junction, or can be reached via back roads from Tanah Lot.

ACCOMMODATION   YEH GANGGA BEACH

Soori Bali Kelating village ☎ 0361 894 6388, ⓦ sooribali .com. Gorgeous minimalist villas and "residences", all with private pools, which either enjoy direct Indian Ocean or mountain and ricefield views. The complex also has three dining options, a 24hr gym, library, luxury spa and infinity pool. $654

Waka Gangga Jl Pantai Yeh Gangga, Sudimara village

☎ 0361 416256, ⓦ wakahotelsandresorts.com. A small professionally run, Balinese-owned hotel with ten circular bungalows and two pool villas scattered across terraced rice paddies, constructed from natural materials (including thatched alang alang roofs) and boasting panoramic views of the ocean and ricefields. $162

Pura Tanah Lot

Signposted 19km west of Seminyak, 9km south of Tabanan • Daily 7am–8pm • Adult/child Rp60,000/30,000, plus Rp5000/Rp2000 parking for a car/bike • ☎ 0361 880361, ⓦ tanahlot.net • You might find a bemo direct from Denpasar's Ubung terminal. However, you're more likely to have to go first to Kediri, served by Ubung (Denpasar)–Gilimanuk buses and bemos. From Kediri bemo station, bemos (30–45min) run fairly regularly in daylight hours, more frequently in the morning. Otherwise, you can charter transport around the parking area, prices to Kuta–Legian will be around Rp220,000

Marooned on a craggy, wave-lashed rock just off the southwest coast, **PURA TANAH LOT** exists simultaneously as one of the island's holiest temples for the Balinese and one of its most famous sights for tourists. Fringed by white surf and black sand, its multitiered shrines are an unofficial symbol of Bali, appearing on countless souvenirs.

However be warned that just getting to the site is an exercise in extreme patience, as access roads are woefully inadequate and traffic jams (particularly in the late afternoon) are infamous. The volume of coach tours and sprawl of tawdry souvenir stalls and warung around the temple will do nothing for your sense of spirituality either. Then there's the fact that more than a third of Tanah Lot's island is artificial, a product of a Japanese-funded renovation programme in the 1980s. So, perhaps the greatest surprise is that Tanah Lot remains a striking sight if you arrive early enough to avoid the coach tours. It might be best to skip the sunset, however.

Pura Tanah Lot is said to have been founded by the Hindu priest **Nirartha**, who sailed to Bali from Java during the sixteenth century. Legends describe how he was drawn to the site by a light that beamed from a holy spring. A local priest was less impressed and demanded this rival holy man leave. In response, Nirartha meditated so hard that he pushed the rock he was sitting on out into the sea, creating Tanah Lot "island". They say he dedicated his new retreat to the god of the sea and transformed his scarf into poisonous snakes to protect the place.

The site

Because of its sacred status, only devotees are allowed to climb the stairway carved from the rock face and enter the compounds; everyone else is confined to the grey beach

5

beneath the rock (which gets submerged at high tide). When the waters are low enough, you can take a sip of **holy water** (*air suci*) from the spring that rises beneath the temple rock (donation requested). Otherwise, your best option is to climb up to the mainland **clifftop** for the best viewing angle.

During the day, most people loiter at the cliff-side restaurants immediately above the temple rock, but if you follow a clifftop path northwest instead, you'll get a panoramic view of the Bukit plateau on Bali's southernmost tip. The coast path continues north past small shrines and wild grey sands to eventually reach Yeh Gangga, about two hours' walk away. Every evening (7pm; Rp50,000) the temple complex hosts a performance of the **Kecak dance** in its wonderfully atmospheric setting. Good luck trying to see that from behind the massed visitors.

There's an **information office** located in the parking area (daily 7am–7pm) and an ATM plus several moneychangers among Tanah Lot's surrounding stalls.

Pejaten

About 6km northeast of Tanah Lot, **PEJATEN** village is known for manufacturing Balinese roof tiles and roof-crown ornaments (*ketu*). Of more interest to tourists is the Pejaten **ceramic ware**, designed with cute frog, gecko and monkey embellishments and glazed in pastel greens, blues and beiges. You'll find Pejaten ceramics sold in the big resorts in southern Bali, but should get better prices and a bigger choice here; kilns are all over the village, each fuelled by coconut husks, which lie in piles along the roadside – about as industrial as rural Bali gets. Try the outlet of **Tanteri Ceramic** (Mon–Fri 8am–5pm, Sat & Sun noon–5pm; US$3; ☎0361 831948, ⓦmuseumtanteribali.com), a respected producer that also has a museum with four hundred years of pottery on display. It's in Banjar Simpangan in the village centre.

Alas Kedaton Monkey Forest

Daily 8.30am–6pm • Rp15,000, children Rp10,000 • ☎0361 814155 • Access is via Kediri: either take a bemo from Denpasar's Ubung terminal to Kediri, then charter one for the final 3km, or drive to Kediri and follow signs for Marga

The long-tail macaques at **Alas Kedaton Monkey Forest**, 3km north of the Kediri junction, are less aggressive than many of their cousins elsewhere in Bali. That said, there's still a lot of monkey business going on so safeguard items like sunglasses and mobile phones. The forest here is home to many flying foxes too. Beware of getting landed with a (human) guide – their main concern will be steering you to the souvenir stalls on the edge of the temple car park.

Mengwi

It's altogether missable today, but the town of **MENGWI**, 8km east of Tabanan and 18km northwest of Denpasar, has a glittering history as the capital of a once-powerful kingdom. From the early seventeenth century until the late nineteenth, the rajas of Mengwi held sway over an extensive area, comprising parts of present-day Badung, Tabanan and Gianyar districts. Their fortunes eventually waned and in 1885 the kingdom of Mengwi was divided between Badung and Tabanan. Descendants of the royal family still live in the Mengwi area – one of their palaces, **Puri Taman Sari** (see below) in nearby Umabian, is now a luxury homestay – while the town is just to the west of the important **Pura Taman Ayun**.

ACCOMMODATION	MENGWI

Puri Taman Sari Umabian, 5km northwest of Pura Taman Ayun ☎0361 742 1165, ⓦpuritamansari .com. In a hamlet, this *puri* (palace) owned by Agung Prana, visionary member of a Mengwi noble family, is a chance to get far off the usual tourist trail. The pick of several tranquil accommodation options are the suites overlooking rice terraces. Cultural activities include offerings or gamelan and dance lessons. Access is via Denkayu on the Mengwi–Bedugul–Singaraja road. **§152**

Pura Taman Ayun

East off main Mengwi–Singaraja road · Daily 7am–6pm · Rp20,000; sarong not required · The temple is easily reached by bemo from Denpasar's Ubung terminal (30min)

The state temple of the former kingdom of Mengwi, **Pura Taman Ayun** is thought to have been built by Raja I Gusti Agung Anom in 1634. Designed as a series of terraced courtyards, the complex is surrounded by a moat to symbolize the mythological home of the gods, Mount Meru, floating in the cosmic ocean. The **inner courtyard** is encircled by its own little moat and is inaccessible to the public except at festival time, although the surrounding wall is low enough to give a reasonable view of the two-dozen multitiered **meru** within. The most important shrines are the three that honour Bali's holiest mountains; their positions within the courtyard correspond to their locations on Bali in relation to Mengwi. So, the eleven-roofed structure in the far northwest corner represents Gunung Batukaru; the nine-roofed *meru* halfway down the east side symbolizes Gunung Batur; and Batur's eleven-roofed neighbour honours Gunung Agung. The Batur *meru* has only nine tiers because the mountain is significantly lower than the other two.

Sangeh Monkey Forest

Sangeh · Daily 9am–6pm · Entry by donation · Sangeh is served by bemos from the small Wangaya terminal in central Denpasar; with your own transport it is an easy drive from Mengwi, 15km southwest, or around an hour from Ubud

Monkeys have a special status in Hindu religion, and a number of Balinese temples boast a resident troupe, respected by devotees and fed and photographed by tourists. The 14-hectare **Monkey Forest** (Bukit Sari) in the village of **Sangeh**, 21km north of Denpasar on a minor northbound road that connects Denpasar with Kintamani via Petang village, is the most atmospheric, its inhabitants the self-appointed guardians of **Pura Bukit Sari**.

According to local legend, the forest was created when the monkey king Hanuman attempted to squash Rama's enemy Rawana between two halves of Mount Meru. They say that part of the mountain fell to earth at Sangeh with hordes of Hanuman's simian retainers still clinging to the trees. The mossy grey-stone **temple** among sacred nutmeg trees was built during the seventeenth century. It's out of bounds to everyone except the monkeys, but beyond the walls you can see a huge Garuda statue, stone-carved reliefs and tiered, thatched *meru*. The place is at its best in late afternoon, when the tour groups leave and the place can assume an almost ghostly aspect. Take heed of the warnings: keep cameras and jewellery out of sight and remove all food from bags and pockets.

MEET THE FAMILY: TUNJUK

The tiny, traditional village of **Tunjuk**, 9km north of central Tabanan, hosts an interesting "village life" programme for tourists organized through **Taman Sari Buwana** (adult/child $68/34 including transfers and lunch; reserve ahead on ☎0361 742 5929, ☜balivillagelife.com). You'll have a chance to visit the local elementary school and a typical house compound that is home to fifteen different families (all related). Other activities include a rice-farming demonstration, local walks and cooking. Overnights stays are also possible. All money contributes directly to the village economy.

5

Gunung Batukaru and around

Much of inland southwest Bali lies in the shadow of massive **GUNUNG BATUKARU** (sometimes spelled Batukau; 2276m), the second-highest mountain on the island after Gunung Agung, and one of the holiest. Beautiful **Pura Luhur Batukaru** temple on the lower slopes is the focus of many pilgrimages.

Gunung Batukaru and its hinterland forms the **wettest** region of Bali, and the dense tropical rainforest on upper slopes has been designated a nature reserve, making this a rewarding area for **birdwatching**. Combine the rainfall with rich volcanic soils on lower gentler slopes and you have some of the most fertile agricultural land on the island. The area could have been tailor-made for rice-growing and the ancient terraces around **Jatiluwih** are some of the most scenic in all of Bali.

As if picture-postcard scenery wasn't reason enough to visit, there are some lovely rural hideaways (see p.230) up here: comfort in **Wongayagede**, eco-chic in **Sarinbuana** or organic escapism near **Jantiluwih**.

Wongayagede

Remote and scenic, the area around **WONGAYAGEDE** village is a pleasant enough spot to lose a half-day, with opportunities to explore the countryside or even trek up Gunung Batukaru. About 500m from its southern edge, where it merges into **Tengkudak**, lies the Catholic **church** (*gereja*) of St Martinus de Pons, which draws a congregation from a handful of local families. It's usually locked, but the facade is an interesting example of Balinese Christian architecture, with Christian motifs carved onto the red-brick facade and a four-tiered Hindu-style *meru* tower instead of a spire.

Pura Luhur Batukaru

End of the road, 2km north of Wongayagede • Daily dawn–dusk • Rp20,000 donation, includes sarong and sash

Quiet except for a resident orchestra of cicadas, frogs and cats, **Pura Luhur Batukaru** is one of Bali's nine directional temples (*kayangan jagat*) – the guardian of the west that justifies its epithet of the "Garden Temple". The grassy courtyards are planted with flowering hibiscus, Javanese ixora and cempaka shrubs, and the forests of Gunung Batukaru press against the compound's perimeters; monuments are encrusted with moss and a web of

---

CLIMBING GUNUNG BATUKARU

Because of the sacred status of Gunung Batukaru, most villagers only make the long trek up the **summit** temple once a year for their village's temple ceremony. A few tourists also **make the ascent** up the extinct volcano, but it's quite an undertaking: a guide is essential and the best months are June to August, with the November–March rainy season usually being too slippery underfoot. A knowledgeable guide will also know the viewpoints in the dense **rainforest** and will be able to point out the flora and fauna, perhaps even the resident rhesus monkeys. Shade and low cloud make the conditions damp whatever the season, so bring warm clothes, rainwear and decent shoes.

Of the several **routes** up Gunung Batukaru, the most accessible start from hotels in Sarinbuana (see opposite), Wongayagede (see above) and Sanda (see p.241). The Sarinbuana route is the easiest (about 4hr to the top) and Sanda the most taxing (about 6hr), though all three routes converge at a point known as Munduk Ngandang for the final two-and-a-half-hour slog to the **summit**. On a clear day the crater of Batukar, lakes of Bedugul, Agung and Batur and two volcanic peaks in East Java and Rinjani in Lombok are all visible. **Camping** near the top is an option, giving you the advantage of being there for sunrise. The descent from the summit usually takes three to five hours.

Guides for Batukaru treks are best arranged through local hotels. Would-be guides also hang around Pura Luhur Batukaru but they tend to ask for absurd fees and unnecessary "permits". Expect to pay a guide about Rp400,000 for an overnight trip to the summit, more if you need transfers to the trail, food and water.

5

paths fans out to shrines set in the forest. The proximity of the forest means you may see **birds** including green woodpecker-like barbets, scarlet minivets, olive-green grey-headed flycatchers and possibly even scarlet-headed flowerpeckers in the treetops.

Pura Luhur Batukaru is thought to have become a holy site in the eleventh century and was later consecrated by the rajas of the kingdom of Tabanan, who made it into their state temple and dedicated shrines to their ancestral gods. Many of the thatched *meru* inside the **inner sanctuary** still represent a particular branch or ancestor of the Tabanan royal family. The most important shrine, though, is a seven-tiered pagoda dedicated to Mahadewa, the god of Gunung Batukaru. To the east of the main temple compound, a large square **pond** has been dug to represent and honour the gods of nearby Danau Tamblingan, which lies immediately to the north of Gunung Batukaru. Pura Luhur continues to play an important role in the lives of Balinese Hindus. Members of local *subak* groups draw holy water from the pond for agricultural ceremonies, and at the annual Galungan festivities, truckloads of devotees travel long distances to pay their respects and make offerings.

In deference to Pura Luhur's sacred status, strict **rules of admission** are posted at the entrance. Aside from the usual prohibitions against menstruating women and the recently bereaved, Batukaru also bars pregnant women and "ladies whose children have not got their first teeth". A stipulation against "mad ladies/gentleman" has been recently dropped.

Jatiluwih road

Toll is Rp45,000 per adult, Rp20,000 per child, Rp5000 per car

About 2.5km south of Pura Luhur, a road branches east from Wongayagede towards **JATILUWIH**; it's a slow, very rough route through forest that occasionally parts for panoramas over the gently sloping rice terraces. The reason you're here is the oldest and most complex system of rice terraces on the island. Arguably the most beautiful, too – so celebrated is the scenery that Jatiluwih hamlet has christened the entire area. Inevitably, it has been designated a tourist site, which means every visitor pays a steep toll to drive through. Yet this is the Bali of postcards: vivid green terraces like contour lines, lush banana trees and palms, fields of chilli peppers and tomato plants, and farmers in pointed woven hats.

Eventually the road arrives at the **Senganan** road junction. The quickest route to the north and south coasts is the northeast (left) fork that feeds into the main Denpasar–Bedugul–Singaraja artery at Pacung. For a slower, scenic route back to Tabanan, take the southbound (right) fork via the market town of **Penebel**.

Sarinbuana

The little village of **SARINBUANA** is tucked away on the southwestern slopes of Gunung Batukaru. It's just a few kilometres west of Wongayagede, but feels more remote. The relative lack of visitors only adds to the appeal of the **eco- and community-focused accommodation** (see p.230) hereabouts. A climate that is cooler at 750m altitude than the sweltering plains below helps, too. These rainforest retreats are not for everyone – if you value traditional hotel amenities or are nervous of nature, which is omnipresent, they aren't for you. For everyone else they are tiny pieces of paradise; a chance to utterly escape that deserves a few nights at least.

GETTING AROUND   GUNUNG BATUKARU AND AROUND

By car or motorbike This area is inaccessible without your own transport or unless you're on a tour. Be aware that signposts and 3G coverage are both sketchy so try to source a decent map and check routes with locals.

On a tour Many agencies in south Bali resorts offer trips to Pura Luhur Batukaru, usually taking in the Jatiluwih rice terraces. SeeBali Adventures uses the area for mountain-biking ($68) and motorbike and quadbike tours (both $88; ⓦ seebaliadventures.com).

5

ACCOMMODATION AND EATING

WONGAYAGEDE

Prana Dewi Signposted 1km north of Wongayagede village ☎ 0361 736654, ⓦ balipranaresort.com. If peace and quiet is your thing, then this resort among former rice terraces is your place, with rustic rooms and bungalows that enjoy views to Gunung Batukaru. There's a 20m spring water pool and the restaurant (9am–9pm) serves fresh dishes such as *mie goreng* (main Rp40,000–65,000) made from home-grown organic red rice and vegetables. Regularly hosts yoga retreats and can provide trekking guides. Cash only. Doubles Rp730,000, bungalows Rp810,000

JATILUWIH

★**The Organic Farm** Signposted from Senganan junction ☎ 0813 5337 6905, ⓦ theorganicfarmbali .com. An environmentally sensitive slice of rural paradise, this Dutch-owned organic farm has a terrific café with local and Indonesian dishes such as curry of *tempeh*, tofu and vegetables, served with Indian bread (Rs75,000). Very simple bungalows (no running water) are available in one of the farm worker's homes. Two nights minimum, reservations essential. Per night Rp200,000

SARINBUANA AREA

Bali Eco Stay Kanciana village, 5km south of Sarinbuana ☎ 0813 3804 2326, ⓦ baliecostay.com. This organic venture has five wooden bungalows with deep verandas and stunning views, one of postcard-perfect ricefields. There's a pool for swimming at a nearby waterfall and power is supplied by a small hydroelectric scheme. Offers cultural classes (including cooking or basket-weaving), massage, trekking and mountain-biking, and there's a restaurant with utterly glorious views. $120

Bali Lush Manikyang vilage, 5km north of Selemadeg junction ☎ 0812 3772 1427, ⓦ balilush.com. A lot of care and attention has gone into the design of this rural hideaway, engulfed by rice terraces and boasting a heart-shaped pool. The four traditional-style, beautifully appointed rooms are built from recycled teak, and there's fine walking during the day and stargazing after dark. Rp684,000

★**Sarinbuana Eco Lodge** ☎ 0828 9700 6079, ⓦ baliecolodge.com. Run by committed environment-alists, this wonderful eco-lodge has jungle-chic bungalows in a rainforest clearing that make the most of the surround-sound of nature and pristine forest views. As a genuinely community-conscious project, it grows organic fruit and veg – meals in the restaurant are fresh and delicious – and organizes workshops in massage, permaculture, cookery and woodcarving. Guided walks and mountain-bike trips are also on offer. Yes it's isolated (wi-fi is limited to the restaurant area), but that's entirely the point. Two nights minimum. Per night $70

Balian Beach and the west

Few tourists venture further west than Tanah Lot, but the stretch of coast beyond Tabanan holds some nice surprises at the black-sand beaches of **Balian** and **Medewi**. Just beyond Medewi, the spectacular cliffside temple of **Pura Rambut Siwi** is almost as stunningly located as Tanah Lot but far less crowded with visitors. Note that the main coastal road is plagued by very heavy traffic – take extra care.

The scenery in the **far west** is generally dry and rugged. Cloud-capped, forested mountains hold very few villages and much of the land is protected by Bali's Forestry Department, with the most important habitats conserved as **Bali Barat National Park**. It's the only national park on the island, explored by few tourists, but it can be rewarding for birdwatchers and snorkellers – some of Bali's best coral fringes **Pulau Menjangan (Deer Island)**.

Balian Beach

Having continued inland from Tabanan, the road to Gilimanuk finally drops down to the coast, affording sea views to southeast Java and occasional panoramas of paddy fields inland. About 10km west of Antosari, the Gilimanuk road zips through **Lalang Linggah**, the village closest to **Balian Beach**, a spiritually charged spot at the mouth of the Balian river (Sungai Balian). Its caves and headlands are frequented by priests and shamen for rituals (indeed *balian* means healer or shaman in Bahasa Indonesia) – and now tourists.

As ever in Bali, **surfers** got here first – Balian Beach has the most consistent left-hand breaks in west Bali, with larger waves breaking behind off a shelf and gentler peaks

CLOCKWISE FROM TOP LEFT BALI BARAT NATIONAL PARK (P.234); SANGEH MONKEY FOREST (P.227); PEMUTERAN BEACH (P.238); PURA LUHUR BATUKARU (P.228) >

5

inshore. Board rental is widely available for around Rp70,000 a day. But whether you're a surfer or not, you may well find this mellow village the most relaxed escape on the west coast. There's no hustle, no tourist shops – just low-key accommodation, a few warung and a beach bar, and the sense of a shared secret. Get here soon, though, as construction is increasing.

The caveat to all this is that a vicious **rip** inshore makes most of the beach too dangerous for casual swimmers; heed local advice or be content to paddle at low tide. Surfers should also be aware that bull sharks (which are attracted by the river) are probably here all year round and there have been occasional attacks (one a year on average). After heavy rainfall the beach can be a mess, the gushing river depositing lots of plastic rubbish from inland along the coast.

Ocean aside, there are a few tracks to explore inland through fields of rice and banana plantations; you could also enjoy hiking up the Balian river or just heading west along 30km of grey-sand wild beach – **Mejan Beach**, 1km west, could define escapism. Yoga and meditation retreats are also operating in Balian with groups hiring local hotels or villas.

Note that there's a "tourism admission" **fee** of Rp5000 to enter Balian.

ARRIVAL AND INFORMATION   BALIAN BEACH

By bemo All Ubung (Denpasar)–Gilimanuk buses pass through Lalang Linggah; they take about 1hr 15min from Ubung or about 30min from Medewi. Coming from the north coast you can take any Seririt–Ubung bemo as far as Antosari and then change onto the Ubung–Gilimanuk service. It's about 800m from the main road to the beach.

By charter A car to Kuta or the airport costs around Rp350,000.

Banks and exchange There's an ATM on the highway and several place including *Pondok Pitaya* change money.

ACCOMMODATION AND EATING

All the following are accessed via the side road that turns sharply south off the Gilimanuk road. Most are signposted and none is more than a 5min walk from the sea. All hotels except homestays have restaurants, and there are also a few warung behind the beach and on the highway.

Gajah Mina Side road right off descent to beach ☎0812 381 1630, ⍟gajahminaresort.com. This spa hotel is a good upmarket option, with twelve rough-walled antique-furnished bungalows secluded in tropical garden compounds that include a 27m pool. The in-house *Naga* restaurant serves French cuisine, Indonesian and Thai dishes (mains from 75,000). $125

Istana Balian On descent to beach ☎0878 6209 5656, ⍟istanabalian.com. Australian/Indonesian-owned place with a selection of very well presented rooms, some above the restaurant with sweeping coastal views and others in the garden. There's a pool and the popular bar-restaurant (a popular hangout for sports events) serves great western grub. Rp600,000

Made's Homestay On left before descent to the beach ☎0812 396 3335. A good budget base, this simple place at the top of the hill to the beach remains a comfortable stay, with clean, spacious cold-water-and-fan rooms close to the beach. Rp200,000

Pondok Pisces On descent to beach ☎0813 3879 7722, ⍟pondokpiscesbali.com. Long-running place with real character thanks to the use of natural materials, including antique doors and traditional furniture. There are two locations: just above the beach and in a garden beside the Balian river. Also home to *Tom's Garden Cafe* (mains Rs36,000–62,000) which offers good international dishes, fresh tropical juices and wine by the glass (Rs50,000). Check the website for special packages. Doubles Rp360,000, bungalows Rp580,000

★**Pondok Pitaya** Behind the beach ☎0819 9984 9054, ⍟pondokpitaya.com. This attracts surfing couples and families for its unbeatable location overlooking the waves – a great spot to laze by the lovely pool or enjoy the relaxed restaurant – and a range of accommodation. Basic "Surfer Suite" rooms have hut-style castaway cool; the better houses, which have been imported from Java then rebuilt here, sleep up to seven. Also runs yoga classes (Rp125,000) twice daily and there's good Japanese food in the *Sushi Surf* café. Doubles Rp780,000, bungalows (for four) Rp1,620,000, houses (for seven) Rp2,090,000

★**Surya Homestay** Side road right off descent to beach ☎0813 3868 5643, ✉wayan.suratni@gmail .com. This is a pleasant place just off the hill to the beach with accommodation facing onto a garden of banana trees and chickens. The fan-cooled rooms, all with verandas, offer modest style and modern(ish) cold-water bathrooms. Rp180,000

Medewi

5

MEDEWI village sits on the main Tabanan–Gilimanuk road at kilometre-stone 72 and is famous for its surf – a left-hand wave peels off a cobblestone point, larger at the back with a smaller inshore wave for novices. Its black-sand **beach** is used primarily by local fishermen, but is fronted by a small enclave of accommodation catering mainly to **surfers**: the light current and fairly benign waves make this a popular spot for novices. That said, since the village is effectively just a 300m street, there's little else here for non-surfers save for the appeal of the wild beach.

As it skirts the coastline, the 25km stretch of road between Lalang Linggah and Medewi Beach crosses more than a dozen rivers which stream down from the Batukaru mountains to water kilometre after kilometre of lush land. **Rice paddies** dominate the landscape, some even dropping to the shoreline, but this area is also a big producer of coconuts, vanilla pods, cloves, cocoa beans and coffee.

ARRIVAL AND DEPARTURE
MEDEWI

By bemo or bus Medewi is served by frequent bemos and buses (about 2hr from Ubung) – those that head towards Gilimanuk can drop you at the turn.

ACCOMMODATION AND EATING

Brown Sugar Beachside, 2km west of central Medewi ☎ 0819 1639 1970, ⓦ brownsugarcamp.com. A lovely sociable place run by a welcoming team with attractive, clean rooms in thatched timber cottages, all with cold-water bathrooms. Offers surf lessons for beginners (there's a break right offshore) as well as a chillout pavilion, ding repairs, surfboard store and great café-resto. **Rp225,000**

CSB Beach Inn Signposted off the main road about 600m east of central Medewi ☎ 0813 3866 7288. A simple losmen with eighteen spacious, en-suite fan and better a/c rooms (Rp275,000) that offer views over ricefields; a 300m track leads down to the beach. Expect an early wake-up call from the local mosques. **Rp150,000**

Kelapa Retreat Pekutatan, 5km east of central Medewi ☎ 0361 805 3535, ⓦ kelaparetreat.com. This small beach resort is in a different league of style (and cost) from anything else in the area. One- and two-bed villas offer comfortable minimalism and modern furnishings – think international-hotel style rather than individual boutique character. Has a pool and spa, naturally. Online deals are usually less than half the hotel's (absurd) official rack rates. **$393**

Mai Malu ☎ 0365 470 0068, ⓔ elga.rumley@yahoo .com. Simple, bright, spotless and with fans and cold-water bathrooms as standard – the first accommodation option on the road to the beach is arguably the pick of Medewi's cheapies. However traffic noise is an issue. **Rp125,000**

Medewi Surf Homestay ☎ 0812 362 3182, ⓦ medewi surfhomestay.com. A welcoming Austrian-Balinese homestay, 800m inland from the beach, and surrounded by ricefields. Offers fan-cooled rooms and cold-water bathrooms in a two-storey wooden house. Geared at those staying for a week or more; resident masseur Ugis is a serious talent. **Rp260,000**

Puri Dajuma Cottages Pekutatan, 3km east of central Medewi ☎ 0365 470 0118, ⓦ dajuma.com. The most relaxing retreat in the area, this seafront hotel has new suites and roomy modern-rustic bungalows; not luxurious but all with a/c, hot water and garden bathrooms, the best sited just behind the beach. The whole place is set in a tropical garden, with a pool, spa and *hammam*. **$137**

Pura Rambut Siwi

Sixteen kilometres west of Medewi • Daily dawn–dusk • Donation Rp20,000; including sarong • Reached via Denpasar–Gilimanuk bemos or buses, which drop you at the head of the 750m access road to the temple

When the sixteenth-century Hindu priest Nirartha sailed across from Java, he paused at this spot and pronounced it a holy site. On leaving, he donated a lock of his hair to the villagers, who duly erected a temple and named it **Pura Rambut Siwi**, "the temple for worshipping the hair", which is now highly revered by the Balinese.

Nirartha's hair along with some of his clothing is enshrined in a sandalwood box deep inside the central three-tiered *meru* in the inner courtyard; it's inaccessible to casual visitors but can seen from the south-facing **kori agung** (gateway). Built in tiers of red brick and ornamented with fierce stonecarvings of open-mouthed Bhoma, the gateway gives direct access to the cliff face and frames a superb view of the Bali Strait. The figure that stands in the stairway, staring out to sea with an arm raised, is said to be looking

5

BULL RACES IN BALI

Bull races or *makepung* (literally "chasing around"), using carts like chariots, is a sport introduced to Bali by migrant Madurese farmers and now celebrated by statues island-wide. In Western Bali, race tracks on beaches, village tracks, even football fields, are cleared in late July and races are staged most Sundays until mid-November. There are **seven tracks** spread across the district: Tuwed, on the main road 10km west of Negara, has one of the main circuits. For details try the Jembrana Government Education, Cultural and Tourism Office in Negara (Jl Surapati 1, Negara; Mon–Fri 8am–5pm; ☎0365 41210 ext 224) but be aware that sourcing information can be as much of an adventure as seeing a race. And prepare for an early start; races begin between 7am and 9am.

---

sorrowfully at Java to bemoan the ascendance of Islam over the Hindu kingdom of Majapahit. Gently stepped garden terraces of frangipani and palm trees connect the outer gateway with the **shrine to Dewi Sri**, goddess of rice and of water (and hence prosperity), which balances on the cliff edge. Descending the rock-cut steps to the charcoal-black-sand beach, you'll find a string of tiny **cave temples** tucked into the cliff face to the left of the stairway.

Negara

If the coastal region from Tabanan to Medewi is little seen, that beyond is practically terra incognita, with most tourists hurrying towards ferries at Gilimanuk then on to Java. This is the least populated area of Bali, with only one town, **NEGARA**. Formerly the home of the Jembrana royal family, it remains the administrative capital of Jembrana district, as its wide boulevards suggest. Its other claim to fame is as the heartland of Balinese **bull races** (see box above).

Bali Barat National Park

While the rest of Bali seems to be caught up in a frenzy of development, 190 square kilometres at the westernmost tip is protected as the **Bali Barat National Park (Taman Nasional Bali Barat)**. It's an area that encompasses savanna, rainforest, monsoon forest, mangrove swamp and coral reef, with a corresponding diversity of life. The roll call of animals here is impressive with 160 species of birds present, including a small population of endangered **Bali starling**, Bali's one true endemic creature. This was also the province of the Bali tiger until the last one was shot in 1937.

By far the biggest attraction is **Pulau Menjangan (Deer Island)**, whose spectacular **coral reefs** draw snorkellers and divers from all over Bali. On dry land, encroachment and illegal tree-felling has degraded some of the forest and the rarely trekked **trails** are only worth it for the reasonably rewarding birdwatching and a sense of isolation. If it's scenery you're after, the

5

central volcanoes are more rewarding. Bear in mind, too, that hefty park admission charges and steep fees for guides (who are mandatory) add up to a costly visit.

Pulau Menjangan (Deer Island)

Pulau Menjangan is accessed from Labuan Lalang. Boats are rented through the national park office roughly from 7am to 2pm (visibility is best in the morning); they hold up to ten people and prices should be Rp400,000 for 2–3hr, which includes 30min travel each way. On top of this you'll need to pay Rp75,000 for a national park guide (who you don't really need), a steep Rp200,000/ person park entry fee, Rp75,000/person/hr national park snorkelling fee and Rp5000 for insurance. You can also rent mask, fins and snorkel from the office for Rp50,000/set. All in – boat rental, guide, fees and gear rental – expect to pay at least Rp1,000,000/two people/3hr

If you only see one part of the Bali Barat National Park, make it **Pulau Menjangan (Deer Island)**, a tiny uninhabited island 8km off the north coast. The island is fringed by some of best **coral reefs** in Bali, offering superb snorkelling and wall dives, though recent coral bleaching and marine pollution have affected the site. The easiest way to visit is an organized dive trip from the north-coast resorts of Pemuteran (see p.238) or Lovina (see p.206), although a group of snorkellers could head to Labuan Lalang, the access port for Menjangan, and club together to rent a boat. You can also source a **guide** here – a prerequisite of a visit as the island is part of the national park.

Snorkelling boats anchor off Menjangan's southeastern corner and you could bring food for a picnic on the beach there. There's little to see on the flat sandy island itself save for a large shrine to the elephant god Ganesh; you could circle it in an hour or so if you're keen.

Pura Jayaprana

Roadside 1km west of Labuan Lalang • Daily dawn–dusk • Entry by donation; includes sash and sarong

Pura Jayaprana temple itself, which lies to the west of Labuan Lalang, is unimpressive, but its location at the top of a long flight of steps is superb, with panoramas of Pulau Menjangan and its aqua seas. Pura Jayaprana enshrines the grave of an eponymous local seventeenth-century folk hero who was murdered because the king wanted to marry his wife; the wife then committed suicide rather than marry the king. The couple's grave is in the inner courtyard.

ARRIVAL AND INFORMATION   BALI BARAT NATIONAL PARK

By bemo or bus All buses and bemos on the Ubung (Denpasar)–Gilimanuk and Singaraja–Gilimanuk routes go past the national park headquarters at Cekik (see below), while those on the latter pass Labuan Lalang (for Pulau Menjangan).

Tourist information The national park headquarters (Mon–Fri 8am–4pm; ☎ 0365 61060) is in Cekik, beside the Denpasar–Gilimanuk–Singaraja T-junction, 3km south of Gilimanuk. A second office is at Labuan Lalang (daily 8am–3pm), where boats depart for Pulau Menjangan.

It has little visitor information besides a topographical map of the park and modest displays on flora and fauna.

Guides and permits Anyone who enters Bali Barat National Park must be accompanied by a park guide and pay for a permit (Rp200,000). Guides don't need to be booked in advance and all speak English – we can recommend Putu Tattoo (☎ 0813 3859 8396). Fees are negotiable, but expect to pay around Rp400,000/2hr trek for up to two people (Rp600,000/three to five people); and from Rp750,000/two people for lengthy birdwatching treks.

ACTIVITIES

BIRDWATCHING

If your main interest is birdspotting, your guide will steer you towards the Prapat Agung Peninsula, where the monsoon forest harbours a large bird population, including flocks of the common yellow-vented bulbul and the loud-chirping black-naped oriole. Other possible sightings include parakeets and fantails; the green jungle fowl; the pinky-brown spotted dove, which has a distinctive

call; the black drongo, completely black save for its red eyes; and the tiny, yellow-breasted sunbird. With a huge slice of luck, you might see the park's last few Bali starlings. Treks usually start at dawn. It is also possible to explore the peninsula by boat and walking or by safari tour, taking a vehicle along the beach for 15km each way (3–6hr; Rp1,000,000/two people). All options can be arranged at the park headquarters.

5

DIVING IN BALI BARAT NATIONAL PARK

The clear, shallow water between the mainland and Pulau Menjangan is protected from excessive winds and strong currents by the Prapat Agung Peninsula, and its **reefs** are in pretty good health, despite some damage. The reefs form a band 100m to 150m wide around the coastline, offering plenty of **dive sites** with drop-offs of 40m to 60m and first-class wall dives. Visibility is superb, ranging from 15m to 50m – as so many of the walls top out near the surface, the snorkelling is good too. While larger pelagic species aren't common visitors, the area is phenomenally rich in sea fans, barrel sponges, sea corals and all manner of soft and hard corals, and is a haven for masses of **reef fish**, nudibranchs, moray eels and other reef dwellers. Reef sharks are regularly seen. Popular sites include **Garden Eel Point** and **Pos II**, or **Anker Wreck**, an old wooden *prahu* at 45m, for more experienced divers.

TREKKING

The toughest hike in the park is the trail between Gunung Klatakan and Gunung Bakingan (7hr; Rp900,000/two people). From the Sumber Klampok ranger post, it ascends the slopes of Gunung Klatakan and Gunung Bakingan, before returning to the main road a few kilometres east of Sumber Klampok. For the most part, you're in tropical rainforest thick with ferns, vines, spiky-stemmed rattan and pandanus palms, plus epiphytic orchids. You're unlikely to spot much wildlife, but you'll probably hear the black monkeys in the canopy, and may stumble across a wild boar. The most dramatic of the birdlife here are the hornbills. Other birds include multicoloured banded pitta, dollarbirds, mynah and the red-and-green jungle fowl. Best in dry season, treks generally start at 5/6am or 4pm. Shorter treks (3hr; Rp450,000/two people) don't tend to be that rewarding given the cost. Note the coastal flats around Teluk Terima bay, west of the Labuan Lalang jetty, are sometimes tainted by plastic pollution, but the wildlife-spotting can be rewarding: if you start early enough, sea eagles, dollar birds, plus monkeys, deer and metre-long iguanas can be seen.

BOAT TRIPS

The most relaxing way to experience the park is on a boat trip around the mangroves of Gilimanuk Bay. Small boats for two people cost around Rp600,000 for 2hr (and when you factor in additional fees for guide, national park entry and other costs you're doubling that). Look out for fiddler crabs – they say their claws are so strong they can open a can of beans – and possibly amphibious mudskipper fish adapted to breathing out of the water and with pectoral fin "legs". Crab-eating or long-tailed macaques hang out along the shore, too, hunting for fruit, mussels, small mammals and crabs (they're very good swimmers and divers). You might also spot some dark-grey Pacific reef egrets. The only downside is that every plastic bottle in Java and other debris seem to get washed into the area from the Bali Strait.

ACCOMMODATION AND EATING

The closest guesthouse to the national park headquarters in Cekik is *Pondok Wisata Lestari* near Gilimanuk. There's a rudimentary campsite at the national park headquarters; well, a field with a toilet nearby (Rp100,000).

The Menjangan 17km marker Gilimanuk–Singaraja road ☎0362 94700, ⓦthemenjangan.com. Just east of Labuan Lalang, this retreat in the national park offers smart rooms in a forest lodge around a pool or more chic beach villas in an eco-resort within the park. It's an activity base too, with opportunities for trekking, riding, kayaking, snorkelling and diving. There are two restaurants: *The Tower* (7.30am–11pm) is a 28m structure with superb forest views to go with regional specialities (from Rp70,000) while the *Pantai* is on the beach and perfect for seafood. Guests can enjoy the barefoot bar and spa, and all facilities are also open to non-residents. $145

Nusa Bay Menjangan Inside national park ☎0361 484 085, ⓦwakahotelsandresorts.com. Accessed by a short boat ride from Labuan Lalang harbour, this lovely hotel is good value considering its sublimely peaceful beachfront location inside the national park. Its well-equipped villas are dotted between trees and you'll have deer, monkeys and monitor lizards for neighbours. There's good snorkelling just offshore and a spa (30min treatments from Rp155,000). $118

★ **Santi Sari** ☎0815 571 7629, ⓦsantisarihotel.com. East of the park boundary area near Banyuwedang, this small coastal boutique hotel has an effortless easy elegance, both in atmosphere and in its suites – which are flooded with light and boast hand-carved four-poster beds and stupendous bathrooms. A Mediterranean-accented gourmet restaurant (9am–11pm) features fish and vegetarian dishes such as pan-fried sea bass with risotto (Rp220,000). The coastal and mountain views are great and, with an adults-only policy, it doesn't come much more peaceful than this. $308

Gilimanuk

On the tip of Bali, **GILIMANUK** is more of a transit point to Java than a destination. A 24-hour ferry service shuttles across the Bali Strait, so there's no reason to stop except to see the silhouettes of Java's volcanoes across the water or to fry your palate with a spicy plate of *betutu* chicken (see below). The **Bali Strait** is a notoriously difficult stretch of water to negotiate due to treacherous currents. Despite this, it is occasionally swum; the world record, set by a Californian expat in May 2006, is 29 minutes and 30 seconds. During the ice ages, it's likely that a land bridge connected the two islands, which both rest on the continental plate known as the Sunda shelf, enabling humans and other animals to walk between the two. The **Museum Manusia Purba** (Mon–Fri 8am–4pm; donation requested; ☎0365 61328) displays the skeletons and grave finds from a Neolithic settlement here. Don't get too excited (though the museum staff will by your arrival).

GILIMANUK

ARRIVAL AND DEPARTURE
GILIMANUK

By bemo or bus Gilimanuk's bus and bemo terminal is opposite the ferry terminal and sees frequent services to and from various destinations: Denpasar's Ubung terminal via the southwest coast; Singaraja via Lovina; Padang Bai; and Amlapura. Services operate around the clock to Denpasar and Singaraja and from 4am to 4pm to Amlapura.
Destinations Amlapura (5hr); Cekik (10min); Denpasar (Ubung terminal; 4hr); Kediri (for Tanah Lot; 2hr 45min); Labuan Lalang (25min); Lovina (2hr 15min); Medewi (2hr); Negara (1hr); Padang Bai (5hr 15min); Pemuteran

(1hr); Seririt (2hr); Singaraja (Banyuasri terminal; 3hr); Tabanan (3hr).
By boat Ferries shuttle between Bali and Ketapang (East Java) 24hr a day (every 10min; around 45min including loading and docking). Ticket prices are cheap: Rp8000/foot passenger; Rp22,000/motorbike. Note nearly all car-rental agencies prohibit their vehicles from leaving Bali. In Ketapang, the Banyuwangi Baru train station is about 100m north of the ferry terminal for services to Surabaya, Probolinggo and Yogyakarta. The long-distance bus terminal is Sri Tanjung, 2km south of Ketapang.

ACCOMMODATION AND EATING

There's no reason to overnight in town – it's a grubby port and sleeping options reflect this.

Ayam Betutu Men Tempeh Terminal Lama ☎0365 61178. Among the many warung serving *ayam betutu* in the old bemo station, this smarter restaurant is well worth visiting. Certainly there's more meat on its chickens – marinated with a mouth-blasting mix of garlic, galangal, turmeric and chilli and served with extra

sambal (Rp35,000). Daily 9am–6pm.
Pondok Wisata Lestari Main road, 2km south from port or 1.5km north from national park headquarters ☎0365 61504. Standard rooms are tatty at this simple place so it's worth paying Rp250,000 for a Deluxe, which are a little smarter and have a/c. **Rp125,000**

The north coast

It's a lovely drive east from the tip of Bali; the road tracks along a narrow strip of the **northwest coast** for sea views on one side and mountains on the other. The terrain becomes more interesting with sharp peaks inland as far as **Pemuteran**, a peaceful beach haven offering plenty of opportunities for snorkelling and diving. Continue east and

5

you'll soon reach an even smaller hideaway at **Ume Anyar**, before the road divides: head east for Lovina (see p.206) and Singaraja (see p.211) or south for the cool, refreshing hills around **Sanda** and **Belimbing**. The north coast also opens up a number of back roads that cut across the interior (see p.241).

Pemuteran and around

PEMUTERAN lives a double life as a fishing village and a holiday getaway. It remains a pleasantly low-key area, especially as the shoreside accommodation seems to make an effort not to upset the village ambience. Alongside idling on the beach – a ribbon of black and biscuit-colour sand which arcs for 1km or so – Pemuteran is known for its **snorkelling** and **diving**. More than a dozen reefs are within easy reach of the shore – Pemuteran has the largest shallow-reef area in Bali – and seas are calm so there's a site to suit all abilities; indeed the number is increasing through an innovative reef-growing programme (see box, p.290). The marine life is varied, too; from turtles, giant clams and rays at the larger scale down to tiny nudibranchs and glass shrimp via corals, fans, sponges and fish such as grouper, sweetlips, pipefish, surgeonfish, triggerfish and wrasse. Most divers and snorkellers based in Pemuteran will take at least one trip to nearby **Pulau Menjangan**, something offered by every dive centre here.

With its cool sea breezes, temperate climate and moderately fertile soil, the stretch of the northwest coast between Pemuteran and **Seririt**, 40km to the east, is ideal for **vines** (Bali's main wine-producer, Hatten Wines, has a vineyard in this area; see p.240) and **pearl** cultivation.

Reef Seen Aquatics turtle hatchery

Daily 8–11am & 1–5pm • Rp25,000 donation • ☎ 0362 93001, ⓦ reefseenbali.com

Reef Seen Aquatics runs a **turtle-hatching** project at its dive centre, with young green, Olive Ridley and hawksbill turtles kept in seawater tanks until they are old enough to be released. All species have nesting sites in the Pemuteran area, but are endangered and their eggs are illegally harvested by locals. To combat this, Reef Seen purchases eggs from villagers for a little above market price and the turtles

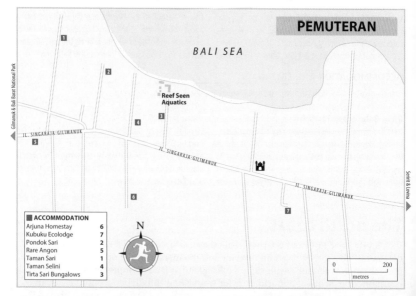

PEMUTERAN

BALI SEA

Reef Seen Aquatics

JL. SINGARAJA-GILIMANUK

ACCOMMODATION

Arjuna Homestay	6
Kubuku Ecolodge	7
Pondok Sari	2
Rare Angon	5
Taman Sari	1
Taman Selini	4
Tirta Sari Bungalows	3

N

0   200
metres

DIVING AND SNORKELLING AROUND PEMUTERAN

Local people and local dive operators have, in recent years, developed a real understanding of the **environmental value** of the reefs and considerable efforts have been made to repair earlier damage caused by the bad practices of local fishermen and unavoidable environmental factors. One initiative was the Karang Lestari Pemuteran project (ⓦglobalcoral.org), just off the Pemuteran shore, using the pioneering "**Biorock**" process (see box, p.290), which encourages new growth by continuously passing a low electrical current through the stony coral, causing minerals to build up at about four times the normal speed. There are now over seventy separate Biorock reefs in Pemuteran – an incredible coral reef restoration project – though coral bleaching due to El Niño in 2016 has affected growth and visibility can be a bit murky around the installations. The **Reef Gardeners** is an initiative to train local people as divers to maintain the Biorock structures, carry out work to maintain the health of the reefs and establish new sites.

Of the naturally occurring sites, **Canyon Wreck**, featuring a 30m wooden Bugis schooner resting in a coral canyon, is among the more dramatic. Of the artificially created sites, the **Ships Graveyard**, where three fishing boats have been sunk to attract coral growth and fish life, is one area that features Biorock structures and is suitable for snorkellers as well as divers. **Temple Garden** consists of a 4m-high temple gateway and ten large statues, which have been submerged to provide a stunning underwater landscape as they are now beautifully covered in fans and attracting all sorts of marine life.

The **map** at Reef Seen Aquatics dive centre gives a good overview of all the sites.

DIVE CENTRES

Pemuteran's **dive centres** cover diving and snorkelling locally and off Pulau Menjangan; some also go to Gilimanuk's Secret Bay, to Puri Jati near Seririt and even to Tulamben on Bali's east coast. Most do night dives, nitrox diving and macro-photography trips.

Two boat **dives** on the Pemuteran reefs averages Rp1,100,000, including all equipment. Two-dive trips to Pulau Menjangan cost about Rp1,350,000 (excluding national park fees). **Snorkelling** trips average Rp220,000 per person to the Pemuteran reefs (2hr, plus equipment rental) or about Rp400,000 per person to Menjangan (6hr, excluding park entrance and other fees of around Rp275,000). You can also rent fins and masks from many hotels, businesses and dive shops for around Rp100,000/day.

Bali Diving Academy Pemuteran Taman Sari ⓣ0361 270252, ⓦscubali.com.
Kubuku Dive Kubuku EcoLodge ⓣ0812 3760 2825, ⓦkubukuhotel.com.
Reef Seen Aquatics ⓣ0362 93001, ⓦreefseen bali.com.
Sea Rovers Dive Hotel Adi Assri ⓣ0811 385 7118, ⓦsearovers.net.
Werner Lau Pondok Sari ⓣ0362 92337 and Matahari Beach Resort ⓣ0812 385 9161, ⓦwernerlau.com.

are hatched and reared before being set free off the Pemuteran coast; many thousands have been released in the last two years. However, some environmental organizations are opposed to turtle hatcheries because it's feared that removing turtle eggs from their sandy nests (and preventing them from hatching naturally) could affect their ability to navigate the ocean successfully and ultimately return to their nesting beach. In an ideal world, perhaps in a decade or two, there will be no need for a hatchery in Pemuteran at all. If you do drop by, turtle feeding time is at 4.30pm.

Pura Agung Pulaki

Main road 7km east of Pemuteran • Daily dawn–dusk • Entry by donation; includes sash and sarong

The temple of **Pura Agung Pulaki** sits on top of a weathered cliff, making for a good viewpoint. The temple's history dates back to the sixteenth-century Javanese priest Nirartha, but the buildings are modern and overrun by grey macaques. Most bemo drivers stop here on their first trip of the day to make an offering at the temple's roadside shrine and get sprinkled with holy water by the attendant priest.

5

Atlas Pearl Farm

Penyabanga village, 10km east of Pemuteran, Jl Nelayan, signposted 700m off the main road • Tours on request (45min; Rp60,000, children under 14 free) • Shop open 9.30am–5pm • ☎ 0361 732769, ⓦ atlassouthseapearl.com.au

At the end of a dirt track to the coast, the **Atlas Pearl Farm** is your place should you be in the market for a $2000 necklace, or pretty $250 choker or simply a $149 pendant, or are just interested in learning about the process through a video of pearl seeding. Tours are available on request – you'll learn about the four-year growing process and how to distinguish fake pearls from the real deal.

Hatten wines

Sanggalangit village, 12km east of Pemuteran, signposted 400m off the main road • Tours Rp60,000 • Open Mon–Sat 10am–4.30pm • ☎ 0812 3964 5077, ⓦ hattenwines.com

Bali's biggest winery is spread over 35 hectares near the village of Sanggalangit, and offers a tour of its vineyards and of course tastings. Two French grape varieties, Alphonse-Lavallée and Belgia are grown, along with local grapes for sparkling wines.

Ume Anyar

About 1.5km short of Seririt you reach the village of **UME ANYAR**, where signs point you north off the main road to the accommodation. The local beach, sometimes known as **Puri Jati**, or PJ, is famous for **muck-diving** – the practice of diving in muddy- or sandy-bottomed bays in search of marine life. It's rich in juvenile fish and rare species and particularly good for macro-photography, so several dive operators around Bali run trips here.

ARRIVAL AND DEPARTURE

PEMUTERAN AND AROUND

By bemo or bus All Gilimanuk–Singaraja buses and bemos pass through Pemuteran and will drop you in front of your hotel. If arriving from Ubud or south-coast resorts, it's fastest to take a tourist shuttle bus to Lovina then hop on to a bus or bemo.

Destinations Gilimanuk (1hr); Labuan Lalang (for Pulau Menjangan; 30min); Lovina (1hr 45min); Singaraja (Banyuasri terminal; 2hr 15min).

ACCOMMODATION AND EATING

All Pemuteran accommodation is accessed from the Gilimanuk–Singaraja road; the most attractive places occupy beachfront land. Real cheapies worth recommending are very thin on the ground – try the lanes inland from the highway. For eating, there are hotel restaurants, cafés and warung on the beachfront and main drag.

PEMUTERAN

Arjuna Homestay Jl Arjuna ☎ 0362 343 7304, ⓦ arjuna-homestay.com. Upmarket homestay with sixteen lovely rooms (fan or a/c) on two levels, with balcony or terrace, which overlook a pool and garden. There's a sense of quality evident (the bedlinen and furnishings are classy) and you'll find a dive shop and restaurant here too. $30

Kubuku Ecolodge ☎ 0362 343 7302, ⓦ kubukuhotel .com. Run by a fun team, this smart place is arranged around a pool that's open to mountain views. Well-maintained rooms have verandas and outdoor showers. There's a good dive school here too. $45

Pondok Sari ☎ 0362 94738, ⓦ pondoksari.com. Spacious accommodation, all with a/c and garden bathrooms, in a mature tropical garden that runs to the beach. There's a low-chlorine pool and spa, and the Werner Lau dive centre is based here. A Biorock reef lies offshore. $98

Rare Angon ☎ 0362 94747, ✉ rareangon@yahoo.co.id. Indonesian crafts, outdoor bathrooms and traditional cottages (with fan or pricier a/c options) lend more Balinese character than usual to this garden homestay. Although situated across the main road, it is just 200m from the beach. $28

Taman Sari ☎ 0362 93264, ⓦ balitamansari.com. Has an enormous range of accommodation in a spread down to the beach, from rooms and suites to luxurious pool villas, all with traditional carving and art. There are two pools, a beachside restaurant and spa. Studios $133, villas $228

Taman Selini ☎ 0362 94746, ⓦ tamanselini.com. Small, elegant outfit secluded at the end of a mature garden so that all eleven bungalows have beach views. Style behind the antique doors is traditional and classy: four-posters in the bedrooms, large garden bathrooms, and day beds on verandas. There's a good-sized pool which faces the Java Sea, plus a restaurant rightly renowned for its excellent Greek dishes. $86

Tirta Sari Bungalows ☎ 0877 6213 2123, ⓦ tirtasari bungalow.com. Peaceful, good-value little spa retreat with comfortable, artistically decorated Superior bungalows in an immaculate small garden. Standard options are furthest from the beach, Deluxe around the pool are the closest and smartest. One-hour massages start at just Rp100,000 in the spa. $32

UME ANYAR

Ganesha Bali Retreat and Villas ☎ 0821 4530 4627, ⓦ ganesha-bali.com. Spacious, well-equipped villas with views of rice paddies or the sea, plus a lovely spa, pool

and restaurant, all set back from the sandy shore. Chinese and herbal medicine, as well as spa treatments, are the specialities here and there are medicinal herbs growing in the grounds. $135

Zen Resort Bali ☎ 0362 93578, ⓦ zenresortbali.com. A short stroll from the beach, with fine views over vineyards to the sea, this place has an extensive programme of Ayurvedic therapies and yoga – book a "Stress Release" package for a blissful week-long recharge. Rooms with a/c are stylishly modern – "Sunset" have large terraces and sunken patio baths – and there's a beautiful pool, plus an in-house diving centre. $150

The Antosari Road

The **road from Seririt** to the south coast commands some breathtakingly scenic views as it crosses through the mountains, rice-growing valleys and small hilltop villages of Bali's central spine. Seven kilometres south of Seririt, the road branches southeast for Mayong and Danau Tamblingan. On the southbound road, the first great viewpoint comes 12km south of Seririt, after **Busung Biu**, where you can stop in a lay-by to admire the vista of rice terraces tumbling down into the valley, framed by the peaks of Gunung Batukaru to the southeast.

The road divides at the village of **Pupuan**, 22km south of Seririt, the site of a 100m-high waterfall called **Blahmantung**. Despite the height, the falls are less than spectacular, only really worth visiting in February or March when water levels are high from several months of rain. The 1.7km-long access road is steep and rutted, signed just beyond the southernmost limit of Pupuan; you can walk it in about half an hour.

Pupuan to Pekutatan (via Tista)

From Pupuan, one route takes you on a slow, twisting course southwest via the ridgetop settlements of **Kemoning** – where you can veer south, via Ceking and Bangal, to arrive just west of Balian Beach (see p.230) – and **Tegalasaih**, then south through clove plantations to **Tista**. Beyond Tista, the road parallels the Pulukan River and soon passes through the middle of an enormous sacred fig tree at **Bunut Bolong**, a famous local sight but not worth a special trip. About 10km south of the tree, you arrive at **Pekutatan** on the main Tabanan–Gilimanuk road, 2km east of Medewi Beach(see p.233).

Pupuan to Antosari (via Sanda and Belimbing)

The easterly branch of the road from Pupuan drops through glorious scenery, affording moutainscapes of Gunung Batukaru to the east. On the way, you'll pass dozens of **coffee plantations**, many protected by spindly-looking *dadap* ("coral") trees – dead leaves fall to act as fertilizer for the coffee plants, while the roots prevent soil erosion. **Cacao** is also a big crop here, as are **cloves**, which you may see drying on mats.

Continuing south the route passes **Sanda** village, about 30km from Seririt, then you roll through the village of **Belimbing**, set in a pretty valley, before hitting the Denpasar–Gilimanuk highway at **Antosari**, 16km west of Tabanan.

Lombok

GUNUNG RINJANI

Lombok

Located 35km due east of Bali, Lombok has long been the poor cousin in terms of tourism statistics and global allure compared with its superstar island neighbour. But with southern Bali increasingly gridlocked and overdeveloped, attention has inevitably shifted to Lombok, which can match Bali for physical beauty, if not artistic heritage. Visually it's stunning, with astonishing landscapes defining the north of the island, home to fecund volcanic foothills, and also the deep south whose staggering coastline of largely untouched surf beaches is a revelation. Culturally, Lombok is mainly Islamic and offers a very different experience for the visitor from Bali, with large tracts of unadulterated wilderness and a lot less traffic and commerce. Things are changing in pockets – down south, around Kuta, there's definitely an upswing in tourism– but overall the island's essential cultural character remains largely intact.

Measuring 80km by 70km, Lombok is slightly smaller than Bali. The mountainous **north** is dominated by the bulk of the sacred volcano **Gunung Rinjani**, at 3726m one of the highest peaks in Indonesia and a popular trekking destination. Most of the population lives in the **central plains**, in a broad, urbanized corridor that runs right across the island from the capital, **Mataram**, in the west, to the port of **Labuhan Lombok** in the east. Lombok's largely agricultural **economy** is focused around this region, producing rice, cassava, cotton, tobacco (a major export), soya beans and chilli peppers. The provincial government is encouraging diversification on Lombok, with **tourism** as one of several potential growth industries.

The main focus of Lombok's tourism has always been along its western coast, with the resort of **Senggigi** a convenient hub, and the shoreline to the north encompassing a string of stunning bays. But in the last few years interest in the wild **south coast**, centred on the small but growing surfers' resort of **Kuta**, has taken off with independent travellers. **Sekotong** and **the southwest peninsula**, with its many enticingly tranquil white-sand islets known as the **Southwest Gilis** are also increasingly popular.

Despite the many attractions, the **tourist presence** on Lombok is nowhere near as pervasive as on Bali. The island hosts a few hundred thousand foreign tourists a year, compared to the almost five million annual visitors that descend on Bali. As a result it's easy to find remote villages, unspoilt coastline and people still living traditional lives. **Facilities** are improving across the island – you'll find chic and luxurious accommodation in Senggigi, Pantai Sire, Southwest Gilis and around the Kuta area – but elsewhere choices are fewer and simpler.

SELONG BLANAK

Highlights

❶ Lombok pottery From egg cups to urns, Lombok's beautiful, distinctive pots make great souvenirs. **See p.253 & p.274**

❷ The southwest Gilis A dozen tropical islands offering excellent snorkelling, diving and plenty of tranquillity. **See p.257**

❸ Senggigi Lombok's main resort has the best dining and nightlife on the island, several good beaches nearby and a wild coastline to the north to explore. **See p.258**

❹ Gunung Rinjani The toughest mountain climb in either Lombok or Bali, but you can also just admire the view from the foothills. **See p.266**

❺ Tetebatu A chance to experience Sasak village life on Rinjani's southern slopes, with pretty views and enjoyable waterfall hikes. **See p.270**

❻ South coast beaches Blinding curves of white sand against wild green hills, world-class surfing and stunning bays such as Selong Blanak. **See p.279**

HIGHLIGHTS ARE MARKED ON THE MAP ON PP.246–247

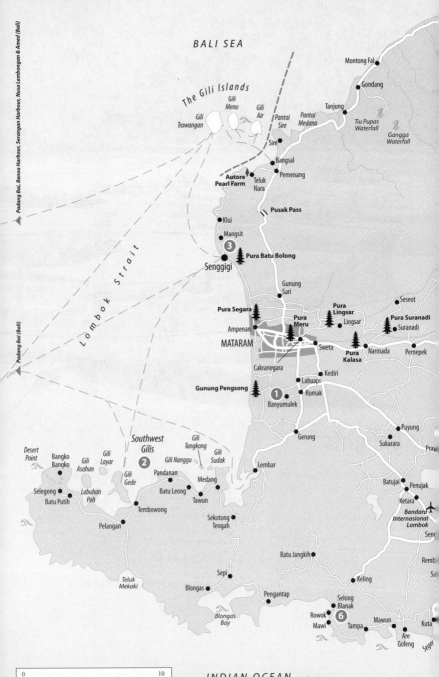

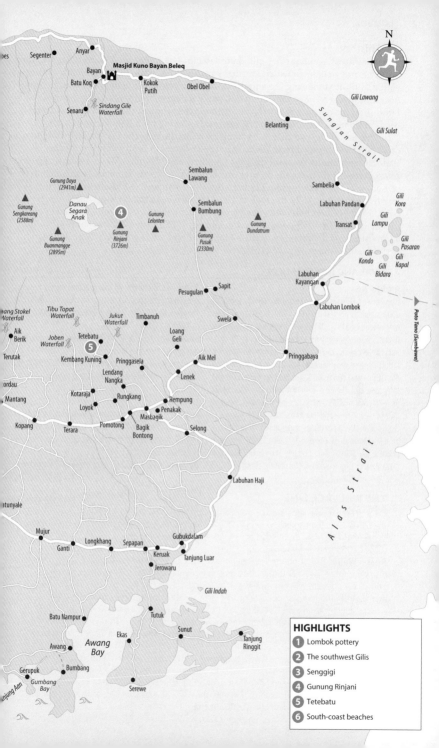

Segenter
Anyar
Bayan
Masjid Kuno Bayan Beleq
Batu Koq
Kokok
Putih
Obel Obel
Senaru
*Sindang Gile
Waterfall*
Gili Lawang

Belanting

Sungian Strait

Gili Sulat

*Gunung Daya
(2941m)*

*Gunung
Sengkareang
(2588m)*

*Danau
Segara
Anak*

Sembalun
Lawang

Sambelia

Labuhan Pandan

*Gili
Kora*

④

*Gunung
Lelonten*

Sembalun
Bumbung

Transat

*Gili
Lampu*

*Gunung
Buanmangge
(2895m)*

*Gunung
Rinjani
(3726m)*

*Gunung
Pusuk
(2330m)*

*Gunung
Dundatrum*

*Gili
Kondo*

*Gili
Pasaran*

*Gili
Kapal*

*Gili
Bidara*

Labuhan
Kayangan

Pesugulan

Sapit

*ang Stokel
Waterfall*

*Tibu Topat
Waterfall*

*Jukut
Waterfall*

Timbanuh

Labuhan Lombok

Poto Tano (Sumbawa)

Aik
Berik

*Joben
Waterfall*

Tetebatu

Swela

Loang
Geli

Terutak

⑤

Kembang Kuning

Pringgasela

Aik Mel

Pringgabaya

ordau

Lendang
Nangka

Lenek

Mantang

Kotaraja

Rungkang

Rempung

Loyok

Penakak

Kopang

Pomotong

Masbagik

Terara

Bagik
Bontong

Selong

Labuhan Haji

Alas Strait

atunyale

Mujur

Longkhang

Sepapan

Gubukdalam

Ganti

Keruak

Tanjung Luar

Jerowaru

Gili Indah

Batu Nampur

Tutuk

Ekas

Sunut

Awang

*Tanjung
Ringgit*

Gerupuk

Bumbang

*Awang
Bay*

*Gumbang
Bay*

Serewe

njung Aan

HIGHLIGHTS

① Lombok pottery

② The southwest Gilis

③ Senggigi

④ Gunung Rinjani

⑤ Tetebatu

⑥ South-coast beaches

Brief history

The majority of Lombok's 3.4 million inhabitants are indigenous Muslim **Sasaks**. Their history is not well documented but many converted to Islam in the sixteenth century, with a minority following the animist-influenced Wetu Telu branch (see box, p.266). About fifteen percent of the population are of **Balinese** origin, practising Balinese Hinduism, introducing themselves as Balinese even though their families may have been on Lombok for several generations, and speaking both Balinese and Sasak.

The history of the two islands has long been interlinked. The east Balinese kingdom of Karangasem invaded west Lombok in the seventeenth century and established a Balinese community that still thrives in modern-day Mataram. West Lombok's Balinese rulers extended their dominion over east Lombok, and were later also granted control of Karangasem by the invading Dutch. But the disempowered Sasaks of east Lombok fought back and in 1894 the Dutch seized the chance to take control, bringing the entire island of Lombok (and Karangasem) under colonial rule until Indonesian independence. In 1958 Lombok and neighbouring Sumbawa became jointly administered as the province of **Nusa Tenggara Barat**, or NTB (West Nusa Tenggara), with Mataram the provincial capital.

ARRIVAL AND INFORMATION — LOMBOK

BY PLANE

Bandara Internasional Lombok (BIL) Lombok's international airport (☎0370 615 7000) is 35km southeast of Mataram, near Praya. It's served by only two international flights: Singapore on Silk Air and Kuala Lumpur on Air Asia, but has domestic flights to nine Indonesian airports, including seven daily flights to Bali, 30min away, with Lion Air, Garuda and Wings Air. When booking flights, use the IATA code LOP. There's a currency exchange office (daily 9am–11pm), an ATM centre with five machines, a tourist office desk and hotel and tour desks.

Destinations Denpasar (Bali; 7 daily; 30min); Jakarta (Java; 14 daily; 2hr); Kuala Lumpur (9 weekly; 3hr); Singapore (1 daily; 2hr 30min); Solo (1 daily, 1hr 15min); Surabaya (Java; 8 daily; 1hr), Yogyakarta (1 daily; 1hr 20min).

Taxis The taxi counters all charge approximately the same rates for the most popular destinations: Mataram Rp90,000; Senggigi Rp220,000; Bangsal around Rp250,000; Kuta Rp130,000.

Buses Every 60–90min, DAMRI public buses run from the airport via Mataram (stopping at the Mandalika bus terminal, Rp20,000) to central Senggigi (Rp30,000); the DAMRI information desk at the exit sells tickets.

BY BOAT

Depending on where you want to go in Lombok, and how well you can cope with the rough seas, flying from Bali is often a much more comfortable option, at approximately the same price.

By ferry An hourly slow ferry operates 24hr between

THE WALLACE LINE

Bali and Lombok are separated by the 35km-wide Lombok Strait, which is more than 1300m deep in places. An imaginary boundary, the **Wallace Line**, runs through it, marking a division between the distribution of Asian and Australasian wildlife.

The boundary is named in honour of the nineteenth-century British naturalist **Sir Alfred Russel Wallace**. He suggested that during the ice ages, when the levels of the world's oceans dropped, animals were able to range overland from mainland Asia all the way down through Sumatra and Java to Bali, but were halted by the deep waters of the Lombok Strait. Similarly, animals from the south could roam only as far as Lombok on the other side of the strait.

Some evidence supports his theory. Bali and the islands to the west have creatures mostly common to **mainland Asia** (rabbits, monkeys, tigers), while the wildlife on Lombok and the islands to the east is more characteristic of **Australia and New Guinea** (parrots, marsupials, platypuses and lizards).

However, research has since shown that many animal species are common to both Bali and Lombok; for example, you're likely to see crab-eating macaques and silver leaf monkeys both in Bali Barat National Park and on the slopes of Gunung Rinjani. Today naturalists refer not to Wallace's Line but to a zone of transition from the Asian type of animal life to the Australasian; in honour of Sir Alfred, this is known as "**Wallacea**".

Padang Bai and Lembar, taking 4hr–4hr 30min. Tickets are Rp40,000/person; motorbikes Rp112,000 (including two people); cars from Rp733,000 (including passengers). Perama (w peramatour.com) runs a cheap, though slow, daily car ferry-and-bus combo from Senggigi to various destinations on Bali using this connection (6–8hr; Rp130,000). The ferry from Poto Tano on Sumbawa takes 1hr 30min to reach Labuhan Lombok in east Lombok and operates round the clock (see p.274).

By fast boat Fast boats run from Benoa, Sanur and Padang Bai on Bali, and from Nusa Lembongan, to the Gili Islands, Bangsal, Teluk Nara/Teluk Kodek (both near Bangsal) and Senggigi. Tickets for most fast boats to Lombok include road transfers from major Bali resorts; costing Rp480,000–790,000 and the sea crossing takes 1–2hr; the calmest conditions are usually in the morning. It's a good idea to check the safety record of operators before purchasing a ticket, especially in rough weather, as there have been accidents on this route. In bad weather services can be suspended for several days. The website w gilibookings.com lists all connections. Reliable daily services from Padang Bai and south Bali include Blue Water Express (t 0361 895 1111, w www.bluewater-express .com); Gili Getaway (t 0813 3707 4147, w giligetaway .com); Giligili (t 0361 763306, w giligilifastboat.com); Island Getaway (t 0878 6432 2515); Marina Srikandi (t 0361 729818, w marinasrikandi.com); and Scoot Cruise (t 0361 285522, w scootcruise.com).

TOURIST INFORMATION
For local features and current information, consult the fortnightly *The Lombok Guide* magazine (w thelombok guide.com).

West Lombok

West Lombok – stretching from **Sekotong** and the southwest peninsula through the port of **Lembar** to the city of **Mataram**, then north to the established resort of **Senggigi** and its satellite beaches – has Lombok's biggest concentration of tourist facilities.

Mataram

MATARAM is Lombok's principal city and the capital of Indonesia's Nusa Tenggara Barat province, or NTB (which comprises Lombok and the neighbouring island of Sumbawa). A sprawl of half a dozen districts, the city stretches about 8km west to east and is just 5km south of the tourist resort of Senggigi. Sights are thin on the ground and accommodation unappealing, so most visitors come for just a few hours, chiefly to browse the **markets** and perhaps a shopping mall, or to sample some authentic Sasak food.

The administrative centre is **Mataram** itself, a district of broad, tree-lined avenues and imposing government buildings, including the immigration office, but not much else of interest. Immediately to the east, **Cakranegara**, or Cakra (pronounced *chakra*), is the commercial heart of the city and centres around the buzzing **Mataram Mall**. Cakra was the capital of Lombok in the eighteenth century, during the height of Balinese ascendancy on the island, and is still the most Balinese area of the island. Two of the city's main sights – **Puri Mayura** and **Pura Meru** – date from the Balinese period. In the far west of the city, closest to Senggigi, the old port town of **Ampenan** flourishes around the mouth of the Kali Jangkok. This is the most traditional and atmospheric part of the city, with narrow streets and a maze of shophouses once inhabited by Chinese and Arab traders, plus the chaotic **Kebon Roek market**. The regional museum is here.

Museum Negeri Nusa Tenggara Barat

Jl Panji Tilar Negara 6, Ampenan • Tues–Thurs & Sun 8am–2.30pm, Fri 8–11am, Sat 8am–12.30pm • Rp5000 • t 0370 632159

The **Museum Negeri Nusa Tenggara Barat** focuses on the history, geology and culture of Lombok and Sumbawa and is worth a brief visit, even if English-language information is scant. Highlights include a scale model of Rinjani, collections of local textiles and sacred *kris* (daggers) and displays about the daily lives of Lombok's Sasak and Balinese people.

6

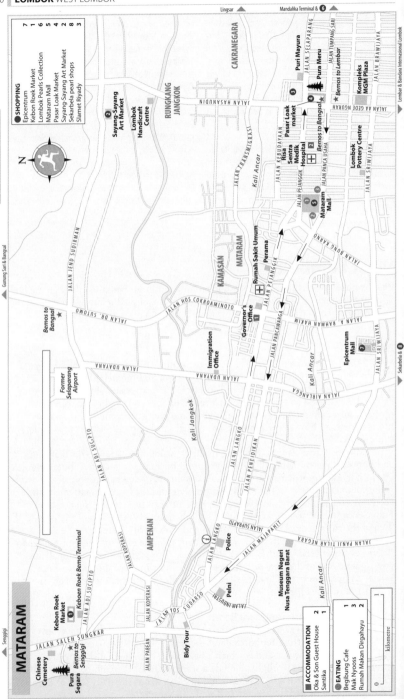

MATARAM

Lingsar ▲   Mandalika Terminal & ⑥ ▲

CAKRANEGARA

RUNGKANG
JANGKOK

Sayang-Sayang
Art Market

Lombok
Handicraft
Centre

Puri Mayura

Pura Meru

JALAN SELAPARANG

JALAN TUMPANG SARI

JALAN BRAWIJAYA

Bemos to Lembar ▶

Kompleks
MGM Plaza

JALAN AA GEDE NGURAH

Lembar & Bandara Internasional Lombok ▶

JALAN HASANUDIN

Pasar Loak
market

Bemos to Bangsal ◀

Risa
Sentra
Medik
Hospital

JALAN KEBUDAYAAN

JALAN PEJANGGIK

Lombok
Pottery Centre

JALAN PANCA USAHA

JALAN SRIWIJAYA

Mataram
Mall

JALAN TRANSMIGRASI

Kali Ancar

JALAN BUNG KARNO

Gunung Sari & Bangsal ▲

JALAN JEND SUDIRMAN

N

Bemos to
Bangsal ★

JALAN DR. SUTOMO

JALAN HOS COKROAMINOTO

KAMASAN   MATARAM

Rumah Sakit Umum

Perama

Governor's
Office

Immigration
Office

Former
Selaparang
Airport

JALAN UDAYANA

JALAN UDAYANA

JALAN PEJANGGIK

JALAN PANCAWARGA

JALAN A. RAHMAN HAKIM

Kali Ancar

Epicentrum
Mall

JALAN SRIWIJAYA

Sekarbela & ⑧ ▶

JALAN AIRLANGGA

Kali Jangkok

JALAN LANGKO

JALAN PENDIDIKAN

Kebon Roek
Market

Kebon Roek Bemo Terminal

JALAN ADI SUCIPTO

JALAN KOPERASI

AMPENAN

JALAN LANGKO

JALAN SUPRAPTO

JALAN LANGKO

Police

Pelni

Museum Negeri
Nusa Tenggara Barat

Kali Ancar

JALAN PANJI TILAR NEGARA

JALAN MAJAPAHIT

JALAN INDUSTRI

JALAN YOS SUDARSO

JALAN KOPERASI

JALAN PABEAN

Chinese
Cemetery

Pura
Segara ★

JALAN SALEH SUNGKAR

Bemos to
Senggigi ★

Bidy Tour

Senggigi ▲

0   1
└─────────┘
kilometre

Pura Meru

Jl Selaparang, Cakranegara • Daily 7am–5pm • Donation of Rp20,000 expected; sarong and scarf available

Pura Meru, also known as Pura Mayura, is the largest Balinese temple on Lombok. It was built in 1720, during the period when the Balinese ruled west Lombok, in an attempt to unite the various Hindu factions on Lombok. The *candi bentar* (split gate) displaying scenes from the Ramayana is well worth lingering over. Watch out for pushy guides requesting inflated fees for their services.

ARRIVAL AND DEPARTURE   MATARAM   6

By plane See p.248.

By bus or bemo If you're arriving by bus or bemo from anywhere except Senggigi, you'll come into Mandalika bus terminal, Lombok's main transport hub. It's in the suburb of Bertais, on the eastern edge of the city, and is sometimes known as the Bertais terminal or even, confusingly, as the Sweta terminal because that's the suburb where it used to be located. As well as transport to destinations around Lombok, Mandalika also runs long-distance a/c buses from and to major Indonesian cities. For those catching a bemo out of Mataram to Lembar (for Sekotong or boats to Bali), there's a conveniently central pick-up point in Cakranegara, just south of the market on Jl AA Gede Ngurah; bemos for Pemenang (for onward travel to Bangsal and boats to the Gili Islands) pick up just around the corner, near Pura Meru on Jl Tumpang Sari. Arriving from Senggigi, you'll come into the Kebon Roek terminal in Ampenan. If travelling to Senggigi or on to Mangsit, there are frequent bemos throughout the day until about 6pm; pick them up on Jl Saleh Sungkar, just north of the turn-off to the Kebon Roek terminal.

Destinations Bayan (for Gunung Rinjani; 2hr 30min); Labuhan Lombok (2hr); Lembar (45min); Pemenang (for Bangsal/the Gili Islands; 1hr 20min); Pomotong (for Tetebatu; 1hr 15min); Praya (for Kuta; 40min); Senggigi (30min).

Travel agents Shuttle-bus, tourist-boat and long-distance-bus tickets to destinations on Lombok, Bali and beyond from Perama, Jl Pejangglk 66 (daily 8am–10pm; ☎0370 635928, ⍟peramatour.com). Air tickets and tours from Bidy Tour, Jl Ragi Genap 17, Ampenan (☎0370 632127).

GETTING AROUND

By bemo Bright-yellow city bemos (Rp3000) ply numerous routes between the Kebon Roek and Mandalika terminals until late evening.

By taxi Blue Bird taxis (☎0370 627000, ⍟bluebirdgroup .com) are plentiful; the initial pick-up charge is Rp5000.

By bike or motorbike *Oka & Son Guest House* (see below) rents out bicycles (from Rp40,000/day) and motorbikes (Rp60,000/day).

INFORMATION

Tourist office The regional tourist office (Provincial Tourist Service for West Nusa Tenggara, Dinas Kabudayan Dan Pariwisata NTB, Jl Langko 70, Ampenan; Mon–Fri 7am–7pm; ☎0370 640471) is unfortunately of limited use, only handing out promotional brochures. The tourism desk at the airport is not always staffed.

ACCOMMODATION

Oka & Son Guest House Jl Repatmaja 5 ☎0819 1600 3637. A reasonable, if dated, budget option, on a quiet street halfway between Pura Mera and the Mataram Mall. A small Balinese-style courtyard has two rows of rooms, some of them with hot water. Rp160,000

Santika Pejanggik 32 ☎0370 617 8888, ⍟santika .com. A modern business hotel opposite the Governor's Office. The rooms are a/c and well designed if a little bland. There's a small swimming pool. $65

EATING

After dark, a **night market** of food stalls lines Jl Pejanggik, just east of Mataram Mall.

Begibung Cafe Mataram Mall, Jl Pejanggik. Serves up fine Sasak food including spicy *ayam goreng taliwang* (huge portions for Rp48,500), veggie dishes for around Rp16,000 and fruit juices. Daily 10am–9pm

Mak Nyooss Jl Panca Usaha. A lively street-food noodle restaurant, where students mingle with office workers and shop staff. A tasty portion of *mie ayam* chicken noodles costs from Rp10,000, and sometimes there's live music. Daily 8am–10pm.

Rumah Makan Dirgahayu Jl Cilinaya 19 ☎0370 637559. A large local restaurant near the Mataram Mall with a big Indonesian menu. Excellent for cheap eats; try the chicken sate with *lontong* rice cake for Rp20,000. Daily 7am–9pm.

6

THE PEARLS OF LOMBOK

Lombok is becoming increasingly recognized as a good place to buy cultured pearls (*mutiara*). **Golden South Sea pearls** are farmed around the coast, especially in southwest and west Lombok. These saltwater pearls are always expensive and they're sold by the gram (large South Sea pearls often costing $100 apiece), but quality varies considerably, so for these you're best off going to a reputable outlet, in Mataram for example, rather than buying off an itinerant vendor. The Autore Pearl Farm near Bangsal has tours and a reasonably priced shop (see p.264). Beach hawkers often sell the cheaper imported Chinese **freshwater pearls**, which are available in many colours.

SHOPPING

Epicentrum Jl Sriwijaya, ⓦ lombokepicentrum.com. This vast new mall 1km south of the centre has a huge selection of local and international brands including the likes of Billabong and Levi's, fast food chains and a good food court. There's a cinema and lots of electronic stores in the basement level. Daily 10am–10pm.

Kebon Roek Market Jl Adi Sucipto. Of Mataram's many markets, Kebon Roek in Ampenan is the most frantic, packed with stalls selling food, household goods and all the necessities of daily life. Daily 7am–5pm.

Lombok Pearls Collection Jl Achmad Yani 2, Selagalas ⓣ 0370 673450. Follow the lead of domestic tourists, who flock to buy good-quality locally cultivated South Sea pearls, as well as imported freshwater pearls. Just east of Cakranegara. Daily 9am–6pm.

Mataram Mall Jl Pejanggik 47. This mall has a department store, Hero supermarket, computer and phone shops, Western fast-food outlets and cafés and (most usefully for anyone about to climb Rinjani) trekking

outfitters selling local-brand Rei walking boots, fleeces and sleeping bags. Daily 9am–9pm.

Pasar Loak Market Jl Selaparang. Slightly less hectic than that at Kebon Roek, Cakranegara's main market selling fruit, vegetables, daily necessities and some crafts is in the heart of the city. Daily 7am–5pm.

Sayang-Sayang Art Market Jl Jend Sudirman. The best one-stop craft centre, with stalls selling a big variety of handicrafts ranged around a car park. Daily 9am–6pm.

Sekarbela pearl shops For cheaper pearls, try the suburb of Sekarbela, 2km south of Mataram, whose pearl shops line the main road west from the junction of Jl Gajah Made and Jl S Kaharudin. Mon–Sat 8am–6pm.

Slamet Riyady Jl Tanun 10 ⓣ 0370 631196. The *ikat* showroom and workshop Slamet Riyady, just off Jl Hasanudin, produces high-quality *ikat* cloth very similar to that woven on Bali (see box, p.155), and you can also watch it being produced on site (except on Sundays). Mon–Fri & Sun 8am–6pm, Sat 8am–2pm.

DIRECTORY

Banks and exchange ATMs can be found in the malls and all along Jl Pejanggik.

Consulates The closest consulates are on Bali (see p.25).

Dentist Dr Darmono, at Jl Kebudayan 108, speaks English (Mon–Fri 8am–noon & 5–9pm; ⓣ 0818 367749).

Hospital The best hospital is the private Risa Sentra Medik Hospital, close to Mataram Mall at Jl Pejanggik 115

(ⓣ 0370 625560). The public hospital, Rumah Sakit Umum, Jl Pejanggik 6, has a daily tourist clinic (9–11am; ⓣ 0370 623498).

Immigration office Kantor Imigrasi, Jl Udayana 2, Mataram (Mon–Fri 8.30am–3pm; ⓣ 0370 632520). Expect to have to make two visits for your extension to be finalized; the process can take up to a week.

Around Mataram

Within easy reach of Mataram are several worthwhile attractions, including the **potteries of Banyumulek**, the formal gardens at **Taman Narmada**, the Hindu-Muslim temple of **Pura Lingsar** and the monkey-infested forest along the road north to Pemenang.

Gunung Sari and Pemenang

Heading north out of Mataram on the Pemenang road, it's a couple of kilometres to **GUNUNG SARI**, the location of a lively morning market. From here the road is very scenic, twisting upwards through lush, towering forest to **Pusuk Pass**, then down again for 10km to the plains and the village of **PEMENANG**, near Bangsal, the port for the Gili Islands (see p.284). Monkeys gather expectantly in groups along the roadside, and strategically located stalls sell bananas.

Banyumulek

Any Lembar-bound bemo from Mandalika terminal will drop you at the junction at Rumak, close to the enormous mosque, Masjid Jami' Asasuttaqwa, from where it's 1km west to the Banyumulek showrooms on foot or by cidomo

The village of **BANYUMULEK**, about 7km south of Mataram, is one of the main **pottery** centres on the island, its access road filled with workshops and showrooms including the recommended outlet Berkat Sabar (daily 8am–5pm; ☎0370 681556). The range of designs is impressive – engraved, painted and plain, taking in everything from teacups to metre-high vases – and the pots come from all over Lombok as well as Banyumulek itself, though they're not especially cheap. Potters work on site and packing and shipping services are offered.

6

Taman Narmada

Jl Raya Narmada • **Gardens** Daily 7.30am–5.30pm • Rp10,000 plus Rp20,000 for optional guide • **Swimming pool** Mon–Thurs & Sat 7.30am–5.30pm • Rp10,000

In the market town of **Narmada**, about 7km east of Mataram, the **Taman Narmada** gardens are very popular with local families, especially at weekends. Built in 1805, they include a replica of Gunung Rinjani and its crater lake, made for the raja when he became too old to climb the real volcano to make his offering to the gods. More cynical commentators claim that he built the lake to lure local women to bathe while he watched from his pavilion. The grounds are extensive, and there's a public swimming pool and a Balinese temple, **Pura Kalasa**. The gardens are on the south side of the main Mataram–Labuhan Lombok highway, opposite the bemo terminal and daily market.

Pura Lingsar

Daily 8am–6pm • Admission by donation; optional guides Rp20,000 • Take a bemo from the Mandalika terminal to Narmada, then change on to a Lingsar bemo

Pura Lingsar, 5km northwest of Narmada, is used by Hindus as well as the Muslim Wetu Telu and is the site of one of Lombok's most enjoyable **festivals**. The temple was founded around 1714 and rebuilt in 1874; its highest, northernmost courtyard is the Hindu one, guarded by fierce monsters at the *candi bentar*, while the Wetu Telu area has a pond overlooked by a vivid statue of Wisnu, home to well-fed holy eels, which emerge for hard-boiled eggs brought by devotees. On the full moon of the seventh Sasak month (Nov or Dec), the local Hindu and Muslim communities cement their amicable coexistence and then ritualize their rivalries in a ceremony known as the **Perang Topat** or **Ketupat War**. Proceedings open with a procession, the presenting of offerings and prayers, and culminate in a good-humoured mock battle involving the raucous hurling of *ketupat* (packets of rice wrapped in leaves) and eggs at each other. Everyone participates, most wearing formal dress, and everyone gets splattered. Tourists are welcome to enjoy the spectacle.

Benang Stokel falls

Daily 8am–5pm • Admission Rp90,000 for foreigners and includes a guide to escort you to all waterfalls • Road access to Benang Stokel is complicated and poorly signed, and may be best done with a local driver; turn north off the main trans-island highway at Pancordau, 17km east of Mataram, and continue uphill via the village of Terutak (4km) to the village of Aik Berik, site of the falls car park, 11km from Pancordau

If you're into waterfalls, or need an excuse for a very scenic drive through a landscape of rice terraces and tobacco fields that's reminiscent of Bali several decades ago (with added mosques), head for **Benang Stokel falls**, 30km northeast of Mataram. The trail to the falls is also the opening stretch of a challenging six-hour **hike** up to the crater rim of **Gunung Rinjani**, the least frequented of the routes up Lombok's majestic volcano (see p.266).

An easy ten-minute trail from the car park through light forest gets you to the unexceptional twin 10m-high cascades and bathing pool of Benang Stokel, a hugely popular spot on Sundays, when it's busy with food stalls and probably best avoided. Continue along an undulating forest trail for another 45 minutes to reach the prettier, net-like spray of **Benang Kelambu falls**.

Lembar

The main port for Bali is the huge natural harbour of **LEMBAR**, 22km south of Mataram. The port has a reputation for **hassle**, with new arrivals being intimidated by transport touts loitering in the car park, so many tourists find it easier to prebook **through-transport from Bali**, buying tickets that include the ferry and then a shuttle bus to Senggigi, Kuta or elsewhere. The town swarms with traffic; there is no reason to linger.

6

ARRIVAL AND DEPARTURE

Ignore the **transport touts** and simply walk straight on through the car park (where there's a BRI ATM), turning right after 300m at the T-junction for the bemo and taxi ranks.

By boat Ferries to and from Padang Bai operate round the clock (see p.248). If you're buying a ferry ticket for Bali, do so at the checkpoint booths, not from anyone else. Tickets for Pelni ferries can be bought on the day of departure from the port, or in advance from the Pelni office in Mataram (Jl Industri 1, Ampenan; Mon–Fri 9am–4pm, Sat 9am–noon; ☎0370 637212, ⓦwww.pelni.co.id).

By shuttle bus Perama and other shuttle-bus operators wait for pre-booked guests in the port car park.

By bemo Public bemos run from the bemo rank just beyond the car park to Mataram's Mandalika terminal (roughly hourly 6am–noon, then less frequently; 40min; Rp15,000) and Sekotong (regularly from 6am–5pm; 1hr; Rp25,000). For other destinations in the southwest you'll probably have to charter: about Rp220,000 to Tawun or Rp350,000 to Bangko Bangko.

By taxi Taxis, whether pre-booked (Blue Bird ☎0370 627000, ⓦbluebirdgroup.com) or for hire, must wait at the rank 300m outside the port, near the *Tidar* hotel. A taxi to Senggigi should cost about Rp230,000, to Kuta about Rp270,000.

ACCCOMMODATION

Tidar ☎0370 681022. Basic accommodation in a row of quirky bungalows and an adjoining restaurant (daily 8am–10pm, meals Rp25,000), 600m from the ferry jetty, down the main road. Staff are used to travellers arriving at all hours. **Rp130,000**

The southwest peninsula

Remote and beautiful, with an attractive shoreline and thirteen picture-perfect white-sand islets just offshore, the **southwest peninsula** – sometimes referred to as **Sekotong**, after one of the main settlements – is still little visited. But the **snorkelling** is excellent, with arguably the most pristine coral in Lombok, and there's good **diving** and famously world-class **surfing** at Bangko Bangko's Desert Point. Accommodation is widely dispersed, and most visitors come simply for a day's snorkelling, but there are rooms for every budget and more in the pipeline. The main village centres are

THE SOUTHWEST PENINSULA

◼ ACCOMMODATION							
Cocotinos	2	Kokomo Gili Gede	4	Papalagi Resort	7	Sulaeman's	9
Desert Point Lodges	11	Krisna	5	Pearl Beach Resort	3	Via Vacare	6
Gili Nanggu Bungalows	1	Palm Beach Gardens	12	Secret Island Resort	10	Villa Yukie	8

SEKOTONG'S GOLD RUSH

The Sekotong region used to be one of Lombok's poorest, but its fortunes changed in 2008 following the discovery of **gold**. A mining company had found deposits but was scuppered by a bylaw that prohibited gold-mining on Lombok, so illegal freelancers immediately moved in, some with experience at mines in neighbouring Sumbawa but most novice chancers from the Sekotong area. At its peak, some three thousand people mined for gold, with makeshift camps popping up on the hillsides and roadside rock-grinding machines in every hamlet. As a result, many households could afford motorbikes or even new concrete houses. But the cost to the environment and public health has been high; tunnel collapses have killed many, and the use of mercury in the filtering process has polluted many sites and led to children with crippling birth defects.

Mining with **mercury** is officially banned but it remains in use and several hundred miners are still active in the mountains. Corrupt police are paid bribes so miners can access gold-rich hillsides. It seems that the exhaustion of the easily reached seams has done more to curb mining activities than any governmental efforts.

6

Sekotong Tengah and **Pelangan**, with **Tawun**, **Tembowong** and **Labuhan Poh** the easiest places to organize boats.

Tawun

Beyond **Sekotong Tengah**, the peninsula's principal settlement, and **Medang**, the views of the **southwest Gilis** become ever more enticing as you reach the harbour village and sweeping white-sand bay of **TAWUN** (also spelt Taun), 19km from Lembar. This is a convenient place to organize boat rides and **snorkelling trips** out to the **islands** that are visible from the shore. Just 1.5km west of Tawun harbour is the Balinese-Sasak village of **Batu Leong**, where there's a decent choice of accommodation and good swimming in the calm, shallow waters.

Pandanan and Tembowong

A kilometre west of *Cocotinos* (see p.256), you'll come to **PANDANAN**, where you'll find the blue-roofed *Sundancer* resort. About 700m west of *Sundancer* (400m east of the Balai Budidaya Laut marine research complex), a dirt track snakes seawards, bringing you to the gorgeous sandy peninsula of **Elak Elak** (or Ela Ela), with great swimming and a sand spit at its northern tip that allows you to walk to miniature **Gili Genting** at low tide. **Tembowong**, 5km west of Pandanan, provides access to **Gili Gede**.

Pelangan

PELANGAN, 2km west of Tembowong, 33km from Lembar and 13km from Bangko Bangko, is the largest village in this part of the peninsula. The coast here is beautifully tranquil, with views to the nearby headland and across to Gili Gede, though in the wet season swimming's not so great because of the rivers that empty into the bay.

Labuhan Poh and around

From Pelangan, the road skirts the dramatic, almost circular bay, enclosed by forested hills and headlands, and takes in views of islands fringed with white sand. Accommodation is strung out along a 2.5km stretch of road around the villages of **LABUHAN POH** and **Batu Putih**, about 5km west of *Bola Bola*, less than 8km from Bangko Bangko. Just offshore is pretty little **Gili Asahan**.

Bangko Bangko and Desert Point

Beyond Batu Putih, the road continues 2km west through a protected forest to Selegong village, where the sealed road ends. It's another 1km to an unsigned junction; the right fork takes you to the fishing village of **BANGKO BANGKO**, 2.5km down the stony but passable track. Continue through the village to a wild beach with views of Nusa Penida. The left fork takes you via a much rougher 2km track to the **surf break** at **Desert Point**. From mid-May to September, and again in December, hundreds of surfers converge here from across the globe in search of its famously long barrels.

ARRIVAL AND INFORMATION   THE SOUTHWEST PENINSULA

Transport is scarce on the peninsula, and it's less stressful, and sometimes cheaper, to take a taxi or prebook transport via your accommodation; all of them can then arrange motorbike rental locally (from Rp50,000/day).

By bemo It's 46km from Lembar to Bangko Bangko at the tip of the peninsula. The route is served by public bemos from Lembar, but service is sporadic.

Banks and exchange The closest ATM is in Lembar, but some hotels will change money for you.

ACCOMMODATION AND EATING

Staff at most places in this region can arrange motorbike rental and snorkelling trips (around Rp350,000/boat).

BATU LEONG

Cocotinos ☎0819 0797 2401, ⊛cocotinos-sekotong .com; map p.254. This luxurious resort fronts its own 300m-long white-sand coral bay 1km west of Batu Leong. It's an attractive set-up, with 36 cheerfully contemporary a/c rooms and villas. There's a sea-view pool, a spa, the Odyssea Divers centre (see box below) and a restaurant. Rates can drop by half during quiet times. **$198**

Krisna ☎0818 0369 4450, ⊛krisnabungalow.com; map p.254. Fine value, this beachfront place has modern bungalows around a small garden facing the shore. Four of the six rooms have uninterrupted views of three Gilis from their verandas (you pay more for a/c), while all have cold-water bathrooms. There's a small pool and the restaurant offers Western and Indonesian dishes (from Rp27,000). **Rp275,000**

Villa Yukie ☎0878 6518 0119, ⊛lombokhomestay .com; map p.254. A charming family-run homestay with attractive beach-view rooms and some new a/c garden rooms under construction. All are well presented, with attractive furnishings and a veranda or terrace. **Rp280,000**

PELANGAN

★**Palm Beach Gardens** ☎0818 0374 7553, ⊛mister knittel.magix.net/public/home.html; map p.254. Set in a coconut grove, with loads of space to enjoy, these five exceptionally good-value bungalows all have sea views, fans and cold-water bathrooms. There is internet access, a good restaurant, snorkel trips and the German owner is well informed about Lombok life. **Rp150,000**

LABUHAN POH AND AROUND

The 13km stretch of road between Pelangan and Bangko Bangko, at the end of the peninsula, only has a few hotels for the tourists and surf enthusiasts that make it this far; booking accommodation ahead is a good idea. Though not all have formal restaurants, they all provide meals on request.

Desert Point Lodges Labuhan Poh ☎0877 6518 3303, ⊛desertpointlodges.com; map p.254. Laidback Indo/ Dutch-owned place with four lovely wood, thatch and bamboo *lumbung* in a flower garden across from the beach. Diving trips with Dive Zone, snorkelling and fishing

---

DIVING AND SNORKELLING IN SOUTHWEST LOMBOK

There's first-class snorkelling and diving in southwest Lombok, with famously pristine coral and very few people to share it with. Of the many local sites, **Gili Layar** is great for snorkelling and also for macro-photographers; it's frequented by turtles, has masses of fish and very good coral. At **Gili Nanggu** there's very good snorkelling right from the beach. **Gili Rengit** is good for novice divers and has a lovely beach; **Medang** has coral stairs and nudibranchs; and **Batu Gendang**, near Desert Point, rewards experienced divers with eagle rays, sharks and Napoleon wrasse.

DIVE CENTRES

Snorkelling can be arranged through any accommodation and with boat captains at any of the village harbours. For **diving**, expect to pay from $74 for two dives. Centres can organize dive-and-stay packages and snorkelling trips. The best season is March to September; the dive centres wind down activities from December to March when visibility is bad.

Odyssea Divers Cocotinos ☎0819 0797 2401, ⊛odysseadivers.com. An upmarket dive centre.

Dive Zone ☎0819 0785 2073, ⊛divezone-lombok .com.

excursions are offered and the restaurant serves great local food. Book ahead. **Rp250,000**

Pearl Beach Resort Gili Asahan ☎ 0819 0724 7696, ⓦ pearlbeach-resort.com; map p.254. This tranquil place on a secluded bay on the east side of mellow Gili Asahan has wonderful shore-side bungalows with fans and hot water; inland there are bamboo cottages (Rp690,000)

with cold water. A good spot for kayaking, and diving with Dive Zone, based nearby. Book ahead for rooms and transport from Labuhan Poh. **Rp1,190,000**

Sulaeman's Batu Putih ☎ 0817 578 7539; map p.254. A very basic, low-key homestay offering eight rudimentary rooms with cold water, some sharing bathrooms. **Rp170,000**

The southwest Gilis

The three tiny islands of Gili Nanggu, Gili Tangkong and Gili Sudak are each encircled by white-sand beaches and are good for swimming. Lovely little **GILI NANGGU** (Rp5000 entry), a twenty-minute boat ride from Tawun, has excellent snorkelling, with lots of fish. It sees the most visitors, and suffers from a bit of a rubbish problem as a result. There are shady trees and lounging *berugaq* on the shore, as well as a restaurant and thatched-hut **accommodation**. East of Gili Nanggu lies very quiet, uninhabited **GILI TANGKONG**. East again, **GILI SUDAK** has decent snorkelling at the reef just off its golden beach and a simple **restaurant** grilling fish for day-trippers.

Tembowong, about 12km west of Tawun, provides access to **GILI GEDE**, the southwest's largest island, measuring about 4km from north to south. The island has half a dozen fishing hamlets around its coast with a few paved footpaths and only a handful of motorbikes; walking around it takes about four hours. The shore is fringed with a mix of beaches and mangrove, offering fine views to the mainland hills and other nearby islands. Electricity is limited on the island, and tap water is brackish.

Only a few of the islands are inhabited; there is tourist accommodation on Gili Nanggu, Gili Gede, **Gili Layar** and **Gili Asahan**, which has a tiny fishing village and a pearl farm, while Gili Sudak has a couple of restaurants.

ARRIVAL AND DEPARTURE | THE SOUTHWEST GILIS

By boat from Bali A new fast boat connection operated by Gili Getaway (☎ 0813 3707 4147, ⓦ giligetaway.com) direct from Bali to the Southwest Gilis and then connecting to the northern Gilis is opening up this region. It sails at 10.30am daily (Rp675,000) from Serangan, Bali to Gili Gede then continues to Senggigi and the northern Gilis before making a return trip to Bali.

By boat from Lombok Expect to pay Rp100,000/person to charter a boat, otherwise boatmen charge from Rp15,000/

person on the public service from Tembowong to Gili Gede. To get to Tembowong it's about Rp250,000 by taxi from either Mataram or Lembar, or about Rp25,000 by public bemo from Lembar, with departures between 6am and 3pm. Day-trips from Tawun taking in three of the islands costs about Rp300,000/boat (up to six people), plus Rp50,000 to rent a snorkel set; a transfer to Gili Nanggu is Rp125,000. Captain Rabin speaks English (☎ 0817 570 2031). Senggigi tour operators offer one-day boat-trips to the islands.

ACCOMMODATION AND EATING

GILI NANGGU

Gili Nanggu Bungalows ☎ 0370 623783, ⓦ gilinanggu .com; map p.254. The only operation in lovely Nanggu, with a dozen small cottages and *lumbung* bungalows on the southern tip of the tranquil island. The larger garden-view a/c bungalows at the rear have fresh water. Yes everything is pricey, including the restaurant (meals around Rp60,000), but you're paying for the isolation. Snorkelling gear is available and canoes can be rented for trips to the neighbouring islands. **Rp550,000**

GILI GEDE

Kokomo Gili Gede ☎ 0819 0732 5135, ⓦ kokomogili gede.com; map p.254. Really upping the stakes in Gede,

this gorgeous stylish new beachfront resort has beautifully built bungalows, villas and a spa. Dining is a delight – the restaurant has amazing seafood (try the seafood antipasti, Rp105,000) and its menu features imported meats and great salads, while the in-house bakery pumps out perfect croissants. **$156**

Papalagi Resort ☎ 0823 4140 6944, ⓦ thepapalagi .com; map p.254. This new place has tiled fan-cooled rooms and two lovely *lumbung* bungalows (Rp1,000,000) with a/c and sea views from their front decks. Prices include free use of snorkelling gear and breakfast. **Rp500,000**

Secret Island Resort ☎ 0818 0376 2001, ⓦ secret islandresort.com; map p.254. A quiet resort run by a jazz-loving American, with budget rooms and bungalows dotted around the southern tip of the island; there are also two quirky recycled teakwood bungalows built on a jetty over the water. Kayak rental is included with longer stays. It has charm but is a tad ramshackle, and a little more TLC would help (perhaps in the future as the place is for sale). **Rp250,000**

Via Vacare ☎ 0812 3732 4565, ⓦ viavacare.com; map p.254. Perfect for really unwinding, this beautifully designed retreat is dedicated to "the art of doing nothing".

The huge bungalows all have sea views and *mandi*-style bathrooms, electricity is limited to three hours a day and there's no wi-fi. Check out the backpackers' dorm with mattresses and nets (Rp200,000/person) for a cheap deal. Delicious meals are eaten communally and are included in the price, together with a pick-up from Tembowong, snorkel gear and yoga sessions. However the Dutch owner is (also) trying to sell the place, so things might change by the time you read this. **$66**

Senggigi and around

Once Lombok's premier beach resort, **SENGGIGI** is these days in limbo, its greyish beaches trumped by the idyll of the easily accessible white-sand Gili Islands, and the nearby airport closed to be replaced by the new one near Praya. The resort still attracts a loyal clientele of Australian and European tourists and there's a community of expats, but only in high season is there a bustle about the place. It's not all bad news, however:

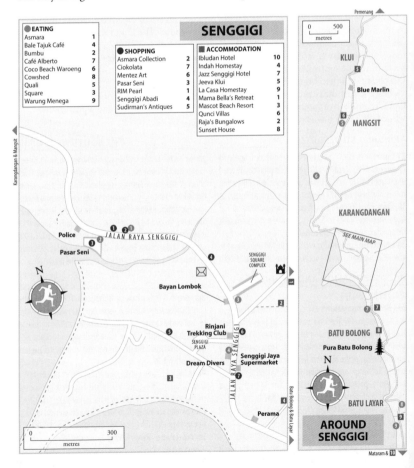

SENGGIGI

● EATING
Asmara	1
Bale Tajuk Café	4
Bumbu	2
Café Alberto	7
Coco Beach Waroeng	6
Cowshed	8
Quali	5
Square	3
Warung Menega	9

● SHOPPING
Asmara Collection	2
Ciokolata	7
Mentez Art	6
Pasar Seni	3
RIM Pearl	1
Senggigi Abadi	4
Sudirman's Antiques	5

■ ACCOMMODATION
Ibludan Hotel	10
Indah Homestay	4
Jazz Senggigi Hotel	7
Jeeva Klui	5
La Casa Homestay	9
Mama Bella's Retreat	1
Mascot Beach Resort	3
Qunci Villas	6
Raja's Bungalows	2
Sunset House	8

AROUND SENGGIGI

SENGGIGI FESTIVAL

The annual **Senggigi festival** is well worth making the effort to get to, featuring several days of Lombok cultural performances, including classical dances, traditional stickfighting (*peresean*), costumed parades and music. It's usually, but not always, held in July, in Senggigi Square: check dates at ⓦ thelombokguide.com.

there are some good hotels and restaurants in central Senggigi, and the outer beaches at **Batu Bolong** (a 10min walk south), and **Mangsit** and **Klui** (4–6km north) are genuinely appealing. The coastline is indisputably handsome, its 10km series of sandy, swimmable bays curving deeply between a sequence of dramatic headlands. And Senggigi still has the best tourist facilities on mainland Lombok: its many tour agencies and restaurants, plus its transport connections, dive centres and souvenir shops continue to make it a convenient base.

Pura Batu Bolong

Jl Raya Senggigi, 2km south of central Senggigi • Daily 7am–7pm • Donation • Any bemo to Mataram can drop you off

Senggigi's one sight is the lovely little Balinese temple **Pura Batu Bolong**, which crowns a promontory at the southern end of Batu Bolong beach. It's built over an archway in the rock, the hole through which virgins were once supposedly sacrificed to appease the gods. Nowadays, when the tide is right, it offers access to Batu Layar Beach and its famous fish restaurant *Warung Menega* (see p.263).

ARRIVAL AND DEPARTURE

SENGGIGI AND AROUND

By plane Senggigi is 50km from Lombok's international airport. A taxi or hotel transfer to Senggigi costs around Rp225,000. The DAMRI airport bus stops on the main road by the art market; buses depart every 60–90min, taking 90min to get to the airport; tickets are Rp30,000.

By shuttle bus For longer-distance travel from tourist centres in Bali and Lombok (including the Gili Islands), tourist shuttle buses and boat/bus combinations are often the most economical option. Perama (ⓣ 0370 693007, ⓦ peramatour.com) offer a good service but do not always run if business is slow. Guesthouses club together with shuttle bus operators to share rides. Sample fares are Senggigi to Mataram Rp25,000; to Bangsal Rp60,000; to the airport, Kuta (Lombok) or Tetebatu Rp125,000.

Destinations Candidasa (Bali; 3 daily; 6hr); Ngurah Rai Airport & Kuta (Bali; 2 daily; 9hr); Kuta (Lombok; 2 daily; 2hr); Sanur (Bali; 2 daily; 8hr 30min); Tetebatu (2 daily; 2hr); Ubud (Bali; 2 daily; 8hr).

By bemo Coming from Mataram, bemos depart at least every 20min from the Kebon Roek terminal in Ampenan until about 6pm and run as far as Mangsit, so are also useful for travelling around the greater Senggigi area: central Senggigi to Mangsit should cost Rp5000.

Destinations Mangsit (10min); Mataram (Ampenan; 20min).

By boat Direct fast boats from Senggigi's beach to the Gili Islands and on to Padang Bai or south Bali (with connecting shuttles to Ubud and Kuta) are offered by several operators. Many don't actually leave from Senggigi but use road transfers to harbours including Teluk Nare (nearer the Gilis) from where boats depart. Schedules change frequently and are best checked locally in Senggigi or online at ⓦ gilibookings.com. Operators include Gili Getaway (ⓣ 0813 3707 4147, ⓦ giligetaway.com) and Scoot Cruise (ⓣ 0361 285522, ⓦ scootcruise.com), which also has a direct fast boat to Nusa Lembongan and Sanur (2.30pm). Tickets to the Gili Islands cost from Rp200,000; to Bali it's Rp375,000–700,000 depending on the company and season. Perama and other transport operators offer shuttles to Gili Trawangan via Bangsal for Rp150,000. It's also worth asking Senggigi's dive centres for transfers to the Gili Islands; Dream Divers (see p.260) charge Rp150,000/person.

Destinations Gili Islands (direct boats 4 daily; 30min; via Bangsal 2hr); Nusa Lembongan (Bali; 2hr 15min); Padang Bai (Bali; 2hr); Sanur (Bali; 2hr 30min).

GETTING AROUND

By taxi Blue Bird (ⓣ 0370 627000, ⓦ bluebirdgroup.com) meter taxis are plentiful in Senggigi and can be flagged down or booked ahead; the 5km ride from Mangsit to central Senggigi should be about Rp22,000.

By car or motorbike Rental cars and motorbikes are widely available.

On a tour All agencies offer tours round Lombok – nearly everywhere on the island is accessible on a day-trip – but

6

it's more fun to design your own by hiring a car and driver. A highly recommended local driver/guide is Made Minggir (☎0819 9988 8910, ✉madetravel10@yahoo.com); expect to pay Rp450,000/day. Perama (daily 7.30am–10pm; ☎0370 693007, ⓦperamatour.com) is an excellent outlet for car and motorbike rental and tours to Komodo.

ACTIVITIES

Cycling Rinjani Trekking Club (☎0370 693202, ⓦinfo2 lombok.com) organizes various Lombok cycle day-trips, taking in villages, beaches, forests and ricefields, from $25–65/person.

Diving and snorkelling There's no diving near Senggigi so all dive centres ship their clients to the Gili Islands or Sekotong Bay for the day (1–2hr away); a two-dive package costs around $80. Reputable local dive centres include Blue Marlin (☎0370 693719, ⓦbluemarlindive.com) at *Holiday Resort Lombok* on Mangsit Beach and Dream Divers, in central Senggigi (Jl Raya Senggigi ☎0370 693738, ⓦdreamdivers.com). If you're on Lombok primarily for the diving, however, it's cheaper and more time-efficient to base yourself on the Gilis or in Sekotong Bay instead. Most dive centres will take accompanying snorkellers for about $20 ($10 for under-10s) and may provide a dedicated snorkelling guide on request.

Trekking Rinjani Trekking Club, Jl Raya Senggigi Km8 (☎0370 693202, ⓦinfo2lombok.com) is a reputable agent for Rinjani trekking packages, and can also arrange much less strenuous hiking day-trips and expeditions to Sumbawa and Flores. Numerous agents in Senggigi (with very similar names) sell trekking packages, but it's worth checking current advice before signing up (see box, p.268).

ACCOMMODATION

CENTRAL SENGGIGI

In central Senggigi there's plenty happening, with restaurants, bars and tour agents on your doorstep. The two sandy bays, to the north and south of the Senggigi Beach promontory, are fine for swimming at all but the highest tides, though outside July, August and the Christmas holidays you may find it's just you and the indefatigable hawkers.

★**Mama Bella's Retreat** Jl Arjuna Tiga 11 ☎0370 692293, ⓦmamabellaslombokretreat.com. A short walk from the centre, but a world away in ambience, this delightful garden hideaway has gorgeous, very well-presented a/c rooms with minibars, satellite TV and verandas that face a central pool. It's run by a welcoming Australian couple; though no children under 12. Located up a narrow side road; turn right after the main mosque. **$42**

Mascot Beach Resort Jl Pantai Senggigi ☎0370 693365, ⓦmascotresort.com. A central but tranquil place with cottage-style a/c and hot-water bungalows set around spacious sea-front lawns; the cheapest are fan-cooled and close to the road. There's a good restaurant and pool overlooking the sea. **Rp600,000**

Raja's Bungalows Gang Arjuna 1 ☎0812 377 0138, ✉rajas22@yahoo.com. Located up a quiet lane in a lush semi-rural spot, but very close to the centre (and mosque – for that early wake-up call). Inside the small, walled compound the five fan-cooled bungalows are nicely furnished and have open-roofed cold-water bathrooms. The owners are very helpful indeed and will sort out onward transport. **Rp260,000**

TAKE THE ROAD TO PEMENANG

With your own transport, the spectacular **coastal road north** from central Senggigi to Pemenang (24km) makes a great day out, passing through small villages set behind sweeping, invariably empty bays and stands of coconut palm. Wending up and over the steep headlands that separate the bays you get fine views of the Gili Islands – three tiny white-rimmed specks in a turquoise sea – and across to Gunung Agung on Bali. First of the beaches is **Karandangan**, with its charcoal-black sand, Sunday seafood warung and a good restaurant; **Mangsit** and **Klui** both have great beaches, with accommodation; then there's Malimbu, the especially pretty whitish-sand **Nippah**, and Teluk Kodek and Teluk Nara (for fast boats to the Gilis and Bali, and with pearl farms offshore). There are occasional warung along the route, good for drinks and snacks, and there's nothing to stop you **swimming** off any of the lovely crescents of sand – except on Sundays, you'll likely be the only one in the water.

Pemenang marks the turn-off to Bangsal (for public and shuttle boats to the Gili Islands). A couple of kilometres beyond Pemenang you reach the beautiful beach at **Sire** and its cluster of deluxe accommodation (see p.265).

6

BATU BOLONG & SOUTHERN BEACHES

The swimming's good off the steeply raked grey-sand beach at Batu Bolong and it's just a 10min walk south of central Senggigi, via either the road or the beach (tide permitting).

Ibludan Hotel Jl Raya Senggigi ☎ 0370 750 1634, ⓦ ibludanlombok.wixsite.com/ibludanhotel. Boasting a lush tropical garden and large saltwater pool, this new place has very stylish, spotless and comfortable rooms, plus a library, great staff and friendly owners. It's 300m inland from the beach, about 5km south of central Senggigi. **Rp565,000**

Indah Homestay 500m off Jl Raya Senggigi, Kampung Loco ☎ 0813 3710 3930, ⓔ indah.homestay.lombok @gmail.com. Tucked away down a lane, off the northern side of the main drag by the *Graha Beach* hotel, this quiet homestay has six very neat, clean fan-cooled rooms and is run by a friendly Dutch/Indonesian couple who can arrange transport, motorbikes and laundry. **Rp200,000**

Jazz Senggigi Hotel Jl Palem Raja 2A ☎ 0370 692323, ⓦ jazzsenggigihotel.com. Just inland from the beach, this modern hotel has a/c accommodation including a good dorm and budget twin room (both with shared bathrooms) as well as posher doubles with en-suites and a veranda. There's a bar-restaurant, good pool and staff are helpful. Dorm **Rp200,000**, twins **Rp400,000**

La Casa Homestay Gang Pura Melase, Tanah Embet, Batu Layar ☎ 0370 692105, ⓔ lacasa.lombok@yahoo .com. Welcoming, very inexpensive French-run budget option, set amid coconut groves and paddy fields, 300m inland from the main road opposite the *Jayakarta* hotel.

The simple rooms grouped around a pretty garden have fans and cold-water bathrooms. **Rp140,000**

★**Sunset House** Jl Raya Senggigi 66 ☎ 0370 692020, ⓦ sunsethouse-lombok.com. Fronting the beach on Batu Balong, this well-managed place has enormous rooms with sea (and sunset) views, huge beds, contemporary decor and all the trimmings – a/c, satellite TV, big breakfasts and use of the generously sized beachside pool. **$62**

MANGSIT AND KLUI

With just half a dozen beachfront hotels, a couple of tiny shops and a mosque, the beach is the focus at Mangsit, 4km north of central Senggigi; it has a small reef for fair snorkelling at the northern end. Bemos shuttle into central Senggigi until 6pm. White-sand Klui, north over the headland from Mangsit, is very quiet.

Jeeva Klui Jl Raya Klui 1 ☎ 0821 5000 0800, ⓦ jeeva klui.com. Stylish boutique resort on lovely Klui beach with a stunning infinity pool, spa and fitness centre. Most of the "suites" have sea views through their picture windows, and there are fine vistas of Bali's Gunung Agung. **$187**

★**Qunci Villas** Jl Raya Mangsit ☎ 0370 693800, ⓦ qunci villas.com. Occupying a prime beach plot, this elegant, design-conscious hotel has rooms in separate zones divided by tropical gardens so intimacy is retained. Guests get the run of three shoreside pools, an excellent spa, lounge bar and a couple of restaurants. Rooms and suites are done out in cool, understated limestone and with original art on the walls. Staff are super-helpful, and the whole place ticks over as efficiently as a Swiss timepiece. **$144**

EATING AND NIGHTLIFE

As you'd expect, central Senggigi has the biggest concentration of **restaurants**, but Batu Bolong, with its candlelit tables and flaming torches on the beach, is the most atmospheric place to eat after dark. On Sundays **local warung** serve seafood from the sea-view shacks near Batu Bolong temple, as they do all along the beach at Karandangan, and every evening at sunset, stalls sell barbecued sweetcorn on the headland just north of the *Sheraton Senggigi*. **Senggigi nightlife** is mostly either restaurants with live music or dodgy karaoke places (not listed here) catering to male domestic tourists. During Ramadan all tourist places remain open. Many restaurants offer free shuttles within the Senggigi area in the evenings.

CENTRAL SENGGIGI

★**Asmara** Jl Raya Senggigi ☎ 0370 693619, ⓦ asmara -group.com. This long-standing, family-friendly Senggigi favourite serves good German and Indonesian dishes including steak (with green pepper gravy, crushed garlic potatoes and green beans wrapped in bacon), great *Wiener schnitzel* (Rp97,000) and good kids' meals. There's a library and kids' toys too. Shuttle service after 6.30pm. Daily 8am–11pm.

★**Bale Tajuk Café** Jl Raya Senggigi ☎ 0819 0731 3455. Offering fine value and a cosy ambience, this cheerful place has a big menu of Indonesian, Sasak and Western food (most mains around Rp45,000) – try the

ayam taliwang (spicy Sasak-style chicken, Rp55,000) or *pepes ikan* (fish cooked in banana leaf, Rp55,000). A big Bintang beer is Rp38,000. Daily 10am–10pm.

Bumbu Jl Raya Senggigi ☎ 0370 693166. Hot, Thai-inspired curries are the thing here, from classic red and green curries (Rp58,000) to good seafood dishes. Steaks and sandwiches too. Near the Pasar Seni (see opposite). Daily 9am–11pm.

Square Jl Raya Senggigi ☎ 0877 6529 4866, ⓦ square lombok.com. Fine dining and contemporary design make this Senggigi's destination restaurant. There's *begibung*, a mix of regional West Nusa Tenggara dishes, and the likes of slow-cooked lamb shank on mashed potato with

6

STREET HAWKERS

Walk along the beach or eat at a streetside restaurant in central Senggigi and you'll be approached by one or more of the local **hawkers** selling sarongs, pearls, T-shirts, paintings, more pearls, tours, transport and yet more pearls. It can be irritating, but it's worth bearing a few things in mind. Despite the tourist gloss, many people in Lombok are poor. Employment opportunities are few, not least because you need either a considerable amount of money, or well-placed connections, to secure many jobs, from government positions to jobs in hotels and restaurants. Family land is often insufficient to support all the people dependent on it. Working as a hawker in Senggigi is a way of trying to escape the cycle – a reality that admittedly is not the first thing that comes to mind when you're faced with the umpteenth request of the day to "just have a look please".

caramelized shallot and mint oil – or splash out on the five-course gourmet set dinner. Mains are upwards of Rp150,000. Daily 10.30am–10.30pm.

BATU BOLONG AND BATU LAYAR

Café Alberto Jl Raya Batu Bolong ☎0370 693039. Deservedly popular beachfront Italian restaurant with its own swimming pool and fantastic sunset views. The Italian menu includes home-made seafood spaghetti (Rp75,000), small wood-fired pizzas, good bread and desserts. Round off your meal with a sip of complimentary *limoncello*. Daily 7.30am–midnight.

Cowshed Jl Raya Senggigi ☎0370 693909. Big barn of a pub ideal for Aussie comfort grub like pies (try the beef and Guinness, Rp85,000), an all-day brunch or really meaty burgers (Rp70,000). Doubles as a drinking den for expats and a good venue to watch sports events. Call for a free pick-up, and they'll also subsidize your taxi home at the end of the night. Daily 8am–11.45pm

Warung Menega Batu Layar Beach ☎0370 663 4422. Unpretentious beach warung that does delicious seafood sold by the weight or good-value set meals (from Rp100,000). Fresh lobster, prawns, crab, clams, snapper and barracuda are cooked on coconut-husk barbecues. Daily noon–1am.

KARANDANGAN AND MANGSIT

★**Coco Beach Waroeng** Karandangan Beach ☎0817 578 0055. Excellent Indonesian home-style cooking in classy *berugaq* on the edge of a coconut grove, just back from the dark-sand beach. Many ingredients are freshly picked from the adjacent garden, and highlights include *kare singkong* (tapioca leaf in coconut milk, Rp30,000) and squid, either cooked in ink or with spicy *sambal* sauce. Food is served on banana leaves or from earthenware bowls. Free transport on weekdays 6–8pm. Daily noon–10pm.

Quali Jl Raya Mangsit (Qunci Villas) ☎0370 693800, ⓦ quncivillas.com. *Qunci*'s classy, romantic seafood restaurant is perfect for a memorable meal of grilled fish or expertly spiced and prepared local seafood. Dine by the shore below Lombok's dramatic evening skies, or with daytime views of Bali's Gunung Agung. Daily 7am–11pm.

SHOPPING

Asmara Collection Jl Raya Senggigi ☎0370 693109. Good-quality handicrafts, jewellery and textiles, and a few antiques all at fixed prices. Daily 9am–9pm.

Ciokolata Jl Raya Senggigi ⓦ ciokolata.com. Attractive designer cotton-print resortwear and swimwear. Daily 10am–9pm.

Mentez Art Jl Pantai Senggigi ☎0812 373 5132. The gallery of prolific Javanese artist Bang Bang, who paints abstract and figurative oils and acrylics on mostly Sasak and Balinese themes. Mon–Sat noon–10pm.

Pasar Seni Jl Raya Senggigi. The main tourist art market at the northern end of town has stalls and a few attractive shops selling beachwear, sarongs, pearls, jewellery and artefacts. Daily 8am–10pm.

RIM Pearl Jl Raya Senggigi. A showroom with a variety of local South Sea pearls and imported freshwater pearls. Daily 11am–11pm.

Senggigi Abadi Jl Raya Senggigi. One of several small supermarkets stocking all the necessities, postcards and snacks. Daily 8am–9pm.

Sudirman's Antiques Jl Raya Senggigi ☎0370 693025. Long-established, reasonably priced outlet for Indonesian crafts and antiques. Call ahead to check the opening hours. Mon–Sat 10am–6pm.

DIRECTORY

ATMs There are many ATMs along Jl Raya Senggigi and in Batu Bolong but none in Mangsit.

Doctor At the *Senggigi Beach Hotel* (☎0370 693210; 24hr). The closest hospitals are in Mataram (see p.252).

Police Next to the Pasar Seni (see above). Call ☎0370 632733.

North Lombok

The focus of any visit to **north Lombok** is **Gunung Rinjani**, Lombok's highest and most sacred volcano. Climbing the mountain is a popular though very challenging undertaking that takes a minimum of two days, but there are plenty of alternative attractions in the area, not least the dramatic mountain scenery, several waterfalls that can be accessed on short hikes, and a couple of traditional Sasak villages. It's perfectly possible to visit the Rinjani area on a day-trip from Senggigi, but if you're reliant on public transport you'll need to stay over – and you generally get the clearest views of the mountain in the early morning. There's accommodation in the villages at the start of the mountain trails, as well as some luxurious hotels on the beautiful **north-coast beaches**. Approaching Rinjani from the south, you'll find a couple of inviting villages in the foothills offering a chance to enjoy rural life, gentle treks and exhilarating mountain views.

Bangsal to Bayan

Gunung Rinjani is usually accessed via the **coast road** that runs north from Pemenang, near **Bangsal** (25km north of Senggigi and 27km north of Mataram), the harbour for public boats to the Gili Islands. Lombok's best hotels occupy beaches along here and there are a couple of waterfalls, a traditional Sasak village and Lombok's oldest mosque, all of which can be woven into a day-trip from Senggigi.

Autore Pearl Farm

Teluk Nare • Daily 9am–5pm; tours 10am–3pm • Tours Rp180,000 • ☎ 0370 684 4895, ⦿ pearlautore.com.au

The **Autore Pearl Farm**, along the main road 4km west of Bangsal, is a working pearl farm (see box, p.252) with an enticing jewellery shop on stilts above the water. The fascinating one-hour **tours** (best booked in advance) take in the lab rooms where South Sea oyster larvae are hatched and fed with Tasmanian plankton and the racks where the small shells are placed to grow, and visitors also see the surgical operation whereby a pearl nucleus is placed inside a grown oyster and a grown pearl harvested from another.

Pantai Sire

The longest white-sand **beach** on Lombok, **Pantai Sire**, 6.5km north of Bangsal, is a blindingly beautiful 2km strand of sand and coral, with ultra-calm waters, reasonable swimming at high tide (wear shoes to avoid sea urchins), lots of fish around the reefs about 100m offshore and fine sunrise views of Rinjani. The fairways of the nearby eighteen-hole **Lombok Golf Kosaido Country Club** (☎0370 640137; from $85) run down to the beach.

Tiu Pupas and Gangga waterfalls

Beyond Pantai Sire, the coast road continues north via **Tanjung**, the district capital of north Lombok (with **ATMs**). Beyond is the village of **Gondang**, the access point for **Tiu Pupas waterfall**, about 7km inland via a very rough track. The falls are glorious, tumbling 40m down a semicircular, sheer rock face into a deep pool. In the dry season (May–Nov), however, the water reduces to a trickle. The trio of cascades at **Gangga waterfalls**, also known as **Selelos**, is about an hour's challenging trek beyond Tiu Pupas, through forest and ricefields and via the riverbed, bamboo bridges and a cave; guides will show you the way.

Segenter

West of Anyar, signs point inland and uphill to the traditional Sasak village of **SEGENTER**, a 2km drive off the main road through dry expanses of cashew plantation; bemos drop off along the main road. The village is a more authentic and rewarding experience than the traditional villages around Kuta, and you will be guided round it (donation expected). The traditional part of the village comprises a grid of very simple, mud-floored bamboo-and-thatch huts and the occasional open-sided *berugaq* (general-purpose hut). You'll be taken inside one of the houses to see the eating platform, stone hearth and the *inan bale*, a small house-within-a-house where newlyweds spend their first night, but which is otherwise used to store rice (see p.330).

Bayan

Four kilometres southeast of Anyar, the village of **BAYAN** is the site of Lombok's oldest mosque, **Masjid Kuno Bayan Beleq**, located on the eastern edge of the village, 1km east of the junction with the road to Senaru. Continuing east, the main road winds 8km through the foothills of Gunung Rinjani, offering fine views of the volcano and soon giving way to the arid terrain of the east of Lombok. From the junction village of **Kokok Putih**, also known as Kalih Putih, buses run to the Sembalun valley, an alternative access-point for treks up Rinjani. The main road around the north coast continues for another 10km to Obel Obel and on to the east coast.

6

Masjid Kuno Bayan Beleq

Open only for special prayer ceremonies

Said to date from before 1700, around the time when Islam probably first arrived on Lombok, **Masjid Kuno Bayan Beleq** is strikingly simple in design, its profile reminiscent of a volcano, constructed entirely from timber, woven bamboo and palm thatch, atop a foundation of stones. It has been renovated of course, but apparently in the original style. You can't go inside but you can peek through the holes in the bamboo walls to see the mud floor and the bamboo torches, which light the interior during the few festival days when the mosque is used. This whole area, around the foothills of Gunung Rinjani and the sacred mountain itself, is a stronghold of the Wetu Telu branch of Islam (see box, p.266), and Masjid Kuno Bayan Beleq has a central role.

ARRIVAL AND DEPARTURE

BANGSAL TO BAYAN

By boat Bangsal is Lombok's main port for the Gili Islands (see p.284). All public transport between Mataram and points around the north coast passes through Pemenang; from here it's a 1.5km cidomo ride (Rp10,000) or a shadeless walk to Bangsal's port.

By shuttle bus If you're coming from Senggigi to Bangsal, there's no bemo service so you'll either have to use Perama's 7.30am shuttle bus or take a taxi.

By bemo Bemos from Mataram or Pemenang terminate at the market in the small town of Anyar, on the main road beyond the Segenter turn-off. Bemos from here to Bayan and Senaru (see p.269) are most frequent in the morning, so you may have to charter one (about Rp160,000), or rent an ojek (Rp30,000). Coming from Labuhan Lombok and the east, you'll change bemos at the turn-off in Bayan.

Destinations From Bayan: Mataram (Mandalika; 2hr 30min); Pemenang (2hr); Senaru (20min).

ACCOMMODATION AND EATING

BANGSAL

Arnel ☎ 0370 630486, ⓦ arnel-restaurant.com. This quiet Dutch-Indonesian guesthouse with the *Padang Salero Mingang* restaurant is a good place in otherwise scruffy Bangsal to have a meal and spend the night. Its bungalows in the garden behind the restaurant are clean and modern while Rinjani treks can be arranged. A 10min walk or short cidomo ride along the road from Bangsal to Pemenang. **Rp250,000**

PANTAI SIRE AND PANTAI MEDANA

A new "ultra luxury" resort, the *Legian Lombok* is scheduled to open on Sire beach in 2017 with commodious guest rooms, eight villas and five private Joglo houses, each equipped with an infinity pool.

Lombok Lodge ☎ 0370 662 2926, ⓦ thelomboklodge .com. An exquisite beachfront hotel overlooking Pantai Medana offering a more intimate experience than its neighbours, with just nine villas set in a lush garden around a stunning pool. The in-house Frangipani Spa is one of Lombok's best, and yoga sessions can be organised for guests. An all-day breakfast and gourmet meals at the excellent restaurant are included in the rates. **$512**

The Oberoi ☎ 0370 613 8444, ⓦ oberoihotels.com. Luxury landmark hotel with accommodation in huge, beautifully appointed thatched villas, all with courtyard dining areas and many with private pools. Park-like palm-filled grounds edge the shore of Pantai Medana beach and there's a dive centre, tennis court, gym, generous pool and offshore reef. $412

★**Tugu** ☎0370 612 0111, ⌖tuguhotels.com. An astonishing creation, this fantasy hotel with a towering temple-like restaurant fronts Pantai Sire and is the perfect romantic getaway. Its suites and rooms fuse colonial, village and Chinese aesthetics and there's a huge infinity pool and vast grounds to explore. Their impressive *Bale*

Kokok Pletok restaurant serves outstanding Indonesian and western food (mains from Rp200,000). $286

TANJUNG
Rinjani Beach Resort ☎0819 3677 5960, ⌖rinjani beach.com. A kilometre beyond the Pantai Medana turnoff, this tranquil if isolated place enjoys a beachfront location, and its thatch-and-bamboo bungalows (most are Rp900,000) are priced for mere mortals compared with its luxury neighbours. There's a small pool and restaurant. Backpacker rooms **Rp300,000**, bungalows **Rp900,000**

Gunung Rinjani and around

The **climb** up majestic, forested **GUNUNG RINJANI** (3726m), taking in the magnificent crater lake of **Danau Segara Anak**, is the most taxing and rewarding trek on either Bali or Lombok. Most climbs start from either **Senaru** or **Sembalun Lawang**, on the northern slopes. If you want to reach the summit, Sembalun Lawang is the best starting point. If you just want to see Danau Segara Anak from the crater rim, the easiest access is from Senaru. Other upland villages south of Rinjani, notably **Sapit** and **Tetebatu**, make pleasant rural bases with opportunities for gentle hikes as well as facilities for arranging Rinjani climbs.

Climbing Gunung Rinjani

The 3726m **summit** of **Gunung Rinjani** is reached by relatively few trekkers; the majority are satisfied with a shorter, less arduous hike to the **crater rim** (2641m). From here there are fabulous views of the vast turquoise crater lake, **Danau Segara Anak**, which measures 8km by 6km, and the perfect, sometimes smoking, cone of **Gunung Baru** rising from it. It is also possible to descend to the lakeside and ease aching muscles in scalding **hot springs**. The lake is considered to be the abode of the gods, and Wetu Telu pilgrims come on nights of the full moon, while Balinese Hindus make offerings to the lake during the Pekelem festival (at the full moon of the fifth Balinese month, often in Nov).

WETU TELU

Followers of **Wetu Telu** – which translates as "three times", possibly referring to the number of daily prayer-times – adhere to the central tenets of Islam, such as belief in Allah as the one God and Muhammad as his prophet, but diverge significantly from the practices of orthodox Muslims, who, because they pray five times a day, are known as "Wetu Lima".

For the Wetu Telu, the older traditions of **ancestor worship and animism** persist and there are many similarities with Balinese Hindu beliefs and practices; both worship at Pura Lingsar, and Wetu Telu believe that **Gunung Rinjani** is the dwelling place of the ancestors and the supreme god, and make pilgrimages to the mountain. There are many Wetu Telu villages around Rinjani, including **Bayan**, whose ancient mosque is especially important (see p.265). Many Wetu Telu observe a three-day fast rather than the full month of **Ramadan**. The most important Wetu Telu rituals are **life-cycle ceremonies** associated with birth, death, marriage and circumcision, as well as rituals connected with agriculture and house-building. Their central annual festival is **Maulid**, Muhammad's birthday.

Throughout their history, the Wetu Telu have been subjected to varying degrees of pressure to conform to mainstream Islamic ideas. During the civil unrest in 1965, anyone less than scrupulously orthodox was in danger of being regarded as communist and there were attacks against the Wetu Telu. These days many Wetu Telu profess to follow orthodox Islam while also carrying out their Wetu Telu observances under the label of *adat*, customary practices.

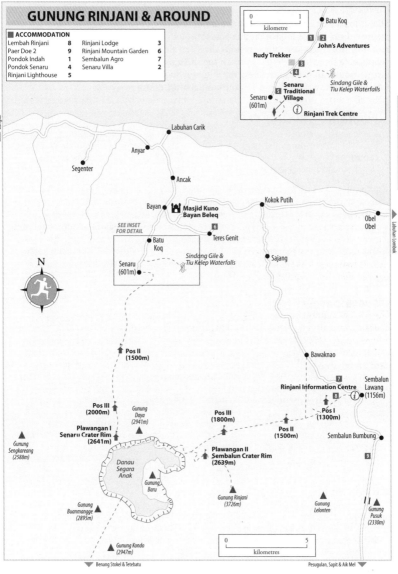

GUNUNG RINJANI & AROUND

ACCOMMODATION

Lembah Rinjani	8	Rinjani Lodge	3
Paer Doe 2	9	Rinjani Mountain Garden	6
Pondok Indah	1	Sembalun Agro	7
Pondok Senaru	4	Senaru Villa	2
Rinjani Lighthouse	5		

Having lain dormant since 1906, Gunung Baru **erupted** in August 1994, closing the mountain for several weeks, and there have been several smaller eruptions since. The Gunung Rinjani cone itself has been inactive since 1901, apart from a few periodic puffs of smoke. However, the mountain should be treated with respect, and its weather is notoriously unpredictable.

Sadly trash is a huge problem on all routes up the mountain and the situation gets worse every year. All campsites are a mess, the human waste and discarded food attracting scavenging mice, rats, flies and monkeys.

The routes

The shortest trek is **from Senaru to the crater rim** (two days, one night). This starts at the top of the village (601m) and ascends through forest to **Pos II** (1500m) and **Pos III** (2000m); you then leave the forest for the steep slog up to the rim (2641m). Most people take six to seven hours to reach the sheltered camp area, from where it's about thirty minutes to the rim the next morning for sunrise, with classic views across Segara Anak to Gunung Baru. You can return to Senaru the same way.

6

PLANNING A RINJANI TREK

The mountain is **closed to trekkers** during the wettest months of the year, usually from late December to late March, and may be out of bounds at other times if the authorities consider conditions to be too risky, though some unscrupulous companies simply take hikers up via illegal entrances. Trekking at any time of year is not for the frail or unfit. A guide is essential and you must **register** at the Rinjani Trek Centre at Senaru or at the trailhead in Sembalun Lawang and pay the national park admission fee (Rp150,000, included in organized hikes) when you set off. Take a photocopy of your passport photo page too.

It is highly advisable to bring your own **walking boots** (trainers aren't suitable, though locals manage in flip-flops!). Other essential equipment includes a seriously **warm**, **windproof jacket** (summit temperatures can drop to freezing at night), a hat and gloves, a head torch that leaves your hands free, and loads of snacks and sweets (even if food is provided). Pack lists can be found on trekking operators' websites. Some trekking companies rent clothes and gear, or you can buy your own at the Mataram Mall (see p.252). Make sure that a mobile phone is available in your party for emergencies.

BOOKING A TREK

Agents in every tourist centre on Lombok, including Gili Trawangan and Senggigi, and even some on Bali, will offer to sell you a Rinjani trek. But choose carefully: this is a serious climb and there have been fatalities due to poor equipment (including lack of sufficiently warm gear) and reckless disregard for safety. As there have been reports of fake agencies on Bali and the Gili Islands copying the names of established operators to sell inferior packages, it's best to deal directly with renowned trek organizers in **Sengiggi** and the trailhead villages of **Senaru** and **Sembalun Lawang** via their websites.

The **Rinjani Trek Management Board** (RTMB; ⓦ rinjaninationalpark.com) coordinates and licenses trekking facilities on the mountain and is supposed to clear litter and train porters. On its website it posts when the park is officially closed. The price of **organized treks** depends on the number of people in the group and the **level of service** – budget, standard or deluxe. There's plenty of competitive pricing going on, though corners are likely to be cut if you bargain too hard; insufficient food and unbearably thin sleeping bags are common complaints. Whatever your chosen service level, you should get a guide, porters, sleeping bags, tents, meals and water. Before you book, be sure to get specific details of exactly **what is included** in the price. **Prices** are from about $110 per person for the crater-rim trek from Senaru (two days, one night), joining a budget group of up to ten people, or about $140 for the rim and lake (three days, two nights). Think twice before booking a trek much cheaper than this. Doing the same routes in a group of two with "standard" service will cost around $160 for the two-day and $220 for the three-day trek; with deluxe service it's about $190 for two days, $260 for three.

TREKKING GUIDES

Senaru is by far the busiest trekking centre, with hundreds of local guides and porters. **Sembalun Lawang** is much quieter and has far fewer trek organizers. Ask at the *Lembah Rinjani* guesthouse (see p.273); there are also agents based in **Senggigi**.

John's Adventures Senaru ☏ 0817 578 8018, ⓦ rinjanimaster.com.

Rinjani Trekking Club Senggigi ☏ 0370 693202, ⓦ info2lombok.com.

Rudy Trekker Senaru ☏ 0818 0365 2874, ⓦ rudytrekker.com.

STT Rinjani ☏ 0819 1777 4082, ⓦ rinjanisttlombok.com.

The most popular trek is a longer version of the above: **from Senaru to the crater rim and down to the lake** (three days, two nights). From the crater rim, a path (2hr) descends into the crater to the lake (2050m). It is steep and scary at the top, with metal handrails and occasional ropes, but gets better. You can bathe in the lakeside hot springs and will probably camp nearby, walking back to Senaru the next day.

You can also combine **the lake and summit from Senaru** (four days, three nights). From the lake, a different path (3hr; pretty steep) climbs to the rim on the Sembalun side and a site called **Plawangan II** (2639m), where everyone aiming for the summit overnights. From here it's an extraordinarily steep haul up to the summit of Rinjani (3726m; another 3–4hr, usually done for sunrise, then 2hr back down to Plawangan II). Trekkers usually descend via the shortest route, to Sembalun Lawang.

The **shortest route to the summit** is to climb **from Sembalun Lawang** (two days, one night). It takes seven to eight hours from Sembalun Lawang (1156m) to Plawangan II and you attack the summit the next morning (if you've any energy left!) before returning to Sembalun.

The most complete exploration of the mountain involves a round trip **from Sembalun Lawang to Senaru, via the summit and the lake** (three days, two nights). This gets the most exhausting ascent over while you are fresh and enables you to soak tired muscles in the hot springs afterwards. Longer trips of up to six days, featuring the "milk caves" and hot springs around the lake as well as the summit, are also possible.

Senaru and Sembalun Lawang are by far the most common trailheads, but hardcore hikers can also take a route up the southwestern flank **from Benang Stokel**, the site of two well-known waterfalls about 28km northeast of Mataram (see p.253). This trail takes you up to the crater rim, via dense forest (6hr), and then down a very steep path to the southern side of the lake (3hr), and is likely to be a lot quieter than the main routes. The return route is the same, unless you want to tackle the summit, in which case you need to arrange to get paddled across the lake to the Sembalun side.

Batu Koq and Senaru

The small, contiguous villages of **BATU KOQ** and **SENARU**, south of Bayan (about 80km from Mataram), are the main centre for Rinjani treks, full of guesthouses and trekking organizers. With cool temperatures and fine views of the mountain, they're also a pleasant destination in their own right.

Other than Rinjani itself, Senaru's main attractions are its waterfalls. The impressive 25m-high **Sindang Gile falls** (Rp115,000 for up to four people including guide and Tiu Kelep falls) is reached via a twenty-minute hike along a path that begins just south of *Pondok Senaru* bungalows (see p.272). Another hour's challenging uphill slog gets you to **Tiu Kelep** falls, where the water pours down in a double horseshoe. You should probably take a dip here; local belief is that you become a year younger every time you swim behind the falls. Longer local treks such as the **Senaru Panorama Walk** (3hr; Rp160,000/person) take in the falls and are guided by women from the village; you'll probably get the best price if you arrange them through the Rinjani Trek Centre (see p.272).

Within a fenced compound a few metres from the Rinjani trailhead, at the end of the road and almost next door to the Rinjani Trek Centre, is Senaru's original **Sasak village** (entry by donation), whose residents still live in simple, traditional houses of bamboo and thatch, similar in design to those at Segenter. A villager will show you around.

Sembalun Lawang

Thirty kilometres southeast of Senaru, set in a high, flat-bottomed mountain valley filled with market gardens growing potatoes and chillies, **SEMBALUN LAWANG** is a very quiet village that's known chiefly as a trailhead for one of the main routes up Gunung Rinjani. There are several more gentle local **treks** as well: the leisurely Sembalun Village Walk to Sajang Waterfall (4hr; Rp120,000 or $10/person), the Sembalun Wildflowers

Walk (includes an overnight camp; best May–Oct; from around $100 depending on group size), and the full-day jungle hike over Pegasingan Hill to Obel Obel on the north coast ($90/two people). The area is also known for **handweaving**, and it's possible to visit local weavers. For all treks, ask at one of the village **guesthouses**.

Sembalun Bumbung

As you continue south from Sembalun Lawang towards Sapit, market gardens proliferate until the valley closes in. Some 4km south of Sembalun Lawang, the village of **SEMBALUN BUMBUNG** clusters round the mosque in the shadows of the surrounding mountains. From Sembalun Bumbung, the mountain road winds for 15km across Gunung Pusuk to Pesugulan, the turn-off for Sapit; there's a fine valley viewpoint at the pass, then it's mostly forest, inhabited by grey macaques and rare ebony leaf monkeys. Rockfalls are common, so the road is sometimes closed.

Sapit

Situated on the southern slopes of Gunung Pusuk, 10km south over the pass from Sembalun Bumbung and a refreshing 800m above sea level, the small village of **SAPIT** makes a quiet retreat with views down to the east coast and over to Sumbawa. Tobacco-growing is the main industry round here, and Philip Morris the big employer; fields are dotted with red-brick drying towers. With basic **guesthouses** in the village, this is a good chance to get away from tourist crowds; staff will fill you in on **trails** to nearby waterfalls and natural swimming pools and can organize Rinjani treks.

Tetebatu and around

Scenically situated on the southern slopes of Gunung Rinjani, 50km east of Mataram (11km north of the main cross-island highway), the little town of **TETEBATU** enjoys fine views of the mountain across terraced fields lush with rice in the rainy season and tobacco in the dry; tall, red-brick drying towers for the tobacco are visible at every turn. At an altitude of about 600m, the area is cool but not cold and Tetebatu makes an excellent base from which to appreciate small-town life and explore the centre of the island. You can also arrange ascents of Rinjani here.

Tiny Tetebatu has no sights of its own, though on a clear morning the views north to Rinjani are exhilarating. The main street has plenty of small *kios* to browse, mostly selling everyday necessities and fresh food.

The waterfalls

The main local attraction is the **trek** through ricefields to the local monkey forest and **Jukut waterfall** (entry Rp20,000), where the water streams down a towering jungle-clad rock face into a pool 20m below. Any guesthouse can organize this as a six-hour return

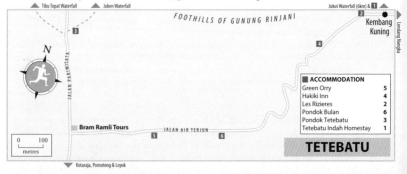

6

trip for around Rp170,000 per person including ticket. With your own transport you can also travel by road to the falls car park (6km), from where it's 1.5km on foot. The twin cascades of **Tibu Topat**, northwest of the village, are a pretty alternative, with a sunlit pool for swimming: the three-hour return trek through the fields costs Rp100,000 per person. Also to the northwest, **Joben waterfall**, or Otak Kokok Gading, is small and much less impressive.

Kotaraja and Loyok

With transport you can explore the town of **Kotaraja**, about 5km south of Tetebatu, which is known for its **blacksmiths** and for its traditional **stickfighting**, *peresean* (see box, p.259), held in August, and nearby **Loyok**, a centre for **bamboo basketware**.

ARRIVAL AND DEPARTURE

BY SHUTTLE BUS
Perama offers shuttle transport from Senggigi and Mataram to Tetebatu, with a minimum of two passengers (Rp140,000; ⓦ peramatour.com).

BY BEMO OR BUS
To Senaru Bemos along the north-coast road stop at Anyar or Bayan for connections to Senaru (see p.269).
To Sembalun Lawang You can reach Senaru via a steep and badly maintained 16km road from Kokok Putih on the north-coast road, or from Sapit 16km to the south. Bemos from Kokok Putih cost Rp25,000; from Sapit they're Rp18,000. There are also irregular pick-ups plying these

GUNUNG RINJANI AND AROUND

routes (you stand in the back with villagers and hold on for dear life). Drivers charge about Rp350,000 to drive between Senaru and Sembalun Lawang.
Destinations Aik Mel (2hr); Kokok Putih (1hr); Sapit (1hr).
To Sapit Sapit is served by bemos and a daily bus from Mataram; there are also bemos from Aik Mel on the cross-island highway (17km).
Destinations Aik Mel (1hr); Sembalun Lawang (1–2hr).
To Tetebatu Bemos and buses from Mataram will get you to Pomotong on the main road, from where it's about 10km to Tetebatu: either take a bemo to Kotaraja then an ojek, or an ojek all the way.

GETTING AROUND AND INFORMATION

In Tetebatu you can arrange motorbike rental (Rp50,000), cars with driver (Rp400,000/day) or bicycle rental at *Green Orry* (see opposite).

Banks and exchange ATMs can be found at regular intervals along the main cross-island highway.
Tours In Tetebatu, Bram Ramli (Jalan Pariwisata; ☏ 0877 6305 0044, ⓔ bramadv@gmail.com) is a recommended

guide for hikes to the waterfalls or beyond.
Trekking information The Rinjani Trek Centre at the trailhead at the southernmost limit of Senaru has information about the treks and maps of the mountain.

ACCOMMODATION AND EATING

BATU KOQ AND SENARU
Accommodation, with one notable exception, is spread for several kilometres along the road through Batu Koq and Senaru. Places on the east of the road generally have the best views towards the mountain. Most can arrange local hikes and trekking guides and will store your stuff while you climb.

Pondok Indah ☏ 0878 6543 3344, ⓦ greenrinjani .com/pondok-indah-senaru.htm; map p.267. A row of basic rooms set in a pleasant garden overlooking a rambutan fruit plantation. Base for Green Rinjani treks, which plants a tree on the mountain during every hike. **Rp200,000**
Pondok Senaru ☏ 0370 622868, ⓔ tiwipondoksenaru @yahoo.com; map p.267. The biggest place in the area, often thronged with hikers in high season. Offers a range of decent bungalows, some with hot water, in a pretty garden with good views and easy access to the waterfalls. Has a

large restaurant with panoramic views too. **Rp240,000**
Rinjani Lighthouse ☏ 0878 6424 1941, ⓦ rinjani lighthouse.mm.st; map p.267. This German-owned, eco-friendly guesthouse at the quiet southern end of Senaru is the most relaxed guesthouse in the village, with mountain views from the garden and lovely wooden rooms with hot water and verandas. There's also a good restaurant and a traditional family house, sleeping six people. **$32**
Rinjani Lodge ☏ 0819 0738 4944, ⓦ rinjanilodge .com; map p.267. Enjoying sweeping views of the volcano down to Lombok's coast strip, this upmarket lodge has very

smart rooms, trimmed with modish wooden panelling and boasting limestone-walled bathrooms. There's an infinity pool (which is opened to non-guests, making things noisy on weekends). **Rp1,000,000**

★**Rinjani Mountain Garden** ✆0818 569730, ✉rinjanigarden@hotmail.de; map p.267. More of farmstay than a hotel (there are resident turkeys, chickens, geese and even a huge hornbill), this gorgeous remote spot is run by a German couple and is ideal for families. Choose from stylish recycled-wood bungalows, simple bamboo *pondok* huts with shared bathrooms, and fully equipped tents. The garden has panoramic views and a natural spring-fed pool while the home-cooking is outstanding and a real highlight, from smoked fish to tropical fruit salads. Access is via the very rough road to Teres Genit, 4km east of Bayan; phone ahead for a Bayan pick-up. Senaru is 1hr walk away. **Rp260,000**

Senaru Villa ✆0812 3781 4445, ⓦrinjanimaster.com; map p.267. This ungainly looking concrete hotel has modern a/c rooms and hot-water bathrooms and is the base for John's Adventures for Gunung Rinjani treks (see p.268). The open-air restaurant has mountain and rice paddy views. **Rp650,000**

SEMBALUN LAWANG

Lembah Rinjani ✆0818 0365 2511, ⓦsites.google .com/site/lembahrinjani; map p.267. A good base with clean, if plain, twins and doubles with verandas facing the mountain, located 200m along the Rinjani trail. The cheaper cold-water rooms are supplied with hot-water buckets for bathing. There's a restaurant too, with Indonesian and international dishes (around Rp35,000); give them notice and they'll provide cold beers so you can celebrate the end of your trek. **Rp350,000**

Sembalun Agro ✆0819 9788 0373, ⓦsembalunagro .com; map p.267. The best accommodation in the valley is just north of the village along the main road; the modern rooms in this hotel all have sweeping views, hot water and satellite TV. The restaurant serves tasty beef sate (Rp30,000) and *gado-gado* (Rp20,000) and has a small shop with trekking food. **Rp425,000**

SEMBALUN BUMBUNG

Paer Doe 2 ✆0819 1771 4514; map p.267. This basic but charming guesthouse has seven traditional wooden *geleng* huts, with cold-water bathrooms, sprinkled across the hillside amid chilli gardens. There's also one large modern room. It's a kilometre south of the village. **Rp250,000**

SAPIT

Balelangga ✆0818 0363 1997, ⓦbalelangga.com. Just below the large mosque, this guesthouse is 700m past *Hati Suci* and has simple bungalows with impressive views across the plantations towards the sea. **Rp240,000**

Hati Suci ✆0370 636545, ⓦdesa-sapit.com. The first guesthouse you'll pass when coming from the main road, *Hati Suci* has simple cold-water bungalows in lovely gardens cascading down from the restaurant. The restaurant serves Indonesian classics. **Rp170,000**

TETEBATU AND AROUND

Green Orry Jl Air Terjun ✆0376 632233, ✉green orryinn@yahoo.com; map p.270. This long-running place is quite pricey for the quality of accommodation but there's always space here. Choose from well-furnished, modern rooms and optional hot water, or spacious new *lumbung* bungalows in the compound. All have views across paddy fields towards Rinjani. **$52**

Hakiki Inn Jl Air Terjun ✆0818 0373 7407, ⓦhakiki -inn.com; map p.270. A very rustic set-up with eight bare-bones *lumbung*-style bungalows and a few single huts set in a garden encircled by paddy fields, about 1km from the village centre. **Rp150,000**

★**Les Rizieres** Jl Raya Tetebatu ✆0859 0313 8111, ⓦles-rizieres.com; map p.270. Charming new French guesthouse that offers fine value and a warm ambience. Rooms are simple yet attractive with colourful bedspreads, the owners serve delicious meals, and there's a large garden and views of ricefields and Rinjani. Dorm **Rp150,000**, doubles **Rp270,000**

Pondok Bulan Jl Air Terjun ✆0878 6592 3240; map p.270. A tiny place whose basic rooms have good bath-rooms and rural views away from the volcano, towards south. **Rp200,000**

Pondok Tetebatu Jl Pariwisata ✆0818 0576 7153; map p.270. With views of Rinjani from the pretty garden, thick mattresses and cheery decor, the bungalows here are a reliable choice. Pricier rooms have hot water. There's a restaurant serving Indonesian and international dishes. **Rp230,000**

Tetebatu Indah Homestay North side of village ✆0822 3653 4942; map p.270. A very welcoming homestay owned by Bram, an English-speaking local and his family, who really look after guests and can organize tours at fair rates. Rooms are basic but clean with *mandi*-style hot-water bathrooms. It's a great place to learn about village life in Lombok. **Rp160,000**

DIRECTORY

Banks and exchange There's a BNI ATM in Senaru just up from *Pondok Semaru*. John's Adventures in Senaru (see box, p.268) can exchange money; some trek organizers will take credit cards.

6

East Lombok

With an arid climate, sparse population and few facilities, **east Lombok** doesn't entice many visitors, although if you're heading to or from Sumbawa (see p.248) you'll pass through the port of **Labuhan Lombok** (75km east of Mataram). The one reason to linger is the prospect of good snorkelling at the uninhabited islands off **Labuhan Pandan**.

While in east Lombok, don't miss the principal **mosque** in **Masbagik**, Masjid Al-Jami Al-Akbar: it's on the main trans-Lombok highway, in the heart of this busy town, and is one of the largest in Lombok. Across the road, cash-starved travellers staying in Tetebatu or Sapit will find an **ATM**. Signed south off the highway, 1.5km east of Masbagik's mosque, is the **pottery-producing** village of **Penakak**, whose road is lined with large and small outlets selling a vast array of pottery from all over Lombok.

Beyond the radar of most foreign tourists, the isolated little beach of **Pantai Pulo Lampu**, 13km north of Labuhan Lombok, near the village of Transat, is popular with locals at weekends but otherwise very quiet. Its main attraction is access to the two groups of uninhabited **islands** just off the coast. The most southerly group – **Gili Lampu**, **Gili Kondo** and **Gili Bidara** – have sandy beaches as well as coral walls and attract plenty of fish. Further north, the larger islands of **Gili Sulat** and **Gili Lawang** are surrounded by coastal mangrove but have lots of coral.

ARRIVAL AND DEPARTURE EAST LOMBOK

By shuttle bus If booked ahead, Perama Tour will do private transfers from Labuhan Lombok to Kuta, Tetebatu or Senggigi – it's around Rp500,000/car for a maximum of four passengers (☎ 0370 693007, ⍟ peramatour.com).

By bus Buses travel the length of the trans-Lombok highway from Mataram's Mandalika terminal to Labuhan Lombok; some continue to the ferry terminal (for

boats to Sumbawa).

Destinations Bayan (2hr); Kopang (for Praya; 1hr); Mataram (Mandalika; 2hr); Sembalun Lawang (2hr 30min).

By bemo Bemos from Labuhan Lombok to Pantai Pulo Lampu will drop you on the main road for the 500m walk down to the beach.

ACCOMMODATION

There are no recommendable places in Labuhan Lombok itself, so it's best to head just north up the coast to Labuhan Pandan or push on to Mataram or Tetebatu.

Pondok Gili Lampu Jl Pantai Pulo Lampu ☎ 0819 1812 3389. Basic wood-and-thatch bungalows and smarter Deluxe options (Rp350,000) in a garden behind the restaurant and beach. The enthusiastic manager arranges boat trips to the islands for snorkelling or fishing (from Rp375,000/boat for up to six people), and can organize "desert-island" camping trips too. Rp150,000

Pondok Siola Jl Raya Sambelia, Labuhan Pandan ☎ 0819 9776 9364, ✉ pondoksiola@gmail.com. Excellent beachfront place with dreamy views over a black-sand beach east towards Sumbawa. Well-built concrete bungalows are equipped with verandas and quality beds, mattresses and linen. The family owners can set up good snorkelling trips and there's tasty local grub served in the restaurant. Rp320,000

South Lombok

Interest in the utterly spectacular **south coast** of Lombok is starting to take off. It's extraordinarily beautiful, with kilometre upon kilometre of white-sand bays backed by wild, forested hills and washed by some of the most rewarding surf on the island. **Kuta** is the main tourist centre, centrally positioned for exploring the fabulous coastline to the west and east. **Inland**, there are worthwhile textile workshops at Sukarara, plus a couple of traditional Sasak villages at **Sade** and **Rembitan**.

Outside the peak periods of July, August and late December, Kuta and the south are still relatively quiet, but the opening of the new **Bandara Internasional Lombok**,

NYALE FESTIVAL

Celebrated on Lombok and the more distant islands of Sumba and Savu, the annual Bau Nyale, or **Nyale Festival**, is all about the sea worm, *Eunice viridis*, known locally as **nyale**. The worms live attached to rocks in the ocean, but at roughly the same time every year, on the nineteenth day of the tenth Sasak month (Feb or March), they begin their sexual cycle and release brightly coloured male and female sexual parts, which rise to the surface ready for fertilization, turning the ocean into a seething mass of fluorescent spaghetti. The number of worms is believed to indicate the success of the next rice harvest and draws huge crowds to celebrate the festival. Around a hundred thousand people travel to Kuta's Seger beach and other south-coast beaches to gather the worms – which are believed to be aphrodisiacs – and to enjoy traditional singing, dancing, poetry and a re-enactment of the Putri Mandalika **legend**. This tells how the beautiful Princess Mandalika, distraught because of the number of suitors who were fighting over her and loath to upset any of them and risk plunging her country into war, flung herself into the sea where her hair was changed into *nyale* sea worms.

6

15km north, has channelled travellers to this coast in ever increasing numbers. There's not quite a tourist boom as yet, but Kuta is certainly developing, and swathes of the coast have been set aside for hotel resorts.

Praya and around

The market town of **PRAYA**, 22km southeast of Mataram and 26km north of Kuta, is a transport hub for the south, though with the new airport highway, buses from Mataram to the new airport and shuttle buses to Kuta bypass the town completely.

Sukarara

The village of **SUKARARA**, about 8km west of Praya, produces the widest range of textiles on Lombok, weaving highly coloured *songket* cloth on backstrap looms and *ikat* cloth on foot looms (see box, p.155). A sarong-and-scarf set can take up to five months to weave and designs are so numerous and complex that girls and boys start learning at the age of seven; young women must be skilled weavers in order to be considered marriageable. There are a number of textile shops in Sukarara and in neighbouring Puyung.

ARRIVAL AND INFORMATION
PRAYA AND AROUND

By bemo or bus Buses and bemos from Mataram's Mandalika terminal drop off at the bus terminal, 3km northwest of the centre, where there are onward buses to Sengkol and Kuta.

Destinations Kuta (1hr); Mataram (Mandalika; 30min).

Banks and exchange There are many ATMs in the town.

EATING AND SHOPPING

Lesehan Asr Jl Basuki Rachmad, Praya. A good restaurant near the police and fire stations. Very popular with office workers, it serves delicious local food, including grilled fish and *kangkung pelecing* for Rp35,000. Daily 8am–11pm.

Patuh Art Shop Sukarara. A local weaving cooperative with an enormous range of textiles; on request they will show you the weavers at work. It's 2km south of the junction with the main Praya road. Daily 9am–6pm.

Kuta and around

Youthful, laidback and surferish, **KUTA** is for the time being still pretty low-key – not too much more than a scruffy fishing village with guesthouses, tourist restaurants and a few upscale alternatives. The pace of change is definitely increasing however, with more upmarket accommodation and dining options available than ever before, but they're mostly small-scale. However all this may (or may not) change with the construction of

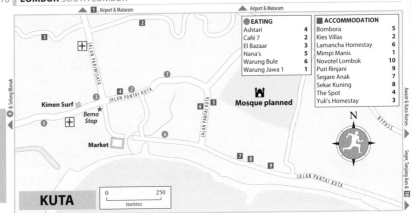

KUTA

a colossal new mosque in the next few years – as locals seek to capitalize on Islamic and domestic tourism – as well as plans for new resort hotels from international hotel brands. The catalyst for Kuta's new-found attention has been the opening of Lombok's new international airport, just 15km to the north.

For the moment there is plenty for all to enjoy. **Surfers** return year after year to pursue the perfect wave, most famously at **Gerupuk**, **Mawi** and, more remotely, at **Ekas**. The **beach** at Kuta is not that appealing, with very persistent hawkers – but at least the proliferation of illegal beach-shack stalls and restaurants has been halted after they were all bulldozed. There's also a busy little Sunday **market** to enjoy (a smaller market is held on Wednesdays). For a swim and a sunbathe you're better off heading to the breathtakingly gorgeous sandy bays nearby, notably **east** at Tanjung Aan and west at **Mawun**, though always ask locally about currents, which can be treacherous. To access the beaches and get the best out of the area you need a car or motorbike – the surrounding roads are now much improved but still cursed by potholes heading towards Gerepuk and beyond Selong Blanak to the west.

Sade and Rembitan traditional villages

Daily 8am–5pm • Rembitan suggested Rp15,000 donation and Rp20,000 for compulsory guide; Sade admission by donation, guides demand around Rp50,000

North of Kuta on the Sengkol road are a couple of traditional **Sasak villages** that welcome tourists. Of the two, the northernmost, **REMBITAN**, 7km from Kuta, is the more authentic and the less grasping; with a good guide you may learn a lot. As with other such villages in north Bali, the thirty homes here are simple, low-roofed windowless constructions, with mud and buffalo-dung floors, bamboo walls and thatched roofs. Some have satellite TV but bathrooms are communal. Villagers farm soya beans and rice and weave cloth and make basketware, some of which is for sale.

The other traditional village is **SADE**, 1km south. It sees hordes of visitors, is more of a shopping and photo opportunity, and has a reputation for hassle.

ARRIVAL AND GETTING AROUND   KUTA AND AROUND

By plane Book airline tickets through *Segare Anak* (see p.278).

By shuttle bus Perama (agency in the *Segare Anak* hotel; ⓦperamatour.com) operates a shuttle service to Kuta from the Gili Islands, Senggigi, Lembar and Mataram (minimum two people; Rp275,000). Other travel agency bus transfers are widely advertised in Kuta; a trip to the airport is

Rp160,000; Mataram or Lembar port Rp140,000; Senggigi Rp150,000; Bangsal Rp180,000; Bali destinations including fast boat cost Rp600,000–750,000.

By bus and bemo Buses and bemos serve Kuta from Mataram's Mandalika terminal with a change at Praya's bus station; the number of bemos has declined in recent years however.

Destinations Praya (1hr); Sengkol (30min).
By motorbike, car or bike Motorbikes are available to rent everywhere from Rp50,000. Bicycles and cars are harder to come by: ask at *Mimpi Manis* or *Yuli's Homestay*.

It's important to avoid a widespread local scam for fake damage claims from freelance rental touts by only renting from your accommodation.

ACTIVITIES

Fishing Mimpi Manis (☏0818 369950, �🌐mimpimanis .com) runs excellent half-day fishing trips (Rp1,200,000, up to three people) and overnight fishing camps. Most anglers come back with more than enough fish for a good barbecue.

Horseriding Explore the area on guided horseback trips with Kuta Horses (☏0819 1599 9436, �🌐horseridinglombok .com) for Rp450,000/hr or around Rp1,700,000/day.

Surfing This is the main deal in Kuta and is possible year-round. Selong Blanak is sandy and good for beginners, and novices can also usually surf Gerupuk; Mawi is a swell magnet. Several surf shops, including the long-established Kimen Surf (☏0370 655064, �🌐kuta-lombok.net) can

repair and rent boards and offer lessons for beginners (Rp500,000/4hr) and trips (half-day from Rp650,000) to Mawi or Are Goling, including boat. They can also arrange surf-and-stay packages to Desert Point.

Yoga The *Ashtari* restaurant (☏0877 6549 7625, ⌨ashtari lombok.com) has up to five daily yoga classes, in hatha, vinyasa flow and power styles for Rp100,000/75min, or ten classes for Rp700,000. The yoga deck overlooking the ocean is truly spectacular. Poolside Yoga at the *Kuta Baru Hotel* (Jl Pantai Kuta; ⌨facebook.com/KutaBaruPoolside Yoga) charges exactly the same rates, has two daily classes and is more centrally located – but does not have that view from *that* deck.

ACCOMMODATION

There's almost no on-the-beach accommodation and no real sea views but most places are an easy stroll from the water. Theft from rooms is an occasional problem: always lock your room and outside-bathroom door, including when you're asleep inside. Accommodation options are expanding quickly, with many new places under construction. Try to book ahead for July and August and late December, when rooms are harder to find.

Bombora Jl Pantai Kuta ☏0370 615 8056, ✉bombora bungalows@yahoo.com. A really attractive place with six pretty wooden bungalows (with fan or a/c) and a large deluxe bungalow with kitchen. All rooms are dotted around a small pool, with decking, and shaded by coconut palms. The owners lead surf trips around Indonesia. **Rp400,000**

Kies Villas ☏0370 615 8222, ⌨kiesvillaslombok.com. Changing the game in Kuta, these very upmarket studios, suites and villas tick all the right contemporary boxes with

stylish interiors and sleek design including original art and gorgeous outdoor showers. Book a Sasak-style *lumbung* if want more of a local feel. There are two pools. **$96**

Lamancha Homestay Jl Pantai Kuta ☏0370 615 5186. Run by a welcoming village family, there are ten rooms here. The simplest have bamboo walls and squat toilets; newer, pricier ones with a/c are more robust and nicely furnished. **Rp170,000**

★**Mimpi Manis** Jl Pariwisata ☏0818 369950, ⌨mimpi manis.com. Owned by a very welcoming Balinese-English

---

DIVING AND SNORKELLING IN SOUTH LOMBOK

The two areas for **diving** in the south are good at different times of year and are always very quiet; it's also possible to reach dive sites in the southwest around Sekotong on a day-trip (see p.254).

Kuta sites are best from October to March and are good for novices. The area is known for its pelagics and its manta rays (around March). At Gili Medas, in front of the *Novotel*, you'll encounter pygmy seahorses and manta rays; Mawun Slope and Tanpa have plentiful coral. Mawun is the only real option for **snorkellers**. Remote **Blongas** (see p.279), west of Selong Blanak, can be dived year-round but it's open ocean and is only for experienced divers and Advanced certification. It's famous for rays (devil, mobula and eagle rays), schooling barracuda and hammerheads.

DIVE CENTRES

Dive Zone Belongas Bay Lodge ☏0819 0785 2073, ⌨divezone-lombok.com. This centre in remote Blongas Bay also organises dives around Kuta.

Scuba Froggy Kuta ☏0878 6426 5958, ⌨scuba froggy.com. Charges from $70 for two all-inclusive dives.

6

family who have lived in Kuta since 2004, this tiny spotless homestay, 2km north of the beach (with free daytime transport), is very good value – though it's is on a busy junction. There's a fan-cooled dorm with five beds, and choice of private rooms (one has a/c), all (except the dorm) with DVD players. The owners are extremely well informed about Lombok and sometimes share meals and beers with guests. Dorm Rp100,000, doubles Rp150,000

Novotel Lombok ☎0370 653333, ⊛novotellombok .com. Kuta's top hotel is stunningly located on its own stretch of white-sand beach, a 15min walk from Seger beach and 3km by road from central Kuta. It's designed to resemble a thatch-roofed village, with over 100 tastefully decorated rooms, some with private pools. There's a large seafront pool and a spa, plus lots of activities such as diving and kayaking. $142

Puri Rinjani Jl Pantai Kuta ☎0370 615 4849, ⊛therinjanikutalombok@gmail.com. Right by the beach these recently renovated and clean, good-quality bungalows all have hot water and a/c. There's an inviting pool and a large restaurant with seaviews. Rp580,000

Segare Anak Jl Pantai Kuta ☎0370 654846, ⊛kuta lombok.com. Long-established place with a selection of

rooms in many different styles and standards. Bottom-end options are very basic (with squat toilets) but some of the mid-priced ones are good quality and a few have a/c. There's a dinky pool and travel services. Rp170,000

Sekar Kuning Jl Pariwisata ☎0370 654856. A cheapie offering basic rooms with fans and cold-water bathrooms and some a/c options (Rp250,000). The decor isn't fancy and rooms (in two-storey blocks) could be a tad cleaner, but are a good size and some of the upstairs ones have partial sea views. Rp150,000

The Spot ☎0370 615 8100, ⊛thespotbungalows.com. Small, attractive bamboo and thatch bungalows (each with a private deck and hammock), as well as a grassy communal area for socializing and a small bar-restaurant. Rp180,000

★**Yuli's Homestay** Jl Pariwisata ☎0819 1710 0983, ⊛yulishomestay.com. An extremely well-run and well-maintained popular place that has expanded considerably in the last few years. It's owned by a charming New Zealand-Lombok couple and has spotless rooms – all with a/c and cold-water bathrooms – dotted around a huge grassy plot with two pools. There's a shared hot shower block and a communal kitchen too. Breakfast is cooked to order, filling and delicious. Rp400,000

EATING

Portions are large and prices generally reasonable at Kuta's restaurants, not least because of the surfers who return year after year. **Nightlife** mostly consists of a couple of local bands that play at one or other of the restaurant bars several nights a week.

★**Ashtari** ☎0877 6549 7625, ⊛ashtarilombok.com. Occupying a spectacular panoramic hilltop position 3km west of central Kuta on the Mawun road, with breathtaking views over the Kuta coastline, this boho hangout is a great place to chill. The (fairly healthy) menu lists fine breakfasts, focaccia sandwiches (Rp50,000), grilled fish and salads, juices and cake. Seating is on cushions, and board games and magazines are available. They also run excellent yoga sessions here (see p.277). Daily 6.30am–8.30pm.

Café 7 Jl Pantai Kuta ☎0817 575 5808. Good, hearty servings of pasta, plus pizzas, deep-fried prawns (Rp45,000) and cocktails (Rp50,000). There's often a nice relaxed buzz in the evening, with shisha pipes and live music on Monday and Friday. Daily noon–11pm.

★**El Bazaar** Jl Raya Kuta 5 ☎0819 9911 3026. El Bazaar offers excellent Middle Eastern food including tagines and kebabs as well as an outstanding meze platter (Rp75,000) which takes in pita bread, hummus, couscous, carrots with honey and mustard dressing, cumin potatoes in olive oil

and baba ganoush, and is almost enough for two. Also serves espresso coffee. Daily 7.30am–11pm.

Nana's Jl Mawun 16. Nana's is recommended for excellent, affordable Indonesian food, including vegetarian nasi pecel (tofu, rice, tempeh, veg and peanut sauce) and a killer "banana beng beng" dessert, prepared with a Beng Beng chocolate bar. Daily 8am–11pm.

★**Warung Bule** Jl Pantai Kuta ☎0823 4098 7828, ⊛warungbulelombok.com. The premises look pretty ordinary but wait till you taste the seafood, all at deliciously good-value prices, cooked by a chef who worked at the Novotel for seven years. Highlights include lobster, mahi mahi and prawns in two sauces (Rp260,000) and mushroom "cappuccino" soup (Rp35,000). There are cheaper mains, too – and a bit of a sea view. Daily 10am–11pm.

Warung Jawa 1 Jl Pantai Kuta. A simple open-fronted warung serving great, cheap Javanese food and Indo classics; try their grilled mahi mahi or village chicken (both Rp30,000). Daily 8am–11pm.

DIRECTORY

Banks and exchange Kuta has several ATMs and many hotels will change cash.

Clinic Lombok International Medical Service is a private clinic and pharmacy with two outlets in Kuta, near the main crossroads and 550m north of the village centre on

Jl Pariwisata (daily 7am–11pm; ☎081 835 3343). The nearest hospital is in Praya.

Police 500m north of central Kuta, near Yuli's Homestay.

Post Segare Anak is a postal agent; the nearest post office is in Sengkol.

West of Kuta

The coast **west of Kuta** has some of the loveliest beaches on Lombok, though to explore it, you'll need your own transport. It's still mostly wilderness alongside the road towards Sepi, peppered with occasional hamlets; as you near Selong Blanak there are tobacco and ricefields too. All **beaches** are signed and all charge for parking (usually Rp10,000 for cars, Rp5000 for motorbikes). Except where stated they all have some **shade**, in *berugaq*, plus at least one tiny **stall** selling water, soft drinks and perhaps packet noodles. Most are quiet during the week.

6

Are Goleng and around

The road west out of Kuta climbs for a couple of kilometres, passing the *Ashtari* restaurant (see opposite) and its panoramic vistas. Some 7km out of Kuta a rough 2km-long dirt track heads to the coast and the village of **ARE GOLENG**. The beach here is about 400m long and known for its excellent right-hand reef break, but a river empties into the bay and it's not one for sunbathers or sightseers.

The next beach west from Are Goleng is the awesomely beautiful **Mawun**, 9km from Kuta, a fabulous semicircular bay embraced by green headlands. It's usually calm and great for swimming and snorkelling, but has limited shade.

West from Mawun, the surf breaks at **Mawi** are some of the most famous, most challenging and busiest in the area. The beach is small, however, and not as pretty as many, and you wouldn't come here for swimming. The turn-off is about 12km from Kuta; the road to the beach is very rough indeed, degenerating into a gnarly dirt track for the final 500m. Even on a trail bike it's tough going, scooter riders should take it easy.

Selong Blanak

The magnificent beach at **SELONG BLANAK**, 15km from Kuta, is a vast sweep of empty sand that stretches 2km west from the fishing village of the same name. Backed by green hills and framed by fine views of **Tomangomang** and **Serangan** beaches (both accessible by tracks), it offers excellent swimming and safe surfing for novices, who appreciate its sandy bottom. There are a few surf shacks by the sand where local instructors rent boards (from Rp80,000) and offer lessons (Rp150,000/hour).

Sepi and Blongas Bay

Up to Selong Blanak the road is fine, but further west to the seaweed-farming village of Pengantap (18km) and on to **Sepi** (23km), it requires four-wheel-drive during the rainy season and great care at all times.

From Sepi another road takes you 11km north to Sekotong Tengah (see p.255), but easiest access to **Blongas Bay**, 1km west, is by boat. Blongas offers challenging diving (see box, p.277) and isolated accommodation. The "road" marked on several maps west to Teluk Mekaki is a very rough track, more suited to a trail bike.

GETTING AROUND
WEST OF KUTA

There are no buses or bemos along this route. If you're travelling between Kuta and Sekotong, it's faster to drive via the airport highway and Lembar than via Selong Blanak. Occasional robberies of motorbikes have occurred on the road beyond Selong Blanak, and though incidents have decreased in recent years, check the situation first in Kuta. Always pay the parking fee (which offers some security) and consider taking a local guide with you as driver or passenger.

ACCOMMODATION AND EATING

★**Laut Biru Cafe** Selong Blanak ☎ 0821 4430 3339, ⓦ sempiakvillas.com/laut-biru-bar-restaurant. *Sempiak Villas* runs this stunning open-sided shore-side café-restaurant, with tasteful white furniture and a hip feel.

There are good breakfasts, seafood (from Rp60,000) and all the espresso coffee options you'll need to recharge after a session in the surf offshore. Daily 8am–10pm.
Sempiak Villas Selong Blanak ☎ 0821 4430 3337,

ⓦ sempiakvillas.com. A tiny upmarket boutique enclave of octagonal wooden villas set on a steep hill overlooking the beach. The villas vary in size but all have a/c, a laptop for watching films, stereo and kitchenettes, and there's a pool and restaurant. Rp1,400,000

East of Kuta

Beyond the *Novotel*, the road **east of Kuta** is bad in places, passing some curiously unfinished mega-resort driveways, but for sunbathers the beach at Tanjung Aan is well worth the trip, while surfers head further on to Gerupuk for world-class wave action and some of the cheapest accommodation in the area. A fifteen-minute walk from the *Novotel* beach takes you across the inlet and via the grassy-hummocked headland grazed by local cows to the white-sand beach of **Seger**. It's a popular surf spot, with a warung and some shade; currents permitting, it can also be good for swimming. In a different league, though, are the gloriously pretty twin crescents of **Tanjung Aan**, 5km from Kuta. The usually calm **Aan**, on the west side of the offshore outcrop, is perfect for swimming and (partially shaded) lounging; **Pedau**, to the east, has a **rip tide**. There are two cafés (8am–9pm) that offer shaded parking, grilled fish, parasols and drinks, plus the occasional sarong hawker.

Beyond Tanjung Aan, the fishing village of **Gerupuk**, 8km from Kuta, sits on the western shores of Gumbang Bay. Lobster is the main source of income here, but with five famously good **surf breaks** within a fifteen-minute boat ride, surf-tourism is also important; surf shops rent boards and arrange boats to the breaks (Rp80,000/person). From Gerupuk, you can look across the huge bay to **Bumbang** on the eastern shore and rent a boat for snorkelling or to get to Ekas (Rp700,000 for a day-trip; 90min each way).

The thriving fishing village of **Awang**, 16km east of Kuta, is worth the trip to see scenic **Awang Bay**, also known as **Ekas Bay**, with views east across to Ekas and south to the open sea. Boats to Ekas can be chartered for about Rp330,000 return.

ACCOMMODATION AND EATING   EAST OF KUTA

GERUPUK
Edo Homestay ☎0818 0371 0521, ✉gerupuksurf @yahoo.com. A selection of clean, tiled fan-and-cold-water rooms above a shore-side café and surf shop, across the road from the mosque. The *Edo* harbour-front restaurant opens daily 7am–10pm. Rp180,000

Lakuen Beach Bungalow ☎0822 3276 6543. Now under new ownership, this place is being steadily upgraded. Its stylish a/c villa-style concrete *lumbung* all have contemporary furnishings, polished wooden floors, kitchenette and outdoor hot-water bathrooms and there's a cool pool. Book through ⓦbooking.com. $46

Seamonkees ☎0819 1739 2574. Offers very cheap, fan-cooled rooms with en-suite cold-water bathrooms and a restaurant (daily 7am–9pm) selling local grub (meals from Rp25,000). Rp130,000

Ekas and the southeast peninsula

Lombok's isolated **southeast peninsula** is way off the beaten track. Travel isn't easy but the coastal views are startling and there's good surfing and some unique accommodation.

The road to the peninsula leaves the southern highway at **Sepapan** and splits at **Jerowaru** – turn right at the southern end of the village, 4km from the highway. To continue south, turn left after another 1.5km at the Masjid Al-Muntaha mosque in the village of **Tutuk**. Carry on south for 5km to reach a major junction, signed straight on for **Tanjung Ringgit** – a very remote beach at Lombok's southeastern tip – and right for another 7.5km to **EKAS**.

ARRIVAL AND DEPARTURE   EKAS AND THE SOUTHEAST PENINSULA

By bemo or boat Irregular bemos link Ekas and the main road at Sepapan but the most comfortable way to get there is by boat from Awang.

ACCOMMODATION

Heaven on the Planet Ekas ☎0812 3768 0189, ⓦsanctuaryinlombok.com. This remote, deluxe resort consists of two sections, 20min walk apart: a variety of clifftop chalets and villas with fantastic views, and six further rooms and a beautiful spa at beach level near the Inside Ekas surf break. Both areas have a pool and restaurant, for guests only. Full-board rates include transport from the airport, watersports equipment (including kite- and windsurfers) rental, boats to the waves and a massage every second day. $123

Jeeva Beloam Tanjung Ringgit ☎0815 4740 4686, ⓦjeevabeloam.com. You can't get further away from things than at this stunning beach camp in a private cove at the southeastern point of Lombok. The eleven large cabins are made with recycled wood and *alang-alang* thatch, with open-air bathrooms and a/c in the evening. A few are set on the beach, the rest on the hillside. Apart from watersports, hiking and biking, the only thing you can do is relax. Room rates include full board and airport transfers, a 1hr 30min drive away. $285

6

The Gili Islands

GILI MENO

The Gili Islands

Fringed by dazzling white-sand beaches, turquoise waters and reefs that teem with turtles and fish, the trio of tiny Gili Islands just off Lombok's northwest coast are strikingly beautiful and have exploded in popularity in the last decade. With no motorized vehicles allowed on any of the islands (just horse carts and bicycles), and swathes of the dusty interiors still taken up with coconut plantations and sandy tracks, the Gilis are as close as you can get to living the tropical dream. Island life here can be incredibly seductive, and most visitors revel in long days spent snorkelling the reefs, eating fresh seafood and enjoying the spectacular views, with the volcanic profiles of Bali and Lombok filling the horizon.

7

Gili Trawangan, the most developed of the three, has become a premier tourist destination with its stunning white sand beaches, easy access from Bali and mass of affordable yet quite sophisticated places to eat, drink and party. Families, honeymooners and backpackers are all well catered for, though budget travellers should note that ultracheap **accommodation** is scarce on any of the islands. Prices soar from June to September and over Christmas; booking ahead is essential during these periods, when you'll be lucky to get the simplest room for under Rp350,000. Overdevelopment is also an issue, and you can expect to encounter noise (and debris) from the island's construction frenzy.

Diminutive **Gili Meno**, next east from Gili Trawangan, is the smallest and quietest of the Gilis, with a limited number of places to stay and no nightlife except a laidback bar or two. East again, **Gili Air** falls somewhere in between, with plenty of restaurants and bars but a much larger population of islanders to balance out the tourist influx.

Prices on the islands are generally higher than on Bali and mainland Lombok due to the high transport costs, and are continuing to increase as local land prices boom and more luxurious hotels open.

All three Gili Islands – "Gili" actually, and tautologically, means "Island" in Sasak – have only really been settled since the 1970s, mostly by Sasaks from mainland Lombok and Bugis fishermen from Sulawesi. Island culture reflects these roots and all three islands are **Muslim**. Alcohol is for sale throughout, though you should be culturally sensitive near mosques (avoid boozing outside) and expect nightlife to be toned down a notch during Ramadan. Local people are very used to seeing scantily clad Westerners but you should cover up when you move away from the beach.

The tourism influx has altered Gili culture in other ways too. In a bid to preserve marine life, scuba diving schools pay the islanders not to fish over the coral, and this has led to a return of top predators including white- and black-tip reef sharks and the year-round presence of turtles. Biorock, a reef regeneration project, has also been a great success, and the Gilis' coral is now in better condition than it was back in the 1990s.

ARRIVAL AND DEPARTURE   THE GILI ISLANDS

Frequent boats run to the Gili Islands from Bali and Lombok; depending on the operator, you may need to change on Gili Trawangan for Gili Meno and Gili Air. Public and charter boats between the Gilis are plentiful. Though the islands have

Diving and snorkelling off the Gili Islands p.287
Biorock: the DIY reef p.290

Trawangan turmoil p.291
Mushrooms and moonshine p.294

DIVING, GILI MENO

Highlights

❶ Scuba diving The Gili's reefs are a delight to explore underwater, with healthy coral, dramatic drop-offs and prolific sealife at dive sites such as Secret Reef. **See p.287**

❷ Other watersports The Gilis are not exclusively about scuba: learn to freedive, take out a kayak – or there's even some surf from time to time. **See p.287 & p.290**

❸ Partying in Gili T Bar hop along the island's east coast then hit one of the designated party venues for dancing until (nearly) dawn. See p.294

❹ Sunset watching The islands' west coasts are a dream at sunset; from bars such as *The Exile*, the great cone of Bali's Agung volcano and setting sun is a spellbinding sight. **See p.295**

❺ Mellow Meno To experience the Gilis of yesteryear you don't need to time travel: just hop on a boat to easy-going Meno, a Gili without the crowds. **See p.295**

❻ Lounging by the shore Kick back on the beach: either horizontal in a hammock or reclined in a beanbag at somewhere chilled like *Mirage Bar*. **See p.299**

HIGHLIGHTS ARE MARKED ON THE MAP ON P.286

jetties, most boats dock on the beach so you'll probably get your feet wet. Flying to Lombok and taking a boat across to the islands costs roughly the same as the fast boats, and is the only option in rough weather; between December and February all boat traffic from Bali can be suspended for days.

FROM BALI

BY PLANE

The most comfortable and safest option from Bali is to fly to Lombok's international airport (30min), then take a taxi to either of the (neighbouring) harbours of Teluk Kodek or Teluk Nare (2hr; Rp280,000) and charter a boat (around $30/one-way) to the Gilis.

BY FAST BOAT

The quickest way to get to the Gili Islands from Bali is to take one of the many fast boat services. Keep in mind that the channel between Bali and Lombok is open ocean, and that it can get very rough in bad weather, so beware of rogue operators that risk the crossing with substandard equipment; only book with trusted companies. Morning departures are usually calmer; in the afternoon choppy seas can make the crossings uncomfortable.

Fast boats depart from several harbours around south and east Bali – Benoa, Sanur, Padang Bai, Nusa Lembongan and Amed – and tickets usually include transfers from hotels all over southern Bali. The sea crossing takes 1hr 30min–2hr in a fast boat, and all-inclusive tickets average Rp675,000; in low season prices go down to around Rp450,000.

Operators Tickets can be bought online or at any tour agent in any tourist centre. Alternatively, the websites ⓦwww.gilibookings.com and ⓦgili-fastboat.com have links to most companies, though dealing directly with the operator can be cheaper. Reliable fast-boat companies include: Blue Water Express (☏0361 895 1111, ⓦblue water-express.com); Gili Getaway (☏0813 3707 4147, ⓦgiligetaway.com); Gili Gili (☏0361 763306, ⓦgiligili fastboat.com); and Scoot Cruise (☏0361 271030, ⓦscoot cruise.com).

BY SLOW BOAT

The cheapest but most time-consuming option is to take the public car ferry from Padang Bai to the west Lombok port of Lembar, then continue by bemos to Bangsal for the

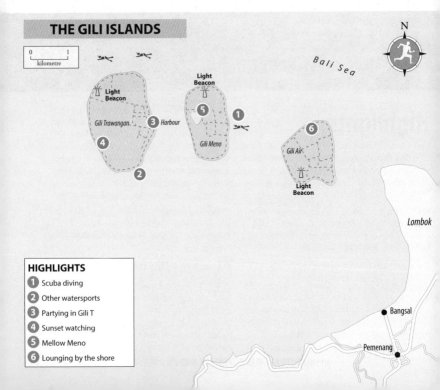

THE GILI ISLANDS

N

Bali Sea

0   1
kilometre

Light Beacon

Light Beacon

Gili Trawangan ③ Harbour

⑤

①

④

Gili Meno

⑥

Gili Air

②

Light Beacon

Lombok

Bangsal

Pemenang

HIGHLIGHTS

① Scuba diving
② Other watersports
③ Partying in Gili T
④ Sunset watching
⑤ Mellow Meno
⑥ Lounging by the shore

DIVING AND SNORKELLING OFF THE GILI ISLANDS

The **snorkelling** and **diving** around the Gili Islands is rewarding and accessible, with two dozen sites within half an hour's boat ride, including drop-offs, slopes and drift dives. The islands are fringed by **coral reefs**, and the Biorock coral regeneration programme has created house reefs all the way down Gili Trawangan and Gili Menos's east coasts (see box, p.290); visibility averages 15–25m. **Turtles** are common and the prolific **fish** life includes reef sharks, cuttlefish, moray eels, lobsters, wrasses and bumphead parrotfish. Among the most popular local **sites** are Shark Point, Meno Wall, Turtle Heaven, Deep Halik, Manta Point and the deep Secret Reef; as they're so close, dive centres tend to send boats to at least three different sites a day, which gives lots of choice and flexibility.

There are also some **freediving** schools. Breath-hold diving (without tanks or scuba gear) is an exhilarating sport, with no bubbles between you and the fish, though you should always take a course with professionals before attempting it yourself.

DIVE CENTRES

Dive centres on the Gili Islands charge similar **prices**, around $75 for two dives, though standards do vary; a list of established centres is below. Most offer dive-and-stay packages and many sell good-quality dive gear. All divers and snorkel-trippers off the Gili Islands are requested to pay a one-off **reef tax** of Rp50,000 to the Gili Eco Trust (wgiliecotrust.com), which works to protect local reefs (see box, p.290). There is a **recompression chamber** in Mataram at Kantor Kesehatan Pelabuhan, Jl Adi Sucipto 13B, Apenan (24hr hotline ☎0370 660 0333) but the chamber in Denpasar (see p.92) is the preferred option.

Dive companies can take accompanying **snorkellers** for about $15, or you can join one of the daily glass-bottomed boat trips to sites around all three Gilis, with a stop for lunch on Gili Air (Rp95,000/person including mask and snorkel); many shops, especially those on Gili Trawangan, sell tickets. Backpackers' liveaboard boat trips from Gili Trawangan to Komodo are widely advertised and cost from $180 for three or four days. For a more casual shore-based snorkel, gear is readily available for Rp25,000–50,000 a day. If you're snorkelling or swimming off the beach, be warned that local **offshore currents** are hazardous and can carry you further than you intended. Though the islands look temptingly close, do not attempt to swim between them; there have been drownings.

Blue Marlin Dive shops in all three islands: ☎0370 613 2424 (Gili Trawangan), ☎0370 639980 (Gili Meno), ☎0811 391636 (Gili Air), wbluemarlin dive.com. The Gili's original dive school. Known for technical diving and tri-mix and rents out closed-circuit rebreathers.

Divine Divers Gili Meno ☎0852 4057 0777, wdivine divers.com. In a great, quiet spot on the west coast; offers PADI courses up to Divemaster.

Freedive Gili Gili Trawangan ☎0370 619 7180, wfreedivegili.com. Asia's foremost freediving school,

run by UK record holder Mike Board with SSI courses from $285. Has a 25m-long practice pool and is also home to Gili Yoga.

Lutwala Dive ☎0877 6549 2615, wlutwala.com. Based on the north coast, this 5-star PADI centre has small groups and does lots of instructor training.

Manta Dive Gili Trawangan ☎0878 6555 6914, wmanta-dive.com. Offers both PADI and SSI courses.

Trawangan Dive Gili Trawangan ☎0370 614 9220, wtrawangandive.com. Works with the Gili Eco Trust and can offer conservation specialities.

public boat to the Gilis. Perama shuttle buses make use of this connection, linking Bali's main tourist centres to those on Lombok.

FROM LOMBOK

On Lombok, the main port for the Gili Islands is Bangsal (see p.265); here you'll find the cheapest and most frequent service to and from all three islands (Rp9000–12,000 on public boats), but it's famous for its hassle. Keep your cool – the Gilis are worth it. Taxis and shuttle buses stop at the car park and barrier 500m from the harbour, from

where you can either walk or take a cidomo; expect to pay Rp8000/person and Rp8000/large bag. The ticket office (8am–5.30pm) for all boats to the islands is on the seafront, to your left once you reach the harbour; ignore all other sellers and only buy your ticket from this large, clearly signed building, which displays a printed price list covering public boats, shuttles and charters. Ideally, get your own bag onto and off the boats; if you can't, negotiate with the porters before you let them touch the bags – and be clear whether you're talking about rupiah or dollars, and for one bag or for the whole lot. Since public services are now so frequent, few people these days bother with the expensive option of chartering a boat.

By public boat to the Gilis Public boats to Gili Air (25min; Rp9000), Gili Meno (30min; Rp11,000) and Gili Trawangan (45min; Rp12,000) leave from Bangsal throughout the day, setting off when full between 7.30am and 5pm. The only public boats with fixed departure times are the 2pm and 5pm boats to Gili Meno. Speedboat charter services to the Gilis are also available (around Rp500,000). There are also direct fast boats from Senggigi to the Gilis (see p.259).

Returning by public boat from the Gilis Returning from the Gilis, Perama shuttle boats depart the islands

about 8am and take you to Bangsal, where they're timed to connect with prebooked through-transport to destinations including Mataram/Senggigi (Rp150,000 inclusive), Lembar (Rp200,000), Kuta, Lombok (Rp275,000), Kuta, Bali (Rp450,000) and Ubud, Bali (Rp450,000). This option is cheaper than using a taxi and avoids having to negotiate with transport touts at Bangsal. In Bangsal, shuttle buses and metered taxis wait near the barrier, a short walk or cidomo ride away. If you plan to travel by metered taxi (Blue Bird ☎0370 627000, ⓦbluebirdgroup.com; Express ☎0370 635968, ⓦexpressgroup.co.id), it's a good idea to phone ahead and reserve. Expect to pay Rp120,000 for a taxi ride to Senggigi.

GETTING AROUND AND INFORMATION

By boat The "hopping island" boat service between all three Gili Islands does one circuit (Air–Meno–Trawangan–Meno–Air) in the morning 8.30–10am, and another in the afternoon 3–4.30pm, which makes day-trips straightforward; the islands are 10–20min apart. The fare is Rp25,000 and tickets are sold at each harbour. If you don't want to wait for a boat, charters are available in all the islands, ask around at each harbour, and cost around Rp275,000/boat.

Tourist information The excellent bimonthly *Gili Life* magazine (ⓦgililife.com) is widely available for free on all three Gili Islands as well as at many cafés and hotels

on Bali and Lombok; it has good maps, articles with a focus on nature conservation, interviews with locals, tide tables and practical information.

Police There are no police on the islands, although Satgas (island security) on Gili Trawangan has a role in tourist security: it's the job of the *kepala desa*, the headman who looks after Gili Air and Gili Meno, and the *kepala kampung* on Gili Trawangan, to deal with any problems. Ask at your accommodation, or one of the dive centres. If you need to make a police report (for insurance purposes, for example), go to the police on the mainland (at Tanjung or Mataram).

Gili Trawangan

The largest and most built-up of the islands, with a permanent population of around three thousand, **GILI TRAWANGAN** (Gili T) is enjoyably buzzy; in parts on its east coast, it's even a little congested (see box, p.291). Once a backpackers' party island, it now appeals to all ages and budgets, with A-frame huts at the bottom end of the scale and – as ground prices increase rapidly – an increasing number of private villas and boutique resorts at the top. There are dozens of beachside restaurants and bars to choose from, and tour agents can organize everything from kayaking and horseriding to diving and snorkelling. Or you can simply go for the sybarite's option: lazing on the beach by day, living it large in the party venues by night.

A sandy track encircles the island and a tangle of paths crisscrosses it, with a few sections concreted. As the island is just 2.5km long by 1.75km wide you can **walk** around it in about two hours, or **cycle** it in less than an hour (pushing through the occasional stretches of deep sand). Development is encroaching inland, but there are still wide areas of dry scrub and coconut plantations. The 100m **hill** in the southwest has fine views of Gunung Agung on Bali, though trees obscure things somewhat.

The liveliest area to stay is the **east coast**, in particular the strip south of the harbour, known as **central**, which is wall-to-wall bungalows, restaurants and dive shops. The lush white sands, clear waters and plentiful fish along the built-up east coast north of the harbour makes it busy with snorkellers and sunbathers during the day, though it's calmer after dark. The **north coast**, about twenty-five minutes' walk from the commercial centre, is quieter, and places here have more spacious grounds, though rocks are exposed here at low tide (when the sea is too shallow for swimming). Over on the **west coast** some large resorts have opened in recent years, mainly geared at vacationing Indonesians, but here a large rocky shelf all but prevents access to the sea at any time. Head just a few metres inland from the east coast and you're in the **village**, dotted with corner shops between islanders' homes, a couple of mosques and the cheapest places to stay on the island. When everything else is booked out, this is the area to wander in search of a room.

Stalls and **shops** along the east coast and in the small art market (*pasar seni*) sell daily necessities, beachwear, fashions and secondhand books.

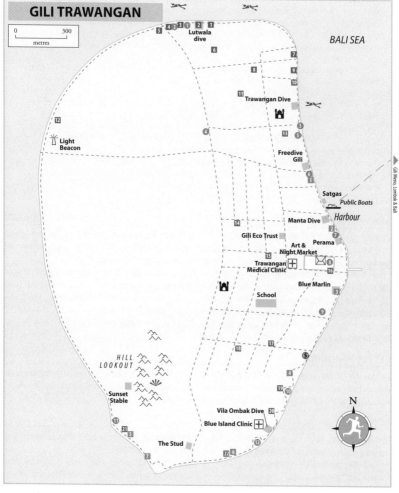

7

■ ACCOMMODATION		Le Petit Gili	16	Vila Ombak	20	Kayu Cafe	7	■ DRINKING AND
Alam Gili	1	Luce d'Alma Resort	6	Villa Almarik	7	Kikinovi	8	NIGHTLIFE
Desa Dunia Beda	5	Lutwala	2	Wilson's Retreat	4	Ko-ko-mo	12	Blue Marlin	3
Edy Homestay	18	M Gili	14			Pesona	9	Evolution	1
The Exile	21	Marta's	17	● EATING		Piluq Café	4	The Exile	5
Gili Beach Bum Hotel	13	My Mate's Place	11	Banyan Tree	6	Scallywags	10	Paradise Sunset	7
Gili Hideaway	8	Pondok Santi	22	Café Gili	3	Wilson's Retreat	2	Sama Sama	2
Gili Nyepi	15	Samba Villas	10	Casa Vintage	11			Santi Lounge	6
Good Heart	9	Scallywags Resort	19	Horizontal	5			Tír Na Nóg	4
Karma Kayak	3	Vila Julius	12	Karma Kayak	1				

7

BIOROCK: THE DIY REEF

Gili Trawangan has seen intense development in recent years, and inevitably the escalating demand on island resources has come at a price. The **Gili Eco Trust** was established in 2002 to address the most pressing environmental and social issues, and to involve islanders, business owners, expats and tourists in a sustainable future for the island.

The trust's most high-profile project to date has been the planting of **Biorock** installations to **regenerate the reef** around Gili T, counteracting degradation caused by anchor damage, fish-bombing and bleaching, and hindering erosion. Biorock frames are steel-grid structures that are fed a continual low-voltage electric current; this causes the minerals in the seawater to crystallize into limestone, and coral then begins to grow along the steel bars at up to six times faster than normal, further stimulated by the grafting of live coral fragments. It's possible to take a special dive course in Biorock and underwater conservation at a couple of Gili T's dive centres.

Biorock and the other work of the Gili Eco Trust is financed in part by a small, one-off **reef tax** that every diver and snorkel-tripper on Gili Trawangan is encouraged to pay. The trust works alongside Satgas, the local island security organization. Another important initiative has been the forging of an agreement with fishermen that restricts fishing to designated zones and uses boat moorings. The trust has also instigated improvements in rubbish collection and **recycling**, environmental education at island schools and the treatment of cidomo horses. Divers also clear (illegally) discarded fishing nets from corals to prevent reef fish getting entangled. A weekly (Friday at 5pm) **beach cleanup** is run in conjunction with the dive centres and island headman, offering a free beer to those who participate.

To find out more about the Gili Eco Trust, drop by the office just inland from the night market, or visit the website (⊚ giliecotrust.com).

ARRIVAL AND DEPARTURE   GILI TRAWANGAN

By boat Boats from Bali, mainland Lombok and the other Gilis dock either at the pier on the east coast or a few hundred metres further north. Most east-coast and village destinations can be reached on foot in 5–10min and the north coast is a 25min walk; or else hop on a cidomo. Boats to Gili Meno, Gili Air, Lombok and Bali leave from either the pier or the nearby harbour. Buy fastboat tickets from agents, public-boat tickets from the Karya Behari office at the harbour, and shuttle bus/boat tickets to destinations on Lombok and Bali from Perama (daily 8am–10pm; ☎ 0370 638514, ⊚ peramatour.com) or one of many other agents.

Destinations Amed (Bali; daily; 1hr); Bangsal (several times daily; 45min); Gili Air (2 daily; 40min); Gili Meno (2 daily; 20min); Nusa Lembongan (Bali; daily; 1hr 45min); Padang Bai (Bali; 4–10 daily; 2hr); Sanur (Bali; 4–10 daily; 2hr); Senggigi (3 daily; 45min–2hr 30min).

GETTING AROUND

By cidomo Cidomo (horse carts) are the island taxis and meet all boats. They are very expensive considering the distances involved, with a minimum charge of around Rp75,000 and around Rp150,000 for a ride to the west coast.
By bike Rental bikes are available all over for around Rp35,000/day.

ACTIVITIES

Cooking classes Learn to cook Indonesian dishes like *gado-gado*, steamed fish and sweet rice balls, and then eat your own creations. Try Gili Cooking Classes at the art market (☎ 0877 6324 8215, ⊚ gilicookingclasses .com), which has three classes per day, or *Sweet & Spicy* near the *Egoiste* restaurant (☎ 0819 1722 6344, ⊚ gili cookingschool.webs.com); prices are from Rp275,000–400,000/person.
Horseriding There's horseriding (from Rp300,000) around the island with The Stud (☎ 0878 6179 1565, ⊚ robbedelphine@yahoo.fr) and Sunset Stable (☎ 0859 3501 2836).

Kayaking *Karma Kayak* (see p.292) offers guided kayaking day-trips (Rp350,000).
Surfing The Gilis are not a big surf destination but there are reef breaks off Kokomo in Trawangan and off the southern tip of Gili Air. Southern or southwestern swells are necessary; both are fast righthanders. Local surfers around Trawangan's art market rent boards.
Trekking Rinjani treks can be organized through Gili T agents, though are best arranged via reputable operators in Senggigi and Senaru.
Yoga Excellent daily yoga classes are offered by Freedive Gili (Rp90,000; ☎ 0878 6579 4884, ⊚ giliyoga.com).

TRAWANGAN TURMOIL

Such is the island's popularity, a **construction boom** has beset the island's east coast, where there's an unbroken strip of restaurants, minimarts, travel agencies, bars and dive shops. Even worse, despite regulations prohibiting building on the beach, virtually all businesses ignored local laws and put up illegal structures right over the gorgeous white sand shore – by 2015 the island looked a mess. After years of threats, the authorities finally moved in with diggers and cleared virtually the entire strip in February 2017, opening up the beach to all, though some concrete and wooden foundations remained. Restaurants and bars were being allowed to place tables and chairs on the sand at the time of research, though nothing else. It remains to be seen if this situation will continue, or whether businesses will attempt to colonize swathes of beach again.

ACCOMMODATION

There are very few hotels right on the beach. Those that do enjoy a shore-side location rarely have rooms with direct sea views; nowhere, however, is more than a few minutes' walk away from the sea. Note that many places along the east coast and in the village are **noisy**, whether from late-night bars or the mosques' early-morning calls to prayers – head north or west for more peace. The groundwater on Gili T is brackish so showers are often salty; however upmarket hotels and guesthouses import **fresh water**. Despite the growing number of places to stay on Gili T, accommodation is at a premium, and most places charge wildly inflated prices during the peak periods. Renting a **private villa** for a week or two is becoming increasingly popular. Note that hostels are officially banned in Gilis, due to opposition from guesthouse owners, though some places remain hostels in all but name. **Dorms** are permitted, but with no more than three beds in one room.

CENTRAL AND THE EAST COAST

Gili Beach Bum Hotel ☎ 0877 6526 7037, ⓦ gilibeach bum.com. Popular backpackers' lodge, by the beach and close to all the action. The very spacious a/c en-suite dorms have good security (doors are secured by a pin-coded lock), lockers and clean facilities and there's a rooftop bar with regular movie screenings and parties. A decent breakfast buffet is included. Dorms **Rp200,000**

Good Heart ☎ 0370 6130225, ⓦ goodheartresort.com. Attractive *lumbung*-style wood-and-palm bungalows, with either garden or seaviews, all with a/c, TV and hot water. There are also some contemporary "villas" which are equipped with all mod cons, though these are a little generic. Rates plummet in low season by at least sixty percent. **$150**

Le Petit Gili ☎ 0878 6585 5545, ⓦ www.facebook.com /LePetitGili. The three a/c rooms here have real charm with four-poster beds and quirky decor, but are in the thick of the action, so expect noise. Bike and snorkel rental is included in the price, as is breakfast in the restaurant downstairs. **Rp680,000**

Samba Villas ☎ 0370 619 4818, ⓦ sambavillas.com. A compound with large, stylish rooms overlooking an attractive garden that's planted with native fruit trees, and a lovely three-bedroom villa. There's a small pool and a good beachfront restaurant. **Rp1,312,000**

Scallywags Resort ☎ 0370 614 5301, ⓦ scallywags resort.com. A well-designed little hotel where each room has a/c, DVD player and contemporary furnishings; some have private plunge pools and ocean views. Showers are solar-powered and a desalination system produces drinking water for the sinks. A good-sized pool and highly popular waterfront restaurant (see p.294) complete the picture. **Rp1,312,000**

Vila Ombak ☎ 0370 614 2336, ⓦ hotelombak.com. Occupying a large chunk of the southern seafront, this established upscale hotel has facilities including two pools, a spa and a dive shop. Most accommodation is in contemporary concrete two-storey *lumbung* (some with downstairs bathrooms), though there are some seriously swanky two-bed villas with private pools too. **Rp2,000,000**

Villa Almarik ☎ 0370 613 8520, ⓦ almarik-lombok .com. More of a traditional hotel than most on the island, with large, Bali-style cottages, all with a/c and hot fresh-water showers, the brightest and most modern being the "superior", mid-priced ones. There's a big pool, a dive centre and sunloungers on the beach across the track. **Rp2,300,000**

THE VILLAGE AND INLAND

Edy Homestay ☎ 0878 6562 4445, ⓔ ebungalows bananaleaf@yahoo.com. A good budget choice with eight neat, clean rooms, some designed in *lumbung* style, in a friendly compound in the village. Hot water and a/c are available. **Rp275,000**

Gili Hideaway ☎ 0812 374 4578, ⓦ gilihideaway.com. A gorgeous little garden enclave, run as a home-away-from-home by a genial UK-Sasak couple. The two types of bungalows (all with fans and cold water only) are in two separate compounds with their own pool; the superior bungalows are thoughtfully outfitted. There are also lounging *berugaq*, books and board games. **$58**

Gili Nyepi ☎ 0853 3749 1996, ⓦ gilinyepi.com. Just a short stroll from the harbour, these four delightful bungalows are set in a pretty garden and have private verandas, a/c, attractive furnishings and spacious bathrooms. It's owned by a welcoming Dutch-Indonesian couple who

7

look after their guests well and is deservedly popular – book ahead. **Rp650,000**

Luce d'Alma Resort 🕿 0370 612 1777, 🌐 lucedalma resort.com. This luxurious boutique hotel is well inland from the shore (around 400m) but its enormous 80m saltwater pool certainly compensates. Each of the elegant, wood-floored rooms opens onto the pool and all have DVD players and freshwater bathrooms with tubs. There's a gym, restaurant and bicycles are available for guests. **$186**

M Gili 🕿 0822 4765 3384, 🌐 m-gili.com. In the heart of the village, this well-designed hostel has a small pool and its dorms are all in muted colours, with thick mattresses, ample plug sockets, good a/c and clean, hot-water en-suites. In terms of atmosphere it's more laidback than party hard. Dorms **180,000**

Marta's 🕿 0812 372 2777, 🌐 martasgili.com. Joanna (from the UK) and her Sasak husband Marta run this welcoming guesthouse. The great-quality two-storey rooms have attractive wooden carvings and all come with a/c and hot water; some can sleep families. Verandas with day beds look onto the garden and pool. It is close to the village mosque, however, so be prepared for the early-morning call to prayer. **$63**

My Mate's Place 🕿 0818 0577 9466, 🌐 mymatesplace gili.com. This party hostel is the largest in the island, with a social zone strewn with beanbags, lively bar and fun vibe (though no pool). Dorms are a/c and have big lockers. Draws a young crowd and its snorkelling trips are popular. Dorms **200,000**

THE NORTH AND WEST COASTS

Alam Gili 🕿 0370 613 0466, 🌐 alamgili.com. Delightful wood-and-thatch a/c bungalows, including one fabulous seaview room, all with attractive Balinese-style furnishings in a quiet garden. Most have fans, all have hot freshwater showers and there's a tiny pool. **$75**

★Desa Dunia Beda 🕿 0370 614 1575, 🌐 desadunia beda.com. This fine hotel's huge plot of land is dotted with salvaged 150-year-old Javanese *joglo* (grand) and *kampung* (village) homes: the supremely spacious wooden bungalows come with antique furniture and four-poster

beds, though only some have a/c and most have saltwater showers. There's a pool and you're steps from the shore, with good snorkelling on your doorstep. **$122**

The Exile 🕿 0819 0722 9053, 🌐 theexilegilit.com. Affordable accommodation on the quiet side of the island is in short supply, but *The Exile* offers good value for money with an eclectic collection of huts, bungalows and rooms dotted around a large plot, all with outdoor bathrooms and some with a/c. **Rp450,000**

Karma Kayak 🕿 0818 0559 3710, 🌐 karmakayak.com. Run by two welcoming Dutch women (one a champion kayaker), this place has attractive, individually styled rooms with hot freshwater showers. It's across from the beach, with loungers and beanbags on the sand, and kayaking trips are available. The beachside restaurant is beautifully set up, and serves great tapas and sangría. **$62**

★Lutwala 🕿 0370 619 4835, 🌐 www.lutwala.com. A wonderfully peaceful place, with highly attractive a/c rooms in a small block at the rear of a landmark villa. There's also an a/c budget bungalow (Rp130,000) but these beds are usually taken with diving students. Guests get the run of a lovely garden, two pools, beachfront bar for sunset drinks and a dive centre that is one of the best in the Gilis. **Rp845,000**

Pondok Santi 🕿 0819 0705 7504, 🌐 pondoksanti .com. A stunning collection of oh-so spacious villas, set well back from the coastal road in expansive grounds shaded by coconut trees – perfect for those who enjoy their privacy. There's gourmet dining, a gorgeous pool area, and staff are efficient and helpful. They also organise very classy sunset boat trips on a 25m wooden cruiser. **Rp2,945,000**

Vila Julius 🕿 0819 1603 4549, 🌐 villajulius.com. This stunning white modernist villa has seven minimalist a/c and fan rooms with open-air showers, hardwood floors and hip furnishings. The shoreline is a few steps out front, and there's a pool. **Rp1,300,000**

Wilson's Retreat 🕿 0370 612 0060, 🌐 wilsons-retreat .com. Named after the volleyball in the *Cast Away* film, this gorgeous small resort has eight spacious suites and two villas with private pools and stunning interior design. There's a fantastic restaurant too (see p.294). **Rp2,000,000**

EATING

With a mass of restaurants to choose from, half the fun is wandering slowly down the main drag, trying to decide which to go for. Alternatively, from sunset onwards, head for the popular **night market** in front of the art market, where *kaki lima* handcart stalls serve up cheap and authentic food – *ayam bakso* (chicken soup), *nasi campur*, seafood and *nasi goreng* are all on offer, from Rp15,000 – which you can eat at the tables set out in front.

CENTRAL, VILLAGE AND THE EAST COAST

Banyan Tree 🕿 0878 6239 1308. A great spot for a budget-friendly feed, with an excellent *nasi campur* (Rp25,000) and salad bar. The (more pricey) healthy-eating menu features dishes like peanut and tofu stir-fry, dip platters and smoothie bowls (from Rp55,000) that include

lots of berry goodness. Daily 7am–8pm.

Café Gili 🕿 0813 1694 4000. The loungers under the casuarina trees are the big draw here, set out on a pretty stretch of beachfront, with views across to Gili Meno. In the afternoon they light up the barbecue and grill fish like snapper (around Rp85,000) or jumbo prawns. Daily 8am–11pm.

7

★**Horizontal** ☎0370 639248, ⓦthegiliislands.com. One for the hipsters, this sleek lounge-style place has a magnificent beachfront plot and serves accomplished western and Indonesian food, including great breakfasts and ocean-fresh seafood. The British owner is one of the Gili's biggest characters and the cocktails are superb: happy hour is 4–7pm. Daily 7am–midnight.

Kayu Cafe ☎0878 6547 2260. Charming café with paninis, salads, pasta, healthy juices and snacks plus some of the best bread and cakes in the Gilis – try their Oreo cheesecake. There's fine coffee and the interior is a/c. Daily 7am–8pm.

Kikinovi ☎0819 1592 5729. A vivacious grey-haired lady cooks up ten pots or so of cheap local food every lunchtime and sells it from her small cornershop warung by the art market. There are plenty of vegetarian choices; a veggie *campur* is just Rp20,000. Daily 10am–4pm.

Ko-ko-mo ☎0370 613 4920, ⓦkokomogilit.com. A fine choice for a special meal, *Ko-ko-mo* offers gourmet dining on crisp white tablecloths and a terrific menu that takes in lots of seafood (oysters are usually on the menu, along with imported scallops) as well as tenderloin beef (Rp190,000), rack of lamb (Rp185,000) and lobster. Daily 8am–11pm.

Pesona ☎0370 612 3521, ⓦpesonaresort.com. A popular Indian place that includes tandoori dishes, nan bread and papadums, rogan josh, biriani and dosas; reckon on Rp120,000 for a really good feed. You eat on low tables with cushions for seating and shisha pipes are available too. Daily noon–1am.

★**Pituq Café** ☎0812 3677 5161, ⓦfacebook.com /Pituqcafe. Some of the best food in the island is served at this modest-looking backstreet vegan place in the village. There's a global menu, with lots of Indonesian influence, expect creations such as "sesamia" (soy-rice noodles with oyster mushrooms and pak choy and baby aubergine). Most dishes are Rp45,000–60,000 and the desserts are

also excellent. It's hot here – little breeze enters the compound – but worth it. Daily 9am–10pm.

Scallywags ☎0370 614 5301, ⓦscallywagsresort.com. Fantastic seafood barbecues in the evenings – buy the fish at market price and get potatoes and unlimited salad to go with it (from Rp90,000) – plus open sandwiches, innovative salads, good tapas platters and ribs. Candlelit tables are set on the beach in the evening. Daily 7am–1am.

THE NORTH AND WEST COASTS

★**Casa Vintage** ☎0819 1724 3808. Wonderful boho-chic beach café with painted driftwood furniture and a barefoot vibe. The menu has a strong Carib character, with specials chalked up on a blackboard that might include jerk chicken, Jamaican fried dumplings and Kingston kebab (all around Rp80,000). You'll find excellent fresh juices and, as the name suggests, there are racks of vintage clothes to browse. Daily 8am–10pm.

Karma Kayak ☎0818 0559 3710, ⓦkarmakayak.com. Right on the beach, under the trees, this is a great place to chill out for a few hours and is a prime spot for sunset viewing from May to mid-September. There are beanbags, loungers and tables on the sand, and good tapas on the menu – calamari, *patatas bravas*, tapenade and *baba ghanoush* among them (Rp19,000–35,000). Wash it all down with a jug of sangría. Daily 7am–11pm.

★**Wilson's Retreat** ☎0370 612 0060, ⓦwilsons -retreat.com. One of the best dining spots on the Gilis, *Wilson's* has a French chef who changes the international menu served at this open-air restaurant every few days, with fish and seafood to the fore. Besides French, inter-national and tapas dishes, there's a fantastic breakfast menu (till noon, Rp181,000). A candlelit dinner on the beach is possible, too. Daily 7am–11pm.

NIGHTLIFE AND ENTERTAINMENT

The southwestern side of the island is wildly popular for drinks around sunset when big crowds gather for photos at the beach swing near *The Exile*. For a mellower vibe at sundown head to *Karma Kayak* or neighbouring spots. Gili T's **famous nightlife** revolves around a handful of venues which take turns to host large parties a few times a week (from about 10pm till 3am or later), though there are plenty of alternatives.

Blue Marlin ☎0370 613 2424, ⓦbluemarlindive.com. The big upstairs dancefloor above the dive centre is the

popular Monday-night party venue. There are several bars and DJs play deep house and trance. Daily 7am–midnight.

MUSHROOMS AND MOONSHINE

After some bad **accidents with bootleg alcohol** containing poisonous methanol – including several deaths – the bars and restaurants that are members of Gili Trawangan's entrepreneur association **APGT** have tightened purchasing policies for alcoholic drinks, only buying from trusted suppliers; look for the acronym on the menu. It's still wise to be wary of cocktails that are too cheap to be true – or simply stick to beer, which is always safe. The **drugs scene** of a few years ago has quietened down and doesn't dominate all island nightlife, though magic mushrooms are widely available. Be aware that penalties for the possession, use or trafficking of illegal drugs in Indonesia are severe (see p.45).

Evolution Just north of the harbour ☎ 0819 0720 2796, ⓦ facebook.com/nduevolution. Hosts big party events several nights a week with house, r'n'b and hip hop DJs. Check their Facebook page for events. Daily 8am–1am or later.

★ **The Exile** ☎ 0819 0707 7475, ⓦ theexilegilit.com. This cool west coast joint plays reggae all day, every day. There's a relaxed bar beneath the palm trees with potent mojitos, plenty of spots to lounge around on the beach and well-priced food too. Join the drum circle at sunset. Daily 8am–midnight.

Sama Sama ☎ 0370 621106. Known for its good live music, especially reggae, this bar is recommended for its great atmosphere, service and parties on Saturday. Bands play nightly at 9pm. Daily 8pm–1am.

Paradise Sunset One of Gili T's favourite sunset-viewing points, where a beach bar sells fine mocktails, cocktails (Rp60,000) and Bintang as well as tapas, snacks and rotisserie chicken. Daily 8am–10pm.

Santi Lounge At Pondok Santi ☎ 0819 0705 7504. Uber stylish yet relaxed lounge with the best cocktails (around Rp125,000) in the Gilis, well-selected electronic tunes and a cool crowd. It makes a wonderful escape from the madness up the coast. Daily noon–11pm.

Tír Na Nóg ☎ 0370 613 9463, ⓦ tirnanoggili.com. Yes an Irish pub in the tropics is a cliché, but the "land of youth" is a perennially popular and lively beachside bar. It's a big barn of a place with bottled Guinness, darts, movies and sports TV plus comfort food. There are nightly DJs (usually cheesy) from 10pm and it's the main party venue every Wednesday. Daily 8am–1am.

DIRECTORY

Banks and exchange There are ATMs all around the island. Changing money is possible, but rates are better on the mainland. Some dive companies offer advances on Visa and MasterCard, but you'll pay up to ten percent for this.

Clinic Trawangan Medical Clinic (☎ 0370 666 6696, ✉ trawanganmedicalclinic@gmail.com), signposted down the alley south of the art market, is open 24hr. Blue Island Clinic (☎ 0819 990 5701, ⓦ blueislandclinic.com) is located at *Vila Ombak*. The nearest hospital is in Mataram (see p.252).

Post There's a postal agent in the art market (Mon–Fri 9am–4pm).

Gili Meno

GILI MENO, 2km long and just over 1km wide, is the smallest and most tranquil of the islands, with a local population of around five hundred. There's plenty of space for horizon-gazing, some gorgeous deserted beaches and a delightfully mellow, barefoot vibe pervades. It takes about two hours to gently stroll around the island, with views across to Gili Air and Lombok from the east and to Trawangan and Bali's Gunung Agung to the west. As on the other Gilis, there's no motorized transport, just a few cidomos (horse carts); bicycles aren't widely available, but ask at your accommodation.

The **snorkelling** is good, especially between *Reef* and *Kontiki* on the east coast, as well as on the northwest at the Meno Wall, near *Diana Café*, and down at the disused Bounty jetty. Check locally for advice on currents (see box, p.287).

The **shop** at *Rust* (daily 8am–11pm) sells basic necessities, including a few over-the-counter medicines. Sasak handicrafts and pots are sold at a stall between *Kontiki* and *Biru Meno*.

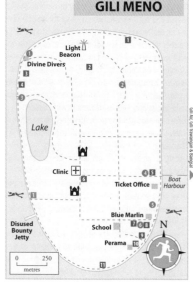

■ ACCOMMODATION		● EATING	
Biru Meno	11	Bibi's Café	6
Gazebo Meno	10	Diana Café	3
Gili Gila	6	Karma	4
Jepun Bungalows	7	Pojok No Five Star	2
Mahamaya	4	Rust	5
Mallias Bungalows	9	We'be	1
Reef	5		
Shack 58 & 59	1	■ DRINKING	
Sunset Gecko	3	Sasak Café	1
Villa Nautilus	8		
Villa Ottalia	2		

7

ARRIVAL AND DEPARTURE

By boat The harbour is on the southeast corner of Gili Meno, within walking distance of the main cluster of accommodation options; cidomos provide transport for around Rp80,000. Buy tickets for the "hopping boat" (see p.288) at the harbour office and for fast-boat connections at harbourside outlets. You can also charter a local boat owner to take you to another Gili for $15/one-way. Shuttle bus/boat tickets to destinations on Lombok and Bali can be bought from Perama (based in the *Kontiki* hotel, south of the harbour); other shuttle-bus tickets are also widely advertised.

Destinations Bangsal (3–4 daily; 30min); Gili Air (2 daily; 20min); Gili Trawangan (2 daily; 20min).

ACCOMMODATION

Accommodation on Meno is less flashy than on Trawangan: few budget places have a/c and there's some roughness around the edges, so things can feel quite rustic even though you're mostly paying well above backpacker prices. Prices fluctuate dramatically and in high season (June–Sept and over Christmas), you need to book ahead.

Biru Meno ☎ 0813 3975 8968, ⊕ birumeno.com. Balinese-owned and -designed bungalows, just back from the beach near the southern tip of the island, a 10min walk from the harbour. All the bungalows have large verandas, a/c and cold-water bathrooms. **$95**

Gazebo Meno ☎ 0370 635795, ⊕ gazebogilimeno.com. Large, attractive fan and a/c coconut-wood bungalows (with brackish, cold-water bathrooms) set in a large, shady seafront garden with (a somewhat murky looking) pool. **Rp864,000**

Gili Gila ☎ 0812 9149 1843, ⊕ facebook.com/gilimeno hostel. Run by a fun French crew, this quirky bamboo, thatch and stick hostel-style set-up in the middle of the island utilizes lots of recycled timber; original design touches include a sunken eating area and cool social zone with beanbags. There are fan and a/c dorms as well as private rooms. Dorms **Rp110,000**, doubles **Rp220,000**

Jepun Bungalows ☎ 0819 1739 4736, ⊕ jepun bungalows.com. Well-furnished rooms and *lumbung*-style bungalows in a garden, most with wooden floors, glass doors and bamboo beds. All rooms come with fresh-water showers, some have a/c and there's a restaurant. **$58**

Mahamaya ☎ 0888 715 5828, ⊕ mahamaya.co. A stylish, family-friendly resort on the western side of the island, with beachfront villas and seven spacious pool-view rooms, all with modern artworks and a/c. Service is great, there are two pools (one for kids) and guests get gratis access to snorkelling gear, bikes and kayaks. **$155**

Mallias Bungalows ☎ 0879 1732 3327, ⊕ malliasgili .com. Centrally located, the beach-shack bungalows here, with fans and cold water, are right on the sand, enjoying unparalleled sea views though they are somewhat dated. Inland there are a few garden-view *lumbung* bungalows. Also has a popular restaurant. **Rp630,000**

Reef ☎ 0370 630982, ⊕ karmaroyalgroup.com. The ten excellent *lumbung* bungalows at this friendly place all have sea and Lombok views, thoughtfully equipped a/c interiors, open-air living rooms and comfy verandas with hammock chairs. **$188**

Shack 58 & 59 ☎ 0813 5357 7045, ⊕ shack58.net. In near isolation just back from the beach on the northeastern side of the island, these two villas offer privacy and peace, both with sitting-room gazebos. The accommodation is far from being shack-like and is beautifully appointed with a/c, fridges, DVD players and garden bathrooms. There's also a (leftfield luxe) bamboo shack with open sides and rustic chic style. No children. **€90**

★ **Sunset Gecko** ☎ 0813 5356 6774, ⊕ thesunsetgecko .com. An inspiring, eco-conscious one-off, with strikingly innovative wood-and-bamboo architecture by the beach on the northwest coast. There are a few basic single rooms in the house and some cheap A-frame bungalows (all sharing bathrooms) plus some standout two-room, two-storey "big huts" with awesome sea views. Minimum two nights. **Rp280,000**

Villa Nautilus ☎ 0370 642143, ⊕ www.villanautilus .com. Stylishly modern and light villas, constructed with an abundance of natural materials and with glass doors opening on to the decks; all have a/c and hot water. There's a café-restaurant too. **$130**

★ **Villa Ottalia** ☎ 0361 736384, ⊕ lesvillasottaliagili .com. The best address on the northern side of the island, the wonderful bungalows and villas here have been fashioned from recycled timber and bamboo yet boast all the luxury a sybarite could desire: DVD/TV, fast wi-fi, a/c and minibar. There are free bikes for guests, a huge pool and good restaurant too. **Rp1,386,000**

EATING

Bibi's Café ☎ 0370 642143, ⊕ www.villanautilus.com. The inviting restaurant attached to *Villa Nautilus* serves excellent pizzas (from Rp60,000) baked in a wood-fired oven, breakfasts and grilled chicken. Daily 7am–10pm.

Diana Café ☎ 0813 5355 6612. A totally chilled feet-in-the-sand experience with hammocks, cushions and fine views on the west coast. The basic menu of Indonesian standards has good seafood and tasty *olah-olah* (vegetables, coconut and water spinach, Rp35,000) as well as cocktails with local liquor (Rp35,000). Daily 8am–10pm.

Karma ☎ 0370 642340. This gorgeous bamboo pavilion (at the *Reef* hotel) is right by the beach and has a limited menu (meals from Rp60,000) of Mediterranean and Indonesian food such as salad with chicken satay and Sumatra-style *rendang* curry. Daily 7am–11pm.

Pojok No Five Star ☎ 0821 4448 8331. Tiny rustic place with just five tables where the chef cooks up a storm with well-seasoned, delicious local dishes (seafood fried rice is Rp25,000) at very modest prices. You'll almost certainly have to wait for a table in the evening. Mon–Wed & Fri–Sun noon–10pm.

Rust ☎ 0821 4677 6430, ⊕ rustgilimenobungalows

.com. Renowned for its fresh seafood barbecues (from Rp60,000), which you can eat in breezy *berugaq* pavilions on the beach. Daily 8am–11pm.

We'be ☎ 0819 1608 5278. With beanbags on the sand, this is a great sunset spot (best viewing between May and Sept). There's good local food such as *urap-urap* (vegetables in coconut sauce, Rp30,000) and fresh grilled fish, plus cocktails made with imported alcohol (most Rp50,000ish). From 8pm a band plays acoustic music. Daily 8.30am–midnight.

DRINKING

Sasak Café West coast, not far from the saltwater lake. This reggae bar and restaurant is a perfect spot to lounge the day away and snorkel on the reef right in front. The food (curries, sandwiches) is not remarkable but the cocktail list

(most are Rp35,000) is worth dipping into; many creations are named after Marley songs – try a *Stir it Up* (with dark rum, lime and ginger ale). Daily 8am–11pm.

DIRECTORY

Banks and exchange There are a few ATMs on the island, and you can change money in the harbour area,

where Blue Marlin also does credit card cash advances.

Gili Air

Closest to the Lombok mainland, **GILI AIR** stretches about 1.5km in each direction and has the largest permanent population of the three islands (around two thousand people). Though tourism is important here, and increasingly so, village life and homes dominate the heart of the island, giving Gili Air a more Indonesian atmosphere than Gili Trawangan, while still being more sociable and livelier than Gili Meno. **Accommodation** is spread around most of the coast but is concentrated in the southeast, which has the most popular beach and excellent snorkelling; ask locally about currents, which can be strong. Countless tracks, some of them paved, cross the interior and allow you to explore beyond the tourist perimeter into the many coconut plantations and *kampung* (villages) with their mosques, flower-filled gardens and grazing cows.

If you're coming to Air just for the day, a good place to head for is the lovely stretch of **beach** on the east side of the island, around *Scallywags*, which is less than ten minutes' walk from the harbour. The restaurants here make enjoyable places to spend the day, with shaded lounging *berugaq*, fine views across to Lombok and snorkels for rent.

The island is ringed by a partially paved track, shadeless and very soft in some places. It takes a couple of hours to complete a circuit on foot, and doing it by **bicycle** is also a lot of fun. As with the other Gilis, there's excellent **diving** offshore.

ARRIVAL AND DEPARTURE
GILI AIR

By boat Boats cover routes to and from Bali, Lombok and the other Gilis (see p.286); they arrive and depart from the harbour in the south. You can buy boat tickets at the harbour counter and Perama tickets from their office

nearby, opposite *Villa Karang Hotel* (daily 8am–5pm; ☎ 0370 638514, ⊕ peramatour.com).
Destinations Bangsal (roughly hourly; 20min); Gili Meno (2 daily; 20min); Gili Trawangan (2 daily; 40min).

GETTING AROUND

By cidomo These horse carts meet all boats, charging from Rp80,000.

By bicycle Bicycle rental costs from Rp25,000/day. Ask at your accommodation for the nearest bike-rental outlet.

TOURS AND ACTIVITIES

Cooking courses Gili Cooking Classes (☎ 0877 6506 7210, ⊕ gilicookingclasses.com). Three daily classes are

offered, allowing you to get a feel for Indonesian cuisine. The introductory option is US$21, while "Super Six"

7

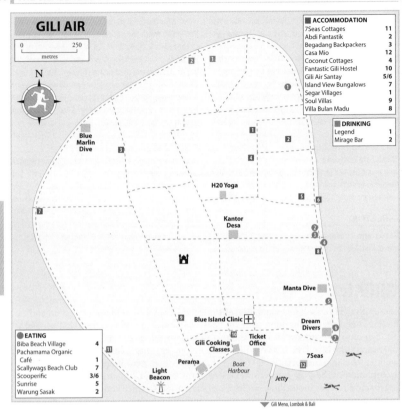

GILI AIR

0 — 250
metres

N

Blue
Marlin
Dive

H20 Yoga

Kantor
Desa

Manta Dive

Blue Island Clinic

Dream
Divers

Gili Cooking
Classes

Ticket
Office

7Seas

Perama

Boat
Harbour

Light
Beacon

Jetty

Gili Meno, Lombok & Bali

ACCOMMODATION

7Seas Cottages	11
Abdi Fantastik	2
Begadang Backpackers	3
Casa Mio	12
Coconut Cottages	4
Fantastic Gili Hostel	10
Gili Air Santay	5/6
Island View Bungalows	7
Segar Villages	1
Soul Villas	9
Villa Bulan Madu	8

DRINKING

Legend	1
Mirage Bar	2

EATING

Biba Beach Village	4
Pachamama Organic Café	1
Scallywags Beach Club	7
Scooperific	3/6
Sunrise	5
Warung Sasak	2

(US$31) includes preparing *ayam taliwang*, a fiercely spicy Sasak chicken dish.

Diving Reputable dive centres include 7Seas (☎0370 647779, ⓦ7seas-international.com), which has tech diving courses, Dream Divers (☎0370 634547, ⓦdreamdivers.com) and Manta Dive (☎0813 3778 9047, ⓦmanta-dive-giliair .com). All three have training pools.

Snorkelling Snorkelling trips to offshore reefs are widely advertised (Rp90,000).

Yoga Classes (Rp100,000/drop-in) including Hatha, Yin and flow at H20 Yoga (☎0877 6103 8836, ⓦh2oyogaand meditation.com) are held in their bamboo pavilion, just inland from *Gili Air Santay*. Four- and eight-day packages are available.

ACCOMMODATION

7Seas Cottages ☎0370 647779, ⓦ7seas-international .com. Large shore-side resort offering a wide selection of accommodation: attractive a/c rooms and cottages, fan-cooled backpacker dormitories and a two-bed luxury villa (Rp3,500,000). There's a gym, pool, dive school and restaurant by the beach. Dorms **Rp100,000**, doubles **Rp450,000**

Abdi Fantastik ☎0370 636421. A long-running rustic place in a fine location on the east coast; the mainly wood-and-thatch bungalows are basic but have fans and sea views, and there are sitting areas overlooking the water. **Rp375,000**

Begadang Backpackers ☎0857 7275 5287, ⓦbegadangbackpackers.com. A well-organized new hostel located inland (off the northwest coast) well away

from the bustle of the harbour and main strip. Choose from deluxe dorms with four or eight beds, a/c and hot-water en-suite bathrooms (from Rp200,000), fan-cooled budget dorms or (tiny) bamboo huts. Best of all there's a superb (mushroom-shaped) pool, surrounded by decking and large *berugaq*. Dorms **Rp180,000**, huts **Rp250,000**

Casa Mio ☎0370 646160, ⓦvillacasamio.com. A burst of sophisticated creativity on the southwest coast, where the four ample-sized thatched bungalows and rooms all have artistic decor, a/c, DVD players and bathrooms with fresh water. There's an inviting chill-out lounge by the shore and a generous healthy breakfast is included. **US$128**

★**Coconut Cottages** ☎0370 635365, ⓦcoconuts

-giliair.com. A lovely Scottish/Indonesian-run hideaway, 80m from the sea, whose comfortable fan and a/c bungalows (all with hot-water bathrooms) are secreted among a delightful tropical garden, with hammocks for enjoying the birds and butterfly life. **Rp440,000**

Fantastic Gili Hostel ☎0877 2966 6957, ⓦfantasticgili group.com. Built almost entirely from bamboo, this popular hostel has smallish ceiling-fan-cooled dorms (with four or five beds) and mozzie nets. It's a short walk from the harbour, and the staff running the place are helpful and offer good island info. Dorms **Rp125,000**

Gili Air Santay ⓦgiliair-santay.com. A popular family-run spot with good-quality traditional thatched cottages (and newer a/c options) in a shady garden 100m from the central east coast, plus *berugaq* on the beach for relaxing. **Rp400,000**

Island View Bungalows West coast ☎0877 6526 5737. If you're after isolation, this rustic family-run place is perfect. Set in a coconut grove facing the beach on the quiet western side of the island, these bungalows come with fans or a/c,

private verandas and hot-water bathrooms. There are also three very smart new options with four-posters and a contemporary feel. Note the sea here is very shallow and only really swimmable at high tide. **Rp525,000**

Segar Villages ☎0818 0526 2218, ⓦsegarvillages .blogspot.de. Attractive fan or a/c bungalows set around a huge garden (complete with grazing cows!) and a small saltwater pond. Breakfast is served on the roof of the reception building by the beach. **$60**

Soul Villas ☎0878 6426 3636, ⓦsoulvillasgiliair.com. Around 300m inland from the harbour, a quiet coconut grove houses these five modern deluxe rooms with thatched roofs and outdoor bathrooms surrounding a small pool. **$65**

Villa Bulan Madu ☎0819 0733 0444, ⓦbulan-madu .com. Five luxurious and spacious villa-style cottages, decorated with textiles and boasting a/c, freshwater bathrooms, kitchenette, French windows and wrap-around verandas. Each has its own generous private flower garden, complete with *berugaq* and dining table. **Rp1,425,000**

EATING

Biba Beach Village ☎0819 1727 4648, ⓦbibabeach .com. This Italian has a romantic setting, with tables under the shore-side trees, and serves authentic cuisine, including freshly baked focaccia, home-made pasta and gnocchi, seafood and pizza from a wood-fired oven. Expect to pay upwards of Rp120,000 per person. Daily 7.30am–10pm.

★**Pachamama Organic Café** ☎0878 641 5210, ⓦwww.pachamamagiliair.com. A lot of effort and love goes into the cooking and presentation at this pretty café. Its healthy-eating menu (reckon on Rp50,000 a feed) features global classics including Vietnamese-style rice paper rolls and mushroom burritos, while the *tempeh* rice bowls have more of a local flavour. You'll also find superb smoothies, juices and coffee. Daily 10am–9pm.

Scallywags Beach Club ☎0370 614 5301, ⓦscallywags resort.com. A well-run establishment with comfy seating and a prime beach plot serving lip-smackingly good

sandwiches, salads (Caesar salad Rp55,000), grilled meats, pasta dishes and fresh seafood barbecues (from Rp75,000) every night. Daily 8am–11pm.

★**Scooperific** ☎0878 6201 7270. Delicious full-cream milk *gelato* ice cream, *sorbettos* and milkshakes, made in Lombok and sold from a number of kiosks around Gili Air. Also serves excellent crepes and fine coffee. Daily 8am–10pm.

Sunrise ☎0819 1601 0360, ⓦwww.sunrisegiliair.com. Enjoys a stunning beachfront location with tables directly facing the aqua blue sea. It's a perfect setting for a chef salad (Rp75,000), Mediterranean kebab (Rp85,000) or chicken quesadillas. There's also a large inland café area where you'll find a dangerous cake cabinet (try the white chocolate mousse). Daily 8am–10pm.

Warung Sasak A family-run beachside warung, and one of the last locally owned shorefront places on the island. Most dishes are Rp25,000–50,000: try *ikan parapek*, fish with spicy yellow curry, or barbecued snapper. Daily 7am–10pm.

DRINKING AND NIGHTLIFE

★**Legend** Chilled north-coast bar and restaurant whose coral mobiles, *berugaq* seating and regulation Rasta accessories make it a nice, quiet spot to while away an afternoon. On Wednesday this is the main party venue, with live music from 7–11pm and then a deep house or trance DJ until 3am. Expect hearty portions of Indo and Euro standards, including an especially good *nasi goreng*

(Rp35,000), and there's barbecued seafood too. Mon, Tues & Thurs–Sun 7am–11pm, Wed 7am–3am.

Mirage Bar There's good sunset-viewing at this north-coast bar, with beanbags and seating angled for the best panoramas. Musically they keep things subtle and relaxed with ambient soundscapes and electronica. Also has a pool table. Mon–Thurs & Sat 9am–11pm, Fri 9am–3am.

DIRECTORY

Banks and exchange There are several ATMs by the harbour; money can be changed at some shops but rates are poor; some dive shops can forward cash from credit cards for a 6–10 percent fee.

Clinic The Blue Island Clinic is just inland from the harbour (24hr; ☎0819 9970 5703, ⓦblueislandclinic.com); the closest hospital is in Mataram.

Post There's no post office on the island.

RANGDA, QUEEN OF THE DEMONS

Contexts

History

Bali and Lombok, two tiny islands, have been buffeted by powerful empires throughout history, and their fortunes have often been tied to those of their larger neighbours, Java and Sumbawa. More recently they have been subsumed in the fate of the vast Indonesian archipelago. Relations between Bali and Lombok have often been turbulent, and the origins of their present cultural, religious and economic differences are firmly rooted in past events.

Beginnings

Homo erectus, a distant ancestor of modern man, arrived in Indonesia around half a million years ago during the **ice ages**. At this time glaciers advanced from the polar regions and the levels of the oceans fell, exposing **land bridges** between the islands and the land masses of Southeast Asia and Australia. Homo erectus moved across these land bridges into and through Indonesia. The fossilized bones of "Java Man" from this period were found in Central Java and stone axes and adzes have been discovered on Bali.

Homo sapiens appeared around forty thousand years ago and were cave-dwelling hunter-gatherers whose rock paintings have been found in the far east of the archipelago. The **Neolithic** era, around 3000 BC, is marked by the appearance of more sophisticated stone tools, agricultural techniques and basic pottery. Remains from this period have been found at Cekik, in the far west of Bali.

From the seventh or eighth centuries BC, the **Bronze Age** spread south from southern China. The Indonesian archipelago is famous for bronze casting; decorated drums have been found throughout the area. Bali's most famous example, and the largest drum found anywhere in Southeast Asia, is the **Moon of Pejeng**, nearly 2m long and housed in a temple near Ubud. **Stone sarcophagi** from this period are on display in the Bali Museum in Denpasar and the Museum Arkeologi Gedung Arca in Pejeng.

Early traders and empires

From at least 200 BC, **trade** was a feature of life across the archipelago. The earliest written records in Bali, metal inscriptions, or *prasasti*, dating from the ninth century AD, reveal significant Buddhist and Hindu influence from the Indian subcontinent, shown also by the statues, bronzes and rock-cut caves at Gunung Kawi and Goa Gajah.

The most famous event in early Balinese history occurred towards the end of the tenth century when a princess of East Java, **Mahendradatta**, married the Balinese king **Udayana**. Their marriage portrait is believed to be depicted in a stone in the Pura Tegeh Koripan near Kintamani. Their son, **Erlangga**, born around 991 AD, later brought the two realms together until his death in 1049.

500,000 BC	40,000 BC	800–600 BC	Ninth century AD
Homo erectus arrives in Indonesia	Homo sapiens appear; their rock paintings have been found in eastern Indonesia	The Bronze Age spreads from China into Indonesia; bronze drums from this period include Bali's Moon of Pejeng	Bali's earliest written records reveal Buddhist and Hindu influences

Intensive rice farming was possible from the ninth century onwards in Bali as a network of *subak* water channels were established, connecting communities and under the supervision of priests in water temples.

In the following centuries, control of Bali was won by the Javanese and then wrested back by Balinese rulers. By 1300 Bali was being ruled domestically by **King Bedaulu**, based in the Pejeng district east of Ubud.

Little is known of **Lombok's** ancient history, although it is known that the kingdom of Selaparang controlled an area in the east of the island for a period.

The Majapahit

One of the most significant dates in Balinese history is 1343 AD, when the island was colonized by **Gajah Mada**, prime minister of the powerful Hindu **Majapahit** kingdom of East Java. Establishing a court initially at Samprangan in eastern Bali and later moving to Gelgel, he introduced a caste system and Balinese who did not accept this established their own villages. Their descendants, known as the **Bali Aga** or Bali Mula, the "original Balinese", still adhere to ancient traditions and live in separate villages, such as Tenganan near Candidasa and Trunyan on the shores of Danau Batur.

Throughout the fifteenth century, **Islam** gained influence on Java and when the Majapahit fell in 1515, many of its Hindu followers – priests, craftsmen, soldiers, nobles and artists – fled to Bali, flooding the island with **Javanese cultural ideas** and reaffirming Hindu practices.

It is unclear why Islam did not expand to Bali, especially as it moved further east to Lombok, Sulawesi and Maluku. It could be that Islam spread along trade routes: with poor harbours and few resources, Bali was largely bypassed (although there are small Muslim communities on the island).

An ancient text detailing the history of the Majapahit dynasty lists **Lombok** as part of its empire, and the villages in the Sembalun valley on the eastern flanks of Gunung Rinjani consider themselves directly descended from the Majapahit dynasty, claiming the brother of a Majapahit raja is buried in the valley.

Bali's Golden Age

During the reign of **Batu Renggong**, who became king, or **dewa agung** (literally "great god") in 1550, the Gelgel kingdom ruled an empire from Blambangan in Java in the west to Sumbawa in the east. This period coincided with a cultural renaissance in Bali and, as a result, is often referred to as the **Golden Age**. The Javanese Hindu priest **Nirartha** achieved a great following on Bali at this time.

Eventually, the glory faded and other kingdoms within Bali rose to prominence, most notably **Gianyar** under Dewa Manggis Kuning in the seventeenth century.

Foreigners and trade

Lacking the spices of the eastern isles, Bali appears not to have been in the mainstream of the archipelago's early trading history. The **Chinese** visited Bali, which they knew as Paoli or Rice Island, in the seventh century, but by this time trade had been established on nearby islands for a thousand years. Bali became known to **Europeans** at the end of

950	Tenth century	1300
A network of water channels (*subak*) is developed across Bali, allowing intensive rice cultivation and indicating close village cooperation	Princess Mahendradatta of East Java marries the Balinese king Udayana. Their son brings the two realms together until 1049	Bali is ruled domestically by King Bedaulu

the fifteenth century when Portuguese, Spanish and English explorers came in search of the lucrative Spice Islands. They marked Bali on their maps as Balle, Ilha Bale or Java Minor, but sailed on by.

The first documented contact between Europeans and the Balinese occurred in the sixteenth century. The **Portuguese**, having won the race for the Spice Islands, dispatched a ship from Malacca in 1588, aiming to construct a trading post on Bali. The ship hit a reef just off Bali and sank. The survivors were treated kindly by the *dewa agung* but not permitted to leave the island. Portuguese attempts at establishing contact were not repeated.

On February 9, 1597, four **Dutch** ships under the command of Commodore Cornelis de Houtman anchored off Bali and three sailors landed at Kuta. Among them was Aernoudt Lintgens, whose report of his experiences is the first account by a Westerner of the island. The other two crew members were reportedly so entranced that they did not return to the ship.

The Dutch came again in 1601, when Cornelis van Heemskerk arrived with a letter from the prince of Holland requesting **formal trade relations**, which the *dewa agung* accepted. The VOC, or **Dutch East India Company**, was formed in 1602, and its headquarters founded in Batavia (modern-day Jakarta) in 1619, from where the Dutch trading empire expanded as far as Sumatra, Borneo, Makassar and the Moluccas.

From then until the beginning of the nineteenth century, Bali was largely ignored by Europeans, as it produced little of interest to them. The exception was **slaves**, who were sold through Kuta to Dutch merchants from Batavia and French merchants from Mauritius.

The situation in Lombok

During the seventeenth century, the west of Lombok was invaded by the **Balinese** from Karangasem in the far east of Bali; the **Makassarese** of Sulawesi, who had conquered Sumbawa in 1618, also invaded eastern Lombok. The first major conflicts between these two outside powers occurred in 1677 when the Balinese, assisted by the indigenous **Sasak** aristocracy, defeated the Makassarese.

From the end of the seventeenth to the mid-nineteenth century, the Balinese struggled to secure control over Lombok. In 1775, **Gusti Wayan Tegah**, who had been placed on the throne by the raja of Karangasem, died, and disagreements over the succession resulted in four rival principalities in the west vying for control: Pagasangan, Pagutan, Mataram and Cakranegara. Meanwhile, the Sasak aristocracy in the east of the island faced little interference in their affairs.

Eventually, in 1838, the raja of Mataram, **Ratu Agung K'tut**, triumphed over the other principalities and brought the east of Lombok under his control. Astutely, he also provided four thousand troops to support the Dutch in their fight against Karangasem in eastern Bali. This ensured the defeat of the ruling dynasty in Karangasem, for which service the Dutch gave him the right to put his own nominee on the Karangasem throne.

Dutch incursions

By the mid-1830s, the Dutch interest in Bali had intensified. Bali was ruled by that time by a number of kingdoms, recognizable today as the regencies named after them: Badung,

1343	Sixteenth century	1550	1588
Bali is colonized by East Java's Hindu Majapahit kingdom. Texts indicate that Lombok was part of the Majapahit empire during this period	Islam gains in influence on Java and when the Majapahit kingdom falls in 1515, many Hindus flee to Bali	Bali enjoys its Golden Age	Portuguese sailing ship reaches Bali but is shipwrecked offshore

Bangli, Buleleng, Jembrana, Karangasem, Klungkung, Mengwi and Tabanan. The Danish trader **Mads Lange** had set up a trading post in Kuta supplying rice to British-held Singapore. The Dutch started trading with Bali, with the aim of gaining political control before the British. In 1839 they established an agent in Kuta with the agreement of the raja of Badung. In 1840, the Dutch envoy, **Huskus Koopman**, began a series of visits with the long-term aim of gaining Dutch sovereignty over the island.

The Dutch also wanted to abolish Balinese *tawan karang* or reef rights, which had been a long-term grievance. The Balinese had always asserted their right to goods salvaged from shipping wrecked on the island's reefs, much of which was Dutch. The plundering of the Dutch vessel *Overijssel*, wrecked on the Kuta reef on July 19, 1841, particularly outraged the Dutch.

By 1843 Koopman had made **treaties** with the kingdoms of Badung, Klungkung, Buleleng, Karangasem and Tabanan, agreeing to a Dutch trade monopoly. The rajas failed to realize that they had also given the Dutch sovereignty over their lands and surrendered reef rights. Following Koopman's retirement, a new commissioner arrived in 1844 to finalize the treaties, but it soon became apparent that there were huge differences in Dutch and Balinese understandings. Most kingdoms did ratify the treaties, but **Buleleng** and **Karangasem** stood firm. A further Dutch mission came the following year, including a military officer whose brief was to assess the Buleleng defences. At a meeting in Singaraja in May 1845, Gusti Ketut Jelantik, brother of the rajas of Buleleng and Karangasem, stated, "Not by a mere scrap of paper shall any man become the master of another's lands. Rather let the *kris* decide."

The First and Second Dutch Military Expeditions

On June 26, 1846, the **First Dutch Military Expedition** arrived off the Buleleng coast with 3500 men. On June 28, the military force landed and marched into Singaraja. The rajas of Buleleng and Karangasem eventually surrendered, agreeing to Dutch sovereignty and to paying costs for the victor's military expedition.

The Dutch departed, believing they had achieved their objectives, and left behind a small garrison until the compensation was paid. However, this fitted in with Jelantik's plan, and he continued to prepare for future battle. Meanwhile, nothing was paid to the Dutch, and ships that foundered continued to be plundered. On March 7, 1848, the governor-general of the Dutch East Indies sent ultimatums demanding compensation, payment of war debts, the destruction of defence works and the delivery of Jelantik to them. These were ignored, and the **Second Dutch Military Expedition** arrived off the northern coast at Sangsit on June 8, 1848, with almost three thousand troops. Having quickly overcome the defences on the coast, the well-armed force marched towards **Jagaraga** where Jelantik had organized his army of around sixteen thousand, armed largely with *kris* (daggers) and lances. The Dutch were eventually put to flight and around two hundred Dutch soldiers were killed or wounded. The Balinese suffered more than two thousand casualties but on June 10, 1848, the Dutch sailed back to Batavia.

The Third Dutch Military Expedition

The following year, during the **Third Dutch Military Expedition**, the Dutch used almost their entire military force in the Indies to overcome the Balinese. Around seven thousand troops landed in Buleleng on April 4, 1849. Negotiations failed and on April 15 the

1597	Seventeenth century	1601
Aernoudt Lintgens, a Dutch sailor, writes the first account by a Westerner of Bali	The Golden Age fades and other regional kingdoms rise to prominence	Bali accepts the Dutch request for formal trade relations

Dutch attacked the fortress at Jagaraga and defeated the Balinese with the loss of only about thirty men to the Balinese thousands. Jelantik and the rajas of Buleleng and Karangasem fled east. With four thousand additional troops from Lombok, the Dutch attacked Karangasem first. On their arrival at the palace on May 20, the raja of Karangasem, Gusti Gde Ngurah Karangasem, along with his family and followers, all committed **puputan** (ritual suicide). The raja of Buleleng, accompanied by Jelantik, fled to the mountains of Seraya, where they were killed in further fighting.

Dutch troops then headed west towards Semarapura where the local king, the *dewa agung*, signed an **agreement** on July 13, 1849. The Balinese recognized Dutch sovereignty and accepted that *tawan karang* was prohibited, while in return the Dutch agreed to leave the rajas to administer their kingdoms and not to base garrisons on the island. A feast on July 15 sealed the agreement.

The strengthening of the Dutch position

The Dutch regarded themselves as having sovereignty over the whole island but initially left the kingdoms of the south and the east largely alone, basing themselves in the north and placing Dutch controllers over the rajas of Buleleng and Jembrana.

From their administrative capital in **Singaraja**, the Dutch improved irrigation, planted coffee as a cash crop, and outlawed slavery and the tradition of *suttee*, whereby widows would throw themselves on their husbands' funeral pyres. They also quelled **local rebellions**, such as the 1864 uprising in the village of Banjar, close to modern-day Lovina.

Meanwhile, with the Dutch concentrated in the north, the kingdoms of Klungkung, Badung, Gianyar, Mengwi, Bangli and Tabanan in the south were weakened by internal conflicts and fighting with each other. The rajas increasingly turned to the Dutch for protection from their neighbours.

Rebellion and the Dutch in Lombok

In Lombok, meanwhile, Ratu Agung K'tut continued to rule. The **west** of the island was relatively harmonious, but in the **east** the frustrated Sasak aristocracy deeply resented their Balinese masters and there were failed rebellions in 1855 and 1871. In 1872, Ratu Agung K'tut was succeeded by his younger brother, **Ratu Agung Ngurah**.

The **rebellion of 1891** was more successful. For many years, Ratu Agung Ngurah had vied with the *dewa agung* of the Balinese kingdom of Klungkung over claims to the title of Supreme Ruler of Bali. In 1891 he decided to take action, but his demand for several thousand Sasak troops was met with resistance in **Praya**, and a local Sasak aristocrat was executed. On August 7, 1891, several thousand Sasaks surrounded and burned the palace of the Balinese district chief and rebellion spread quickly. By September 22, 1891, Balinese rule had been overthrown throughout eastern Lombok.

Hostilities between the Balinese and the Sasak aristocracy dragged on, gains being made and then lost, until 1894, when the Dutch army landed in West Lombok.

On the night of August 25, 1894, Balinese forces attacked the Dutch camp in the **Mayura Palace** at Cakranegara, where around nine hundred soldiers were camped. The Dutch escaped with heavy casualties, but they soon received reinforcements and, aided by the Sasaks from the east, proved too strong for the raja. Mataram was razed to the ground. Some members of the royal family surrendered while others committed *puputan*.

1677	1775	1830–45
Western Lombok is invaded by the Balinese, while the Makassarese of Sulawesi attack eastern Lombok. In 1677, the former, helped by the Sasak aristocracy, defeat the latter	Lombok monarch Gusti Wayan Tegah dies and four different factions fight to gain control	Dutch interest in Bali intensifies; the Balinese lose their land and reef rights

The Dutch took control of the entire island, including the district of Karangasem on Bali, which had been under the raja's control.

Further confrontation in south Bali

The Dutch had wanted to emphasize their control of the **south of Bali** for many years, but it wasn't until the beginning of the twentieth century that they made their move. On May 27, 1904, a schooner, the *Sri Kumala*, under Dutch protection, hit the reef just off Sanur. The owner complained to the Dutch Resident in Singaraja that copper and silver coins had been stolen from the ship. The Resident decreed a **blockade** of Badung and ordered that the raja of Badung, Gusti Gde Ngurah, should pay compensation.

The situation continued until July 1906, when the Dutch threatened military action. Dutch forces landed at Sanur, and by September 20, 1906, had advanced to **Badung** (modern-day Denpasar). Gusti Gde Ngurah realized defence was useless and arranged the traditional **puputan**. An eyewitness account from a Dutch observer, Dr van Weede, in his book *Indies Travel Memories*, describes the event:

The ruler and the princes with their followers, dressed in their glittering attire, with their krises girded on, of which the golden hilts were in the form of Buddha statues and studded with precious stones; all of them were dressed in red or black and their hair was carefully combed, moistened with fragrant oils. The women were wearing the best clothes and accessories that they had; most of them wore their hair loose and all had white cloaks. The prince had his palace burned down and had everything that was breakable destroyed.

When at nine o'clock it was reported to him that the enemy had penetrated Denpasar from the North, the tragic procession of 250 people started to move; each man and woman carried a kris or long lance, also the children who had the strength to do it, while the babies were carried in their arms. Thus they walked to the north along the wide road bordered by tall trees, meeting their destruction.

The prince walked in front, carried on the shoulders by his followers according to custom, and silently ... until all of a sudden, at a turning in the road, the dark line of our infantry was visible before them. Immediately a halt was commanded and Captain Schutstal ordered the interpreters to summon the arriving party to a halt with gestures and with words. However, these summons were in vain, and in spite of the repeated warnings the Balinese went over to a trot.

Incessantly the Captain and the interpreters made signs, but it was in vain. Soon they had to realize that they had to do with people who wanted to die. They let them approach to a hundred paces, eighty, seventy paces, but now they went over to a double quick step with couched lances and raised krises, the prince always in front.

A longer delay would have been irresponsible in view of the safety of our men, and the first salvo was given; several killed men remained at the place. One of the first to fall was the ruler; and now one of the most horrible scenes one could imagine took place.

While those who were saved continued the attack, and the shooting on our part for self-defence remained necessary, one saw lightly wounded give the death-blow to the heavily wounded. Women held out their breasts to be killed or received the death blow between their shoulders, and those who did this were mowed down by our rifle fire, other men and women got up to continue the bloody work. Also suicides took place there on a big scale, and all seemed to yearn for their death: some women threw as a reward for the violent death which they desired from them gold coins

1846–49	1855–91	1894
After three bloody conflicts, in 1849 the Dutch eventually secure sovereignty over northern Bali	After a series of failed rebellions, in 1891 the Sasak aristocracy in eastern Lombok overthrow their Balinese rulers	The Dutch take over Lombok; forced labour, harsh taxes and many cases of virtual starvation follow

*to the soldiers, and stood straight up in front of them, pointing at their heart, as if they wanted to be hit there; if no
shot was fired they killed themselves. Especially an old man was busily stepping over the corpses, and used his kris left
and right until he was shot down. An old woman took his task and underwent the same fate, however, nothing
helped. Always others got up to continue the work of destruction.*

This scene was repeated later the same day at the palace of the prince of **Pemecutan**.
Estimates of the number of people killed that day vary between four hundred and two
thousand. Having defeated Badung, on September 27, the Dutch marched on to **Tabanan**,
where the raja and crown prince surrendered and were imprisoned, where they both
committed suicide rather than face exile.

The completion of Dutch control

On April 28, 1908, Dutch troops in **Semarapura** witnessed a scene similar to the
Badung *puputan* two years earlier. Reports tell how the *dewa agung* stabbed his royal
kris into the ground expecting its power to rent the ground asunder or bring torrential
rain to destroy the enemy. Nothing happened and around two hundred members of
the royal household committed suicide that day; the remainder were exiled. At this
point the raja of **Bangli** realized a pretext would soon be found to attack him and, in
October 1908, requested that his kingdom should have the same status as Gianyar and
Karangasem and become a Dutch Protectorate. When this was approved in January
1909, the whole of the island of Bali came under **Dutch control**.

Colonial rule

The *puputan*s of 1906 and 1908 caused a stir in Europe and the United States and
pressure was put on the Dutch to moderate their policies. They ruled with a philosophy
they called the **Ethical Policy**, which was claimed to uphold Balinese values. Traditional
rulers remained as regents under Dutch authority, although not all of the old royal
families were amenable to this; in Buleleng, it was not until several generations after
the Dutch conquest that an obliging member of the royal family could be found.

Under the Dutch, engineers, doctors and teachers were introduced to the colony and
Bali was spared the less enlightened **agricultural policies** that had turned large parts of
Java into plantations. Big businesses were discouraged from Bali, although the steamship
line KPM began encouraging **tourism** on the island from 1924 onwards.

Lombok under the Dutch

The situation on **Lombok** deteriorated markedly following the Dutch victory in 1894,
and brought the population to the point of starvation more than once. The Dutch
were determined to rule profitably: they taxed the population harshly and introduced
compulsory labour for projects such as road-building. In addition to land tax, there
were **taxes** on income and on the slaughter of animals. These were initially payable in
local currency, but eventually they were demanded in Netherlands Indies currency
(NIC). The Chinese rice-exporters were one of the few groups on the island who
traded in NIC, and increasing amounts of rice needed to be sold to raise money for
taxes. Consequently, a high proportion of food grown on the island was exported,

1904–09	1924	1942–49
The Dutch attack southern Bali, provoking mass *puputan*s. By 1909 the Dutch rule all of Bali	The arrival of a steamship line heralds the start of Western tourism in Bali	Japanese forces occupy Bali during World War II, and the Dutch are expelled. In 1945, President Sukarno declares independence for Indonesia, resulting in a prolonged armed conflict

and local rice consumption dropped by a quarter. By 1934, it was estimated that a third of the population were **landless and destitute**.

World War II and independence

Following the bombing of the US Pacific Fleet in Pearl Harbor on December 7, 1941, Japan entered **World War II** and moved quickly through Asia. The **Japanese** fleet arrived off Sanur on February 18, 1942, were unopposed on their march to Denpasar and took control of Bali without a fight. Java and Sumatra had fallen by March 9 and the Dutch were expelled from the country.

The Japanese **occupation** was hard but it showed the occupied islanders that the Dutch colonialists could be defeated. Throughout the war years, the idea of liberation grew and, on August 17, 1945, three days after the Japanese surrender, Indonesia made its **Declaration of Independence** in an announcement by President **Sukarno**. Some Balinese were strong supporters of independence but many were uncertain about joining a republic dominated by Islamic Java.

The fight for independence

Returning to their colony in March 1946 the **Dutch** faced ferocious fighting on Java. On Bali guerrilla forces, the most famous of which was led by **I Gusti Ngurah Rai**, harried the Dutch relentlessly, despite suffering immense losses in a famous battle near Marga in Tabanan. Ngurah Rai is remembered as a hero: Bali's airport is named after him.

However, the Dutch were also under a different sort of attack. The US questioned the Dutch expenditure of Marshall Plan aid (money allocated to European countries for reconstruction after the war) on fighting to keep the Indies. Finally, in January 1949, the UN Security Council ordered the Dutch to negotiate. In December 1949, the United States of Indonesia was legally recognized, dissolving the following year to form the **Republic of Indonesia**, with Sukarno as president.

The Sukarno years

The early years of independence were not kind to Indonesia. The economic situation was disastrous as inflation, corruption and mismanagement ran riot. Martial rule was instituted and 1963 saw a catastrophic war against Malaya.

Although Sukarno's mother was from Bali, the Balinese felt neglected by the government in Jakarta, which, in turn, was suspicious of the islanders' Hinduism. Sukarno visited his palace at Tampaksiring regularly, with a huge entourage that demanded to be fed, entertained and then sent away with gifts. During the 1960s, a groundswell of resentment against the government grew in Bali. The Balinese began to believe that a state of spiritual disharmony had been reached, and a huge purification ceremony, **Eka Dasa Rudra**, was held in 1963 against the backdrop of a rumbling Gunung Agung (see box, p.163), which eventually erupted and laid waste to much of the east of the island.

Later events in Jakarta piled disaster upon disaster in Bali. In 1965 **Major-General Suharto** seized power after a mysterious attempted coup that was blamed on the communist party (PKI). It unleashed a bloodbath in the country with actual or suspected members of the PKI and their sympathizers the main targets, along with the

1949	1963	1965
The Indonesians achieve independence	The Balinese stage a major purification ceremony while Gunung Agung rumbles in the backround	Suharto seizes power, unleashing a bloodbath across Indonesia. Around 150,000 people on Bali and Lombok are killed. As president, Suharto holds power for thirty-one years

Chinese population. At least half a million people were killed across Indonesia: an estimated hundred thousand on Bali and fifty thousand on Lombok. Around two hundred thousand were imprisoned, mostly without trial, more than half of them for ten years or more while their families were stigmatized well into the 1990s. Suharto officially became the second president of Indonesia in March 1968, a position he held for over thirty years.

Indonesia under Suharto

Suharto's **New Order** policy of attracting foreign investment, curbing inflation and re-entering the global economy was largely successful. It was helped enormously by Indonesia's massive **natural resources** of copper, tin, timber and oil. The **economic situation** of the country improved and the material prosperity of the average Indonesian rose.

However, the economic benefits came with a price as alongside this the government acquired almost complete control. **Political opposition** was crushed and the **media** silenced. Corruption was rife and the policy of transmigration, which moved landless people from Java and Bali to outlying, less-densely populated Indonesian islands, caused enormous ethnic strife. In every election from 1971 to 1997 the government party, Sekretariat Bersama Golongan Karya, known as **Golkar**, won the majority of seats in the House of Representatives and then re-elected Suharto as president.

The **economic crisis** of the late 1990s that decimated the economies of Southeast Asia savaged Indonesia as well. Prices of imports (including food) rose sharply, and a series of riots in early 1998, centred on Java, targeted Chinese businesses – long the scapegoats of Indonesian unrest. The violence spread to Lombok, where there were many deaths during days of rioting and several churches (many Chinese Indonesians are Christian) were torched in Mataram and Ampenan. Gradually, Indonesian anger turned against President Suharto and his family, who were seen to have been the biggest winners in the Indonesian economic success story.

Student rioting in May 1998 led to more widespread unrest and, eventually, to **Suharto's resignation** on May 21. He spent the ten years until his death on January 27, 2008, dodging corruption charges – in 2000 he was judged as unfit to stand trial. Transparency International, an international anticorruption NGO, estimates that he stole $15–35 billion, possibly topping the worldwide list of corrupt politicians. Suharto's influence still endures across Indonesia, with his sons and daughters having controlling interests in many industries such as oil and gas, telecommunications and toll roads across the nation. The family also own vast chunks of prime real estate in Bali and Lombok including luxury tourist hotels in Nusa Dua, Jimbaran and Sanur.

After Suharto

Following Suharto proved a tough job. The next two presidents, **B.J. Habibie** and **Abdurrahman Wahid**, lasted only short periods of time and on July 23, 2001 **Megawati Sukarnoputri** became president. Megawati – darling of the Balinese, to whom she is known simply as Mega – was regarded in Bali with something approaching fanaticism, based on the fact that her maternal grandmother (Sukarno's mother) was Balinese. Starting her presidency on a wave of optimism, she proved an ineffectual leader.

Late 1990s	2001	2004
Indonesia suffers during the Asian economic crisis. Following widespread unrest, Suharto resigns in 1998	Megawati Sukarnoputri becomes Indonesia's first (and only) female president	Susilo Bambang Yudhoyono wins the country's first direct presidential elections

Indonesia hit the world headlines on **October 12, 2002**, when **bombs** planted in the heart of tourist Bali, at the *Sari Club* and *Paddy's Irish Bar* in Kuta, exploded, killing more than two hundred people, the majority of them tourists but with dozens of Indonesian victims also. A third bomb exploded outside the US consulate in Denpasar. The attacks were carried out by members of the Islamic militant organization Jemaah Islamiah. After hugely public and drawn-out trials, three men were executed in November 2008 and in 2012 bombmaker Umer Patek was sentenced to twenty years in prison for his role in the attacks. Further bombings in Jakarta in 2003, 2004 and 2009 and Jimbaran and Kuta in 2005 emphasized to Indonesians and the wider world that anti-Western jihadi forces represent an ongoing threat in the largest Muslim nation in the world.

Whatever Megawati's failings, she did lay the foundations for Indonesia's first-ever **direct presidential election** in 2004, in which 114 million voters across almost fourteen thousand islands voted her out of the job in favour of **Susilo Bambang Yudhoyono**, commonly known as **SBY**.

With 61 percent of the vote Yudhoyono was the clear winner and outside the country he received international approval for his peace deal with the Aceh separatists. He was re-elected with another landslide victory in 2009, as Indonesia weathered the global financial crisis far better than many of its neighbours, though corruption remained endemic.

Indonesia elected a relatively youthful Javanese businessmen-turned-politician **Joko Widodo** in 2014, on a mandate to tackle corruption. The first president not from an elite politicial or military background, Joko has been faced with a difficult balancing act trying to stimulate the country's economy while facing reduced income from the key commodity and mining sectors. He has also had to deal with pressure from conservative Islamic groups seeking stricter laws on the sale of alcohol and changes to the school curriculum. On islands including Hindu Bali, these measures have raised wider concerns about growing intolerance and creeping Islamization, as well as their effect on communities when the religion is not dominant.

Significant challenges remain ahead for Indonesia. Inflation, unemployment, corruption, terrorism and nepotism concern every citizen – of whom more than twelve percent live below the poverty line.

2002–09	2014	2016
In 2002, Islamic militants carry out bombings in Bali. Further attacks take place in Jakarta in 2003, 2004, 2009 and 2016 and in Bali in 2005	Joko Widodo elected Indonesian president on a mandate to tackle corruption, modernize economy and infrastructure	Bali enjoys a record year for tourism with almost five million foreign visitors, including soaring numbers from China and India

Religion

Some ninety percent of Balinese are Hindus, with Islam the dominant minority faith, practised mostly in the west and north by migrants from Java. The reverse is true on Lombok, where around 85 percent of the population is Muslim, with Balinese Hinduism followed mainly in the west by those of Balinese heritage. There are also small numbers of Buddhists and Christians, mostly from the Chinese community.

Religious activity permeates almost every aspect of **Balinese** life. Each morning, tiny palm-leaf offerings are laid down for the gods and spirits who need twenty-four-hour propitiation; in the afternoons, processions of people parade the streets en route to temple celebrations, towers of fruit and rice cake offerings balanced on their heads.

While Islam is as pervasive on **Lombok** as Hinduism is on Bali, it has a much more austere presence. You'll hear the call to prayer five times a day, and streets are often deserted on Fridays around noon, when a large proportion of the population go to the mosque. Marriage and circumcision are celebrated, but the exuberant festivals of Balinese Hinduism have no Muslim equivalents.

Balinese Hinduism

Though it's not a proselytizing faith, **Balinese Hinduism** is a demanding one, which requires participation from every citizen. Despite certain obvious similarities, Balinese Hinduism differs dramatically from Indian and Nepalese Hinduism. Bali's is a blend of theories and practices borrowed from Hinduism and Buddhism, grafted onto the far stronger indigenous vision of a world that is populated by good and bad spirits.

Early influences

The **animism** of the Stone- and Bronze-Age Balinese probably differed very little from the beliefs of their twenty-first-century descendants, who worship sacred mountains and rivers and conduct elaborate rituals to ensure that the souls of their dead ancestors are kept sweet. In among these animist practices are elements borrowed from the **Mahayana Buddhism** that dominated much of Southeast Asia in the eighth century – certain Buddhist saints, for example, some of which are still visible at Goa Gajah, and a penchant for highly ornate imagery. The strongest influences arrived with the droves of **East Javanese Hindu priests** who fled Muslim invaders en masse in the early sixteenth century. High-caste, educated pillars of the Majapahit kingdom, these strict followers of the Hindu faith settled all over Bali and quickly set about formalizing the island's embryonic Hindu practices. Balinese Hinduism, or **agama Hindu** as it's usually termed, became the official religion, and the Majapahit priests have, ever since, been worshipped as the true Balinese ancestors.

As Bali's Hinduism gained strength, so its neighbouring islands turned towards Islam, and Bali is now a tiny Hindu enclave in an archipelago that contains the biggest Islamic population in the world. Hindu Bali's role within the predominantly Muslim Indonesian state has always been problematic. As part of its code of national law, or **Pancasila**, the Jakarta administration requires that all Indonesian faiths be monotheistic and embrace just one God – a proviso that doesn't sit easily with either Hindu or animist tenets. The compromise decided on by Bali's Hindu Council was to emphasize the role of the supreme deity, **Sanghyang Widi Wasa** (who manifests himself as the Hindu Trinity of Brahma, Siwa and Wisnu); this convinced the Ministry of Religion that Bali was essentially monotheistic, and in 1962 Balinese Hinduism was formally recognized by Jakarta.

The beliefs

At the root of *agama Hindu* is the understanding that the world – both natural and supernatural – is composed of opposing forces. These can be defined as good and evil, positive and negative, pure and impure, order and disorder, gods and demons, or as a mixture of all these things, but must in any event be balanced. The desire to achieve **equilibrium** and harmony in all things dictates every spiritual activity. **Positive forces**, or *dharma*, are represented by the gods (*dewa* and *bhatara*), and need to be entertained and honoured with offerings, dances, beautiful artworks, fine earthly abodes (temples) and ministrations from devotees. The **malevolent forces**, *adharma*, which manifest themselves as earth demons (*bhuta*, *kala* and *leyak*) and cause sickness, death and volcanic eruptions, need to be neutralized with rites and special offerings.

Ritual uncleanliness (*sebel*)

To ensure that malevolent forces never take the upper hand, elaborate purification rituals are undertaken for the exorcism of spirits. Crucial to this is the notion of **ritual uncleanliness** (*sebel*), a state which can affect an individual (during a woman's period, for example, or after a serious illness), a family (after the death of a close relative, or if twins are born), or even a whole community (a plague of rats in the village ricefields, or a fire in village buildings). The whole island can even become *sebel*, and **island-wide exorcisms** are held every new year (Nyepi) to restore the spiritual health of Bali and all its people. The 2002 Kuta bombing caused the whole island to become ritually unclean, and as well as a huge purification ceremony at Ground Zero a month after the attack, exorcism rites were performed simultaneously across the island. Other regular, very elaborate island-cleansing rituals are performed every five, ten and 25 years, climaxing with the centennial *Eka Dasa Rudra* rite, which is held at the mother temple, Besakih. In addition, there are all sorts of **purification rituals** (*yadnya*) that Balinese must go through at various significant stages in their lives (see p.331).

Holy water

The focus of every purification ritual is the ministering of **holy water** (*agama Hindu* is sometimes known as *agama tirta*, the religion of holy water). Ordinary well or tap water can be transformed into holy water by a *pedanda* (high priest), but water from certain sources is considered to be particularly sacred – the springs at Tirta Empul in Tampaksiring and on Gunung Agung, for example, and the water taken from the lakeside Pura Danu Batur.

As the main sources of these life-giving waters, Bali's three great **mountains** are also worshipped: the highest, and the holiest, of the three is Gunung Agung, site of Bali's most sacred mother temple, Besakih; Gunung Batur and Gunung Batukaru also hold great spiritual power. Ever since the Stone Age, the Balinese have regarded their mountains as being the realm of the deities, the sea as the abode of demons and giants, and the valleys in between as the natural province of the human world. From this concept comes the Balinese sense of direction and **spatial orientation**, whereby all things, such as temples, houses and villages, are aligned in relation to the mountains and the sea: **kaja** is the direction towards the mountains, upstream, and is the holiest direction; **kelod** is the downstream direction, the part that is closest to the sea and therefore impure.

Karma, reincarnation and enlightenment

Finally, there are the notions of karma, reincarnation and the attaining of enlightenment (*moksa*). The aim of every Hindu is to attain **enlightenment**, which unites the individual and the divine, and brings liberation from the endless cycle of death and rebirth; it is only attainable by pure souls, and can take hundreds of lifetimes to attain. Hindus believe that everybody is **reincarnated** according to their **karma**, a kind of account book that registers all the good and bad deeds performed in the past lives of a soul. Karma is closely bound up with caste and the notion that an individual should accept rather than challenge their destiny.

The gods

All Balinese **gods** are manifestations of the supreme being, **Sanghyang Widi Wasa**, a deity who is often only alluded to in abstract form by an empty throne-shrine, the *padmasana*, that stands in the holiest corner of every temple. Sanghyang Widi Wasa's three main aspects manifest themselves as the Hindu trinity: Brahma, Wisnu and Siwa.

Brahma and Wisnu

Brahma is the Creator, represented by the colour red and often depicted riding on a bull. His consort is the goddess of learning, **Saraswati**, who rides a white goose. As the Preserver, **Wisnu** is associated with life-giving waters; he rides the Garuda (half-man, half-bird) and is honoured by the colour black. Wisnu also has several avatars, including **Buddha** – a neat way of incorporating Buddhist elements into the Hindu faith.

Siwa, Durga and Ganesh

Siwa, the Destroyer, or more accurately the Dissolver, is associated with death and rebirth, with the temples of the dead and with the colour white. He is also represented as a phallic pillar or lingam, and sometimes in the manifestation of **Surya**, the sun god. Siwa's consort is the terrifying goddess **Durga**, whose Balinese personality is the gruesome widow-witch **Rangda**, queen of the demons. The son of Siwa and Durga is the elephant-headed deity **Ganesh**, generally worshipped as the remover of obstacles.

Lesser deities

Among the many lesser deities or *dewi* (*dewa* if male) are **Dewi Sri**, the goddess of rice, worshipped at tiny shrines in the paddy fields and celebrated at significant stages throughout the agricultural year; and **Dewi Danu** (more formally known as Ida Batara Dewi Ulun Danu), the goddess of the crater lakes. Dewi Danu is honoured with temples at lakes Bratan, Batur and Tamblingan, and is so important to rice growers as a source of vital irrigation that annual pilgrimages are made to all three temples.

The demons

Demons also come in a variety of manifestations. The forces of evil are personified by a cast of **bhuta** and **kala**, invisible goblins and ghosts who inhabit eerie, desolate places like the temples of the dead, cemeteries, moonless seashores and dark forests. Their purpose is to wreak havoc in the human world, causing horrible lingering illnesses, ruinous agricultural and economic disasters and entering villagers' minds and turning them insane. But they are not invincible and can be appeased with **offerings** just as the gods can – the difference being that the offerings for these demons consist mainly of dirty, unpleasant, unattractive and mouldy things, which are thrown on the ground, rather than placed respectfully on ledges and altars. Demons are notoriously greedy, too, and so the Balinese will often waste a dash of *arak* (rice liquor) on the ground before drinking, or drop a few grains of rice to the floor when eating.

Various other strategies are used to repel, confuse and banish the *bhuta* and *kala*. Most entrance gates to temples and households are guarded by fierce-looking statues and ugly demonic images designed to frighten off even the boldest demon. Many gateways are also blocked by a low brick wall, an **aling-aling**, as demons can only walk in straight lines, and so won't be able to zigzag around it. *Bhuta* and *kala* get particular pleasure from entering a person's body via their various orifices, so certain temples (especially in the north) have covered their walls in pornographic carvings, the theory being that the demons will have so much fun penetrating the carved simulation orifices on the outside walls that they won't bother to try their luck further inside the temple compound.

The leyak

In addition to the unseen *bhuta* and *kala*, there are the **leyak**, or witches, who take highly visible and creepy forms, morphing into headless chickens, bald-headed giants, monkeys with rows of shiny gold teeth, fireballs and riderless motorbikes. *Leyak* can transform themselves effortlessly, and most assume the human form during the daytime, leading outwardly normal lives. Only at night do they release their dark spirits to wreak havoc on unsuspecting islanders, while their human shell remains innocently asleep in bed. Even in their human form, *leyak* cannot be killed with knives or poisons, but they can be controlled by harnessing the white magic practised by shamanic *balian* (traditional healers) and priests.

The temples

The focus of every community's spiritual activity is the **temple**, or *pura*, a temporary abode for the gods that's open and unroofed to invite easy access between heaven and earth.

To outsiders, Balinese temples can seem confusing, even unimpressive: open-roofed compounds scattered with shrines and altars, built mainly of limestone and red brick, and with no paintings or treasures to focus on. But there are at least twenty thousand temples on the island and many do reward closer examination. Every structure within a temple complex is charged with great symbolic significance, often with entertaining legends attached, and many of the walls and gateways are carved with an ebullience of mythical figures, demonic spirits and even secular scenes. Note that when **visiting a temple**, you must be appropriately dressed (see p.38), even if there's no one else in the vicinity.

Every *banjar*, or neighbourhood, in Bali is obliged to build at least three temples. At the top of the village – the *kaja*, or holiest end – stands the **pura puseh**, the temple of origin, dedicated to the community's founders. For routine spiritual activities, villagers worship at the **pura desa**, the village temple, which always stands at the heart of the village. (In some communities, the *pura puseh* and the *pura desa* are combined within a single compound.) The trio is completed by the **pura dalem**, or temple of the dead, at the *kelod* (unclean) end of the village, which is usually dedicated either to Siwa or to the widow-witch Rangda.

Bali also has nine directional temples, or **kayangan jagat**, which protect the entire island and all its people. They're located at strategic points across Bali, especially on high mountain slopes, rugged cliff faces and lakeside shores: Pura Ulun Danu Batur is on the shores of Danau Batur (north); Pura Pasar Agung on Gunung Agung (northeast); Pura Lempuyang Luhur on Gunung Lempuyang (east); Goa Lawah near Candidasa (southeast); Pura Masceti near Lebih (south); Pura Luhur Uluwatu on the Bukit (southwest); Pura Luhur Batukaru on Gunung Batukaru (west); Pura Ulun Danu Bratan on the shores of Danau Bratan (northwest); and Besakih on Gunung Agung (centre). The most important of these is **Besakih** – the mother temple – as it occupies the crucial position on Bali's holiest and highest mountain, Gunung Agung; the others are all of equal status, and islanders are expected to attend the anniversary celebrations (*odalan*) of the one situated closest to their home.

Temple layout

Whatever the size, status or particular function of a temple, it follows a prescribed layout. All Balinese temples are oriented *kaja–kelod*, and are designed around two or three courtyards, each section divided from the next by a low wall punctuated by a huge, and usually ornate, "split" gateway, the **candi bentar**.

In many temples, particularly in northern Bali, the **outer courtyard** (*jaba*) and **middle courtyard** (*jaba tengah*) are merged into one. These courtyards represent the transition zone between the human and the divine worlds, containing thatched pavilions or **bale** (pronounced "ba-leh") for the preparation of offerings, cockfights (see box opposite) and the less sacred dance performances (such as those for tourists). The **kulkul** or drum tower is also here, housing the wooden bell ("drum") used to summon villagers to meetings and festivals. Entry to the extremely sacred **inner courtyard**, *jeroan*, is via an imposing covered gateway, the three-doored **kori agung** or **paduraksa**, whose central door is kept locked, opened only for the deities at festival times. The *jeroan* houses all the **shrines**: the small,

COCKFIGHTS

Certain Hindu rituals require the shedding of fresh sacrificial blood to placate evil spirits, so every temple's purification ceremony is prefaced by a **cockfight**, which attracts massive crowds and even larger bets. Providing you wear suitable temple dress, tourists are welcome to attend, but make sure you can stand the gore.

Prize cocks can earn both their owners and the temple tidy sums of money – and plunge losing gamblers into debilitating debt – and you'll see men of all ages and incomes preening their birds in public. When not being pampered, the birds are kept in bell-shaped bamboo baskets, often in quite noisy public places such as by the roadside, to train them not to be scared or distracted when in the ring.

Fights generally take place in the temple's special cockfighting pavilion or *wantilan*. Complicated **rules** written on ancient manuscripts specify the days on which fights may take place, and describe the detailed classification system under which the birds are categorized. Before the fight, a lethal 11- to 15cm-long blade, or *taji*, is attached to the left ankle of each bird. This is considered a sacred weapon and cockfights are meant to be won and lost by skilful use of the *taji*, not just by brutish pecking. Fights last for a maximum of five rounds, and the winning bird is the cock who remains standing the longest – even if he drops dead soon after. The owner of the winning cock gets the body of the losing bird plus his opponent's share of the central fund.

thatched, red-brick structures dedicated to a particular deity or ancestor are *gedong*; the distinctive, elegant pagoda-style towers with multitiered roofs thatched with thick black sugar-palm fibre are **meru**, after the sacred Hindu peak Mount Meru (in East Java), home of the gods. A *meru* always has an odd number of roofs (three, five, seven, nine or eleven), the number indicating the status of the god to whom it is dedicated. All offerings are brought to the inner courtyard, the most sacred dances are performed within its confines, and prayers are held in front of the shrines. The *jeroan* is quite often out of bounds to the lay community and opened only during festivals.

Temple festivals

Aside from the daily propitiation of the household spirits, *agama Hindu* requires no regular act of collective worship, daily mass or weekly service, and so, for much of the year, Bali's twenty thousand temples remain deserted, visited only by the village priest (*pemangku*) and perhaps the occasional curious tourist. But this all changes on the occasion of the temple's anniversary celebrations, or **odalan**, a three-day devotional extravaganza held at every temple either once every 210 days – every Balinese calendar year – or once every 354–356 days (the *saka* year). As there are at least three temples in every community, any visitor who spends more than a week on the island will be certain to see some kind of festival. Most temples welcome tourists to the celebrations, provided they dress respectably (see p.38), wear the temple sash and don't walk in front of praying devotees.

The more important the temple, the more dramatic the *odalan* celebrations. But whatever the size, the purpose is always to invite the gods down to earth so that they can be entertained and pampered by as many displays of devotion as the community can afford. In the days before the *odalan*, the *pemangku* dresses the temple statues in **holy cloths**, either the spiritually charged black-and-white *kain poleng*, or a length of plain cloth in a symbolic colour. Meanwhile, the women of the community begin to construct their offering towers, or *banten*, and to cook ceremonial food.

Odalan are so important that everyone makes a huge effort to return to their home village for their own temple festival, even if they live and work far away; most employers will automatically give their Balinese staff time off to attend. **Celebrations** start in the afternoon, with a procession of ceremonially clad women carrying their offerings to the temple. Sometimes the gods will temporarily inhabit the body of one of the worshippers, sending him or her into a trance and conveying its message through gestures or words.

Elsewhere in the temple compound, there might be a cockfight and some gamelan music, and sacred dances are regularly performed. After dark, a shadow play, *wayang kulit*, is often staged.

As well as the temple anniversary celebrations, there are numerous island-wide religious festivals, the most important of which are Nyepi and Galungan-Kuningan (see p.32).

Offerings

The simplest **offerings** are the ones laid out every day by the women of each house, and placed at the household shrine, at the entrance gate, and in any crannies thought to be of interest to *bhuta* and *kala*. These offerings, called **canang**, are tiny banana-leaf trays, pinned together with bamboo splinters and filled with a symbolic assortment of rice, fruit, flowers and incense. The flowers are always red or pink, to represent the Hindu god Brahma, and white for Siwa, with the green of the banana leaf symbolizing Wisnu. Though it's still common for women to make their own *canang*, an increasing number buy theirs at the market. Offerings for the gods are always placed in elevated positions, either on specially constructed altars or on functional shelves, but those meant for the demons are scattered on the ground. When the devotee places the gods' offering, she sprinkles holy water over it and wafts the incense smoke heavenwards. This sends the essence of the *canang* up to the appropriate god and ensures that he comes down immediately to enjoy it. Once the essence has been extracted, the *canang* loses its holiness and is left to rot.

In the run-up to festivals and celebrations, the women of each *banjar* band together to create great towers of fruit and rice cakes, tiny rice-dough figurines and banners woven from palm fronds. The most dramatic of these are the magnificent **banten**, built up around the trunk of a young banana tree, up to 3m high. *Banten* cannot be reused, but once they've done service at the temple they can be dismantled and eaten by the families who donated them.

On the occasion of major island-wide festivals, such as Galungan-Kuningan, or at the Balinese New Year, Nyepi, Bali's villages get decked out with special banners and ornamental poles, designed to attract the attention of the deities living on Gunung Agung and to invite them onto the local streets. The banners, known as **lamak**, are amazing ornamental mats, often up to 3m long and woven in bold symbolic patterns from fresh green banana leaves. The most common design centres round the **cili** motif, a stylized female figure thought to represent the rice goddess Dewi Sri, with a body formed of simple geometric shapes and wearing a spiky headdress. Seven days before the great Galungan festival begins, special bamboo poles, or **penyor**, are erected along the streets of every village, each one bowed down with intricately woven garlands of dried flowers and palm leaves, which arch gracefully over the roadway. Attached to the *penyor* are symbolic leafy tassels, and offerings of dried paddy sheaves and coconut shells.

Lombok and Islam

Indonesia is the largest **Muslim** nation in the world, and almost ninety percent of its population follow the faith. On Lombok, 85 percent of the islanders are Muslim, and most of the remainder are Balinese Hindus. A tiny minority of Lombok's Muslims adhere to **Wetu Telu** (see box, p.266) but as it is not officially recognized, numbers of followers are unknown.

On Lombok, most women dress modestly, wearing a *hijab* (headscarf which covers the hair) or *jilbab* (hair and neck), but may combine this with anything from Arabian-style ankle-length robes to tight-fitting jeans. The centre and east of the island are more conservative and devout, but even here you'll see some women without head-coverings and relatively few with their entire body covered. The **mosque** is the centre of the Muslim faith, and prayers on Friday at noon pretty much empty the villages of men (women often do not attend this service). Those planning to visit a mosque should be aware of the expected etiquette (see p.38). Many new, extremely grand concrete mosques are under construction throughout the island and driving around the interior you'll be regularly stopped by bucket-shakers asking for donations for mosque renovations. Thousands of islanders every year manage to afford the many millions of rupiah needed for a pilgrimage to Mecca.

It is still unclear exactly how **Islam came to Indonesia**, but it seems likely that it spread along trade routes, probably via traders from Gujarat in India who had converted to Islam in the mid-thirteenth century, and by the sixteenth century had reached Lombok. Traditionally, the arrival of Islam in **Java** is thought to have more exotic roots, brought by nine Islamic saints or *wali sangga*, one of whom is believed to be buried near Rembitan in the south of Lombok.

The most influential modern-day **Islamic social organization** on Lombok is Nahdlatul Wathan, which was founded in east Lombok by Guru Pancor in the 1930s. It now runs more than seven hundred Islamic schools in Lombok and Sumbawa and has many adherents among government officials. Significantly, the current provincial governor, Zainul Majdi (popularly known as Guru Bajang, or "Young Teacher"), is Guru Pancor's grandson.

Traditional music and dance

Music and dance play an essential part in daily Balinese life, and as a visitor you can't fail to experience them, either at a special tourist show, in rehearsal or at a temple festival. Ubud and its neighbouring villages have long had a reputation for their superb dance troupes and gamelan orchestras, and villagers supplement their incomes by doing regular shows in temple courtyards and village compounds. Although not exactly authentic – most shows comprise a medley of highlights from the more dramatic temple dances – the quality is generally high and spectators are given English-language synopses. Ubud is also the place to take lessons in the performing arts. To see wholly authentic performances you'll need to find out about imminent temple festivals or attend rehearsals, most of which take place in the local *banjar* after sundown; you'll probably be welcome to watch. Lombok also has a vibrant tradition of music and dance, rarely witnessed by casual visitors to the island, since it's associated almost exclusively with religious practices.

Balinese performing arts

Traditionally, **Balinese** dancers and musicians have always learnt their craft from the experts in their village and by imitating other performers. Since the 1960s, however, arts students have also had the option of attending a government-run high school and college dedicated to the performing arts. Denpasar's month-long **Bali Arts Festival** (see p.32) showcases the best in the performing arts, staging both new and traditional works by professional arts graduates and village groups.

Balinese gamelan music

The national music of Bali is **gamelan**, a jangly clashing of syncopated sounds described by the writer Miguel Covarrubias as being like "an oriental ultra-modern Bach fugue, an astounding combination of bells, machinery and thunder." The highly structured compositions are produced by a group of twenty-five or more musicians playing a variety of bronze percussion instruments – gongs, metallophones and cymbals – with a couple of optional wind and stringed instruments and two drums. All gamelan music is written for instruments tuned either to a five- or (less commonly) a seven-tone scale, and most is performed at an incredible speed: one study found that each instrumentalist played an average of seven notes per second.

"Gamelan" is the Javanese word for the bronze instruments, and the music probably came over from Java around the fourteenth century. The Balinese adapted it to suit their own personality, and now the sounds of the Javanese and Balinese gamelan are distinctive even to the untrained ear. Where Javanese gamelan music is restrained and rather courtly, Balinese is loud and flashy, boisterous and speedy, full of dramatic stops and starts. This modern Balinese style, known as **gong kebyar** (*gong* means orchestra, *kebyar* translates, aptly, as lightning flashes), has been around since the early 1900s, emerging at a time of great political upheaval when the status of Bali's royal houses was irreparably dented by Dutch colonial aggression. Until then, Bali's music had been as palace-oriented as Javanese gamelan, but in 1915 village musicians from northern Bali gave a public performance in the new *kebyar* style, and the trend spread like wildfire,

DISCOGRAPHY OF TRADITIONAL MUSIC

All the following are available to download. Alternatively, try any of the tourist CD shops on Bali, or Ganesha Books in Ubud (⟨w⟩ganeshabooksbali.com).

Angklung 1 Sidarkarya (Maharani; ⟨w⟩bali-maharani.com). Ceremonial classics played by a small, light, processional gamelan orchestra.

Bali: Gamelan and Kecak (Nonesuch; ⟨w⟩nonesuch.com). A fine cross-section, including *gong kebyar*, *gender wayang*, Kecak and *genggong*.

Degung Instrumental: Sabilulungan (Maharani; ⟨w⟩bali-maharani.com). Not strictly Balinese, but played in every tourist restaurant and shop, this is typical Sundanese (West Javan) *degung* featuring the softer gamelan and a prominent bamboo flute.

Gamelan Gong Kebyar of "Eka Cita" Abian Kapas Kaja (King World Music Library; ⟨w⟩farsidemusic.com). A terrific example of the Balinese *kebyar* style.

Gamelan Semar Pegulingan: The Heavenly Orchestra of Bali (CMP; ⟨w⟩discogs.com). Sonorous recording of the gentle, older gamelan from Kamasan.

Music for the Gods (Rykodisc; ⟨w⟩discogs.com). Fascinating music from the 1940s, recorded by anthropologists Bruce and Sheridan Fahnestock.

with whole orchestras turning their instruments in to be melted down and recast in the new, more exuberant, timbres.

Gamelan orchestras are an essential part of village life. Every *banjar* that can afford to buy a set of instruments has its own *seka* or **music club**, and there are said to be 1500 active *gong kebyar* on the island. In most communities, the *seka* is open only to men (the all-female gamelan of Peliatan is a rare exception) but welcomes players between the ages of eight and eighty. There's special *gong* music for every occasion – for sacred and secular dances, cremations, *odalan* festivities and *wayang kulit* shows – but players never learn from scores (few *gong* compositions are ever notated), preferring instead to have it drummed into them by repetitive practice. Whatever the occasion, *gong* players always dress in the ceremonial uniform of their music club, and make appropriate blessings and ritual offerings. Like dancers, musicians are acutely conscious of their role as entertainers of the gods.

Although the *gong kebyar* is by far the most popular style of music and orchestra in Bali, there are more than twenty different ensemble variations. The smallest is the four-piece **gender wayang**, which traditionally accompanies the *wayang kulit* shadow-play performances; the largest is the old-fashioned classical Javanese-style orchestra comprising fifty instruments, known as the **gamelan gong**. Most gamelan instruments are huge and far too heavy to be easily transported, so many *banjar* also possess a portable orchestra known as a **gamelan angklung**, designed around a set of miniature four-keyed metallophones, for playing in processions and at cremations or seashore ceremonies. There are also a few "bamboo orchestras", particularly in western Bali, where they're known as **gamelan joged bumbung** and **gamelan jegog**, composed entirely of bamboo instruments such as split bamboo tubes, marimbas and flutes.

Traditional dance-dramas of Bali

Most Balinese **dance-dramas** have evolved from **sacred rituals**, and are still performed at religious events, with full attention given to the devotional aspects. Before the show, a *pemangku* sprinkles the players and the performance area with holy water, and many performances open with a Pendet, or welcome dance, intended for the gods. The exorcist Barong-Rangda dramas continue to play a vital function in village **spiritual practices**, and the Baris dance re-enacts the traditional offering up of weapons by village warriors to the gods to invest them with supernatural power. Some of the more secular dance-dramas tell ancient and **legendary stories**, many of them adapted from the epic Hindu morality tales, the Ramayana and the Mahabharata (see box, p.321), which came from India more than a thousand years ago. Others are based on **historical events**, embellishing the romances and battles of the royal courts of Java and Bali between the tenth and the fourteenth centuries.

There are few professional **dancers** in Bali; most performers don costumes and make-up only at festival times or for tourist shows. Dancers learn by imitation and repetition and personal expression has no place, but the skilful execution of traditional moves is much admired and trained dancers enjoy a high status.

Female dancers keep their feet firmly planted on the ground, their legs and hips encased in restrictive sarongs that give them a distinctive forward-angled posture. They express themselves through a vocabulary of controlled **angular movements** of the arms, wrists, fingers, neck and, most beguilingly, the eyes. Each pose and gesture derives from a movement observed in the natural rather than the human world. Thus, a certain type of flutter of the hand may be a bird in flight, a vigorous rotation of the forearms the shaking of water from an animal's coat. Dressed in pantaloons or hitched-up sarongs, the **male dancers** are much more energetic, emphasizing their manliness by opening shoulders and limbs outwards, keeping their knees bent and their heads high.

Most dramas are performed either within a temple or palace compound. The **costumes and masks** give immediate clues to the identity of each character – and the action that is to follow. Some are performed in a combination of contemporary Bahasa Indonesia and the ancient literary Kawi language, while others stick to modern speech, perhaps with a few humorous English phrases thrown in for the tourists.

Baris

The **Baris** or **Warrior Dance** is most commonly performed as a solo by a strutting young man who cuts an impressive figure in a gilded brocade cloak of ribboned pennants. He enacts a young warrior's preparation for battle, goading himself into a courageous mood, trying out his martial skills, showing pride at his calling and then expressing a whole series of emotions, much of it through his eyes.

Barong-Rangda dramas

Featuring the most spectacular costumes of all the Balinese dances, the **Barong-Rangda dramas** are also among the most sacred and important. Essentially a dramatization of the eternal conflict between good and evil, they take various forms but nearly always serve as ritualized exorcisms.

The mythical widow-witch character of **Rangda** represents the forces of evil, and her costume and mask present a frightening spectacle. The **Barong** is much more lovable, a shaggy-haired creature with bug-eyes and a mischievous grin, a cross between a pantomime horse and a Chinese dragon. The Barong Ket (lion) is his most common persona, but you might also see Barong Macan (tiger), Barong Bangkal (wild boar) and Barong Celeng (pig). All Rangda and Barong **masks** are invested with great sacred power and treated with extreme respect.

Barong-Rangda dramas can be self-contained, as in the Calonarang, or just one symbolic episode in the middle of a well-known story. Whatever the context, the format tends to be similar. Rangda is always called upon by a character who wants to cause harm (unrequited love is a common cause). She generally sends a minion to wage the first battles, and is then forced to appear herself when the opposition calls in the Barong, the defender of the good. In this final confrontation, the Barong enters first, occasionally joined by a monkey who teases him and plays tricks. Suddenly, Rangda appears, fingernails first, from behind the central gateway. Flashing her magic white cloth, she harasses the Barong, stalking him at every turn. When the Barong looks to be on his last legs, a group of village men rush in to his rescue, but are entranced by Rangda's magic and stab themselves instead of her. A priest quickly enters before any real injury is inflicted. The series of confrontations continues, and the drama ends in a typically Balinese stalemate: the forces of good and evil remain as strong and vital as ever, ready to clash again in the next bout.

THE MAHABHARATA

Like its companion piece the Ramayana, the **Mahabharata** is an epic moral narrative of Hindu ethics that came to Indonesia from India in the eleventh century. Written during the fourth century AD by the Indian poet Vyasa, the original poem is phenomenally long – more than a hundred thousand verses. The **Balinese version** is translated into the ancient poetic language of Kawi and written on sacred *lontar* books kept in the Gedong Kirtya library at Singaraja. Its most famous episodes are known to every Balinese and reiterated in paintings, sculpted reliefs, *wayang kulit* dramas and dances.

THE PANDAWAS AND THE KORAWAS

At the heart of the story is the conflict between two rival branches of the same family, the Pandawas and the Korawas, all of them descendants of various unions between the deities and the mortals. The five **Pandawa brothers** represent the side of virtue, morality and noble purpose, though they each have their own foibles. The eldest is **Yudhisthira**, a calm and thoughtful leader with a passion for justice, whose one vice – an insatiable love of gambling – nonetheless manages to land the brothers in trouble. Then comes **Bhima**, a strong, courageous and hot-headed fighter, whose fiery temper and earthy manner make him especially appealing to the Balinese. The third brother, **Arjuna**, is the real hero; not only is he a brave warrior and an expert archer, but he's also handsome, high-minded and a great lover. Arjuna's two younger brothers, the expert horseman **Nakula** and the learned **Sahadeva**, are twins. Their rivals are their cousins the **Korawas**, who number a hundred in all, and are led by the eldest male **Durodhana**, a symbol of jealousy, deviousness and ignoble behaviour.

AN EARLY EPISODE

An early episode in the Mahabharata tells how the Pandawa boys are forced by the usurping Korawas to give up their rightful claim to the throne. Banished to the mountains for a minimum of thirteen years, the Pandawas grow up determined to regain what is theirs. Meanwhile, both families engage in countless adventures, confrontations with gods and demons, long journeys, seductions and practical jokes. A particular favourite is the exploit known as **Bhima Swarga**, in which Bhima is dispatched to Hell to rescue the souls of his dead father and stepmother. While there, he witnesses all sorts of horrible tortures and punishments, many of which are graphically depicted on the ceilings of Semarapura's Kerta Gosa. When Bhima returns to earth with the souls of his relatives, he's immediately sent off to Heaven in search of the holy water needed to smooth his dead parents' passage there. This episode is known as **Bhima Suci** and features the nine directional gods, as well as a dramatic battle between Bhima and his own godly (as opposed to earthly) father, Bayu.

Finally, a full-scale battle is declared between the two sets of cousins. On the eve of the battle, Arjuna suddenly becomes doubtful about the morality of fighting his own family, and confides as much to his friend and charioteer Krishna. Actually an avatar of the Hindu god Wisnu, Krishna then launches into a long theological lecture, in which he explains to Arjuna that the action is the all-important factor, not the result, and that because Arjuna is of the warrior caste, his duty is to fight, to act in a manner that's appropriate to his destiny. This episode of the Mahabharata is known as the **Bhagavad Gita**, and encapsulates the core Hindu philosophy of caste, and the notions of karma and destiny. Duly persuaded, Arjuna joins his brothers in battle, and at the end of eighteen bloody days the Pandawa brothers are victorious.

The **Calonarang** is an embellished version of the Barong-Rangda conflict, grafted onto an ancient legend about the daughter of a witch queen whom no one will marry because they're scared of her mother. The witch queen Calonarang is a manifestation of Rangda who, furious at the lack of suitors for her daughter, demands that her followers wreak destruction in all the villages. This drama is acted out on a regular basis, whenever there are considered to be evil forces and impurities affecting the community, and sometimes the whole neighbourhood takes part, the men parading with hand-held *kulkul* drums and the women filing in to make offerings at the temple shrines.

There's also an unusual human version of the Barong, called **Barong Landung** ("Tall Barong"), which feature two huge puppets. The forbidding male puppet represents the malicious giant from Nusa Penida, Jero Gede; the far sweeter-looking female is the smiling Jero Luh. Together they act out a bawdy comic opera, which also has exorcist purposes.

Kecak

Sometimes called the **Monkey Dance** after the animals represented by the chorus, the **Kecak** gets its Balinese name from the hypnotic chattering sounds made by the a cappella choir. Chanting nothing more than "cak cak cak cak", the chorus of fifty or more men uses seven different rhythms to create the astonishing music that accompanies the drama. Bare-chested, and wearing lengths of black-and-white-check *kain poleng* cloth around their waists and a single red hibiscus behind the ear, the men sit cross-legged in five or six tight concentric circles. The **narrative** itself is taken from a core episode of the Ramayana, centring around the kidnap of Sita by the demon king Rawana, and is acted out in the middle of the chorus circle, with one or two narrators speaking for all the characters.

Although frequently attributed to the German artist and musician Walter Spies, the main creative force behind the Kecak was the famous Baris dancer **I Wayan Limbak**, who lived in Bedulu in Gianyar. In 1931, he developed the chants from the Sanghyang trance dances, in which the chorus chants the "cak cak cak" syncopation as part of the trance-inducing ritual, and created accompanying choreography to flesh out the episode from the Ramayana.

THE RAMAYANA

Written in Sanskrit around the fourth century BC, the 24,000 verses that comprise the **Ramayana** have since fired the imaginations of writers, artists, dramatists and theologians right across Southeast Asia. Like the other great Hindu epic, the Mahabharata, the Ramayana has been translated into the classical Javanese Kawi language and transcribed on to sacred *lontar* texts.

GOOD AND EVIL

It's essentially a morality tale, a dramatization of the eternal conflict between the forces of good (*dharma*) and the forces of evil (*adharma*). The forces of good are represented by Rama and his friends. **Rama**, the hero, is a refined and dutiful young man, handsome, strong and courageous, who also happens to be an avatar of the god Wisnu. Rama's wife, **Sita**, epitomizes the Hindu ideals of womanhood – virtue, fidelity and love – while Rama's brother, **Laksmana**, is a symbol of fraternal loyalty and youthful courage. The other important member of the Rama camp is **Hanuman**, the general of the monkey army, a wily and athletic ape who is unfailingly loyal to his allies. On the opposing side, the forces of evil are mainly represented by the demon king **Rawana**, a lustful and devious leader whose retainers are giants and devils.

The story begins with Rama, the eldest son of the king, being banished to the forests for thirteen years, having been cheated out of his rightful claim to the throne by a scheming stepmother. Sita and Laksmana accompany him, and together the trio have various encounters with sages, giants and seductresses.

SITA'S ABDUCTION

The most crucial event in the epic is the **abduction of Sita** by Rawana, a crime that inspires the rather unwarlike Rama to wage battle against his enemy. A favourite subject for dances and carvings, the episode starts with Sita catching sight of a beautiful golden deer and imploring her husband Rama to catch it for her. The golden deer turns out to be a decoy planted by Rawana, and the demon king duly swoops down to abduct Sita as soon as Rama and Laksmana go off to chase the animal. The distraught Rama determines to get Sita back and, together with Laksmana, he sets off for Rawana's kingdom. En route he meets Hanuman, the monkey general, who agrees to sneak him into Sita's room at Rawana's palace and **give her Rama's ring**. Eventually, Rama, Laksmana, Hanuman and his monkey army all arrive at Rawana's palace and, following a big battle, Sita is rescued and Rawana done away with.

Legong

Undoubtedly the most refined of all the temple dances, the **Legong** is an acquired taste, characterized by the restrained, intricate weavings of arms, fingers, torsos and heads. It's always performed by three prepubescent girls who are bound tightly in sarongs and chest cloths of opulent green or pink, with gilded crowns filled with frangipani blossoms on their heads. The Legong is considered the acme of Balinese femininity and Legong dancers have always enjoyed a special status, a reputation that endures long after they retire at the onset of menstruation. In the past, many a Legong dancer has ended up as a raja's wife or, later, as an expatriate artist's muse.

The dance evolved from a highly sacred Sanghyang trance dance and takes several different forms. By far the most common is the **Legong Keraton** ("Dance of the Court"), based on a classical twelfth-century tale from Java. It tells the story of King Laksem, who is holding a princess, Rangkesari, captive against her will. Rescue is on the way in the form of Prince Daha, who plans to wage battle against King Laksem. The princess tries to dissuade the king from going to war, but he sets off anyway. As he leaves he is attacked by a raven, an extremely bad omen, after which he duly loses the battle and is killed.

The **performance** begins with a solo dance by a court lady, known as the *condong* (dressed in pink and gold). She picks up two fans from the ground in anticipation of the arrival of the two *legong* (literally "dancer"). Dressed identically in bright green and gold, the two *legong* enact the story, adopting and swapping characters with no obvious distinction. The *condong* always returns as the raven, with pink wings attached to her costume. The final fatal battle is never shown on stage.

Sanghyang: trance dances

The state of **trance** lies at the heart of traditional Balinese dance. In order to maintain the health of the village, the gods are periodically invited down into the temple to help in the exorcism of evil and sickness-inducing spirits. The deities reveal themselves by possessing certain individuals, sometimes communicating through them with words, which may have to be interpreted by a priest, and sometimes taking over the whole physical being so that the medium is moved to dance or to perform astonishing physical feats. The chosen medium is put into a trance state through a combination of priestly chants and protective mantras, intoned exhortations by the a cappella choir, and great clouds of incense wafted heavenwards to attract the gods' attention. Trance dances are traditionally only performed when the village is suffering from a particularly serious bout of sickness or ill fortune – the versions that are reproduced at tourist shows have none of the spiritual dynamism of the real thing, though it is said that performers do sometimes slip into trance.

One of the most common trance dances is the **Sanghyang Dedari**, in which two young girls become possessed and perform a complicated duet with their eyes closed; though they have never learnt the steps, the girls usually perform in sync, sometimes for up to four hours. In the Sanghyang Dedari performed at tourist shows, however, the girls have almost certainly rehearsed the dance beforehand and probably do not enter a trance state at all. They wear the same tightly bound green and gold sarongs as the Legong dancers, and perform to the haunting backing vocals of an a cappella chorus of men and women.

In the **Sanghyang Jaran** (Horse Deity), one or more men are put into a trance state while the temple floor is littered with burning coconut husks. As they enter the trance, the men grab hold of wooden hobbyhorse sticks and then gallop frantically back and forth across the red-hot embers as if they were on real horses. The all-male Kecak chorus fuels the drama with energetic a cappella crescendos until, finally, the exhausted hobbyhorse riders are awoken by the priest.

Topeng: mask dances

In the **Topeng** or **Mask Dance**, the performer is possessed by the spirit of the mask (see box, p.140). Before every entrance, the Topeng actor sprinkles holy water on his mask and recites a mantra. Women never participate in Topeng: female roles are played by men.

Topeng **storylines** usually centre around popular folk tales or well-known historical episodes, and the characters are immediately recognizable. One of the most popular is the **Topeng Tua**, a touching solo in which an elderly retired first-minister recalls his time in the king's service. His mask is fringed with straggly white hair and beard, and his gait is frail and wavering. Another favourite tourist Topeng is the **Frog Dance** – performed to the evocative music of the Balinese jew's harp or *genggong* – which tells how a frog turns into a prince. In the **Jauk**, the soloist portrays a terrifying demon-king who leaps mischievously about the stage as if darting from behind trees and pouncing on unsuspecting villagers. His red or white mask has bulging eyes and a creepy smile and he flashes his long fingernails menacingly throughout.

Wayang kulit: shadow-puppet shows

Wayang kulit or **shadow-puppet shows** are typically staged as entertainment following weddings, cremations or temple *odalan*. The stories are often taken from the Mahabharata, but improvisation and topical jokes keep the art alive and a skilled and witty *dalang* (puppeteer), nearly always a man, can attract huge crowds and keep them entertained into the early hours. The performance takes place behind a white cloth screen illuminated by flaming torches and may star as many as sixty different **wayang** (puppets), generally made from buffalo hide and mounted on a stick. Visitors can see the workshops of some well-known *dalang* in Sukawati (see p.139).

Amazingly, the **dalang** not only manipulates each of his many *wayang* himself, but speaks for each one of them as well, displaying an impressive memory for lines and an extraordinary range of different voices. At the same time he also conducts the special four-piece orchestra, the *gender wayang*. Unsurprisingly, *dalang* are greatly revered and considered to have great spiritual power.

The torchlit **screen** represents the world in microcosm: the puppets are the humans that inhabit it, the torch represents the sun, and the *dalang* acts as god. Puppets representing good characters always appear to the right of the *dalang*; evil ones appear on his left. A leaf-shaped fan-like puppet, symbolizing the tree of life, marks centre stage and is used to indicate the end of a scene as well as to represent clouds, spirits and magical forces.

Lombok music and dance

Lombok has a rich heritage of music and dance. The indigenous Sasak traditions have been subject to many influences, both Hindu and Islamic, direct from Bali and Java, and through Buginese and Makassarese traders. The resulting melange of puppetry, poetry, song and dance is varied, but largely inaccessible to tourists. **Cultural shows** are very rare, except for during the annual **Senggigi Festival** (see box, p.259), held in September, but you may stumble across a wedding or other celebration.

Lombok's gamelan music

Lombok's traditional **gamelan** music is similar to Bali's, though some of the orchestras are different. The **gamelan gong Sasak** resembles the *gamelan gong*, but may be combined with the bamboo xylophones of the **gamelan grantang**. The **gamelan oncer** is also widely used, and accompanies the Gendang Beleq dance.

Gamelan tawa-tawa and **barong tengkok** are used in processions at weddings and circumcision ceremonies. The usual gongs and drums are accompanied by eight sets of cymbals attached to decorated lances. The gamelan *barong tengkok* from central Lombok actually has gongs suspended within a Barong figure. **Gamelan rebana** consists of up to twenty different drums, which mimic the traditional sound of gamelan music, but without the use of bronze instruments. More unusual is the **gamelan klentang**, made up entirely of iron instruments. Other musical ensembles that are seen on the island include **kecimol** and **cilokaq**, consisting of an oboe (*preret*), flutes, lutes, violins and drums, and are often played to accompany Sasak poetry.

Lombok's performance and martial arts

In contrast to the huge academic interest in Balinese performing arts, Sasak **dances** have been studied far less.

Of the various **public dances**, the **Gendang Beleq** was traditionally used to send off soldiers heading into battle and to welcome them home again. It is performed to the distinctive rhythm of huge drums (*gendang*) and is these days staged to welcome VIPs. The **Batek Baris**, which is performed in Lingsar and elsewhere, has dancers wearing costumes mimicking Dutch army uniforms and carrying wooden rifles while they lead a procession to the sacred springs. At the Nyale Festival near Kuta the Putri Mandalika legend is re-enacted to large crowds (see box, p.275); the popular **Kemidi Rudat** retells the *Thousand and One Nights* stories, complete with colourful characters and clowns; the **Telek** is based on the tale of a princess who falls in love with a humble man; and the **Kayak Sando** (with masks) dramatizes the Panji stories from Java in which a prince undergoes numerous adventures while searching for his lost bride.

Local, village-based dances include the **Gandrung** of central Lombok, a demonstration of love performed by a solo female dancer who selects a man to join her, and the **Tandak Geroq**, staged in east Lombok to celebrate the end of the harvest. There are also **trance dances** such as the **Suling Dewa**, accompanied by flutes and song, which is particular to north Lombok and used to induce spirits to enter the local shaman and bless the village. The **Pepakon**, from east Lombok, causes the sick to become possessed so that their illness can be removed from them.

More a martial art than a performing art, but still a massive spectator draw, **peresean**, or **stickfighting**, involves two men attacking each other with long rattan canes, with only a goatskin shield to defend themselves. The aim is to draw blood from the head – and it's all for real, as the injuries show. Every schoolboy learns the art of *peresean* and contests are staged between village teams. The best time to see a stickfight is on August 18, the day after Independence Day: Narmada, east of Mataram, and Kotaraja near Tetebatu are both famous centres. You can also see *peresean* at the Senggigi Festival (see box, p.259).

Modern Balinese music

The last twenty years has seen an explosion in the popularity of modern Balinese music – in Bali itself, throughout Indonesia, and even abroad. Uniquely in Indonesia, Balinese musicians no longer need to go to Jakarta to make their name, but can use Bali as a gateway to national and international recognition. More and more relatively small local bands, musicians and DJs are now playing overseas without first hitting the big time in the Indonesian capital.

There are two main genres of modern Balinese music: **Balinesia**, in which the Balinese artists sing in Indonesian, and **Balibali**, in which they sing in Balinese. Albums by musicians from both genres outsell their Western competition in Bali (though piracy has severely dented all markets), and concerts are often as well attended as those of the major national (mainly Javanese) bands. The cultural impact of this boom has been significant. Instead of feeling marginalized and crowded out by Java, Balinese youth now have a channel through which they can express themselves and their disappointment with the political elite and endemic corruption. There is also a renewed pride in the Balinese language, whose "cool" status has been given a big boost by artists singing in Balinese.

The **indie scene** actively encourages creativity, especially in the young (a big contrast with the repressively conformist years under Suharto's rule), and has opened people's eyes to the possibility of doing something different from the Balinese norm. This is reflected in the trend for all things punk and alternative, from independent clothing shops (*distros*) selling original fashion and music-related paraphernalia, to chopper-style motorbikes and low-rider pushbikes.

Balinesia

Balinesia emerged in the mid-1980s with rock bands that favoured covers – AC/DC, Rainbow and Def Leppard were all popular in Bali – and drew large crowds.

But the Balinesia breakthrough came in 2003 when the first big Balinese band, punk-rock-styled **Superman Is Dead (SID)**, released their debut album, *Kuta Rock City*, with a major label, Sony Music Indonesia. They were the first Balinese band to make it big outside Bali and the first to record mostly in English (with about thirty percent of their songs in Indonesian). Having toured Australia, and participated in the legendary Warped Tour around the USA in 2009, they went on to break into the US Billboard chart.

Grunge band **Navicula** is the second-biggest Balinesia band on the island and one of the most successful grunge/alternative bands in Indonesia. Their focus on social and environmental issues and flower-power fashion style has them tagged as new hippies. Their latest album, *Tatap Muka*, is largely acoustic and was recorded at Ubud's Setia Darma museum.

Another star is virtuoso guitarist **Balawan** and his band, Batuan Ethnic Fusion. They skilfully combine jazz and Balinese music, using gamelan instruments, *kendang* (traditional drums) and bamboo flutes alongside guitars, modern drums and keyboards. A master of finger-tapping, Balawan is the only guitarist in Indonesia who plays a double-neck guitar with two independent hands (eight-finger touch style). He frequently performs overseas, mainly in Europe and Asia. Balawan is also involved in a Hindu/spiritual project called **Nyanyian Dharma**, in which he and other famous Balinese musicians sing in Sanskrit and promote peace and love around Indonesia and abroad.

One of Balawan's collaborators on Nyanyian Dharma is the increasingly famous world music singer **Ayu Laksmi**. She began as a "lady rocker" in the late 1980s but has since embraced jazz fusion. Her 2011 world music album, *Svara Semesta*, on which she sang in five languages – including Sanskrit, Kawi and Balinese – was a nationwide hit and rated as one of Indonesia's best albums of the year.

Other notable local music artists include pioneer rockabillies **The Hydrant**, who have a significant fanbase in Bali and Java and are an exciting band to see live, with European tours under their belt. There's also the amazing trumpeter **Rio Sidik**, "psychobilly" band **Suicidal Sinatra** (mixing punk and rockabilly) and punk collective **Scared of Bums**. They are all massive in Bali and have enjoyed a similarly positive reception nationwide – especially Rio, who, with his world music band **Saharadja**, has already travelled the world and can sometimes still be heard playing in Kuta, Seminyak and Ubud.

Balibali

The **Balibali** phenomenon is unique in Indonesia: its artists sing exclusively in Balinese, and the music tends to be edgy and controversial. Its appeal is not as limited as you might expect, as there are tightknit Balinese communities also in Lombok, Kalimantan, Sumatra and Sulawesi. Interest in Balibali peaked between about 2003 and 2008, but its big-name artists still attract significant audiences.

Balibali began with folk-style bands in the 1960s and came of age in the mid-1980s, when several artists released pop-rock-style albums in Balinese and began writing more risqué lyrics, perhaps due to new Western influences. But the big shake-up came in 2003 when Lolot 'N Band released *Gumine Mangkin*. **Lolot**, the singer, was a complete original of the genre with his punk-rock attitude and confrontational Balinese lyrics, totally unlike the plaintive style common to the genre. He invented so-called alternative

---

DISCOGRAPHY

Modern Balinese music is hard to find outside Indonesia, but within Bali the best sources are major **record-store** chains such as Disc Tarra, local music shops and *distro*s. The following are popular albums from major local artists.

PUNK ROCK/ALTERNATIVE ROCK

The Hydrant *Bali Bandidos* (Balinesia; a few lyrics in English)
Lolot *Pejalan Idup* (Balibali)
Nanoe Biroe *M3tamorforia* (Balibali)
Painful by Kisses *The Curse of…* (Balinesia; some lyrics in English)
Superman Is Dead *Sunset di Tanah Anarki* (Balinesia; Sony Music Indonesia)

GRUNGE/METAL

Navicula *Salto* (Balinesia; some lyrics in English)
Parau *Somatoform* (Balinesia; a few lyrics in English)

JAZZ/WORLD MUSIC

Ayu Laksmi *Svara Semesta* (Balinesia; some lyrics in English)
Riwin *My Sexy Life* (Balinesia; a few lyrics in English)

REGGAE

Joni Agung & Double T *Melalung* (Balibali)

HIP-HOP

[XXX] *Sangut Delem* (Balibali)

ELECTRONICA

Discotion Pill *Amphetamine* (Balinesia; lyrics mostly in English)

POP

Dek Ulik *Rindu Ngantosang Janji* (Balibali)

rock in Bali and pushed the boundaries with songs such as *Bangsat* (Bastard), a social protest anthem against the grasping Indonesian authorities.

Nanoe Biroe is another Balibali rock star, commanding a legion of fanatical followers known as "Beduda" who see him as a hero, or even a prophet. All over Bali, you'll come across young men wearing "President of Beduda" T-shirts, bearing a Nanoe version of the famous Che Guevara silhouette. "Beduda" is Balinese for dung beetle and so the dreadlocked Nanoe has cleverly positioned himself as the leader of marginalized people.

But perhaps the biggest of them all are **[XXX]**, Balibali's first hip-hop band. Their unique approach, Balinese rapping and great voices have made them an enduring act. The island's top reggae artists are **Joni Agung & Double T**; their records go down well all over Bali and Joni is a local celebrity. Pop diva **Dek Ulik** is especially popular with Balinese women. Her debut album of 2005, *Rindu Ngantosang Janji*, sold more than fifty thousand copies, a first for a Balinese female soloist.

Venues and festivals

The main live music **venues** for Balinese bands are in Kuta and Denpasar, and are detailed in the relevant accounts in the Guide. For gig **listings** check the free fortnightly English-language magazine *The Beat* (Ⓦthebeatbali.com). You can also hear Balinesia and Balibali artists on the many dedicated local music radio stations.

Modern music **festivals** in Indonesia used to depend solely on corporate sponsorship but now get a little more support from regional government. Among the highlights, **Soundrenaline** always involves lots of local bands. The annual **Denpasar Festival**, held in downtown Denpasar (Dec 28–31), has a special stage presenting the best local bands, while **Kuta Karnival** (on Kuta Beach) is usually held in September (see p.32) and features a stimulating mix of Bali and national band line-ups.

Village life and traditions

Most people on Bali and Lombok live in villages. People employed in the cities or tourist resorts may well commute and even those whose villages are far away still identify with them and return for particular festivals each year.

Balinese village layout

Orientation in Bali does not correspond to the compass points of north, south, east and west. The main directions are **kaja** (towards Gunung Agung, dwelling place of the gods) and **kelod** (away from the mountain). The other directions are *kangin* (from where the sun rises), and its opposite, *kauh* (where the sun sets).

All Balinese villages are oriented *kaja–kelod* and the locations of the three village temples, *pura dalem*, *pura puseh* and *pura desa* (see p.314), are determined on this axis.

House compounds

Each Balinese **house compound** is built within a confining wall. When a son of the family marries, his wife usually moves into his compound, so there are frequently several generations living together, each with their own sleeping quarters, but otherwise sharing the same facilities. Most domestic activities take place outside or in the partial shelter of **bale** (raised platforms with a roof). The different structures of the compound are believed to reflect the human body: the family shrine (*Sanggah Kemulan*) is the head, the *bale* are the arms, the courtyard is the navel, the kitchen and rice barn are the legs and feet, and the rubbish tip, located along with the pig pens outside the *kelod* wall, is the anus. The Traditional Balinese House museum in Tabanan (see p.224) is a good example of a typical compound.

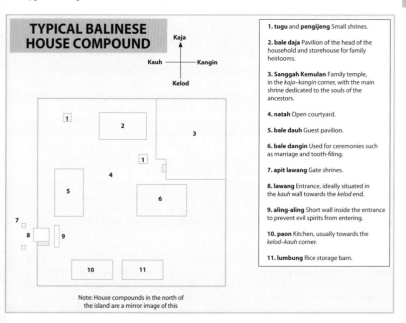

TYPICAL BALINESE HOUSE COMPOUND

Kaja ↑

Kauh —— Kangin

Kelod

1. **tugu** and **pengijeng** Small shrines.

2. **bale daja** Pavilion of the head of the household and storehouse for family heirlooms.

3. **Sanggah Kemulan** Family temple, in the *kaja–kangin* corner, with the main shrine dedicated to the souls of the ancestors.

4. **natah** Open courtyard.

5. **bale dauh** Guest pavilion.

6. **bale dangin** Used for ceremonies such as marriage and tooth-filing.

7. **apit lawang** Gate shrines.

8. **lawang** Entrance, ideally situated in the *kauh* wall towards the *kelod* end.

9. **aling-aling** Short wall inside the entrance to prevent evil spirits from entering.

10. **paon** Kitchen, usually towards the *kelod–kauh* corner.

11. **lumbung** Rice storage barn.

Note: House compounds in the north of the island are a mirror image of this

Initially all prospective house-builders consult an expert in the Balinese calendar to choose auspicious days for buying land and beginning construction. The architect or master builder (*undagi*) follows rules laid down in ancient texts, taking a series of **measurements** from the body of the **head of the household** and using these to calculate the exact dimensions of the compound. Before building starts, offerings are placed in the foundations so that work will proceed smoothly. When the building work is finished, further ceremonies must take place before the compound can be occupied. The final ceremony is the **melaspas**, an inauguration ritual that "brings the building to life".

Lombok's Sasak villages

Balinese people living on Lombok retain their traditional house compounds, as do the Bugis people, who have settled along Lombok's eastern and southern coasts and live in wooden houses constructed on tall piles. The indigenous **Sasak** people of Lombok also have their own architectural style.

Traditional Sasak villages, such as those at Segenter and Senaru in northern Lombok, and Rembitan and Sade in southern Lombok, are walled enclosures, with a gateway that is closed at night. **Houses** are made of bamboo with a thatch roof that slopes almost to the ground and floors of mud and dung; they may have none or only a few windows, with a veranda on at least one side. Traditionally, the cooking hearth and eating area are inside the house; a walled-off room, the *inan bale*, is used for storage but is also the place where newlyweds spend their first night.

The symbol of Lombok, the **lumbung rice barn**, with its bonnet-shaped roof, is a feature in the south of the island. They are built in rows, on four piles, with a thatch roof and a single opening high up. A circular wooden disc, the *jelepreng*, on each post stops rats climbing up to the rice. Underneath each post, old Chinese coins (*kepeng*) are buried for good luck and protection.

In the last few years thatched *lumbung*-style cottages have become wildly popular as (faux-traditional) tourist bungalows in the Gili islands, and even in Bali and Lembongan, though many hoteliers equip them with a/c and mod cons rather than devices to keep out rodents.

Balinese Village organizations

The smallest unit of social organization in each Balinese village is the **banjar** or neighbourhood. Each adult male joins the local *banjar* when he marries; his wife and children are also members but only the adult men attend meetings. The largest *banjar* in Denpasar may have five hundred heads of household, the small rural ones just fifty.

Typically, the *banjar* meets monthly in the meeting house, the **bale banjar**, to discuss anything of relevance to the neighbourhood, for example land issues, temple ceremonies or the gamelan orchestra. Although there is a head of the *banjar* (*kliang*), all decisions are reached by consensus.

The *banjar* has considerable authority. If residential land in the area is left vacant for a period of time, it will revert to the *banjar* for redistribution. If members neglect their duties, they can be fined or even expelled from the village. This is a particularly powerful threat among people where communal life is at the heart of their existence. Expulsion also means the loss of the right to burial and cremation within the village.

The subak

Much of the daily life of a village revolves around the *sawah*, or **ricefields**. The local organization controlling each irrigation system is the **subak**; these have existed on Bali since the ninth century, and are made up of all the farmers who use the water in that system. The maintenance of the irrigation system, along with complex planning that ensures every farmer gets adequate water, is coordinated by the *kliang subak*. Any *subak* with plans that have a wider impact or cause potential conflict with another *subak* – such as changing dry fields to wet – consults the regional water temples and, ultimately, the **Jero Gede**, chief priest of Pura Ulun Danu Batur, whose decision is final.

The **Subak Museum** (see p.224) is well worth a visit for more information on this unique aspect of Balinese life. In 2012, UNESCO added the Balinese *subak* system to its World Heritage list as being of outstanding value to humanity.

Balinese life-cycle celebrations

On **Bali**, rituals and ceremonies are carried out at important points in an individual's life for purification and to ensure sufficient spiritual energy for good health.

The first life-cycle ritual, **pegedong-gedongan**, takes place about six months after conception, when the foetus has a human form, and emphasizes the hope for a long, healthy life. Subsequent **birth rituals** focus on the placenta, which is buried inside a coconut wrapped in sacred white cloth near the gateway of the parents' household. A rock is placed over the spot to protect it, and regular offerings are made there.

Following the birth, the parents and child are regarded as unclean (*sebel*), and cannot participate in religious practices. For the mother and baby, this lasts 42 days; for the father, it lasts until the baby's umbilical cord drops off, when the **kepus pungsed** ritual is carried out. The cord is wrapped in cloth, placed in an offering shaped like a dove and suspended over the baby's bed, along with a small shrine dedicated to Sanghyang Panca Kumara, son of Siwa, who is invoked as the child's protector. There are further ceremonies at twelve and 42 days and then, after 105 days, it's time for **telubulan**, a large, elaborate ceremony at which the child is named and may be given an amulet to guard against evil spirits.

The child's **first birthday**, *oton*, occurs after 210 days – a Balinese year in the *wuku* calendar (see p.32). This is the first occasion that the child is allowed contact with the ground, and it may be accompanied by a ritual hair-cutting ceremony. The next ceremony, **maketus**, takes place when the child's milk teeth fall out. Sanghyang Panca Kumara, who has been protecting the child since birth, is relieved of his duties, and the child is now guarded by the family ancestors.

Tooth filing

The **tooth-filing ritual**, *mapandes*, which preferably takes place before marriage, is a huge celebration with guests, music and lavish offerings. It is considered vital, and the elderly, and even the dead, have been known to have their teeth filed if they have never had it done previously. The aim is to remove coarse behaviour from the person and rid them of lust, greed, anger, drunkenness, confusion and jealousy, in order that they will lead a better life and be assured a more favourable reincarnation. The upper canine teeth or fangs and the four teeth in between are filed down.

Marriage

There are two **marriage** options. The most correct is *mamadik*, when the marriage is agreed between the two sets of parents and a huge financial outlay for lavish ceremonies is involved. Much more common is *ngerorod* or *malaib* – elopement. The man and woman run off and spend the night together, not so secretly that nobody knows, but with sufficient subterfuge that the girl's parents can pretend outrage. The following morning the couple are married in a private ceremony. More elaborate rituals and a reception may be hosted later the same day by the boy's parents. The girl's parents will not be invited as there is supposed to be bad feeling between the two sides. However, three days later the two sets of parents meet at the *ketipat bantal* ceremony and are reconciled.

Cremation

The ceremony that visitors to Bali are most likely to witness is **cremation** (*pengabenan* or *palebonan*). The Balinese believe that the soul inhabits a temporary receptacle, the

---

TRADITIONAL HEALERS

Known as *balian* in Bali and *dukun* in Lombok, **traditional healers** are a vital adjunct to Western medicine on the islands. Illness is believed to stem from a lack of balance between the patient and the spirit world; for example, a patient may have paid insufficient respect to a god. There are many different kinds of *balian* including the practical and medical like *balian tulang* (bonesetters), *balian manak* (midwives) and *balian apun* (masseurs). More spiritual healers include *balian taksu*, mediums who enter a trance to communicate with the spirit world and *balian kebal*, who work with charms and spells, making love potions and magical amulets to protect the wearer against spiritual attack. *Balian* are also consulted to find out which ancestral souls have been reincarnated in the bodies of newborn babies, and which days are auspicious for certain events.

---

body, during life on earth. After death, the body must be returned to the five elements of solid, liquid, energy, radiance and ether to ready the soul for reincarnation.

Following death, the body is usually buried, sometimes for years, while the **preparations** for the cremation are made. Poorer families often share in the cremation ceremonies of wealthier families as costs are crippling. The entire extended family and *banjar* is involved in preparations. Animals are slaughtered, holy water acquired and gamelan, dancers and puppet shows organized. An animal-shaped, highly decorated sarcophagus is built to hold the body. The cremation tower, representing the Balinese universe, supported by the turtle, Bedawang, and the two *naga*, Basuki and Anantaboga, is also built, with tiers similar to the roofs on the *meru* in temples. A *bale* at the base of the tiers houses an effigy of the dead person.

Accompanied by the bamboo **gamelan angklung**, the sarcophagus and cremation tower are carried to the cemetery and twirled around many times en route to ensure that the soul is confused and cannot return home to cause mischief for the family. At the cremation ground the sarcophagus and tower are burned and the ashes taken to the sea or to a stream that will carry them to the ocean. Further ceremonies are needed after three days and twelve days, finishing with the ritual of *nyagara-gunung* when the family take offerings to important sea and mountain temples.

Sasak life-cycle ceremonies

Some of the ceremonies performed in Sasak communities on **Lombok** are associated with the more orthodox adherents to Islam, while others are associated only with Wetu Telu followers (see box, p.266). The Wetu Telu **birth ceremony** of *adi kaka* is similar to the Balinese one involving the placenta. A few days after birth, the **naming ceremony** of *buang au* or *malang mali* takes place. A ritual **hair-cutting ceremony**, *ngurisang*, is also obligatory for a young child, although the age it takes place is variable.

The most important ceremony for a Muslim boy is his **circumcision** (*nyunatang*), which often takes place in the Muslim month of the Prophet Muhammad's birthday, accompanied by much ceremony and feasting.

There are three **marriage** options in Sasak culture: a marriage arranged by the families, one between cousins, or an elopement. Whichever occurs, the man's family pays a price for the bride, who moves to their house. During the wedding ceremony, the couple are often carried on a sedan chair and accompanied by a gamelan orchestra.

Under the laws of Islam, the dead are **buried**, rather than cremated. According to Wetu Telu custom, the dead are ritually washed and wrapped in a white sarong, carried to the cemetery and buried with the head towards Mecca. A death in the family sets in motion a whole cycle of rituals. The most important is **deena nitook**, seven days after the death, **nyatus** after a hundred days, and the final event, **nyiu**, a thousand days after death, when the grave is sprinkled with holy water, commemorative stones are placed on it and offerings such as toothbrushes and clothes are made to ensure the deceased is comfortable in heaven.

The impact of tourism

Debates about the effects of tourism on Bali and Lombok have been running for almost a century. In the 1920s and 1930s, soon after the first tourists arrived, some local commentators decried visitors who took photographs of bare-breasted Balinese women and damaged island roads with their motor cars. In fact, nostalgia for a more peaceful Bali is even older; a Javanese mystic who visited Bali in 1500 complained that it was no longer quiet enough to practise meditation.

The history of tourism

Tourism in Bali effectively started in 1924 when KPM, the Royal Packet Navigation Company, established weekly **steamship services** connecting Bali with Batavia (Jakarta), Singapore, Semarang, Surabaya and Makassar, with visitors to Bali using the government rest-houses dotted around the island. Bali received 213 visitors that year, and the numbers, with a few blips, have continued to rise ever since; the island had almost five million foreign visitors in 2016, plus similar numbers of Indonesian tourists.

In 1928, KPM opened the island's first **hotel**, the *Bali Hotel* in Denpasar; an air link to Surabaya began in 1933; a daily ferry between Java and Gilimanuk launched in 1934; and the airport at Tuban opened in 1938. By the 1930s several thousand tourists were visiting Bali each year, some of whom settled there. Artists, such as Walter Spies and Miguel Covarrubias, and anthropologists, including Margaret Mead and Gregory Bateson, focused on the artistic and religious aspects of Balinese life and, through their writing, painting, photography and filmmaking enhanced the worldwide image of Bali as a paradise.

The Japanese occupation during World War II, followed by the struggle for independence, halted the tourist influx, but under President Sukarno and later President Suharto, the **promotion of tourism** became official government policy. The inauguration of **Ngurah Rai Airport** in 1969 marked the beginning of mass tourism; it is now Indonesia's second-busiest airport after Jakarta.

In 1972, the government-owned **Bali Tourist Development Corporation (BTDC)** was formed and built the resort of **Nusa Dua**, aimed at closeting high-spending tourists away from local people. However, the tourists didn't all stay hidden away. By the 1970s, **Kuta** had become a surfing hub and local villagers turned their homes into small hotels. Not everyone was happy; the surfers were labelled as hippies, drug addicts and practitioners of free love, and the negative impact of tourism on the island was contemplated fearfully.

There was also concern about the **over-commercialization** of arts and culture for tourist consumption. Dances, for example, were shortened and changed to suit tourist tastes; it was a rare visitor who could enjoy a five-hour performance. In the 1970s the annual Bali Arts Festival was inaugurated to encourage the Balinese to appreciate their own culture.

Nevertheless, the advance of tourism continued. In 1971, about 33 percent of the island's income was derived from tourism; by 2016, it was approaching 70 per cent, boosted by the success of the film *Eat Pray Love* and booming numbers from China and India. Bali is one of Indonesia's wealthiest provinces, with average income exceeding that on neighbouring Java.

Brand Bali

Bali has an extremely high **global profile** and is regularly voted one of the top island destinations in the world. This image, however, was sorely tested by the terrorist attacks of 2002 and 2005. Without Bali's high profile and the international interest in the island, it is unlikely that it would have held any interest for the bombers.

Following the Kuta bombing on October 12, 2002, the island emptied of tourists overnight. However, when it was discovered that the bombers were Muslims, the Hindu population of Bali made no moves against Muslim communities or individuals on the island. Many Balinese interpreted the bombing as an indication that the gods were angry and on November 15, 2002, a huge purification ceremony was carried out. The annual commemoration ceremony has always been an interfaith service.

With an estimated eighty percent of the population relying on tourism for their living in some way or another, the economy nosedived. By June 2003, a World Bank report estimated that the average Balinese income had dropped by forty percent. The fate of Lombok, inextricably linked to that of its more famous neighbour, mirrored Bali's exactly. However, within a year there were signs of recovery aided by messages to the world that Bali was safe and needed tourists to return and support the island. When bombers struck again on October 1, 2005, in Kuta and Jimbaran, tourist arrivals plummeted again. Still, once again, Bali recovered and tourist numbers now far exceed those before the bombs. Indeed, such is Bali's worldwide appeal that the challenge is now managing the millions, a crisis of popularity shared with the likes of Venice, Rome and Barcelona in Europe or Angkor Wat in Cambodia.

Economy versus culture

Whatever the **economic benefits** to the island, in studies by Universitas Udayana (the University of Bali), some Balinese people described tourism as a tempest. Particular concerns related to tourism damaging **religion**; they condemned the desecration of temples by tourists and the fact that Balinese involved in the industry neglected their religious duties.

Even when tourism is thriving, the financial advantages are unevenly spread and there remain significant pockets of poverty on the island. Similarly, profits from multinational hotel chains flood out of the island. Equally concerning to many Balinese, the island is now a magnet for migrants from across Indonesia. Some people describe Kuta Beach as *universitas pantai*, the beach university. Although many of the traders, from all across Indonesia, have no formal education, they end up as skilled, multilingual communicators with sales skills second to none. Some tourist businesses prefer to employ non-Balinese rather than cope with Balinese staff needing to take time off to attend religious ceremonies.

However, as families grow, many people in Bali can no longer earn a living from agriculture; the tourist sector offers opportunities at all levels, and Bali is now an exporter of skilled staff for the hospitality industry. Commentators have noted that the increased wealth of the Balinese is very often spent in highly traditional ways – in particular, on elaborate religious ceremonies.

Environmental concerns

Tourism also generates major **environmental concerns**. It is estimated that ten square kilometres of agricultural land are lost to tourist development every year. Rice cultivation,

---

RESPONSIBLE TOURISM ORGANIZATIONS

Many organizations are working to raise awareness of the impact of tourism throughout the world and to encourage responsible travelling.

Ethical Traveler ⓦ ethicaltraveler.org
Indonesian Ecotourism Network ⓦ indecon.or.id
Responsible Travel ⓦ responsible-travel.org
Tourism Concern ⓦ tourismconcern.org.uk

so prevalent in Bali, depends heavily on water; one five-star hotel room is estimated to consume five hundred litres of water each day. Recent fears relate to the Balinese water table being polluted by saltwater due to overuse and uncontrolled development.

Global awareness of the environmental problems of **golf courses** is established, while particular concerns have arisen about the effects of tourist developments on the island's **coral reefs**. But perhaps the most pressing concern is the poor air quality and pollution that affects the Denpasar-Kuta-Legian-Seminyak conurbation in southern Bali. Thousands of new **vehicles** head out onto a woefully inadequate road network each month and at times the entire region is gridlocked. Few Balinese choose to ride public transport, and with cheap loans virtually everyone can afford a motorbike. The **rubbish** problem is another huge issue and visible for every visitor to see; many villagers simply chuck plastic into rivers, which end up dumping waste onto the island's beaches and into the ocean, while discarded construction materials fringe roadsides.

Social changes

Social change has inevitably followed the influx of tourism. Michel Picard, author of *Bali: Cultural Tourism and Touristic Culture*, suggests Bali has now become a "**touristic culture**" whereby the Balinese have adopted the tourists' perceptions of themselves and their island as their own, and have "come to search for confirmation of their 'Balinese-ness' in the mirror held to them by the tourists".

The situation in Lombok

A trickle of tourists started arriving on **Lombok** in the 1980s and local people set up small losmen around Senggigi, the Gili Islands and, later, around Kuta. By 1989, there were over 120,000 visitors annually and, though the figures are now over 800,000, many of those only stay in the Gili Islands, and numbers are still a fraction of those visiting Bali.

Lombok's fortunes are closely tied with those of Bali, and visitor numbers plummeted following the 2002 and 2005 bombings. As on Bali, however, Lombok tourism has since revived. Indeed, one tiny, atypical corner – the **Gili Islands** – is booming, raising widespread concern about the social and environmental sustainability of unregulated development on its tiny land mass. Islanders and expats are actively addressing this under the auspices of the impressive Gili Eco Trust (see box, p.290), and the island has become the subject of a surprising number of academic studies on island tourism.

To date, the issue of sustainable tourism on "mainland" Lombok hasn't been so pressing, not least because there's limited **political appetite** for tourism on Lombok. Many Sasaks (and Westerners) consider the gap between conservative Muslim morals and those of foreign visitors to be unacceptably wide, while the tourist job market has been increasingly dominated by better-qualified Balinese. Rural Sasak people in particular, forced out of education due to poverty, have a limited chance of landing well-paid work. Though the current provincial governor of Nusa Tenggara Barat, Guru Bajang, is seen as pro-tourism, there are virtually no hotels or facilities in the conservative east of the island, despite a long coastline and several idyllic offshore islands.

The opening of Lombok's new **airport** in 2011 near Kuta in south Lombok has brought more flights to Lombok – though not the number of international connections hoped for. Investment is evident around Kuta, but so far the big hotel brands are sitting on land they've acquired. On the plus side, the airport has resulted in the much-needed upgrading of roads across south Lombok and, if tourist development is carefully and inclusively managed, could boost the economy of one of the island's poorest regions.

There's recently been an attempt to target Islamic tourism, and it's hoped that Muslims from the Middle East and other corners of Indonesia will visit a vast new mosque that's planned for Kuta. However how this will sit with the town's growing surf and backpacker scene, its bars and party culture, is difficult to see.

Books

While plenty has been written on the culture, temples and arts and crafts of Bali, there has been little coverage of Lombok. We have included publishers' details only for books that may be hard to find outside Indonesia. Ganesha (ⓦganeshabooksbali.com) in Ubud offers an online ordering service. Titles marked ★ are particularly recommended; "o/p" means out of print.

TRAVEL

Elizabeth Gilbert *Eat, Pray, Love*. This insightful, funny journey of self-discovery, now a bestseller and a film, climaxes in Ubud with various life-changing encounters of the sensual and spiritual kind.

★**William Ingram** *A Little Bit One O'Clock: Living with a Balinese Family*. Warm, funny, warts-and-all portrait of the author's life with an Ubud family in the 1990s. Both the author and his adoptive family still live in Ubud.

★**Louise G. Koke** *Our Hotel in Bali* (o/p). The engaging true story of two young Americans who built the first hotel on Kuta beach, in 1936. Some of the book's photos are displayed in Ubud's Neka Art Museum.

★**Elizabeth Pisani** *Indonesia, Etc.: Exploring the Improbable Nation*. A terrific state-of-the-nation account of Indonesia today from a fluent Indonesian speaker and on-off resident. Pisani explores virtually every nook and cranny of the country and debates all the important issues in an engaging, often humorous manner.

Adrian Vickers (ed) *Travelling to Bali: Four Hundred Years of Journeys* (o/p). One-stop anthology with accounts by early Dutch, Thai and British adventurers, excerpts from writings by the expat community in the 1930s, and the musings of late twentieth-century visitors.

CULTURE, SOCIETY AND HISTORY

Susan-Jane Beers *Jamu: The Ancient Indonesian Art of Herbal Healing*. Fascinating look at the role of herbal medicine (*jamu*) in Indonesia.

Kathryn Bonella *Hotel K: The Shocking Inside Story of Bali's Most Notorious Jail*. Extraordinarily revealing exposé of Kerobokan Prison, the corrupt system that sustains it and the tourists and locals who end up doing time there. Bonella followed it up with a wider exposé of the Bali drugs world, *Snowing in Bali*.

★**Miguel Covarrubias** *Island of Bali*. An early classic (first published in 1937) in which the Mexican artist and amateur anthropologist explores everything from the daily routines of his adopted village household to the philosophical significance of the island's arts, drama and music.

★**Dr A.A.M. Djelantik** *The Birthmark: Memoirs of a Balinese Prince* (o/p). Fascinating autobiography of the son of the last raja of Karangasem, who was born in east Bali in 1919, became Bali's most influential doctor, and lived through Dutch rule, World War II, the eruption of Gunung Agung and the communist killings.

Fred B. Eiseman Jr *Bali: Sekala and Niskala Vols 1 and 2*. Seminal, essential, wide-ranging anthologies of cultural and anthropological essays by an American expat.

Cameron Forbes *Under the Volcano: A story of Bali*. A compelling picture of Bali from a former foreign correspondent based on interviews with islanders and foreign settlers. Covers the ritual suicides of the colonial era as well as the twentieth-century bombings.

David J. Fox *Once a Century: Pura Besakih and the Eka Dasa Rudra Festival* (Penerbit Sinar Harapan, Citra, Indonesia). Fabulous pictures and a readable text make this an excellent introduction to Besakih. The book includes accounts of the 1963 Eka Dasa Rudra festival and the eruption of Gunung Agung.

Gregor Krause *Bali 1912* (January Books, New Zealand). Reprinted edition of the original black-and-white photographs that inspired the first generation of arty expats to visit Bali. The pictures were taken by a young German doctor and give unrivalled insight into Balinese life in the early twentieth century.

Jeff Lewis and Belinda Lewis *Bali's Silent Crisis: Desire, Tragedy, and Transition*. Especially interesting on the unresolved trauma of the 1965 massacres and Bali's troubled relationship with the greater Indonesian° state.

Anna Mathews *The Night of Purnama* (o/p). Moving description of village life focusing on events in the Iseh area in the 1960s, including the eruption of Gunung Agung. Written with a keen realization of the gap between West and East.

Michel Picard *Bali: Cultural Tourism and Touristic Culture*. Fascinating, readable but ultimately depressing analysis of the effects of tourism upon the people of Bali.

★**Robert Pringle** *A Short History of Bali*. An incisive history from the prehistorical era to the 2002 bomb, focusing on society, culture and the environment.

★**K'tut Tantri** *Revolt in Paradise*. The extraordinary, if embellished, story of British-born Muriel Pearson, who became an active member of the Indonesian independence movement between 1932 and 1947, for which she was tortured by the Japanese.

Adrian Vickers *Bali: A Paradise Created*. Detailed, intelligent and highly readable account of the outside world's perception of Bali, the development of tourism, and how events inside and outside the country have shaped the Balinese opinion of themselves as well as outsiders' view of them.

ART, CRAFTS AND MUSIC

Edward Frey *The Kris: Mystic Weapon of the Malay World*. Small but well-illustrated book outlining the history and making of the *kris*, along with some of the associated myths.

John Gillow and Barry Dawson *Traditional Indonesian Textiles*. Beautifully photographed and accessible introduction to Indonesia's *ikat* and batik fabrics; a handy guide if you're thinking of buying cloth in Bali or Lombok.

Brigitta Hauser-Schaüblin, Marie-Louise Nabholz-Kartaschoff and Urs Ramseyer *Balinese Textiles*. Thorough and gloriously photographed survey of Balinese textiles and their role within contemporary society.

★ **Garrett Kam** *Perceptions of Paradise: Images of Bali in the Arts* (Yayasan Dharma Seni Neka Museum, Bali). Ostensibly a guide to Ubud's Neka Art Museum, this is actually one of the best introductions to Balinese art.

Jean McKinnon *Vessels of Life: Lombok Earthenware*. Exhaustive and fabulously photographed book about Sasak life, pottery techniques and the significance of the items they create in the lives of the women potters.

Idanna Pucci *Bhima Swarga: The Balinese Journey of the Soul*. Brilliantly produced guide to the Mahabharata legends. Illustrated with glossy colour photographs and including descriptions of the stories.

Anne Richter *Arts and Crafts of Indonesia* (o/p). A guide to the fabrics, carvings, jewellery and other folk arts of the archipelago, with some background on the practices involved.

Michael Tenzer *Balinese Music*. Well-pitched introduction to the gamelan.

LIFESTYLE

Gianni Francione and Luca Invernizzi Tettoni *Bali Modern: The Art of Tropical Living*. A celebration of modern Balinese architecture, from the tasteful to the ostentatious.

Rio Helmi and Barbara Walker *Bali Style*. Sumptuously photographed paean to all things Balinese, from bamboo furniture to elegant homes.

William Warren and Luca Invernizzi Tettoni *Balinese Gardens*. This exploration of the role of the garden in Balinese culture is gorgeously photographed.

Made Wijaya and Isabella Ginanneschi *At Home in Bali*. The beautiful homes of Bali's beautiful (mainly expatriate) people.

FOOD AND COOKERY

Heinz von Holzen *Street Foods of Bali*. The longtime Bali resident, chef and restaurateur provides a beautiful evocation of Balinese food including plenty of background information, pictures and recipes.

Janet DeNeefe *Fragrant Rice*. The Australian cofounder of Ubud's *Casa Luna* (see p.127) paints an enticing picture of life with her Balinese husband and family, interweaving her observations with recipes for local dishes.

NATURAL HISTORY

John MacKinnon *Field Guide to the Birds of Borneo, Sumatra, Java and Bali*. The most comprehensive field guide of its kind.

★ **David Pickell and Wally Siagian** *Diving Bali: The Underwater Jewel of Southeast Asia*. Beautifully photographed and detailed account.

FICTION

★ **Nigel Barley** *Island of Demons*. Delightful, fictionalized account of the early expats in Bali told in the distinctive (imaginary) voice of Rudolf Bonnet, by turns sad, petulant, generous and tetchy, but never boring.

★ **Diana Darling** *The Painted Alphabet*. Charming reworking of a traditional Balinese tale about young love, rivalry and the harnessing of supernatural power.

Garrett Kam *Midnight Shadows* (o/p). A teenage boy's life in 1960s Bali is turned upside down first by the devastating eruption of Gunung Agung and then by the vicious, divisive, anti-communist violence that swept the island.

Odyle Knight *Bali Moon: A Spiritual Odyssey* (o/p). Riveting tale of an Australian woman's deepening involvement with the Balinese spirit world through her romance with a young Balinese priest. Apparently based on true events.

Christopher J. Koch *The Year of Living Dangerously*. Set in Jakarta in the last year of President Sukarno's rule, leading up to the 1965 takeover by Suharto and the subsequent violence, this story compellingly details ethnic, political and religious tensions that are still apparent in Indonesia today.

Putu Oka Sukanta *The Sweat of Pearls: Short Stories about Women of Bali* (o/p). Though all the stories in this collection were written by a man, the vignettes of village life are enlightening, and the author is a respected writer who spent many years as a political prisoner.

Language

You'll hear an exciting mix of languages in Bali and Lombok: the national language of Indonesia, known locally as Bahasa Indonesia and in English as Indonesian, as well as the indigenous languages of Balinese and Sasak (on Lombok), which are just two of more than seven hundred native languages and dialects spoken throughout the Indonesian archipelago. In practical terms, Indonesian will help you to communicate effectively, and everyone on the islands is at least bilingual, but a few words of Balinese or Sasak used appropriately will get you an extra warm welcome.

Bahasa Indonesia

Until the 1920s, the lingua franca of government and commerce was Dutch, but the independence movement adopted a form of Bahasa Malay as a unifying language and by the 1950s this had crystallized into **Bahasa Indonesia**, which is taught in every school and understood throughout Bali and Lombok.

Bahasa Indonesia is written in Roman script, has no tones and uses a fairly straight-forward grammar, making it relatively easy to get to grips with. There are several pocket-sized **phrasebooks**, including one published by Rough Guides, and any number of apps. Among many downloadable **teach yourself** courses, you could try Talk Now DL Indonesian (@eurotalk.com). A good **dictionary** is the *Tuttle Concise Indonesian Dictionary*. The best Indonesian language schools are in Denpasar and Ubud.

Grammar and pronunciation

For **grammar**, Bahasa Indonesia uses the same subject-verb-object word order as in English. The easiest way to make a question is simply to add a question mark and use a rising intonation. **Nouns** have no gender and don't require an article. To make a noun **plural** you usually just say the noun twice; thus *anak* (child), *anak-anak* (children). **Adjectives** always follow the noun. **Verbs** have no tenses: to indicate the past, prefix the verb with *sudah* (already) or *belum* (not yet); for the future, prefix the verb with *akan* (will).

VOWELS AND DIPHTHONGS

a is a cross between f**a**ther and c**u**p
e as in **a**long; or as in p**ay**; or as in g**e**t; or sometimes omitted (eg *selamat* is pronounced "slamat")
i as in bout**i**que; or as in p**i**t
o as in h**o**t; or as in c**o**ld
u as in b**oo**t
ai as in f**i**ne
au as in h**ow**

CONSONANTS

Most consonants are pronounced as in English, with the following exceptions:
c as in **ch**eap
g is always hard, as in **g**irl
k is hard, as in English, except at the end of the word, when you should stop just short of pronouncing it. In written form, this is often indicated by an apostrophe; for example, beso' for *besok*.

GREETINGS AND BASIC PHRASES

The all-purpose greeting is **Selamat** (derived from Arabic), which communicates general goodwill. If addressing a married woman, it's polite to use the respectful term **Ibu** or **Nyonya**; if addressing a married man use **Bapak**.

Good morning (5–11am)	Selamat pagi	**Good evening (after 7pm)**	Selamat malam
Good day (11am–3pm)	Selamat siang	**Good night**	Selamat tidur
Good afternoon (3–7pm)	Selamat sore	**Goodbye**	Selamat tinggal

See you later	Sampai jumpa lagi	clean/dirty	bersih/kotor
Have a good trip	Selamat jalan	cold	dingin
Welcome	Selamat datang	expensive/inexpensive	mahal/murah
Enjoy your meal	Selamat makan	fast/slow	sepat/lambat
Cheers (toast)	Selamat minum	foreigner	turis
How are you?	Apa kabar?	friend	teman
I'm fine	Bagus/Kabar baik	good/bad	bagus/buruk
Please (requesting)	tolong	hot (water/weather)	panas
Please (offering)	silakan	hot (spicy)	pedas
Thank you (very much)	Terima kasih (banyak)	how?	berapa?
You're welcome	Sama sama	hungry/thirsty	lapar/haus
Sorry/excuse me	Ma'af	ill/sick	sakit
Never mind/no worries	Tidak apa apa	married/single	kawin/bujang
What is your name?	Siapa nama anda?	men/women	laki-laki/perempuan
My name is …	Nama saya …		or wanita
Where are you from?	Dari mana?	no (with noun)	bukan
I come from …	Saya dari …	not (with verb)	tidak (or tak)
Do you speak English?	Bisa bicara bahasa Inggris?	open/closed	buka/tutup
I don't understand	Saya tidak mengerti	tired	lelah
Do you have …?	Ada …?	very much/a lot	banyak
I want/would like …	Saya mau …	what?	apa?
I don't want it/No thanks	Tidak mau	when?	kapan?
What is this/that?	Apa ini/itu?	where?	dimana?
another	satu lagi	who?	siapa?
beautiful	cantik	why?	mengapa?
big/small	besar/kecil	yes	ya
boyfriend or girlfriend	pacar		

DIRECTIONS AND GETTING AROUND

Where is the …?	Dimana …?	to drive	mengendarai
I'd like to go to the …	Saya mau pergi ke …	entrance/exit	masuk/keluar
How far?	Berapa kilometre?	ferry	ferry
How long?	Berapa jam?	fuel (petrol)	bensin
How much is the fare to …?	Berapa harga karcis ke …?	horse cart	dokar/cidomo
		hospital	rumah sakit
Where is this bemo going?	Kemana bemo pergi?	hotel	losmen
When will the bemo/ bus leave?	Bila bemo/bis berangkut?	market	pasar
		motorbike	sepeda motor
Where is this?	Dimana ini?	motorbike taxi	ojek
Stop!	Estop!	near/far	dekat/jauh
here	disini	pharmacy	apotik
right	kanan	phone office	wartel/kantor Telkom
left	kiri	police station	kantor polisi
straight on	terus	post office	kantor pos
airport	lapangan terbang	restaurant	restoran/rumah makan/ warung
bank	bank		
beach	pantai	shop	toko
bemo/bus station	terminal	taxi	taksi
bicycle	sepeda	ticket	karcis
bus	bis	tourist office	kantor turis
car	mobil	village	desa
city/downtown	kota	to walk	jalan kaki
to come/go	datang/pergi		

ACCOMMODATION AND SHOPPING

How much is …?	Berapa harga …?	**air-conditioning**	ac (pronounced "a say")
a single room	kamar untuk satu orang	**bathroom**	kamar mandi
a double room	kamar untuk dua orang	**breakfast**	makan pagi
Do you have a	Ada kamar yang	**fan**	kipas
cheaper room?	lebih murah?	**hot water**	air panas
Can I look at the room?	Boleh saya lihat kamar?	**mosquito net**	kelambu nyamuk
to sleep	tidur	**swimming pool**	kolam renang
to buy/sell	membeli/menjual	**toilet**	kamar kecil/wc
money	uang		(pronounced "waysay")
is there …?	apakah ada…?		

NUMBERS

0	nol	30, 40, 50, etc	tigapuluh, empatpuluh,
1	satu		limapuluh
2	dua	100	seratus
3	tiga	200, 300, 400, etc	duaratus, tigaratus,
4	empat		empatratus
5	lima	1000	seribu
6	enam	2000, 3000, 4000, etc	duaribu, tigaribu,
7	tujuh		empatribu
8	delapan	10,000	sepuluhribu
9	sembilan	20,000, 30,000,	dua puluhribu,
10	sepuluh	40,000, etc	tiag puluhribu,
11	sebelas		empat puluhribu
12, 13, 14, etc	duabelas, tigabelas,	100,000	seratusribu
	empatbelas	200,000, 300,000,	dua ratusribu, tiga
20	duapuluh	400,000, etc	ratusribu, empat ratusribu
21, 22, 23, etc	duapuluh satu,	1,000,000	sejuta
	duapuluh dua,	2,000,000, 3,000,000,	dua juta, tiga juta,
	duapuluh tiga	4,000,000, etc	empat juta

TIME AND DAYS OF THE WEEK

What time is it?	Jam berapa?	**month**	bulan
When does it open/close?	Kapan dia buka/utup?	**year**	tahun
3.00	jam tiga	**today/tomorrow**	hari ini/besok
4.10	jam empat lewat	**yesterday**	kemarin
	sepuluh	**now**	sekarang
4.45	jam lima kurang	**not yet**	belum
	seperempat	**never**	tidak pernah
6.30	jam setengah tujuh	**already**	sudah
	("half to seven")	**Monday**	Hari Senin
… in the morning	… pagi	**Tuesday**	Hari Selasa
… in the afternoon	… sore	**Wednesday**	Hari Rabu
… in the evening	… malam	**Thursday**	Hari Kamis
minute/hour	menit/jam	**Friday**	Hari Jumaat
day	hari	**Saturday**	Hari Sabtu
week	minggu	**Sunday**	Hari Minggu

MENU READER

GENERAL TERMS

		evening meal	makan malam
to eat	makan	**menu**	daftar makanan
breakfast	makan pagi	**I am vegetarian**	Saya seorang vegetaris
lunch	makan siang	**I don't eat meat**	Saya tidak makan daging

knife	pisau
fork	garpu
spoon	sendok
plate	piring
glass	gelas
drink	minum
without ice, please	tolong tanpa es
without sugar, please	tolong tanpa gula
cold	dingin
hot (temperature)	panas
hot (spicy)	pedas
sweet-and-sour	asam manis
fried	goreng
delicious	enak
I want to pay	Saya injin bayar

MEAT, FISH AND BASIC FOODS

ayam	chicken
babi	pork
bakmi	noodles
buah	fruit
es	ice
garam	salt
gula	sugar
ikan	fish
itik	duck
jaja	rice cakes
kambing	goat
kare	curry
kecap asam	sour soy sauce
kecap manis	sweet soy sauce
kelinci	rabbit
kepiting	crab
nasi	rice
petis	fish paste
sambal	hot chilli sauce
sapi	beef
soto	soup
telur	egg
tempeh	soya bean cake
tenggiri	king mackerel
udang	prawn
udang karang	lobster

EVERYDAY DISHES

ayam goreng	fried chicken
bakmi goreng	fried noodles with vegetables and meat
bakso	meatball soup
botok daging sapi	spicy minced beef with tofu, *tempeh* and coconut milk
cap cai	mixed fried vegetables

es campur	fruit salad and shredded ice
gado-gado	steamed vegetables with a spicy peanut sauce
ikan bakar	grilled fish
ikan goreng	fried fish
ikan pepes	spiced fish steamed in banana leaf
jaffles	toasted sandwiches
kangkung	water spinach
krupuk	rice or cassava crackers, usually flavoured with prawn
lalapan	raw vegetables and *sambal*
lontong	steamed rice in a banana-leaf packet
lumpia	spring rolls
nasi campur	boiled rice served with small amounts of vegetable, meat, fish and sometimes egg
nasi goreng	fried rice
nasi pecel	steamed green vegetables with a spicy peanut sauce and rice
nasi putih	plain boiled rice
nasi sela	steamed rice and sweet potato
pisang goreng	fried bananas
rendang	spicy coconut curry with beef, chicken or pork
rijsttafel	Dutch/Indonesian spread of six to ten different meat, fish and vegetable dishes with rice
rujak	hot, spiced fruit salad
rujak petis	vegetable and fruit in a spicy peanut and shrimp sauce
tahu goreng telur	tofu omelette
sate	meat or fish kebabs served with a spicy peanut sauce
sayur bening	soup with spinach and corn
sayur lodeh	vegetable and coconut-milk soup
urap-urap/urap timum	vegetables with coconut and chilli

BALINESE SPECIALITIES

ayam betutu	steamed chilli-chicken
babi guling	roasted suckling pig

betutu bebek	smoked duck	sum-sum	bone marrow
lawar	raw meat, blood and spices	tumbek	rice flour, coconut milk and palm-sugar dessert, wrapped in coconut leaves
megibung	Balinese *rijsttafel*		
sate languan	ground fish, coconut, spices and sugar cooked on a bamboo stick	usus	intestines
		wajik	sticky rice and palm-sugar sweet

SASAK SPECIALITIES

ayam taliwang	fried or grilled chicken served with a hot chilli sauce	**FRUIT**	
		apel	apple
		buah anggur	grapes
beberuk	raw aubergine and chilli sauce	jeruk manis	orange
		jeruk nipis	lemon
cerorot	rice-flour, palm-sugar and coconut-milk sweet, wrapped into a cone shape	kelapa	coconut
		mangga	mango
		manggis	mangosteen
		nanas	pineapple
geroan ayam	chicken liver	nangka	jackfruit
gule lemak	beef curry	pisang	banana
hati	liver	semangkha air	watermelon
kelor	vegetable soup		
lapis	rice-flour, coconut-milk and sugar dessert, wrapped in banana leaves	**DRINKS**	
		air jeruk	orange juice
		air jeruk nipis	lemon juice
		air minum	drinking water
olah olah	mixed vegetables and coconut milk	arak	palm or rice spirit
		bir	beer
pangan	coconut milk and sugar dessert	brem	local rice wine
		kopi	coffee
paru	lungs	kopi bal	black coffee
pelecing	chilli sauce	kopi susu	white coffee
sate pusut	minced beef and coconut *sate*	susu	milk
		teh	tea
sayur nangka	young jackfruit curry	tuak	rice or palm beer

Bahasa Bali

The Balinese language, **Bahasa Bali**, has three main forms: High (*Ida*), Middle or Polite (*Ipun*) and Low (*Ia*). The form the speaker uses depends on the caste (see box, p.39) of the person he or she is addressing and on the context. If speaking to family or friends, or to a low-caste (Sudra) Balinese, you use **Low Balinese**; if addressing a superior or a stranger, you use **Middle or Polite Balinese**; if talking to someone from a high caste (Brahman, Satriya or Wesia) or discussing religious affairs, you use **High Balinese**. If the caste is not immediately apparent, then the speaker traditionally opens the conversation with the euphemistic question "Where do you sit?", in order to elicit an indication of caste. However, in the last couple of decades there's been a move to popularize the use of Polite or Middle Balinese and to disregard the caste factor.

Despite its numerous forms, Bahasa Bali is essentially a **spoken language**, with few official rules of grammar and hardly any textbooks or dictionaries. However, there is the *Tuttle Concise Balinese Dictionary*, available internationally. All phrases and questions given below are shown in the Middle or Polite form, unless otherwise stated.

USEFUL WORDS AND PHRASES

What is your name?	Sira pesengan ragane?	house	jeroan
Where are you going?	Lunga kija?	husband	rabi
Where have you been?	Kija busan?	no	tan, nente
How are you?	Kenken kebara?	rice	pantu, beras, ajengan
How are things?	Napa orti?	to sleep	sirep sare
(I'm/everything's) fine	Becik	small	alit
I am sick	Tiang gelem	wife	timpal, isteri
What is that?	Napi punika?	yes	inggih, patut
bad	corah	0	kosun
big	ageng	1	siki, diri
child	putra, putri	2	kalih
to come	rauh, dateng	3	tiga
delicious	jaen	4	pat
to eat	ngajeng, nunas	5	lima
family	panyaman, pasa metonan	6	nem, enem
food	ajeng-ajengan, tetedan	7	pitu
friend	switra	8	kutus
to go	lunga	9	sia
good	becik	10	dasa

Sasak

The language of Lombok is **Sasak**, a purely oral language that varies quite a lot from one part of the island to another. However, even a few words of Sasak are likely to be greeted with delight. The following should get you started.

There's no Sasak equivalent to the Indonesian **greetings** *Selamat pagi* and the like. If you meet someone walking along the road, the enquiry "Where are you going?" serves this purpose even if the answer is blatantly obvious.

USEFUL WORDS AND PHRASES

Where are you going?	Ojok um bay?	frightened	takoot
Just walking around	Lampat-lampat	heavy/light	berat/ringan
I'm going to Rinjani	Rinjani wah mo ojok um bay	hot	beneng
		hungry	lapar
Where is …?	Um bay tao …?	husband/wife	semame/senine
How are you?	Berem bay khabar?	nothing	ndarak
I'm fine	Bagus/Solah	thirsty	goro
And you?	Berem bay seeda?	tired	telah
What are you doing?	Upa gowey de?	today	djelo sine
How many children do you have?	Pira kanak de?	tomorrow	djema
		yesterday	sirutsin
See you (I'm going)	Yak la low	none	ndarak
No problem	Nday kambay kambay	0	nol
Go away!	Nyeri too!	1	skek
big/small	belek/kodek	2	dua
brother/sister	semeton mama/ semeton nine	3	telu
		4	empat
child/grandchild	kanak/bai	5	lima
dark/light	peteng/tenang	6	enam
daughter/son	kanak nine/kanak mame	7	pitook
delicious	maik	8	baluk
fast/slow	betjat/adeng-adeng	9	siwak
friend	kantje	10	sepulu

Glossary

adat Traditional law and custom.

alang-alang Tall, tough, sharp-edged Imperata cylindrical grass widely used for thatching roofs.

aling-aling Low, freestanding wall built directly behind a gateway to deter evil spirits.

Arjuna The most famous of the five heroic Pandawa brothers, stars of the Mahabharata.

bale Open-sided pavilion found in temples, family compounds and on roadsides, usually used as a resting place or shelter.

bale banjar Village *bale* used for meetings.

balian (or **dukun**) Traditional faith healer, herbalist or witch doctor.

banjar Neighbourhood. Also refers to the neighbourhood association or council to which all married men are obliged to belong; membership averages one hundred to five hundred.

Barong Ket Mythical lion-like creature who represents the forces of good.

Barong Landung Ten-metre-high humanoid puppets used in temple rituals and dances.

bemo Local minibus transport.

berugaq The Sasak equivalent of a Balinese *bale*: an open-sided "resting" pavilion in family compounds and on roadsides and beaches.

Bhoma (or **Boma**) The son of the earth and repeller of evil spirits.

bhuta (and **kala**) Invisible demons and goblins, the personification of the forces of evil.

Calonarang Exorcist dance-drama featuring the widow witch Rangda.

candi Monument erected as a memorial to an important person, also sometimes a shrine.

candi bentar Split gateway in a temple compound.

cidomo Horse-drawn cart used as a taxi on Lombok.

dalang Puppet-master of *wayang kulit* shadow plays.

danau Lake.

desa Village.

dewa/dewi God/goddess.

Dewi Pertiwi Earth goddess.

Dewi Sri Rice goddess.

dokar Horse-drawn cart used as a taxi.

dukun See *balian*.

dulang Wooden stand/pedestal used for offerings.

endek *Ikat* cloth in which the weft threads are dyed to the final pattern before being woven.

Erlangga (sometimes **Airlangga**) Eleventh-century king from East Java, son of Rangda.

Galungan The most important Bali-wide holiday, held for ten days every 210 days in celebration of the triumph of good over evil.

gamelan Orchestra or music of bronze metallophones.

Ganesh Hindu elephant-headed deity, remover of obstacles and god of knowledge.

gang Lane or alley.

Garuda Mythical Hindu creature, half-man and half-bird, and the favoured vehicle of the god Wisnu.

gedong Building.

genggong Crude bamboo wind instrument, played like a jew's harp.

geringsing Weaving technique and cloth, also known as double *ikat* because both the warp and the weft threads are dyed to the final design before being woven.

gunung Mountain.

Hanuman Monkey-god and chief of the monkey army in the Ramayana story; an ally of Rama's.

Ida Batara Dewi Ulun Danu (also just **Dewi Danu**) The goddess of the lakes in the centre of the island.

ikat Cloth in which the warp or weft threads, or both warp and weft threads, are tie-dyed to the final pattern before being woven: see also *endek* and *geringsing*.

jalan (**Jl**) Road.

joglo Traditional Javanese wooden house, usually made from teak

jukung Traditional wooden fishing boat with outriggers.

kain poleng Black-and-white checked cloth used for religious purposes, symbolizing the harmonious balancing of good and evil forces.

kaja Crucial Balinese direction (opposite of *kelod*), which determines house and temple orientation; towards the mountains, upstream.

kala See *bhuta*.

kantor pos General Post Office.

kantor telkom Government telephone office.

Kawi Ancient courtly language of Java.

kayangan jagat Highly sacred directional temple.

Kebo Iwa Mythical giant credited with building some of Bali's oldest monuments.

Kecak Spectacular dance-drama often referred to as the Monkey Dance.

kelod Crucial Balinese direction (opposite of *kaja*), which determines house and temple orientation; towards the sea, downstream.

kepeng Old Chinese coins with holes bored through the middle.

ketu Terracotta crown-shaped roof ornament.

kori agung See *paduraksa*.

kris Traditional-style dagger, with scalloped blade edges, of great symbolic and spiritual significance.

kulkul Bell-like drum made from a large, hollow log slit down the middle and suspended high up in a purpose-built tower in temples and other public places.

Kumakarma Brother of the demon king, Rawana, in the Ramayana story.

Kuningan The culmination day of the important ten-day Galungan festivities.

Legong Classical Balinese dance performed by two or three prepubescent girls.

leyak Witches who often assume disguises.

lontar Palm-leaf manuscripts on which all ancient texts were inscribed.

losmen Homestay or guesthouse.

lumbung Barn used for storing rice, raised high on stilts above a platform, and with a distinctive bonnet-shaped roof.

Mahabharata Lengthy Hindu epic describing the battles between representatives of good and evil, and focusing on the exploits of the Pandawa brothers.

mandi Traditional scoop-and-slosh method of showering, sometimes in open-roofed bathrooms.

meru Multitiered Hindu shrine with an odd number of thatched roofs (from one to eleven), which symbolizes the cosmic Mount Meru.

moksa Spiritual liberation for Hindus.

naga Mythological underwater deity, a cross between a snake and a dragon.

nusa Island.

odalan Individual temple festival held to mark the anniversary of the founding of every temple on Bali.

ojek Motorcycle taxi.

padmasana The empty throne that tops the shrine-tower, found in every temple and dedicated to the supreme god Sanghyang Widi Wasa.

paduraksa (or **kori agung**) Temple gateway to the inner sanctuary, like the *candi bentar,* but joined together rather than split.

Pancasila The five principles of the Indonesian constitution: belief in one god; the unity of the Indonesian nation; guided democracy; social justice and humanitarianism; and a civilized and prosperous society. Symbolized by an eagle bearing a five-part crest.

paras Soft, grey volcanic tuff used for carving.

pasar Market.

pasar seni "Art market" selling fabrics and non-foodstuffs, and sometimes artefacts and souvenirs.

pawukon See *wuku.*

peci Black felt or velvet hat worn by Muslim men.

pedanda High priest of the Brahman caste.

pemangku Village priest.

perada Traditional gold, screen-printed material used for ceremonial garb and temple *umbas.*

prahu Traditional wooden fishing boat.

prasasti Ancient bronze inscriptions.

pulau Island.

puputan Suicidal fight to the death.

pura Hindu temple.

pura dalem Temple of the dead.

pura desa Village temple.

pura puseh Temple of origin.

puri Raja's palace, or the home of a wealthy nobleman.

raksasa Mythical Hindu demon-giant with long teeth and a large club, often used to guard temple entrances.

Rama Hero of the Ramayana and an avatar of Wisnu.

Ramayana Hugely influential Hindu epic, essentially a morality tale of the battles between good and evil.

Rangda Legendary widow-witch who personifies evil and is most commonly depicted with huge fangs, a massive lolling tongue and pendulous breasts.

Rawana The demon king who represents the forces of evil (Rama's adversary in the Ramayana).

raya Main or principal ("Jalan Raya Ubud" is the main Ubud road).

saka Hindu calendar, which is divided into years made up of between 354 and 356 days and runs eighty years behind the Western Gregorian calendar.

Sanghyang Widi Wasa The supreme Hindu god; all other gods are a manifestation of him.

Saraswati Goddess of science, learning and literature.

sarong The anglicized generic term for any length of material wrapped around the lower body and worn by men and women.

sawah Ricefields.

sebel Ritually unclean.

shophouse Shuttered building with living space upstairs and shop space on ground floor.

Siwa (Shiva) Important Hindu deity; "The Destroyer" or, more accurately, "The Dissolver".

sok Square-lidded basket used for offerings or storage.

songket Silk brocades often woven with real gold or silver thread.

subak Irrigation committee or local farmers' council.

suttee Practice of widows choosing to burn themselves to death on their husbands' funeral pyres.

swastika Ancient Hindu and Buddhist symbol representing the wheel of the sun.

teluk Bay.

Topeng Masked dance-drama, performed with human masks.

tuak Rice or palm wine.

wantilan Large pavilion, usually used for cockfights and dance performances.

wartel Phone office.

warung Food stall or tiny streetside restaurant.

wayang kulit Shadow-puppet play.

Wisnu (Vishnu) Important Hindu deity – "The Preserver". Usually shown with four arms, holding a disc, a conch, a lotus and a club, and often seated astride his vehicle, the Garuda.

wuku (or **pawukon**) Complex Balinese calendar system based on a 210-day lunar cycle.

Small print and index

Rough Guide credits

Editor: Neil McQuillian
Layout: Nikhil Agarwal
Cartography: Swati Handoo
Picture editor: Phoebe Lowndes
Proofreader: Stewart Wild
Managing editor: Andy Turner
Senior editor: Helen Abramson

Assistant editor: Divya Grace Mathew
Production: Jimmy Lao
Cover photo research: Marta Bescos
Editorial assistant: Aimee White
Senior DTP coordinator: Dan May
Programme manager: Gareth Lowe
Publishing director: Georgina Dee

Publishing information

This ninth edition published October 2017 by
Rough Guides Ltd,
80 Strand, London WC2R 0RL
11, Community Centre, Panchsheel Park,
New Delhi 110017, India
Distributed by Penguin Random House
Penguin Books Ltd, 80 Strand, London WC2R 0RL
Penguin Group (USA), 345 Hudson Street, NY 10014, USA
Penguin Group (Australia), 250 Camberwell Road,
Camberwell, Victoria 3124, Australia
Penguin Group (NZ), 67 Apollo Drive, Mairangi Bay,
Auckland 1310, New Zealand
Penguin Group (South Africa), Block D, Rosebank Office
Park, 181 Jan Smuts Avenue, Parktown North, Gauteng,
South Africa 2193
Rough Guides is represented in Canada by DK Canada, 320
Front Street West, Suite 1400, Toronto, Ontario M5V 3B6
Printed in Singapore
© Rough Guides 2017
Maps © Rough Guides

360pp includes index
A catalogue record for this book is available from the
British Library
ISBN: 978-0-24128-067-6
The publishers and authors have done their best to
ensure the accuracy and currency of all the information
in **The Rough Guide to Bali & Lombok**, however,
they can accept no responsibility for any loss, injury, or
inconvenience sustained by any traveller as a result of
information or advice contained in the guide.
1 3 5 7 9 8 6 4 2

MIX
Paper from
responsible sources
FSC www.fsc.org FSC™ C018179

Help us update

We've gone to a lot of effort to ensure that the ninth
edition of **The Rough Guide to Bali & Lombok** is
accurate and up-to-date. However, things change –
places get "discovered", opening hours are notoriously
fickle, restaurants and rooms raise prices or lower
standards. If you feel we've got it wrong or left
something out, we'd like to know, and if you can

remember the address, the price, the hours, the phone
number, so much the better.

Please send your comments with the subject line
"**Rough Guide Bali & Lombok Update**" to mail@uk
.roughguides.com. We'll credit all contributions and send
a copy of the next edition (or any other Rough Guide if you
prefer) for the very best emails.

A ROUGH GUIDE TO ROUGH GUIDES

Published in 1982, the first Rough Guide – to Greece – was a student scheme that became a
publishing phenomenon. Mark Ellingham, a recent graduate in English from Bristol University,
had been travelling in Greece the previous summer and couldn't find the right guidebook.
With a small group of friends he wrote his own guide, combining a contemporary, journalistic
style with a thoroughly practical approach to travellers' needs.

The immediate success of the book spawned a series that rapidly covered dozens of
destinations. And, in addition to impecunious backpackers, Rough Guides soon acquired a
much broader readership that relished the guides' wit and inquisitiveness as much as their
enthusiastic, critical approach and value-for-money ethos. These days, Rough Guides include
recommendations from budget to luxury and cover more than 120 destinations around the
globe, from Amsterdam to Zanzibar, all regularly updated by our team of roaming writers.

Browse all our latest guides, read inspirational features and book your trip at **roughguides.com**.

ABOUT THE AUTHOR

Iain Stewart first visited Bali and Lombok in the 1990s and has returned to both islands regularly ever since in search of the perfect coral reef, palm-fringed beach and *nasi goreng*. He has visited most corners of Indonesia, which ranks as perhaps his favourite country (there are a few other contenders). He lives close to the beach in Brighton, UK, and has written several other books for Rough Guides including Guatemala and Ibiza.

Acknowledgements

Iain Stewart Thanks to all the Rough Guide team in the UK, particularly Neil McQuillian for his patient and astute editing. To Guy Somers for his many contacts in Bali and Lombok and the tour of his unique lodgings, John Hardy in Ubud, Stuart MacDonald, the World Diving team in Lembongan, Fern Perry and Ewan in the Gilis. Deep down south I was kindly assisted by Yuli and Mike and Gemma and Made in Kuta, Lombok. This book is what it is thanks to the years of expertise of Rough Guides authors Lucy Ridout and Lesley Reader.

Photo credits

All photos © Rough Guides, except the following:
(Key: t-top; c-centre; b-bottom; l-left; r-right)

1 Robert Harding Picture Library
2 AWL Images: ImageBROKER
4 Corbis: Design Pics/Dave Fleetham
5 Alamy Stock Photo: Evgeny Ermakov
9 Corbis: 145/John W Banagan/Ocean (tl); Art in All of Us/Anthony Asael (tr). **Getty Images**: John W Banagan (bl). **Photoshot**: TTL (br)
11 Alamy Stock Photo: hemis.fr/MOIRENC Camille (c). **Corbis**: Victor Fraile (t). **Dreamstime.com**: Rigo Hidayat (b)
12 Getty Images: www.zoomion.ch/Dennis Stauffer
13 Alamy Stock Photo: WaterFrame (c). **Dreamstime.com**: Erikj57 (b). **Getty Images**: John W Banagan (t)
14 Alamy Stock Photo: Matthew Williams-Ellis. **AWL Images**: Michele Falzone (b)
15 Alamy Stock Photo: Michele Falzone (cr). **Corbis**: Remi Benali (cl). **Getty Images**: Dan Ballard (t); Medioimages/Photodisc (b)
16 Corbis: SuperStock/James May (c); Macduff Everton/Science-Faction (b)
17 AWL Images: Michele Falzone (br). **Corbis**: Blaine Harrington III (tl). **Getty Images**: John W Banagan (bl). **Picfair.com**: Stockimo (tr)
18 Corbis: Thierry Tronnel (t). **Getty Images**: Daniel Frauchiger, Switzerland (bl). **Picfair.com**: PageTwoTravel (br)
19 Corbis: Lauryn Ishak (c); JAI/Niels van Gijn (t). **Dreamstime.com**: Mikhail Dudarev (b)
20 Corbis: 2/John Harper/Ocean
22 Getty Images: Edmund Lowe Photography
52–53 Getty Images: Jason Childs
55 Alamy Stock Photo: southeast asia
69 Cocoon Beach Club Bali (bl). **Dreamstime.com**: Pavel Aleynikov (t)

108–109 Corbis: Craig Lovell
111 Alamy Stock Photo: devi
137 Corbis: Robert Harding World Imagery/Bruno Barbier (br); xPACIFICA (t)
148–149 Corbis: JAI/Michele Falzone
151 Corbis: Louie Psihoyos
171 Corbis: JAI/Michele Falzone (t)
190–191 Corbis: JAI/Michele Falzone
193 Corbis: JAI/Michele Falzone
205 Alamy Stock Photo: Eagle Visions Photography/Craig Lovell (tr). **Corbis**: GUIZIOU Franck/Hemis (tl)
218–219 Corbis: Robert Harding World Imagery/Gavin Hellier
221 Dreamstime.com: John Anderson
231 Alamy Stock Photo: Poelzer Wolfgang (tl). **Corbis**: Hemis/CHAPUT Franck (br); JAI/Michele Falzone (bl). **Dreamstime.com**: David Steele (tr)
242–243 Getty Images: Andras Jancsik
245 Alamy Stock Photo: travelib Indonesia
261 Alamy Stock Photo: Stefano Politi Markovina (tl); Marvin Minder (tr). **Corbis**: Robert Harding World Imagery/Jochen Schlenker (b)
271 AWL Images: Hemis (b). **Corbis**: Robert Harding World Imagery/Jochen Schlenker (t)
282–283 Alamy Stock Photo: hemis.fr/GUIZIOU Franck
285 Getty Images: Randi Ang
293 Alamy Stock Photo: Giles Moberly (tr); Aurora Photos/Thomas Pickard (tl). **Picfair.com**: Stockimo (b)
300 Picfair.com: Alfonso Rahardja

Cover: *Woman walking through rice terraces* **Getty Images**: Stone/Martin Puddy

Index

Maps are marked in grey

Map symbols

The symbols below are used on maps throughout the book

Chapter division boundary	Point of interest	Spring
Motorway	Parking	Waterfall
Main road	Post office	Surf break
Minor road	Information centre	Mountain peak
Pedestrianized road	Internet access	Mountain range
Steps	Hospital	Lighthouse
Coastline	Fuel station	Reef
Ferry	International ATM	Cave
Footpath	Golf course	Statue/memorial
Bemo/bus stop	Snorkelling	Boat
International airport	Viewpoint/lookout	Military checkpoint
Bridge	Gate/park entrance	Ranger station

Museum
Birdwatching
Wildlife park
Balinese temple
Chinese temple
Mosque
Church (town maps)
Market
Building
Park/forest
Beach
Mangrove swamp/marsh

Listings key

Accommodation

Eating/beach club

Drinking and nightlife/live music

Shopping

ROUGH
GUIDES

ESCAPE
THE EVERYDAY

ADVENTURE BECKONS
YOU JUST NEED TO KNOW WHERE TO LOOK

roughguides.com